W9-CHP-530

RENEWAL THEOLOGY

RENEWAL THEOLOGY

Salvation, the Holy Spirit, and Christian Living

J. Rodman Williams

Academie Books Grand Rapids, Michigan
Zondervan Publishing House

RENEWAL THEOLOGY: SALVATION, THE HOLY SPIRIT, AND CHRISTIAN LIVING
Copyright © 1990 by J. Rodman Williams

Academie Books is an imprint of Zondervan Publishing House
1415 Lake Drive, S.E., Grand Rapids, Michigan 49506.

Library of Congress Cataloging in Publication Data

Williams, J. Rodman (John Rodman)
    Renewal theology : Salvation, the Holy Spirit, and
  Christian living
        p.   cm.
    Bibliography: p.
    Includes indexes.
    ISBN 0-310-24190-1
    1. Theology, Doctrinal.   2. Pentecostalism.   I. Title.
  BT75.2.W54 1990
  230'.046—dc20   89-32108
                                                            CIP

Edited by Gerard Terpstra

Printed in the United States of America

90 91 92 93 94 95 / AF / 10 9 8 7 6 5 4 3 2 1

To the Spirit of Truth

CONTENTS

ABBREVIATIONS

AB	*Anchor Bible*
ASV	American Standard Version
BAGD	Bauer, Arndt, Gingrich, and Danker, *Greek-English Lexicon of the New Testament*
BDB	Brown, Driver, and Briggs, *Hebrew-English Lexicon of the Old Testament*
BDF	Blass, Debrunner, and Funk, *A Greek Grammar of the New Testament*
EBC	*Expositor's Bible Commentary*
EDT	*Evangelical Dictionary of Theology*
EGT	*Expositor's Greek Testament*
HNTC	*Harper's New Testament Commentary*
IB	*Interpreter's Bible*
ICC	*International Critical Commentary*
IDB	*Interpreter's Dictionary of the Bible*
ISBE	*International Standard Bible Encyclopedia, Revised Edition*
JB	Jerusalem Bible
KJV	King James Version
LCC	*Library of Christian Classics*
LXX	Septuagint (Greek Old Testament)
NASB	New American Standard Bible
NCBC	*New Century Bible Commentary*
NEB	New English Bible
NICNT	*New International Commentary of the New Testament*
NICOT	*New International Commentary of the Old Testament*
NIDNTT	*New International Dictionary of New Testament Theology*
NIGTC	*New International Greek Testament Commentary*
NIV	New International Version
RSV	Revised Standard Version
TDNT	*Theological Dictionary of the New Testament*
TNTC	*Tyndale New Testament Commentary*
TOTC	*Tyndale Old Testament Commentary*
TWOT	*Theological Wordbook of the Old Testament*
UBS	United Bible Societies Greek New Testament
WBC	*Word Bible Commentary*
WBE	*Wycliffe Bible Encyclopedia*
ZPEB	*Zondervan Pictorial Encyclopedia of the Bible*

PREFACE

Renewal Theology: Salvation, the Holy Spirit, and Christian Living is a treatise on the Christian faith. It begins with a consideration of the way of salvation from the calling of God to final perseverance. Next, the person and work of the Holy Spirit, His coming, and the gifts of the Spirit are given attention. The book concludes with a discussion of Christian living.

The opening chapters on salvation deal with the heart of the Christian faith. This section concerns how God's work of redemption in Jesus Christ becomes effective for mankind. How do we enter on the way of salvation and continue in it? In this connection particular attention is given to the doctrines of regeneration, justification, and sanctification. I have written this section on salvation with the strong conviction of the need for fuller biblical, theological, and practical understanding in these areas.

The next chapters discuss many aspects of the activity of the Holy Spirit that call for special attention in our time. After some reflection on the identity and nature of the Holy Spirit, I turn to a study of His unique work of enabling and empowering. The coming of the Holy Spirit, next considered, is the critical center of this section of the book. I deal with the phenomenon of tongues after that. Next I write in some detail about the gifts of the Holy Spirit and focus on the ninefold manifestation of these gifts. My concern in this matter is to give a thorough biblical presentation of these spiritual gifts in their nature and function and to demonstrate their relevance for today.

The study in the aforementioned area of the Holy Spirit has particular bearing on the charismatic renewal in our time. As a participant in that renewal since 1965, I have long been concerned with its biblical and theological orientation. I trust that what is said in the section on the Holy Spirit will provide both an elaboration and a critique of many of the emphases in this renewal. Also it is my hope that both participants and nonparticipants will find this portion of the book helpful.

The final chapter on Christian living, which deals with doing God's will, walking in the light, and following the way of love, provides an ethical climax to this volume of *Renewal Theology*.

Renewal Theology: Salvation, the Holy Spirit, and Christian Living is the second of two volumes. The first is entitled *Renewal Theology: God, the World, and Redemption*. Although volume 2 does not necessarily presuppose the use of volume 1, there is undoubtedly value in reading and studying what has preceded. Incidentally, there are footnotes in this volume that refer to volume 1, and it may prove helpful to follow them up. I also call attention to the preface in the first volume for further orientation to the writing of both volumes.

Finally, I extend appreciation to Regent University for the sabbatical leave that provided time for the research and writing of this volume. In this regard I express special thanks to Pat Robertson, Chancellor; Bob Slosser, President; Carle Hunt, Vice President for Academic Affairs; and Jerry Horner, Dean of the College of Theology and Ministry. As with volume 1, I am grateful for the careful reading of the manuscript by my colleagues in the School of Biblical Studies, John Rea and Charles Holman, and for the helpful suggestions they made. Mark Wilson has again been of great help in the initial editing of my material and in providing the several indexes. Also I offer thanks to Gerard Terpstra of Zondervan Publishing House for his invaluable work in the final editing of the material in this volume. My wife, Jo, has again been extremely helpful in putting all this material on computer and, even more, has been a constant source of challenge and encouragement.

This second volume of *Renewal Theology* is dedicated to "the Spirit of truth" (John 16:13). I sincerely hope that all who read these pages will be led more deeply into the truth that He alone can reveal.

1

Calling

In the last several chapters of volume 1 we have discussed the person and work of Jesus Christ: His incarnation, vicarious sacrifice, and exaltation. Their main thrust has been His entrance into the world as Savior: "To you is born this day in the city of David a Savior, who is Christ the Lord" (Luke 2:11). The question now before us is this: How does the work of Christ as Savior become effectual for us? How is His great redemption applied to us?

Surely it would be a serious mistake to say that what Jesus Christ did depends basically on us. This is not the case, for "God was in Christ reconciling the world to himself" (2 Cor. 5:19). Thus He accomplished something at the cross objectively for all mankind. However, it would also be a serious mistake to view the work of reconciliation and redemption as becoming effective without our participation. This is far from the truth. God has done everything on His part, but you and I must receive it, else we are still in our sins.

Hence, we come now to the critical matter of how the redemption through Christ becomes effective on our behalf. We begin our consideration of salvation

with the doctrine of *calling:* God calls us to salvation.

I. PRELIMINARY—THE WORD "CALLING"

A. A Variety of Usages Unrelated to Salvation

The word "calling" or "call" may be used in a number of ways not directly related to salvation. It may mean to *name* as in the Scripture, "You shall call his name Jesus" (Matt. 1:21). Or it can signify to *summon:* "They called together the whole battalion" (Mark 15:16). Also there is the meaning of *designate* or *appoint:* "Paul . . . called to be an apostle" (Rom. 1:1). Further it may signify a *vocation:* "Let every man abide in the same calling wherein he was called" (1 Cor. 7:20 KJV). The last of these—calling as "vocation"—is common in secular usage, i.e., one's calling or vocation in life, but at the same time it suggests some dimension beyond human decision.

B. General Calling to Salvation

In this connection the particularly relevant Scripture is Matthew 22:1–14, the parable of the marriage feast. Jesus told of a king who prepared a marriage feast for his son and then sent out his servants "to call those who were invited" (v. 3). All those invited spurned the invitation—some made light of it going off to farm and business, others abused and killed the servants. The king destroyed the murderers, and then sent other servants into the thoroughfares to invite as many as they found (v. 9). So they came, although one man entered without a wedding garment and as a result was cast into "outer darkness." The final word of Jesus in this parable is that "many are called, but few are chosen" (v. 14).

This parallels God's word through Isaiah: "When I called you did not answer, when I spoke, you did not listen," and the result: "I will destine you to the sword, and all of you shall bow down to the slaughter" (Isa. 65:12). God called, but the response was negative. Thus they were not God's "chosen."[1]

In a similar way, though not directly related to salvation, Jesus called many to follow Him in His ministry. But not all responded positively. Whereas some immediately followed Him,[2] others turned away. The account in Luke 9:57–62 depicts one person after another who found the cost too great or who would not give the call priority in

their lives ("Lord, let me first go and bury my father . . . let me first say farewell to those at my home") and thus did not become Jesus' disciples. They were called but decided not to follow.

The call of God therefore does not always bring about an affirmative response. Many are called to the marriage feast, to heed God's word, to accept Christ's invitation, but some do not respond; indeed only a few do. Thus the summary word: many are called but few are chosen—or, according to the Greek text, many[3] are *kletoi* (called) but few are *eklektoi* (called out, elect, chosen).

The general call of God is sometimes described as the universal call of God. In the words of Calvin, "There is a universal call, by which God through the external preaching of the word, invites all men alike. . . ."[4] All men are called to salvation, whatever their responses.

C. Effectual Calling to Salvation

This call of God is our basic concern, for it relates vitally to the area of salvation. It is sometimes described as "effectual calling," that is to say, the calling of God that is effectual unto salvation.[5] This is the most frequent use of the word "call" in the New Testament.

---

[1] As Isaiah 65:15 shows: "You shall leave your name to my chosen for a curse."

[2] Matthew 4:18–22; Mark 1:16–20; Luke 5:1–11; John 1:40–42.

[3] "Many" (Gr. *polloi*) in this context (Matt. 22:14) should be understood in an inclusive sense. It is not as if some are not called ("many" thus taken as exclusive); rather the call is to all people. According to J. Jeremias, "Mt. 22:14 contrasts the totality of those invited with the small number of the chosen. God's invitation . . . embraces all without restriction" (article on πολλοί in TDNT, 6:542—also see article by John Rea on "the many" in WBE, 2:1075). "Many" in this comprehensive sense may be especially noted by comparing Matthew 20:28—"The Son of man came . . . to give his life a ransom for many"—with 1 Timothy 2:6—" . . . who [Christ] gave himself a ransom for all." Hence the many who are called are the many, i.e., the all for whom Christ gave His life as a ransom. In sum: the call of God is a general call to all mankind (as the next paragraph above assumes).

[4] *Institutes*, III.24.8, Beveridge trans. Calvin adds, ". . . even for those whom he designs the call to be a savour of death." We will discuss Calvin's view in this connection later.

[5] Effectual calling is "that calling of the living, sovereign, and almighty God which makes us partakers of the life eternal which Jesus Christ earned for us" (Carl F. H. Henry, *Basic Christian Doctrines*, "Effectual Calling," 179).

Here we may note a number of biblical references. Two particularly stand out. Peter writes, "But you are a chosen race, a royal priesthood, a holy nation, God's own people, that you may declare the wonderful deeds of him who called you out of darkness into his marvelous light" (1 Peter 2:9). In the words of Paul, "Share in suffering for the gospel in the power of God, who saved us and called us with a holy calling" (2 Tim. 1:8–9). We have been "called out of darkness"; God has "saved us and called us." Both are expressions of that calling of God wherein salvation comes about. A few other Scriptures may be added: "God is faithful, by whom you were called into the fellowship of his Son" (1 Cor. 1:9); "Lead a life worthy of the calling to which you have been called" (Eph. 4:1); " . . . holy brethren, who share in a heavenly call" (Heb. 3:1); "He called you through our gospel, so that you may obtain the glory of our Lord Jesus Christ" (2 Thess. 2:14); "The God of all grace, who has called you to his eternal glory in Christ . . ." (1 Peter 5:10).

In all these cases, the "called" ones are the "saved" ones. They have entered into a totally new sphere of fellowship with Christ and a sharing in His eternal glory.

II. BACKGROUND

Our consideration now will relate to God's calling of those who are in Christ—who have received salvation through Him—hence effectual calling. What is its background?

A. God's Gracious Purpose

Let us continue with the words of Paul in 2 Timothy 1:9—"God, who saved us and called us with a holy calling, not in virtue of our works but in

virtue of his own purpose and the grace which he gave us in Christ Jesus ages ago. . . ." God's calling to salvation has nothing to do with our works, for our works can never achieve salvation. If the calling were based on works, no one would ever be saved, since all the works of everyone are laden with sin. Thus the calling is fully based on grace—God's unmerited love given to us in Christ Jesus—and that grace is in conjunction with God's purpose. In another statement Paul writes that we are "called according to his purpose" (Rom. 8:28).

The gracious purpose of God reaches far back: it existed "ages ago," or literally, "before times eternal."[6] Thus it is an aspect of God's eternal purpose. Paul writes elsewhere of "the eternal purpose which he has realized in Christ Jesus our Lord" (Eph. 3:11). Hence both God's action in Jesus Christ and the grace we have received through Him go back into God's purpose in eternity.

I should add that God's gracious purpose for salvation is an aspect of His total purpose for all things. Paul speaks of "the purpose of him who accomplishes all things according to the counsel of his will" (Eph. 1:11). At the very heart of that overall purpose is God's ultimate intention to head up everything in Christ. For Paul had just spoken of the "mystery of his will, according to his purpose which he set forth in Christ" as "a plan for the fulness of time, to unite all things in him, things in heaven and things on earth" (Eph. 1:9–10). God's gracious purpose for salvation is grounded in this universal purpose of God.

B. God's Choosing

The background of God's calling to salvation is also His choosing. Let us

---

[6]The Greek phrase in 2 Timothy 1:9 is *pro chronōn aiōniōn,* "before the beginning of time" (NIV); "from all eternity" (NEB, NASB); "before the world began" (KJV).

return to 2 Thessalonians and notice Paul's previous words: "God chose you from the beginning to be saved, through sanctification by the Spirit and belief in the truth. To this he called you through our gospel . . . " (2:13–14). Thus behind God's calling is His choosing.

Further, this choosing is "from the beginning." What takes place in the present, namely, the calling to salvation, had its origins long ago.

Nowhere is this more vividly expressed than in Ephesians 1:4—"He [God] chose us in him [Christ] before the foundation of the world." Thus we are again "before times eternal"—the eternity that precedes the creation of the world. Even as God's grace and purpose were given to us in Christ Jesus from all eternity, likewise God has chosen us before there ever was a world.

Incidentally, we should pause for a moment to consider the extraordinariness of this statement. This is the only biblical reference to what God did before the foundation of the world. Here the one amazing thing, we are told, is that He "chose us in Christ"! *Prior* to Genesis 1:1 ("In the beginning God created . . . ") was our eternal choosing or election[7] in Jesus Christ!

This marvelous fact highlights two things. First, the call of God is wholly a matter of His prevenient grace: His grace eternally preceded our call to salvation. God's free mercy is thereby vividly declared.[8] It is not that we have chosen Him, but He has chosen us. The words of Jesus to His disciples are quite relevant: "You did not choose me, but I chose you and appointed you" (John

15:16). The response necessary on our part is not to an indifferent God. Far from it, He has already—long prior to our response—reached out and chosen us.[9]

Second, it provides an unshakable basis for our call and salvation. Since God's call reaches us out of eternity and stems from His purpose and action (choice) before the world began, a foundation is provided that nothing else can give. Works, once again—even the best of them—can have absolutely nothing to do with it, since works belong to time. How splendid it is to know that the calling to salvation is based on nothing in us but wholly on the prior purpose and action of Almighty God.

The precursor of this calling to salvation is found in the Old Testament, where Israel is called to be a holy nation and is chosen by God for that purpose. "For you are a people holy to the LORD your God; the LORD your God has chosen you to be a people for his own possession" (Deut. 7:6). This choice has nothing to do with Israel's own qualifications, but lies wholly in God's grace: "It was not because you were more in number than any other people that the Lord set his love upon you and chose you, for you were the fewest of all peoples; but it is because the Lord loves you, and is keeping the oath which he swore to your fathers" (Deut. 7:7–8). The calling of Israel was based on God's election of grace.

Another word used in the New Testament in connection with God's choosing or electing is *predestining*. After Paul writes about God's choosing us in Christ before the foundation of the

---

[7] The terms are essentially interchangeable.

[8] "When the call is coupled with election, in this way scripture sufficiently suggests that in it nothing but God's free mercy is to be sought" (Calvin, *Institutes,* III.24.1, Beveridge trans.).

[9] "The eternal election means that God's Word of Love which now reaches [= calls] me in Jesus Christ, reaches me out of Eternity, that it goes 'before' my existence, and my decision, as that which makes it possible" (Emil Brunner, *The Christian Doctrine of God,* 318).

world, he adds, "In love He predestinated[10] us to adoption as sons through Jesus Christ to Himself" (Eph. 1:4–5 NASB). Hence, predestining points to the same prior action of God, with the emphasis more particularly on God's *sovereign action* in the choosing or electing. Predestining also points more directly to the *end* to which we are called. Later in Ephesians 1 Paul speaks of our "having been predestined according to his purpose . . . to the end that we . . . should be to the praise of His glory" (vv. 11–12 NASB). Having noted these things—the broader meaning of God's sovereign action and the larger meaning of direction—we now observe that the word "predestine" may serve for "choose" or "elect."

This is illustrated in Romans 8:28–30. Paul first speaks of calling: "those . . . who are called according to his [God's] purpose." He then proceeds to say, "For those whom he foreknew he also predestined to be conformed to the image of his Son. . . . And those whom he predestined he also called. . . ." The end of this sequence is glorification: "Those whom he called he also justified; and those whom he justified he also glorified." Again both God's sovereign action is stressed—quite strongly through the whole sequence of events—and the ultimate intention: glorification.

In passing, it is important (in the light of many misinterpretations) to observe that the word "predestine" or "predestinate" is never used in the New Testament to refer to anything other than the arena of salvation—(as we have noted), adoption of sons, living to the praise of God, glorification—or matters connected with these realities.[11] Accordingly, a view of "double predestination"—a predestination referring to death and damnation as well as to eternal life[12]—has utterly no basis in Scripture. This does not mean that there is no death or damnation,[13] but such does not belong to God's predestining action, which (as we have noted) refers only to the general arena of salvation.

C. God's Foreknowledge

We proceed next to another factor in the background of calling, namely, foreknowledge. Here we recall Paul's words in Romans 8: "For those whom he foreknew he also predestined . . . " (v. 29). Significantly God's predestining (choosing, electing) is of persons "whom he foreknew." Peter in the salutation of his first letter similarly addresses the scattered believers as those "who are chosen according to the foreknowledge of God the Father" (1 Peter 1:1–2 NASB). These two Scriptures, from Paul and Peter, underscore the fact that God's elect are personally foreknown by Him; He does not choose or predestine them as abstract entities but as real persons.

---

[10] The Greek word is *proorisas*.

[11] Predestine (Gr. *proorizō*) occurs six times in the New Testament. Four instances deal directly with salvation, all of which we have noted: Romans 8:29, 30; Ephesians 1:5, 11. The other two are Acts 4:28: "to do whatever Thy hand and Thy purpose predestined to occur" (referring to the action of Herod, Pilate, the Gentiles, and the Jews), and 1 Corinthians 2:7: "We speak God's wisdom in a mystery, the hidden *wisdom*, which God predestined before the ages to our glory" (quotations from the NASB). The last two deal with matters related to salvation.

[12] As held particularly by Calvin: "All [men] are not created on equal terms, but some are preordained to eternal life, others to eternal damnation; and accordingly, as each has been created for one or other of these ends, we say that he has been predestinated to life or to death" (*Institutes*, III.21.5, Beveridge trans.).

[13] Although there is no "double predestination" in Scripture, there is a "double destination": eternal life and eternal death. See Excursus I, pp. 18–22.

We may observe specific illustrations of this. First, Israel is spoken of by Paul as a people whom God foreknew: "God has not rejected his people whom he foreknew" (Rom. 11:2). As God's chosen people in the Old Testament, they were foreknown by Him; God in His infinite knowledge and love[14] knew Israel before He chose them. Second, and quite remarkably, Jesus Himself is described by Peter as "foreknown before the foundation of the world" (1 Peter 1:20 NASB). Jesus was also God's Chosen,[15] but like Israel and Christian believers, He was foreknown before the world was made.

A pertinent Scripture relevant in this connection is Psalm 139, which begins: "O LORD, thou hast searched me and known me" (v. 1). It continues later: "Thy eyes beheld my unformed substance; in thy book were written, every one of them, the days that were formed for me, when as yet there was none of them" (v. 16). The psalmist says that God foresees, as in a book, everything about us as well as everything we do. His love, His grace, is indeed particular and detailed. Likewise, we may add, does God foreknow those whom He chooses. It is this foreknowledge that fills His election with profound and personal meaning. So can the psalmist cry: "How precious to me are thy thoughts, O God! How vast is the sum of them!" (v. 17).

Before leaving the relationship of God's foreknowledge to election (or predestination), it is important to observe that Scripture nowhere suggests that God's election is based on foreknowledge in the sense of God's knowing ahead what someone will do and then basing His election on that knowledge.[16] This was not true of Israel in the Old Testament or of Jesus as God's Chosen in the New Testament, and correspondingly it is not true of the Christian believer. The idea of election as based on what God foresees in human action is actually alien to the whole biblical witness.

EXCURSUS I:
ADDITIONAL OBSERVATIONS
ABOUT ELECTION

1. Election is not to be understood in the New Testament as a limitation by which only so many *can* believe—as if God's grace were discriminate—but that all who *do* believe have their faith grounded in eternity.[17] To say that "God chose us in Christ before the foundation of the world" is not to say that he reprobated others (thus preordained their death—Calvin; or passed them by—a later, more moderate Calvinism) but to say with glad conviction that our faith is based on the infinitely solid rock of God's prior action and foreknowledge. Thus it is a matter of

---

[14] Recall Deuteronomy 4:37 where the only reason given for God's choice of Israel was His love for them.

[15] E.g., Luke 9:35—"This is my Son, my Chosen."

[16] The view of post-Reformation Dutch theologian James Arminius (1560–1609). Arminius held that God's election was based on His foreknowledge of our decision to accept His offer in Christ, hence our faith. See *The Writings of James Arminius,* 1:247–48. Henry Thiessen, following Arminius, writes, "By election we mean that sovereign act of God in grace whereby He chose in Christ Jesus for salvation all those whom he foresaw would accept Him" ("Election and Vocation," 54, in *The New Life,* Millard J. Erickson, ed.). Calvin (prior to Arminius) had already asked, "How can it be consistently said, that things derived from election are the cause of election?" (*Institutes,* III.22.3, Beveridge trans.). Calvin, I believe, at this point is entirely correct.

[17] Election is not selection in the New Testament. In the Old Testament God did select a particular people; now election relates to all who believe in Christ.

great joy. Paul says, "[We] have been destined and appointed to live for the praise of his glory" (Eph. 1:12)!

2. Election does not rule out human responsibility. There is nothing automatic about it. As we noted earlier, "Many are called, but few are chosen." There must be the response of faith. However, when this response does occur, the calling is an "effectual calling,"[18] both because of man's faith and because of his grounding in the prior purpose and action of God. The very fact that there is a call of God (the "general" or "universal" call) that does not always result in salvation is by no means due to any withholding on the part of God, for Scripture makes it clear that "God our Savior . . . desires all men to be saved and to come to the knowledge of the truth" (1 Tim. 2:3–4). The failure is due to people's turning away from God's purpose for them. It is indeed possible to reject God's purpose,[19] to turn from the light: "Light has come into the world, and men loved darkness rather than light" (John 3:19). Election coerces no one nor rules anyone out but is the firm background for all who in faith respond to God's glorious grace.

3. Election consequently is to be held in close correlation with faith. It is not because we are elected that we are able to believe (Calvinism)[20] nor are we elected on the basis of foreseen faith (Arminianism)[21] but that *we are elected as believers*. God "chose us in him" — in Jesus Christ — "before the foundation of the world." This Ephesians passage from the outset is addressed to "believers incorporate in Christ Jesus" (1:1 NEB). Hence when Paul proceeds to say that "God chose us in Christ before the foundation of the world," he speaks of believers and no one else. Thus there is no choice outside our being "in Christ." Consequently, all that the New Testament has to say about election is addressed to believers and is relevant only in connection with them.[22] If one, even for moment, steps outside the correlation of election and faith, the situation becomes meaningless. Election is related only to those "in Christ"; outside Him there is no election. Again, it is "those who love him [God], who are called according to his purpose" (Rom. 8:28). Thus it is the people of faith who are the elect people of God.[23]

---

[18]The language, e.g., of the Westminster Confession of Faith (chap. X, "Of Effectual Calling"). There is no mention, however, in the WCF of effectual calling as including the response of faith.

[19]As did the Pharisees and the lawyers: "The Pharisees and the lawyers rejected the purpose of God for themselves" (Luke 7:30).

[20]Calvin speaks of election as "the parent of faith" (*Institutes,* III.22.10, Beveridge trans.), hence election produces or brings about faith.

[21]See note 16.

[22]A verse that particularly bespeaks the close connection between believing and election is Titus 1:1, which begins: "Paul, a servant of God, and an apostle of Jesus Christ, according to the faith of God's elect" (KJV).

[23]Election and faith may be depicted as the two poles of the arch of salvation.

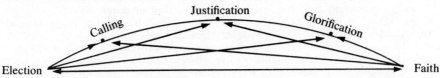

The arrows point out both the integral connection between election and faith and their relations to the other moments in salvation.

What about persons outside this correlation of election and faith? Their situation seems to be thus: God yearns for their salvation as well, and Jesus Christ died for them all. It is reprehensible to speak of a limited atonement, that is to say, that Christ died only for those whom God elected to salvation. Christ did not come into the world to save some and condemn others, but to save all. The only barrier is man's own disbelief: "This is the condemnation, that . . . men loved darkness" (John 3:19 KJV). Thus general calling is the calling of God's outreaching love that would take every person to Himself. He has no hidden agenda, by which He has already decided to save some and reprobate or bypass the others. There is *no* predestination to death. God's purpose is never destruction. Those who do not believe will go into darkness, but this is not God's desire. They go, not because God did *not* choose them before the foundation of the world, but because in spite of His great love and act of reconciliation they do not choose to receive it in faith.

Let us note further that God's saving action in Jesus Christ is shown in the New Testament to bring about both positive and negative results. According to Luke 2:34, Simeon prophesied, "Behold, this child [Jesus] is set for[24] the fall[25] and rising of many in Israel" (KJV). This does not mean that Christ came in order that people might both fall and rise, for earlier Simeon had said, "Mine eyes have seen thy salva-tion . . . a light for revelation to the Gentiles, and for glory to thy people Israel" (2:30, 32). Christ came that people might rise rather than fall; He came as Savior and not also as Destroyer. However, His very coming precipitates a crisis in which some fall and others rise. Similarly God says in Romans 9:33: "Behold, I am laying in Zion a stone that will make men stumble, a rock that will make them fall; and he who believes in him will not be put to shame"[26] (compare 1 Peter 2:6).[27] Again there is a twofold result. While the text may suggest that Christ came to bring about people's stumbling and falling, this is not the case. Peter gives the real reason: "they stumble because they disobey the word, as they were destined to do" (v. 8).[28] The stumbling is due to disobedience, *not* to God's predetermination; the destining is not due to God's prior decision, but to their disobedience of the word.

The gospel proclamation itself brings about a twofold result. Paul writes in 2 Corinthians 2:15–16 that "we are the aroma of Christ to God among those who are being saved and among those who are perishing, to one a fragrance from death to death, to the other a fragrance from life to life." The same gospel (always good news with the same "aroma")[29] is the fragrance of death to one, of life to another. Is this due to the gospel? Not at all, for the gospel is for life, not for death. Is this because God withholds saving grace from the dying? Not at all: it is the same

---

[24] The Greek word is *keitai:* "appointed for" (NASB); "destined to cause" (NIV); "destined to be" (NEB). The idea of destiny is clearly contained.

[25] The Greek word is *ptōsin;* "fall, falling . . . lit. of the collapse of a house" (BAGD), "downfall—that many may fall and bring upon themselves ruin" (Thayer).

[26] Paul here conflates two texts, Isaiah 8:14 and Isaiah 28:16 (after the LXX). He seeks to emphasize Israel's faithlessness in spite of her election.

[27] Peter speaks of the stone as "a cornerstone chosen and precious."

[28] Peter also quotes the two verses from Isaiah in verses 6 and 8. In verse 7 he quotes a related passage from Psalm 118:22. His emphasis, however, is that the twofold result is evidenced in Gentiles as well as Jews.

[29] The Greek word is *euōdia,* "sweet savour" (KJV).

grace, the same beautiful fragrance. But some die *because they are not able to receive it*.[30] The gospel is for them, tragically, a fragrance unto death.

On this latter point, there are persons whom Paul describes elsewhere as "vessels of wrath fitted[31] to destruction" (Rom. 9:22 KJV). This might seem to suggest that "the vessels of wrath" were fitted beforehand by God to be such vessels. However, the larger context about "the vessels of mercy, which he has prepared beforehand for glory" (v. 23) excludes this interpretation. The vessels of wrath were not "prepared beforehand" for destruction, but "fitted" thereto because of their condition.

To summarize, there *are two destinations, but not two predestinations.* Christ came to save, not to condemn, to bring life, not to bring death. Yet His very coming brings about both falling and rising, destruction and salvation. He is the light that draws, the light that repels (John 3:19–21); a precious cornerstone and a stone of stumbling;[32] a fragrance that brings life and a fragrance that brings death. But none of this— the falling, the repulsion, the stumbling, the death—is due to God's decree but to *what is in man himself.*

Let us emphasize this latter point: what is in man himself. We earlier quoted the words of Simeon about "this child" being "set for the fall and rising of many." Shortly thereafter Simeon added, "that thoughts out of many hearts may be revealed" (Luke 2:35). In other words, the fall and rising are a revelation of people's innermost disposition—the thoughts of their hearts— and they respond accordingly. Hence, the falling and rising are not the revelation of an eternal decree of God regardless of man's situation; rather the very falling and rising are due to the condition of the heart.

God ordains life, and He ordains death. In the one case, it occurs through faith, and in the other, through unbelief. Moreover, God unquestionably remains sovereign over both those who believe and those who disbelieve. Nothing occurs outside His ultimate control and disposition. He is the sovereign Lord of life and death, of heaven and hell, of this age and all that may occur in the ages to come. *But,* let us never say that the destiny of man, any man, has been fixed by God in eternity and for eternity. The ordination of life is for those who believe in His only Son Jesus Christ, the ordination of death for those who spurn His unspeakable gift of love.

In Jesus Christ—to close with the magnificent words of Paul—"*it is always Yes*" (2 Cor. 1:19). There is a No, but it is outside Him. Let us therefore proclaim the Yes of Christ with great joy to all mankind.

---

[30] This is not too different from the old adage: "What is one man's food is another man's poison."

[31] The Greek word is *katērtismena;* the RSV has "made," NIV and NASB, "prepared." The RSV, NIV, and NASB translations too much imply that God directly made or prepared beforehand vessels of wrath for destruction. "Fitted"—or other possibilities such as "ready" or "ripe for"—better convey the meaning that the destruction is also due to the nature of the vessel itself. EGT has "perfected, made quite fit or ripe." Moffatt translates as "ripe and ready to be destroyed." Everett F. Harrison, while using the word "prepared," writes, " 'Prepared for destruction' designates a ripeness of sinfulness that points to judgment unless there is a turning to God, yet God is not made responsible for the sinful condition. The preparation for destruction is the work of man who allows himself to deteriorate in spite of knowledge and conscience" (EBC, 10:107).

[32] "Every one who falls on that stone will be broken to pieces; but when it falls on any one it will crush him [or "crush him to pieces" (Thayer)]" (Luke 20:18).

EXCURSUS II: ADDITIONAL OBSERVATIONS ABOUT FOREKNOWLEDGE

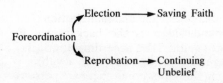

A *neglect* or *misapprehension* of foreknowledge leads to a serious misunderstanding regarding the doctrine of salvation. *Each* must be carefully guarded against.

1. If one moves from God's eternal purpose to election neglecting to consider foreknowledge, the result will be that of arbitrary election: a "decree" of election. In Calvinistic theology the stress falls on this decree. It is set not against the background of foreknowledge but of absolute foreordination, the foreordination of all things. The decree of election is then viewed as a special application of this general decree. This may be diagramed as follows:

Foreordination ⟶ Election ⟶ Saving Faith

Hence against the background of absolute foreordination, the decree of election goes forth and necessarily brings about faith and salvation. Furthermore, since absolute foreordination rather than foreknowledge is the background—and not all people believe—and since there can be faith only if there has been election, then there must be another decree of reprobation,[33] whether the decrees were before or after the Fall.[34] Thus:

In both cases above saving faith is viewed as the result of election: it is an election *to* faith and salvation.

2. If, on the other hand, one misapprehends foreknowledge by viewing it as the foreseeing of faith, the result will be that of exaggerating human freedom. Divine election would therefore be based on the human decision of faith. Arminian theology, which represents this viewpoint,[35] stresses foreknowledge in general (counter to foreordination in general of Calvinism). Election is based on the particular foreseeing of those who will believe. This may be diagramed as follows:

Fore-knowl-edge ⟶ Saving Faith ⟶ Election

Here against the background of God's total knowledge, which of course includes those who believe, God's election takes place.

3. To respond to both the neglect of foreknowledge (as in Calvinism) and its misapprehension (as in Arminianism), one needs to emphasize that foreknowledge (not foreordination) is the back-

---

[33] Calvin declares, "There could be no election without its opposite reprobation" (*Institutes*, III.23.1, Beveridge trans.). "Reprobation" refers to God's condemning the nonelect to eternal punishment.

[34] "Supralapsarianism" is the theological term used to express the Calvinistic view that God foreordained *before* the Fall (the "lapse")—indeed before creation—both those elected to salvation and those reprobated to damnation (see n. 12 for Calvin's statement). "Infralapsarianism," a somewhat milder form of Calvinism, holds that God foreordained *after* the Fall—hence from among the sinful mass of humanity—those whom He elected and those whom He reprobated. The term "preterition" was used by later Calvinists to express the idea that God simply passed over (Latin: *praeteritus* = "pass over") those whom He did not elect to salvation: they were allowed to go on their way to just damnation for their sins. Most Calvinist, or Reformed, confessions of faith tend toward infralapsarianism and preterition.

[35] See earlier note 16.

ground of election and that election (not foreknowledge) is the background of saving faith. This, accordingly, may be diagramed in this way:

$$\text{Foreknowledge} \longrightarrow \text{Election} \longrightarrow \text{Saving Faith}$$

This brings us back to the pattern of Paul in Romans 8:29–30: foreknowledge, predestination (= election), and then calling ("effectual"), justification, and glorification—a pattern that occurs with those who truly believe.

III. METHOD

The calling of God to salvation occurs by the ministry of the word and the Spirit. It is the conjoining of these two that God's calling is effectual.

A. Proclamation of the Word

Paul writes that "we preach Christ crucified . . . to those who are called . . . Christ the power of God and the wisdom of God" (1 Cor. 1:23–24). It is through the word about Christ, focused on the cross, that people come to salvation. In a similar vein Peter declares, "You have been born again not of seed which is perishable but imperishable, *that is,* through the living and abiding word of God . . . this is the word which was preached to you" (1 Peter 1:23, 25 NASB).

It is God's intention that through the word of proclamation people be called out of darkness into light, called into the fellowship of Jesus Christ, and called into eternal glory.[36]

The first step, accordingly, is that the gospel proclamation be *heard.* Paul asks, "How are they to believe in him of whom they have never heard?" (Rom. 10:14). If Christ—who He is and

what He has done—is simply not known, there obviously can be no calling unto salvation. Proclaiming the good news, speaking the word of the gospel, is unmistakably primary.

Jesus began His own ministry with proclamation: "Now after John was arrested, Jesus came into Galilee, preaching the gospel of God" (Mark 1:14). He emphasized this matter of hearing in the parable of the sower and the seed, where He began with "Listen!" and ended with "He who has ears to hear, let him hear" (Mark 4:3–9). The problem, as Jesus declared, is that people often hear superficially or only partially. Thus the word brings forth little result. People must be able to hear or salvation cannot occur.

Peter likewise began his message on the Day of Pentecost with these words: "Men of Judea and all who dwell in Jerusalem, let this be known to you, and give ear to my words" (Acts 2:14). A little later he again said, "Men of Israel, hear these words" (Acts 2:22). People must hear, and hear clearly, if there is to be that faith in which salvation occurs.

So it has been down through the ages, even to our present day: the gospel must be heard. In this lies the great challenge, namely, to get people to listen that they may hear and believe. In many cases, as at the beginning, it is a first hearing—as when the gospel is proclaimed in places previously unreached. In others, it is a matter of gaining a true hearing where people have heard in part many times but still have not come to a vital faith. The problem of a surfeit of hearing the gospel without genuine response is also compounded in our day by the multiplicity of voices (both religious and secular) calling out to be heard. If Paul

---

[36]See Scriptures earlier quoted in section I.C., page 15.

could say about many in his audience, "their ears are heavy of hearing" (Acts 28:27), how much more has this become a fact in our time!

Hence the whole area of communication—*how* to get the gospel message across—has become an increasingly critical matter. In the local church the "sermon monologue" doubtless will continue to hold a high priority and thus needs very careful homiletical consideration: effective content, style of delivery, and the like. However, in an age of multimedia communication the proclaimer of the good news should be sensitive to many other forms such as story, dialogue, and dramatic presentation.[37] In missions the subject of contextualization has assumed major importance.

Of much greater significance is the proclamation of the gospel accompanied by "signs and wonders," so that the word is visibly confirmed by miracles of healing, deliverance, and the like.[38] One cannot see a soul being saved, whereas the healing of a lame or blind person cannot be easily over-looked. In the early church "they went forth and preached everywhere, while the Lord worked with them and confirmed the message by the signs that attended it" (Mark 16:20). Communication with confirmation—how better can the gospel be proclaimed!

Second, if there is to be a hearing there must of course be one who *proclaims* the message: "How can they hear without someone preaching[39] to them?" (Rom. 10:14 NIV). Thus basic to hearing is the proclamation of the gospel. There is no more important—or more "beautiful"—function than that, according to Paul (quoting Isaiah): "How beautiful are the feet of those who preach good news!" (Rom. 10:15).

The proclaimer of the message is basically a witness: "You shall be my witnesses" (Acts 1:8).[40] He stands firmly on the original witness of the biblical apostles and prophets, and with that witness confirmed in his own experience, he seeks to proclaim the truth. He speaks as one who has also seen and heard, and thus has the weight of inner authority and conviction.

---

[37] Lest these seem like innovative and somewhat flighty ways of proclamation, let us call to mind that Jesus almost constantly preached in story form ("Indeed he said nothing to them without a parable"—Matt. 13:34); that Paul, in addition to a sermonic method, spent hour upon hour, arguing and dialoguing with his audiences (see, e.g., Acts 17:2: "Three weeks he argued with them"; Acts 17:17: "He argued in the synagogue . . . and in the market place every day"; Acts 19:8: "for three months . . . arguing and pleading about the kingdom of God"). Dramatic presentation was not lacking in an Old Testament Hosea (see Hosea 1) or Ezekiel (see, e.g., Ezek. 4–5), and in a New Testament Agabus (Acts 11:27–30; 21:10–11). Indeed, the whole life of Jesus (and to a degree of Paul) was a dramatic presentation of the gospel. Such liturgical activities as baptism and the Lord's Supper continue as visible demonstrations of the gospel.

[38] Such an emphasis is represented by John Wimber in his books *Power Evangelism* and *Power Healing*.

[39] The Greek word is *kērussontos*. Hence, "preaching" is a better translation than "preacher" (as in KJV, RSV, NASB). "Preacher" conveys overmuch the note of an office rather than an action or activity. But even "preaching" may not be the best translation since the verb *kērussō* means basically to "announce," "make known by a herald," "proclaim aloud," "speak of," "spread the story widely" (BAGD). Since "preaching" has tended to signify for many "to exhort in an officious or tiresome manner" (Webster), other ways of translating *kērussō* would seem to be valuable in our time. The NEB translates Romans 10:14: "And how hear without someone to spread the news?"

[40] Although these words were spoken to those who beheld Jesus as resurrected and then became witnesses of His resurrection (see Acts 1:22; 3:15; 4:33; 5:32), the words in a larger sense may be used to refer to the total witness to the gospel (see also Acts 14:3; 22:20).

This is the role not only of an official proclaimer (evangelist, pastor, teacher), but also of everyone who belongs to Christ. All are urged to proclaim the word, to bear witness, to share the good news. It may not, and will not, always be sermons from a pulpit or even on a street corner, but often the simple, unostentatious conversation about Jesus and the new life in Him.

The focus must always be on Jesus Christ, for He is the Word made flesh and our word made real. We are to proclaim the whole Christ—all that He is and has done—but with the emphasis always where the apostle put it: "Jesus Christ and him crucified" (1 Cor. 2:2). Peter's first gospel proclamation to the Jewish nation[41] is the original example, since everything he said focused on Christ: it began, continued, and ended there. So it must be with us today.

Finally, those who proclaim the message must be *sent*. Immediately following the words "How are they to hear without someone preaching to them?" Paul adds, "And how can men preach unless they are sent?" (Rom. 10:15). This brings to mind also the words of the risen Christ, "As the Father has sent me, even so I send you" (John 20:21).

On the one hand, this applies in a special way to those who are called by God to a particular "ministry of the word."[42] Paul, for example, was "called . . . to be an apostle" (1 Cor. 1:1 and elsewhere). An apostle is, by definition, one "sent out."[43] Hence, he stood under a special commission. So today we speak properly of a "call to the ministry" or "the ministry of the word," and affirm that there is such a unique calling. The office of "apostle," incidentally, even in New Testament times was not coterminous with the twelve apostles,[44] nor has it actually ever been so down through the centuries.

But again, any believer regardless of office may be sent by God to proclaim the gospel. Surely this was true also in New Testament times in that such "nonapostles" as Philip (who came to be known as "the evangelist" [Acts 21:8]) and Stephen—both "deacons"[45]—were unmistakably also "sent" by God. Many others "who were scattered [by persecution] went about preaching[46] the word" (Acts 8:4). Surely, as the first to move beyond Jerusalem, they were "sent" by God. So it has been for almost two thousand

---

[41] Acts 2:22–36. Peter's words preceding this (vv. 14–21) are not proclamation of the gospel but explanation of what had just happened to himself and the other disciples in the "outpouring" of the Holy Spirit (vv. 1–4).

[42] As in Acts 6:4. The apostles appointed a number of men to "serve tables" (v. 2) so that they might "devote" themselves "to prayer and to the ministry of the word."

[43] The Greek word is *apostolos,* from *apostellō,* to "send out" or "away."

[44] For example, others mentioned as "apostles" include Barnabas (Acts 14:14); James, "the Lord's brother" (Gal. 1:19); and Andronicus and Junias, Paul's "kinsmen and . . . fellow prisoners" (Rom. 16:7).

[45] Stephen and Philip were among those appointed by the twelve apostles to "serve tables" (literally, to "deacon [*diakonein*] tables") so that the apostles would be free for the "ministry" (literally, the "deaconing"! [*diakonia*]) of the word (Acts 6:2). However, their table service could not confine them, for soon Stephen and Philip turned to proclaiming the word (Stephen: Acts 6:8–7:53; Philip: Acts 8:5–40). Surely they were "sent" by God and therefore, in a broad sense, performed an "apostolic" ministry.

[46] The Greek word is *euangelizomenoi,* "bringing the good tidings of" (NASB mg).

years: "ordinary" believers also being used to proclaim the gospel.

Whereas there is no official limitation regarding those sent, it should be added, however, that one dare not proclaim the message in a given situation unless God sends him. Peter was sent primarily to the Jews, Paul to the Gentiles;[47] within their commissions there were particular persons and places to whom they were sent. This remains the case since God prepares the way. The messenger bears witness to those whom God has made ready.

The importance of this needs much emphasis. The Christian—every Christian—is commissioned by God to bear witness to the truth in Christ; *everyone is sent*. However, this *does not necessarily mean that a person is sent to everyone*. There can be much harm done, much confusion, much sense of failure if the witness is not under God's command and direction. The attitude should always be that of "Here am I! Send me,"[48] and then going to those to whom the Lord sends.

"How can they preach unless they are sent?" When they are sent, the next words ring forth with glad affirmation: "How beautiful are the feet of those who preach good news!" (Rom. 10:15).

B. Application by the Holy Spirit

There must be the application by the Holy Spirit of the word proclaimed if people are to be effectively called to salvation.

We have earlier noticed Peter's statement about being "born again" by the proclamation of the good news. Prior to this statement, however, Peter speaks of "the things which have now been announced to you by those who preached the good news to you" as having been done "through the Holy Spirit sent from heaven" (1 Peter 1:12). The proclamation of the word was through the agency of the Holy Spirit. Paul writes in similar fashion to the Thessalonians: "Our gospel came to you not only in word, but also in power and in the Holy Spirit and with full conviction"[49] (1 Thess. 1:5). The Spirit applying the word is the power that effectuates salvation. Without such activity of the Holy Spirit even the most plausible and compelling message will have absolutely no value in bringing about salvation.[50] Where the Holy Spirit is active in proclamation, He is verily the divine agent in salvation.

Jesus Himself began His ministry only after being anointed by the Holy Spirit. There is no record in the Gospels of any proclamation by Him until the Holy Spirit "descended upon him" (Luke 3:22). Then Jesus "full of the Holy Spirit . . . was led by the Spirit . . . in the wilderness" (4:2), and after that "returned in the power of the Spirit into Galilee" (4:14) to begin His ministry. When He came to Nazareth, He declared the fulfillment of a word in Isaiah: "The Spirit of the Lord is upon me, because he has anointed me to preach good news . . . " (4:18; cf. Isa. 61:1). Jesus' proclamation throughout

---

[47] Jesus declared to Paul, "I will send you far away to the Gentiles" (Acts 22:21). Paul compared his ministry with Peter's thus: "I [Paul] had been entrusted with the gospel to the uncircumcised, just as Peter had been entrusted with the gospel to the circumcised" (Gal. 2:7).

[48] This was the response of young Isaiah to the voice of the Lord: "Whom shall I send, and who will go for us?" (Isa. 6:8).

[49] Incidentally, the words immediately before are: "We know, brethren beloved by God, that he has chosen you; for. . . . " Note the close correlation between election and saving faith (which was discussed earlier).

[50] "Without this activity of the Holy Spirit, who writes the word in man's heart, God's Word itself is but an empty letter" (Heinrich Heppe, *Reformed Dogmatics*, 517).

His ministry was accordingly in the power of the Holy Spirit.

Moreover, after His death and resurrection Jesus announced to His disciples that "repentance and forgiveness of sins should be preached in his name to all nations" (Luke 24:47). However, He also commanded them, "Stay in the city, until you are clothed with power from on high" (Luke 24:49). Hence, to be effective unto repentance and forgiveness the proclamation must go forth in the "power from on high"—the power of the Holy Spirit.

This is precisely what happened, beginning on the Day of Pentecost. The anointing came as it had come upon Jesus three years before: "They were all filled with the Holy Spirit" (Acts 2:4). Shortly after that, through Peter as spokesman, the proclamation of salvation was sounding forth. Paul later was likewise "filled with the Holy Spirit" (Acts 9:17) and "immediately he proclaimed Jesus" (9:20). Thus it was that "through the Holy Spirit sent from heaven" the good news was declared by one person after another.

Now all of this has been reviewed in some detail because of the urgency to stress that if the calling of God to salvation is to be effective, it must go forth in the power of the Holy Spirit. Proclamation, witness, sharing the good news no matter how capably, earnestly, even fervently[51] done, cannot be effective without this anointing "from on high."[52]

The reason for this is apparent. The calling to salvation is far more than a human call: It is God himself through Jesus Christ moving in a life and effecting the supernatural miracle of a new creation. The word is essential—as in the beginning of the first creation ("And God said, 'Let there be . . . ' "). But even as it took the Spirit of God "moving over the face of the waters" (Gen. 1:2) for the earth to be formed and enlivened, so it is with the new creation. Since man has fallen from his primal estate and become "dead in trespasses and sins" (Eph. 2:1 KJV), the renewed moving of the Holy Spirit's power is the only hope to bring him to life again.

The continuing significance of this is that all who proclaim the word of God unto salvation must rely utterly on the power and efficacy of the Holy Spirit. The word remains important (there can be no minimizing of this), but even the most persuasive speech is totally ineffective without the dynamism of the Holy Spirit. As Paul said to the Corinthians, "My message and my preaching were not in persuasive words of wisdom[53] but in demonstration of the Spirit and of power"[54] (1 Cor. 2:4 NASB). So it

---

[51]Apollos, "an eloquent man, well versed [or "mighty," Gr. *dynatos*] in the scriptures . . . [and] instructed in the way of the Lord" (Acts 18:24–25), is a possible case in point. He was also "fervent in spirit" and "spoke and taught accurately the things concerning Jesus" (v. 25). However, something was lacking, for "he knew only the baptism of John." When Priscilla and Aquila heard him speaking "boldly in the synagogue," they sensed something was missing and "took him and expounded to him the way of God more accurately" (v. 26). This "way" surely went beyond "the baptism of John" and its lack of the Holy Spirit (see Acts 19 for others who likewise had experienced only "John's baptism" and knew nothing about the availability of the Holy Spirit). Accordingly, Apollos' fervency in spirit needed the additional fervency of the Holy Spirit.

[52]Without a similar anointing, even well-intended and highly organized evangelistic outreaches become little more than human efforts.

[53]Paul thus distanced himself from the dependency on rhetoric and subtlety that was the manner of Greek oratory.

[54]This may mean more than the Spirit's empowering the word; it could also include the word's being accompanied by "signs and wonders" of the Holy Spirit. For in a summary of

continues today; every proclamation of the word that is truly effectual must be under the Spirit's anointing and power.

IV. RESPONSE: FAITH

The response to God's calling in which salvation occurs is *faith*. Accordingly, this (as I have previously described it) may be termed saving faith. Without such faith, regardless of what God has done, there can be no salvation.[55]

A. Inception

Faith[56] comes about through the unity of word and Spirit. Paul, after declaring that his message and preaching were done in the demonstration of the Spirit (1 Cor. 2:4), added, " . . . that your faith should not rest on the wisdom of men, but on the power of God" (v. 5 NASB). Hence, faith is the result of the word, the message, going forth in the power of the Spirit.

Faith, therefore, goes back to God's action. It is not grounded in a human decision to believe. If that were so, salvation would be based on man's activity rather than God's. However, God reaches out to man—the initiative is totally on His side—and offers him an accomplished redemption in Jesus Christ. Man needs only to receive what God has done. This reception is the response of faith.

God's grace (His "gracious purpose"),[57] therefore, is the source, and faith the human instrument. In the striking words of Ephesians 2:8, 9— "For by grace you have been saved through faith; and this is not your own doing, it is the gift of God—not because of works, lest any man should boast." Similarly Paul wrote to the Philippians, "It has been granted to you on behalf of Christ . . . to believe on him" (1:29 NIV). Salvation originates in grace: it is God's gift, God's grant. It is channeled through faith. Grace, however, is clearly the primary reality.

No one, therefore, can make himself believe. It is not a matter of working up faith—as some have said, "to believe the unbelievable." It is not a human leap in the dark in the hope that what the Bible speaks about is true and perchance one may secure it for himself. Nor is faith a decision based on human reasoning and attempted proof; it has a far more solid basis than rational and empirical evidence. Moreover, faith, rather than reaching out and hoping to secure God's promise by passionate human effort, *is itself,* according to Hebrews 11:1, "the assurance of things hoped for, the conviction (or the "proof"[58]) of things not seen." Faith is not a human effort to believe but the inward assurance and conviction that results from God's presence and action.

Faith, accordingly, is man's response. Faith is made possible by God, but the faith, the believing, is not God's

his years of proclaiming the gospel Paul elsewhere wrote, "Christ has wrought through me to win obedience from the Gentiles, by word and deed, by the power of signs and wonders, by the power of the Holy Spirit" (Rom. 15:18-19).

[55]"Saving faith," consequently, does not mean that faith effectuates salvation. It is rather the human corollary to God's calling and election (as previously described). Still, without faith God's calling does not issue in salvation. It may be called "saving" to signify its necessity for salvation. Also this differentiates it from faith that is a special gift of God to the believer for doing mighty works (e.g., see 1 Cor. 12:9).

[56]By "faith," from here on, I mean "saving faith."

[57]Recall II.A., page 15.

[58]The Greek word is *elenchos*. BAGD gives "proof," "proving" as the first translation (prior to "conviction"). Thayer, likewise, states that *elenchos* means "a proof, that by which a thing is proved or tested."

but man's. A human being is fully engaged in the activity of faith.

Let us now turn to the nature of this faith.

B. Nature

Faith may be spoken of as containing three elements: knowledge, assent, and trust. We will consider these in turn.

1. Knowledge

Faith begins in the apprehension of God's redeeming work in Jesus Christ. It is a matter of hearing, hence understanding, the gospel and thereupon believing. In the words of Paul, "Faith comes from hearing the message, and the message is heard through the word of Christ" (Rom. 10:17 NIV). The "word of Christ" must be proclaimed, heard, and understood if faith is to eventuate.

This principle is well-illustrated in Peter's sermon on the Day of Pentecost (Acts 2:22–36). His message is basically informational; he tells his audience about Jesus Christ, His life, death, and resurrection. Peter begins by saying, "Men of Israel, hear these words." They must hear, that is, know about Jesus Christ, if they are to come to faith and salvation. Thus again, "faith comes from hearing"; it occurs through a true hearing about Christ.

Faith, accordingly, is not blind; indeed, a blind faith is not faith at all. Faith begins at the point of apprehending what God has done in Jesus Christ. This does not mean wide-ranging knowledge (this may occur later), but a simple understanding that through Jesus Christ there is salvation. The blinders are removed, and in resulting faith a person moves into the way of salvation.

It is important to stress the knowledge component of faith. In some mystical forms of religion, ignorance is touted as the way of salvation. Knowledge, presumably, is the barrier to spiritual unity with the great Unknown (or Unknowable). Hence, the human mind is to be set aside in the search for oneness with the Ultimate. Such forms of religion usually have no historical rootage in a divine act of redemption. Thus no knowledge is necessary: it is a matter of achieving mystical unity. From a biblical perspective, however, some knowledge is essential to faith and salvation.

We need to add quickly that knowledge is not in itself sufficient for salvation. One may be well informed about the things of God, including His work of redemption in Christ, and still be far from God. James writes, "You believe that God is one; you do well. Even the demons believe—and shudder" (James 2:19). To "believe that God is one" is good: "you do well." But such knowledge obviously is by no means enough: the demons also so believe.[59] Likewise, there may be knowledge about Jesus Christ and even His work of redemption but without such knowledge leading to salvation. Knowledge in and of itself has no saving significance.

Nonetheless, knowledge is the beginning point of faith. For there must be a basic understanding of the gospel message for salvation to occur.

2. Assent

Faith continues with assent to the word of the gospel. It is not only an apprehension of the message, but also an acknowledgment of it. It is saying yes to what is proclaimed.

Assent means the recognition of the truth of the gospel and of the personal need for Christ's saving work. Assent represents a growing realization that the gospel is for the one who hears it; it is knowledge passing into acknowledg-

---

[59] Demons mentioned in the Gospels also knew who Jesus Christ was. E.g., recall the demonic outcry to Jesus in Mark 1:24—"I know who you are, the Holy One of God."

29

ment. What begins as a mental perception now becomes a matter of genuine personal concern. It is assent to God's offer of salvation in Jesus Christ.

We must be careful to distinguish such assent from assent to doctrinal belief. There is sometimes a tendency in orthodoxy to identify faith with assent to a body of doctrine. Faith in that case is viewed as right belief, and salvation as assent to the doctrines of the church. For example, the Athanasian Creed begins: "Whoever will be saved: before all things it is necessary that he hold the Catholic Faith."[60] Therein salvation is said to depend on holding "the Catholic Faith"—namely, the body of doctrine set forth in the creed that follows. However important and correct the doctrines may be, it is surely an error to hold that salvation comes by orthodox affirmation and assent. Faith that saves is not directed to a body of doctrine but to Christ Himself in the gospel.

In relation to this latter point, let us recognize, nonetheless, that in the New Testament faith occasionally refers in a general sense to the gospel. Examples include Galatians 1:23—" 'He who once persecuted us is now preaching the faith he once tried to destroy' "; 1 Timothy 4:1—"In later times some will depart from the faith . . . "; Jude 3—"Contend for the faith which was once for all delivered to the saints." Such statements about "the faith" are quite important, for they do stress that there is a corpus of Christian truth.[61] However, it is *not* assent to this doctrinal content of the faith that is salvific. Rather, it is assent of mind and heart to the grace of God in Jesus Christ.

Faith that passes into acknowledg-

ment and assent is a critical second element in the occurrence of salvation.

3. Trust

Faith, lastly, is trust. Faith begins in knowledge, deepens in assent, and is completed in trust. It is the critical and final element in saving faith.

Faith as trust is complete reliance on God's promise in the gospel; it is total confidence in the mercy of God in Jesus Christ. Faith means to *believe in*.

Faith hears the word of the gospel and believes in it. Faith, accordingly, is reception of God's truth. After Peter's sermon at Pentecost, the Scripture reads that "those who received his word were baptized" (Acts 2:41). To believe the word means to trust in it and to depend on it as the way of salvation. Paul writes the Corinthians, "I preached to you the gospel, which you received, in which you stand, by which you are saved" (1 Cor. 15:1–2). It is firm reliance on the truth of the gospel.

But faith is more than believing in the good news; it is believing in the one whom God has sent, even Jesus Christ. It is not only receiving the word; it is also receiving *the Word*. According to John 1, the Word came into the world, and "to all who *received him,* who *believed in* his name, he gave power to become children of God" (v. 12). To believe in His name is to receive Him— and this means trust. The most vivid statement of this is in John 3:16—"For God so loved the world that he gave his only Son, that whoever believes in him should not perish but have eternal life." Hence, even beyond believing in His name, the heart of faith is belief in Jesus Christ personally—"in him." This in the profoundest sense is trust.

---

[60] See Philip Schaff, *The Creeds of Christendom,* vol. 2, *The Greek and Latin Creeds,* 66–71.

[61] Hence, there is value in church creeds, confessions, and various doctrinal statements. There is such a reality as *the* faith that calls for understanding, propagation, and defense. But *the* faith is *not* saving faith.

To trust in Jesus signifies the reposing of all confidence in Him. It is the kind of personal commitment that gives up any and all reliance on the self and looks wholly to Jesus Christ. It is the conviction that He is totally trustworthy, that in Him and Him alone is to be found full salvation, and that one must surrender all[62] to Him as Savior and Lord.

C. Climax

The climax of faith is union with Christ.[63] It is we in Christ and Christ in us. Faith is that kind of intimate relationship.

1. In Christ

One of the striking emphases of the New Testament is that all the blessings the believer knows are due to his being "in Christ" or "in Christ Jesus." Paul writes, "Blessed be the God and Father of our Lord Jesus Christ, who has blessed us in Christ with every spiritual blessing in the heavenly places" (Eph. 1:3); and after that he depicts the magnificent panorama of our being originally chosen "in him" (v. 4), redeemed "in him" (v. 7), and finally sealed "in him" (v. 13). This emphasis on being "in him," i.e., in Christ, is predicated on Paul's opening salutation to the Ephesians as "believers incorporate in Christ Jesus" (v. 1 NEB).[64] To be in Christ is to be incorporated by faith into Him.

This truly is the climax of faith. For faith is not only a matter of trust in Christ, thus of Christ as the object of faith; it is also—and most profoundly—the reality of being united with Him.[65] The climax of believing in Christ is being in Him.

Many biblical texts speak of being in Christ. Paul writes in Romans about being "alive to God in Christ Jesus" (6:11), and says later that there is "no condemnation for those who are in Christ Jesus" (8:1). In 2 Corinthians Paul declares, "If any one is in Christ, he is a new creation" (5:17), and in Ephesians are these words: "In Christ Jesus you who once were far off have been brought near in the blood of Christ" (2:13). All such texts emphasize that being in Christ is the very heart of faith.

Moreover, being in Christ is a unity of relationship. It is to be one with Him so that life finds its center in Him. Accordingly, this is not a unity of essence so that the believer loses his identity in Another.[66] Rather, it is a vital union in which the believer is constantly being invigorated and renewed by the life of Christ. The result, therefore, is not loss of personhood but

---

[62] The old acronym for F-A-I-T-H is still a good one: Forsaking All I Trust Him.

[63] The importance of this union with Christ is emphasized by Calvin: "Though we may be redeemed by Christ, still, until we are ingrafted into union with him by the calling of the Father, we are darkness, the heirs of death, and the enemies of God" (Institutes, III.14.6, Beveridge trans.).

[64] The Greek phrase pistois en Christō Iēsou. This could be translated as "faithful in Christ Jesus" (so KJV, RSV, NASB, NIV). However, the idea here is not so much that of faithfulness in Christ or even of Christ being the object of faith as it is of being in Him, namely, of being united with Him. As F. F. Bruce says, "The phrase 'in Christ' is incorporative—that is to say, it does not point to Christ Jesus as the object of belief but implies that the saints and the believers are united with him, partakers together of his new life" (The Epistles to the Colossians, to Philemon, and to the Ephesians, NICNT, 251).

[65] The preposition "in" as found in the expression "believing in Christ" (e.g., John 3:16) is eis, signifying "into," that is, into Christ as object of faith. The Greek preposition used for "in Christ" is en, which conveys much more the unitive sense.

[66] As in a mysticism where the goal is absorption into the divine. (Recall my earlier statement about some forms of mysticism.)

its true fulfillment in Jesus Christ. Some analogy of this is found on the human level where in marriage a man and woman become "one flesh" (Gen. 2:24). Rather than suffering a loss of identity, they find themselves fulfilled in each other.

Moreover, being in Christ is a spiritual union. As Paul puts it, "He who is united to the Lord becomes one spirit with him" (1 Cor. 6:17). The human spirit is joined with the Spirit of Christ so that Christ's Spirit operates in and through the believer's spirit. Consequently, on the deepest level of human nature there is oneness with Jesus Christ.

2. Christ in Us

The other side of the relationship brought about through faith is Christ in us. One of the most dramatic statements regarding this is the affirmation of Paul in Galatians 2:20—"I have been crucified with Christ; it is no longer I who live, but Christ who lives in me; and the life I now live in the flesh I live by faith in the Son of God, who loved me and gave himself for me." Christ lives in the believer—by faith.

Here, indeed, there is paradox. For in one sense the believer is dead—"crucified with Christ"—and no longer lives. Christ is the One who lives in him. Yet, in another sense, the believer lives—"I now live"—through faith in Christ. One truly lives when Christ lives in him.

Christ in us is also a mystery. Paul writes to the Colossians concerning "the glory of this mystery, which is

Christ in[67] you, the hope of glory" (1:27). There is no way of adequately comprehending the truth of Christ in the believer; hence, it is a mystery and indeed a glorious one.

But now we must also realize that Christ is in the believer through the Holy Spirit. Or, to put it another way, the dwelling of Christ in the believer is identical with the indwelling of the Spirit. In Romans Paul interchangeably uses these expressions: "the Spirit," "the Spirit of God," and "the Spirit of Christ"—all in reference to Christ's dwelling within (8:9–11).[68] Hence, Christ in us is not a bodily reality but a spiritual presence.

Faith, we now add, is the medium through which this occurs. Paul prays for the Ephesians "that Christ may dwell in your hearts through faith" (3:17). By faith the believer is united to Christ so that He comes to dwell within the heart, which is the center of human existence.

3. We in Christ and Christ in Us

Finally, faith is a union both of our being in Christ and of Christ's being in us. There is an inseparability of each from the other. One of the most expressive New Testament images is that of the vine as Christ and believers as branches: "I am the vine, you are the branches" (John 15:5). The branches are inseparably united to the vine and the vine to the branches. Another New Testament picture is that of the head and the body (e.g., Eph. 4:12, 15). Christ is the head and believers are His body.[69] The two, head and body, are

---

[67]The Greek preposition *en* could also be translated "among" (as in NEB mg) since Paul's words "how great among [*en*] the Gentiles" immediately precede "the glory of this mystery." However, "among" hardly seems appropriate for the second *en,* since the reference is to "Christ *en* you" as "the hope of glory." It is not Christ *among* people but *in* them, that is the hope of the glory to come.

[68]For a fuller discussion of this, see the next chapter, "Regeneration," III.A., "The Agency of the Spirit," pages 37–39.

[69]Paul speaks of "building up the body of Christ" and thereafter states that "we are to grow up in every way into him who is the head."

totally joined and function as one. Another metaphor also found in Ephesians is that of husband and wife wherein the two "become one" (5:31). Husband and wife ideally function in a mutuality of life together.

Truly the climax of faith is union with Christ. It is such a response to God's calling that the believer is in Christ and Christ in the believer. This is the meaning of faith in its fullest dimension.

2

Regeneration

At the heart of the reality of salvation is the doctrine of regeneration. As in the doctrine of effectual calling, the whole of salvation is included. Regeneration points particularly to the inward change that occurs in those who come to salvation.

I. DEFINITION

Regeneration means essentially rebirth: it is re-generation. Hence regeneration is a being born again or anew. The classic New Testament passage is these words of Jesus: "You must be born again"[1] (John 3:7 NASB). We may also note Peter's words to Christians "you have been born again" (1 Peter 1:23 NASB).[2] Paul declares to Titus that God "saved us . . . by the washing of regeneration[3] and renewing by the Holy Spirit" (Titus 3:5 NASB). These three passages stand out in their testimony to regeneration; and the last (in Titus) specifically relates this to salvation.

It is apparent that this is a *spiritual* rebirth. It is not a second physical birth,[4] but a rebirth that is spiritual. Jesus emphasized this in His words just prior to those about rebirth: "That which is born of the flesh is flesh, and that which is born of the Spirit is spirit" (John 3:6). Thus, through the Holy Spirit there is spiritual rebirth. The Old Testament looked forward to this. God spoke through Ezekiel concerning Israel: "I will give them one heart,[5] and put a new spirit within them" (Ezek. 11:19; see also 36:26). Jeremiah says: "I will

---

[1]The Greek word is *anōthen*. It is translated "again" also in the KJV and NIV; as "over again" in NEB. The RSV has "anew." It is also possible to translate *anōthen* "from above" (as in John 3:31 and 19:11). According to BAGD, the expression "*gennethenai anōthen* is purposely ambiguous and means both born from above and born again."

[2]Literally, "having been born again" or "regenerated." The Greek word is *anagegēnnēmenoi* (the "again," *ana*, being included in the participle).

[3]The word for "regeneration" here is *palingenesias* (from *palin*, "again," and *genesis*, "birth"). The only other New Testament use of *palingenesia* is in Matthew 19:28, referring there to the regeneration of the world in the *eschaton*.

[4]As, for example, in various religions that affirm reincarnation, i.e., the rebirth of the soul in a new human body or other forms of life.

[5]Or "a new heart" (RSV mg).

give them a heart[6] to know that I am the Lord" (Jer. 24:7). And the psalmist prays, "Create in me a clean heart, O God, and put a new and right spirit within me" (Ps. 51:10). Although the language of the Old Testament is not precisely that of rebirth, it points in the direction of a spiritual renovation for which the word "regeneration" is the fulfillment.

Regeneration, however, cannot be limited to one area of human nature. It is not only that the spirit, or heart, is made new, but the person himself is thereby *a new being*. As noted, Paul writes that God "saved *us*"—not just our spirits—as persons: *we* have been born again. Paul writes similarly elsewhere, "If any one is in Christ, he is a new creation; the old has passed away, behold, the new has come" (2 Cor. 5:17). The person is a new creature. This is the wonder of regeneration.

II. IMPORTANCE

Regeneration is an *imperative*. Again, in the words of Jesus: "You *must* be born again," that is, if you desire to see or enter the kingdom of God. Jesus had said to Nicodemus, "Truly, truly . . . unless one is born again, he cannot see the kingdom of God"; also "unless one is born of water and the Spirit, he cannot enter into the kingdom of God" (John 3:3 and 5 NASB).[7] Rebirth is the only way.

The human situation outside of re-generation is indeed a bleak one. Paul speaks in Romans of how people's minds have become darkened, their hearts impure, and their actions perverse (1:21–32). Hence, despite the fact that there are accomplishments of the mind, affections of the heart, and innumerable human activities, many of which are surely noteworthy, the pallor of death is on all. For Paul says elsewhere to believers: "You he made alive, when *you were dead* through the trespasses and sins in which you once walked" (Eph. 2:1–2). This, tragically, goes all the way back to the first man who by disobeying the word of God became spiritually dead (Gen. 2:17). In this way "sin came into the world through one man and death through sin, and so death spread to all men because all men sinned" (Rom. 5:12). The only hope for a human race spiritually dead is spiritual rebirth. And the marvel is that such a regeneration has become possible through Jesus Christ!

The message of the possibility of spiritual rebirth has never been more timely than today. In countless numbers of people there is the desire for something radically new to happen in their lives. They have tried many things, but whether successful or not, they often have a feeling of emptiness and confusion[8] at the center of all their efforts and activities. "If there were some way of starting over again,[9] not

---

[6]"Heart" and "spirit" thus are used interchangeably. Despite different nuances of meaning, they both basically refer to the inner life, the center of human personality.

[7]"The kingdom of God" is the sphere of salvation. Hence, it is essentially the same thing to say that one cannot see salvation and enter into it except through rebirth.

[8]Walter Lippmann some years ago wrote of the insight of higher religion that "unregenerate men can only muddle into muddle" (*A Preface to Morals*, 251).

[9]The following lines by an unknown author catch up the feeling of many:

I wish that there were some wonderful place
Called the land of beginning again
Where all our mistakes
And all our heartaches
Could be left like a shabby old coat at the door
And never put on again.

just repeating the same old mistakes, but to live truly meaningfully . . . if there really were a rebirth. . . . '' It is quite extraordinary how the language of "born again" is so current in our time: "born-again Christian"[10] is mentioned even in the public media, and a large number of Americans now speak of themselves as "born again."[11] Born again—rebirth—regeneration—such language doubtless is touching a vital nerve and bespeaks the contemporary interest in a reality of critical importance.

III. MEANS

But how is regeneration possible? How can such a miracle occur? To answer we need to consider basically two things: the Spirit and the word.[12] By the Holy Spirit and the word rebirth may occur.

A. The Agency of the Spirit

Regeneration is primarily the work of the Holy Spirit. We have already noted that Jesus said, "That which is born of the flesh is flesh, and that which is born of the Spirit is spirit." Hence, the second birth is by the Holy Spirit. Since this is a *spiritual* birth, there is no other possibility: it must come from the Holy Spirit.

This means a rebirth from God Himself. Accordingly, it is to be born "of God." According to the Gospel of John, it is to be "born, not of blood nor of the will of the flesh, nor of the will of man, but of God" (1:13). In John's first letter he spoke several times of the Christian as one "born of God" (3:9; 4:7; 5:4, 18).

It is clearly a supernatural birth—from God Himself.

It is significant to recall that even Jesus Himself was born of the Holy Spirit. According to the angelic messenger to Joseph, "that which is conceived[13] in her [Mary] is of the Holy Spirit" (Matt. 1:20). However, this of course was not his regeneration, but His generation. Nonetheless, Christ as the one to be first born of the Spirit, hence supernaturally, becomes the precursor of all who after Him, and because of Him, will be reborn of the Spirit, thus also supernaturally.

Only the Holy Spirit can bring about the marvel of regeneration. Even as in the original generation of the heavens and the earth it was the Spirit of God who moved across the dark waters and brought forth life, so in regeneration that same Spirit brings forth new life. Now the Spirit, who goes forth in the proclamation of the Word,[14] moves upon human beings who are in darkness and death and brings them to life again. This is the greatest miracle that any person can ever experience, for while one remains the same person, he is born anew in the whole of his being. It happens by the agency of the Spirit of the living God.

Before leaving the matter of the role of the Holy Spirit in regeneration, we need also to consider the significance of "water" and "washing." It will be recalled that Jesus, according to John 3:5, not only spoke of being born of the Spirit but also of being born of water: "Truly, truly, I say to you, unless one is born of water and the Spirit, he cannot enter the kingdom of God."

---

[10] Despite the tautology. A Christian is either "born again" or no Christian at all.

[11] According to one Gallup Poll, three in ten Americans (31 percent) describe themselves to be "born-again" Christians. However correct this figure, the significant fact is that the nomenclature of "born again" has become current.

[12] As was the case in our consideration of "Calling" (chapter 1). See the previous chapter, section III, "Method," pages 23–26.

[13] The Greek word is *gennēthen,* literally, "begotten" or "born."

[14] As described in chapter 1, IV.C.1.

"Water" here seems clearly to point to water baptism.[15] Indeed, just following this discourse with Nicodemus, the text reads: "After this Jesus and his disciples went into the land of Judea; there he remained with them and baptized" (v. 22). Water (in vv. 5 and 22) suggests cleansing, which indeed is one aspect of his new birth.[16] Similarly, as noted, Paul writes in Titus 3:5 of "the washing of regeneration and renewal in the Holy Spirit." Since "washing"[17] refers to the "bath" of baptism, the water of baptism is closely related to regeneration. This could have Old Testament connections with the Book of Ezekiel in which the Lord declares, "I will sprinkle clean water on you, and you will be clean. . . . I will give you a new heart and put a new spirit in you; I will remove from you your heart of stone and give you a heart of flesh. And I will put my Spirit in you" (36:25–27 NIV). Even as stated by Paul and Jesus, water precedes Spirit and is preparatory to the action of the Spirit.

It is significant to observe, however, that in relation to regeneration, water and the Spirit are not of equal importance. First, in the words just quoted from Ezekiel, regeneration clearly follows the sprinkling of water. Second, although the words of Jesus taken in themselves seem to suggest regeneration through both water and Spirit, nonetheless in his next statement, "That which is born of the flesh is flesh, and that which is born of the Spirit is spirit," Jesus did not mention water at all.[18] Hence while water is related to regeneration, the regeneration of the heart is actually by the Holy Spirit. Third, whereas the words of Paul speak of the "washing" or "bath," the actual regeneration and renewal[19] come from the Holy Spirit. Both regeneration and renewal are by the Holy Spirit. Baptism in all these cases points symbolically to the inward cleansing and renewal of the Holy Spirit.

A highly important conclusion may now be stated: there is no teaching of "baptismal regeneration" in the Bible. The water itself in baptism does not

---

[15]It is sometimes suggested that the phrase "born of water" has no reference to baptism. Nicodemus had just asked Jesus, "How can a man be born when he is old? Can he enter a second time into his mother's womb and be born?" (v. 4). To this Jesus replied, "Unless one is born of water and the Spirit, he cannot enter the kingdom of God" (v. 5). Jesus could have been referring to natural birth. For example, in rabbinic Hebrew "water" sometimes refers to semen (see C. K. Barrett, *The Gospel According to John,* 209; Leon Morris, *The Gospel According to John,* 217–18); thus "born of water" could refer to procreation. If this is what Jesus meant, he was saying that not only is a person born of water naturally, but he must also be born supernaturally. However, I hardly think that this is what Jesus intended, since "born of water" also refers to entrance into the kingdom of God: "Unless one is born of water and the Spirit, he cannot enter the kingdom of God."

[16]See hereafter. Incidentally, some persons hesitate to say that Jesus is referring to water baptism in v. 5 because such might imply baptismal regeneration. F. F. Bruce speaks contrariwise: "It is a pity when reaction against the notion of baptismal regeneration . . . leads to complete overlooking of the baptismal allusion in the words of Jesus" (*The Gospel of John,* 84–85). Jesus is definitely not affirming baptismal regeneration, since regeneration occurs essentially by the Spirit (as succeeding words in v. 8 clarify: "born of the Spirit").

[17]The Greek word is *loutrou.* The word *loutron* = "*bath, washing* of baptism" (BAGD). *Loutron* is "used in the N.T. and in eccles. writ. of *baptism*" (Thayer).

[18]Cf. the words of Jesus as reported in Mark 16:16: "He who believes and is baptized will be saved; but he who does not believe will be condemned." Baptism, which appears coordinate with belief for salvation in the first statement, is not mentioned in the second. The weight clearly is on belief, not baptism.

[19]The word translated "renewing" or "renewal" is *anakainoseōs* and refers to "the spiritual rebirth of men" (BAGD).

bring about rebirth.[20] Nor is there any suggestion that the Holy Spirit invests baptismal waters with regenerative power. Furthermore, regeneration may also occur without water baptism at all—as is apparent from a number of scriptural evidences.[21] Baptism is important, but it must not be viewed as in any way effecting regeneration. It is essential that we be fully aware that the Holy Spirit throughout remains the agent.

B. The Word Implanted

Regeneration, although immediately the work of the Holy Spirit, occurs through the implanting of the word. Remember these words of Peter: "You have been born again," to which he adds, "not of seed which is perishable, but imperishable, *that is,* through the living and abiding word of God. . . . And this is the word which was preached to you" (1 Peter 1:23, 25 NASB). We have previously discussed the role of the word in preaching.[22] Here we observe that it is "the living and abiding word of God," hence the living word that abides within, through which rebirth occurs. It is the word of the gospel that has penetrated to the inner being and as seed therein is activated by the Holy Spirit to bring forth new life.[23]

The importance of the implanted word was emphasized by Jesus Himself. In one of His parables Jesus spoke of a man sowing seed (Mark 4:3–9) and how some of the seed fell along the path, some on rocky ground, some among thorns, but also some "into good soil . . . [which] brought forth grain, growing up and increasing and yielding thirtyfold and sixtyfold and a hundredfold" (v. 8). The "good soil" signifies the heart open to receive the word that goes "into" it, and finding lodgment therein brings forth new life in increasing abundance. James, the brother of Jesus, writes, "Of his [God's] own will he brought us forth by the word of truth that we should be a kind of first fruits of his creatures" (1:18). It is by the implanted word, the word of the gospel, "the word of truth," that the Holy Spirit works the miracle of regeneration.

In the matter of the proclamation of the word,[24] we must now stress the importance of continued witness to it until the word finds entrance into the hearts of those who hear. To be sure, there are many whose hearts seem as hard as the stony ground and appear little likely to receive the word (as in Jesus' parable). However, we may also recall the powerful declaration of the Lord to Jeremiah: "Is not my word like

---

[20] First Peter 3:21 might seem to suggest such: "Baptism . . . now saves you, not as a removal of dirt from the body but as an appeal to God for a clear conscience, through the resurrection of Jesus Christ." The meaning is not that baptism in and of itself saves: it is rather "through the resurrection of Jesus Christ." The NIV puts it clearly: "It [baptism] saves you by the resurrection of Jesus Christ."

[21] E.g., Peter preached to the Gentiles in Caesarea and the Holy Spirit fell upon them, an unmistakable evidence of their regeneration. Only after that were they baptized (Acts 10:44–48; cf. 11:14–18). Also note Paul's words: "I am thankful that I baptized none of you except Crispus and Gaius. . . . For Christ did not send me to baptize but to preach the gospel" (1 Cor. 1:14, 17). These words clearly imply preaching resulting in salvation but without baptism. For a fuller discussion of baptism see pages 283–87.

[22] In the preceding chapter, "Calling."

[23] Witsius, early Reformed theologian, writes of regeneration as "the hyperphysical act of God, by which the elect man who is spiritually dead is imbued with new, divine life . . . from the incorruptible seed of God's word, fecundated by the transcendent power of the Spirit." Quoted in Heppe's *Reformed Dogmatics,* 518.

[24] Again, see chapter 1, "Calling."

fire . . . and like a hammer which breaks the rock in pieces?'' (Jer. 23:29). This may well be considered a challenge for continuing to bear witness especially in light of God's promise, ''I will remove from you your heart of stone and give you a heart of flesh'' (NIV).[25] The word that finally gets into the stoniest of hearts can be the word that makes the heart new!

This leads us also to emphasize again the ''sowing'' of the word in every way possible. For example, this is quite pertinent in the preparation of a child for the time when the Holy Spirit will bring him into salvation. Here is the importance of parents, Sunday school teachers, and pastors—indeed all who contribute to the planting of the word in the child's heart. The child is increasingly exposed to the word of the gospel and penetrated by it.[26] The word sown in the heart and activated by the Holy Spirit will surely bring forth salvation.

IV. OCCURRENCE

Regeneration relates to the total person in his heart, mind, and will. We have lately been focusing on the heart, for this is the center of needed change. However, the change includes also the mind and the will. According to the Great Commandment: ''You shall love the Lord your God with all your heart, and with all your soul, and with all your mind, and with all your strength'' (Mark 12:30).[27] In order to fulfill this commandment a total life-changing occur-

rence is necessary. Let us consider this in more detail.

A. Illumination

As was previously mentioned, the mind has been darkened by sin and evil. Accordingly, there is first need for *illumination* in order to apprehend the gospel of salvation. Paul writes that ''the god of this world has blinded the minds of the unbelievers, to keep them from seeing the light of the gospel of the glory of Christ'' (2 Cor. 4:4). This darkness, this blindness, can be overcome only by interior illumination. For the believer this has happened, for ''the God who said, 'Let light shine out of darkness,' . . . has shone in our hearts to give the light of the knowledge of the glory of God in the face of Christ'' (2 Cor. 4:6). The glory of God in the face of Christ: this is what the ''born again'' person knows through the light shining in his heart!

Because sin has darkened the mind, the illumination must, secondly, show man his desperate plight and his need for salvation. As the primary illustration of this, Peter's first sermon, on the Day of Pentecost, not only declared God's gracious action in Christ but also confronted the audience with their evil deed: ''This Jesus . . . you crucified and killed'' (Acts 2:23). The message climaxes with the words: ''Let all the house of Israel therefore know assuredly that God has made him both Lord and Christ, this Jesus whom you cru-

---

[25] These words from Ezekiel 36:26, previously quoted, are similarly found in Ezekiel 11:19.

[26] The Old Testament particularly speaks of the role of the parent in this connection: ''These words which I command you . . . shall be upon your heart; and you shall teach them diligently to your children, and shall talk of them when you sit in your house, and when you walk by the way, and when you lie down, and when you rise. And you shall bind them as a sign upon your hand, and they shall be as frontlets between your eyes. And you shall write them on the doorposts of your house and on your gates'' (Deut. 6:6–9). If this was important for the words of the law, how much more for the word of the gospel!

[27] The words of Jesus in Mark 12:30 (parallels in Matt. 22:37 and Luke 10:27) are essentially a quotation from Deuteronomy 6:5 (words preceding the quotation in footnote 26).

cified'' (Acts 2:36). Through such straightforward address in the power of the Spirit, Peter's hearers were brought to a more vivid awareness of their sin and evil. The blinders were removed under the stark and awful realization that they had put to death the Lord of glory. Peter's exposure of their sinful situation was essential if they were to come through to salvation. Paul's commission by the exalted Christ is another illustration of this: "I send you to open their[28] eyes, that they may turn from darkness to light and from the power of Satan to God" (Acts 26:17–18). Eyes must be opened to know one's serious need if there is to be a turning from darkness to light.

Let this point be emphasized: for regeneration to occur, a person must know that he is lost. This is more than merely a sense that one has made some mistakes. It is rather a sharp awareness that before a holy and loving God one is a sinner in desperate plight and needing salvation.[29] It is to know that one's whole life, whatever the outer appearance, is turned away from true devotion to God and turned in upon itself. It is to realize that in one's natural condition a person is without hope and "without God" (Eph. 2:12). The "god of this world," Satan, is the master of lies and deception so that people are blinded and even lulled into false security, not knowing that the way of the world is the way of death and destruction. Eyes must be opened by the word of God through the power of the Spirit so that people may move from darkness into light.[30]

This word of God includes the message of God's righteous and just requirements. These He has declared in His commandments, especially in the Decalogue; in the words of Jesus, especially in the Sermon on the Mount; and elsewhere in the Scriptures. It is unmistakably set forth that God not only requires external righteousness—such as not murdering, not committing adultery, not stealing, but also internal, such as not hating, not lusting, not falsely vowing.[31] Even more, the requirement goes far beyond the external by commanding love for one's enemies.[32] Such is the righteousness that God expects in His human creatures.[33] When this word truly opens one's eyes, there can be no pretense of innocence: a person knows, however much he may try to avoid it, that his condition before God and His righteousness is hopeless.

The realization of lostness is all the more intensified under the impact of the word, which declares that every sin is against God personally. If the psalmist could cry out, "Against thee, thee only, have I sinned, and done that which is evil in thy sight" (51:4), how much more must one who hears the message of Christ come to realize that he is guilty too. It is not only that some people two thousand years ago were responsible for putting to death the Lord of glory, but also you and I are— and every person is. "Were you there

---

[28] Referring to "the people" (the Jews) and "the Gentiles" who had just been mentioned.

[29] Witness these words of Augustine before his conversion: "For I felt that I was still the captive of my sins, and in my misery I kept crying 'How long shall I go on saying "tomorrow, tomorrow"? Why not now? Why not make an end of my ugly sins at this moment?' " (Confessions, Pine-Coffin trans., 8.12).

[30] Barth writes that a person now "sees what he did not previously see as a blind man, hears what he previously could not hear as a deaf man. . . because it was present to him only outwardly and not inwardly" (Karl Barth, Church Dogmatics IV/3, 512).

[31] Matthew 5:21–37.

[32] Matthew 5:38–47.

[33] Matthew 5:48—"You, therefore, must be perfect, as your heavenly Father is perfect."

when they crucified my Lord?"[34] The only possible answer, however terrible, must be yes. For in the actions of those who nailed Him to the tree it was not just Jews or Romans but all mankind collectively represented. Your sin, my sin, your guilt, my guilt—this is staggering beyond all imagination.

There can be no escaping the fact that "none is righteous, no, not one" (Rom. 3:10).[35] But to *know* this personally is necessary if one is to come into salvation. Hence, there must be an illumination of the human condition by the word of God. For it is only when a person knows he is a lost sinner that a radical change can occur.

Actually, the world, for all its knowledge, is a vast realm of spiritual darkness. Paul speaks of it as a "dominion[36] of darkness" (Col. 1:13). The wonder, however, for believers is that "He [God] has delivered us from the dominion of darkness and transferred us to the kingdom of his beloved Son." Surely such deliverance begins with the opening of blind eyes to the truth about God, about sin and evil, and the marvelous way God has wrought our salvation.[37]

We may close this section with the words of the blind man whose eyes Jesus opened: "Though I was blind, now I see" (John 9:25). This is the glad testimony of all whose eyes have been opened to the grace of God in Jesus Christ.

B. Conviction

For regeneration to take place there must also be a conviction of sin. This is more than illumination (which is basically a matter of the mind); it is an action of the Spirit that brings about a profound inner sense of guilt before God. It is a deep conviction of one's sinfulness and evil.

Doubtless the most striking illustration of conviction is that of the consequence of Peter's sermon at Pentecost: "Now when they heard this they were cut[38] to the heart, and said to Peter and the rest of the apostles, 'Brethren, what shall we do?'" (Acts 2:37). Rather than fighting back, or seeking to justify themselves, as well they might have under the accusation that they had put to death the long-hoped-for Messiah, they came under such conviction of sin and guilt that they could only cry out for help: "Men and brethren, *what shall we do?*" (KJV).

Let us ponder this phrase, "cut to the heart." The physical heart is the central vital organ of the body, circulating blood throughout. The heart spiritually is the innermost spring of human personality, hence such biblical expressions as "out of it [the heart] are the issues of life" (Prov. 4:23 KJV)[39] and "the words that the mouth utters come from the overflowing of the heart" (Luke 6:45 NEB). But alas, the tragedy of the human condition is that the heart has become hardened to the things of God. So does the Lord cry forth in the Old Testament: "The sin of Judah is

---

[34] A line from the gospel song that goes by that title.

[35] These words, quoted freely by Paul from Psalm 14:3, refer to Jew and Gentile alike.

[36] The Greek word is *exousias,* "domain" (NASB, NEB).

[37] Hence this is a matter of knowledge. Recall what was said on page 29 about the fact that faith begins with knowledge. Indeed, illumination of the mind (the subject of the present section) and the beginning of faith as knowledge are identical moments in the initial stage of salvation (or regeneration).

[38] The Greek word is *katenygēsan,* "pierced" (NASB). The word is used only here in the New Testament and conveys the idea of feeling a sharp pain, thus being "pierced," "stabbed," "smitten" in heart. (KJV "pricked" does not sufficiently convey this deep note.)

[39] Or "from it flow the springs of life" (RSV, NASB); "it is the wellspring of life" (NIV).

written with a pen of iron; with a point of diamond it is engraved on the tablet of their heart" (Jer. 17:1). Jesus Himself, in the presence of the Pharisees, was "grieved[40] at their hardness of heart" (Mark 3:5). Paul speaks of mankind as having a "hard and impenitent heart" (Rom. 2:5). Man's only hope in this lamentable situation is that somehow his heart can be so cut, pierced, and smitten as to come under conviction of sin and evil until (like the Jews at Pentecost) there is a desperate outcry for help and salvation.

Let us be careful to understand this correctly. Conviction of sin is far more than a feeling of misery or remorse. There are countless numbers of people who may—and often do—feel sorrow and pain, their lives being on the edge of despair. There may be occasional, even continuing, remorse for actions they have done. Paul speaks of a "worldly grief"[41] that only "produces death" (2 Cor. 7:10). It is "a sorrow of the world," which many know, but it contains no real conviction of sin. Judas doubtless felt remorse for what he had done to Jesus; indeed, he cried out, "I have sinned in betraying innocent blood" (Matt. 27:4), but there was no "godly grief [that] produces a repentance that leads to salvation" (2 Cor. 7:10). Rather Judas went out and hanged himself. Many in the world also experience "worldly grief" that sometimes leads even to suicide. But they have no genuine conviction of sin, no "godly grief," the grief and sorrow toward God that leads to salvation.

Only the Holy Spirit can bring this about. In the words of Jesus: "He . . . will convict[42] the world concerning sin" (John 16:8 NASB). No human persuasion, regardless of how pointed and direct, can produce the deep inward realization of one's sinful condition before God. The *Holy* Spirit, verily the Spirit of holiness, probing the inner recesses of the human heart, is like a light exposing all that is evil, impure, and ungodly. What previously may never have been sensed as sin is now experienced in all its heinousness. Indeed, to put it more succinctly, the Holy Spirit utilizes the implanted word (the word of God's holiness and righteousness) and brings the sinner under the judgment that prepares the way for salvation.

We have now arrived at a critical turning point. For here we observe that this very conviction of sin not only signifies a deep realization but also brings about a profound internal change. For the "cutting" of the heart is not only a cutting *into* but also a cutting *away*! Let us, in this connection, first recall the word of God as spoken through Moses to Israel: "The LORD your God will circumcise your heart and the heart of your offspring, so that you will love the LORD your God with all your heart and with all your soul, that you may live" (Deut. 30:6). Physical circumcision—the cutting away of the flesh as required in the Abrahamic covenant—is the precursor of the circumcision of the heart—the cutting away of sin that will result in spiritual life. Thus Paul is able to say, "Circumcision is a matter of the heart"

---

[40]The Greek word is *syllypoumenos*, literally, "deeply grieved"; NIV reads "deeply distressed."

[41]The Greek phrase is *hē tou kosmou lupē*, literally, "the grief ['sorrow' (KJV)] of the world."

[42]Instead of "convince" (RSV) or "reprove" (KJV). The Greek word is *elenxei*. According to TDNT (2:74), it means "to show someone his sin and to summon him to repentance," hence "convict." The NIV translation, "convict the world of guilt in regard to sin," conveys the idea excellently.

(Rom. 2:29), and it occurs "by the Spirit."[43] Thus we behold the office of the Holy Spirit in the "circumcision" that brings eternal life. And this includes Jew and Gentile alike, for to quote Paul again: "Neither [fleshly] circumcision counts for anything, nor uncircumcision, but a new creation" (Gal. 6:15).

The point now is—and it is an extraordinary one indeed—that the "circumcision" of the heart is possible through Jesus Christ! And it occurs through faith in Him[44] whereby His Spirit in transforming power performs the miracle of cutting away the old to make the heart ready for a total change.

To conclude: all this happens when the Holy Spirit so applies the word that there is a profound conviction of sin. For when the heart is pierced through with the realization of the heinousness of one's sin and guilt, the miracle of regeneration soon follows.

Finally, we need to raise two questions in relation to our Christian witness to others:

First, do we so witness as to let the Holy Spirit through the word bring about conviction? Are people "cut to the heart"? Is there profound sorrow over sin? We read in Scripture that Peter, after his threefold denial of Christ, "went out and wept bitterly" (Luke 22:62). Does this happen today? Is there a growing sense of the intolerable burden of sin that is being carried around? Do people so hear our testimony to the righteousness of God that they become convinced that all their righteousness is like "filthy rags" (Isa. 64:6 KJV) and nothing but judgment awaits? But along with this, do they apprehend the mercy of God, the everlasting mercy, that in Jesus Christ is poured out to bring forth salvation?

Second, are we willing to let conviction deepen? If the Spirit is to probe the inmost recesses of the heart, this may take time as He pierces through one layer after another, breaks through one barrier after another. This, incidentally, is the advantage of revival meetings over several days, even weeks, in which there can be growing conviction of sin, for sometimes people need time to "come under conviction." Do we make the "mourner's bench" available to them? Or are we so eager to get people to "accept" Christ that we fail to ascertain whether it is a matter of the heart? For, in the words of Paul, a "man believes with his heart" (Rom. 10:10). But has the heart been probed under a profound conviction of sin, so much that, like the tax collector, one who hears may "beat his breast, saying, 'God, be merciful to me a sinner!'" (Luke 18:13)?

C. Repentance

The climactic moment that makes for regeneration is the moment of repentance. For it is in repentance that a person turns from the old to the new, from darkness to light, from the dominion of Satan to the power of God, from the way of destruction to the way of eternal salvation.

Here it is important to stress the grace and mercy of God to the convicted sinner; namely, that if he now turns to God, he will be fully received. God has no desire to condemn anyone for his sinfulness but to save him from it: "God sent not his Son into the world to

---

[43] Thus NASB, NIV, NEB. The RSV has "spiritually"; KJV, "in the spirit"; the Greek phrase is *en pneumati*. Although any of these translations is possible, the context suggests "by the Spirit."

[44] This faith is more than knowledge that the Spirit of Christ can accomplish this radical change; it is also assent to His doing it. (See chapter 1, IV.B.2 with the concluding statement about "faith that passes into acknowledgment and assent.")

condemn the world; but that the world through him might be saved" (John 3:17 KJV). While there must be both an awareness of sin and a deep conviction of guilt, this is not to bring a person under condemnation. It is rather to prepare the way for a life-transforming return to God through Jesus Christ. Truly the righteous and holy God finds all sin intolerable, but—and this is the wonder of the Gospel—He gladly receives back to Himself the repentant sinner.

In the Old Testament there is frequently the call to Israel to repent, to return to God. One of the most powerful statements is that of Solomon concerning Israel: "If they sin against thee . . . so that they are carried away captive to a land far or near; yet if they lay it to heart . . . and repent . . . saying, 'We have sinned, and have acted perversely and wickedly'; if they repent with all their mind and with all their heart . . . then hear thou from heaven . . . and forgive thy people" (2 Chron. 6:36–39). There must be a full recognition of sinfulness—"We have sinned . . . perversely and wickedly." There must also be a profound conviction of heart—"if they lay it to their heart." And there must be withal a total repentance: "if they repent with *all their mind* and *all their heart*." It is of vital significance and importance that after Solomon's prayer God said to him, "If my people who are called by my name humble themselves, and pray and seek my face, and turn from their wicked ways, then I will hear from heaven, and will forgive their sin and heal their land" (2 Chron. 7:14). This is the climax: not only must there be an awareness and conviction of sin (as Solomon called for); there must also be *a turning* from it—"from their wicked ways." For it is in the turning from sin that repentance reaches its culmination. A turning to God that does not stem from awareness and conviction will surely be superficial;[45] an awareness and conviction that does not result in turning will inevitably be incomplete. Repentance therefore climaxes in the *will*: it is a movement of the whole self away from sin to God. Further, it occurs in the assurance that God will forgive: "I will hear from heaven, and will forgive their sin."

Despite the call of God in the Old Testament for repentance (for example, "Turn back, turn back from your evil ways; for why will you die, O house of Israel?" [Ezek. 33:11]), there never was a full turning. Doubtless, this failure was deeply grounded in both spiritual blindness and hardness, a condition that goes back to the beginning of human history. Man as such is a fallen creature, one who (as Paul puts it) has become "futile in . . . thinking" with "senseless minds . . . darkened" (Rom. 1:21).[46] Hence, although God discloses the way that leads to life, Israel neither fully comprehended nor ever truly walked in it. Whether God lovingly sought to bring Israel back to himself[47] or harshly declared His righteous judgments of destruction and death (as quoted in Ezekiel), there was no ade-

---

[45] The words of 2 Chronicles 7:14 are frequently used today in calling people (sometimes a nation) to repentance. Surely this is good. However, if there is not a prior realization of what sin is (its contravening of God's holiness and righteousness) and a deep conviction of human perverseness and unrighteousness, there can be no genuine turning to God. Incidentally, this is doubtless the reason why many of the well-intended appeals for repentance accomplish so little: those addressed are not existentially prepared for it.

[46] Paul speaks elsewhere of "the Gentiles" (people at large) as living in "the futility of their minds . . . darkened in their understanding, alienated from the life of God . . . [with] hardness of heart; they have become callous" (Eph. 4:17–19).

[47] E.g., in Hosea 2:14–23.

quate response from His people. So the Old Testament ends.[48]

With the dawning of the New Testament era of the gospel, life-transforming repentance at last becomes a possibility. The call to repentance was present from the outset as John the Baptist proclaimed, "Repent, for the kingdom of heaven is at hand" (Matt. 3:2). Multitudes came to the Jordan River to be baptized, "confessing their sins" (3:6), and thereupon received stern admonition from John to "bear fruit that befits repentance"[49] (3:8). The Baptist's proclamation, however, was only preparatory for the coming of Jesus. After John's arrest, Jesus likewise called for repentance,[50] but with the decisive sense of fulfillment: "Jesus came into Galilee, preaching the gospel of God, and saying, 'The time is fulfilled, and the kingdom of God is at hand; repent, and believe in the gospel'" (Mark 1:14–15). The "gospel of God," for which John prepared the way, makes possible a repentance that is life-transforming.[51] Although Jesus continued to call for repentance throughout His ministry,[52] it is only after His death and

resurrection that the gospel proclamation can elicit a genuine and total repentance.

We come once more to Pentecost and the message of Simon Peter. We have noted how Peter declared Jesus' life, death, and resurrection with the result that the assembly was brought under profound conviction of sin, crying out, "Brethren, what shall we do?" Next we observe Peter's reply: "Repent, and be baptized every one of you in the name of Jesus Christ for the forgiveness of your sins" (Acts 2:38). While the word "repent" is not different from that spoken by Old Testament prophets, by John the Baptist, or even by Jesus Himself, the vast difference is that radical repentance[53] is finally possible. It at last is a "repentance unto life";[54] it is the doorway into the kingdom, it is entrance into eternal life.

What brings about this profound repentance? Surely it is the message that in Jesus Christ there is forgiveness of sins. For the Jerusalem multitude this meant that in spite of their heinous sin in crucifying the Lord of glory,[55] they

---

[48]This is not to discount, for example, the confession of sin made by the Israelites returned from exile. According to Nehemiah 9:2, "the Israelites separated themselves from all foreigners, and stood and confessed their sins and the iniquities of their fathers." However, the changes refer largely to such matters as mixed marriages, Sabbath observance, and temple obligations (see especially Neh. 10:28–39). There was no radical repentance that led to life.

[49]See, e.g., the practical instructions to the multitudes, to the tax collectors, and to the soldiers in Luke 3:10–14.

[50]See Matthew 4:17 where Jesus is recorded as speaking the identical message of John: "Repent, for the kingdom of heaven is at hand."

[51]Although people repented under John's preaching, the repentance had no life-changing character. John in his ministry spoke of "the ax . . . laid to the root" (Luke 3:9), but he had no way of rooting out the sin. It was only when "the gospel of God" was proclaimed that people could come to genuine repentance.

[52]Early in His ministry Jesus said, "I have not come to call the righteous, but sinners to repentance" (Luke 5:32). These words bespeak His continuing concern.

[53]The root of sin (see earlier note) is eradicated in radical repentance ("radical" is from the Latin word *radix* = "root").

[54]Later, after the Gentiles at Caesarea heard the gospel and believed, it was said of them, "Then to the Gentiles also God has granted repentance unto life" (Acts 11:18). Thus it was "repentance unto life" for both Jews and Gentiles.

[55]Paul speaks of Jesus Christ as "the Lord of glory" in 1 Corinthians 2:8. Also cf. James 2:1.

could receive forgiveness. Indeed, by faith in the very One they had sinned against so terribly, they might now be granted full forgiveness. Such an extraordinary message of God's grace in Christ—a message, not of condemnation (which they knew they deserved), but of mercy and compassion—had the power to lead them from conviction of their sin into total repentance. Amazing grace: God forgives in spite of all that we have done! With the overwhelming realization of that fact, they could repent with all their mind and all their heart, turn from their wicked ways, and enter into salvation.[56]

Repentance and forgiveness are closely related in the gospel message. Jesus Himself had instructed His disciples that "repentance and forgiveness of sins should be preached in his name to all nations, beginning from Jerusalem" (Luke 24:47). "In his name" means that through Christ and because of what He has accomplished, repentance and forgiveness may be received. And "beginning from Jerusalem"[57] implied that this message is to be proclaimed everywhere else. Hence, it means that the message is just as relevant today to all the peoples of the

world as it was in Jerusalem twenty centuries ago.

Let me be specific. The heart of the gospel is this: no matter how great our sins, God pours forth forgiveness through Christ to those who truly repent. If God could forgive those who were actually involved in the crucifixion of His Son two thousand years ago— the greatest sin ever—then His forgiveness is available to you and me. As we hear that message in faith, become convicted of our sinfulness, acknowledge our desperate need of salvation, and turn from our sins to God, we enter into salvation. Verily it is "repentance that leads to salvation,"[58] it is "repentance until life."[59] It is life-transforming repentance.

Repentance, we may now emphasize, is a *turning* from the old to the new. While it includes the mind[60] and heart, as we have seen, it is an action of the will. It is the climactic moment in regeneration in which the whole person turns to move in a totally new direction. Further, this turning stems from an abhorrence[61] of the sin and evil that has held one fast, and represents a 180-degree change from the old life to a new life.[62] This means a radical break with

---

[56] Recall Solomon's words (earlier quoted) to Israel: "If they repent with all their mind and all their heart . . . and turn from their wicked ways, then I will . . . forgive their sin." *What Israel could never fully do is at last possible through Jesus Christ.*

[57] We have already noted the initial proclamation in Jerusalem: "Repent and be baptized in the name of Jesus Christ for the forgiveness of your sins." Peter again appealed to the Jews in Acts 3:19: "Repent, then, and turn to God, so that your sins may be wiped out [i.e., forgiven]" (NIV). Later Peter and his fellow apostles declared: "God exalted him [Christ] at his right hand as Leader and Savior, to give repentance to Israel and forgiveness of sins" (Acts 5:31).

[58] Recalling 2 Corinthians 7:10.

[59] Recalling Acts 11:18.

[60] The word for "repentance" in all the accounts we have quoted is from the Greek word *metanoia*. Literally, this means "a change of mind" (mind = *nous*). Hence, the mind is involved (as in the Old Testament words "if they repent with all their mind") and so is the heart ("if they repent with all their heart"). However, *metanoia* points more in the direction of the will.

[61] According to Thayer, *metanoia* means "heartily to amend with abhorrence of one's past sins."

[62] Repentance with such a change is memorably set forth in Jesus' parable of the prodigal

the past—old ways, old habits, old attitudes—and entrance into a glorious new world in which Christ is Savior and Lord.

This brings us to another term, namely, *conversion*. Conversion means a turning from sin and a turning to God. The word repent" in itself conveys the note of conversion.[63] But "repent" in Scripture may also be used in conjunction with another word that specifically means turn, as, for example, in Peter's words: "Repent, then, and turn[64] to God, so that your sins may be wiped out" (Acts 3:19 NIV). Paul uses similar language to describe his mission to Jews and Gentiles: that "they should repent and turn to God" (Acts 26:20). Both repentance and turning express the idea of conversion. Conversion, however, may suggest even more vividly than repentance this idea of a total alteration,[65] the turning of an individual from the old life of sin and evil to the new life of God.

Hence, the term "conversion" may express in itself the occurrence of salvation as in Acts 15:3, "the conversion[66] of the Gentiles." In that case, conversion is not only the act of repentance in which the climactic moment leading to regeneration occurs (following upon illumination and conviction); it is also a way of speaking of the totality of salvation. Accordingly, conversion may stand for both salvation and regeneration.[67] Nothing else need be added.

The word conversion also may be used to express the whole idea of repentance and faith in which salvation occurs. Later in Acts Paul spoke of "testifying both to Jews and to Greeks of repentance to God and of faith in our Lord Jesus Christ" (20:21). Repentance and faith[68] may accordingly be viewed as the constituents of the conversion referred to in Acts 15:3. Since to convert, to turn, is two-sided, repentance and faith may well express both aspects that make up the totality of salvation.

Now to return specifically to the word "repentance," it is important on the practical side to give opportunity for repentance to be expressed. We have spoken earlier about the need for allowing conviction to deepen so that a person's inmost being is probed by the Holy Spirit. In regard to repentance it is

---

son (Luke 15:11–32). When the son "came to himself" (v. 17), he turned back to his father in repentance and received complete forgiveness.

[63] The call to repentance is the call to conversion. According to TDNT, *metanoia* means "convert, conversion" (9:999).

[64] The Greek word is *epistrepsate* (from *epi*, "to," and *strephō*, "turn"). The KJV translates as "be converted" which, while properly speaking of conversion, wrongly uses the passive voice instead of the middle or reflexive voice. Conversion is *not a being converted but a converting*, a turning to God.

[65] This is true in secular usage also. To convert, e.g., may mean to alter the physical or chemical nature of one form into another.

[66] The Greek word is *epistrophēn*.

[67] Conversion, accordingly, is neither the result of regeneration nor prior thereto. Louis Berkhof regards conversion as *"that act of God whereby He causes the regenerated sinner . . . to turn to Him in repentance and faith"* (*Systematic Theology*, 483), hence results from regeneration. Millard J. Erickson, on the other hand, declares that "the biblical evidence favors the position that conversion is prior to regeneration" (*Christian Theology*, 3:932). Both views fail to recognize the integral nature of regeneration and conversion.

[68] There is no priority of one over the other. Previously under "Calling" I discussed that we are called to faith in Jesus Christ. Nothing was said about repentance in regard to calling; however, it is apparent that the very act of faith is a turning to Christ *from* something else, namely, the old life. Since a turning from is the basic idea in repentance, Paul refers to repentance and faith in that order (cf. Heb. 6:1, which speaks of "a foundation of repentance from dead works and of faith toward God").

quite important that a person give outward evidence of his turning to Christ. For example, this can mean coming forward in response to an evangelist's invitation to give public expression to one's faith. Since repentance involves the will, action is needed. "O Lamb of God, I come, I come,"[69] not only sung but also enacted, can represent that climactic moment of repentance when by the very act of walking down an aisle, the old life is left behind and a new life with Christ is begun. Most importantly, there needs to be the outward confession of the lips. For when such confession is from a believing heart, it is not only a verbal demonstration of repentance; it is also an essential expression. As Paul puts it: "If you confess with your lips that Jesus is Lord and believe in your heart that God has raised him from the dead, you will be saved" (Rom. 10:9). Confession with the lips—the culmination of repentance—is the final moment that leads to salvation.

One further word about repentance: it is a gift from God. This needs to be stressed because so much has been said about various actions involved in repentance that the impression could be given that repentance is basically a human work. Repentance, to be sure, is very much an act of human beings; however, it can occur only through God's gracious enabling. I have before quoted the words "repentance unto life"; now let us note the fuller statement: "To the Gentiles also God has granted repentance unto life" (Acts 11:18). Regarding this granting (or giving) we may also recall these words of

Peter about Jesus: "God exalted him at his right hand as Leader and Savior, to give repentance to Israel and forgiveness of sins" (Acts 5:31). Repentance, along with forgiveness, is God's wondrous gift.

Repentance, accordingly, is not doing penance by which we may hope to achieve a relationship with God. We may be forever grateful that such is not the case, for we could never be sure that we had done enough. Repentance, rather, stems from God's gracious deed in Jesus Christ whereby our eyes are enlightened, our hearts convicted, *and* our wills enabled to turn away from sin and bondage to eternal life and liberty. Thanks be unto God!

Lastly in the act of repentance there is such a turning from sin to Christ that one is united with Him. Immediately following Peter's message at Pentecost to repent, he added, "And be baptized every one of you in the name of Jesus Christ" (Acts 2:38). To be baptized points to an immersion in Christ so that the person who is baptized is thereby identified with Him.[70] Hence the climax of repentance is union with Christ: the believer in Christ, and Christ in the believer.[71] Truly this is repentance unto life.

Christ in the believer and the believer in Christ is a spiritual union. It is a union with the Spirit of Christ, the Holy Spirit, so that the believer is in the Spirit and the Spirit in him. The Holy Spirit, who has been the primary agent in regeneration, now becomes the resident factor in the believer's life. Such a one, to use Paul's language, is "a temple of the Holy Spirit" (1 Cor. 6:19). The believer operates out of a

---

[69] Words from the hymn "Just as I Am, Without One Plea."

[70] Paul writes that "as many of you as were baptized into Christ have put on Christ" (Gal. 3:27).

[71] Accordingly, the climax of faith and repentance is the same. In chapter 1, "Calling," I wrote of the climax of faith as union with Christ. Since faith and repentance are two sides of the same activity—faith being a "turning to" Christ and repentance a "turning from" sin—they both culminate in union with Christ.

new center, not his own spirit but the Spirit of the living God. Indeed, this is the very touchstone of being a Christian: "Any one who does not have the Spirit of Christ does not belong to [literally, "is not of"] him" (Rom. 8:9). Paul elsewhere urges the importance of self-examination in this connection: "Examine yourselves to see whether you are in the faith; test yourselves. Do you not realize that Christ Jesus is in you—unless, of course, you fail the test?" (2 Cor. 13:5 NIV). *The one essential thing that marks the true Christian is that the Holy Spirit, the Spirit of Christ, dwells within.* Nothing else can substitute. For it is only by the presence of the indwelling Spirit that all things become new.

V. RESULT: A NEW CREATURE

In regeneration a person becomes a new creature. He is no longer born of the flesh, but of the Spirit: "If any one is in Christ, he is a new[72] creature[73]; the old has passed away, behold, the new has come" (2 Cor. 5:17). One is still the same person, but the old in terms of the former sin-dominated existence is no longer there: all things have become new.

A. A New Being

Regeneration brings about a radical alteration in man's being—his heart, his mind, his will. This may be described in terms of a changed heart, a renewed mind, and a liberated will.

1. A Changed Heart

Regeneration occurs primarily in the central area of man's being, namely, his heart or spirit. In this deepest level of human existence there is a decisive change.[74] In the Old Testament period God had spoken through the prophet Ezekiel to His people: "A new heart I will give you, and a new spirit I will put within you; and I will take out of your flesh the heart of stone and give you a heart of flesh" (Ezek. 36:26). This signifies a radical alteration.

First, we may speak of a *cleansing* of the heart. The heart of sinful man is the source of many evils. In the words of Jesus: "Out of the heart come evil thoughts, murder, adultery, fornication, theft, false witness, slander" (Matt. 15:19). The heart, accordingly, needs to be washed clean. This occurs through what Paul calls "the washing of regeneration" (Titus 3:5).[75] When regeneration occurs, the heart is cleansed basically of every kind of evil. The Gentiles who had experienced "repentance unto

---

[72] The Greek word for "new" in 2 Corinthians 5:17 is *kainos*. *Kainos* refers to what is new in quality or nature. In that sense the new as *kainos* is not the appearance of something that did not exist before but the making new or renovating of what was already there. (*Kainos* is quite different from another word for new, *neos*. According to Johannes Behm in TDNT, *neos* signifies "what was not there before," "what has only just arisen or appeared," what is "new in time or origin"; *kainos,* "what is new and distinctive," "new in nature," what is "essentially different from the old divine order" [3:447, 449]. Similarly, according to Thayer, *neos* "denotes the new primarily in reference to time, the young, the recent"; *kainos* "denotes the new primarily in reference to quality, the fresh, the unworn" [article on καινός]. The new, consequently, may also be spoken of as the "renewed" (as in the "renewed mind"), but so renewed as to be qualitatively different from what was before.

[73] Substituting "creature" (as in KJV, NASB) for "creation." The Greek word *ktisis* can be translated either way. Paul also speaks of "a new *ktisis*" in Galatians 6:15: "For neither circumcision counts for anything, nor uncircumcision, but a new *ktisis.*"

[74] Emil Brunner writes, "Regeneration consists in this, that in this invisible core of personality the great, eternally decisive change takes place that 'Christ is formed in us' through the death of the old man and the creation of the new . . . " (*Dogmatics*, 3:273–74).

[75] Recall the earlier discussion in III.A about this verse.

life'' were later described by Peter as having had their hearts cleansed: "He [God] made no distinction between us and them, but cleansed their hearts by faith"[76] (Acts 15:9). Thus their hearts were made clean before God.

This cleansing of the heart is a wondrous aspect of regeneration. Recall that the psalmist cried out, "Behold, thou dost desire truth in the innermost being [i.e., the heart]. . . . Purify me with hyssop, and I shall be clean; Wash me, and I shall be whiter than snow" (51:6–7 NASB). These words, probably spoken by David after his sins of adultery and murder,[77] call for the deepest kind of cleansing. We may, therefore, be all the more grateful that through repentance from sin and faith in Christ the heart of any person may receive a full cleansing. One may be "born again"—the slate made clean and a new life stretching ahead![78]

Second, there is the inscribing of God's *law* on the heart. One of the chief problems in the Old Testament period was the inability of people to keep God's law. The Israelites, regardless of all their efforts, never lived up to God's command: it was inscribed on stones but not on their hearts. Hence, one of the great promises of a future covenant was, "I will put my law within them, and I will write it upon their hearts" (Jer. 31:33, cf. Heb. 8:10). Thus the partakers of the new covenant have God's law newly inscribed[79] on their

hearts so that they can truly do what God commands.

This is one of the most beautiful aspects of regeneration. The old and impossible struggle to keep God's law, the continual turning from God's command to pursue one's own ends, the inward conflict brought about by the failure to live up to conscience—all such is essentially done away with by God's transforming the heart. I have earlier referred to the "circumcision of the heart," the cutting away of the old. Now we speak of the cutting in of the new, the inscribing of God's law so that we are able to fulfill God's law and purpose.

Third, there is a *unification* of the heart. Ezekiel prophesied this to Israel: "I will give them one heart" (11:19), hence an "undivided heart" (NIV). This implies a heart that will no longer be torn by many, often contrary, affections and emotions, but a heart that is united before God. In Jeremiah is this promise: "I will give them one heart and one way" (32:39), hence "singleness of heart and action" (NIV translation). We may also look back to the psalmist (possibly David) who prayed, "Teach me thy way, O LORD, that I may walk in thy truth; unite my heart to fear thy name" (86:11). This uniting, this singleness makes possible the fulfillment of the Great Commandment, which begins: "Hear, O Israel: The LORD our God, the LORD is one"[80] (Deut. 6:4 NIV).

---

[76] Repentance and faith are again seen to be closely related.

[77] Adultery in relation to Bathsheba; murder in connection with having Uriah, Bathsheba's husband, killed (see 2 Sam. 11).

[78] This does not mean that no taint of sin and evil remains. As I will discuss later (chapter 4, "Sanctification"), despite the new birth and the Spirit's indwelling, there is still the "flesh" and an ongoing warfare between Spirit and "flesh." Nonetheless, whatever the struggle that lies ahead, the radically new has begun in regeneration.

[79] There is the natural law written on the hearts of all men (see Rom. 2:15: "What the law requires is written on their hearts"). The conscience attests this; however, because of man's fallen and sinful nature, he does not truly obey God ("no one does good, not even one" [Rom. 3:12]). Thus there is needed a new and lasting inscription.

[80] The RSV reads, "The LORD our God is one Lord" but has the NIV reading in the margin. The NASB is almost identical with the NIV.

Then follows: "And you shall love the LORD your God with all your heart" (v. 5).[81] Even as the Lord is one, so the heart must be one that we may love God unitedly and totally. Truly, through the miraculous act of regeneration we are given a new heart, a heart that is one and single, that we may love God with all our being.

Also in regard to the other part of the Great Commandment, "You shall love your neighbor as yourself," as cited in the New Testament,[82] it is apparent that this can be done only from singleness of heart. The earliest Christian believers were said to be "of one heart and soul" (Acts 4:32). Their fervent oneness was the result of the uniting of their hearts through faith in Christ. Prior to their becoming new creatures in Christ, the state of people is that of separation and estrangement from others. Through the wonder of new birth, there is at last the realization of a unity that binds people together in genuine love and concern.

2. A Renewed Mind

Regeneration is also, quite importantly, a matter of the mind: the mind is renewed. Paul writes, "In reference to your former manner of life, . . . lay aside the old self . . . and . . . be renewed in the spirit of your mind" (Eph. 4:22–23 NASB). This refers to such a basic effect on the mind that it is actually made new[83] in the sense that it takes on a totally different attitude[84] or orientation from what it had before. As we have observed, before regeneration persons are blind to the things of God.

Paul speaks of how in their sinful condition people "became futile in their thinking and their senseless minds were darkened" (Rom. 1:21). This does not mean that the mind of a sinful person is incapable of thinking; such an idea would be absurd in light of all the accomplishments in civilization made possible through human mental faculties. But Paul's words do declare that in regard to the knowledge of God and His ways—which is the truly critical knowledge—unregenerate man is utterly incompetent.

Let us recall for a moment the strong biblical emphasis on the knowledge of God. Through the prophet Jeremiah the Lord said, "Let not the wise man glory in his wisdom, let not the mighty man glory in his might, let not the rich man glory in his riches; but let him who glories glory in this, that he understands and knows me" (Jer. 9:23–24). To understand, to know God is the all-important matter; in comparison with such knowledge all human knowledge pales. Yet, tragically, no such true knowledge remains. In the words of another prophet, Hosea, "There is . . . no knowledge of God in the land" (Hosea 4:1).[85] Furthermore, there is no way by human wisdom to gain that knowledge. According to Paul, "the world by wisdom knew not God" (1 Cor. 1:21 KJV). What, therefore, is of supreme importance in knowledge, namely, that concerning God, is not known by mankind.

Here, then, is to be seen the critical importance of the Old Testament promise in which God declares, "No longer will a man teach his neighbor, or a man

---

[81] Jesus recalled the words of Deuteronomy 6:4–5 in Mark 12:29–30; cf. Matthew 22:37; Luke 10:27.

[82] Matthew 22:38; Mark 12:31; Luke 10:27.

[83] The Greek word translated in Ephesians 4:23 as "renewed" (*ananeousthai*) means "to take on a new mind" (Thayer). The NIV and NEB translate it "be made new."

[84] The NIV translation of Ephesians 4:23 continues: "to be made new in the attitude of your minds."

[85] Although these words were spoken particularly in regard to Israel, they undoubtedly also have universal relevance.

his brother, saying, 'Know the LORD,' because they will all know me, from the least of them to the greatest" (Jer. 31:34 NIV; cf. Heb. 8:11). *They will all know me.* And it turns out, according to the New Testament witness, that this happens to all those who through Jesus Christ become new creatures. Renewed in their minds, they truly know God.

Indeed, Paul declares (and surely this is an extraordinary statement) that "we have the mind of Christ" (1 Cor. 2:16). This means that because Christ dwells in believers, they have basically a new mental outlook. Rather than their thoughts and knowledge being rooted in themselves, they now have a new source: Jesus Christ. By no means do regenerated persons invariably view things from the perspective of Christ, for there is much of the flesh that remains.[86] However, because of the indwelling Spirit of Christ, His mind, His attitude, is ever present and ready to be expressed through the committed believer.[87]

Finally, the renewal, or making new, of the mind means that all of life is viewed in a new perspective. Rather than seeing everything from the aspect of the self—its interests and ambitions—the primary devotion is to God, His will, His word, His purpose. Further, there is a fresh orientation to other people and a new desire to reach out to them in thoughtfulness and concern.

When the old self has been laid aside, and there is a renewal "in the spirit of the mind" and the mind of Christ becomes the controlling source, all things truly are new and different.

3. A Liberated Will

Regeneration also includes the liberation of the will from its bondage to sin and evil. Shortly before the words about regeneration in Titus 3:5 Paul spoke of his—and our—former condition: "We ourselves were once foolish, disobedient, led astray, slaves to various passions and pleasures, passing our days in malice and envy, hated by men and hating one another" (v. 3). This is a sad, but true picture of the human predicament: "slaves" we were,[88] in bondage to all these evils—and with no hope of ever escaping or changing. But then, Paul adds, "When the goodness and loving kindness of God our Savior appeared, he saved us . . . by the washing of regeneration" (vv. 4–5). We were saved from this terrible bondage, brought into a new life of freedom in Christ.

In another place Paul speaks about regeneration in relation to people whom he describes as "fornicators . . . idolaters . . . adulters . . . effeminate [by perversion] . . . homosexuals . . . thieves . . . covetous . . . drunkards . . . revilers . . . swindlers" (1 Cor. 6:9–10 NASB). Then Paul adds, "And such were some of you; but you were washed . . . " (v. 11).[89] The washing of regeneration! No longer is one in bondage to a terrible past, even if it was sexual immorality and perversion, coveting and stealing, drunkenness and abusiveness. Free at last!

One of the sadder things about the old life—even if the evils were not as gross as those just described—is the utter human inability to break from the

---

[86] Paul, after saying, "We have the mind of Christ," in the next verse calls the Corinthian believers "men of the flesh . . . babes in Christ" (1 Cor. 3:1) because of the strife and jealousy among them.

[87] Hence, this calls for an ongoing renewal. See Chapter 4, "Sanctification."

[88] In Romans 6:6 Paul likewise describes our former condition in terms of slavery: we were "enslaved to sin" (also see v. 20: "You were slaves of sin").

[89] The verse continues, "You were sanctified . . . you were justified." Justification and sanctification will be considered in the next two chapters.

past. Perhaps we were not aware of how much the chains of evil bound us; but if we did become aware, no amount of exertion could turn our lives around. Paul speaks of being "sold under sin," and he expressed what that meant for him: "I do not do what I want, but I do the very thing I hate" (Rom. 7:14–15). So he cries out, "Wretched man that I am! Who will deliver me from the body of this death?" (v. 24). And the answer—glowingly stated: "Thanks be to God through Jesus Christ our Lord!" (v. 25). Verily, this is *the* deliverance that surely comes through Christ.[90]

This liberation is from all that binds man, including the forces of darkness. Paul speaks of his commission from the risen Lord to Jews and Gentiles thus: "to open their eyes so that they may turn from darkness to light and from the dominion of Satan to God" (Acts 26:18 NASB). Unredeemed man is not only in slavery to sin, he is also in bondage to the source of sin, the devil. When therefore one is born again, it is a tremendous liberation from the power and dominion of Satan into light and freedom. In writing the Colossians Paul declares, "He [God] has delivered us from the dominion of darkness and transferred us to the kingdom of his beloved Son" (1:13).

Many a person has become so engrossed in sin that sin is far more than a matter of bondage to his own passions and pleasures; it is more profoundly a bondage to the power of Satan. But, praise God, there is emancipation even here! For Christ in his work of redemption has broken the power of Satan.

Hence, when we are united to Him in faith and are regenerated, there is a full and joyful liberation. The born-again person has at last been freed from the dominion of Satan and now lives in the kingdom of Christ.

It is a blessing to be on a new path of obedience to the will of God. One may—and often will—stumble and fall; however, the believer is free to walk in the way of Christ.

A messianic Psalm contains these words: "I delight to do thy will, O my God; thy law is within my heart" (40:8). These words are totally fulfilled only in Jesus Christ. For, according to Hebrews, "when Christ came into the world, he said . . . 'Lo, I have come to do thy will, O God' " (10:5, 7). At every point in Jesus' life and ministry there was the continual, "Thy will be done." Since the born-again person is now in Christ and Christ in him, his will is basically set in Christ's pattern. It is a will of obedience, not disobedience; it is a will of delight to do the will of God.

Paul speaks of "doing the will of God from the heart" (Eph. 6:6). This is the glad way of the new man who belongs to Christ.

B. A New Nature

Regeneration also means the birthing of a new nature. Rather than the old self of sinful disposition, attitudes, and impulses, there emerges a self whose nature is basically new. In the words of Paul, "Behold, the new has come" (2 Cor. 5:17). These words surely apply to a new nature in man.[91]

---

[90] Many New Testament commentators view Romans 7:14–25, not as referring to Paul's regeneration, but to his continuing struggle as a Christian with sin (see, e.g., F. F. Bruce, *Romans*, TNTC, 256–73). I agree, however, with James Denney that "the experience described is essentially that of his [Paul's] pre-Christian days" (EGT, 2:641). To be "sold under sin" can hardly refer to the regenerate person who has been essentially delivered from sin!

[91] As 2 Corinthians 5:21 suggests: " . . . so that in him we may become the righteousness

The "old man"[92] —man's unregenerate self—is foreign to God and His nature. When regeneration occurs, the nature or character of God becomes operative in the new man. According to 2 Peter 1:4, we have become "partakers of the divine nature,"[93] that is, sharers in God's holiness, love, truth—indeed, all that represents the divine nature. Similarly in 1 John 3:9 it is said of the regenerate person, one "born of God," that "God's nature[94] abides in him." Indeed, according to John, there is such a radical change in the reborn man that sin becomes foreign to his new nature: "No one born of God commits sin; for God's nature abides in him, and he cannot sin because he is born of God" (1 John 3:9).[95] Sin becomes unnatural to the born-again person,[96] for it is totally out of character with the divine nature abiding within and the new life that has begun.

Since God's nature is that of holiness, love, and truth,[97] man's new nature shows forth the same. Likewise since original man, Adam, before the Fall was not a sinner, he reflected God's nature (or character) in all these ways.[98] Hence, the person born again will show forth the same; he will be a new creature in holiness, love, and truth. Let us examine this in more detail.

1. Holiness

The new nature is, first, that of holiness and righteousness. So Paul writes, "Put on the new nature,[99] created after the likeness of God in true righteousness and holiness" (Eph. 4:24). The regenerate person is one whose inmost being is now inclined to righteousness and holiness. There is a reorientation in which the governing disposition is that of righteousness. Consequently, his desire is to walk blamelessly before the Lord.

Indeed, Paul elsewhere calls this new person a "slave of righteousness": "You who were once slaves of sin . . . having been set free from sin, have become slaves of righteousness" (Rom. 6:17–18). Such a strong statement is entirely appropriate, because the new man in Christ has a totally different orientation. Previously, everything he did, whether wittingly or unwittingly,

---

of God." (For further discussion of this righteousness, see the next chapter, "Justification.")

[92]This is the language of the KJV in Ephesians 4:22 and Colossians 3:9.

[93]This does not mean that we share in God's *being*. Regeneration does not signify any kind of merger of man with God; there is no absorption into deity. The word translated "nature," *physis*, does not refer to being but to "natural characteristics" (Thayer).

[94]The Greek word is *sperma*, literally "seed" (as in KJV, NIV, NASB, NEB). Some interpreters view the "seed" as the word, some others as the Spirit. According to I. H. Marshall, "most commentators take 'seed' to refer to a divine principle of life which abides in the believer" (*The Epistles of John*, NICNT, 186). Perhaps "nature" is the best translation, as the reference, I believe, is not only to a divine principle of life but also to the divine nature indicated by the word "seed."

[95]The NIV translates: "No one who is born of God will continue to sin, because God's seed remains in him; he cannot go on sinning, because he has been born of God." This translation removes any idea of sinless perfection. For further discussion of this matter see chapter 4, "Sanctification," 88–89n.29.

[96]This does not mean that a person will not do the unnatural, i.e., sin; indeed, we often do just that (see John 1:8: "If we say we have no sin, we deceive ourselves, and the truth is not in us"). Still, such an action is basically contrary to the new nature.

[97]See vol. 1, chapter 3, "God."

[98]For a fuller discussion of this see vol. 1, chapter 9, "Man."

[99]The Greek phrase is *kainon anthrōpon*, literally, "new man." The NASB and NIV translate the phrase "new self."

was under the domination of sin; now it is under the domination of righteousness. Again, the new person will not always act in righteousness (for there is no one who does not sin), but he will be basically mastered by a new passion: to fulfill the charge of righteousness and holiness.

So John declares: "Every one who does right[100] is born of him" (1 John 2:29). The doing of righteousness is the nature of a person born of God.

2. Love

The new nature is also characterized by love. Shortly before Paul's words that any person in Christ is a new creature (2 Cor. 5:17), he declared that "the love of Christ controls us" (v. 14). Christ's love expressed in dying for us, Paul adds, is also for the purpose that "those who live might live no longer for themselves but for him who for their sake died and was raised" (v. 15). In 1 John are similar, and quite succinct, words: "We love, because he first loved us" (4:19).

This very love is a vital element in the life of the reborn person. Again in the language of 1 John: "He who loves is born of God and knows God. He who does not love does not know God; for God is love" (4:7–8). The love is agape,[101] an outgoing love that has replaced self-love (the natural condition of sinful man) with love for and devotion to God and to Christ. It is also a love that reaches out to other persons whatever their status or situation.

The regenerate person, accordingly, is at last in the position to fulfill the great commandments: "You shall love the Lord your God with all your heart, and with all your soul, and with all your mind, and with all your strength" and "You shall love your neighbor as yourself" (Mark 12:30–31). One born of God—having a changed heart, a renewed mind, and new strength,[102] and one whose newborn nature is grounded in love—has the capacity to love God and his neighbor in a total kind of way.

Since love is the very nature of God—"God is love" (1 John 4:8)— and God's nature abides in one born of God, then to exhibit love is a natural expression. Or to put it a bit differently, since Christ through His Spirit dwells within, His love may be freely shed abroad. Love is the new way of life of the newborn child of God.[103]

It is exciting to realize that through the origination of the new person, the person through whom God's love can be expressed, a new force has been released in the world that can alter every relationship. Natural man, to be sure, knows of passionate love, which

---

[100]The Greek word is dikaiosynēn, literally, "righteousness."

[101]In the quotation from 1 John 4:7–8 the Greek noun for love is agapē: God is agapē. The verbs for love are from agapaō. Agapaō, the verb, is occasionally used in the New Testament to refer merely to an act of human love or affection; however, the noun agapē invariably refers to divine love (God's love of persons or their love of God) or the outgoing love for others that God's love makes possible.

[102]We have previously talked about a changed heart and renewed mind. "New strength" refers to the will liberated from bondage.

[103]This does not mean that the regenerate person invariably exercises love; far from it. As will be discussed later (in chapter 4, "Sanctification"), the continuing "flesh" of man wars against every godly expression and activity of the new man. This surely includes love. Moreover, love is to be an ever-growing reality in the life of the child of God; no new Christian fully loves. This is why Paul speaks of love as a "fruit" of the Spirit (Gal. 5:22)— and fruit may take long to ripen and mature. In another place Paul prays that believers may "know the love of Christ which surpasses knowledge" (Eph. 3:19).

seeks in another its fulfillment;[104] he may indeed experience affection or friendship in human relationships.[105] But none of this operates on the level of *agape* love that is wholly selfless in relation to God and one's fellowman.

3. Truth

The new nature, finally, is marked by truth. The Holy Spirit who dwells within all those born of God is "the Spirit of truth." Jesus spoke to His disciples about "the Spirit of truth, whom the world cannot receive, because it neither sees him nor knows him," and then added: "You know him, for he dwells with you, and will be in you" (John 14:17). So it is that in John's second letter the apostle speaks of believers as those who "know the truth . . . the truth which abides in us and will be with us for ever" (vv. 1–2). Paul writes similarly about this truth to Timothy: "Guard the truth that has been entrusted to you by the Holy Spirit who dwells within us" (2 Tim. 1:14).

Hence the person born of God has a knowledge of truth of which the world knows nothing. He knows the truth about God, about Christ, about salvation, about life and death, and about the world to come—all the things that are of ultimate importance.[106]

Furthermore, since God has "brought us forth by the word of truth" (James 1:18), lying and deception belong to prior days. Those born of God have entered upon a new path of speaking and doing the truth in every relationship. So Paul writes: "Once you were darkness, but now you are light in the Lord; walk as children of light" (Eph. 5:8). To be "light in the Lord"

means to be so enlightened by truth that it is natural to walk steadfastly in it. They are those, as Paul elsewhere says, who "in the midst of a crooked and perverse generation . . . shine as lights in the world" (Phil. 2:15).

The new thing about the regenerate person is that truth marks his nature. He may, and sometimes does, slip into untruth, deception, falsehood (the old life out of which he came), but there has been an internal basic alteration so that he now naturally walks in the truth.

On one occasion Jesus declared, "Believe in the light [namely, in Jesus Himself], that you may become sons of light" (John 12:36). To be a son of light is to be one who radiates truth in both being and action. This is a high mark of those who are born from above.

C. A New Life

Finally, through regeneration there is entrance into a new life. In the language of Paul it is to "walk in newness of life" (Rom. 6:4). This truly is such life as one has never known before.

To be born again is actually to pass from death to life. Paul writes the Ephesians, "And you he made alive, when you were dead through . . . trespasses and sins" (2:1). Before being made alive, what passed for life was actually death—not physical of course, but spiritual. Ever since Adam's fall the human race has been walking in spiritual death. Now there is spiritual life.

First, there is *aliveness to God*. In the striking words of Paul, "You also must consider yourselves dead to sin and alive to God in Christ Jesus" (Rom. 6:11). Alive to God! Before Christ came and brought new life, people in general

---

[104]Often expressed by the Greek word *eros* in nonbiblical literature. The word "eros" is not found in the New Testament.

[105]Often expressed by the Greek word *philia* in nonbiblical literature. It is found only once in the New Testament—in James 4:4 where reference is made to "friendship with the world."

[106]Paul couples salvation and knowledge of truth in 1 Timothy 2:4: "[God] desires all men to be saved and to come to the knowledge of the truth."

were dead to God and the things of God. They were "without hope and without God in the world" (Eph. 2:12 NIV).[107] Now through the miracle of rebirth there is aliveness to God and His ways.

The awareness of God's presence becomes a new fact in the believer's life. Before rebirth, people, like sinful Adam, are shut out from fellowship with their Maker, so that strive as they may, there is no way back into the presence of God. Now all has changed, for regeneration is to be born of God, to be a child of God, and thereby to live in His presence. As John writes, "Our fellowship is with the Father and with his Son Jesus Christ" (1 John 1:3). This is the meaning of being "alive to God in Christ Jesus": new life in the presence of God.

To be alive to God is a fulfillment of the deepest need of human nature. The "death of God,"[108] that is, the deadness of man to God, is the ultimate tragedy, for that death darkens all of life's activities. For without God there is no ultimate meaning to life's pursuits: it is all "sound and fury, signifying nothing." On the other hand, aliveness to God means that our human existence, which was made for God (and without which all is futile), is at last being fulfilled. Man is now truly human again because he is back in connection with his Creator!

The wonderful sense of God's hand in all that transpires becomes a reality. Although there may not always be understanding, there is now the realization of God's providence, His sustaining care, His presence even in times of suffering and seeming defeat. For to be alive to God is to be alive to the One who in Christ Jesus has said, "Lo, I am with you alway, even unto the end of the world" (Matt. 28:20 KJV).

Second, and this follows from the preceding, the new life a believer knows is one of *true happiness*. The "pursuit of happiness" is not only an expressed goal in the United States Declaration of Independence; it is also what people everywhere seek after. The natural man pursues it in terms of such earthly satisfactions as wealth, success, pleasure, recognition, and security. But none of these really satisfies the deeper longings for the things of God; moreover, any such attainment can with a change of fortune quickly pass away. True happiness is to be found only through the new life in Christ.

For one thing, there is abundant life in Jesus Christ. On one occasion Jesus declared, "I came that they may have life, and have it abundantly" (John 10:10). In such abundance is the highest possible happiness. There may or may not be earthly abundance, but that does not really matter, for the new life in Christ is one of continuing spiritual blessings. There is the highest happiness of knowing God's salvation through Jesus Christ, and along with this the blessedness of His Holy Spirit's continuing presence to comfort and guide. There is also the blessing of fellowship with other believers. This fellowship is far deeper than any earthly association or even that within human families: it is the fellowship of those who have been brought to life by Christ, and who know a rich experience of fellowship with one another. This is true happiness.

Again, in Christ there is profound and abiding joy. Jesus, on the same occasion, also declared, "These things I have spoken to you, that my joy may be

---

[107] Paul writes these words particularly in reference to Gentiles.

[108] This modern-day expression originating with Friedrich Nietzsche in the nineteenth century says nothing, of course, about God's demise but much about the inward condition of man.

in you, and that your joy may be full"[109] (John 15:11). The natural man in his pursuit of happiness never knows the joy Christ brings. Primarily there is the joy of salvation: it is truly the "great joy" (Luke 2:10) that was promised at the birth of Christ. Hence, all who are born again have entered into this joy beyond all earthly measure. Through the ancient prophet the Lord had declared, "With joy you will draw water from the wells of salvation" (Isa. 12:3). But also it is a continuing joy that does not depend on outward circumstances. Paul wrote, "Rejoice in the Lord always; again I will say, Rejoice" (Phil. 4:4), and added shortly after, "I have learned, in whatever state I am, to be content" (v. 11). These words written from a Roman prison (see Phil. 1:7, 12–17) declare the extraordinary joy, regardless of circumstance, of one who truly belongs to Jesus Christ. The believer in Christ knows the joy of the Lord. This is true happiness.

Once more, there is victory through Christ. In the words of John, "Everyone born of God overcomes the world" (1 John 5:4 NIV); in the language of Paul, "We are more than conquerors through him who loved us" (Rom. 8:37). One who has not experienced the new life in Christ is still in the bondage of sin, still under the control of Satan, still haunted by the fear of death and judgment. The pursuit of happiness, therefore, is constantly frustrated by these insuperable negative forces. But

for the born-again person all is changed: the bondage to sin gone, the control of Satan broken, the fear of death and judgment dissipated. In the continuing words of Paul, "Neither death, nor life, nor angels, nor principalities, nor things present, nor things to come, nor powers, nor height, nor depth, nor anything else in all creation, will be able to separate us from the love of God in Christ Jesus our Lord" (vv. 38–39). Christ has triumphed, and we share His victory! This is true happiness.

Third, and finally, the new life is *life eternal*. Not only is there new life now but also it never ends. Following the words of Jesus to Nicodemus, "You must be born again" (John 3:7 NASB), the Scripture reads: "For God so loved the world that he gave his only Son, that whoever believes in him should not perish but have eternal[110] life" (v. 16). To be born again is to enter by faith in Jesus Christ into eternal life. Truly such life begins now—and it is life indeed—but the final glory is that such life never ends. This is the ultimate happiness.

We close with the memorable words of Peter: "Blessed be the God and Father of our Lord Jesus Christ! By his great mercy we have been born anew [or "again"] to a living hope through the resurrection of Jesus Christ from the dead, and to an inheritance which is imperishable, undefiled, and unfading, kept in heaven for you" (1 Peter 1:3–4). Amen and amen!

---

[109] See further chapter 12, II, "Fullness of Joy."
[110] The Greek word is *aiōnion*, "everlasting" (KJV).

3

Justification

In the area of salvation one of the critically important doctrines is justification.[1] This doctrine has to do with salvation in terms of man's *standing* before God. One who has experienced salvation has a new relationship to God: he is justified.

I. BACKGROUND

The doctrine of justification concerns God's way in salvation of dealing with man as unrighteous. God, who is righteous in all His ways, demands of His human creature a reciprocal righteousness. But man does not respond affirmatively; indeed, because of his sinful nature he cannot and will not. Yet there is no way to avoid the demand of God that he walk in righteousness.

Hence, this is the original crisis, for no man can live a life that truly reflects the righteousness of God.

The burning question is simply this: How can any person stand before a righteous and holy God? When God is recognized for who He is, a human being can only cry out, "Woe is me!"[2] For there comes the vivid realization that "all our righteousnesses are as filthy rags."[3] All that we do, even "our righteousnesses," is unclean in His holy and pure presence.

This situation is the case for all people. It may be more obviously true for those who are given to immorality: those who constantly defy God, live in lustful passion, and abuse their neighbors. If confronted by the Righteous

---

[1]Martin Luther, who brought this doctrine to the forefront in the Reformation, spoke of it as "the test of a standing or falling church." In his commentary on Galatians 3:13 Luther wrote: "As I often warn . . . the doctrine of justification must be learned diligently. For in it are included all other doctrines of our faith; and if it is sound, all the others are sound as well" (*Luther's Works*, 26:283). John Calvin, while discussing regeneration first, nonetheless spoke very highly of justification as "the principal ground upon which religion must be supported" (*Institutes*, III.11.1, Beveridge trans.). There can be no doubt that justification was *the* doctrine that most deeply separated Protestantism from Roman Catholicism at the time of the Reformation.

[2]As Isaiah cried out in the presence of the thrice-holy God ("Holy, holy, holy is the LORD of hosts"). See Isaiah 6:1–5.

[3]Isaiah 64:6 (KJV).

One, who bids all persons to honor Him, to live in purity and holiness, and love their fellow human beings, there can only be great anxiety and fear. Indeed, the overall situation seems hopeless: they simply have no genuine righteousness to respond to the righteousness of God. Their manner of life merits only God's judgment.

The plight, however, is no better for those who may be called moral persons. These are the ones who seek generally to keep God's commandments, obey the laws of the land, or at least follow after the scruples of their consciences. They seem to belong to an entirely different category from the immoral (as described above) and would indeed be classified by most people as good and righteous. However, in the presence of the holy Lord of heaven and earth, all their deeds are immediately shown to be darkened by sin: there is no true worship of God, no clear inner conscience, no pure love of neighbor. Some such persons may even strive to achieve a righteousness that God will find acceptable, but it is to no avail. They still fall short of what God requires, and therefore likewise stand under judgment.[4]

It is with such matters that Paul deals in Romans 1:18–3:20. In those verses the apostle sets forth the unrighteousness of all men, Jew and Gentile alike. Paul first speaks about the wickedness of men in general: how they turn from God's own revelation of Himself in nature, hence suppress the truth, and how, as a result, God gives them over to ways of immorality and unrighteousness (1:18–32). Paul then declares that Gentiles are inexcusably unrighteous, for in addition to natural revelation, they have the law written on their hearts (2:1–16). But so are Jews who, having the law of Moses, nonetheless constantly break it and thereby render their circumcision invalid (2:17–29). The result is, in Paul's words, that "all men, both Jews and Greeks, are under the power of sin, as it is written: 'None is righteous, no, not one'" (3:9–10).[5] Hence, "no human being will be justified in his [God's] sight by works of the law" (3:20).

The situation, then, is extremely serious for all people: on the one hand, God demands righteousness; on the other, none can give it because of the power of sin.

From all appearances man's plight is indeed hopeless. The only hope from the human side would seem to be that of living a life of such a caliber of righteousness that God would be able to accept it. But such attempted justification by human deeds is not possible because of who God is, what He requires, and man's sinful condition. The other possible hope might be that God, knowing human frailty and disposition to evil, would simply overlook it and receive man in spite of his sinfulness to Himself. But such is even more impossible, for God as totally holy, righteous, and pure, cannot act in such an arbitrary fashion.

---

[4]This was Luther's problem. As a young monk, he had strenuously sought God's approval through fasting, penance, vigils, mortifications, prayers, strictness of life and morals. As Luther himself said, "If ever a monk got to heaven by his monkery it was I." But it was all to no avail: more and more he came to realize that nothing he did could measure up to God's righteous demand. "My situation was that, although an impeccable monk, I stood before God as a sinner troubled in conscience, and I had no confidence that my merit would assuage him. Therefore I did not love a just and angry God, but rather hated and murmured against him." Luther, "impeccable monk," was utterly destitute before God. (Quotations from *Here I Stand: A Life of Martin Luther* by Roland H. Bainton, 45, 65.)

[5]This is a free quotation from Psalm 14:1. Reference might also be made to Psalm 143:2: "No man living is righteous before thee."

II. MEANING

Before proceeding further, we do well to consider the meaning of the word "justification." In the New Testament it is the usual translation of the Greek word *dikaiōsis*. *Dikaiōsis* may also be rendered "acquittal."[6] In one instance "justification" is the translation of *dikaiōma*.[7] The verb "justify" (also "justifies," "justified") is the translation of the Greek verb *dikaioō*. Some form of *dikaioō* is found most frequently in Romans and Galatians.[8] The usual meaning of the term, especially as found in the writings of the apostle Paul, is to "pronounce or declare righteous."[9]

The striking feature about the word "justification" (both in substantive and verbal forms) is its declaratory aspect: it does not mean to make righteous or just but, as noted, to declare or pronounce righteous.[10] Hence, one who is justified is one who is declared by God to be righteous. It is not the justification of the righteous but of the unrighteous! Paul speaks of God as He "who justifies the ungodly" (Rom. 4:5). There is nothing in sinful man that merits God's approbation. Accordingly, it is not the righteous (there are none), but the unrighteous whom God justifies.

Here we might pause to marvel and wonder. We have previously commented on the extremely serious nature of the human situation, namely, that God demands righteousness in man but that man is by no means able to comply. There is no way by which man can justify himself.[11] Moreover, God being holy and righteous cannot simply overlook sin, nor can man do enough that is good to make himself acceptable to God.[12] Now what we are saying—or better, the gospel proclaims—is that God in an extraordinary manner declares the sinner to be righteous!

How this can occur will be considered later. For the moment, we need simply to rejoice in the wonder of it all. Hear this: we do not have to prove ourselves before God, we do not have to be anxious about His final judgment against us,[13] we do not need to struggle

---

[6]*Dikaiōsis* appears only twice, both times in Romans: 4:25: "who [Christ] was put to death for our trespasses and raised for our justification"; and 5:18: "one man's act of righteousness leads to acquittal and life for all men." In the latter verse KJV, NIV, and NASB, instead of "acquittal," translate *dikaiōsis* "justification."

[7]In Romans 5:16: "The free gift following many trespasses brings justification." The KJV, NIV, and NASB likewise have "justification."

[8]Fifteen times in Romans, eight times in Galatians.

[9]"To declare, pronounce, one to be just, righteous, or such as he ought to be" (Thayer); "to be acquitted, be pronounced and treated as righteous" (BAGD).

[10]There are instances in the New Testament where *dikaioō* has the related meanings of "vindicate" (e.g., Luke 7:35; 1 Tim. 3:16) and "free" (e.g., Acts 13:39; Rom. 6:7). However, *dikaioō* never means "to make righteous." In Luke 7:29 the people "justified God"; they could not "make" God righteous, only declare that He is just.

[11]The Pharisees are the primary New Testament example of those who seek to justify themselves, but God sees beneath the surface. In the words of Jesus to the Pharisees: "You are those who justify yourselves before me, but God knows your hearts; for what is exalted among men is an abomination in the sight of God" (Luke 16:15).

[12]Paul could even say, "I am not aware of anything against myself, but I am not thereby acquitted ['justified" KJV]" (1 Cor. 4:4).

[13]Justification unmistakably includes the future as well as the present: the present declaration of righteousness will also be heard on the final day of judgment. George E. Ladd, speaking of justification as "an eschatological doctrine," adds, "The issue of the final judgment will be either a declaration of righteousness that will mean acquittal from all guilt, or conviction of unrighteousness and subsequent condemnation" (*Theology of the New*

to achieve something God will somehow find acceptable. Rather, He declares us to be righteous. In Him we are righteous—not we who are godly, but we who are ungodly; not we who have climbed the mountain heights of righteous living, but we who are struggling on the plains, and sometimes in the muck and mire, of unrighteous living. There is nothing, absolutely nothing, in us—whether we be the most moral or the most immoral of people—that makes this possible. God pronounces us righteous, though we are not: this is the glory and wonder of the gospel message.

III. ASPECTS

Now we move on to observe that there is a double aspect (or two aspects) of God's declaratory righteousness. On the one hand, there is the nonimputation of sin; on the other, there is the imputation of the righteousness of Jesus Christ.

A. The Nonimputation of Sin

We begin with the words of the rejoicing psalmist: "Blessed is the man to whom the LORD imputes no iniquity" (32:2). In Paul's discussion of justification in Romans, he quotes these words thus: "Blessed is the man to whom the Lord will not impute sin" (4:8 KJV). This nonimputation of sin may also be called the *nonreckoning* of sin or the *nonaccounting* of sin.[14] This means that although sins are still there, God does not hold them against us.

One of the great Pauline statements to this effect is that of 2 Corinthians 5:19—"God was in Christ, reconciling the world unto himself, not imputing[15] their trespasses against them" (KJV). This nonimputation of sin stands at the very center of God's act of salvation through Jesus Christ.

We pause again briefly to marvel and rejoice. God does not impute our sins against us. Although they be as a great mountain, though they be a vast number, though they be black as night, God does not impute, does not count, them against us. We cannot pretend sins are not there—and surely God makes no such pretense—but they are not charged to our account. We may shudder at some thought of a heavenly account book, with column upon column of entries against us, and sense the horror of God's coming condemnation. But, praise God, the record is clear; there are no such entries. Somehow, somewhere, they have all been removed.

How significant are the later words of Paul in Romans 8:33–34: "Who shall bring any charge against God's elect? It is God who justifies; who is to condemn?" And the answer implied is: "*No one.*" In the Book of Revelation the devil is depicted as the accuser of believers, one who "accuses them day and night before our God" (12:10). However, his accusations (e.g., "You are a sinner and have no hope." "You are condemned whether you admit it or not") cannot stand. God does not accuse; Christ does not condemn. Who, therefore, shall bring *any* charge against

---

Testament, 441). However, we would add, the primary emphasis of justification lies in the present.

[14]The RSV in Romans 4:8 reads, "Blessed is the man against whom the Lord will not reckon his sin." The NASB reads, "BLESSED IS THE MAN WHOSE SIN THE LORD WILL NOT TAKE INTO ACCOUNT"; NIV: "will never count against him"; NEB: "does not count against him." The Greek word variously translated "impute," "reckon," "account," or "count" is *logisētai.*

[15]"Not counting" (RSV, NASB, NIV).

God's elect, God's people?[16] Again, and even stronger, the answer implied is: "*Absolutely no one.*" For since it is God who justifies, who can there be to condemn?

The nonimputation of sins also means the *forgiveness* of sins. Paul's quotation from Psalm 32 (above) actually mentions forgiveness first: "Blessed are those whose iniquities are forgiven, and whose sins are covered" (Rom. 4:7). This, then, is followed by the statement about not imputing sins.[17] Hence forgiveness is the same as nonimputation, though the latter term does help to give the concept of forgiveness further clarification.[18] On the other hand, the beauty of the word forgiveness is its deeply personal quality.

Many Old Testament passages speak vividly of God's forgiveness. For example, Psalm 130:3-4—"If thou, O Lord, shouldst mark iniquities, Lord, who could stand? But there is forgiveness with thee, that thou mayest be feared [or 'revered' NEB]." Isaiah 43:25—"I, I am He who blots out your transgressions for my own sake, and I will not remember your sins." Micah 7:18-19— "Who is a God like thee, pardoning iniquity and passing over transgression . . . ? Thou wilt cast all our sins into the depths of the sea." However, even beyond all such expressions, there is to be a future forgiveness of sins. Through the prophet Jeremiah, God declares that in days to come He will make "a new covenant" (31:31). The climactic words are: "I will forgive their iniquity, and I will remember their sin no more" (v. 34). In all such Old Testament passages forgiveness is truly the nonimputation of sins, and this truth is conveyed through the imagery of blotting out, not remembering, passing over, casting into the depths of the ocean. How blessed are those who are thus forgiven, whose sins are no more imputed to them!

In Jesus' ministry also forgiveness of sins has a vitally important place. He said to a paralytic, "My son, your sins are forgiven" (Mark 2:5); to a sinful woman, "Your sins are forgiven" (Luke 7:48); to a woman taken in the act of adultery, "Neither do I condemn you; go, and do not sin again" (John 8:11);[19] to His disciples at the Last Supper, "This is my blood of the [new][20] covenant, which is poured out for many for the forgiveness of sins" (Matt. 26:28); and on the cross He spoke these memorable words: "Father, forgive them; for they know not what they do" (Luke 23:34). More-

---

[16]This includes self-condemnation. According to 1 John 3:19–20, "By this we shall know that we are of the truth, and reassure our hearts before him whenever our hearts condemn us; for God is greater than our hearts."

[17]This form—forgiveness, then nonimputation—is a Hebrew poetic parallelism of ideas in that both refer in different ways to the same reality. Paul, accordingly, follows this parallelism.

[18]According to Gottlob Schrenk (art. on δικαιοσύνη) in TDNT, "It is important to Paul not merely to speak of forgiveness but by means of δικαιοσύνη to give to forgiveness a precision grounded, enlarged and deepened in divine right" (2:205). Significantly, Paul, outside the quotation from Psalm 32, nowhere in Romans speaks directly of forgiveness. His concern (as Schrenk suggests) is that forgiveness be understood in relationship to God's righteousness. This, incidentally, is why I have dealt with nonimputation before forgiveness.

[19]Although John 8:1–11 is not found in most of the ancient manuscripts, this passage so much expresses the attitude of Jesus that I do not hesitate to include it in a total picture of Him. Regarding the passage, it may be noted here that though the word "forgiveness" is not used, Jesus' statement of noncondemnation amounts to the same thing.

[20]Some ancient manuscripts have "new." However, whether "new" was in the original text or not, it is doubtless implied. Jesus' words unmistakably point to the fulfillment of the prophecy in Jeremiah.

over, after His death and resurrection, Jesus declared to His disciples that "repentance and forgiveness of sins should be preached in his name to all the nations" (Luke 24:47). It is apparent that forgiveness of sins is at the heart of Jesus' ministry and that forgiveness along with repentance[21] is to be the focus of gospel proclamation thereafter.

It follows that in the preaching of the early church, forgiveness of sins is often declared. Peter on the Day of Pentecost proclaimed, "Repent, and be baptized every one of you in the name of Jesus Christ for the forgiveness of your sins" (Acts 2:38). Shortly after that Peter, along with the other apostles, declared that God has "exalted him [Jesus] at his right hand as Leader and Savior, to give repentance to Israel and forgiveness of sins" (Acts 5:31). A number of years later Peter preached the gospel for the first time to the Gentiles, saying, "Every one who believes in him receives forgiveness of sins through his name" (Acts 10:43). After that, Paul declared, "Through this man forgiveness of sins is proclaimed to you" (Acts 13:38). Finally, Paul asserted that his mandate from Jesus regarding Jew and Gentile alike was to "open their eyes, that they may turn from darkness to light and from the power of Satan to God, that they may receive forgiveness of sins" (Acts 26:18).

A further word about repentance should be added here. God does not impute our sins to us; He freely forgives. But only those who are truly repentant can receive this forgiveness (recall the words about repentance *and* forgiveness in the words of Christ and Peter). I have previously discussed in some detail the nature of repentance,[22] so I will not repeat that here except to emphasize its necessity in the reception of forgiveness. The Scripture that best illustrates this and its relationship to justification is Luke 18:9–14, the parable of the Pharisee and the tax collector. The Pharisee represents, according to Jesus, those who "trusted in themselves that they were righteous," hence, justified themselves ("God, I thank thee that I am not like other men"). However, the tax collector in contrition cried out, "God, be merciful to me a sinner!" "This man," said Jesus, "went down to his house justified rather than the other." It was the tax collector's repentance and humbleness of spirit that led to his justification, even God's forgiveness. His sins were not imputed to him; he, not the Pharisee, was righteous before God.[23]

Now back again to forgiveness of sins: here we are at the very heart of the gospel. For the good news is that however great the sin, however deep the sense of guilt, however heavy the condemnation that may be felt, there is total forgiveness.[24] If Peter could

---

[21] I will discuss repentance shortly.

[22] See chapter 2, "Regeneration," IV.C, pages 44–50.

[23] The words of Psalm 32:1, "Blessed is he whose transgression is forgiven," quite possibly are words of David following God's forgiveness for his sins of adultery and murder. David repented: "I have sinned against the LORD," and received God's forgiveness: "The LORD also has put away your sin" (2 Sam. 12:13).

[24] There is one exception, namely, blasphemy against the Holy Spirit. Jesus declared, "All sins will be forgiven the sons of men, and whatever blasphemies they utter; but whoever blasphemes against the Holy Spirit never has forgiveness, but is guilty of an eternal sin—for they had said, 'He has an unclean spirit' " (Mark 3:28–30; cf. Matt. 12:31–32; Luke 12:10). As the larger context shows, this sin was that of the scribes and Pharisees who deliberately and maliciously attributed to Christ the work of the devil. Thus one may even blaspheme

charge the multitude in Jerusalem with putting to death the Messiah—"this Jesus . . . you crucified and killed by the hands of lawless men" (Acts 2:23)—and thereafter proclaim to these same people forgiveness, then there is no limit to God's forgiveness. For surely if the most heinous crime ever committed, the crucifying of the Son of God, could be forgiven, then forgiveness is unlimited. Idolatry, sexual perversion, murder, theft, adultery, false witness, slander, betrayal of others, lust—and on and on—every single sin, both in its fullest dimension and minutest detail, may be totally forgiven by Almighty God.

When we are aware of this, we are able all the more to say with the psalmist and Paul, "*Blessed* are those whose iniquities are forgiven, and whose sins are covered; *blessed* is the man to whom the Lord will not impute sin." The forgiveness of sins, the nonimputation of sins: blessed beyond measure are all who have received this grace from God!

B. Imputation of the Righteousness of Jesus Christ

The other aspect of God's declaratory righteousness (and this is the positive side) is that our righteousness is found in Jesus Christ. God does not impute our sins to us; rather He imputes to us the righteousness of His Son, Jesus Christ. Christ is our righteousness! So Paul states in 1 Corinthians 1:30—"By His doing you are in Christ Jesus, who became to us wisdom

from God, and righteousness and sanctification, and redemption" (NASB). Clearly Christ has become many things for us: here we focus on the marvel that He "became to us . . . righteousness."

We might at this juncture call to mind a beautiful word in the Old Testament given through the prophet Jeremiah: "Behold, the days are coming, says the LORD, when I will fulfill the promise I made to the house of Israel and the house of Judah. In those days and at that time I will cause a righteous Branch to spring forth for David; and he shall execute justice and righteousness in the land. In those days Judah will be saved and Jerusalem will dwell securely. And this is the name by which it will be called: 'The LORD is our righteousness' "[25] (Jer. 33:14–16). What an extraordinary and meaningful name! Not that the city is called "righteous," but "the LORD is our righteousness."

Returning to the New Testament again, let us hear other words from Paul that express some of his deepest feelings about Christ's righteousness. After reviewing how in regard to "righteousness under the law" he was "blameless" (Phil. 3:6),[26] Paul shortly after adds, "For his [Christ's] sake I have suffered the loss of all things, and count them as refuse, in order that I may gain Christ and be found in him, not having a righteousness of my own, based on law, but that which is through faith in Christ" (3:8–9). This is not a righteousness that is my own, or our own, but that which comes from Jesus Christ.

In summary, this declaratory right-

God, fight against Christ and His church, spurn all truth and righteousness, commit the most debased act of immorality possible to mankind—all such horrible sins are forgiveable. But to blaspheme against the Holy Spirit shows a conscience so perverse and hardened as never to be able to receive forgiveness. (See also vol. 1, chapter 11, "The Effects of Sin," page 256, including n. 54). It is knowingly to call light darkness, to claim Christ to be the ally of Satan, and to identify a work or act of the Holy Spirit as demon-inspired.

[25] The Hebrew phrase is *Yahweh Ṣidqēnû*.

[26] Even as Martin Luther was an "impeccable monk," Paul, long before him, was "blameless." Luther's had to rediscover what Paul had attested, namely, that the only righteousness that counts is that which comes from Jesus Christ.

eousness is not only a matter of nonimputation of our sins, as important as that is though still basically a negative, but also the imputing to us of the righteousness of Christ. That means a perfect righteousness, nothing lacking, all complete: His purity, His obedience, His integrity, His humility, His love—all this and more, making up His righteousness. It is all ours by virtue of Jesus Christ.

When God looks at us, He beholds us clothed in the righteousness of His Son, and each of us is complete in Him. "Yes, but," I may reply, "there is too much sin and evil in me." The answer from heaven by God the Father is that all is covered by His Son; hence, I am righteous in Him. There is not even a tawdry little bit that remains. *It is as if I had never sinned.*[27] For even as I have been acquitted of all sin, so do I stand complete in His righteousness.[28]

We may summarize the doctrine of justification at this point by saying that it highlights the wonder of the good news that we do not have to achieve righteousness to be acceptable to God. It is not on the basis of any righteousness that we may have or gain that salvation occurs. Rather, by humbly accepting God's forgiveness and looking to Christ for all righteousness, we enter upon the way of salvation.

Before proceeding further, I should make clear that imputation of the righteousness of Christ is far different from an infusion of righteousness. It would be a serious mistake to assume that we are justified by virtue of God's putting righteousness within us. Although such may seem proper (why should God justify anyone except on the basis of some given righteousness?), it is not God's way of justification. Doubtless one reason for this is that even though the righteousness should be given by God—a righteousness we did not have before salvation—we would be inclined to focus more on what we are than on giving God all the glory. Further, such an instilled righteousness would never be complete in this life (sin continues to some degree in the most righteous of persons);[29] hence, we would never fully know the deep peace of being totally right with God. To sum it up, justification is not making righteous, but declaring righteous by virtue of Jesus Christ. The difference is of great importance in understanding and living the Christian life.[30]

IV. GROUND

The ground of our justification is God's act of redemption in Jesus Christ. So Paul writes, "Since all have sinned and fall short of the glory of God, they are justified by his grace as a gift, through the redemption which is in Christ Jesus, whom God put forward as an expiation by his blood" (Rom. 3:23–25). Justification is grounded in the costly deed of redemption.

---

[27] A popular, but meaningful, way to put this is to say that the word "justified" in part spells this out: "just-as-if-I'd" never sinned.

[28] Quite appropriate are the words of the chorus:
He is all my righteousness,
I stand complete in Him and worship Him,
Jesus Christ the Lord.

[29] This will be discussed further under "Sanctification."

[30] Calvin has a valuable discussion of infused righteousness, designated as "essential righteousness," in the *Institutes,* III.11.5–12. He is arguing with Osiander, a Lutheran theologian, and calls his view of essential righteousness a "monstrosity" that "deprives pious minds of a serious sense of divine grace" (5). Calvin also argues that this "heresy" (10) confuses regeneration (in which there is truly a given righteousness) with justification (11). (Osiander was also criticized by his fellow Lutheran theologians [especially Melanchthon], and his views were later repudiated in the Lutheran *Formula of Concord,* Article III.)

We now need to emphasize this point lest there be some misapprehension about justification as God's declaratory righteousness. It is by no means a casual matter to speak of God's declaring the sinner righteous and imputing to him the righteousness of Christ. God is not like some absolute earthly monarch who by a stroke of the pen decrees whatever He wills or changes the laws if He so likes. The holy and righteous God does not play fast and loose so as to pronounce righteous what is actually unrighteous without some alteration of the situation. In saying this, the question may naturally arise, Does this not then call for some change in man's condition? Is not some basic righteousness—at least a bit of it—required for God to declare man righteous (God perhaps supplementing His declaration with some infused righteousness)? In accordance with a moral universe, how can God possibly justify anyone without some evidence of moral character, good works, and the like? Is not some radical change necessary?

Now to respond: there has been a profound alteration of the human situation, but *not* by sinful man. God does not act casually, contrary to His own righteousness, in justifying man. Rather in extraordinary fashion His righteousness is vindicated through his redemptive act in Christ Jesus. Shortly prior to the words in Romans (quoted above) Paul declared, "Now the righteousness[31] of God has been manifested" (3:21). And this manifestation of God's righteousness was not in man himself but in the redemption wrought by Christ. It was at the cross that God so altered the human situation that man could truly be declared righteous.

Here we turn to the words of Paul in 2 Corinthians 5:21—"For our sake he [God the Father] made him [Christ] to be sin who knew no sin, so that in him we might become the righteousness of God." What an extraordinary, mind-boggling statement! First, Christ, the truly righteous One—the *only* righteous One—*made* to be[32] *sin*. There at the cross of Calvary Jesus Christ, Son of God and Son of Man, took upon Himself the sin of the whole world—every sin of every person of every time and place, so that in a real and terrible way he became totally identified with sin. Christ the wholly righteous One became Christ the wholly sinful One! Second, all this was done that we might become the righteousness of God in Him. Observe that Paul does not say that we might become righteous but the righteousness of God in Him. Here truly is the wondrous deed of God that lies behind justification: Christ's dying in our place. He took all our sin to Himself and in return gave to us His righteousness.

For a full elaboration of justification let us look again at Romans 3:23–24. First, justification is an act of God's grace: we have been "justified by his grace as a gift." In fact, justification must be by grace—i.e., God's unmerited favor—or not at all, since all people are sinners without any possible way of achieving salvation. Second, justification is based on Christ's redemption, His death bringing about mankind's release from bondage to sin and evil. Hence, the person who experiences justification is one who has been redeemed by Christ. It is not that a person has become righteous, but as one who has been brought back by Christ from the realm of darkness into light, he is declared righteous or for-

---

[31] The Greek word is *dikaiosynē*. It is significant that this comes from the same Greek root as *dikaiōsis* (justification).

[32] There is actually no "to be" in the Greek text; *hamartian epoiēsen* is literally "he made sin." This all the more staggers the mind.

given. This is why Paul so closely relates redemption to the forgiveness of sins. As Paul says elsewhere: "He [God] has delivered us from the dominion of darkness and transferred us to the kingdom of his beloved Son, in whom we have redemption, the forgiveness of sins" (Col. 1:13–14). This is not an infused righteousness so that man is now righteous in himself, but a positive one in which his abode is no longer in the kingdom of darkness but in the kingdom of Christ. Third, and climactically, this redemption has occurred through "an expiation [or "propitiation"][33] by his blood." The word translated "expiation" is from a Greek word that originally referred to the lid or cover on the ark of the covenant. This cover was also called the "mercy seat."[34] On this cover of the ark the blood of the sin offering was sprinkled annually on the Day of Atonement. However, since the blood of an animal could not really suffice for redemption ("It is impossible that the blood of bulls and goats should take away sins" [Heb. 10:4]), Christ in His death "entered once for all into the Holy Place, taking not the blood of goats and calves but his own blood, thus securing an eternal redemption" (Heb. 9:12). It was an amazing act of expiation, so that by Christ's atoning sacrifice both a way of extinguishing the guilt and paying the penalty for sin occurred. In this way eternal redemption was secured.

Similarly Paul says elsewhere that "in him [Christ] we have redemption through his blood, the forgiveness of our trespasses, according to the riches of his grace" (Eph. 1:7). Since forgiveness is one way of speaking about justification, justification is through Christ's blood. This is precisely the language of Paul in Romans 5:9—"We are now justified by his blood." Justification is no light matter to God: it cost Him the death of His only Son.

But we dare not stop with the death of Christ, for if He had remained dead, there would be no justification. The powers of evil and darkness would have prevailed, and man would still be in his sins. This is why Paul says in Romans 4:25 that Christ "was put to death for our trespasses and raised for our justification." "Raised for our justification"! It is the righteousness of a triumphant Christ, a living Christ, that is now ours.

To return, finally, to the central point: the ground—and the only ground—of justification is our redemption through Jesus Christ. Based on the marvel of God's grace ("by grace as a gift"), we have been redeemed through the sacrifice of Christ. Since He bore our sins in that sacrifice, they are no longer imputed to us; since by His sacrifice our guilt and punishment have been taken away, we are now accounted righteous before God. It is through the grace of redemption that we stand justified in the presence of Almighty God.

Before proceeding further, we do well to observe that the righteousness imputed to us in justification is more than an alien righteousness. Surely God justifies the ungodly and the unrighteous by not imputing to us our sins but imputing to us the righteousness of Christ, so that we are declared righteous. Yet it is also a quite important fact that by the death of Christ we are *constituted* as righteous. In a real sense, righteousness does not simply cover

---

[33] The Greek word is *hilastērion*. See my earlier comments on these two possible translations in volume 1, 360n.18.

[34] *Hilastērion* is usually translated "mercy seat" in Hebrews 9:5.

us—thus remaining basically alien to us; it becomes our new constitution.[35]

Paul speaks of this in Romans 5, where he compares Adam and Christ. The apostle first states that "the judgment following one trespass brought condemnation, but the free gift following many trespasses brings justification" (v. 16). Adam's sin of disobedience, Paul adds, has "led to condemnation for all men" whereas Christ's "act of righteousness leads to acquittal[36] and life for all men" (v. 18). Then—and here is the pertinent verse—Paul declares, "For as by one man's disobedience many were made sinners, so by one man's obedience many will be made righteous" (v. 19). The obedience referred to is doubtless Christ's "act of righteousness,"[37] namely, His willing death on the cross;[38] by this many are "made righteous." The translation "made righteous" might be better translated "constituted[39] righteous," that is to say, established as righteous. Hence, in justification there is a basic sense in which God not only declares the sinner righteous but also constitutes him as such. He becomes what God has pronounced him to be.

On this latter point recall the words earlier quoted: ". . . that we might become the righteousness of God." The word "become"[40] also contains both ideas, the declarative and the actual:[41] we become in a vital sense what God declares us to be. The new standing in Christ is also a new being: the opening door into a new life!

V. INSTRUMENT—FAITH

Everything thus far said about God's declaratory righteousness and its ground in redemption becomes effective only through faith. We have dealt with the objective side of justification, namely, that it is basically a declarative act of God that in no way depends on our righteousness and is made possible through the redemption in Jesus Christ. To that we contribute absolutely nothing. But now we have reached the critical subjective point, namely, it is through faith that this justification becomes effective for us.

Indeed, Paul highlights this in Romans prior to his presentation of the unrighteousness of man in 1:18–3:20. In Romans 1:16–17 Paul declares, "I am not ashamed of the gospel: it is the power of God for salvation to every one who has faith, to the Jew first and also to the Greek. For in it the righteousness of God is revealed through[42] faith for faith; as it is written, 'He who through

---

[35] At this point the doctrines of justification and regeneration tend to merge.

[36] The Greek word is *dikaiōsin,* literally, "justification."

[37] The Greek word is *dikaiōmatos,* literally, "righteous act."

[38] Cf. Philippians 2:8: He "became obedient unto death, even death on a cross."

[39] As, e.g., in Weymouth's *New Testament in Modern Speech.* The relevant Greek word is *katastathēsontai* (from *kathistēmi*). Thayer, in loco, has "to set down as," "to constitute." There is both the declarative sense and the effective sense in the Greek word. This means that what *declares* a person's righteousness in some sense also *makes* him that. The English word "constitutes" well conveys both meanings. John Murray puts it succinctly: "Justification is a constitutive act, not barely declarative" (*Romans,* NICNT, 205). *Kathistēmi* contains both the idea of declaring and rendering, of showing to be and causing to be (again see Thayer).

[40] The Greek word is *genōmetha.*

[41] The KJV translation instead of "become" has "be made." "Be made" conveys (perhaps too strongly) the note of the actual. "Become" (like "constitute") better represents the Greek text and, most importantly, the fuller meaning of justification.

[42] The Greek word is *ek,* more often translated as "by."

faith is righteous shall live.' "[43] The instrument of justification is faith.

Now let us again look at Romans 3:25 and note the words "through[44] faith" (NASB). Justification against the background of God's redemptive work in Jesus Christ is through faith in Christ. A few words later Paul declares, "He himself [God] is righteous and . . . justifies him who has faith in Jesus" (3:26). To be sure that both Jew and Gentile understand this, Paul adds, He "will justify the circumcised by faith and the uncircumcised through faith" (3:30 NASB).[45] It is faith in Jesus all the way—for everyone.

How, we may inquire, do grace and faith relate? Let us recall Paul's previous words that "they are justified by his grace as a gift." Hence, grace is the basis, the source, the origin of our new life. But it is to be received by faith; thus faith is the means, the channel, the instrument. In Ephesians Paul puts it very simply: "By grace you have been saved through faith" (2:8). By grace[46] —through faith. If the language is "justified by[47] faith," this does not mean that faith is the source or condition. It is rather the agent or means by

which justification comes to man. If it is said to be "through[48] faith," the emphasis lies on faith as the instrument or channel. In either case, the basic idea is that there is no justification without faith in Christ. And behind that faith stands the grace of God in Jesus Christ. For, says Paul, "it is by faith, that it might be in accordance with grace" (Rom. 4:16 NASB). Thus harmonious and vital is the relationship between grace and faith![49]

Next there is need to emphasize the urgency of faith. I have spoken about the amazing fact of God's declaratory righteousness, how God justifies even the most ungodly, and that man can make utterly no contribution to what God has done and does. However, until a person responds in faith to God's prior activity, he is still in his sins and unrighteousness. It is not as if God justifies and then a person receives justification in faith; it is rather that God justifies him who has faith. The atonement, to be sure, is an objective work of God in Christ that has occurred regardless of any man's response. It is the ground of God's justifying the sinner. But justification itself occurs only where there is faith that receives it.

---

[43] Or, "the just shall live by faith" (KJV). Luther's turning point was this statement by Paul. "Night and day I pondered until I saw the connection between the justice of God and the statement that 'the just shall live by his faith.' Then I grasped that the justice [or "righteousness"] of God is that righteousness by which through grace and sheer mercy God justifies us through faith. Thereupon I felt myself to be reborn and to have gone through open doors into paradise" (Here I Stand, 65).

[44] The Greek word is dia, usually translated "through" (as also in KJV, NIV, NEB).

[45] The two prepositions translated "by" and "through" are ek and dia. They are used interchangeably in relation to faith here and elsewhere. Note especially Galatians 2:16, where dia is first used, then ek.

[46] Cf. also Titus 3:7 where the language is "justified by his grace."

[47] Usually ek, as in Romans 3:30 above. See also Romans 3:26; 5:1; Galatians 2:16; 3:24 among others.

[48] The Greek word is dia, as in Romans 3:22, 25, 30, 31; Galatians 2:16; Ephesians 2:8 above.

[49] This is a relationship, or correlation, that needs constantly to be borne in mind. Berkouwer puts it well: "The preaching of salvation is perpetually threatened from two directions: on the one hand from an over-estimation of the function of faith, by which the decisiveness of grace is made dependent upon human abilities and capacities, and, on the other hand, from a disruption of the correlation by making salvation so wholly objective that faith loses its decisive role in the correlation" (Faith and Justification, 167).

Now let us examine more closely this matter of faith. In doing so we next observe Paul speaking of Abraham as the original illustration. He writes, quoting from Genesis, " 'Abraham believed God, and it was reckoned[50] to him as righteousness' " (Rom. 4:3).[51] It was not Abraham's deeds, Paul adds, that counted, but his faith. Immediately following this Paul says, "To the one who does not work, but believes in[52] Him who justifies the ungodly, his faith is reckoned as righteousness" (Rom. 4:5 NASB). We noted previously that God justifies the ungodly (we also marveled at it) and stressed the aspect of God's declaratory righteousness. But now the point before us is that God does this to the one who "believes in Him." Such a person does not rely on his own works (however good they may seem to be), but realizing his total need—his "ungodliness"—believes in God and is thereby justified.

Faith, accordingly, is "believing in"; for our salvation it means believing in the One who has accomplished this. In a summary statement on righteousness Paul writes, "It will be reckoned to us who believe in him that raised from the dead Jesus our Lord, who was put to death for our trespasses and raised for our justification" (Rom. 4:24–25). It is not merely a believing in God (for example, that He exists), but in Him as the One who completed the work of redemption by raising Jesus from the dead.[53]

Faith—I must now add—is more than a matter of intellectual assent.

Such faith surely includes this: it is a "believing," hence involves the mind. But it is also a "believing in" and therefore involves the heart. Paul clearly makes this point later in an important statement about justification: "If you confess with your lips that Jesus is Lord and believe in your heart that God raised him from the dead, you will be saved. For man believes with his heart and so is justified, and he confesses with his lips and so is saved" (Rom. 10:9–10). It is not a matter merely of accepting as a fact that God raised Jesus (even Satan accepts that fact), but of believing in what God has done. "Believing in" is therefore trust;[54] it is the grateful response of man's inmost being—his heart—to what God has wrought in the death and resurrection of Jesus Christ. It is this kind of faith, out of which the lips proclaim the lordship of Jesus, that is the vehicle of our justification.

Simply put, the faith by which we are justified is faith in Jesus Christ. Paul earlier in Romans, as we observed, spoke thus: "God justifies him who has faith in Jesus" (3:26). In Galatians Paul writes, "We have believed in Christ Jesus, in order to be justified by faith in Christ" (2:16). This means believing in Him as the expiation for our sins and as the risen Lord; but it is at the same time a matter of personal trust and commitment.

Indeed, faith can now be seen as actually the means of our being *united* with Christ. After speaking about being buried with Christ in baptism (baptism

---

[50]The Greek word is *elogisthē* (see earlier discussion), "counted" (KJV, NEB); "credited" (NIV).

[51]Genesis 15:6 reads, "And he believed the LORD; and he reckoned it to him as righteousness."

[52]The Greek word is *epi*, usually translated as "on" or "upon." Whether "in" or "on" or "upon," the meaning is essentially the same.

[53]Peter similarly writes about the resurrection: "Through him [Christ] you believe in God, who raised him from the dead and glorified him, and so your faith and hope are in God" (1 Peter 1:21 NIV).

[54]Recall the discussion of faith as trust in chapter 1, "Calling," IV.B.3., pages 30–31.

representing death to self and total identification with Christ), Paul declares, "If we have been united with him in a death like his, we shall certainly be united with him in a resurrection like his" (Rom. 6:5). Faith—believing in Jesus Christ—is to be in union with Him. This is why Paul, after several statements about justification by faith in Galatians (2:15–17), movingly declares, "I have been crucified with Christ; it is no longer I who live, but Christ who lives in me; and the life I now live in the flesh I live by faith in the Son of God, who loved me and gave himself for me" (2:20). The climax of faith is this, that we are in Christ and Christ is in us.

All of this leads to some further reflection on the role of faith in justification. We have spoken earlier of the nonimputation of sins and the imputation of Christ's righteousness. Now we are ready to emphasize that it is the person who believes in Christ to whom this righteousness is imputed ("he justifies him who has faith in Jesus"). It is not a matter of an imputed righteousness that is thereafter received by faith, but of such righteousness being imputed to one who now has faith. Moreover, since faith is a believing in and union with Christ, this imputation of righteousness is by no means a pretense or a make-believe, as if God declares about us what really is not so. Rather, by virtue of our union with Christ through faith (Christ thereby living in us), God declares what really is true! Yes, God does justify the ungodly,[55] but only as they are believers in Christ and thereby united with Him. Hence, Christ's righteousness does clothe the sinner[56] and he is in some sense thereby constituted righteous,[57] but this occurs through the faith that unites one to Jesus Christ. This is not by virtue of any accomplished righteousness in ourselves, but totally what we have in Him. We are, then, righteous in Jesus Christ.[58] This does not mean that we are no longer sinners, for indeed *in ourselves* we are. But *in Christ* we are wholly righteous!

In the last several paragraphs I have spoken much about faith and its necessity for justification: we are justified only through faith. Where faith is not present, there is no justification. But now we must not so elevate faith as to make it the cause of justification. We are justified by faith, through faith, but *not on account of faith*. The grace of God is prior to all faith; the work of redemption is the ground of justification. Christ's righteousness precedes any righteousness we may have; hence, faith, for all its importance, is only the channel of God's saving deed. To say that faith justifies[59] is to place too great an emphasis on the place of faith. "He [God] justifies him who has faith in Jesus," Paul says, but faith is

---

[55] The full statement of Paul reads, "To one who does not work but trusts him who justifies the ungodly, his faith is reckoned as righteousness" (Rom. 4:5).

[56] As earlier discussed.

[57] As earlier discussed.

[58] "God treats us as righteous, because we are righteous in so far as we are 'in Christ.' It is not that God treats us 'as if' we were righteous. In Christ we *are* righteous even now" (Alan Richardson, *An Introduction to the Theology of the New Testament*, 237).

[59] Luther in his strong concern to repudiate any idea of works as contributing to justification sometimes puts it that way: "Since . . . works justify no man . . . it is very evident that it is faith alone which, because of the pure mercy of God through Christ and in his Word, worthily and sufficiently justifies and saves the person" (*Selections from His Writings*, John Dillenberger, ed., "The Freedom of a Christian," 70). Luther, to be sure, emphasizes God's "pure mercy" before mentioning justification; however, the statement that "faith . . . justifies" can be misleading. (For the expression "faith alone justifies" also see ibid., 56–57, three times repeated.)

not the cause or source: this rests in God.

One statement in Romans might seem to place the larger emphasis on faith. Paul, referring to the promise to Abraham and his descendants about inheriting the world, declares that the promise is fulfilled "through the righteousness of faith" (4:13). Then Paul adds, "For this reason it is by[60] faith, that it might be in accordance with[61] grace" (4:16 NASB). "By faith," however, does not mean that the promise depends on faith,[62] but that it is by way of the faith that accords with the grace of God that the promise is to be fulfilled. Faith is essential, but is not to be placed above grace.

Further, by overemphasizing faith there is the danger of its becoming a kind of work to be accomplished. Later I will discuss the misplaced stress on works that may lead to anxiety about whether enough has been done to achieve or merit salvation. But a similar anxiety concerning faith may emerge, for example, have I believed enough to be justified? If faith justifies, do I have sufficient faith?[63] It is far better to understand faith not as some act of believing, but purely and simply as a channel. It is an empty one at that, receiving what God has done in Christ. Faith makes no positive contribution (as a work seeks to do), but simply and wholly relies on God's mercy for justification.

In summary, wherever there is realization of sin and repentance, faith in turn is total reliance on God. There is nothing to offer up, to contribute, except our own sinfulness. The only hope is to cleave to the mercy of God and trust Him for entire salvation. We accept what He has wrought in Jesus Christ, and thereby are justified. Faith is merely this thankful acceptance, and thus the way into eternal life.

From all that has been said it is apparent that faith *alone* is the instrument of justification. There is nothing that man can contribute by way of preparation or cooperation. It is "by faith from first to last."[64] The singularity of faith[65] is critical to a proper understanding of justification.[66] Without such an understanding, salvation becomes precariously based. There

---

[60] The Greek word is *ek*.

[61] The Greek word is *kata*.

[62] The RSV translation, "it depends on faith," is misleading.

[63] Calvin writes, "For did faith justify of itself . . . as it is always weak and imperfect, its efficacy would be partial, and thus our righteousness being maimed, would give us only a portion of salvation. We indeed imagine nothing of the kind, but say, that, properly speaking, God alone justifies" (*Institutes,* III.11.7, Beveridge trans.). Later, Calvin calls it "an absurd dogma, that man is justified by faith" (III.11.23).

[64] The NIV translation of Romans 1:17: "For in the gospel a righteousness from God is revealed, a righteousness that is by faith from first to last. . . . "

[65] Luther felt so strongly about this singularity that in his German translation of the New Testament he added the word "alone" to the word "faith" in Romans 3:28.

[66] The Roman Catholic Council of Trent in its reaction against Luther (and other Reformers) set forth a number of "Decrees" and "Canons" including some on justification. Canon 9 reads, "If anyone says that the sinner is justified by faith alone, meaning that nothing else is required to co-operate in order to obtain the grace of justification, and that it is not necessary that he be prepared and disposed by the action of his own will, let him be anathema." In other words, man must do something by way of cooperation (according to chapter V in the "Decree," "co-operating with that grace"): faith alone is not sufficient. Roman Catholicism thereby failed to recognize that man is in no way capable by an act of will to "be prepared and disposed," that man can do nothing except to rely totally on the grace and mercy of God. It is sad that the Roman view puts man back in the anxious condition of wondering if he has done enough to receive justification.

will, again and again, arise the disturbing question: Have I done enough, in addition to believing, to merit justification?

VI. PLACE OF WORKS

Now we come to a consideration of the place of works in justification. Already much has been said to discount works as having any positive role to play. The main point is that all our works are so tainted by sin that they can make no contribution to salvation. Ideally, as Paul declares in Romans, "it is . . . the doers of the law who will be justified" (2:13).[67] However, as he proceeds to show after that, there is no one who really keeps the law; hence, "no human being will be justified in his sight by works of the law" (3:20). Works of the law, thus any works, are ruled out as contributing anything at all to justification.

We may turn first to Ephesians 2:8–10 on this matter of works. Paul therein declares that salvation is not by works and that this deprives anyone of boasting. "For by grace you have been saved through faith; and this is not your own doing, it is the gift of God—not because of works, lest any man should boast" (vv. 8–9). If we were saved[68] by our good works, we might become boastful of our accomplishment. But since salvation is totally of God and wholly a gift through faith, all boasting is eliminated. This is important because humility is what God desires of man; moreover, it is essential to a genuine Christian walk. Second, Paul affirms that good works are a result of our new creation in Christ: "For we are his workmanship, created[69] in Christ Jesus for good works, which God prepared beforehand, that we should walk in them" (v. 10). Good works, accordingly, are the issue of salvation. They are so closely related to the new creation in Christ that they are not merely a consequence. We are created "for"; hence, for the purpose of performing the good works that God has "prepared beforehand."[70] Without such good works our creation in Christ remains unfulfilled.

This leads us to observe how intimately faith and works are related. Although we are justified by faith alone (and that means without works), faith is never alone. For a true faith, a justifying faith, is a faith that works through love. To use the language of Paul in Galatians 5:6: "In Christ Jesus neither circumcision nor uncircumcision is of any avail, but faith working through love." Love is the immediate companion of faith, but this does not mean that it is coeffectual with faith in terms of justification.[71] If so, we are back again with something in man, in this case love, that provides some basis for justification. Love, to be sure, Paul says elsewhere, is "poured into our hearts" (Rom. 5:5) as a result of our justification (v. 1—"since we are justified by faith"), but it is not a shared basis with

---

[67] Paul, at this juncture, is comparing hearing with doing: "It is not the hearers of the law who are righteous before God, but the doers of the law who will be justified." Paul has not yet come to his statements about the gospel meaning of justification.

[68] The terminology of justification is not used in Ephesians; however, the same theme is implicitly here.

[69] This is not the original creation but new creation. See Ephesians 2:15 for further clarification. The Amplified Bible translates as "recreated in Christ Jesus."

[70] The Greek word is *proētoimasen*. This further eliminates any room for boasting: even our good works are those which God has already prepared!

[71] In Calvin's words: "The only faith which justifies is that which works by love . . . but love does not give it its justifying power" (*Institutes,* III.11.20, Beveridge trans.).

faith for justification.[72] It is that which the Holy Spirit, given to the believer, pours into his heart. Love is the sure and certain outflow of a true and living faith.

This becomes apparent in the letter of James. In a discussion of the relation between faith and works James says a number of things. First, he declares that "faith by itself, if it has no works, is dead" (2:17). James prefaces this statement by speaking of someone who says he has faith but no works, and as a result shows utterly no concern to help a needy and hungry person. Such a faith obviously never was real: It cannot save him (v. 14) and by showing no love demonstrates its deadness. We may interpolate by saying that a living faith centered in Jesus Christ is bound to express itself in love; else it is no faith at all. But, again, it is not the loving deed that saves a person; it is rather his relationship to Christ. Second, James declares that "faith apart from works is barren" (2:20).[73] In context, this means again that a faith not

expressing itself in works is as barren as the faith of demons, who believe God is one (v. 19). Their faith is obviously not a living faith (surely no salvation accrues to them), and their works are idle, useless, barren. Third, James attests that Abraham's faith "was *completed* by works" (2:22)[74] in that he offered up his son Isaac. This was the fulfillment, James adds, of the Scripture that says, "Abraham believed God, and it was reckoned to him as righteousness" (v. 23), hence "a man is justified by works and not by faith alone" (v. 24). It is important to observe here that although there is a seeming contradiction with Paul, James is not dealing with works as a way of salvation but with a superficial faith that issues in little or no works at all.[75] Again, a living faith will overflow in good deeds, else it is only a dead faith. Hence, the appropriateness of the final words of James on the subject: "For as the body apart from the spirit is dead, so faith apart from works is dead" (2:26).[76]

---

[72] Here, again, the Council of Trent erred. Under the "Canons" related to justification, Canon 11 states in part: "If anyone says that men are justified either by the sole imputation of the justice of Christ or by the sole remission of sins, to the exclusion of the grace and *the charity* [love] *which is poured forth in their hearts by the Holy Ghost,* and remains [or "is inherent"—Lat. *"inhereat"*] in them . . . let him be anathema." However, we must reply, love is excluded basically from justification. Rather, it is the immediate result in that *one already justified* has the love of God poured into his heart by the Holy Spirit. Trent errs on both sides of justification: it looks for *something plus faith* (see earlier n. 66—a cooperation to obtain justification) or *faith plus something* (love poured forth in the heart as also necessary). Either of these plusses vitiates the gospel of the marvelous free grace of God that is received by faith and faith alone.

[73] The Greek word is *argē:* "idle, useless" (BAGD), "idle," "unprofitable" (Thayer). The NASB and NIV translate it "useless." "Barren" (also NEB translation) well conveys the meaning. (Cf. 2 Peter 1:8 where *argous* is used along with *akarpous* ["unfruitful"]. "Barren" and "unfruitful" are good parallel translations.)

[74] The NEB interestingly reads, "By these actions the integrity of his faith was fully proved."

[75] "James was combating a superficial faith that had no wholesome effect in the life of the professed believer. Paul, on the other hand, was combating legalism—the belief that one may earn saving merit before God by his good deeds" (Donald Burdick, *James,* EBC, 12:185).

[76] Luther in his "Preface to the Epistles of St. James and St. Jude" begins by saying, "I think highly of the epistle of James." However, later he declaims against it, stating that "in direct opposition to St. Paul and all the rest of the Bible, it ascribes justification to works."

Returning to the main theme in Paul about faith working through love, we may say that works are not the ground but the consequence of justification. Works are clear-cut evidence that the faith is a vital faith. Hence, works have demonstrative but not saving value. When John writes in one of his letters, "We know that we have passed out of death into life, because we love the brethren" (1 John 3:14), it is not that love has made the passage but that it is the evidence that it has occurred. Indeed, John says later, "He who does not love does not know God" (4:8)— again not that love justifies or saves,[77] but that if one does not love, it is sure proof that he has not really come to know God. Faith operates through love: it cannot be otherwise.

To use the language of Jesus Himself, "Every sound tree bears good fruit . . . you will know them by their fruits" (Matt. 7:17, 20). A good tree, we might add, is one rooted deep in the soil of faith, and in that is its life and salvation. But the only assurance we have that the tree is good is by seeing the fruit. Surely, this is the proof—good fruits, good works—that salvation, yes, just-ification, has been received. Good works are the fruit of a true and living faith.

VII. RESULTS OF JUSTIFICATION

The primary result of justification is that we become *sons of God*. All human beings are God's creatures: they are made by Him. But those justified are now His sons and daughters, His children. This is our new status in Jesus Christ.

Let us look again at Galatians. Shortly after his statement "that we might be justified by faith" (3:24), Paul adds, "In Christ Jesus you are all sons of God, through faith" (v. 26). Still further on, Paul speaks of this sonship as adoption: "God sent forth his Son . . . to redeem those who were under the law, so that we might receive adoption as sons" (4:4–5). Hence, as sons of God by adoption we may call God "Father"— "Abba! Father!" (4:6). Paul likewise says in Romans, "You have received a spirit of adoption as sons by which we cry out, 'Abba! Father!' " (8:15 NASB).[78] Thus, not only are we declared righteous in justification but we are also adopted into God's family.[79] Conse-

---

Luther adds concerning James, "I therefore refuse him a place among the writers of the true canon of my Bible" (see, e.g., *Selections from His Writings,* 35–36). Luther's deeply personal experience of justification by faith doubtless influenced his mixed attitude toward James. Still, there are many today who find in James a contradiction to Paul, or at least a misunderstanding; e.g., B. S. Easton: "James, of course, misunderstands Paul . . . " (IB, 12:41). Although there are some difficulties in the language James uses, I see no real contradiction or misunderstanding. Paul does stress justification by faith alone, whereas James is saying that if faith is genuine, good works will follow. James is dealing with what might be called operational justification!

[77]To use Paul's and James' terminology. John, neither in his Gospel nor his letters, speaks, as such, of justification.

[78]John, without using the exact language of justification, says much the same thing: "As many as received Him, to them He gave the right to become children of God" (John 1:12 NASB). "Right" is the Greek word *exousin* and signifies a new status (as does justification); "to become" (not "to be") is similar to Pauline language, "that we might become the righteousness of God" (2 Cor. 5:21).

[79]The Westminster Confession of Faith, after a chapter on justification (chap. XI), has a chapter on adoption (chap. XII). This latter chapter begins, "All those that are justified God vouchsafeth, in and for his only Son Jesus Christ, to make partakers of the grace of adoption. . . . " What follows in the Confession is generally what I will be saying in the

quently, there is a new child-to-Father relationship, which is the joyous result of justification. We are in the family of God.

A. Freedom

One of the outstanding results of justification is *freedom*. As the children of God we have been delivered from the slavery of the past. Paul declares, "Through God you are no longer a slave but a son" (Gal. 4:7). We are free people because of Christ.

For one thing this is a freedom from any and all earthly systems. Just prior to Paul's speaking about our adoption as sons, he says, "We, when we were children, were in bondage under the elements[80] of the world" (Gal. 4:3 KJV). "Elements" probably refers to basic forces by which people live and are bound—pagan dieties, ceremonial practices, societal demands, and the like. Formerly captives to the world— this elemental worldly system—we have been set free by Christ. Paul later calls the elementary forces "weak and beggarly elements" (v. 9 KJV), and in this connection refers to the observance of "days, and months, and seasons, and years" (v. 10). All such elemental stuff, whether one is yoked to it as Jew or Gentile, represents bondage to the world. From this, declares Paul, we have been set free!

This bondage to the world is common to all people outside of Christ. We have but to reflect for a moment on our contemporary situation in which people are dominated by the spirit of the age. This refers not so much to obvious sin and evil as to the constant pressures to conform to a worldly outlook that makes idols out of such things as success, pleasure, money, security, and fame. Also there is the ongoing substitution of forms for reality in the religious sphere—observances, rituals, practices—that actually enslave people. From all this, and much more, Christ freed us.

The greatest deliverance, in simple terms, is from bondage to sin. We may turn in this regard to the Book of Acts and hear Paul's words in a sermon: "Let it be known to you therefore, brethren, that through this man [Jesus] forgiveness of sins is proclaimed to you, and by him everyone that believes is freed from everything from which you could not be freed by the law of Moses" (13:38–39). The two words here translated "freed" are derived from the word for "justified,"[81] hence the close approximation of the two. To be justified, accordingly, is to be freed from all sin through the forgiveness of sin. This freedom the Mosaic Law could never give. That law commanded righteousness, but because of man's bondage to sin, there was no deliverance.

There is, finally, a freedom from anxiety in justification. No longer is there cause for concern about one's relationship to God. Such questions as,

---

following pages except that my presentation continues under the heading of "Results of Justification." I do not believe that there is need for a separate doctrinal formulation of adoption, since it is really another aspect of justification, namely, that in justification we are not only declared righteous but also adopted as sons. Both aspects refer to our new standing before God, with the latter, i.e., adoption, highlighting the new family status.

[80]The Greek word is *stoicheia*. According to Thayer, Paul here refers to "the rudiments with which mankind . . . were indoctrinated before the time of Christ, i.e., the elements of religious training, or the ceremonial precepts common alike to the worship of Jews and of Gentiles." These rudiments became forces to which people were enslaved. The RSV rendering of *stoicheia* as "elemental spirits" (which is a possible interpretation of *stoicheia*) points to the power nature of these forces.

[81]Two forms of *dikaioō*. The NIV (like the KJV) translates both words "justified."

Have I done enough to be right with God, enough to please Him, enough to insure salvation? are all done away. God has completely forgiven our sins and declared us righteous in Jesus Christ. Our standing with God, because of Him and His grace, is perfect. There is utterly nothing lacking.

This freedom from anxiety also applies to one's daily Christian walk. Even though there is a right relationship to God, we do sin now and again. Hence, as believers, we may again feel anxious about our situation. Here is where a proper understanding of justification makes for a full freedom from anxiety, namely, that whatever sins we may commit are *already* forgiven. We may and ought to repent of these sins, even more to seek to remove them from our lives,[82] but we do not need to feel condemned. In Jesus Christ there is no condemnation; we are complete in Him, and His righteousness totally envelops us! The burden of sin and guilt is gone forever: we are totally and gloriously free!

B. Peace

Another result of justification is the *peace* that it brings. There is peace with God, peace with others, and peace within.

First, let us reflect on peace with God. At the conclusion of Paul's presentation of justification in Romans 3 and 4, he says, "Therefore, since we are justified by faith, we have peace[83] with God through our Lord Jesus Christ" (5:1). Formerly, we stood under the wrath of God, but, Paul later adds, "now justified by his blood, much more shall we be saved by him [Christ] from the wrath of God" (5:9). We were "enemies" of God (5:10), subject to His wrath and anger, without hope of anything except terrible judgment. Now we are no longer at odds with God, no longer standing under His wrath, no longer hopeless and helpless: we have peace with God. Justified by His blood through faith, we have this marvelous peace!

As sons of God through justification, our status is totally different from what it was before. Previously, as Paul puts it elsewhere, we were "children of wrath" (Eph. 2:3). Now we are children of God, no longer under His wrath, but through Jesus Christ under His peace and salvation. What a blessed change of status!

There is also peace with other people. In the sinful human situation division, hostility, enmity, and the like everywhere predominate. There are insurmountable barriers between people, but, as Paul declares (particularly in reference to Jew and Gentile), through Christ there is peace: "For he is our peace, who has made us both one, and has broken down the dividing wall of hostility" (Eph. 2:14). But this also refers to all categories of people. Shortly after Paul has said (in Galatians) that we are all sons of God through faith, he declares, "There is neither Jew nor Greek, there is neither slave nor free, there is neither male nor female; for you are all one in Christ Jesus" (3:28). This, of course, does not mean that there are no differences and distinctions among people. But where culture and race, sex and social status formerly made for hostility and enmity, these are now transcended by a oneness in Jesus Christ. To be sure, we still see hostility, rancor, and antagonism existing among

---

[82]This will be discussed more fully in chapter 4, "Sanctification."

[83]There is some manuscript evidence for "let us have peace" (in accordance with this, NEB reads, "Let us continue at peace"). However, Paul's prior argument plus the further development in Romans 5 favors "we have peace." So (in addition to RSV) KJV, NIV, NASB translate.

many who call themselves Christians. However, such is contrary to our true life in Christ.

The gospel is the gospel of peace, indeed of "grace and peace." Since God has forgiven and accepted all of us in Jesus Christ, we are challenged thereby to forgive and accept one another. "He is our peace!"

Finally, there is peace within. Among the last words Jesus spoke to His disciples were these: "Peace I leave with you; my peace I give to you; not as the world gives do I give to you" (John 14:27). This is an inner peace that the world can neither give nor take away. It is more than freedom from anxiety (which I have previously discussed); it is a positive sense of deep peace that belongs to those who are justified by faith in Christ. Being united to Him in faith, we find *His* peace deep in our hearts.

It is a peace that stems from being right with God—no longer under His judgment and condemnation—and thus we are at peace within ourselves. We do not need to feel condemnation, for, as Paul asks, "Who is to condemn?" (Rom. 8:34). Since God does not condemn, no one—including Satan, other persons, or even we ourselves—is able to condemn!

At peace with God, our neighbors, and ourselves, we are at peace within.

C. Inheritance

The final result of justification is that we are *heirs* of God's promise. In Galatians, following words about being justified by faith and the statement that we are "all sons of God, through faith" (3:26), Paul declares, "If you are Christ's, then you are Abraham's offspring, heirs according to promise" (v. 29). The promise in the New Testament is clearly that of an *eternal inheritance*.[84]

Later in Galatians we read, "Therefore you are no longer a slave, but a son; and if a son, then an heir through God" (4:7 NASB). The nature of the inheritance is not specified, but that it is "through God" is a matter of decisive importance. On earth we may inherit many things through the action of other people (for example, through their last will and testament), but such pales into insignificance when compared with the fact that we are heirs through God. As no longer slaves but sons, there is a rich inheritance from God our Father.

Next, we observe that not only are we heirs through God but also, as Paul says in Romans, "fellow heirs[85] with Christ" (8:17). Fellow heirs with Christ! In the messianic Psalm 2 God speaks to His Son, saying, "Ask of Me, and I will surely give the nations as Thine inheritance, and the very ends of the earth as Thy possession" (v. 8 NASB). In John 3:35 the text reads, "The Father loves the Son, and has given all things into his hand." So whatever God has given Christ, we are to share as "fellow heirs." In John 17:22 Jesus declared, "The glory which thou hast given me I have given to them"; hence His immeasurable and incomparable glory will also be shared with us!

But the inheritance begins even now! Perhaps nowhere in Scripture is this stated more effectively than in 1 Corinthians 3:21–22: "For all things are yours, whether Paul or Apollos or Cephas or the world or life or death or the

---

[84] Hebrews 9:15 speaks of receiving "the promised eternal inheritance." Hebrews 11:8–10 first speaks of the land as an inheritance, but thereafter adds that Abraham "looked forward to the city which has foundations, whose builder and maker is God." These two passages, viewed together, emphasize that the promise to Abraham ultimately was that of an eternal inheritance.

[85] The Greek word is *synklēronomoi;* KJV: "joint heirs," NIV: "co-heirs."

present or the future, all are yours; and you are Christ's; and Christ is God's.'' Belonging to Christ, we are heirs even now of all valuable things—the rich Christian heritage (Paul, Apollos, etc.), the world in all its extent and wonder, life in all its richness and variety, the present in all its challenge and opportunity. But also the inheritance extends far beyond: for death is ours (we triumph over it), as well as the future beyond the grave—life everlasting. All are ours, for we are Christ's and Christ is God's.

Finally, of course, the glorious inheritance is the life to come. One last word from Paul is surely in order: ''He saved us, not because of deeds done by us in righteousness, but in virtue of his own mercy . . . so that we might be justified by his grace and become heirs in hope of eternal life'' (Titus 3:5, 7). *Justified by His grace*—our theme throughout this chapter—and as a climactic result: we are heirs looking forward to eternal life. Truly we shall sing God's praises forever and ever! Amen.

4

Sanctification

We come next to a consideration of the doctrine of sanctification. Our concern will not only be with salvation in its initial occurrence but also with the wider area of Christian life. Accordingly, we will be viewing sanctification in all its dimensions.

I. MEANING

At the outset it is important to recognize that we are dealing with the matter of holiness.[1] To sanctify means to *make holy* or *be made holy*. Sanctification refers, accordingly, both to an action—sanctifying or making holy, and to a condition or state—being sanctified or made holy. In any event, sanctification has to do with holiness of life.

First, holiness refers to *separation* or *apartness*. In the Old Testament, Israel was called a holy people because of their separation to God from all other nations. So, for example, Deuteronomy 7:6 reads, "For you are a people holy to the LORD your God; the LORD your God has chosen you to be a people for his own possession, out of all the peoples that are on the face of the earth." Israel was a separated people, separated unto the Lord and therefore holy, not because of any intrinsic virtue but simply because of their set-apartness.[2] Israel, consequently, was not like any other people: they belonged exclusively to the Lord.

This matter of separation and apartness is grounded essentially in the reality of God Himself. The oft-repeat-

---

[1] In the English New Testament the Greek word *hagiasmos* is often translated either "sanctification" or "holiness." E.g., 1 Thessalonians 4:3–7 contains *hagiasmos* three times: the NASB translates all three as "sanctification"; the KJV as "sanctification" the first two times, "holiness" the other time; the RSV as "sanctification" the first time, "holiness" the other two times (NIV and NEB shift to a verbal form, namely, "to be holy" in the first instance, and various like renditions thereafter). A similar Greek word is *hagiosynē* (used only in Rom. 1:4; 2 Cor. 7:1; 1 Thess. 3:13) is translated "holiness" in RSV, KJV, NASB.

[2] The Hebrew word for "holiness," *qōḏeš* (or "holy," *qāḏôš*) means initially "apartness" or "separation." TWOT lists "apartness" first. IDB speaks of the "elemental meaning" as "separation" (see article "Holiness"). Louis Berkhof suggests that *qōḏeš* may "derive from the root *qad*, meaning 'to cut,'" thus making "the idea of separation the original idea" (*Systematic Theology*, 527).

ed declaration that God is holy refers primarily to His otherness from everything else.[3] This includes any other gods: "Who is like thee, O LORD, among the gods? Who is like thee, majestic in holiness, terrible in glorious deeds, doing wonders?" (Exod. 15:11). This otherness is also in relation to man: "I am God and not man, the Holy One in your midst" (Hosea 11:9). Since God is thus separate from all else, His people are a people separated to Him and set apart from the rest of mankind. Thereby they are a holy people belonging solely and uniquely to God.[4]

This basic idea of a distinctive holy people carries over into the New Testament in regard to Christian believers. For example, note these words: "But you are a chosen race, a royal priesthood, a holy nation, God's own people" (1 Peter 2:9). "Chosen," "holy," "God's own people"—all fit together. God's people are a "holy people" by virtue of belonging uniquely to Him.[5]

Second, holiness refers to *purity and cleanness*. For holiness means not only separation in the sense of removal from one sphere of existence to another (as Israel from all other nations), but also separation from all that is impure and evil. This again goes back to the holiness of God, for the divine holiness signifies not only God's total otherness from His creation, but also His purity over against all that is common and profane. As the holy God, who is "of purer eyes than to behold evil" (Hab. 1:13), He calls for purity in His people. In the Old Testament this is early

seen in the account of Israel at Mount Sinai. God said to Moses: "Go to the people and consecrate them today and tomorrow, and let them wash their garments . . . for on the third day the LORD will come down upon Mount Sinai in the sight of all the people" (Exod. 19:10–11). The consecration of the people and the washing of their garments points to the necessity of purity and cleanness in the presence of God.

There is much in the Old Testament that relates to ritual holiness. The washing of garments, just mentioned, is but the first of many requirements for Israel in regard to ceremonial cleansing. Such cleansing is required of everything—priests, utensils, the people themselves—all that participates in the worship activity. Furthermore, the call to holiness (as in Lev. 11:44) may be put in terms of not eating foods designated as unclean. Holiness, whether in terms of ritual cleansing or abstention from food, is in such instances a matter of external purity and cleanness.

There is, however, an increasingly strong emphasis on holiness as inward purity. A central feature of the Day of Atonement is that of inner cleansing: "You shall be clean from all your sins before the LORD" (Lev. 16:30 NASB). In addition, there are many expressions elsewhere in the Old Testament relating to the need for inner cleanness and purity. For example, in reply to the question, "Who shall stand in his holy place?" the answer is, "He who has clean hands and a pure heart" (Ps. 24:3–4). Once again, this goes back to

[3]Everett F. Harrison writes, "Judging from the usage of the root *qdš*, the basic idea conveyed by the holiness of God is His separateness, i.e., His uniqueness, His distinction as the Wholly Other . . . the One who stands apart from and above the creation" ("Holiness; Holy," ISBE rev. ed., 2:725).

[4]Indeed, everything associated with God is holy. E.g., the Sabbath instituted by God is "a holy sabbath" (Exod. 16:23); the heaven above is God's "holy heaven" (Ps. 20:6); God sits on His "holy throne" (47:8); and Zion is God's "holy hill" (2:6).

[5]In the New Testament the apostles and prophets are called "holy apostles and prophets" (Eph. 3:5), the Christian calling is a "holy calling" (2 Tim. 1:9), the Jerusalem from above is "the holy city" (Rev. 21:2). See vol. 1, chapter 3, IV.A., pages 59–63.

God Himself who is "of purer eyes than to behold evil." Accordingly, only the pure of heart can stand in His holy presence.

In the New Testament the idea of ritual purity or cleanness is almost totally eclipsed. Jesus in His ministry spoke against those who "cleanse the outside of the cup and of the plate, but inside they are full of extortion and rapacity" (Matt. 23:25; cf. Luke 11:39). On another occasion, after Jesus declared that "whatever goes into a man from outside cannot defile him," the Gospel writer added, "Thus he declared all foods clean" (Mark 7:18–19). In both instances the purity called for is not outward but inward: it is a matter of the heart. Nothing more vividly says this than these words of Jesus in the Beatitudes: "Blessed are the pure in heart, for they shall see God" (Matt. 5:8). Purity in heart—not outward purity—is the way to the Highest.

The purpose of Christ's self-giving, according to Paul, included our purification: "[He] gave himself for us to redeem us from all iniquity and to purify for himself a people of his own who are zealous for good deeds" (Titus 2:14). Unmistakably this refers to inner purification or cleansing, not an outward "cup," but people themselves. Elsewhere Paul writes, "Let us cleanse[6] ourselves from every defilement of body and spirit, and make holiness perfect in the fear of God" (2 Cor. 7:1). It is apparent that purification refers to both body and spirit and relates to the perfection of holiness, or sanctification.

Third, holiness refers to *moral perfection*. In the Old Testament God is declared to be perfect: "This God—his way is perfect" (2 Sam. 22:31; also Ps. 18:30).[7] This is a positive affirmation about God's character, "His way." It is not only that the holy God is without evil in His nature but that He is perfect in all His ways and actions—in righteousness,[8] love,[9] and truth.[10] In the Old Testament perfection was demanded in the sacrificial animals. As an illustration: "When any one offers a sacrifice of peace offerings to the LORD . . . from the herd or from the flock, to be accepted it must be perfect" (Lev. 22:21). That was the external perfection of an animal without bodily blemish. However, in the New Testament the shift is to internal perfection, as especially declared in the words of Jesus: "Therefore you are to be perfect, as your heavenly Father is perfect" (Matt. 5:48 NASB).

The perfection of which Jesus spoke (preceding the "therefore") is spelled out in terms of a sixfold "But I say to you," five of which prohibit anger, lust, divorce,[11] swearing, and retaliation, and the sixth enjoining love of enemies. Prior to these injunctions by Jesus, He had already affirmed the indissolubility of the Old Testament commandments;[12] hence the perfection He declared includes these, *plus* His own statements beginning "But I say to you. . . ."

It is significant that, according to Jesus, this perfection finds its fulfillment in terms of self-sacrificing love. To the rich young ruler who claimed to have kept all the command-

---

[6]The Greek word is *katharisōmen*, "purify" (NIV).

[7]Also cf. Deuteronomy 32:4: "The Rock, his work is perfect."

[8]E.g., "the law of the LORD is perfect" (Ps. 19:7), referring to God's righteousness.

[9]E.g., Paul writes about God's "perfect patience" (1 Tim. 1:16). God's patience, or longsuffering (*makrothymia*), represents His continuing love.

[10]Right after the statement, quoted above, "This God—his way is perfect," are the words "the promise of the LORD proves true."

[11]Except on grounds of unchastity (Matt. 5:32).

[12]"Not an iota, not a dot, will pass from the law until all is accomplished" (Matt. 5:18).

ments, Jesus asserted, "If you would be perfect, go, sell what you possess and give to the poor . . . and come, follow me" (Matt. 19:21). The final perfection is the perfection of love. To this we may well add the words in 1 John 4:12—"If we love one another, God abides in us and his love is perfected in us." The holy God, who is perfect in all His ways, calls His people to perfection.

II. OCCURRENCE

Next we observe that sanctification relates to the beginning, the continuation, and the goal of the Christian life. Thus sanctification is past, present, and future.

A. The Beginning

Sanctification, or holiness, in a primary sense *already* belongs to those who are the people of God. Israel, as previously noted, is a holy people by virtue of their separation from other peoples unto God—"You are a people holy to the LORD your God." Likewise the New Testament people of God are "a holy nation." Holiness, or sanctification, is a bedrock fact of the existence of God's people.

However—and this must immediately be added—sanctification belongs to Christian believers not simply by virtue of their being separated from other people but because of separation and purification from sin. The "holy nation"—referring to Christians—consists of those who (as the verse continues) have been "called . . . out of darkness into his marvelous light" (1 Peter 2:9). Paul writes about those who were previously "immoral . . . idolaters . . . adulterers . . . homosexu-

als . . . thieves . . . greedy . . . drunkards . . . revilers . . . robbers," adding, "such were some of you. But you were washed, you were sanctified, you were justified in the name of the Lord Jesus Christ and in the Spirit of our God" (1 Cor. 6:9–11). This separation from sin is therefore not only a distancing from it,[13] but also an inner purification or a cleansing ("you were washed"). There is both separation and cleansing in sanctification.

It is important to recognize that the source of this sanctification is Jesus Christ. Paul spoke earlier of how Christ is "our wisdom, our righteousness and sanctification and redemption" (1 Cor. 1:30). And this is *an accomplished reality* because of what He has done. According to Hebrews, "we have been sanctified through the offering of the body of Jesus Christ once for all" (10:10), hence by His sacrificial death on the cross. This has happened through the purification of sin by His blood.[14] Hebrews earlier spoke of how in the former covenant "the sprinkling of defiled persons with the blood of goats and bulls and with the ashes of a heifer sanctifies for the purification of the flesh"[15] (9:13). Then the writer adds, "How much more shall the blood of Christ, who through the eternal Spirit offered himself without blemish to God, purify your conscience from dead works to serve the living God" (9:14).

Now all of this refers quite specifically to the beginning of the Christian walk. Even as our justification was at the beginning, so was our sanctification; even as He forgave our transgressions, so did He cleanse us from sin. Not only did He remove from us

---

[13] Sometimes called positional sanctification.

[14] Hebrews 10:29 speaks of "the blood of the covenant" by which one has been "sanctified."

[15] "Flesh" here refers to the outward, external aspect of man "defiled" by ceremonial impurities (e.g., the "ashes of a heifer" refers to Numbers 19 where a person, made "unclean" through contact with a dead body, became clean through the ashes of a slaughtered red heifer mixed with water).

the guilt of sin, but He also purged us of its inner pollution.[16] This happened— and happens—in and through Jesus Christ's death on the cross and is received on our part by putting our faith in Him.

All believers, whatever their present situation, have accordingly been sanctified in Christ Jesus and therefore are *saints*. Paul addressed the church at Corinth as "those who have been sanctified in Christ Jesus, saints by calling"[17] (1 Cor. 1:2 NASB). All Christians, i.e., those "in Christ Jesus," are persons who have been sanctified, and by their very calling[18] are saints.[19] A saint, therefore, is any and every Christian, not some person on a higher level of holiness.[20] We may say "Saint Paul" and "Saint Peter," but just as properly we may say "Saint William" and "Saint Louise" if they are believers. "Sainthood" is proper nomenclature for all God's people. In Christ Jesus we are all holy ones, sanctified and, as such, saints of God.

Moreover, there is a sense in which one may speak of believers as those whom God has *perfected*. In Hebrews 10 the writer speaks, first, of how the Old Testament system of repeated sacrifices "can never . . . make perfect those who draw near" (v. 1). Then later are these words: "By a single offering [of Christ] he has perfected for all time those who are sanctified"[21] (v. 14). This statement underscores the close connection between perfecting and sanctifying. It also doubtless, in looking back to Hebrews 9:14, refers primarily to the conscience, which was said to be purified by the sinless offering of Christ. The Old Testament sacrifices were inadequate in that they could serve only to purify the flesh,[22] whereas the sacrifice by Christ was wholly adequate, since it serves to perfect the conscience. The perfected conscience, accordingly, is a corollary to the perfect self-offering of Jesus Christ, which results in a perfectly restored relationship to God.[23]

In summary, sanctification, whether it is viewed as separating, purifying, or perfecting, is a given reality for all who belong to Christ. We were sanctified in the beginning of our Christian walk.

---

[16]We will later observe that the believer needs ongoing cleansing and removal of pollution; however, it is important, first of all, to emphasize the initial purification through Jesus Christ.

[17]Not "called to be saints" (KJV, RSV) or "called to be holy" (NIV). The Greek reads *Klētois hagiois*, literally, "called saints." Hence, the NASB translation, "saints by calling," is quite proper. "Called to be . . . " may suggest sanctification as wholly future.

[18]The calling to salvation, i.e., "effectual calling." See chapter 1, "Calling."

[19]Paul also addresses the Romans (1:7), the Ephesians (1:1), the Philippians (1:1), and the Colossians (1:2) as "saints." Cf. Hebrews 13:24 and Jude 3. In the Old Testament the whole people of God are likewise often called saints. One among several references is Psalm 85:8: "He will speak peace to his people, to his saints" (NASB reads "godly ones").

[20]According to Roman Catholic theology, "saints" are departed persons who through the ecclesiastical process of canonization are elevated to sainthood and thereby are worthy of special veneration. This view of sainthood, as belonging to only a few, is far different from the biblical picture.

[21]In between are the words of verse 10 (earlier quoted): "We have been sanctified through the offering of the body of Jesus Christ once for all."

[22]Recall Hebrews 9:13 (quoted earlier).

[23]F. F. Bruce writes, "By that same sacrifice Christ has eternally 'perfected' His holy people . . . by it His people have had their consciences cleansed from guilt; by it they have been fitted to approach as accepted worshippers; by it they have experienced the fulfilment of what was promised in earlier days, being brought into that perfect relation to God which is involved in the new covenant" (*Hebrews*, NICNT, 241).

B. The Continuation

Sanctification also relates to the continuing life of the people of God. Under the old covenant it was not enough for Israel to be claimed as a holy people by virtue of their calling; Israel was also called *to* holiness. Thus the Lord said to Moses, "Say to all the congregation of the people of Israel, You shall be holy; for I the LORD your God am holy" (Lev. 19:2). Then follows a number of divine prescriptions—the Ten Commandments and various ordinances—by which this holiness is to be manifested.[24] To be a holy people, therefore, is to walk according to God's command. In the New Testament the people of God are called to an even more extensive holiness: "Like the Holy One who called you, be holy yourselves also in all your behavior;[25] because it is written, YOU SHALL BE HOLY, FOR I AM HOLY"[26] (1 Peter 1:15–16 NASB). "All your behavior" represents a call to total holiness.

Not only is sanctification, therefore, for Christian believers the primary reality of their existence—they have been sanctified from the beginning—but also it is to be a *continuing process*. We have earlier recounted these words of Paul in regard to a number of specified sins: "You were sanctified." However, shortly after that, along with other admonitions, he urges them to "shun immorality" (1 Cor. 6:18). Hence there is an additional call for continuing sanctification or holiness. In his second letter to the Corinthians Paul speaks about the Old Testament call to holiness: "Come out from them, and be separate from them . . . and touch nothing unclean" (6:17, quoting freely from Isa. 52:11). Later he adds: "Beloved, let us cleanse ourselves from every defilement of body and spirit, and make holiness perfect[27] in the fear of God" (7:1). The words are written to believers: "beloved"—including Paul himself—"let us cleanse ourselves." Hence, though they, and Paul, have already been sanctified, there is the call to continuing sanctification.

The reason for such a call is apparent. Believers, although sanctified, are by no means without sin in their lives.[28] According to John, "If we say we have no sin, we deceive ourselves, and the truth is not in us" (1 John 1:8).[29] To use

---

[24] Holiness in the Old Testament was also (as we have observed) a matter of ceremonial cleanness. E.g., see words similar to Leviticus 19:2 (above) in Leviticus 11:44: "I am the LORD your God; consecrate yourselves therefore, and be holy, for I am holy." The context here relates to eating of unclean foods, namely, "to make a distinction between the unclean and the clean and between the living creature that may be eaten and the living creature that may not be eaten" (11:47).

[25] The Greek word is *anastrophē*, "way of life, conduct, behavior" (BAGD). The KJV reads "conversation," which at the time of translation (1611) meant conduct or behavior. Such is obviously an unsatisfactory rendition for our time, since it now seems to limit holiness to speech.

[26] The capital letters in NASB do not signify a special emphasis but an Old Testament quotation (this is the case elsewhere in NASB and is true also of italics).

[27] The Greek phrase is *epitelountes hagiōsynēn*, "perfecting holiness" (KJV, NASB, NIV).

[28] Calvin puts it well in saying that "sin . . . though it ceases to reign, does not cease to dwell" (*Institutes*, III, 3.11 Beveridge trans.).

[29] John's concern, expressed shortly thereafter, is that believers not sin. But if they do, there is help: "My little children, I am writing this to you so that you may not sin [*hamartēte*—aorist tense = commit sin (see NEB)]; but if any one does sin [again aorist], we have an advocate with the Father, Jesus Christ" (1 John 2:1). Further on, John emphasizes that "no one who is born of God will continue to sin [*hamartian ou poiei*—present tense = does not practice sin (see NASB)], because God's seed remains in him; he cannot go on sinning [*ou dynatai hamartanein*], because he has been born of God" (3:9 NIV). The believer

Paul's language again, there is still "defilement of body and spirit"; there remain sinful elements from the former life. Although we have been cleansed (as earlier discussed), cleansing and purification continue to be needed. So John continues by saying to believers: "If we confess our sins, he is faithful and just, and will forgive our sins and cleanse us from all unrighteousness" (1:9). Later in the epistle John states that "every one who . . . hopes in him [Christ] purifies himself as he is pure" (3:3). Cleansing and purification will never cease to be needed. Although we have been "perfected" (as stressed in Hebrews), there is nonetheless a need, in Paul's words, for "perfecting holiness." It is quite significant that Hebrews, with its strong emphasis on the perfection already received (recall 10:14), also says, "Strive for peace with all men, and for the holiness without which no one will see the Lord" (12:14). Holiness is a matter to "strive for" in every believer's life.

Sanctification in this sense refers to *progressive transformation*. Paul writes to the Romans, "I appeal to you therefore, brethren, by the mercies of God, to present your bodies as a living sacrifice, holy and acceptable to God. . . . Do not be conformed to this world but be transformed by the renewal of your mind" (12:1–2). These words are clearly addressed to believers—"brethren";

moreover, the sacrifice called for is "holy."[30] Nonetheless, the call is for nonconformity to the world and an ongoing transformation. Although believers are holy, they are admonished to a continuing self-sacrifice in which this transformation may come about. This is *not* a movement *toward* sanctification (for believers are already holy) but a growth *in* it, a gradual process of transformation. Paul expresses this vividly in writing the Corinthians, "We all, with unveiled face beholding as in a mirror[31] the glory of the Lord, are being transformed into the same image from glory to glory, just as from the Lord, the Spirit" (2 Cor. 3:18 NASB). There is nothing automatic about this ongoing change: it occurs as we behold "the glory of the Lord." But in so beholding His glory, we move from glory to glory! This verily is progressive transformation—the continuance of sanctification.

One further scripture in Hebrews relating to the process of sanctification contains these challenging words: "Therefore, since we have so great a cloud of witnesses surrounding us, let us also lay aside every encumbrance, and the sin which so easily entangles us, and let us run with endurance the race that is set before us" (12:1 NASB). Here, in the imagery of Christian life as a race, there is the laying aside of sin as we move to the finish line. It is not a once-for-all laying aside of sin but a

---

may, and often does, fall into sin, but he will not walk in it. No born-again person—one in whom "God's seed" (or "God's nature" RSV) dwells—continues in sin (the present tense represents ongoing practice). He may commit sins (the aorist tense signifies complete action without reference to duration or repetition), but he cannot practice them [i.e., sin is no longer a habitual matter] because he has a new nature. See Dana and Mantey, *A Manual Grammar of the Greek New Testament,* 195, for a discussion of the Greek tenses here. F. F. Bruce puts it well: "The new birth involves a radical change in human nature; for those who have not experienced it, sin is natural, whereas for those who have experienced it, sin is unnatural" (*The Epistles of John,* 92). It is clear that John is by no means teaching that the regenerate person never commits a sin, only that it is *not natural* to him. But when he does sin, he has an advocate, Jesus Christ.

[30]Recalling the holy status of believers.

[31]"Beholding as in a mirror" is the translation above for *katoptrizomenoi.* The NIV has "reflect"; NEB, "reflect as in a mirror." However, "beholding as in a mirror" seems preferable (see BAGD: "to look at something in a mirror").

continuing activity throughout the whole of life.

Sanctification, accordingly, is not only an accomplished fact—it has happened in our Christian beginning—but also a matter of day-by-day growth in holiness.

C. The Goal

Finally, sanctification is the goal of the Christian life. God would have His people constantly moving toward the goal of complete holiness. This is stated quite trenchantly by Paul thus: "May the God of peace Himself sanctify you entirely; and may your spirit and soul and body be preserved complete, without blame at the coming of our Lord Jesus Christ" (1 Thess. 5:23 NASB). The goal is clear—entire sanctification; the goal to be fulfilled at the coming (Parousia) of Jesus Christ.

The goal of entire sanctification is set forth markedly in Philippians: "And it is my prayer that your love may abound more and more, with knowledge[32] and all discernment, so that you may approve what is excellent, and may be pure and blameless for[33] the day of Christ, filled with the fruits of righteousness" (1:9–11). The goal is purity and blamelessness, and (as in 1 Thess.) for the day of Christ. Paul had earlier said, " . . . being confident of this, that he who began a good work in you will carry it on to completion until[34] the day of Christ Jesus" (1:6 NIV). The process of sanctification is to go on until the Parousia.

There can be little question but that the goal is complete sanctification. James writes: "Let steadfastness have its full effect[35] that you may be perfect[36] and complete, lacking in nothing" (1:4). Peter speaks about "the coming of the day of God" with "new heavens and a new earth in which righteousness dwells" and then adds, "Therefore, beloved, since you wait for these, be zealous to be found by him without spot or blemish, and at peace" (2 Peter 3:12–14). In Hebrews 12:2 Jesus is called "the author and perfecter of our faith" (NIV), thus signifying that perfection is the end in view. Thereafter in Hebrews 12:14 (as earlier quoted) the writer says, "Strive for peace with all men, and for the holiness without which no one will see the Lord." Purity, completeness, perfection, holiness—whatever the wording—is the goal of Christian faith and practice.

This question may now arise: Is this goal achievable in the present life? There can be no question but that the goal is ever present. The quotations in the preceding paragraphs declare this in many ways: "May" this happen, "my prayer" is for this to occur, "I am confident" that it will come to completion, "let steadfastness" continue, "be zealous" for spotlessness and purity— all such expressions point to the high importance of total sanctification. Indeed, one might even draw the conclusion that the New Testament teaches the possibility of entire sanctification in

---

[32] The Greek word *epignōsis* equals "precise and correct knowledge" (Thayer), "decisive knowledge" (TDNT, 1:107), "real knowledge" (NASB).

[33] The Greek word is *eis*. "Until" (NASB, NIV; cf. KJV) is a less adequate translation for this preposition.

[34] The Greek word is *achri*. "Until" is the correct rendering in this instance.

[35] The Greek phrase is *ergon teleion*, literally, "perfect work"; "perfect result" (NASB).

[36] The Greek word is *teleioi*, "mature" (NIV). Although *teleios* can be translated "mature," that word hardly seems satisfactory here. "Maturity" does not necessarily imply "lacking in nothing."

this life.[37] However, the overall tenor of Scripture does not sanction such a conclusion.

First, it is apparent that there is much biblical testimony to the continuance of sin throughout life and the need for moving on to perfection. We have earlier noted the words of John that "if we say we have no sin, we deceive ourselves and the truth is not in us"—a statement that clearly applies to every stage of the Christian walk. Also we have quoted certain words of Paul in Philippians 1 that might suggest the possibility of perfection now. However, Paul speaks further on of himself as not being perfect, but rather pressing on to the goal: "Not that I have already obtained all this, or have already been made perfect, but I press on to take hold of that for which Christ Jesus took hold of me. . . . I press on toward the goal to win the prize for which God has called me heavenward in Christ Jesus" (3:12, 14 NIV). Paul unmistakably disclaims perfection, but at the same time declares that he is pressing on to the goal to which God has summoned him.[38] In Hebrews it is also apparent that although Jesus is "the author and perfecter of faith" and although we are called to strive for holiness "without which no one will see the Lord," there is no suggestion of perfect holiness becoming a reality in this life. Indeed,

in the whole chapter (Heb. 12), contrariwise, there is a continuing encouragement not to grow weary and faint, to accept God's frequent and painful discipline, and to strengthen feeble arms and knees (vv. 3–13)—whereas perfection lies beyond. This comes out particularly where "the heavenly Jerusalem" (v. 22) is spoken of as now the place of "the spirits of righteous men made perfect" (v. 23 NIV). These last words imply that perfection lies only in the world to come. In 1 John the writer speaks of the appearing of Christ (3:2), and adds (as we have observed) that "every one who thus hopes in him purifies himself as he is pure" (3:3). Hence, there should be a continuing personal purification, or cleansing, until the Parousia.

Here we need to interpose that there is a certain "relative perfection"[39] in this life. In the Old Testament Noah is called "a righteous man, blameless in his generation" (Gen. 6:9); Job is said to be "blameless and upright, one who feared God, and turned away from evil" (Job. 1:1); and Daniel is listed along with Noah and Job as a person of "righteousness" (Ezek. 14:14, 20).[40] Yet such righteousness was relative; no one was without sin. But in comparison with others of their time, they were blameless and righteous. In the New Testament Zechariah and Elizabeth are

---

[37] John Wesley affirmed such in his teachings. He wrote that "from the time of our being born again the gradual work of sanctification takes place. . . . We go on from grace to grace . . . we take up our cross, and deny ourselves every pleasure that does not lead us to God. It is thus that *we wait for entire sanctification* [italics mine]" (quoted from *The Scripture Way of Salvation* [1765], as found in *Creeds of the Churches,* ed. John Leith, 363–64). In this "entire sanctification," Wesley adds, "Sin ceases to be" (372). Such total sanctification may be looked for now: "It will come, and will not tarry. . . . Expect it *by faith,* Expect it *as you are,* and Expect it *now!*" (ibid.).

[38] "The apostle denies . . . any sense of final perfection as a present experience . . . he makes it clear that the work of sanctifying grace is progressive, and the *summum bonum* of Christian experience will be reached only at the consummation. . . . If the attainment of perfection is denied, there is equally no quietism or indifferent acquiesence in his present experience. He is concerned to strain every nerve to pursue the ideal before him. . . . " So writes Ralph P. Martin in *The Epistle of Paul to the Philippians,* TNTC, 151–52.

[39] A. H. Strong uses this expression (*Systematic Theology,* 879).

[40] Also see Daniel 6:22, where Daniel says, "I was found blameless before him [God]."

called "righteous" and "blameless" (Luke 1:6), and Paul declares that deacons (1 Tim. 3:10) and elders (Titus 1:5–6) are to be "blameless." Again, all of this is clearly relative in relation to others around them: they still remained sinners. Also there is a certain relative perfection that may be defined as "maturity." For example, Paul writes about attaining to "mature manhood . . . so that we may no longer be children, tossed to and fro and carried about with every wind of doctrine" (Eph. 4:13–14). The word translated "mature,"[41] here and elsewhere, is the same as "perfect" in the previous quotations. However, in this context "mature" or "full grown," is much more adequate. The same is true in 1 Corinthians 14:20: "Be babes in evil, but in thinking be mature"; Philippians 3:15: "Let those of us who are mature[42] be thus minded" (in regard to *not* viewing oneself as "already perfect" but pressing on to the goal); Colossians 1:28: ". . . teaching every man in all wisdom, that we may present every man mature[43] in Christ"; and Hebrews 5:14— "But solid food is for the mature." Maturity is much to be desired and does represent a kind of perfection, in the sense of completeness or full growth, but it is by no means to be understood as moral and spiritual perfection.

Second, there is the biblical affirmation that at the end of this life, whether at death or the return of Christ, there will be complete sanctification. We have already observed the words of Hebrews that in the world to come the spirits of righteous men are made perfect, signifying that perfection belongs to believers after death. And, as certain other Scriptures attest or imply, this will also happen for those who are alive at the Parousia. According to 1 John, "When he appears we shall be like him" (3:2); and to this is added the statement that "every one who thus hopes in him purifies himself as he is pure" (3:3). Hence, in conclusion, whereas purification continues in this life, total likeness to Christ awaits His final coming. We may note also some of the words in the benediction of Jude: "Now to him who is able to keep you from falling and to present you without blemish before the presence of his glory with rejoicing" (v. 24). God is able in the believer's lifetime to guard against falling, but the "without blemish" condition will occur only at the occasion of final glorification. Similar to the words of Jude are Paul's in 1 Thessalonians 3: "May the Lord make you increase and abound in love to one another and to all men . . . so that he may establish your hearts unblamable in holiness before our God and Father, at the coming of our Lord Jesus" (vv. 12–13; cf. Col. 1:22). During this life believers should continue to grow in love for all people (the process of sanctification), whereas at the Parousia there will be the final establishment of perfect holiness.

---

[41] The Greek word is *teleion*. The KJV has "perfect" ("a perfect man") rather than "mature." Such a translation is misleading, since the comparison is not between the perfect and imperfect but between children and fully grown, or mature, people. (John Wesley makes much use of the KJV translation here—"a perfect man"—to emphasize his doctrine of Christian perfection. He writes, "We understand by that scriptural expression, 'a perfect man' . . . one whom God hath 'sanctified throughout in body, soul, and spirit'; one who 'walketh in the light as He is in the light; in whom is no darkness at all: the blood of Jesus Christ having cleansed him from all sin' . . . He is 'holy as God who called' him is holy. . . . This it is to be a perfect man, to be 'sanctified throughout.' " (*A Plain Account of Christian Perfection*, 42–43.)

[42] The KJV and NASB translation of "perfect" is quite unfortunate, because Paul's whole idea is that one who is *teleios* does *not* lay claim to perfection!

[43] Again "perfect" in KJV, NIV.

Finally, it is quite important to distinguish between the goal and the fulfillment of perfection. The goal of growing in holiness should always be before the believer. Indeed, there is no justification for any view that suggests little concern for holy living.[44] We are called by God to be a holy people and that means, as we have seen, progressive sanctification. There is serious error if we do not devote ourselves to growing continually in holiness. However, we err badly if we allow the goal to be claimed as an accomplished end. It is a misreading of God's word, and—this must be emphasized—*a critical danger to the Christian walk*. If we make such a claim, there is terrible deception at work and the forsaking of truth (recall once more: "If we say we have no sin, we deceive ourselves and the truth is not in us"). The person so self-deceived by claiming perfection is open to many dangers such as pride, hypocrisy, blindness, and even despair.[45] Moreover, being presumably beyond sin, such a one may be all the more at the mercy of its subtler and higher manifestations.

Verily we continue to need the acute testimony of the apostle Paul. Although he again and again exhorts believers to continue growing in holiness, he never claimed perfection for himself. Rather it was a matter of *pressing on*—to the goal. He once called himself the "fore-most of sinners" (1 Tim. 1:15);[46] and he also recognized the continuing internal struggle of the flesh against the Holy Spirit in the believer's life (Gal. 5:16–26).[47] Hence, even though we are being transformed into Christ's likeness, we can never claim to have arrived in this life. But—surely and definitely—we must ever move on.

To Paul's testimony might be added a final exhortation from Peter: "But grow in the grace and knowledge of our Lord and Savior Jesus Christ" (2 Peter 3:18). There can be no end in this present life to such growth in sanctification.

III. SCOPE

Sanctification refers to the renewal of the whole person according to the likeness of God.[48]

A. Renewal

The word "renewal" may well be used to reflect the full range of sanctification. Renewal may represent the beginning of sanctification in such a passage as Titus 3:5, which speaks of how God "saved us . . . by the washing of regeneration and renewal[49] in the Holy Spirit." "Regeneration" here refers to the new birth and "renewal" to the sanctification given in the origination of Christian life. There is a renewal of holiness in the first moment of the new life in Christ. Paul refers to this also in Ephesians 4:22–24, where he

---

[44]The popular saying "I'm not perfect, just forgiven" leaves much to be desired. We may—and should—thank God for His mercy and forgiveness in Jesus Christ; but we *dare not* stop there. The saying too easily suggests a lack of concern for holy living.

[45]Pride: "I have now arrived"; hypocrisy: "I am not like other Christians"; blindness: "I find no fault in myself"; despair: "I know I have just sinned, so I feel hopeless."

[46]The context might suggest that Paul is here referring to his pre-Christian days; however, the present tense, "*I am* the foremost of sinners" points to Paul's Christian walk. Cf. Paul's words about himself as "the least of the apostles" (1 Cor. 15:9) and as "the very least of all the saints" (Eph. 3:8).

[47]I will discuss this struggle in some detail hereafter.

[48]Sanctification is defined in the Westminster Shorter Catechism as "the work of God's free grace, whereby we are renewed in the whole man after the image of God, and are enabled more and more to die unto sin and live unto righteousness." "Renewed in the whole man after the image of God" is what we are discussing in this section on "Scope."

[49]The Greek words are *palingenesias* (regeneration) and *anakainōseōs* (renewal).

says, "Put off your old nature[50] . . . and be renewed in the spirit of your minds, and put on the new nature, created after the likeness of God in true righteousness and holiness." Renewal here again refers to the new life—the "new nature"—as one of righteousness and holiness.

Renewal also points to ongoing sanctifiation. It is a process of day-by-day renewing. To this Paul speaks particularly in these words to the Colossians: "Do not lie to one another, . . . seeing that you have put on the new nature, which is being renewed in knowledge after the image of its creator" (Col. 3:9–10). "Being renewed" clearly speaks of a continuing activity. This is equally apparent where Paul exhorts the Romans, "Be transformed by the renewing of your mind" (12:2 NASB). Renewal and transformation are closely linked together.

Renewal implies a continuing "making new." The person who is born again has a new nature; indeed he is a "new creature" (2 Cor. 5:17 NASB). But along with the new, much of the old remains and needs to be dealt with. Hence, an ongoing renewal or rejuvenation is called for so that all areas of the new being will be increasingly conformed to the likeness of God.

B. The Whole Person

In this connection our key scriptural passage is 1 Thessalonians 5:23 (earlier quoted): "Now may the God of peace Himself sanctify you entirely; and may your spirit and soul and body be preserved complete, without blame at the coming of our Lord Jesus Christ" (NASB). We will note particularly the words "entirely"[51] and "spirit . . . soul . . . body."

1. The Spirit

The spirit of a person is the deepest dimension of human nature.[52] As given by God, it is particularly the center of man's being. The spirit is that dimension of the self in which God immediately encounters man. However, as a result of sin man has become estranged in his spirit from God and shut away from His life-giving presence. Thus he has become dead to the things of God. But in and through Jesus Christ, the spirit is alive through righteousness: there is a renewed spirit within. Communication with God becomes reestablished, and the Holy Spirit witnesses to our spirits that we are God's children (Rom. 8:16). Nonetheless—and here we come to the point of sanctification— the human spirit needs to be continually purified and refined. The goal is to be completely transparent to the divine Spirit and to radiate His glory from within.[53]

Hence, there is need for an ongoing purification of the spirit. The words of Paul again come to mind: "Beloved, let us cleanse ourselves from every defilement of body and spirit, and make holiness perfect in the fear of God" (2 Cor. 7:1). In the area of spirit surely much in the believer needs a continuing

---

[50]The Greek phrase is *palaion anthrōpon,* literally, "old man" as in KJV, "old self" (NASB, NIV), "old human nature" (NEB).

[51]The Greek word is *holoteleis.* The KJV and RSV translate it "wholly"; NIV, "through and through"; NEB, "in every part."

[52]See vol. 1, chapter 9, "Man," II.B, pages 210–13. E.g., "The spirit . . . is the very *essence* of human nature."

[53]This operation of the Holy Spirit in the human spirit is basic to the renewal of the mind (to be considered hereafter under "soul"). Paul exhorts (as we have seen) that believers "be renewed in the spirit of . . . [their] minds." Spirit and mind are very closely related; however, since the spirit functions through the mind, the renewal must be primarily in "the spirit" of the mind.

cleansing. There may be pride or haughtiness of spirit that needs reduction to humility, bitterness of spirit that needs a sweetening by God's Spirit, a judgmental spirit that needs to be refined by love, a fretful spirit that needs to be renewed in calmness and peace. To these may be added especially an unforgiving spirit that needs to be released from hardness and ingratitude.

The words of Paul to the Ephesians are a much needed exhortation: "Let all bitterness and wrath and anger and clamor and slander be put away from you, with all malice, and be kind to one another, tenderhearted, forgiving one another, as God in Christ forgave you" (4:31–32).

Here the word "heart" should be mentioned. "Spirit" and "heart" may be used interchangeably; for example, "My spirit faints within me; my heart within me is appalled" (Ps. 143:4). Again in relation to committed sin the psalmist prayed, "Create in me a clean heart, O God, and renew a steadfast spirit within me" (Ps. 51:10 NASB). In terms of needed sanctification this would suggest that defilement of spirit and defilement of heart are essentially the same. It is quite significant that Paul earlier prays for the Thessalonians,[54] "May the Lord . . . establish your hearts unblamable in holiness" (1 Thess. 3:12–13). Purification of heart and spirit belong together.[55]

One further word should be mentioned in this context, namely, "conscience." "Conscience" is placed alongside "heart" in Romans 2:15. Here Paul, speaking of the Gentiles, says that "what the law requires is written on their hearts, while their conscience also bears witness." In 1 Timothy 1:5 he writes, "Our charge is love that issues from a pure heart and a good conscience and sincere faith." Conscience particularly highlights the moral aspect of the heart, hence expressions such as "a troubled heart" and "pangs of conscience"[56] may be used interchangeably. The close approximation of the two terms may further be seen in the frequent biblical concern for both a clean heart and a clear conscience.[57] In terms of sanctification, Hebrews 10:22 puts it directly: "Let us draw near . . . with our hearts sprinkled clean from an evil conscience."

All three of these biblical terms, "spirit," "heart," and "conscience," refer to man in his responsible nature before God. In salvation there has been a renewing of the spirit, an alteration of the heart, a purifying of the conscience.[58] However, although this has occurred essentially (man has a new spirit/heart/conscience), there is the need for further sanctification. It is this area that we will examine shortly. But let us first consider the aspects of man as soul and body.

2. The Soul

The soul can be spoken of as the inner life of man through which the

---

[54] Earlier than the passage in which Paul speaks of entire sanctification of spirit, soul, and body.

[55] Hence, what was said in the previous paragraph about pride, bitterness, judgment, and anger in relation to the spirit also applies to the heart.

[56] As in the RSV and NASB translations of 1 Samuel 25:31. The RSV reads, "My lord [David] shall have no cause of grief, or pangs of conscience, for having shed blood." The NASB, instead of "pangs of conscience," reads "a troubled heart."

[57] See especially Acts 24:16; 1 Timothy 3:9; 2 Timothy 1:3; Hebrews 13:18; 1 Peter 3:16, 21. The words "unblemished" and "good" are also used in other translations.

[58] Hebrews 9:14 speaks of the blood of Christ purifying (or cleansing) the conscience: "how much more shall the blood of Christ . . . purify your conscience from dead works to serve the living God."

spirit expresses itself.[59] Man is a living and conscious soul, or self, as demonstrated in the wide range of his intellectual, emotional, and volitional activity. Accordingly, mind, feeling, and will are all aspects of the soul in action. With the incursion of sin there has been a darkening of the soul, indeed a turning from God in all these vital areas. As salvation has been received, the mind is able again to ponder the things of God, the emotions to sense and enjoy the presence of God, the will to move in harmony with God's purposes. Yet the soul needs further cleansing and strengthening.

a. *The Mind.* Sanctification has to do with an ongoing renewal of the mind. We refer, first, again to the words in Romans 12:2—"Do not be conformed to this world but be transformed by the renewal of your mind." This exhortation is spoken to those who already belong to Christ and thereby have a new mind;[60] however, this mind needs a continual renewing, indeed, a further transforming.[61] The mind may be beset by evil thoughts, corrupt schemes, and worldly plans; the mind may slip away from spiritual concerns into things of the flesh; the mind may not seek a walk in humility after the pattern of Christ. In this latter regard, the words of Paul to the Philippians are urgent: "Let this mind be in you, which was also in Christ Jesus" (2:5 NIV). They are to have the mind and attitude of a servant, humbling themselves and being obedient even unto death.

The renewal of the mind is essential if we are to walk in God's will. Romans 12:2 continues, " ... that you may prove what is the will of God, what is good and acceptable and perfect." To "prove" here means to "prove by testing,"[62] hence to know for a certainty what is God's will, a will that is good, acceptable (or well-pleasing),[63] even perfect. Since sanctification is concerned with the "perfect"—as we have discussed—the renewal of the mind plays a critically important role, for only thereby can the perfect be discerned.

Elsewhere Paul speaks about his intention to "take every thought captive to obey Christ" (2 Cor. 10:5). Although Paul's words refer specifically to the thoughts of those in the world,[64] there is also an implication for his believing readers, for Paul later expresses a fear lest their "thoughts will be led astray from a sincere and pure devotion to Christ" (2 Cor. 11:3). Hence, to take "every thought captive to obey Christ" also expresses a fundamental requirement in the believer's ongoing process of sanctification.

Let me elaborate this latter point further. The believer, while truly having the mind of Christ, may yet be far from subjecting all his thoughts to that mind. This is not only a matter of evil or stray thoughts, but also thoughts that, while seemingly without fault, are not really submitted to the mind of Christ. Since the believer lives in a world that is not guided by that mind, it is easy to fall

---

[59]See vol. 1, chapter 9, "Man," II.C, pages 213–14. Hence "spirit" and "soul" are sometimes in the Scriptures used interchangeably.

[60]Paul writes earlier in Romans 8 that those who are "in Christ Jesus" (v. 1) have their minds "set . . . on the things of the Spirit" (v. 5); cf. 1 Corinthians 2:16: "But we have the mind of Christ."

[61]Since the mind is the organ of knowledge, there needs to be a renewing in knowledge. As we have seen, Paul speaks of our "being renewed in knowledge" (Col. 3:10).

[62] The Greek word is *dokimazein,* "put to the test," hence, "prove by testing" (BAGD).

[63]The Greek word is *euareston.*

[64]2 Corinthians 10:5 reads in full: "We destroy arguments and every proud obstacle to the knowledge of God, and take every thought captive to obey Christ."

into secular ways of thinking with little realization of doing so. The mind-set of contemporary culture—its philosophy, its morals, its values—is not of Christ. Since the believer necessarily lives in such a culture, it takes much rethinking and reshaping for the mind of Christ to pervade all. There is constant pressure to submit to, or at least conform with, the prevailing ethos. Thus, there is the urgency of bringing "every thought captive" to obey Christ. It is unquestionably an ever-continuing struggle, but every success makes it eminently worthwhile.

"Do not be conformed . . . but be transformed by the renewal of your mind." The renewal of the mind is basic to the transformation of all of life.

b. *The Feelings (Emotions, Desires, Passions)*. Sanctification deals also with inward feelings and desires. The Christian has already had a basic victory in this realm. As Paul declares in Galatians, "Those who belong to Christ Jesus have crucified the flesh[65] with its passions and desires" (5:24). The flesh—the carnal nature—has been essentially "crucified," or put to death. There is new life in the Spirit and by the Spirit. However, the flesh still remains (even if no longer as a central, dominating principle); hence there is an ongoing struggle with the Holy Spirit. Paul wrote shortly before: "The desires of the flesh are against the Spirit, and the desires of the Spirit are against the flesh; for these are opposed to each other, to prevent you from doing what you would" (5:17). This area of "the desires of the flesh" calls for much sanctification.

Elsewhere Paul wrote to Timothy that "if any one purifies himself from what is ignoble, then he will be a vessel for noble use, consecrated and useful to the master of the house, ready for any good work," immediately adding, "So shun[66] youthful passions" (2 Tim. 2:21–22). In his letter to Titus, Paul wrote, "The grace of God has appeared, bringing salvation to all men," and then added, "instructing us to deny ungodliness and worldly desires and to live sensibly, righteously and godly in the present age" (2:11–12 NASB). The denial of "worldly desire" is an aspect of the continuing life of sanctification.

We may also recount John's exhortation to believers: "Do not love the world or anything in the world. . . . For everything in the world—the cravings of sinful man, the lust of his eyes and the boasting of what he has and does—comes not from the Father" (1 John 2:15–16 NIV). All such craving and lusting and boasting is a constant temptation for believers, but it must not be indulged in. This calls for a life of daily growth in holiness.

There is much in the realm of the feelings and passions that needs to be sanctified. We have but to mention such things as anger, lust, envy, jealousy, and covetousness to recognize immediately how often these occur in the Christian walk. For example, anger and lust (and here let us go back to Jesus' own teaching) are passions that inwardly break God's law against murder and adultery.[67] The issue deeper than murder is giving vent to anger and hatred; the issue deeper than adultery is allowing oneself to look lustfully at another person. It is such feelings and passions that need continual purging. Indeed,

---

[65] The Greek word is *sarx*, "flesh" ("sinful nature" [NIV], "lower nature" [NEB]). "Flesh" can mean simply the body; however in this verse, and frequently elsewhere, "flesh" refers to the principle of sinfulness at work in every area of human personality.

[66] The Greek word is *pheuge*, "flee from" (NASB), "flee" (KJV, NIV). It is important to note that Paul uses the imperative mood here.

[67] Matthew 5:21–30.

such are included in Jesus' climactic words: "You, therefore, must be perfect, as your heavenly Father is perfect" (Matt. 5:48).

The perfecting of holiness must deal in depth with desires and passions that are not of God.

c. *The Will.* Sanctification also has to do with the will. Before salvation, the will was in bondage to sin. There was an invariable turning from God to sin and evil—man was *not* able not to sin. But with a liberated will through Christ there is a fresh path of freedom ahead. However, there is also the ever-present pull of the world to step back into sinful practices.

In this connection Paul declares, "There must be no filthiness and silly talk, or coarse jesting" (Eph. 5:4 NASB)—all temptations to believers. After that he urges: "Walk as children of light . . . trying to learn what is pleasing to the Lord. And do not participate in the unfruitful deeds of darkness, but instead even expose them" (vv. 8, 10–11 NASB). Believers are challenged as "children of light" to walk in the way of the Lord. Elsewhere Paul writes, "If we live by the Spirit, let us also walk by the Spirit" (Gal. 5:25). The way of the world must not be the Christian way.

There is the constant temptation in the Christian life to fall back into worldly, or pagan, ways. Hence there is a never-ending need to say, "Not mine, O God, but your will be done."

3. The Body

Finally, there must be a sanctification of the body. Prior to the new life in Christ the body was actually a body devoted to sin, but with the crucifixion of our old nature that sinful condition has been essentially destroyed. As Paul puts it: "We know that our old self was crucified with him so that the sinful body[68] might be destroyed, and we might no longer be enslaved to sin" (Rom. 6:6). However, although the body of the believer no longer is controlled by sin, sin is still present and needs cleansing. So it is that Paul says elsewhere (as previously noted), "Let us cleanse ourselves from every defilement of *body* and spirit, and make holiness perfect in the fear of God" (2 Cor. 7:1). Wherever bodily sin is found, there is need for cleansing and purification from it.

One of Paul's strongest statements about bodily sanctification is found in these words: "This is the will of God, your sanctification" (1 Thess. 4:3). Immediately after saying that, Paul dealt with the bodily sins of sexual immorality, saying, "That is, that you abstain from sexual immorality; that each of you know how to possess his own vessel[69] in sanctification[70] and honor" (1 Thess. 4:3–4 NASB). All of this bespeaks the importance of holiness of the body in sexual matters. Just prior to that Paul had spoken about God's establishing the Thessalonians' "hearts unblamable in holiness" (3:13) at the

---

[68] The Greek phrase is *to sōma tēs hamartias*, "body of sin" (KJV, NIV, NASB). As John Murray writes, "The expression 'the body of sin' would mean the body as conditioned and controlled by sin, the sinful body" (*Romans*, NICNT, 220). Paul was not referring to the destruction of the physical body but to the body as sinful—i.e., "the sinful body" (as RSV translates).

[69] The Greek phrase is *to heautou skeuos ktasthai.* The word *"skeuos"* has been interpreted to mean either "body" or "wife." In regard to the former, the NIV translates "control his own body"; in regard to the latter, the RSV reads, "take a wife to himself." "Body" seems the more likely in light of the context. Also, as F. F. Bruce says, "There is no New Testament parallel for calling a man's wife his *skeuos*" (*1 & 2 Thessalonians*, WBC, 83).

[70] The Greek word is *hagiasmō,* "holiness" (RSV), "holy" (NIV).

Parousia; now it is a matter of bodies that need also to be pure. Generally speaking, any form of sexual immorality[71] is included here. Moreover, the emphasis is very strong: *"This is the will of God"*—and to paraphrase, "it is your sanctification of the body."

In another passage Paul deals specifically with the sin of giving one's body to a prostitute. He first asks, "Do you not know that your bodies are members of Christ?" (1 Cor. 6:15). Then comes a crucial question: "Shall I therefore take the members of Christ and make them members of a prostitute?" Paul is adamant in his answer: "Never!" Shortly thereafter Paul says, "You are not your own; you were bought with a price. So glorify God in your body" (vv. 19–20). We were bought at the awesome price of Christ's death; our bodies are now united to Him. How terribly wrong, then, it is to indulge in this sexual immorality, for in so doing we prostitute the body that belongs to Christ. If such a sin does happen, how great the need to "cleanse ourselves" of the "defilement of body" so that we may again glorify God in our bodies.

But there is also another reason why this sanctification of the body is important. In the same passage Paul asks another question: "Do you not know that your body is a temple of the Holy Spirit who is in you, whom you have from God?" (1 Cor. 6:19 NASB). Since the body of a believer is a temple of the indwelling Spirit, it is indeed a heinous sin against the Holy Spirit, the Spirit of holiness, to give over one's body to a prostitute. It is a profanation of the indwelling Holy Spirit of God. All the more desperately cleansing is called for!

To return briefly to Paul's words about the will of God and sanctification in relation to sexual immorality in general (1 Thess. 4:3–4), we now note that Paul concludes his teaching thus: "He who rejects this [instruction] is not rejecting man but the God who gives his Holy Spirit to you" (v. 8 NASB). To reject this teaching, says Paul, is to reject God (whose will is for total bodily sanctification), who freely gives the Holy Spirit. All sexual immorality is a travesty against this gracious gift.[72].

The constant temptation to sexual immorality is surely no less today than in Paul's time. There is, first, the ever-increasing lure to lust[73] in a culture of declining sexual standards: primarily it is this inner temptation that must be dealt with. But, second, in a society becoming more and more hedonistic ("Do it if it feels good"), it is all the harder not to slip into outward forms of immorality. It is urgent, on the path of sanctification, to continue to bear in mind to Whom we belong and that—marvelous to realize—our bodies are temples of God's Holy Spirit.[74]

But now a brief word needs to be spoken about two other related bodily

---

[71] The Greek word translated "sexual immorality" above is *porneia*. The KJV and NEB have "fornication." Fornication, usually defined as sexual intercourse between an unmarried person and one of the opposite sex (whether married or unmarried), is doubtless one important meaning. but *porneia* represents, more broadly, any illicit sexual activity. BAGD, under πορνεία, reads: "prostitution, unchastity, fornication, of every kind of unlawful sexual intercourse."

[72] For more on the gift of the Holy Spirit see chapter 8.

[73] As mentioned in the previous section.

[74] I have not touched on homosexual activity in this section. My concern—following Paul—has been with heterosexual deviations. It is significant that Paul never discusses homosexuality as an issue for Christians. For example, in 1 Corinthians 6:9–10 Paul speaks vigorously against homosexuality, but only as that which some had practiced ("such *were* some of you") prior to their becoming Christians. Homosexuality obviously cannot be—as some would claim today—a "viable Christian lifestyle."

sins—namely, drunkenness and gluttony. In the Book of Proverbs is this practical admonition, "Be not among winebibbers, or among gluttonous eaters of meat; for the drunkard and the glutton will come to poverty" (23:20–21). In the New Testament Paul, speaking against "the works of the flesh," concludes with "drunkenness" and "carousing" (Gal. 5:19, 21). He then warns that "those who do such things shall not inherit the kingdom of God" (v. 21). There is utterly no place for such in the Christian life. On the matter of gluttony, Paul elsewhere speaks of those whose "end is destruction, their god is the belly" (Phil. 3:19).[75] This is a warning against allowing bodily appetites[76] to get out of hand and thus lead to destruction.

A personal word: it is commonplace to hear Christians speak quite strongly against such bodily vices as sexual immorality and drunkenness, but often they are soft on gluttony. However—it needs to be emphasized—overindulgence in food, frequently with results of obesity, bodily ailments, and the like, is no less sinful before God than immorality or drunkenness. Our bodies, indwelt by the Holy Spirit, are in all things—including sex, food, and drink—to show forth the glory of God.

C. The Likeness of God

The intention in the sanctification of the whole person is renewal in the likeness of God. Let us recall Paul's words about "the new nature, which is being renewed in knowledge after the image of its creator" (Col. 3:10). Although the reference is only to knowledge, it is a knowledge in the sphere of the things of God, and hence one aspect of renewal in God's likeness. The more complete renewal is described in Paul's words to the Corinthians (earlier quoted): "But we all, with unveiled face beholding as in a mirror the glory of the Lord, are being transformed into the same image from glory to glory" (2 Cor. 3:18 NASB). The "same image" is the image, or likeness, of the Lord—and this means particularly the Lord Jesus Christ.

The likeness of God is the likeness of Christ. Hence, the ultimate goal of sanctification is transformation into the likeness of God in Christ. Or, to put it another way, it means *conformity to Jesus Christ*. So Paul writes to the Romans: "For those whom he foreknew he also predestined to be conformed to the image of his Son" (8:29). Whereas this conformity begins with the new life in Christ, it is also to be ever growing, with the goal that of likeness to Jesus Christ.[77] Not "conformity to this world" (to recall Paul's words further on in Romans 12), but "conformity to Christ"—this is God's intention!

There can be no higher goal.

IV. METHOD

We come now to a consideration of the method of sanctification. How does sanctification occur? In our reflection on this we will recognize both a divine and human side.

---

[75] The people were at least nominal Christians (see background in vv. 18–19). EGT speaks of them as "professing Christians who allowed their liberty to degenerate into license" (in loco).

[76] Paul also speaks in Romans 16:18 about those who "do not serve the Lord Christ, but their own appetites [literally, "belly"]." Service of the Lord is given up for their own bellies—indeed, again, "their god is the belly."

[77] According to EGT, in loco, "This conformity is the last stage in salvation, as πρόγνω ("foreknew") is the first. The image [or "likeness"] is in import not merely spiritual but eschatological . . . to be conformed to His image is to share His glory as well as His holiness."

A. The Work of God

Sanctification is primarily the work of God: its source is in Him. Sanctification is basically God's doing; it is not a work man can perform in himself. It is not as if a person who has been called, regenerated, and justified[78] (all unmistakably works of God) is thereafter called on to sanctify himself, so that whereas God justifies, man sanctifies.[79] While man's role is an important one, sanctification is not basically his work. Jesus could say, "I sanctify Myself" (John 17:19 NASB), but no one else can.[80] For sinful man, it is God alone who sanctifies.[81]

Let us observe several scriptural references. A number of times in the Old Testament there is this declaration: "I, the LORD, sanctify you" (Exod. 31:13).[82] In the Gospel of John, Jesus prayed to the Father, "Sanctify them in the truth" (17:17). Thus it is the Father who sanctifies. Paul also says, "May the God of peace Himself sanctify you entirely." Further, Paul adds, "Faithful is He who calls you, and He also will bring it to pass" (1 Thess. 5:23–24 NASB).[83] God (the Father) is the *source* of sanctification.

Jesus Christ is the *agent* of sanctification. As we have earlier noted, Paul writes to the Corinthians as those "who have been sanctified in Christ Jesus" (1 Cor. 1:2 NASB) and speaks shortly after that about "Christ Jesus, whom God made our ... sanctification" (1:30). Christ is the agent of sanctification in that, as Hebrews says, "We have been sanctified through the offering of the body of Jesus Christ once for all" (10:10).[84] This is also true of our continuing sanctification. So Paul writes Titus that "our great God and Savior Jesus Christ ... gave himself for us to redeem us from all iniquity and to purify for himself a people of his own who are zealous for good deeds" (Titus 2:13–14). The consummation of this sanctification for God's people—collectively the church—will also come from Jesus Christ; for "Christ loved the church and gave himself up for her ... that he might present the church to himself in splendor, without spot or wrinkle ... that she might be holy and without blemish" (Eph. 5:25, 27).

Finally, it is the Holy Spirit who is the *energizer* of sanctification. Peter writes to believers as those "chosen according to the foreknowledge of God the Father, through the sanctifying work of the Spirit, for obedience to Jesus Christ" (1 Peter 1:2 NIV).[85] This suggests that through His work of sanctification the Holy Spirit prepares believers for obedience to Jesus Christ. Also, Paul speaks of the walk of sanctification in which we seek not to gratify fleshly desires but rather to "walk by the Spirit" (Gal. 5:16, 25). The Holy

---

[78] See our discussion of these matters in previous chapters.

[79] G. C. Berkouwer puts it well in saying that sanctification is not "a series of devout acts and works performed by the previously justified man" (*Faith and Sanctification,* 21).

[80] Indeed, His sanctification was that others might be sanctified—"that they themselves also may be sanctified in truth" (continuation of John 17:19 NASB).

[81] "Sanctification is indeed God's work, for no one can sanctify but He who is Himself the Holy One" (Emil Brunner, *The Christian Doctrine of the Church, Faith, and the Consummation, Dogmatics,* 3:298).

[82] Cf. Leviticus 20:8; 21:8, 15, 23; 22:9, 16, 32; Ezekiel 20:12; 37:28. The wording varies somewhat, but it is "the LORD" each time who sanctifies.

[83] Also cf. Hebrews 13:20–21: "May the God of peace ... equip you with everything good that you may do his will."

[84] Also cf. Hebrews 13:12: "Jesus also suffered outside the gate in order to sanctify the people through his own blood."

[85] Also cf. 2 Thessalonians 2:13: "God chose you from the beginning to be saved, through sanctification by the Spirit and belief in the truth."

Spirit provides the strength for this walk. In the verse where Paul speaks of our "being transformed into the same image from glory to glory," he adds that this happens "from the Lord, the Spirit"[86] (2 Cor. 3:18 NASB). The Spirit is at work to make this transformation complete.

But now a further thing needs to be said about the activity of the Holy Spirit, namely, that His operation is from *within* believers. This is true, first, corporately of believers. Paul speaks to the Ephesians thus: "You [Jew and Gentile together] . . . are of God's household . . . Christ Jesus Himself being the corner stone" and "[you are] growing into a holy temple in the Lord." He adds that they are being "built together into a dwelling of God in the Spirit" (Eph. 2:19–22 NASB). God in the Spirit indwells this "holy temple," the community of believers. Paul also refers to the community as a temple indwelt by the Holy Spirit in 1 Corinthians 3:16–17—"Do you not know that you [plural] are God's temple and that God's Spirit dwells in you?" Then Paul adds: "If any one destroys God's temple, God will destroy him. For God's temple is holy, and that temple you [plural] are." The community of believers is not to be destroyed, for it is God's own habitation in the Spirit.

Second, each believer is also individually indwelt by the Holy Spirit. We have already observed the further words of Paul: "Do you not know that your body is a temple of the Hoy Spirit within you, which you have from God?" (1 Cor. 6:19).[87] This refers to the extraordinary fact that each believer's body is a temple, hence also a

dwelling place of God in the Spirit. Paul writes Timothy: "Guard the truth that has been entrusted to you by the Holy Spirit who dwells[88] in us" (2 Tim. 1:14). A further word from Paul: "But you are not in the flesh, you are in the Spirit, if the Spirit of God really dwells in you." That such indwelling is a fact for the believer, Paul adds, "Any one who does not have the Spirit of Christ does not belong to him" (Rom. 8:9). Anyone who belongs to Christ—marvelous to say—is indwelt by God the Holy Spirit.

Since the Holy Spirit dwells within believers, it follows that His sanctifying work will be an internal operation. It is He who carries forward in depth the work of sanctification. As the Spirit of holiness, He is constantly illuminating the dark areas of the believer's life and ever seeking to bring every aspect of human nature—spirit, soul, body—into conformity with Christ. The Holy Spirit—the *Spiritus Sanctus*— is the sanctifying Spirit. It is His main office to bring the work of sanctification to increasing fulfillment.

B. The Human Task

Sanctification is also the task of man: God does not work without our involvement. It is not that God does so much, say 50 percent, whereas man is called upon to accomplish the rest, the other 50 percent. It is, rather, *God all the way through man all the way.*

We have previously noted the Old Testament word of God that says, "I the LORD, sanctify you." Now we may observe another word: "Consecrate yourselves . . . and be holy; for I am the LORD your God" (Lev. 20:7). God does

---

[86]Or "the Lord who is the Spirit" (RSV; cf. NIV).

[87]Recall that these words are spoken against immoral sexual use of one's body—a heinous sin against the Holy Spirit who dwells within.

[88]The Greek word is *enoikountos* (see also Rom. 8:11).

the basic work of sanctifying,[89] but Israel's consecration is also called for in order to "be holy." In the New Testament it is likewise the case that although God is declared to be the author of sanctification, the believer is definitely challenged to personal consecration. Two scriptural exhortations, earlier mentioned, highlight this: "Beloved, let us cleanse ourselves from every defilement of body and spirit, and make holiness perfect in the fear of God" (2 Cor. 7:1); and "Strive for peace with all men, and for the holiness without which no one will see the Lord" (Heb. 12:14). There must be a human perfecting, a human striving: such is the task of man.

In reflecting on the human task, let us observe both a negative and a positive aspect: on the one hand, there needs to be a constant dying to sin; on the other, a steadfast living toward righteousness. Some words from 1 Peter are particularly relevant: "He himself bore our sins in his body on the tree, so that we might die to sins[90] and live for righteousness" (2:24 NIV). Let us consider the human task under the twofold heading of dying to sins and living for righteousness.

1. Dying to Sins

It is a paradoxical fact about Christian existence that though the believer is to understand himself as "dead to sin"[91] —in that sin no longer dominates him—nonetheless sins do remain, and to those sins he is called upon to die.

This may be understood first as *renunciation* of sins. We may here listen to the words of Paul: "For the grace of God has appeared, bringing salvation to all men, instructing us to deny[92] ungodliness and worldly desires and to live sensibly, righteously and godly in the present age" (Titus 2:11–12 NASB). "Ungodliness" refers to everything in the believer's life that is contrary to God; "worldly desires" signify all those passions that are not directed to the things of God but to the world. All such ungodliness and desires are to be denied—or, put more strongly, to be renounced.

Jesus pointed to a similar renouncement when He said, "If anyone would come after me, he must deny himself[93] and take up his cross daily and follow me" (Luke 9:23 NIV). Denial of the self refers here to the total self that is opposed to the way of Christ: this sinful self must be left behind. It follows that whatever there is of pride, anger, lust, or any other sin, it is to be denied, indeed, renounced. This is by no means a renunciation of the person and his selfhood, as if there were some virtue in self-persecution. Rather it is a renunciation of everything that continues in the self as sin, hence the sinful self. Dying to these sins, moreover, is not a matter of calm repose (as death may be viewed) but of vigorous action. It is as if to say, "I *renounce* each and every sin that operates in my life; I *disown* them

[89] Significantly, in the following verse God adds: "Keep My statutes, and do them; I am the LORD who sanctifies you" (v. 8 NASB).

[90] The Greek word is *hamartias,* a plural. The RSV, NASB, and NEB reading of "sin" is unfortunate, since the problem for the believer is not *sin* but *sins* (as will be discussed later).

[91] Paul writes in Romans 6:11: "So you also must consider yourselves dead to sin and alive to God in Christ Jesus."

[92] The Greek word is *arnēsamenoi* (from *arneomai*—to "deny, repudiate, disown" BAGD), "renounce" (RSV, NEB).

[93] The Greek phrase is *arnēsasthō heauton,* an imperative: "Leave self behind" (NEB). The same Greek words are found in Matthew 16:24 and Mark 8:34 with the omission of "daily." The Gospel of Luke carries Jesus' emphasis of an ongoing activity.

as not belonging to me as a follower of Jesus Christ." This is the complete opposite from denying Christ and disowning him (as Peter was later to do):[94] it is rather to deny and renounce everything that is contrary to Christ and His manner of life.

We must recognize that the Holy Spirit who dwells within is totally opposed to the sinful self—or, in the words of Paul—to the "flesh." Indeed, there is strong internal opposition on each side. "For the desires of the flesh are against the Spirit, and the desires of the Spirit are against the flesh; for these are opposed to each other" (Gal. 5:17). Since the Holy Spirit stands in opposition to the sinful self, this means that every act of renunciation on the part of the believer will be strongly undergirded by the Holy Spirit. Moreover, since this opposition exists, there cannot be any taming of the flesh or compromise with it (or spanking it like an unruly child!). The flesh is wholly evil and must be totally renounced.

Dying to sins may be understood next as *mortification*. Here we turn to the words of Paul in Romans 8:13—"For if you live according to the flesh you will die, but if by the Spirit you put to death[95] the deeds[96] of the body[97] you

will live." Observe two things: first, believers are exhorted to the very serious business of mortifying the evil practices of the body; second, this is to be done by the power of the indwelling[98] Spirit. One should carefully note that it is not the Holy Spirit who performs the task of mortification, though He is clearly the energizer. It is rather the believer himself who *by* that power is to execute the mortification. Hence, the Holy Spirit is not only opposed to the flesh, but He is also the empowering force in the believer's action of ongoing mortification.[99]

This means that not only is the believer to renounce sins (as we have discussed) but also he is to put them to death in the power of the Holy Spirit. For example, when such a sin as jealousy, or anger, or lust is manifest, and the believer feels in the grip of it, then he may declare vehemently some such words as these: "*By the power of the Holy Spirit I put you* (jealousy, anger, lust) *to death!*" Sin should not be permitted to have its way or be allowed to lurk in some hidden corner. If necessary, it should be dragged out screaming, and then slain in the power of the Spirit. Nothing less can suffice when the Christian is dealing with the viciousness of sin.[100]

---

[94] Simon Peter's tragic denial of Christ with cursing and swearing, "I do not know the man" (Matt. 26:74), would never have happened if he had truly denied himself. In all Christian experience it is one or the other: deny self or deny Christ. There is no other alternative.

[95] The Greek word is *thanatoute*, "mortify" (KJV).

[96] The Greek word is *praxeis*. In the present context the connotation is clearly "evil or disgraceful deeds" (BAGD), hence "misdeeds" (NIV) or "base pursuits" (NEB).

[97] "The body" may refer to the physical body; however, more likely it refers to "the body of sin" (recall Rom. 6:6). So writes John Murray: " 'The deeds [or "misdeeds"] of the body' are those practices which the believer must put to death if he is to live' " (*The Epistle to the Romans,* NICNT, 294). Paul, accordingly, is referring to any and all sins.

[98] Paul had just spoken of the Holy Spirit as indwelling (vv. 9–11).

[99] That this mortification is ongoing is suggested by the present tense of *thanatoute*. The NASB translates, "If by the Spirit you *are* putting to death. . . . "

[100] Lest there be some misunderstanding, mortification is not infliction of pain upon oneself (though in the past mortification has often been viewed that way) or the obliteration of personality, but it is the putting to death of those evil forces that wage war against the person. Sin is like cancer in a person: it warrants destruction, even cell by cell, until the deadly disease is no more.

Paul also deals with the subject of mortification in Colossians 3:5. There he writes: "Put to death[101] therefore what is earthly in you:[102] immorality, impurity, passion, evil desire, and covetousness, which is idolatry." This is even stronger, and possibly broader, than the words in Romans 8:13 which contain the conditional statement ("*if* by the Spirit you put to death . . . ") and speak of "the body." Here in Colossians, there is a blunt imperative that relates to the "earthly."[103] When Paul mentions immorality, impurity, etc., these are doubtless only illustrative of whatever in a person needs sanctification. But the important matter again is that the believer is not to tolerate sins: they are to be utterly destroyed.

Here a word is in order regarding confession and contrition. There is much need for the believer to confess his sins, both generally and particularly, and to receive God's forgiveness, for a humble and contrite spirit is pleasing to the Lord. But confession and contrition cannot replace mortification. Many Christians make confession of sin in some such words as "We have sinned and strayed from thy ways like lost sheep. . . . But thou, O Lord, have mercy upon us, miserable offenders. . . . And grant that we may hereafter live a godly, righteous, and sober life."[104] However, there is no suggestion in this prayer of the penitent doing anything about his sins. Truly we must be ever grateful that God does hear a genuine confession of sins and delights to grant pardon. *But* He also expects us to get down to the serious business of mortifying sins—not just confessing them—and moving on in sanctification.

Returning to the passage in Colossians, it is important to observe that the background for mortification is found in the statement "You have died, and your life is hid with Christ in God" (3:3). The believer's true life is no longer earthly but heavenly,[105] and therefore he is able from this heavenly vantage point both to perceive more clearly and to deal more effectively with his sins. In regard to perception there is better perspective: what is earthly is more clearly seen in its nature and shape. Sins can be viewed for what they are—*not* belonging to one's true nature, which is heavenly ("hid with Christ in God"), and in a real sense unnatural and very distant. For that very reason they are all the more detestable and deplorable. As a result the believer should be even more determined to deal with these sins in such manner as to increasingly mortify them. However, the strength comes not from oneself but from Christ in whom the believer's life is hidden. The risen and ascended Lord, victorious over sin and evil, is the source of the believer's continuing victory.

This brings us back again to the Holy Spirit, for Christ now operates on earth through the Spirit's presence and power. Hence, in relation to sins of the self—whether of the spirit, soul, or body—it is in order to deal with them in terms of Christ and the Holy Spirit. Recall that Paul speaks of sanc-

---

[101]"Mortify" (KJV); the Greek word this time is *nekrōsate*.

[102]The NASB rendering is a poor one: "Therefore consider the members of your earthly body as dead." The KJV, NIV, NEB, like RSV, translate as an imperative.

[103]The Greek phrase is *ta meletā epi tēs gēs,* literally, "the members on the earth." This rather unusual construction relates to everything about the believer that is sinful (earthly over against heavenly—see Col. 3:1).

[104]Some of the words in a frequently recited liturgical prayer.

[105]Recall my earlier designation of this as "the ascended life"; see vol. 1, pages 393–95.

tification[106] "in the name of the Lord Jesus Christ and in the Spirit of our God" (1 Cor. 6:11). Thus one may properly—and vigorously—declare about any sin: "*I put you to death in the name of Jesus Christ by the power of the Holy Spirit*!"[107] The believer accomplishes this mortification in the power that the Lord provides through His indwelling Holy Spirit.

Mortification, we need to add, is not a way of coping with sins in general but in particular. As noted, Paul says, "Put to death therefore what is earthly *in you*," and thereupon certain sins are mentioned. Hence, what a believer sees and knows as specifically sinful *in himself*—the sins being named—is to be put to death. Thus when a sin becomes particularly visible[108] and perhaps threatening at a given time, it is then that the believer may in the name of Christ and by the Holy Spirit seek to put it to death.[109] One may know he has a problem, for example, with lust, but it is when the temptation presses in unmistakably and almost overwhelmingly that the believer may then call out for its mortification. Or he may have just succumbed to a particular sin, and now, realizing what has happened, he cries out in anguish of spirit for its total annihilation. In any event, when the believer speaks forth, "I put you to death . . . ," it is by no means a verbal exercise; it is done with the total being.

This leads to the recognition that such mortification may involve much effort. Evil does not easily let go its grasp; hence, it must be dealt with severely. In Hebrews there is this striking statement: "In your struggle against sin you have not yet resisted to the point of shedding your blood" (12:4). These vivid words may well declare the extent to which the believer will sometimes have to go in his battle against sin: it is a fierce struggle even to the shedding of blood.[110] Christ Himself, although He was without sin, was in much agony in Gethsemane as He struggled against the temptation to turn from the Father's will, so much so that "his sweat became like great drops of blood falling down upon the ground" (Luke 22:44). Although this was not the shedding of blood later at Calvary, it was the final struggle of our Lord against the temptation to forsake the way of the Cross. Sin, however viewed, is no light matter: the struggle against it can be bloody indeed.

One further way of dying to sins is through the *putting away* of sins. Shortly after Paul wrote the Colossians to "put to death" the earthly in them, he

---

[106]As well as justification.

[107]Thus expanding the earlier suggested declaration against sin so as to include the name of Jesus Christ.

[108]This may happen not only in one's conscious life but also while dreaming in sleep. Since dreams emerge from subconscious depths, they often are the channels for sin and evil to express themselves. What appears in dreams may be suppressed in ordinary consciousness, but in dreams the dark elements become visible.

[109]A person waking from a dream and perhaps startled by the evil expressed in it may find this a God-given opportunity for mortification. The evil has gotten by the censor of consciousness; it has now exposed itself in its base nature; hence, it is ready for the slaughter!

[110]Many biblical commentators view the words in Hebrews 12:4 as having to do with martyrdom. However, in light of the preceding words in 12:1: "Let us also lay aside every weight, and sin which clings so closely," I believe the struggle is in relation to the power of sin. Sin that "clings closely" often may not be dislodged without a bloody struggle. According to F. F. Bruce "the agonistic language is continued, although it is warfare with sin rather than a race to be run that is now envisaged" (*The Epistle to the Hebrews*, NICNT, 355, n. 55).

added, "But now put them all away: anger, wrath, malice, slander, and foul talk[111] from your mouth" (3:8). To put away is by no means a gentle action: it implies to get rid of them, to cast them off, to be done with them.[112] This suggests an act of the will in which the believer who is caught up in such sins as anger, malice, and the like, throws them off and away. So Paul writes elsewhere: "Let us then cast off[113] the works of darkness" (Rom. 13:12).[114] It is, therefore, not only a matter of attacking sins so that they become dead, that is, mortified, but also a vigorous expulsion of them so that they are no longer present.

Accordingly, in regard to putting away sins, the believer may not only declare about a particular sin, "I put you to death," but also "*I put you away*"—and in the latter case he may add, "*never to return.*" The corpse of the dead sin is not to be allowed to remain but is to be cast far away. Henceforward the believer will have utterly nothing to do with that sin. It is both dead and gone. Indeed, I may add, it is renounced, mortified, and expelled![115]

Again, the putting away of sins cannot be done in the believer's own strength. As with mortification, the strength comes from his life being "hid with Christ in God." Hence, it is from the believer's true place in the heavenly realm and by the power of Him who is "seated at the right hand of God" (Col. 3:10) that the putting away is to be accomplished. Still the believer must do it: he himself is to cast the sin away.

The putting away of sins is continuous throughout one's lifetime. Hebrews 12:1–2 depicts the whole of life as a race of perseverance, and in the running of it we are urged: "Let us also lay aside[116] every weight, and sin which clings so closely, and let us run with perseverance the race that is set before us, looking to Jesus . . . ." Ever and again sins will make their appearance, but we can and must put them away in the strength that Christ provides.

A further word about the role of the Holy Spirit in the believer's "dying to sins" needs to be stated. It is through the indwelling presence of the Holy Spirit that the believer is again and again made conscious of sins. No matter how far he may have gone in renouncing, mortifying, and expelling sins there is never any place at which he may claim arrival at perfection;[117] rather, the Holy Spirit will disclose to him further areas of need. There will surely be growth in holiness with many sins no longer present, but this does not mean that the struggle is all over. Indeed, it is usually only when grosser

---

[111]The Greek word is *aischrologian*, "abusive speech" (NASB).

[112]The Greek word translated in RSV as "put away" (KJV: "put off"; NASB: "put aside") is *apothesthe*. The NIV renders it "rid yourselves"; the NEB after translating it "lay aside" adds "have done with them!"

[113]The Greek word is *apothōmetha* (the same root as *apothesthe*); "lay aside" (NASB), "put aside" (NIV), "cast off" (KJV), "throw off" (NEB).

[114]Cf. also similar statements about casting off (putting away, getting rid of, etc.) in Ephesians 4:22: "Put it ["lay aside" NASB, NEB] your old nature which belongs to your former manner of life"; James 1:21: "Therefore put away ["get rid of" NIV; "away with" NEB] all filthiness and rank growth of wickedness"; 1 Peter 2:1: "So put away ["rid yourselves of" NIV] all malice and all guile and insincerity and envy and all slander."

[115]Renunciation (as previously discussed) may be the first step as the believer renounces everything in the self that evidences sin; mortification can then follow with attack on a particular sin; and finally expulsion, by which the sin is cast totally away, is the climax.

[116]The Greek word is *apothemenoi*, "throw off" (NIV, NEB).

[117]As we have earlier discussed.

sins have been dealt with that subtler sins become apparent in the light of the Holy Spirit. The believer who is far advanced in sanctification is often aware of sins in his life that would scarcely be recognized by another person, nor would he have recognized them himself until other sins were gotten out of the way. The closer one comes to the light, the more exposed are sins that were hardly recognized before. It is the noble saint who knows, as no one else, that he is still a sinner. For the Holy Spirit never ceases to illumine the dark places and to call for further sanctification.

This does not mean, however, that the believer's life is weighted down by sin. First of all, there is the basic and joyous fact that sin does not reign in the believer's life. Through faith in Jesus Christ he has been liberated from the bondage of *sin*; hence no matter where the believer is on the road of sanctification, he can never be burdened by the *sins* that remain. The believer is always victorious in Jesus Christ! Second, from the believer's vantage point in heavenly places, he knows that although sins remain, they do not truly represent his new life with Christ in God. Hence, there is the constant challenge to do everything possible to remove these earthly blemishes. Third, there is ever and again the joyful realization that through his dying to sins some sins no longer exist for him. He can look back on them and praise God for the victory.

Finally, there is the comforting assurance of the Lord's presence all the way. Since He knew far more than we what it was like to struggle against sin, we have His accompaniment, encouragement,

and help in and through every battle. Truly He rejoices with us in every victory. At last, when all the struggle is over, He will complete our sanctification in glory.

2. Living for Righteousness

The other side of the human task in sanctification is living for righteousness. As was noted previously, we are to "die to sins and live for righteousness." To "live for" signifies a steadfast concern for righteous and holy living.

This means, basically, that the believer's life should be undergirded with an intense desire for righteousness. So Jesus declared, "Blessed are those who hunger and thirst for righteousness" (Matt. 5:6). Afterward, in the Sermon on the Mount (Matt. 5–7), Jesus spelled out the nature of this righteousness. At one point He urged, "Seek first his kingdom and his righteousness" (6:33). Accordingly, the believer who will grow in holiness must be a person who both hungers and thirsts after righteousness and gives it the highest priority in his life.

Paul describes this living for righteousness in the vivid metaphor of slavery. Writing to the Romans, he says of them that they who have "been set free from sin, have become slaves of righteousness" (6:18)[118]. Paul then adds, using the imagery of the human body: "Now present your members as slaves to righteousness, resulting in sanctification" (6:19 NASB)[119]. Righteousness should be so much the concern and commitment of the believer that just as he was formerly given over to sin, now he will be given over to righteousness.

---

[118]This essentially is true of every believer. We who were formerly in bondage to sin, hence slaves, "become the righteousness of God" (2 Cor. 5:21). In that sense, we are slaves (free ones!) of righteousness.

[119]The Greek phrase is *eis hagiasmon,* "for sanctification" (RSV). This properly suggests a continuing sanctification.

Thereby he will become truly a slave of righteousness.[120]

With this understanding of living for righteousness as an intense desire for and commitment to righteousness and that such leads to further sanctification, we are ready to consider how the believer is to move forward. How does one live for righteousness?

a. *Obeying God's Word.* We begin with the necessity of giving obedience to God's word. Since God's word expresses His holy and righteous will, living for righteousness means, for one thing, to live according to that word. The psalmist declares, "I have laid up thy word in my heart, that I might not sin against thee" (119:11). The word of God "laid up" in the heart—the center of one's being—is a powerful force in keeping a person from sin and thereby enabling him to walk in holiness.

Since God's word is found authoritatively in Scripture, the Bible contains the primary guidance for righteous living. In the words of 2 Timothy 3:16–17: "All scripture is inspired by God and profitable for teaching, for reproof, for correction, and for training in righteousness, that the man of God may be complete, equipped for every good work." The words "for reproof, for correction, for training in righteousness" all declare the role of Scripture in helping toward holy and righteous living.

Hence, if a believer is to grow in holiness, he must live according to Scripture. First, this points to an immersion in the words of Scripture, so that they are a part of one's daily life. Even as Jesus Himself made use of the Old Testament when tempted by Satan[121] and thereby continued to walk in the Father's will, so the believer must make constant use of Scripture in his ongoing walk. This can happen only through an ever-growing apprehension of God's written word.

Second, this faithful reading of God's word must be constantly supplemented by action. Jesus emphasized this in relation to His own words: "Every one then who hears these words of mine and does them will be like a wise man who built his house upon the rock" (Matt. 7:24).[122] Since words spoken by Christ are now found only in Scripture, His disciples—those who believe in Him—must hear them as if spoken directly today, and then seek to put them into practice. By doing so a believer's "house"—that is, his life and character—is built on a solid rock. He will become increasingly a person of holy and righteous living.

Accordingly, it is urgent both to know the Scripture and to obey what is written in it. The believer who would "live for righteousness" will again and again turn to God's inspired word. For there he will find the basic guide to "training in righteousness,"[123] and he will earnestly seek to live by its admonitions and teachings.

Obedience to God's word also refers to the word, based on Scripture, that may be spoken in a community of

---

[120]Paul writes, a few verses later, that sanctification is a result of becoming "slaves of God" (v. 22): "Now that you have been set free from sin and have become slaves of God [literally, "enslaved to God"], the return you get is sanctification and its end, eternal life." This is actually no different from what Paul had said about being "a slave of righteousness," since God Himself is the epitome of righteousness. To be enslaved to righteousness, in the true meaning of that word, *is* to be enslaved to God.

[121]See Matthew 4:1–11; Luke 4:1–13.

[122]Recall also the words of James: "Be doers of the word, and not hearers only, deceiving yourselves" (James 1:22).

[123]Paul also speaks of training in 1 Timothy 4:7. He admonishes Timothy: "Train yourself in godliness." This applies to all believers who would grow in holiness.

believers. When a pastor or teacher speaks an exhortation that comes from God, it is incumbent on those who hear to obey. In Hebrews is this statement: "Remember your leaders, those who spoke to you the word of God" (13:7). Later this directive is added: "Obey your leaders and submit to them" (v. 17). Hence, the word of God may come from those called especially to minister that word. When that word is spoken, there is the call by God to obedience. Of course, if the exhortation is out of harmony with sacred Scripture, it is not to be accepted as God's word. However, the *truly* proclaimed word[124] is God's word, and by giving heed to it the believer may grow in holiness and righteousness.

God may also speak His word in other situations. In one's prayer time God's word may be spoken and heard. Indeed, the believer should expect to hear from God regularly. In relation to sanctification the Lord may point to some area in a person's life that needs to be dealt with and likewise give directions to be followed. If there is a genuine concern for holiness on the believer's part, he may expect God, the holy and righteous One, to offer such guidance. But it is not only during the prayer time that God may speak. There are other occasions and circumstances in life by which God speaks forth His word, and the alert believer will often hear in them some message from God. For example, one may endure suffering, and the very suffering itself could be a call for deeper obedience.[125]

In summary, to live for righteousness is to live in obedience to God's word. This means basically to live according to Scripture. But however that word may be spoken, the believer's concern should be that of constant attention with earnest determination to follow every leading of the holy God into fuller holiness.

b. *Looking to Christ.* The central focus of living for righteousness is Jesus Christ. In Hebrews where the "race" of life is described, the center of attention is Jesus: "Let us also lay aside every encumbrance, and the sin which so easily entangles us, and let us run with endurance the race that is set before us, fixing[126] our eyes on Jesus, the author and perfecter of faith" (12:1–2 NASB). By fixing their eyes on Jesus—that is, staying constantly focused on Him—believers may increasingly lay aside their sins.

Primarily this means to actively *follow Jesus.* One of the striking features of Jesus' ministry was His call to people to follow Him. The command "Follow me" was spoken at the beginning,[127] during,[128] and at the end of His ministry. The last words in John's Gospel spoken to Peter were "Follow me" (21:22). "Following" meant very clearly to give Jesus a total commitment, so that devotion to Him would be absolutely first in a person's life. The words of Jesus are quite pointed: "If anyone would come after me, he must deny himself and take up his cross daily and follow me" (Luke 9:23 NIV). Not only must there be self-renunciation,[129] there must also be an active, daily

---

[124]This is not necessarily a word from the pulpit. It may be spoken by a fellow believer— e.g., as a word of wisdom or knowledge, a prophecy, or a tongue plus interpretation (see 1 Cor. 12:8–10)—and be likewise truly from God.

[125]Even Jesus "learned obedience through what he suffered" (Heb. 5:8).

[126]The Greek word is *aphorōntes.* According to Thayer, the verb *aphoraō* means "to turn the eyes away from other things and fix them on something."

[127]E.g., see Matthew 4:19; Mark 1:17, 2:14; Luke 5:27; John 1:43.

[128]E.g., see Matthew 8:22; 9:9; Luke 9:59.

[129]As was discussed in the previous section on "dying to sins."

cross-bearing[130] and following of Jesus. In the words of Peter: "Christ also suffered for us, leaving us an example, that ye should follow his steps: Who did no sin, neither was guile found in his mouth: Who, when he was reviled, reviled not again" (1 Peter 2:21–23 KJV). As the true believing disciple follows the steps of Jesus, there will be suffering. But there will also be an increasing likeness to Him in whom there was no guile. When one follows Jesus faithfully, sin and evil become all the more despicable and are more readily set aside.

The psalmist declared, "I keep the LORD always before me" (16:8). "Always before" suggests in daily life a constant looking to the Lord for guidance. So the psalmist added, "Thou dost show me the path of life" (v. 11). By keeping Jesus always before him, the believer sees the true path so that he may walk in it and in this way be increasingly changed. Paul puts it vividly when he writes, "We all, with unveiled face beholding as in a mirror the glory of the Lord, are being transformed into the same image from glory to glory" (2 Cor. 3:18 NASB). Like Moses, believers in Christ who steadily look upon the glory of the Lord begin to reflect that same glory and are more and more changed into His likeness. What an amazing picture of transformation! It is indeed "from glory to glory." There is no limit on earth; the one beholding becomes increasingly like Christ.

This calls for looking constantly to Jesus as the Lord of one's life. Whether it be in the time of prayer and worship or in the midst of busy activity, the believer's controlling devotion should be to Jesus Christ.[131] So to follow One who is the perfection of holiness enables, as nothing else, the breaking away from sin and living to righteousness. This has well been called "the expulsive power of a higher affection."[132] The devotion of the heart to Another, even as in human relations, makes for a strong desire and urgent action to remove every barrier in the way of that relationship. To look continuously to Jesus is the most powerful incentive to holy conduct and living.

Practically speaking, this means turning again and again to Scripture, where the picture of Christ is set forth. As the believer beholds His manner of life in a wide variety of circumstances and seeks truly to follow His example, the whole person will steadily change into His likeness.[133] This is the way of growing in holiness.

We may note again that looking to Christ means that the believer is constantly to *seek after the highest*. In the words of Paul to the Colossians, "Seek the things that are above, where Christ is. . . . Set your minds on things that are above, not on things that are on earth" (3:1–2). The believer, knowing that his life is "hid with Christ in God" (v. 3), is doing only what is natural to his heavenly position in Christ Jesus when he sets his mind on heavenly things. Paul writes in similar fashion to

---

[130]Cross-bearing does *not* mean the usual sicknesses and sorrows that all people suffer at some time; rather it means, as it did for Jesus, the endurance of suffering that the world inflicts on those who truly follow Him.

[131]Paul, in another connection, speaks of the believer being "a slave of Christ" (1 Cor. 7:22). We may recall his similar words about being "slaves to God" (Rom. 6:22).

[132]I am not sure of the source of this expression.

[133]The words of Adolf Köberle in *The Quest for Holiness* are most apropos: "For the formation of the image of God within us, for the renewing of our minds . . . for the control of our emotions, for the determination of the manner and form of our conduct, the contemplation of the teaching, praying, healing, suffering Savior as he is portrayed in Scripture is indispensable" (158).

111

the Philippians: "Finally, brethren, whatever is true, whatever is honorable, whatever is right, whatever is pure, whatever is lovely, whatever is of good repute, if there is any excellence and if anything worthy of praise, let your mind dwell on[134] these things" (4:8 NASB). Truly these are the excellences of Christ Himself. The mind of the believer is to dwell on all of them, and in so doing the mind of Christ will be increasingly formed in him.[135] In this way he will become more and more like the Lord.

Hence, for sanctification to continue, it is imperative for the believer to have his mind set on things above and to have his thoughts dwell on them. This means that he will in no wise allow the base and degrading to occupy his mind but will constantly turn from such to the highest, the noblest, the best. This does not mean that the believer will perfectly express the things that are above; however, there will be such a set of the mind in that direction that every slippage into things earthly will cause inward pain and anguish. For the believer knows that his life is "hid with Christ in God," and that any failure is an unnatural betrayal, even a distortion of his heavenly position.

But seeking after the highest is also to follow Christ in His descent from the highest to the lowest. We have earlier quoted the words of Paul: "Let this mind be in you, which was also in Christ Jesus" (Phil. 2:5 KJV). Paul continues, " . . . who, being in the form of God, thought it not robbery to be equal with God: but made himself of no reputation,[136] and took upon him the form of a servant . . . he humbled himself, and became obedient unto death, even the death of the cross" (vv. 6–8 KJV). The word "mind" may also be translated "attitude";[137] hence, the continuing attitude of a believer should be that of self-emptying (as with Christ) and being a servant of all mankind. Hence, to focus on Christ and the things of Christ means to follow Him in His amazing act of giving up glory and humbling Himself for the sake of others. Shortly before Paul's words about having this mind, or attitude, he writes, "Do nothing from selfishness or conceit,[138] but in humility count others better than yourselves" (v. 3). This (humanly) impossible attitude can come about only through focusing on Christ in His compassionate action of total selflessness and utter humility.

I have reviewed all this to emphasize that sanctification includes the forsaking of selfish concern (the sin of pride and self-centeredness) in a total outgoing attitude of compassionate selflessness and humble concern for others. Sanctification is far more than a life of purity of heart (as basic as that is); it is also a life of humility, love, and self-sacrifice.

This means, finally, the activity of

[134]The Greek word is *logizesthe;* "think (about), consider, ponder, let one's mind dwell on" (BAGD).

[135]The believer already essentially has "the mind of Christ" ("We have the mind of Christ" [1 Cor. 2:16]). However, the believer's mind needs continuing conformation to Christ, as do all other areas of his being. We may recall how deeply Paul yearns for this full formation in regard to the Galatians: "I am again in travail until Christ be formed in you" (4:19).

[136]The Greek word is *ekenōsen,* "emptied himself" (RSV, NASB).

[137]As in the NASB and NIV. The Greek word *phroneite* does not so much mean have "this mind" (above) as "be thus minded" (BAGD). It is the same word used in Colossians 3:2, there translated "set your minds." In Philippians 2:5 "attitude"—understood perhaps as a "set attitude"—may be the best translation.

[138]The Greek word is *kenodoxian,* "vainglory" (KJV).

putting on. As the believer focuses on Christ in His vast act of condescension, his attitude should also gradually change. However, the vigorous activity of putting on, or clothing oneself with, the characteristics of Christ is also needed. Thus Paul writes the Colossians, "Put on[139] a heart of compassion, kindness, humility, gentleness and patience; bearing with one another and forgiving each other . . . beyond all these things put on love, which is the perfect bond of unity" (3:12–14 NASB). To put on is to set one's mind on Christ (3:2), for in doing so there is vision and motive power. Without this mind-set any attempt at putting on such virtues as compassion, humility, and patience would be entirely artificial and empty. But against the background of Christ Himself, the believer is called to the continuing and forceful action of putting on, or clothing himself with, the characteristics and virtues exemplified in Christ.

Let us understand this as vigorous effort. We have previously observed how Paul in Colossians 3:5 speaks strongly about putting to death, or mortifying, various sins: immorality, impurity, evil desire, etc. Now it is after this putting to death and putting away (v. 8)—both essentially negative actions—that Paul speaks of putting on. This suggests that the negative should be followed by the positive, for as sins are put off, there should be immediate concern, no less vital to be sure, for virtues to be put on.

Indeed, this signifies deliberate action. As if dressing in the morning, the believer is to put on one piece after another: the clothing of compassion, kindness, humility, gentleness, patience, forbearance, forgiveness, and love (which binds all the others to-

gether). This kind of action, incidentally, is not dissimilar to Paul's admonishing the Ephesians to "put on the whole armor of God" (6:11). After that he describes, one after another, various pieces of armor that are to be put on (vv. 14–18). The purpose, of course, is quite different: the armor is for the battle against evil forces (v. 12), whereas the clothing is for representing Christ and His character to all persons. Still, deliberate activity is called for; this is implied in the verb "put on."

Practically speaking, this could suggest the zealous effort each day to put on afresh these various virtues. There are many believers who make a practice at the beginning of the day of putting on the whole armor of God, piece by piece, to stand against the world of evil forces. Why not also try the other, and far more significant, even more exciting, activity of putting on the clothing of Christ? One might say, "As I rise in the morning, focused on Christ (the necessary background and power), *I will put on compassion, next kindness, next humility, and so on*—piece by piece." To be sure, there are other virtues besides those Paul lists in Colossians 3:12–14 that may likewise be put on. However, this is surely a good place to begin, and God will indeed honor even the believer's fumbling attempts in such a continuing exercise.

The subject of looking to Christ may be summarized in the phrase *abiding in Him.* Jesus said to His disciples, "Abide in me, and I in you. As the branch cannot bear fruit by itself, unless it abides in the vine, neither can you, unless you abide in me" (John 15:4). The word "abide" brings out especially the note of constancy, a looking to Jesus, that is as continuous as is His life within the believer.[140] By abiding in

---

[139]The Greek word is an imperative: *endysasthe,* "clothe yourselves with" (NIV).
[140]I much appreciate the words of James H. McConkey in his little book, *The Three-Fold*

Jesus, the believer does bear fruit—including the fruit of righteousness—that will continue to multiply.

According to 1 John, "No one who lives[141] in him keeps on sinning" (3:6 NIV)[142]. This signifies that one who abides in Christ has thereby a powerful deterrent to sin. Sin is no longer natural to him as it was before. Now the true life is the life of Christ, one of increasing righteousness and holiness.

Truly to abide in Christ is the capstone of looking to Christ. For looking is not to glance now and then, but to look constantly so that the believer day by day becomes more like his Master and Lord. This, indeed, is the very heart of living for righteousness.

c. *Walking by the Spirit.* Finally, to live for righteousness is to walk by the Spirit. Paul writes to the Galatians: "If we live by the Spirit, let us also walk[143] by the Spirit" (5:25). Because believers have been made alive by the Spirit, they are challenged to walk by that same Spirit.

This means, first, to *walk in freedom.* Paul writes the Corinthians about the "new covenant" which is "not in a written code[144] but in the Spirit; for the written code kills, but the Spirit gives life" (2 Cor. 3:6). Afterward Paul adds, "Where the Spirit of the Lord is, there is freedom" (v. 17). Hence, in terms of sanctification, the believer is no longer operating under a killing written code but under a life-giving Spirit—and this means freedom. In Romans Paul declares, "We serve in the new way[145] of the Spirit, and not in the old way of the written code" (7:6 NIV). This "new way of the Spirit" is no longer the way of the written code, the law, but the way of freedom in the Spirit.

Thus the believer who walks in the Spirit is not (amazing to relate!) under the law. For we also hear Paul declare in Galatians: "If you are led by the Spirit you are not under the law" (5:18). The law, for all its righteous content, could not bring about true righteousness and holiness because it demands what the previously unregenerate person could not do—namely, walk truly in the way of God. At best there could only be an external righteousness;[146] at worst the law produced an anguishing sense of condemnation.[147] The believer

---

Secret of the Holy Spirit: "These three words, LOOKING TO *Jesus,* picture perfectly the posture of the soul that is abiding in Christ. The moon keeps *looking* to the sun, for every gleam of her reflected radiance; the branch keeps *looking* to the vine, for every whit of its life and fruitage; the drinking fountain keeps *looking* to the supplying reservoir, for every drop of water it is to pour out to its thirsting visitors; the arc light keeps *looking* to the great dynamo, for every ray of the stream of light with which it floods the midnight darkness. Even so the child of God . . . must *keep looking to Jesus,* until such abiding in faith becomes the constant attitude of his soul" (p. 106).

[141]The Greek word is *menōn,* "abides" (RSV, NASB, KJV).

[142]The Greek word is *hamartanei.* This present tense refers to a "continuance in sin" (EGT, in loco). See previous note 29. The KJV, "sinneth not," and RSV and NASB, "No one who abides in him sins," are misleading translations.

[143]The Greek word is *stoichōmen.* The NIV translates thus, "Since we live by the Spirit, let us keep in step with the Spirit."

[144]The Greek word is *grammatos,* literally, "a letter" (however, "letter" clearly means the written code, or law, or the Old Covenant).

[145]The Greek word is *kainotēti,* literally, "newness."

[146]Paul could speak of himself prior to his conversion "as to righteousness under the law blameless" (Phil. 3:6), but it was by no means a righteousness of the heart.

[147]According to Paul, the law that says, "You shall not covet," because of sin in himself, "proved to be death" to him (Rom. 7:7, 10). Paul later declares about his new status in Christ, "There is therefore now no condemnation . . . " (Rom. 8:1).

is set free from the law by Christ ("for freedom Christ has set us free"—Gal. 5:1). He is no longer under the law; he walks in the freedom of the Spirit.

Moreover, in the new life of walking by the Holy Spirit, there is for the first time true holiness. As the believer strives after righteousness, it is not a matter merely of his own effort but of the Spirit enabling him to fulfill the righteousness he seeks. Hence, instead of a sense of bondage to a law he could not keep before, there is the freedom in the Spirit that transcends all law and brings about a higher holiness and righteousness.

Now we come to Paul's great statement about the fruit of the Spirit. Shortly after saying that those led by the Spirit are not under the law, Paul declares: "The fruit of the Spirit is love, joy, peace, patience, kindness, goodness, faithfulness, gentleness, self-control; against such there is no law" (Gal. 5:22–23). What the law could never produce, the Holy Spirit brings about. This takes time and much walking by the Spirit, because good and mature fruit may be long in producing. But the results are far beyond what the law could ever bring about. Further, the law cannot be against this fruitage of the Spirit because in such is the true fulfillment of the law[148] and of more than the law ever demanded.[149]

I wrote earlier about putting on such virtues as compassion, kindness, humil-ity, gentleness, and patience, some of which are identical with, or similar to, the fruit of the Spirit. Hence, there is no essential difference between the virtues designated in the clothing and the fruit. However, what may be most significant is the inner direction by the Spirit as to how these virtues are to be exercised. "Putting on" is one thing, how to do this is another—and in this the Holy Spirit is the true guide.[150] Guided by the Spirit of freedom, believers may express these virtues in a great variety of ways so that they increasingly flourish in the believers' lives.

Walking by the Spirit, second, enables the believer *to fulfill the law*. Paul speaks in Romans of how "the just requirement[151] of the law" may be "fulfilled in us, who walk not according to the flesh but according to the Spirit" (8:4). What the law requires (and what could not be accomplished before) can be fulfilled by those who walk according to the Spirit. Hence, although the believer is not under the law[152] (as we have seen), the law does not thereby cease to be. For the law is God's righteous ordinance and an expression of His own nature: it remains firm. The great difference between the old and new covenants is this: since the law is now written on the heart by the indwelling Spirit, the believer can actually do what the law requires. To put it another way, although the believer is now not under the law but under grace ("You

---

[148]Herman Ridderbos writes in reference to Galatians 5:22–25: "The law is not against those who walk by the Spirit because in principle they are fulfilling the law" (*Commentary on Galatians*, NICNT, 208).

[149]Indeed, the very fruit of the Spirit represents the character of Christ being formed in the life of the believer. F. F. Bruce writes, "Living by the Spirit is the root; walking by the Spirit is the fruit, and that fruit is nothing less than the practical reproduction of the character (and therefore the conduct) of Christ in the lives of his people" (*Commentary on Galatians*, NIGTC, 257).

[150]Relevant here may be the earlier-mentioned NIV translation of Galatians 5:25: "Since we live by the Spirit, let us keep in step with the Spirit." To this may be added the NEB rendition: "If the Spirit is the source of our life, let the Spirit also direct our course."

[151]The Greek word is *dikaiōma*. The NIV has "righteous requirements."

[152]I speak here particularly of the moral law as expressed in the Ten Commandments and as further declared in Christ's teachings (especially the Sermon on the Mount).

are not under law but under grace" [Rom. 6:14]), grace does not dispense with law but fulfills it. In a still earlier statement in Romans about justification by faith Paul adds, "Do we then nullify the Law through faith? May it never be! On the contrary, we establish[153] the Law" (3:31 NASB). The law is at last established, given a firm footing, in that it can now become truly operational in the life of a believer.

Furthermore, the law is needed in the life of a believer because of the remnants of sin that invariably remain in him. Although he is now moving in the Spirit, the flesh is still present to seek its own way. In our earlier discussion on "dying to sins" I quoted the words of Paul that "the desires of the flesh are against the Spirit, and the desires of the Spirit are against the flesh; for these are opposed to each other" (Gal. 5:17). Paul then adds: " . . . to prevent you from doing what you would." Although the Spirit does operate within to enable the believer both to transcend the law and to fulfill its just requirements, there is still the opposition of the flesh that prevents a fully free action. Accordingly, the law remains as a needful curb against the desires and passions of the flesh. Even the Spirit-filled believer needs to hear such commandments as "You shall not be angry," "You shall not lust," "You shall not resist one who is evil," "Love your enemies."[154] For the flesh remains antagonistic to all such commands. To say that one does not need such injunctions because he is no longer under law but under grace is wholly unrealistic. Rather the law remains for the believer a necessary constraint on his continuing sinfulness.

But now to return to the affirmative side. The believer moves in the freedom of the Spirit and this enables him for the first time to begin to fulfill the law, thus finding a fresh delight in it. Since it is *God's* law—His way of righteousness and justice—there can now be even a pleasure in its contemplation. If the psalmist could say, "Oh, how I love thy law!" (119:97) in the time of the old covenant, how much more should the Christian be able to rejoice in it! To be sure, there is much more than law in the Christian walk, but in the law basically is set forth God's will and purpose. Thus the grateful believer takes delight in all that God has revealed and gladly seeks to walk according to it.

This means continuing progress in sanctification. For as the believer walks by the Spirit in the fulfilling of the law, he more and more is conformed to the image and likeness of Christ.

The climax of walking by the Spirit is *walking in love*. We have been discussing how walking by the Spirit is both a walking in freedom from the law and, at the same time, a fulfilling of the law. *The reality that unites both freedom and law is love.*

It is quite significant that in Galatians 5 Paul writes first about freedom: "For freedom has Christ set us free" (v. 1); "For you were called to freedom, brethren" (v. 13). Then he adds, "Only do not use your freedom as an opportunity for the flesh, but through love be servants of one another. For the whole law is fulfilled in one word, 'You shall love your neighbor as yourself' " (vv. 13–14). This means, accordingly, that law is not done away with by freedom, but is fulfilled in the commandment to love one's neighbor.[155] This signifies

---

[153]The Greek word is *histanomen*. The NEB translates the last sentence above thus: "By no means: we are placing law itself on a firmer footing."

[154]I am freely paraphrasing Jesus' words in Matthew 5:22, 28, 39, 44.

[155]Cf. Romans 13:10: "Love does no wrong to a neighbor; therefore love is the fulfilling of the law."

that all the commandments in regard to the neighbor are to be fulfilled freely in love. The Christian's freedom, therefore, can be neither a selfish freedom that disregards the other person nor a legalistic action that does only to him what the law requires. For where the love of God operates, there is a free and glad self-giving to all persons that includes but also goes far beyond any requirement of the law.

The supreme example of walking in love was Christ Himself. He freely gave Himself for the sake of all mankind. In correspondence to this, Paul enjoins, "Walk in love, as Christ loved us and gave himself up for us, a fragrant offering and sacrifice to God" (Eph. 5:2). This was a love that went far beyond any requirement of the law, and it was freely and totally given. Followers of Christ are to walk in that same love, and by the strength of His indwelling Spirit it can freely be done.

Those who so love are truly walking by the Spirit. Since there can be nothing higher or greater than the love of Christ, to walk day by day in such a way is to become more and more like Him.

In this our sanctification is made complete.

5

Perseverance

In this chapter we will consider the matter of perseverance in the Christian life. Having reflected on matters relating to the occurrence of salvation,[1] our concern here will be with the subject of continuation in salvation throughout life.

I. PRELIMINARY

A. General Usage

The word "perseverance" may be generally defined as persistence in a state, a course of action, or undertaking often in spite of difficulties, contrary influences, or opposition. Perseverance accordingly particularly signifies steadfastness and endurance.

Regarding steadfastness in the Christian life, Paul speaks of the need to "keep alert with all perseverance"[2] (Eph. 6:18). He also encourages the Colossians to persevere in prayer:

"Continue steadfastly in prayer " (Col. 4:2).[3] Of the early Christians it was said that "they continued steadfastly in the apostles' doctrine and fellowship, and in breaking of bread, and in prayers" (Acts 2:42 KJV). The apostles also said of themselves: "We will devote ourselves to prayer and to the ministry of the word" (Acts 6:4). These are, variously, instances of perseverance in Christian life and ministry.

There is similarly the New Testament note of endurance. In the Book of Hebrews this challenge is given: "Let us run with endurance[4] the race that is set before us" (12:1 NASB). Also, "by your endurance you will gain your lives" (Luke 21:19); "suffering produces endurance, and endurance produces character" (Rom. 5:3–4); "here is a call for the endurance of the saints" (Rev. 14:12). The perseverance (or endurance) of "the saints" lies at the heart of victorious Christian living.

---

[1]In the previous chapters 1–3: "Calling," "Regeneration," and "Justification." Also, as was noted in chapter 4, "Sanctification," sanctification in its beginning is an aspect of the event of salvation.

[2]The noun form *proskarterēsis* is used here. The verb form *proskartereō* can also be translated "to continue steadfastly in," "to be constant in," or "to devote self to."

[3]Cf. Romans 12:12: "Be constant in prayer."

[4]The Greek word is *hypomonēs*. The word "endurance" in the following quotations above is also from *hypomonē,* and so could be translated "perseverance."

B. Special Usage

The word "perseverance" also has a more technical usage, namely, its relation to salvation. Here the concern is not the Christian life in general with the call for steadfastness and endurance, but the arena of salvation. Now that salvation has been received through faith in Jesus Christ, what is the *basis* for persisting therein throughout life, what are the *conditions* of this persistence, and what *conclusions* may be drawn? Is it possible for a person to forfeit his salvation?

Thus we will be focusing on the matter of *persistence in salvation*. The question, in traditional theological language, is that of "the perseverance of the saints." Since all Christians are saints,[5] the concern is not for some special—presumably higher—category of Christians, but relates to all believers. We turn now to the consideration of their perseverance, or persistence, in salvation unto the end of life and the glory that lies beyond.

II. BASIS

The basis, or ground, of perseverance lies in the activity of the Triune God. He has set everything in motion, and He is the sustainer. It is God's work and activity that is the basis of persistence in salvation.

A. God the Father

1. His Will and Purpose

First, it is God's intention that all who truly come to Christ shall remain to the end. Jesus Himself declared, "This is the will of him who sent me, that I should lose nothing of all that he has given me, but raise it up at the last day" (John 6:39). Paul also spoke of his conviction: "I am sure that he who began a good work in you will bring it to completion at[6] the day of Jesus Christ" (Phil. 1:6). It is God's intention that all who belong to Christ, as well as their work, remain and be fulfilled at the end.

2. His Power

What God wills and purposes He is able to fulfill. We turn immediately to the stirring climax in the letter of Jude: "Now to him who is able to keep you from falling[7] and to present you without blemish before the presence of his glory with rejoicing" (v. 24). Our God is able; He has the power to do this.

Another relevant text is 1 Peter 1:5, where the apostle speaks of those "who by God's power are guarded through faith for a salvation ready to be revealed in the last time." Again, it is a matter of God's power that undergirds the salvation to be concluded at the end. The almighty power of God stands guard against every obstacle or enemy that would seek to prevent the Christian from arriving at the ultimate goal.

Our God is able—totally.

3. His Faithfulness

The faithfulness of God also lies behind the perseverance of the believer. Paul writes, "[He] will sustain[8] you to the end, guiltless in the day of our Lord Jesus Christ. God is faithful, by whom you were called into the fellowship of his Son, Jesus Christ our Lord" (1 Cor. 1:8–9). We do not strengthen ourselves; it is God who undergirds and strengthens us. Moreover, in 2 Timothy Paul writes: "If we are faithless, he remains faithful" (2:13). God's faithfulness never wavers whatever may be our faithlessness. One other Scripture

---

[5]By virtue of their sanctification in Jesus Christ (see the previous chapter).

[6]The Greek phrase is *epitelesei achri,* "perfect it until" (NASB).

[7]The Greek word is *aptaistous,* "stumbling" (NASB).

[8]The Greek word is *bebaiōsei,* "keep you strong" (NIV), "confirm you" (KJV, NASB). I have substituted "strengthen" (see BAGD) for "sustain" in RSV.

that is apropos is set against the background of sanctification. In the preceding chapter we noted that Paul wrote, "May the God of peace himself sanctify you wholly." And he immediately added, "And may your spirit and soul and body be kept[9] sound and blameless at the coming of our Lord Jesus Christ. He who calls you is faithful, and he will do it" (1 Thess. 5:23–24). God in His faithfulness will strengthen and keep to the end.

B. God the Son

1. His Safeguarding

In one of His addresses to a critical audience of Jews, Jesus said, "My sheep hear my voice, and I know them, and they follow me." Then He added, "I give them eternal life, and they shall never perish, and no one shall snatch them out of my hand"[10] (John 10:27–28). Similarly, Jesus later said in His prayer to the Father: "While I was with them, I kept them in thy name, which thou hast given me; I have guarded them, and none of them is lost but the son of perdition" (John 17:12). Jesus never fails to safeguard and to safekeep those who belong to him.

2. His Continued Intercession

I have earlier spoken of the high priestly role of the Lord Jesus for His people: "He always lives to make intercession for them." Prior to these words the Scripture reads: "He holds his priesthood permanently, because he continues for ever. Consequently he is able for all time to save those who draw near to God through him, since he always lives to make intercession for them" (Heb. 7:24–25). Jesus, exalted at the right hand of the Father and constantly interceding for those who come to Him, is able to save both now and forever. A clear-cut example of Jesus' intercession to the Father while on earth is found in these words: "Holy Father, keep them in thy name, which thou hast given me" (John 17:11). This is surely the kind of intercessory prayer that the exalted Lord Jesus never ceases to offer at the throne of God.

3. His Unity With Us

Since through faith we have been united with Jesus Christ in His death and resurrection ("If we have been united with him in a death like his, we shall certainly be united with[11] him in a resurrection like his" [Rom. 6:5]), this very union is a strong basis for the continuing of salvation. In another text Paul writes, "You have died, and your life is hid with Christ in God" (Col. 3:3); this means death to the old self and life in this unity with Him. We are so incorporated into Christ as to give a solid ground for persisting to the end.

C. God the Holy Spirit

1. His Abiding Presence

In one of His discourses about the Holy Spirit, Jesus said, "I will pray the Father, and he will give you another Counselor,[12] to be with you for ever" (John 14:16). The fact of the presence of the Holy Spirit "forever" provides a dynamic and continuing basis for enduring salvation.

[9]The Greek word is tērēthein, "preserved" (NASB).
[10]Jesus also added these words, "And no one is able to snatch them out of the Father's hand" (v. 29). Hence, here is a kind of double safeguard!
[11]The Greek word is symphytoi, "planted together" (KJV), "become incorporate with" (NEB).
[12]The Greek word is paraklēton. The Holy Spirit is the Paraclete. Other translations such as "Comforter" (KJV), "Counselor" (NIV), "the Advocate" (NEB), and "the Helper" (NASB) express aspects of the rich meaning in the word paraklētos.

2. His Sealing

Paul writes to the Ephesians of being "sealed with the promised Holy Spirit, [who] is the guarantee[13] of our inheritance until we acquire possession of it" (1:13–14). The sealing by the Spirit, occurring in those who believe in Christ, is the guarantee of their future inheritance. This guarantee, truly a "gilt-edged" basis for the inheritance to come, would insure continuance in salvation until the goal beyond death is reached.

3. His New Life

Finally, through the Holy Spirit we have been "born anew" (John 3:3, 7). By this new birth we have "eternal life" (John 3:16). Moreover, through the Holy Spirit dwelling in us—"he dwells with you, and will be in you" (John 14:17)—the life of God verily is within our life. Hence, born anew to eternal life and indwelt by the Holy Spirit, the believer is on firm ground for a life that will not end at death.

From what has been said in the preceding paragraphs, it is apparent that the Triune God provides in multiple ways the solid basis for persistence in salvation. From the background of the divine action, perseverance takes on the note of preservation:[14] God's preservation of those who belong to Him. Perseverance, accordingly, like other areas of salvation and Christian faith (calling, regeneration, justification, and sanctification) is primarily a work of God.

III. CONDITIONS

Although God Himself has done— and continues to do—everything by way of sustaining the believer to the end, this does not eliminate certain human conditions. Although God's grace is unconditional, there is no unconditional persistence in salvation.[15] A good preparatory warning is that of Paul: "Let any one who thinks that he stands take heed lest he fall" (1 Cor. 10:12).

We turn now to a number of scriptural conditions. Some of these overlap; however, I will treat them separately so as to note the variety of biblical statements regarding conditions.

A. Our Abiding

One of the first requirements is that of abiding or staying close. In his first epistle John writes: "If what you heard from the beginning abides[16] in you, then you will abide in the Son and in the Father. And this is what he has promised us, eternal life" (2:24–25). The promise of eternal life made by God is sure. But abiding in the truth of the gospel, and thereby in Christ and the Father, is necessary for that life to be fulfilled. In Hebrews there is another passage that emphasizes the need for abiding, staying close: "We must pay the closer attention to what we have heard, lest we drift away from it. . . . How shall we escape if we neglect such

---

[13] The Greek word is *arrabōn,* "pledge" (NASB, NEB), "earnest" (KJV), "deposit" (NIV).

[14] " . . . the doctrine of perseverance has to do with divine preservation, with our being preserved for our inheritance" (G. C. Berkouwer, *Faith and Perseverance,* 225).

[15] Berkouwer views the divine preservation (n. 14), with the corollary of perseverance, as basically unconditional. Although he mentions "conditionality," Berkouwer proceeds to speak of "the irresistibility of God's sovereign grace" (ibid., 90). Hence persistence in salvation is sovereignly assured, thus unconditional. I gladly affirm "God's sovereign grace" (though not its "irresistibility"), and God's preservation but not regardless of the human situation. (For a helpful critique of Berkouwer's position see I. Howard Marshall's book, *Kept by the Power of God,* "The Solution of G. C. Berkouwer," 204–6).

[16] The Greek word is *meinē,* "remains" (KJV, NIV), "dwells" (NEB).

a great salvation?'' (2:1, 3). In both of these cases abiding is a matter of remaining in what has been "heard," and that means for us today especially abiding in the words of Scripture.

But also, and of even greater importance, there is the call to abide in Christ Himself. After Jesus gave this message, "You are already made clean by the word which I have spoken to you" (thus the word of salvation), He said, "Abide in me, and I in you" (John 15:3–4). This likewise includes abiding in His words: "If you abide in me, and my words abide in you" (v. 7). The focus unmistakably is on Christ personally and the call to abide in Him.[17]

The result of failure to abide in Christ is a tragic one indeed: "If a man does not abide in me, he is cast forth as a branch and withers; and the branches are gathered, thrown in the fire and burned" (John 15:6). Such a one who does not abide is "cast forth," literally, is "cast outside,"[18] and his future is without hope.

The first condition of persisting in salvation is that of abiding, of staying close to the source, whether this be understood as the word heard and read or the Word who is Christ Himself.

B. Our Continuing

Closely related to the matter of abiding is that of continuing, of remaining steadfast. God has begun the work of salvation in us; now we are to continue in it. This is necessary if we are to arrive at the final goal.

One of the great passages on salvation is Colossians 1:21–22, where Paul says: "And you, who once were estranged and hostile in mind, doing evil deeds, he has now reconciled in his body of flesh by his death, in order to present you holy and blameless and irreproachable before him." Reconciliation has occurred, and its goal is the final presentation before Christ. There is, however, a proviso in the words that immediately follow: "Provided that you continue[19] in the faith,[20] stable and steadfast, not shifting from[21] the hope of the gospel which you heard" (v. 23). A condition is clearly included: "provided that [literally, "if indeed"] you continue . . . ." If we shift, that is move away from the faith and hope that is in the gospel, then we will not be present before the Lord.

In another place Paul speaks of how God in His kindness has granted the Gentiles salvation. The Jews would not listen, but "through their trespass salvation has come to the Gentiles" (Rom. 11:11). This, says Paul, as he writes the Gentile Romans, is "God's kindness to you, provided you continue in his kindness." Then Paul immediately adds, "Otherwise you too will be cut off" (11:22). "Salvation has come," "God's kindness" is there, but by failure to continue, the end is tragic: such persons are "cut off."

Paul also speaks of continuance in his words to Timothy: "Take heed to yourself and to your teaching; hold to[22] that, for by so doing you will save both yourself and your hearers" (1 Tim.

---

[17]The thrust of these words of Jesus is, first, on fruit-bearing and, second, on answers to prayer. He does not speak directly of abiding so that salvation or eternal life may continue. However, the words that follow, quoted in the next paragraph, unquestionably have implications related to that.

[18]The Greek phrase is *eblēthē exō*, "thrown away" (NASB, NIV).

[19]The Greek word is *epimenete*, both here and in other verses quoted after this.

[20]Or, simply, "in faith" (as NASB mg suggests). The NEB and NIV translate the phrase "in your faith."

[21]The Greek word is *metakinoumenoi*, "not moved away from" (KJV, NASB, cf. NIV).

[22]The Greek word is *epimene*, literally, "continue in."

4:16). Only by continuance is there persistence in salvation.

Hence, there is need for continuing, holding fast, if we are to attain the ultimate goal. God in His great love and kindness has wrought our salvation; He has reconciled us to Himself and intends to present us holy and blameless in heaven—*provided that . . . .*

C. Our Enduring

We take a further step in noting also the importance of enduring, or holding on. The moment of salvation to the end of life may cover many days and years—a shorter or longer time. Ordinarily there are many ups and downs. Through it all, whatever may happen, we are called on to endure.

In a memorable passage Paul writes of his concern for God's "elect": "I endure everything for the sake of the elect, that they also may obtain the salvation which in Christ Jesus goes with eternal glory" (2 Tim. 2:10). He then quotes from an early Christian hymn: " 'If we have died with him, we shall also live with him; if we endure,[23] we shall also reign with him' " (vv. 11–12). The reigning "with him" points to the future kingdom, and this will occur "if we endure." Paul immediately adds, "If we deny him, he also will deny us." If we deny Him, Christ at the end will not recognize or claim us. Thus endurance—to the end—is the condition of the final salvation of God's elect.

The Book of Hebrews strikes a similar note in a passage that recounts many sufferings the readers have gone through—public abuse, plundering of their possessions, and the like. Then the writer adds, "Do not throw away your confidence, which has a great reward.

For you have need of endurance, so that you may do the will of God and receive what is promised" (10:35–36). The promise refers to what was earlier mentioned—"a better possession and an abiding one" (v. 34)—in other words, life in the world beyond. If we fail to endure, the end is quite different. The Lord adds these words: "For yet a little while and the coming one shall come and shall not tarry; but my righteous one shall live by faith, and if he shrinks back, my soul has no pleasure in him" (vv. 37–38).[24] This is shrinking back "to destruction" (v. 39 NASB)—a tragic end after so great a beginning.

One further word may be mentioned—and this from the mouth of Jesus Himself: "He who endures to the end will be saved" (Matt. 24:13). While the text here does not necessarily refer to salvation in terms of eternal life (the context concerns tribulation and persecution), nonetheless, since the immediately preceding words are "most men's love will grow cold" (v. 12), there is a strong suggestion of reference to personal salvation.

To summarize, endurance is clearly called for in order to obtain the future salvation, to reign with Christ, to secure the better possession. Truly—in this larger sense—"he who endures to the end will be saved."

D. Our Firmness

It is also important to make firm, or confirm, what has been given us in Jesus Christ. In Hebrews we read, "For we share[25] in Christ, if only we hold our first confidence firm to the end" (3:14). In other words, those who share in Christ both now and in the future are those whose "first confidence" is never

---

[23] The Greek word is *hypomenomen*. See earlier use of this word in reference to Christian life in general. The KJV translates *hypomenomen* as "suffer." However, in this context (and in the next quotation) the idea is more concretely that of enduring or holding on to the end.

[24] The LXX reading of Habakkuk 2:3–4.

[25] The Greek phrase is *metochoi . . . gegonamen*, literally, "we have become sharers."

lost but rather is held firm to the very end.

A somewhat similar statement is found in 2 Peter: "Brethren, be the more zealous to confirm[26] your call and election, for if you do this you will never fall; so there will be richly provided for you an entrance into the eternal kingdom of our Lord and Savior Jesus Christ" (1:10–11).

It is particularly significant to note the need for confirming, or making firm one's "call and election." This clearly implies that calling and election (the background of calling)[27] do not guarantee continuance; rather, this only occurs through our making this firm and thereby having an abundant entrance into God's eternal kingdom.

As to how this "making firm" is to be done, Peter gives a list of qualities of character to be developed. He speaks of supplementing faith in a number of ways: "Make every effort to supplement your faith with virtue . . . knowledge . . . self-control . . . steadfastness . . . godliness . . . brotherly affection . . . love" (1:5–7). Faith is clearly basic. But as these qualities develop and abound, the knowledge of Christ is intensified (1:8), and they make for a confirming of one's call and election.

Further, in this second letter Peter speaks of the tragic situation of those who do just the opposite, some becoming false prophets and false teachers, "denying the Master who bought them, bringing upon themselves swift destruction" (2:1). There are some whose final condition turns out to be worse than their first: "For if, after they have escaped the defilements of the world through the knowledge of our Lord and Savior Jesus Christ, they are again entangled in them and overpowered, the last state has become worse for

them than the first" (2:20). Peter adds sadly, "For it would have been better for them never to have known the way of righteousness than after knowing it to turn back" (2:21). For the true believer, who knows the Lord and Savior, to become entangled again in worldly defilements is far worse than never to have known Him at all. Could there possibly be a stronger warning for the Christian than this: to guard against that worldly defilement wherein one's last state is worse than his first?

How important it is—to return to Peter's earlier words—to confirm, make firm, to firm up, our call and election. For this we should be zealous. In so doing, we shall never fall.

E. Our Faithfulness

Finally, it is necessary that we remain faithful to the end. We have already observed God's faithfulness; now we must hear the call for our faithfulness, our remaining in faith and belief. The words of Christ in the Book of Revelation to the church in Smyrna (and accordingly to all believers) stand out: "Be faithful unto death, and I will give you the crown of life" (2:10). Our faithfulness, all the way, is climaxed with the award of heaven's crown. The importance of this is shown by earlier words of Christ to the church in Ephesus: "I have this against you, that you have abandoned the love you had at first. Remember then from what you have fallen, repent and do the works you did at first. If not, I will come to you and remove your lampstand from its place" (2:4–5). When faithfulness gives way to abandonment, the end is *removal*—with all that the word suggests—unless there is repentance and return.

Another strong warning about re-

---

[26]The Greek word is *bebaian*, "make firm, establish" (BAGD). This word is also used in Hebrews 3:14.

[27]See our discussion of this in chapter 1, "Calling."

maining in faith is found in Hebrews: "Take care, brethren, lest there be in any of you an evil, unbelieving heart, leading you to fall away[28] from the living God" (3:12). This evil, unbelieving heart is one that has become "hardened by the deceitfulness of sin" (3:13), of which the parallel is Israel in the Old Testament (3:7–11). Such a heart has not remained faithful, but has allowed unbelief gradually to come in.

How seriously the situation can deteriorate is further shown in Hebrews 6:4–8. For here the picture is of a full-orbed faith that gives way to apostasy. The Scripture reads, "It is impossible to restore again to repentance those who have once been enlightened, who have tasted the heavenly gift, and have become partakers of the Holy Spirit, and have tasted the goodness of the word of God and the powers of the age to come, if they then commit apostasy,[29] since they crucify again[30] the Son of God on their own account and hold him up to contempt.[31] For land which has drunk the rain that often falls upon it, and brings forth vegetation useful to those for whose sake it is cultivated, receives a blessing from God. But if it bears thorns and thistles, it is worthless and near to being cursed; its end is to be burned." This, indeed, is a tragic picture of persons who have had a comprehensive Christian experience—enlightenment,[32] tasting the heavenly gift,[33] becoming partakers[34] of the Holy Spirit, the powers of the age to come[35]—and then commit apostasy. It actually signifies the crucifying of Christ again

---

[28] The Greek word is *apostēnai,* literally, "to apostatize," hence, to "fall away," "desert," "depart."

[29] Or "and then have fallen away" (NASB), "and after all this have fallen away" (NEB). There is no word "if" in the Greek text. The word for "commit apostasy" or "fall away" is *parapesontas.*

[30] "Again" is not in the RSV; I have added it here. The Greek word is *anastaurountas,* which can be translated simply "crucify" (so in extra-biblical Greek, according to BAGD). However, the prefix *"ana"* can mean "again" (so, according to BAGD, ancient translators and Greek fathers understood it). The NASB, NIV, and KJV convey this note in their translation; not so RSV and NEB. The context, I believe, calls for "crucify again," since it is something apostates do—not the original crucifixion.

[31] The Greek word is *paradeigmatizontas,* "put [Him] to open shame" (NASB).

[32] The Greek word is *phōtisthentas;* cf. Hebrews 10:32; see also 2 Corinthians 4:6. These texts refer unmistakably to the enlightenment of salvation.

[33] The Greek phrase is *geusamenous te tēs dōreas tēs epouraniou. Geusamenous,* translated here as "tasting," means also "to enjoy," "to eat" (cf. Luke 14:24; Acts 10:10; 20:11), thus to "experience" (see Thayer). *Dōrea* is used to refer to the gift of salvation in Romans 5:15, 17; to the "inexpressible gift" of God's "surpassing grace" in Christ in 2 Corinthians 9:15. It also is used in connection with the Holy Spirit in Acts: the "gift of the Holy Spirit" (2:38; 10:45). However, in the present context of "tasting," it seems more likely to refer to the gift of salvation.

[34] The Greek word is *metochous.* Hebrews 3:1 reads: "holy brethren, who share in a heavenly call," literally, "sharers [*metochoi*] of a heavenly calling"; Hebrews 3:14: "for we share in Christ," literally, "we have become sharers [*metochoi*] of Christ." Hence, the reading (in Heb. 6:4) might preferably be "becoming sharers of the Holy Spirit." This points to the profound experience of the Holy Spirit such as is recorded in the Book of Acts (e.g., chaps. 2, 8, 10, and 19), which the early church knew, and which is being experienced afresh in the Pentecostal/charismatic renewal of the twentieth century.

[35] The Greek phrase is *dynameis te mellontos aiōnos.* After becoming sharers of the Holy Spirit is the experience of these *dynameis,* or miracles. Hebrews 2:4 speaks of God's bearing witness "by signs and wonders and various miracles (*dynamesin*) and by gifts of the Holy Spirit." The "gifts of the Holy Spirit" accompanying the gospel in the early church are likewise reappearing on the contemporary scene.

"on their own account," the holding Him up to contempt. The result can be none other than a curse near at hand upon all such—and the end: burning.

All of this demonstrates that even the fullest Christian experience can end in tragic loss. However, to guard against it, the writer of Hebrews, after expressing his persuasion that this will not apply to his readers (because of their "work and the love . . . in serving the saints" [v. 10]), gives a critical prescription: "We desire each one of you to show the same earnestness in realizing the full assurance of hope until the end, so that you may not be sluggish, but imitators of those who through faith and patience inherit the promises" (vv. 11–12). Diligence and earnestness must mark our pilgrimage of faith.

In regard to these five conditions relating to persistence in salvation—our abiding, continuing, enduring, firmness, and faithfulness—we may summarize by saying that what is essential throughout is *faith*. Another relevant passage of Scripture (earlier noted in part) is found in 1 Peter where the apostle first speaks of how "by his great mercy we have been born anew to a living hope . . . and to an inheritance . . . kept in heaven for you." Then he adds, " . . . who by God's power are guarded[36] through faith for a salvation ready to be revealed in the last time" (1:3–5). We are "guarded through faith"; this is the channel through which God's work of preservation is carried forward.

Thus it is possible to say that the various conditions mentioned are all aspects of faith in operation. Faithfulness is obviously just that, but it is also true of the other qualities. Hence, an abiding, continuing, enduring, firm faith

is called for. These are not conditions beyond faith, but are the very dynamics of a living and vital faith in Jesus Christ.

IV. RELATIONSHIP

From all that has been said about basis and conditions in perseverance, there is an unmistakable inner relationship. The basis in the Triune God is exceedingly strong, so much so as perhaps to suggest unconditional preservation. But also there can be no question that the Scriptures also point again and again to the existence of a human side. How are we to relate the two aspects?

Let us observe once more the divine basis and seek to relate it to the human condition. We shall do this in a number of summary statements.

A. God the Father and Believers

God's will, power, and faithfulness are ever present to undergird Christian life and salvation, but He operates through the faith[37] of those who have come to Him. God's intention is always affirmative, to "lose nothing," to "bring to completion"; His power to "keep from falling" is unlimited; His faithfulness to "strengthen to the end" never ceases. But it all operates *through* the one who believes.

For example, the passage in John's Gospel emphasizing the Father's will that the Son should "lose nothing" of all that the Father had given Him (6:39) is set in the context of "he who believes in me" (6:35). Believing, by which one enters upon salvation, is not a once-for-all accomplishment; rather it is a continuing reality. Believing is abiding, continuing, holding fast; it is of such a person that Scripture speaks. God intends that the Son should lose none who have come to salvation (and He

---

[36] The Greek word is *phrouroumenous;* "kept" (KJV), "protected" (NASB), "shielded" (NIV).

[37] Understood as abiding, continuing, enduring, confirming faithfulness.

127

will undergird them all the way), but if the believing *through which God acts* should discontinue, there can be no continuing salvation.

Again, God's faithfulness, by which He will "strengthen to the end," so that even "if we are faithless he remains faithful," does not mean that our faithlessness is of little importance. Indeed, quite the opposite, for the immediately preceding words are "if we deny him, he will also deny us." God's faithfulness operates through our faithfulness (recall the earlier discussion of faithfulness as a human condition), and our faithfulness is nothing other than our continuing in faith.[38]

B. Jesus Christ and Believers

Christ's safeguarding, interceding, and unity with us are very strong factors in the maintenance of our salvation, but again we must remain in faith.

One of the texts quoted that might seem particularly to affirm an unconditional preservation of the Christian has the words, "I give them eternal life, and they shall never perish, and no one shall snatch them out of my hand." It is important again to observe the context, for the immediately preceding words

are "My sheep hear my voice, and I know them, and they follow me" (John 10:27–28). The word "follow," by definition, means to continue in action, to come after, and keep coming after. It is *such* persons who can never perish, and who cannot be "snatched" out of Christ's hand. Neither the world nor the devil nor all principalities and powers together can break a person loose from the Lord's firm grasp and safekeeping. However, if we fail to follow, if we drop out somewhere along the line, we do what no other power can possibly do to us: we remove ourselves from Christ's protection and care—and the results are tragic indeed.[39] Thus, following is simply another way to speak about abiding: to follow Christ is to abide in Christ, and (as earlier quoted) "if a man does not abide in [Him], he is cast forth as a branch . . . thrown into the fire and burned." To follow and to abide are essential—else we too shall perish.

All of this applies likewise in Scriptures that speak of our unity and incorporation with Christ. Upon first reflection it might seem impossible for such a unity with Christ in His death and resurrection ever to be broken. Surely this is a solid basis for enduring

---

[38] I. Howard Marshall writes that in the New Testament "the believer is not told that he is one of the elect and cannot fall away, nor is there any particular character of his faith which indicates that he is the kind of person who cannot fall away. He is simply told to continue in obedience and faith and to trust in God who will keep him from falling. He perseveres by persevering. Perseverance is not some particular quality of faith or something to be added to faith, but the fact that faith continues" (*Kept by the Power of God,* 208).

[39] The case of Judas Iscariot is just that. Jesus in His prayer to the Father (John 17) says, "While I was with them, I kept them in thy name, which thou hast given me; I have guarded them and none of them is lost but the son of perdition" (v. 12). Judas was numbered among those "given" to Jesus by the Father; he was chosen by Jesus as the other eleven apostles were. But somewhere along the way Satan got into him: "the devil having now put into the heart of Judas Isariot . . . to betray him" (John 13:2 KJV). Jesus did speak of Judas earlier as "a devil"—"Have not I chosen you twelve, and one of you is a devil?" (John 6:70 KJV). But he was a devil by defection from his earlier faith (as John 13:2 demonstrates). That Judas became apostate is clear from the later words of Peter (after Judas' suicide) concerning the need to select another apostle "to take the place in this ministry and apostleship from which Judas turned aside [Gr. *parebē,* "by transgression fell" KJV], to go to his own place" (Acts 1:25). This sad record of Judas' life and death is a demonstration that even with Jesus' keeping and guarding (John 17) of those the Father had given Him, such a one could still defect and be lost.

salvation. Nevertheless, once again we must recognize that however great His self-giving to us, it is only through continuing faith that the connection is maintained. Recall that Paul speaks of our being grafted into Christ, hence into a living unity with Him. But then he adds, "You stand fast only through faith" (Rom. 11:20). Following that, he makes the statement about continuation: "else you too will be cut off." Thus a unity with Christ, no matter how dynamic and close, is no guarantee of persevering forever.

Also, it is true that Christ ever makes intercession for His own, and thus by His prayers to the Father undergirds our continuing salvation; hence, "he is able for all time to save." But this does not prohibit our departure from Him. Nothing can overcome us if we continue to look to Him in trust, for His prayers are mighty indeed. But if we give access to Satan (as did Judas), then we can be carried away.

C. The Holy Spirit and Believers

The Holy Spirit's abiding presence, sealing, and new life are also powerful factors in the persistence of salvation. Once again, however, we must note the human situation.

Truly the Holy Spirit has been given to be with us forever. This very presence of God in the Spirit makes for a tremendous force in our bearing witness to Christ, in doing His work, and confronting every circumstance of life. Nonetheless, the New Testament speaks (as we have seen) of those who, though they have become "sharers of

the Holy Spirit," do fall away. Thus the presence of the Spirit may dim. Paul warned the Thessalonians, "Do not quench[40] the Spirit" (1 Thess. 5:19). This implies that the Holy Spirit may be rendered ineffective in a person's life by that person's own actions; hence, the Spirit ceases to be an operative force. "Sharing" is no more.

On the matter of the sealing with the Spirit, our "pledge" or "earnest" of the coming inheritance, it is not impossible to forfeit that pledge. For example, in a business contractual relationship, even though "earnest money" has been given, failure to carry out the terms of the agreement will nullify the contract. Paul writes that "in him [Christ] you . . . were sealed." If we do not remain "in Christ" (by failing to abide, continue, etc.), the sealing is voided, and there is no longer any pledge of a future inheritance.

Finally, in regard to being "born anew" by the Holy Spirit to eternal life, it is important to recognize that this life is related to the operation of faith. Whoever "believes" has "eternal life" (John 3:16), and "believing" signifies continuation.[41] This is apparent from the words of Jesus in John 8:51—"If anyone keeps my word, he will never see death." "Keeping" is not a matter of a moment, but an ongoing process. So unless there is "keeping," one will see death. This is the same as a failure to abide in Christ and His words, which, Jesus later says, results in being "cast forth" (John 15:6). There is no longer life, but death. How important it is, therefore, to realize that while eter-

---

[40]The Greek word is *sbennute,* to "extinguish," "put out" (as a fire); also to "quench," "stifle," "suppress" (BAGD). Although the context of 1 Thessalonians is not directly soteriological, it does suggest that the Holy Spirit may be quenched or extinguished. This then surely affects one's salvation.

[41]In Greek the present tense often means duration, thus the sense here would be "whoever believes, and keeps on believing." See A. T. Robertson, *A Grammar of the Greek New Testament,* 879, on the frequent "durative" significance of the present tense. Robertson says that "the verb and context must decide" whether the meaning is linear or durative. I believe the durative here is the proper understanding.

nal life is God's free gift through faith in Jesus Christ, we must continue to believe. Hebrews, as has been noted, warns against there being "in any of you an evil, unbelieving heart, leading you to fall away from the living God," thus into death. The forsaking of eternal life through unbelief *can* happen.[42] How much more are we called on to remain firm in faith as the final day draws near!

V. CONCLUSIONS
A. The Security of Salvation

Because of all that God is, has done, and continues to do, the salvation of believers is in secure hands. It is not that we have reached out to God and found Him, but that God has reached out and found us. It is not that we hold on to God, but that God holds on to us. Thus the security of believers rests in both God's prevenient and sustaining grace.

Let this be emphasized still more. We can rest assured in the knowledge that it is God's desire that none should ever again be lost. It is not a matter of indifference but of vast importance. He who loved us so much as to send His only Son for our salvation at infinite cost has no other concern than to preserve us to the end. Moreover, there is no limit on His ability and power to accomplish this or on His continuing faithfulness. Also, our Lord Jesus Christ constantly watches over us and

intercedes for us. There is a oneness between Him and us that is very personal and real. Certainly, He who bore our transgressions, died for us, and brought us to life, never ceases to uphold us in great love and compassion. Further, the presence of the Holy Spirit, His inward sealing, and bringing of new life makes for a rich and deep salvation. Also, the Holy Spirit is the constant inward intercessor for all who belong to God.[43] The Triune God—Father, Son, and Holy Spirit—*is* the security of our salvation!

Hence, there is no way of falling out of God's love and care and concern. *Grace is unconditional.* This means that God perseveres, whatever man may do, in the undergirding and sustaining of all who truly believe. God never fails. The security of salvation rests—let it be repeated—not in ourselves, but in Him.

Further, believers may, and often do, sin against God, even grievously. But whenever they turn to God in genuine repentance, there is abundant forgiveness.[44] Truly, "if we [believers] confess our sins, he is faithful and just, and will forgive our sins and cleanse us from all unrighteousness" (1 John 1:9). Thus the fear sometimes expressed that one may have lost his salvation because of a particular sin is groundless. What is needed is not to be "saved again" (salvation can happen only once)[45] but to seek God's forgiveness. If one were

---

[42] It is sometimes said that since we have been "born again" to eternal life it would be impossible to be "unborn." While this is quite true, what is "born again" may die. It is possible that the "twice dead" of Jude 12 refers to such persons (Jude 5 speaks of how God "saved a people out of the land of Egypt" and "afterward destroyed those who did not believe"). In any event, we must "grow up to salvation" (1 Peter 2:2), and this does not automatically happen.

[43] ". . . the Spirit intercedes for the saints according to the will of God" (Rom. 8:27).

[44] The one exception to this is the "sin unto death," which will be discussed later (pp. 132–33).

[45] The Council of Trent contrariwise speaks of a forfeiture of the "grace of justification," which is recoverable through the sacrament of penance. "Those who through sin have forfeited the received grace of justification, can again be justified when, moved by God, they exert themselves to obtain through the sacrament of penance the recovery, by the merits of Christ, of the grace lost" (*Decree Concerning Justification,* chapter XIV). Justification—salvation—rather occurs once only.

to look to himself in his sinful plight, all salvation might seem to have been forfeited. But God, not we ourselves, is our security!

Most important in this matter is the constant reminder that our total security is in God. When we focus on ourselves—the ups and downs of our continuing Christian existence—we may be overwhelmed by a sense of our own inadequacy and sinfulness. Indeed, the more we grow in holiness, the more we become aware of our sinfulness. There may even come times of crying out in despair with the haunting fear that perhaps we have never really known salvation or have now lost it: "Woe is me; for I am undone!" In such a dark situation as this, we need all the more to be reminded that our salvation is in God, not ourselves. For "if we confess our sins, he is faithful and just, and will forgive our sins. . . . "

We must then take a strong stand against any idea of the possible recurrence of salvation. There simply is no "sliding in and out" of salvation: no first, second, third conversion, and so on. Unfortunately, in some quarters there are those who will go forward at every altar call to "get saved again." This may even stem from an exaggerated "saved one minute, lost the next" viewpoint. However, such behavior, if there has been prior salvation, is an offense against the Triune God. What God does He does well, and there can be no possibility or need of repetition. It may be the diabolical ploy of Satan who would delight to convince us that we are no longer God's children; or it could instead be the impurity of the flesh that still resists the Spirit. But

whatever the case, if we turn to God in true repentance and faith, there is abundant forgiveness. Surely we need forgiveness over and over again, but not repeated salvation.

Our security is not in ourselves, but in God. Moreover, there is no earthly security that can begin to compare with it. "Salvation belongs to our God" (Rev. 7:10), and we are totally secure in Him.

B. The Possibility of Apostasy

But because of the fact that the salvation of God operates through faith—a faith that is living—the forsaking of that faith can lead to apostasy. By failing to abide in Christ, to continue in Him and His word, to persevere in the midst of worldly trial or temptation, to make faith firm and strengthen it—thereby allowing unbelief to enter—believers may fall away from God. Thereby they may tragically forfeit their salvation.

Here we may recall the previously quoted warning; "Take care, brethren, lest there be in any of you an evil, unbelieving heart, leading you to fall away [apostatize][46] from the living God" (Heb. 3:12). "Brethren" are here addressed; therefore it is believers who are warned against the development of "an evil heart of unbelief"[47] that leads to falling away, to apostasy from the living God. This warning is surely meant for all Christians, "lest there be in any" of us such evil unbelief and resulting apostasy.[48]

We may also note another Scripture passage that refers directly to apostasy "in later times" and observe again how the reason for this is failure in faith. "In

---

[46] The Greek word is *apostenai*.

[47] The literal translation of *kardia ponēra apistias* in the quotation above.

[48] It is sometimes suggested that such a warning refers only to a hypothetical possibility. This is said from the perspective that no true believer could actually "fall away" from God. Such, however, is contrary to the most obvious meaning of the passage and the immediate context (see prior discussion). Moreover, such an interpretation dilutes the seriousness of the warning.

later times some will depart from [apostatize][49] the faith by giving heed to deceitful spirits and doctrines of demons" (1 Tim. 4:1). This is no light matter, no suggestion of a temporary or partial falling away: this is apostasy[50]—the departure from and the abandonment of faith. Further, it is an urgent warning to those "in later times"—doubtless including, perhaps even climactically, the times in which we live. Truly many "deceiving spirits and things taught by demons" (NIV) are abroad in the world so that even believers are being led astray. Hence, peculiarly in our time we need to hear and heed the grim warning of apostasy.

Such apostasy can occur simply by "drifting away." Here we may recall the statement, earlier quoted, "We must pay the closer attention to what we have heard, lest we drift away from it," followed by the question "How shall we escape if we neglect such a great salvation?" Thus, there is not only a falling away from the living God and from the faith, but also—and included in that—a falling away from salvation. Again we have a warning, in this case of gradual departure, concerning the terrible dangers of neglecting salvation and so leaving it behind.

In addition to a situation of gradual departure from faith and salvation, there is also the real possibility of a particular "sin unto death" that may be committed by a believer. In the words of 1 John: "If any one sees his brother committing a sin not leading to [literally, "unto"][51] death, he shall ask and God will for him give life to those who commit sin not leading to ["unto"] death. There is a sin leading to ["unto"] death; I do not say that he should make request for this" (5:16 NASB).

The nature of this "sin unto death"—or "mortal sin" (RSV)—is not specified. It may be the sin (1 John 4:1–3) of succumbing to the "false prophets" who deny "that Jesus Christ has come in the flesh" (such denial being "the spirit of antichrist"), and thereby of adjuring one's faith. To do so is to inflict a mortal wound on one's spiritual nature: there can be no healing. Possibly it is the same as blasphemy against the Holy Spirit. Jesus warned, "Truly, I say to you, all sins will be forgiven the sons of men, and whatever blasphemies they utter; but whoever blasphemes against the Holy Spirit never has forgiveness, but is guilty of an eternal sin—for they [the scribes] had said, 'He has an unclean spirit'" (Mark 3:28–30). Although this unforgivable sin is spoken of in connection with the scribes, "religious" people, it clearly has a wider reference ("whoever blasphemes") and this could include Christian believers as well. Deliberately to call what is holy "unclean" or of the devil, to declare as evil what is of the Lord, is to so capitulate to Satan and the kingdom of darkness that there is no hope: it is an "eternal sin." Such a person has passed the point of no return. Whether John is referring to blasphemy against the Holy Spirit, the abjuring of Christ, or something else, it is unmistakable that "sin unto death"—"mortal sin"—is that committed by a believer—a "brother."

Moreover, while it is a particular sin, there may well be a long build-up before it is committed. Nonetheless, when it occurs there is a climactic suddenness,

---

[49] The Greek word is *apostēsontai,* "will abandon the faith" (NIV).

[50] There is no such thing as "limited apostasy." The expression is self-contradictory as well as foreign to New Testament teaching. Apostasy means abandonment of faith and thereby of salvation.

[51] The Greek word is *pros. Pros* is likewise the Greek word for the "leading to ["unto"]" in the following two statements.

and a clear recognition of it by the faithful believer. John urges further that one is not even to "make request for" such a person. God will not "give life" to one so hardened; there is no forgiveness. For this is apostasy—irrevocable and eternal.

It is imperative to stress that the biblical picture of what awaits the apostate is indeed a grim one. We have already observed such declarations as "The last state has become worse than the first," "my [God's] soul has no pleasure in him," and that one who does not abide in Christ will like a branch be "cut off," "thrown into the fire and burned." Also the awesome statement "Vengeance is mine, I will repay" (Heb. 10:30) is spoken not to the unbelieving sinner, but to the apostate believer. The fires of eternal judgment, however much they may burn for the one who has refused Christ in the first place, are depicted as even more furious for one who has spurned the Christ in whom he has believed and the Holy Spirit through whom he has received grace.

We must therefore warn against a false sense of security. Truly the security of our salvation is in God, not in ourselves (as we have discussed). But this is not to be interpreted to mean that through our own faithlessness we may not forfeit it. Even in the Old Testament the prophetic word warns, "The LORD is with you, while you are with him. If you

seek him, he will be found by you, but if you forsake him, he will forsake you" (2 Chron. 15:2). These words spoken to people in the Old Covenant are much more poignantly true for us in the New: *because we have been given so much more.* Hence any claim to security by virtue of the great salvation we have in Christ without regard to the need for continuing faith is totally mistaken and possibly tragic in its results.[52] We need to hear the word again and again, "How shall *we* escape if *we* neglect such a great salvation?"

This means, accordingly, that although perseverance in salvation is surely grounded in who God is and what He has done (including the establishment of the new covenant), there is no assured continuance in salvation: apostasy is a real possibility. This is more than just a temporary "backsliding," a temporary falling away: it is total and final.[53] This is by no means God's wish, for, as earlier recounted, His power and faithfulness, Christ's safeguarding and intercession, and the Holy Spirit's presence and sealing are ever present to undergird the believer. However, there must also be continuing faith—with all that that means in terms of abiding, enduring, continuing—or there can be a gradual or sudden falling away: apostasy. A doctrine of "perseverance of the saints" that does not affirm its occurrence through faith[54] is

---

[52] It is sometimes said that such a view affords "a lifetime indulgence for sinning." That may be an extreme statement, but at the least such a view may make for a lax faith and a sad end. Remember that it is neither the "cold" nor the "hot" but the "lukewarm" whom Christ says that He will "spew out" of His mouth (Rev. 3:16).

[53] The Westminster Confession of Faith speaks contrariwise: "They whom God hath accepted in the Beloved, effectually called and sanctified by his Spirit, can neither totally nor finally fall away from the state of grace but shall certainly persevere therein to the end, and be eternally saved" (chapter XVII.I).

[54] This precisely is the error in the Westminster Confession's teaching. The next section (II) reads: "The perseverance of the saints depends not upon their free will, but on the immutability of the decree of election, flowing from the free and unchangeable love of God the Father; upon the efficacy of the merit and intercession of Jesus Christ; the abiding of the Spirit and of the seed of God within them; and the nature of the covenant of grace. . . . "

foreign to Scripture, a serious theological misunderstanding, and a liability to Christian existence.

Another word needs to be added. It is sometimes said that apostasy refers only to those who are not true believers.[55] If persons fall away, this shows that they were not believers in the first place. The biblical text frequently quoted is 1 John 2:19—"They went out from us, but they were not of us; for if they had been of us, they would have continued with us; but they went out, that it might be plain that they all are not of us." However, John is here referring to unbelievers—indeed "antichrists"[56] who have been in the Christian fellowship but who do not in faith truly belong, and who by their defection exhibit this. This, we may add, is by no means limited to John's time. There are many in the church today who are not genuinely believers; some have manifested their infidelity by leaving and even blatantly denying the Christian faith.[57] But as diabolical as this is, it is not apostasy, for they—no more than the *diabolos* (the devil)— were ever actually believers. Apostasy can only mean departure from the faith.

Also, the claim is similarly made by some persons that all the references in Scripture (especially in Hebrews) to those who turn aside describe persons who have not actually received salvation. For example, in Hebrews 6 it is sometimes held that such persons have been intellectually "enlightened" but not "spiritually," that they have only "tasted" salvation but not received, and so on. But on the basis of our earlier discussion of this and other like passages, it is apparent that this is a serious misreading. Often such interpretation is due to the importing of a theological perspective that leads to a false interpretation.[58]

A few other comments are in order. One of the mistakes made by those who affirm the invariable continuance of salvation is the viewing of salvation too much as a "state." From this perspective, to be saved is to enter into "a state of grace."[59] However true it is that one moves into a new realm—whether it is called the kingdom of God, eternal life, or other like expression—the heart of the matter is the establishment of a new relationship with God. Prior to salvation, one was "without God" or "against God," cut off from His presence. Now through Jesus Christ recon-

However true all these ways are as a basis for perseverance, there is no mention of faith. Perseverance, however, is *through* faith, *not without* it.

[55] Apostasy, as earlier observed, means "falling away" in the sense of "departure," "abandonment," hence a forsaking of what one originally had (not what one did not have!). Thus there is already a linguistic self-contradiction in the statement above.

[56] The preceding verse says that "many antichrists have come." It is "they" of whom John speaks in 2:19.

[57] The "antichrists" referred to are those who embody the spirit of the antichrist: "This is the antichrist, he who denies the Father and the Son" (1 John 2:22).

[58] John Calvin is a significant case in point. In his exegesis of Hebrews 6:4–6, though he first speaks of the "enlightenment" or illumination, and "tasting" as pertaining to genuine faith, when he proceeds to deal with the fact that Hebrews speaks also of the same persons as falling away, Calvin does an about-face and refers the language of enlightenment and tasting to "the reprobate" since from his theological perspective it is only the reprobate who can so fall. Calvin states that he cannot see why God "should not grant the reprobate also some taste of his grace, why he should not irradiate their minds with some sparks of his light . . . in some sort engrave his word on their hearts. . . . There is therefore some knowledge in the reprobate which afterwards vanishes away . . . " (*Commentaries, Hebrews*, 138, Beveridge trans.). This is *eis*egesis, not *ex*egesis, and badly in error.

[59] Recall the expression in the Westminster Confession, note 53.

ciliation—"at-one-ment with God"—has occurred. Moreover, the Holy Spirit, who becomes present, is not merely some force or energy but God Himself in a new and intimate relationship. Hence, if a person begins to "drift away," it is not from some static condition or "state" but *from a Person.* It is a personal relationship that thereby is betrayed, broken, forfeited; this is the tragic meaning of apostasy. It is not so much giving up something, even so marvelous as salvation, but the forsaking of a Person. Surely through such an action salvation too is forfeited. But the critical matter is the severing of a relationship with the personal God.

Another comment: all that has been said about the possibility of apostasy is contrary to the expression, sometimes heard, of "once saved, always saved." Salvation, to be sure, is once and for all: there can no more be repetition of it than the once-and-for-all act of redemption through Christ. However, the "onceness" of salvation does not mean its necessary continuance. God surely undergirds it, but since salvation is *both received and continued in faith,* it is also a matter of our faithfulness to the end. To one who has "kept the faith" as Paul did, truly there is "laid up . . . the crown of righteousness" (2 Tim. 4:7–8). So will we likewise be saved in the age to come.

Finally, what has been stated in the preceding paragraphs about the possibility of apostasy is not meant to give it the primary place. The first fact—and glorious indeed—is that our security is in God; that our salvation is based on the Triune God; that it is God—the Father, the Son, and the Holy Spirit—who has made salvation possible for us, and who daily sustains us by His grace. It is a *great* salvation indeed! However, just because it is so great, the New Testament writers are also concerned to warn us of the tragedy of its possible loss.

One senses in all the biblical warnings a compassionate note of hope that none of the dire results should befall believers. For example, at the conclusion of the passage containing warnings regarding those who "commit apostasy" and "crucify the Son of God on their own account" with the result that their "end is to be burned," the writer adds, "But, beloved, we are convinced[60] of better things concerning you" (Heb. 6:9 NASB). Such a conviction, indeed such a hope, set against the background of unmistakable warning is the positive witness of the Christian faith.

C. The Christian Pilgrimage

It would be fitting to close this discussion of perseverance by observing the nature and spirit of what it means to persevere in salvation. We are here concerned, finally, with the Christian pilgrimage from the time of its beginning until its culmination in glory. I will summarize by saying three things.

First, Christian believers are ever to move forward, rejoicing in their great salvation. We need have no feeling of insecurity or anxiety about it, knowing that God Himself is the Author. There is nothing in all the world more firmly based than the salvation a believer has received. Moreover, we know that God's attitude is that of desiring only good for us and never ill. Since God also delights to forgive, when we commit sin we need not hesitate to turn to Him in sincere confession. He will surely cleanse us from all unrighteousness and establish our way. Thus we may every day "with joy . . . draw water from the wells of salvation" (Isa. 12:3).

---

[60]The Greek word is *pepeismetha,* "persuaded" (KJV), "confident" (NIV), "feel sure" (RSV).

Let it be said vigorously: God is not "spying" on us, at every moment watching to see if we have made some mistake for which He can justifiably annul our salvation. Nor is He a neutral figure with the attitude that it makes little or no difference to Him whether we "make it" or not. God—Father, Son, and Holy Spirit—is *totally for us,* and therefore He is with us every step of our journey. He made us the crown of His creation; He redeemed us at infinite cost and therefore yearns over us with immeasurable love and compassion. Accordingly, He will do everything possible to guard us in our pilgrimage until we arrive in glory.

Second, Christian believers are called upon to pay serious heed to the New Testament warnings. These are declared not to create fear and anxiety about God's attitude toward us or to question the genuineness of our salvation, but they are God's own earnest counsel not to neglect what He has given to us. We are forcefully warned that apostasy is possible and that its very occurrence makes for a far worse condition than that prior to salvation. To turn from God who *created* us (which all persons have done from the beginning) brings sin and judgment, but through faith there may be salvation. To turn from the God who *redeemed* us— that is, to commit apostasy—can only bring destruction. God does not desire it: He will remain faithful to the end. But ultimately if we deny Him, He will also deny us; if we do not abide in Christ, we will be cut off.

Hence, we are called upon earnestly *not* to neglect this great salvation. In all the world no other neglect with its possible tragic consequences can compare with it. Such neglect may begin by failures now and then to be faithful in prayer and God's word, by gradually forsaking the assembling of God's people together,[61] by more and more allowing "the defilements of the world" to crowd in, and on and on until the apostasy is complete. Thus Christians are called upon to heed the warnings and also to seriously warn brethren (as, for example, the Book of Hebrews does over and over again) not to take steps that can finally lead to that apostasy from which there is no return. "It is impossible to restore again to repentance. . . ."

Third and finally, we can throughout life move ahead: giving God the glory, rejoicing in salvation from day-to-day, heeding the warnings, and in it all and through it all giving thanks to God for what He has done and what He intends to do. Our great God has redeemed us: we will ever bless Him! He is fully able likewise to keep us to the very end: we will ever praise His name!

Let us close with the beautiful doxology of Jude 24–25:

> Now to him who is able to keep you from falling and to present you without blemish before the presence of his glory with rejoicing, to the only God, our Savior through Jesus Christ our Lord, be glory, majesty, dominion, and authority, before all time and now and for ever. Amen.

---

[61] In Hebrews there is emphasis on "not forsaking our own assembling together" (10:25 NASB) a few verses prior to the statement about "trampling under foot the Son of God."

6

The Holy Spirit

We now begin a study of the doctrine of the Holy Spirit. This area of theology is often the least comprehended. Many persons profess to some knowledge of, or about, God the Father and Jesus Christ but express much uncertainty concerning the Holy Spirit.[1] They may well have heard terminology concerning the Holy Spirit, but they are largely unaware that He really exists,[2] performs such and such a role, and may even be experienced.

I. NAME

A. The Holy Spirit

Since we are discussing the Holy Spirit, it seems logical to begin with reflection on the name itself. Let us consider each word in reverse order.[3]

1. Spirit

The word *spirit* conveys the note of intangibility, incorporeality, thus *immateriality*. The spirit in a person, for example, is other than body and thus has no substantial existence. Spirit is not substance—even substance in its most rarefied or shadowy form. Yet it represents the essential reality of human existence, operating through soul and body. Spirit cannot, like an object, be located, perceived, weighed, dissected: it is immaterial.

In the Scriptures "spirit" is sometimes contrasted with "flesh": "The Egyptians are men, and not God; and their horses are flesh, and not spirit" (Isa. 31:3). Or the contrast is with "flesh and bones": "A spirit has not flesh and bones" (Luke 24:39).

---

[1]Especially is this the case when the nomenclature is "Holy Ghost." The King James Version of the Bible uses this antiquated language as do many familiar liturgies, hymns, and prayers. "Ghost" formerly meant Spirit, but now is associated with the realm of the spectral—hobgoblins, ghouls, and the like. Its continued usage in Christian faith is questionable. Of course, "spirit" is also sometimes used in the same way as "ghost"; however, it is much less subject to misunderstanding.

[2]The disciples whom Paul encountered in Ephesus (Acts 19:2) reported, "We have never even heard that there is a Holy Spirit." Most people today in a country of Christian influence, and presumably everyone in the church, have at least heard of the Holy Spirit; however, that may unfortunately be the limit of their knowledge.

[3]It seems proper to consider first the noun *Spirit,* then the adjective *Holy,* and finally the definite article *the*.

The word *spirit* also signifies *freedom of movement*. Since spirit knows no corporeal limitations, it does not follow a prescribed pattern. "Where the Spirit of the Lord is, there is freedom" (2 Cor. 3:17). Concerning those who are "born of the Spirit," Jesus says, "The wind blows where it wills, and you hear the sound of it, but you do not know whence it comes or whither it goes; so it is with every one who is born of the Spirit" (John 3:8). There is spontaneity and freedom in the Spirit.

The spirit of man is circumscribed by the limitations of a tabernacle of flesh. But with God who has no such limitations, His freedom of spirit is limitless. He is bound in no way to places or things. He does what He pleases: He is totally free. As spirit He may voluntarily limit Himself for a time, as in the Incarnation: "The Word became flesh" (John 1:14). But a voluntary action is no ultimate limitation. The Son is free and offers to all others the freedom that He Himself knows: "If the Son makes you free, you will be free indeed" (John 8:36).

Finally, *spirit* represents *energy, drive,* and *dynamic movement*. Spirit, as noted, is immaterial reality and moves in freedom. But it also signifies vital force. At the inception of creation a force moved over the primeval waters. That force was "the Spirit of God" (Gen. 1:2). Spirit has energy, power, force, and drive. Thus the Holy Spirit overshadows the Virgin Mary and makes her womb capable of bearing the Son of God (Luke 1:35). By the power of the Holy Spirit Jesus casts out demons (Matt. 12:28). And on the Day of Pentecost the Holy Spirit comes in hurricanelike force: the sound from heaven was "like the rush of a mighty wind" (Acts 2:2).

Spirit brings power *(dynamis)*. Those on whom the Spirit comes receive that "dynamite": "You shall receive power *[dynamis]* when the Holy Spirit has come upon you" (Acts 1:8). The Spirit delivers the energy of God.

2. Holy

The word *holy* in the name stresses *sacredness*. The holy is that which is set apart from the common and the ordinary. "I am God and not man, the Holy One in your midst" (Hos. 11:9) is an expression of the otherness of the holy from all things human. Wherever the holy is present, reverence is the proper response. Thus God said to Moses at the burning bush, "Put off your shoes from your feet, for the place on which you are standing is holy ground" (Exod. 3:5). The holy is the hallowed, the sacred.

Holiness also connotes *utter purity and righteousness*. Holiness is the white heat of perfect righteousness that is a consuming fire against any trace of evil or corruption. "Thou art of purer eyes than to behold evil and canst not look on wrong" (Hab. 1:13). Such is the word of the prophet about God; hence, it is true about His Holy Spirit. In the early church the Holy Spirit was dynamically experienced. Ananias and Sapphira, after lying about the sale of property, fell down dead, for they had lied to the Holy Spirit (Acts 5:1–10). The Holy Spirit is wholly pure in Himself and righteous in all His dealings.

Holiness, further, expresses the high note of *majesty* and *glory*. God is One who is "majestic in holiness, awesome in glory" (Exod. 15:11 NIV). In regard to holiness and glory the prophet Isaiah heard the voices of the seraphim crying out, "Holy, holy, holy is the LORD of hosts; the whole earth is full of his glory" (Isa. 6:3). The prophet later spoke of God's "holy and glorious habitation" (Isa. 63:15). Peter wrote of his experience "on the holy mountain" (the Mount of Transfiguration) with Jesus where they "were eyewitnesses of his majesty . . . and the voice [of God] was borne to him by the Majestic

Glory'' (2 Peter 1:16–18). Holiness, majesty, glory—all belong together. This surely is true in the name of the Holy Spirit, for He is "the Spirit of glory" (1 Peter 4:14 NIV).

3. The

Finally, the article *the* speaks quite simply of *singularity* and *uniqueness*. There are many "spirits"—angels, demons, even human (the spirit in man), but there is only "one Spirit" (1 Cor. 12:13). Other spirits are called holy, such as the "holy angels" (Mark 8:38), who are "ministering spirits" (Heb. 1:14). But no such holy spirit is "the Holy Spirit." Christians have sanctified spirits that someday will be spirits perfected in holiness—hence "holy spirits." But we will never be "the Holy Spirit."[4]

"The Holy Spirit" is the source of all freedom and energy, the quintessence of all righteousness and purity: there can be no other.

B. Variations

Thus far we have considered the name "the Holy Spirit." Now it is important to observe a number of variations on this name in the Scriptures.

1. The New Testament

The nomenclature of "the Holy Spirit" is frequently interchanged with other expressions in the New Testament. For example, "Jesus, full of the Holy Spirit, returned from the Jordan, and was led by the Spirit for forty days. . . " (Luke 4:1–2). Here and in many other places "the Holy Spirit"

and "the Spirit" are used interchangeably and synonymously. Frequently, the expression "the Spirit of God" is used in conjunction with "the Holy Spirit." Jesus said that He cast out demons "by the Spirit of God" and thereafter warned about speaking "against the Holy Spirit" (Matt. 12:28, 32).

Sometimes instead of "the Holy Spirit" there are several other expressions used interchangeably. In one verse in Romans Paul speaks of "the Spirit," "the Spirit of God," and "the Spirit of Christ": "But you are not in the flesh, you are in the Spirit, if the Spirit of God really dwells in you. Any one who does not have the Spirit of Christ does not belong to him" (8:9). When He commissioned the Twelve, Jesus spoke to them of "the Spirit of [their] Father" (Matt. 10:20). In similar statements in Mark 13:11 and Luke 12:12 the phrase used is "the Holy Spirit. However, the most common expression by far for the Holy Spirit is simply "the Spirit."[5]

It is apparent that the Holy Spirit, while a distinguishable entity, is inseparable from Christ and the Father. The Holy Spirit is the Spirit of Father and of Son. But also the Holy Spirit is the Spirit of God, hence identical with the reality of God Himself.

2. The Old Testament

In the Old Testament it is significant to observe that the phrase "the Holy Spirit" is not found. The nearest approximation is "your Holy Spirit" and "his Holy Spirit." In Psalm 51 David said, "Do not cast me from your pres-

---

[4]The English expression "the Holy Spirit" may or may not have the article "the" in the Greek. For example, Luke 2:25–26 reads: "The Holy Spirit was upon him. And it had been revealed to him by the Holy Spirit." The first Greek phrase, *pneuma . . . hagion,* has no article whereas the second, *tou pneumatos tou hagiou,* does. This is often the case in the New Testament; e.g., cf. Matthew 22:43 with Mark 12:36 where "David . . . in the Spirit" lacks the Greek article in Matthew but has it in Mark. The note of specificity and uniqueness is there regardless of the presence or absence of the Greek article. Hence all English translations properly read "the Holy Spirit" regardless of the Greek text.

[5]This abbreviated form is used over one hundred times in the New Testament.

ence or take your Holy Spirit from me" (v. 11 NIV). Isaiah the prophet, speaking about the history of Israel in their wilderness journey, declares, "Yet they rebelled and grieved his Holy Spirit. So he turned and became their enemy. . . . Where is he who set his Holy Spirit among them?" (63:10–11 NIV).[6] The distinctive New Testament expression, "the Holy Spirit," seems close at hand, but has not yet been used.[7]

Quite frequently the Old Testament speaks (as the New Testament does later) of "the Spirit" and "the Spirit of God." Genesis 1:2 depicts "the Spirit of God . . . moving over the face of the waters." This expression is found in a number of other places.[8] Numbers 11:26 says, "The Spirit also rested on them [two people prophesying]" (NIV). This shorter form also occurs in other places.[9] A possessive pronoun often occurs in such statements as this: "My Spirit shall not strive with man forever" (Gen. 6:3 NASB); "When thou sendest forth thy Spirit, they are created" (Ps. 104:30); and "If he should take back his Spirit to himself" (Job 34:14).[10] All of these expressions—"the Spirit," "the Spirit of God," "my Spirit," "thy Spirit," and "his Spirit"—speak of a very close relationship between the Spirit and God. This is also the case for "your" and "his Holy Spirit" noted in the previous paragraph.

The most common expression, however, in the Old Testament is "the Spirit of the LORD."[11] For example, "the Spirit of the LORD came upon him" (Judg. 3:10).[12] Significantly, this frequent Old Testament expression is carried over into the New Testament only a few times.[13] One instance occurs in Luke 4:18 when Jesus quotes Isaiah 61:1—"The Spirit of the Lord is upon me." Other instances show that "the Spirit of the Lord" has now become identified with the ascended Christ; for example, Paul writes, "Where the Spirit of the Lord is, there is freedom" (2 Cor. 3:17).[14]

In conclusion, "the Holy Spirit"—a New Testament expression—goes by many other names in the Old and New Testament Scriptures. Whether it is "the Spirit of God," "the Spirit of the Father," "the Spirit of the Lord," "the Spirit of Christ," or simply "the Spirit," it is the same reality.

---

[6]The NASB also capitalizes both Holy and Spirit in all three instances above; the NEB does not capitalize at all; the KJV does not capitalize in Psalm 51, but does so in both Isaiah statements; the RSV capitalizes only Spirit in the three verses. The Hebrew text provides no clue whether or not to capitalize.

[7]Doubtless one of the reasons for the hesitation of many translators to capitalize both "holy" and "spirit" is that it may convey a New Testament understanding not yet fully reached. However, whether capitalized or not in the Old Testament, there is not yet the New Testament terminology, "the Holy Spirit."

[8]See Exodus 31:3; Numbers 24:2; 1 Samuel 10:10; 19:20; 2 Chronicles 24:20; Job 33:4.

[9]See Numbers 11:25–26; 1 Chronicles 12:18; Isaiah 32:15; Ezekiel 2:2; 3:12, 14, 24; 8:3; 11:1; 43:5.

[10]I have capitalized the "S" because the reference is to God. The NIV keeps "spirit" in the main text but reads in the margin "Spirit."

[11]Literally, "the Spirit of Yahweh [YHWH]." English versions generally translate the tetragrammation "YHWH" as "LORD." However, "Jehovah" is found in the ASV, "Yahweh" in the JB.

[12]See also Judges 6:34; 11:29; 14:6, 19; 15:14; 1 Samuel 10:6; 16:13–14; 2 Samuel 23:2; 1 Kings 18:12; 22:24; 2 Kings 2:16; 2 Chronicles 18:23; 20:14; Isaiah 11:2; 61:1; Micah 2:7.

[13]In addition to Luke 4:18 (next mentioned above) see Acts 1:8; 19:6.

[14]Also see Acts 8:39: "The Spirit of the Lord caught up Philip." Throughout the Book of Acts "the Lord" signifies the exalted Christ.

II. TITLES AND SYMBOLS

A. Titles

Next, we observe particularly in the New Testament a number of descriptive titles that are given to the Holy Spirit.

1. The Spirit of Truth

The first title, "the Spirit of truth," is found in the Gospel of John. Jesus in his final discourses uses this expression three times. First: "I will pray the Father, and he will give you another Paraclete,[15] to be with you forever, even the Spirit of truth, whom the world cannot receive, because it neither sees him nor knows him" (14:16–17). Second: "When the Paraclete comes, whom I shall send to you from the Father, even the Spirit of truth, who proceeds from the Father, he will bear witness to me" (15:26). Third: "When the Spirit of truth comes, he will guide you into all the truth" (16:13). That "the Spirit of truth" is the Holy Spirit is apparent from another verse: "The Paraclete, the Holy Spirit, whom the Father will send in my name, he will teach you all things" (14:26).

Several things regarding "the Spirit of truth" stand out from these passages. First, "the Spirit of truth" points to what the world "cannot receive"—a reality incomprehensible to the natural man. Paul writes, "A natural man does not accept the things of the Spirit of God; for they are foolishness to him" (1 Cor. 2:14 NASB). Hence, the Holy Spirit is the source of spiritual truth, which cannot be apprehended without an alteration of the natural man.

It would be a mistake, however, to view "the Spirit of truth" as truth wherever it is known. The world does have knowledge in many areas (and for all this we may be grateful). But it does not have the knowledge of truth that is spiritual and therefore ultimate. Hence, when Jesus speaks of the Spirit of truth coming "to guide . . . into all the truth," He does not refer to truth at large or in toto, but to truth that relates to the spiritual realm.[16]

Furthermore, John earlier records that Jesus Himself is "the way, and the truth, and the life" (14:6). It follows, then, that the "Spirit of truth" will testify of Him: "He will bear witness to me." He will not speak of Himself; He will bear witness totally to the truth incarnate in Jesus Christ.

The Holy Spirit is the Spirit of truth.

2. The Spirit of Holiness

In the Epistles we observe a number of titles for the Holy Spirit. Let us note, first, "the Spirit of holiness." Paul wrote that Jesus was "designated[17] Son of God in power according to the Spirit of holiness by his resurrection from the dead" (Rom. 1:4). It seems obvious to say that the Holy Spirit is "the Spirit of holiness." However, by using the word "holiness," Paul stresses the sanctity

---

[15] I have retained the transliteration of the Greek word *paraklētos*, Paraclete. The word is translated variously in English as "Comforter" (KJV), "Counselor" (RSV, NIV), "Helper" (NASB), "Advocate" (NEB and JB). "Paraclete," in some sense, is a title also; however, since it refers more specifically to a function or activity of the Holy Spirit, we shall discuss it later. "Another" (above) implies that there is already a Paraclete, namely Jesus Himself. F. F. Bruce (*The Gospel of John*, 301–2) writes: "Jesus' mention of 'another' Paraclete implies that they already have one, and this can only be Himself. In 1 John 2:1, indeed, Jesus is called 'our "Paraclete" with the Father.'" The Spirit of Truth, the Holy Spirit, is, however, distinct from Christ.

[16] Of course, God is "the God of truth" (see vol. 1, chap. 3, IV. C.) so that all truth ultimately comes from Him. Thus in the broader sense the Holy Spirit as the Spirit of God is the author and guide into any and every truth. Nonetheless, "the Spirit of truth" in the Fourth Gospel refers to what "the world cannot receive" (John 14:17) or know.

[17] Or "declared" (KJV, NIV, NASB, NEB), Greek *horisthentos*.

of Christ in His resurrection (death could not hold fast the sinless Christ), and by the substantive "Spirit," Paul refers particularly to the role of the Holy Spirit in Christ's resurrection.[18] Hence, by this "Spirit of holiness," Christ was demonstrated to be the "Son of God in power." The "Spirit of holiness" was the profoundest reality in the life of Christ. From His conception by the Holy Spirit[19] throughout His years on earth, He lived a life of perfect holiness.[20] According to that same reality, the Spirit of holiness, He was declared to be "the Son of God in power."

The "Spirit of holiness," accordingly, is both the Spirit that makes holy and the Spirit of resurrection. He is the sanctifying Spirit who would have all persons live in purity before the Lord. And at their death He will give life to those in whom He dwells: "He who raised Christ Jesus from the dead will give life to your mortal bodies also through his Spirit which dwells in you" (Rom. 8:11).

The Holy Spirit is the Spirit of holiness.

3. The Spirit of Life

In Romans Paul also speaks of the Holy Spirit as "the Spirit of life." "For

the law of the Spirit of life has set me free in Christ Jesus from the law of sin and death" 8:2).[21] The Holy Spirit is the Spirit who "gives life." No longer is there bondage to sin, death, and the law.[22] The Holy Spirit has wrought life and freedom for all who belong to Christ.

Moreover, it is now possible by "the law of the Spirit of life" to fulfill "the just requirement of the law" (Rom. 8:4). For if we walk "not according to the flesh but according to the Spirit" (v. 4), this will happen. Whereas the believer has been freed from bondage to the law (the "written code," the "letter"), he is now able by the Spirit of life to fulfill its requirements. How true also are these words of Jesus: "It is the Spirit who gives life; the flesh profits nothing" (John 6:63).[23]

The Holy Spirit is the Spirit of life.

4. The Spirit of Adoption

In Romans 8 Paul later speaks of the Holy Spirit as "the Spirit of adoption": "For ye have not received the spirit of bondage again to fear; but ye have received the Spirit of adoption,[24] whereby we cry, Abba, Father" (v. 15 KJV). Two things are said here: first, we are children of God by adoption; sec-

---

[18] Later in Romans Paul speaks of "the Spirit of him who raised Jesus from the dead" (8:11).

[19] Matthew 1:20; Luke 1:35.

[20] See, e.g., John 8:46; Hebrews 4:15.

[21] I have adopted the NASB marginal reading for my translation. The KJV and RSV translate as "the law of the Spirit of life in Christ Jesus." Both the NIV and NEB follow the NASB margin, but with a slightly different word order. I am convinced that the translation above is more consistent with the idea of the life-giving work of the Holy Spirit.

[22] Paul contrasts the law with the Spirit in 2 Corinthians 3:6: "The written code kills, but the Spirit gives life."

[23] NASB, similarly NIV. The JB, RSV, and NEB have "spirit" instead of "Spirit." Either is possible from the Greek text, for *pneuma* is always lowercase whether referring to spirit or Spirit. The word for "flesh," *sarx*, refers to corporeal existence, whereas in Romans 8:4 (quoted above) *sarx* signifies man's sinful nature. In neither case can the *sarx* bring life.

[24] Likewise NASB and NIV marginal readings: "the spirit of adoption." RSV has "the spirit of sonship," NEB, "a Spirit that makes us sons." The Greek word *hyiothesias* is a legal term meaning "adoption." To be sure, we are "sons" due to adoption into God's family. But if the word "adoption" is replaced by some other term or words, the means whereby this sonship occurs fails to be emphasized.

ond, we have received the Spirit following this adoption. Paul elaborates on this theme in his letter to the Galatians, speaking of our redemption through Christ "so that we might receive adoption as sons" (4:5). Then he adds, "To prove that you are sons, God has sent into our hearts the Spirit of his Son crying 'Abba! Father!'" (v. 6 NEB). "The Spirit of adoption" is the Holy Spirit whom God sends to certify our adoption into the family of God.

It is striking to note that at His reception into our hearts the Holy Spirit cries out—or enables us to cry out—"Abba! Father!" This appellation signifies a deep personal relationship with God established by the Spirit, for "Abba" is the Aramaic name for "Father" used only in the home, especially by a child in addressing an earthly father.[25] It was the term used by Jesus in the Garden of Gethsemane when He prayed in great anguish to the heavenly Father, "Abba, Father, all things are possible to thee; remove this cup from me; yet not what I will, but what thou wilt" (Mark 14:36). Thus "the Spirit of adoption" enables us to address God, not only as "Father," but with the kind of personal feeling that a word like "Dad" or "Daddy" conveys.[26] Truly, what a blessing it is to receive the Holy Spirit into our hearts!

The Holy Spirit is the Spirit of adoption.

5. The Spirit of Grace

The Holy Spirit is also referred to as "the Spirit of grace" (Heb. 10:29). To better appreciate the meaning of this expression, we need to note that the context speaks of one who has "trampled the Son of God under foot, who has treated as an unholy[27] thing the blood of the covenant that sanctified him, and who has insulted[28] the Spirit of grace" (NIV). "The Spirit of grace" is thus the Spirit that has been graciously[29] at work in salvation.

The Holy Spirit makes available all that the Son of God has done to bring about our salvation and new life. It is wholly a matter of grace.

The Holy Spirit is the Spirit of grace.

6. The Spirit of Glory

Peter writes, "If you are reviled for the name of Christ, you are blessed, because the Spirit[30] of glory and of God rests upon you" (1 Peter 4:14 NASB). The Spirit of glory is the Spirit of God[31] and rests particularly on those who suffer for Christ's sake. This suggests that the glory yet to come already rests on those who belong to Christ.

Indeed, wherever the Holy Spirit is,

---

[25]"Abba" was "the form used in prayer and in the family circle" (BAGD). It was "the simple 'speech of the child to its father'" (TDNT, 1:6). According to the early church father Chrysostom, fathers were called "Abba" by their little children (TDNT, 1:6.n12).

[26]There is obviously some danger of disrespect in such familiar language. Indeed when Jesus used it, it "must have sounded familiar and disrespectful to His contemporaries because used in the everyday life of the family" (TDNT, 1:6). TDNT concludes with this application for the believer: "Jewish usage shows how the Father-child relationship to God far surpasses any possibilities of intimacy assumed in Judaism, introducing indeed something which is wholly new." On this matter also see J. Jeremias, *New Testament Theology*, 61–68.

[27]Or "common, ordinary, profane" (BAGD); Greek *koinon*.

[28]Or "outraged" (RSV), "affronted" (NEB), "done despite unto" (KJV). Another possible translation is "shown contempt for." The Greek word is *enybrisas*.

[29]For "the Spirit of grace," the NEB has "God's gracious Spirit."

[30]RSV and KJV have "spirit." NASB (quoted above), NIV, and NEB capitalize Spirit, which seems more appropriate in the context of the verse.

[31]NEB brings this out well in its translation: "that glorious Spirit which is the Spirit of God."

there is glory. In the Old Testament the inauguration of the tabernacle and the temple climaxes when "the glory of the LORD filled the tabernacle/temple" (Exod. 40:35; 2 Chron. 7:1). In the New Testament the climactic moment in the inauguration of the church occurred when "they were all filled with the Holy Spirit" (Acts 2:4). Truly, to be "filled with the Holy Spirit" is to be filled with the glory of God!

The Holy Spirit is the Spirit of glory.

7. The Eternal Spirit

Finally, the Holy Spirit is "the eternal Spirit." The letter to the Hebrews speaks of Christ "who through the eternal Spirit[32] offered himself without blemish to God" (9:14). The sacrifice of Christ was far more than a temporal event: it was an action through the eternal Spirit that wrought our redemption.

The Holy Spirit is without beginning or ending: He is the eternal Spirit.

B. Symbols

Let us next observe a number of symbols of the Holy Spirit. These symbols depict various operations of the Holy Spirit. Since the Holy Spirit is incorporeal and intangible (see above), such symbols (images, representations, or likenesses) give us further insight into the person and work of the Holy Spirit.

1. Wind

Wind is one of the most vivid representations of the Holy Spirit. The creation account in Genesis, which usually reads, "The Spirit of God was moving over the face of the water" (1:2), is sometimes translated "the wind[33] of God was moving. . . ." The Hebrew word rûaḥ and the Greek word pneuma have both meanings. Consequently, only the context can determine the proper translation. John 3:8 is a well-known example of linguistic double entendre: "The wind [pneuma] blows where it wills, and you hear the sound of it, but you do not know whence it comes or whither it goes; so it is with every one who is born of the Spirit [pneumatos]."

Wind as a symbol of the Holy Spirit is strikingly depicted in the coming of the Holy Spirit at Pentecost. Acts 2:2 reads, "And suddenly a sound came from heaven like the rush of a mighty[34] wind, and it filled all the house where they were sitting." This mighty windlike sound was the Holy Spirit: invisible, but nonetheless powerfully felt by all.

Sometimes rûaḥ may better be translated "breath." This is especially the case in Ezekiel's vision of the valley of dry bones. The Lord spoke to the bones: "Behold, I will cause breath[35] to enter you, and you shall live" (Ezek. 37:5). Again the Lord said, "Come from the four winds, O breath, and breathe upon these slain, that they may live" (v. 9). The word "breath" here undoubtedly symbolizes the Spirit of God. After His resurrection Jesus "breathed on them [the disciples] and said, 'Receive the Holy Spirit' " (John 20:22). Breath (breathing) is a clear representation of the Holy Spirit.

Wind or breath is a vivid figure of speech that depicts the Spirit of God as a moving force and divine kind of energy.

---

[32] So also KJV, NIV, NASB. NEB reads: "He offered himself without blemish to God, a spiritual and eternal sacrifice." The NEB reading, however, clearly departs from the Greek text—dia pneumatos aiōniou.

[33] So the NEB and AB. KJV, RSV, NIV, and NASB translate as "Spirit" (RSV footnote has "wind").

[34] Or "violent" (NIV, NAS), "driving" (NEB); Greek biaias.

[35] RSV footnote has "spirit."

2. Fire

Another outstanding symbol of the Holy Spirit is *fire*. That the two are closely connected is seen in this statement about Jesus: "He will baptize you with the Holy Spirit and with fire" (Matt. 3:11; Luke 3:16). The baptism with the Spirit is closely conjoined with fire. And this fire, as the succeeding statements suggest, deals with the consuming of evil: "The chaff he will burn with unquenchable fire" (Matt. 3:12; Luke 3:17).

The two Gospel accounts call to mind another in Isaiah. The picture there is of a coming day "when the Lord shall have washed away the filth of the daughters of Zion and cleansed the bloodstains of Jerusalem from its midst by a spirit of judgment and by a spirit of burning"[36] (4:4). The "spirit [or Spirit] of burning" likely symbolizes the Spirit of God in His role as fire cleansing away evil. The result: "The LORD will create over the whole site of Mount Zion . . . a cloud by day, and smoke and the shining of a flaming fire by night" (4:5). The fire of judgment becomes the flaming fire of glory!

Let us return to the Day of Pentecost in Acts 2. We have already observed the symbolism of wind—the Spirit, like the sound of a rushing mighty wind. Verses 3–4 read, "And there appeared to them tongues as of fire, distributed and resting on each one of them. And they were all filled with the Holy Spirit and began to speak in other tongues, as the Spirit gave them utterance." Here is the fulfillment of the promise: "He will baptize you with the Holy Spirit and with fire." This fire in the mouth and on the tongue would consume the chaff and make salvation possible as the gospel was proclaimed. Thus the Holy Spirit and fire are closely and vitally related.

3. Water

Another striking symbol of the Holy Spirit is *flowing water*. This is portrayed in the statement of Jesus: "If any one thirst, let him come to me and drink. He who believes in me, as the scripture has said, 'Out of his heart[37] shall flow rivers of living water.' Now this he said about the Spirit" (John 7:37–39). Jesus had spoken earlier to the woman of Samaria about "living water" that He would give to everyone (4:10). He added, "The water that I shall give him will become in him a spring of water welling up to eternal life" (v. 14).[38] Accordingly, the "living water" that Jesus gives and that wells up to eternal life when it flows out is the activity of the Holy Spirit. Water overflowing and outpouring: this is a vivid representation of the Holy Spirit.

The scripture that Jesus quoted, while nowhere to be found exactly in the Old Testament,[39] seems to relate particularly to these prophetic words in Isaiah: "Fear not, O Jacob my servant, Jeshurun whom I have chosen. For I will pour water on the thirsty land, and streams on the dry ground; I will pour my Spirit upon your descendants, and my blessing on your offspring" (44:2–3). Thus the natural outflowing of water on a thirsty and dry ground corresponds to the spiritual outpouring of the Spirit of God. Earlier in Isaiah reference was also made to an outpouring of the Spirit: ". . . until the Spirit is poured upon us from on high" (32:15).[40] Again

---

[36] The NIV footnotes that "a spirit" in both cases could be translated "the Spirit."

[37] Or "innermost being" (NASB), Greek *koilias*.

[38] For Old Testament parallels see Isaiah 12:3; 55:1; 58:11.

[39] Other Old Testament allusions include Jeremiah 2:13; Ezekiel 47:9; Zechariah 14:8.

[40] We will have occasion to look later into other passages that depict an outpouring of the Spirit (see chap. 8, "The Coming of the Holy Spirit").

the imagery is that of water pouring down, hence of flowing water.

Other Scriptures that depict flowing water[41] possibly refer to the Holy Spirit. Ezekiel had a vision of the temple from which water issued (47:1–9). Shallow at first, the water deepened into a river in which "everything will live wherever the river goes" (v. 9). Zechariah speaks of the coming day of the Lord with these words: "On that day living waters shall flow out from Jerusalem" (14:8). Finally, the Book of Revelation has the climactic picture of the holy city with "the river of the water of life, bright as crystal, flowing from the throne of God and of the Lamb through the middle of the street of the city" (22:1–2). Such extraordinarily beautiful passages that speak of living, flowing water have a profound spiritual quality that express the very activity of the Spirit of the living God.

4. Dove

Still another memorable symbol of the Holy Spirit is the *dove*. According to all four Gospels, at the baptism of Jesus the Holy Spirit came as a dove upon Him. Luke writes, "The Holy Spirit descended upon him in bodily form, as a dove" (3:22). Moreover, according to John 1:32, "it remained on him."

The full meaning of the dove symbolism is not clear. The dove, however, often represents gentleness[42] and innocence. When Jesus sent forth His twelve disciples He said, "Be as wise as serpents and innocent[43] as doves"

(Matt. 10:16). In Jewish tradition the "voice of the turtledove" (Song of Sol. 2:12) was interpreted as "the voice of the Holy Spirit of redemption." In a similar way the picture of the dove at the initiation of Jesus' ministry suggests the anointing of Christ with the Holy Spirit for the work of redemption.

Other Old Testament pictures come to mind. We have observed in Genesis 1 how the Spirit of God moved over the face of the waters, and that "Spirit" and "wind" are interchangeable terms. The word "moving" may be translated as "hovering" or "brooding,"[44] either of which suggests a bird, possibly a dove,[45] close upon the waters to bring forth life: thus a life-giving Spirit. Also in the Flood narrative it was a dove that Noah sent three times to discover whether the waters had subsided from the face of the earth. The dove is thus a picturesque emblem of life returning to a flood-ravaged world. It represents the Spirit as the "Spirit of life." The dove is also a bird used in the Old Testament sacrifices;[46] hence it may relate to Christ as He who came to offer Himself for the sake of the world.

All in all, the dove as the anointing of One who in gentleness would not "break a bruised reed or quench a smoldering wick" (Matt. 12:20), and who in perfect innocence and purity lived out his days, seems to be the most meaningful understanding of this beautiful symbolism.

5. Seal

The Holy Spirit is also symbolized as a *seal*. Paul uses this language in Ephe-

---

[41]See, e.g., Psalm 46:4; Proverbs 4:23; 18:4.

[42]"Gentle as a dove" is a common phrase, which illustrates my point.

[43]The KJV has "harmless." However, the Greek word is *akeraioi*, which is better translated "innocent" or "pure" (BAGD).

[44]"Hovering" (NIV, NEB, NASB mg); "brooding" (BDB); Hebrew *merahepet*.

[45]One Jewish tradition (Babylonian Talmud *Hagigah*, 15a) translates Genesis 1:2 thus: "The Spirit of God like a dove brooded over the waters."

[46]E.g., Genesis 15:9–10, Leviticus 12:6–8, and Numbers 6:10–11. Also note how the parents of the infant Jesus brought a sacrifice "according to what is said in the law of the Lord [in Leviticus 12:8] 'a pair of turtledoves, or two young pigeons'" (Luke 2:24).

sians 1:13–14: "In him you also, who have heard the word of truth, the gospel of your salvation, and have believed in him, were sealed with the promised Holy Spirit, which[47] is the guarantee[48] of our inheritance until we acquire possession of it." Later in the letter he adds, "And do not grieve the Holy Spirit of God, in whom you were sealed for the day of redemption" (Eph. 4:30).

These passages depict the Holy Spirit as a seal in the sense of designating both God's ownership and His protection. A seal is a mark of ownership and a proof of identity; thus those sealed unmistakably belong to a certain person. When the Holy Spirit is given to the believer, that event is a validation that he belongs to God; it is the ratification of his status in Christ: he is God's inviolable possession. A seal also makes secure: it is a mark of protection placed on something or someone. In the Book of Revelation this word goes forth: "Do not harm the earth or the sea or the trees, till we have sealed the servants of our God upon their foreheads" (7:3). This sealing protects them during great suffering and tribulation. So, likewise, does the Holy Spirit seal a person "for the day of redemption."

The Holy Spirit is also a seal in the sense of being a guarantee or pledge. A seal is a pledge of something not yet received, but is guaranteed to become a possession in the future. So the seal of the Holy Spirit is "the guarantee of our inheritance until we acquire possession of it." As Paul says elsewhere, God "has put his seal upon us and given us his Spirit in our hearts as a guarantee" (2 Cor. 1:22).[49]

The seal may also signify a mark of confirmation and dedication. It is said of Jesus in John 6:27 that "on him has God the Father set his seal." This happened when the Holy Spirit came upon Jesus and the Father declared, "Thou art my beloved Son" (Luke 3:22). This heavenly confirmation and dedication—the sealing by the Holy Spirit—was for Jesus' ministry in the years ahead. So, we may add, likewise the believer who receives the seal of the Holy Spirit is thereby dedicated for ministry in the mission of Jesus Christ.

6. Oil

Finally, the Holy Spirit may be viewed as a heavenly anointing, an unction from on high, the *oil of God*.

In the Old Testament a vivid scene occurred when God said to Samuel concerning the youthful David: " 'Arise, anoint him; for this is he.' Then Samuel took the horn of oil, and anointed him in the midst of his brothers; and the Spirit of the LORD came mightily upon David from that day forward" (1 Sam. 16:12–13). The horn of oil used in the anointing clearly symbolizes the Holy Spirit's consecration of David to the kingship. In Jesus' own case, not long after the Spirit came upon Him at His baptism, He said, "The Spirit of the Lord . . . has anointed me" (Luke 4:18). Hence, the idea of anointing—symbolically with oil—is inseparable from Jesus' own consecration for the total ministry to which He had been called.

Similarly John writes about the believer, "You have an anointing[50] from the Holy One" (1 John 2:20 NIV). Later he adds: "The anointing which you received from him abides in you . . . his

---

[47] Or "who" (NIV, NASB); Greek *hos* or *ho* (UBS).

[48] Or "pledge" (NASB, NEB); "deposit" (NIV); "earnest" (KJV); Greek *arrabōn*.

[49] See footnote 48.

[50] Or "unction" (KJV); Greek *chrisma*. The symbolism of oil for the Holy Spirit became increasingly significant in the early church ceremony of initiation wherein immediately following baptism the chrism of oil was applied to the believer as his consecration in the Holy Spirit.

anointing teaches you about everything" (2:27). Reference undoubtedly is made to the Holy Spirit who (according to John 14:26) "will teach you all things." Thus is the Holy Spirit the heavenly oil (or unction) whereby the believer is anointed and led into all truth.

Oil is a vivid symbol of the anointing of the Holy Spirit.

III. NATURE

Having discussed the identity of the Holy Spirit in terms of name, titles, and symbols, we do well to consider more specifically the nature of the Holy Spirit. Our reflections have largely centered on what the Holy Spirit is like. Let us move on to the question of who, or what, the Holy Spirit is.

A. God

The Holy Spirit is God. Whatever the various names or whatever the titles or symbols, all refer to God Himself. The Holy Spirit is not some reality less than God or other than God: He is God.

1. Divine Recognition and Identification

The Holy Spirit is recognized as God. This is particularly clear in the New Testament with the coming of the Holy Spirit. The Book of Acts, which records this event, recognizes throughout that the Holy Spirit is God. An outstanding example is the story of Ananias and Sapphira, who lied about their property. Peter said to Ananias, "Why has Satan filled your heart to lie to the Holy Spirit?" (5:3). Then Peter added, "You have not lied to men but to God" (v. 4). This is an unmistakable identification of the Holy Spirit with God. Other examples of such identification in the Book of Acts are the declaration of Agabus

the prophet, "Thus says the Holy Spirit" (21:11),[51] and Paul's reference to an Old Testament command of the Lord, "The Holy Spirit was right in saying to your fathers through Isaiah the prophet. . ." (28:25). In all these cases the Holy Spirit, acting in the community of faith, is identified with God.

Throughout His ministry, Jesus referred to the Holy Spirit in language that can only signify deity. On one occasion after casting out demons, He said that this had been done by the Holy Spirit: "It is by the Spirit of God that I cast out demons" (Matt. 12:28). In response to the Pharisees who attributed these exorcisms to the power of Beelzebul, the prince of demons, Jesus replied, "Every sin and blasphemy will be forgiven men, but the blasphemy against the Spirit will not be forgiven. And whoever says a word against the Son of man will be forgiven; but whoever speaks against the Holy Spirit will not be forgiven, either in this age or in the age to come" (vv. 31–32). The Holy Spirit can be no one less than Almighty God.

In the Old Testament the Holy Spirit is not explicitly called God. However, the many references to "the Spirit of the Lord," "the Spirit of God," and to "the Spirit" suggest a recognition of the Holy Spirit as God. On first reflection it might seem that the Holy Spirit is less than, or other than, God from such terminology. Is not the Spirit in such expressions simply an aspect of God (perhaps His inner nature, like the spirit of a man)? However, reference to "the Spirit" is a clear recognition of God Himself.

Let us return to the New Testament. Here we further observe a witness stemming from Christian experience. Paul speaks of believers as "being built

---

[51]The Old Testament language that precedes a prophetic utterance is often "Thus says the LORD." Since "the LORD." is God, and "the Holy Spirit" is used in place of "the LORD" in Acts 21:11, the Holy Spirit is thus identified as God.

together into a dwelling of God in the Spirit" (Eph. 2:22 NASB). "The Spirit" is unmistakably God Himself present among His people. Moreover, every Christian personally enjoys the inner presence of the Holy Spirit and knows that this is nothing less than God taking up residence in his life. Furthermore the believer who knows the experience of being "filled with the Holy Spirit"[52] is acutely aware that the infilling Spirit is none other than God. The fact that gifts—including miracles—are multiplied through this same Holy Spirit is further evidence of the identification of the Spirit with God.[53]

The Holy Spirit is to be unmistakably recognized and identified as God.

2. Divine Perfections

The Holy Spirit also has the perfections of God.[54] This is additional evidence that the Holy Spirit is God. Let us observe these perfections in turn.

First, the Holy Spirit is *omnipresent*. This is vividly stated in Psalm 139: "Whither shall I go from thy Spirit? Or whither shall I flee from thy presence? If I ascend to heaven, thou art there! If I make my bed in Sheol, thou art there! If I take the wings of the morning and dwell in the uttermost parts of the sea, even there thy hand shall lead me, and thy right hand shall hold me" (vv. 7–10). The Spirit of God—the Holy Spirit—is everywhere-present and ever-present. In the New Testament Jesus tells his disciples both present and

future, "The Father . . . will give you another Paraclete, to be with you for ever, even the Spirit of truth" (John 14:16–17). Thus, in a special kind of way, the Holy Spirit is continually present with those who have received Him.

Second, the Holy Spirit is *omniscient*. The prophet Isaiah asks this pointed question: "Who has directed the Spirit of the LORD, or as his counselor has instructed him?" (Isa. 40:13). The clearly implied answer is "No one," for the Spirit has all knowledge. In a memorable passage Paul writes, "The Spirit searches all things, even the deep things of God" (1 Cor. 2:10 NIV).[55] Since the Spirit searches all things, even fathoms[56] all things, truly He is omniscient. One further confirmation: Jesus said to His disciples that when the Spirit came, He would "guide you into all the truth . . . [and] declare to you the things that are to come" (John 16:13). Since the Holy Spirit does this, He lacks no knowledge. He has the omniscience of God Himself.

Third, the Holy Spirit is *omnipotent*. He is identical with Almighty God. This is dramatically set forth in the words of Elihu: "The Spirit of God has made me; the breath of the Almighty gives me life" (Job 33:4 NIV). This is a Hebraic parallelism; hence, "the Spirit of God" and "the breath of the Almighty" are essentially the same. The Spirit of God is omnipotent—all-powerful—and the evidence of this is His work in creation.

---

[52] See chapter 8, "The Coming of the Holy Spirit," for more detail.

[53] According to 1 Corinthians 12:6, "God . . . works all things in all persons" (NASB); according to 1 Corinthians 12:11, "One and same Spirit works all these things" (NASB). Note, again, the identification of God and the Spirit.

[54] See vol. 1, chapter 3, V, "The Perfections of God."

[55] The KJV, like NIV, has "deep things"; RSV and NASB translate the words as "the depths of God" (similarly NEB). The Greek is *ta bathē tou theou*. Though "depths" is the most obvious translation (cf. Rom. 11:33), it may be misleading, for the point is not that the Holy Spirit searches the "depths" of God's being but the "deep things"—i.e., the "secret and hidden wisdom of God" (1 Cor. 2:7).

[56] The word translated "searches" in 1 Corinthians 2:10 might also be rendered "fathoms" (see BAGD). The Greek is *eraunā*.

This calls to mind the words of Paul concerning the spiritual gifts: "One and the same Spirit works[57] all these things" (1 Cor. 12:11 NASB).[58] Although these words do not directly speak of omnipotence, the implication is certainly there. The Holy Spirit "works all these things" as an aspect of His working out of all things.

In summary, the Holy Spirit demonstrates the "alls" or "omnis" of God. He is all-present, all-knowing, all-powerful: omnipresent, omniscient, omnipotent. Truly the Holy Spirit has the perfections of God.

3. Divine Work

The work of the Holy Spirit is the work of God. This was illustrated in a number of preceding statements. Moreover, in our previous discussion of such doctrines as creation, providence, the Incarnation, regeneration, and sanctification, we have observed in various ways the divine Spirit at work.[59] So I will not elaborate this further here.

One point needs to be made, however. Since the Holy Spirit is invariably shown to be doing the work of God (and of that there can be no question), then He must be God. For the picture is never that of one less than God[60] performing God's work; rather the Holy Spirit is God Himself in action.

B. Person

The Holy Spirit is a person. When referring to the Holy Spirit, personal pronouns, such as "He" and "Him," are properly used. The Holy Spirit is not merely a divine influence or power but is a person in His own right.

The personhood of the Holy Spirit becomes fully apparent with the revelation of God in the New Testament, particularly in the Book of Acts and the Epistles. This is due to the fact that the coming of the Spirit follows the Gospel accounts. Only when the Holy Spirit has come is it possible to have a full apprehension of His personal nature.[61] However, as will be noted after this, there are intimations of the Spirit's personhood prior to Pentecost.

1. Personal designations

In the final discourses of Jesus recorded in the Fourth Gospel, the Holy Spirit is referred to several times as "the Paraclete."[62] However the term is translated—"the Comforter," "the Counselor," "the Helper," "the Advocate"—reference is thereby made to a person. Hence, this cannot signify a mere influence or force. Also in John 16:13, though the words for "the Spirit" are neuter,[63] a masculine pronoun follows: "When the Spirit of truth comes, he[64] will guide you into all the truth." Thus, "the Spirit of truth"—

---

[57]The Greek word is *energei*—operates, effects, works.

[58]See footnote 53.

[59]Vol. 1, chapters 5–6, and 13 and chapters 2 and 4 of this volume. However, there are many references to the work of the Holy Spirit in other chapters.

[60]The Holy Spirit is no more a demiurge (Plato's subordinate deity who fashions the world) than is Jesus Christ. (On "demiurge" see vol. 1, chapter 5, pp. 99, 101.)

[61]The same thing essentially is true about the personhood of the Word of God. Only when the Incarnation actually occurs is this made unmistakably clear. The Holy Spirit is the last of the "persons" to be fully disclosed.

[62]See the prior discussion under II.A.1, "The Spirit of Truth."

[63]The Greek words are *to pneuma*.

[64]The Greek word is *ekeinos*. This is quite significant, because the pronoun regularly agrees with the gender and number of the noun to which it refers.

"the Paraclete"—is definitely a person.[65]

It is important to recognize that when the Holy Spirit does come—as the Book of Acts records—He comes as a person. Language such as the "outpouring" and "falling" of the Holy Spirit and being "baptized in" and "filled with" the Holy Spirit[66] therefore does not refer to some impersonal power or force, but rather to the *way* in which He comes. The language thenceforth used in Acts about the Spirit unmistakably refers to the coming of a person. Perhaps the most dramatic example occurs in Acts 13:2: "The Holy Spirit said, 'Set apart for *me* Barnabas and Saul for the work to which *I* have called them.'" Note the two personal pronouns. The Holy Spirit definitely is a person—spiritual, to be sure, rather than corporeal—who, as Jesus promised, had come to be with the church.

One of the most striking features of the contemporary spiritual renewal is the strong sense of the personhood of the Holy Spirit. For many people prior to the renewal the Holy Spirit was little more than an unknown entity.[67] While a doctrinal recognition of personhood may have existed, there was little or no confirming experience. Now the Holy Spirit, dwelling within and moving among the believing community, is known to be a personal reality.

2. Personal Characteristics

We observe next that there are a number of personal characteristics that relate to the Holy Spirit. For example, there is *intelligence*. As we have just noted, when Barnabas and Saul were set apart, the Holy Spirit spoke—"the Holy Spirit said. . . ."[68] Indeed, the Book of Acts constantly shows the Holy Spirit guiding the young church with His wisdom and intelligence. An outstanding example of this occurred at the Jerusalem council, convened to resolve the thorny issue of the circumcision of the Gentiles. After much deliberation by the apostles and elders, a letter was sent to the Gentiles that included the statement "It has seemed good to the Holy Spirit and to us . . ." (Acts 15:28). Thus the Holy Spirit is a person who acts as the primary guide and director of the church. Paul also spoke of "the mind of the Spirit, because the Spirit intercedes for the saints according to the will of God" (Rom. 8:27). The Spirit knows the will of God and makes intercession accordingly.

Next, there is *will*. Paul and Timothy on their second missionary journey were "forbidden by the Holy Spirit to speak the word in Asia" (Acts 16:6). When "they attempted to go into Bithynia, . . . the Spirit of Jesus did not allow them" (v. 7). It was the will of the Holy Spirit that constrained them. Looking back into the Old Testament, we note the words of Genesis 6:3: "My Spirit shall not strive with[69] man forever" (NASB). The Spirit is depicted as struggling with man. The will of the Holy Spirit is also shown in Paul's discussion about the spiritual gifts: "the

---

[65] One can sense in these discourses the breaking through of the climactic revelation of the personhood of the Holy Spirit.

[66] See chapter 8, "The Coming of the Holy Spirit," for more details.

[67] I recall the statement of a newly "Spirit-filled" person, who put it memorably: "For me the Holy Ghost is a ghost no longer!"

[68] Cf. Acts 8:29: "The Spirit said to Philip. . ."; 10:19: "While Peter was pondering the vision, the Spirit said to him. . ."; and 28:25: "The Holy Spirit was right in saying. . . ."

[69] RSV has "abide in," NEB "remain in." The Hebrew is *yādôn*. KJV, like NASB, has "strive with"; NIV reads "contend with." These latter translations contain more of a sense of the will of God's Spirit.

same Spirit . . . apportions to each one individually as he wills" (1 Cor. 12:11).

Likewise, the Spirit is depicted as having *feelings*. In both the Old and the New Testament the Holy Spirit is said to grieve. The prophet Isaiah, rehearsing Israel's false ways, says, "They rebelled and grieved his Holy Spirit" (Isa. 63:10 NIV). And the apostle Paul urges believers, "Do not grieve the Holy Spirit of God, in whom you were sealed" (Eph. 4:30). The Holy Spirit may be grieved because He has feelings. In a profound statement describing the feelings of the Holy Spirit, Paul says that "the Spirit himself intercedes for us with sighs[70] too deep for words" (Rom. 8:26). These "sighs," or "groanings," depict the profound depth of the Spirit's feeling. The Spirit not only searches out "the deep things" but also feels them through and through.

3. Personal Relationships

The Holy Spirit likewise is shown to be personally related to others. The primary example surely is His personal relationship to Jesus. Jesus at the beginning of His ministry was "led by the Spirit for forty days in the wilderness" (Luke 4:1–2).[71] Thus a close relationship is indicated. It is particularly apparent in Jesus' words about "the Spirit of truth": "He will glorify me, for he will take what is mine and declare it to you" (John 16:14). Throughout the Book of Acts the personal relationship of the Holy Spirit to the early Christians is demonstrated. On one occasion Paul said, "The Holy Spirit testifies to me in every city that imprisonment and afflictions await me" (Acts 20:23). Also

we find in the New Testament the expression "the fellowship[72] of the Holy Spirit." Paul closes his letter to the Corinthians with these words: "The grace of the Lord Jesus Christ and the love of God and the fellowship of the Holy Spirit be with you all" (2 Cor. 13:14). This beautiful benediction speaks of a close personal relationship between the Holy Spirit and the Christian community.

This personal relatedness to the Holy Spirit has become very meaningful in the spiritual renewal of our time. The Spirit, to be sure, always points beyond Himself to Christ ("He will glorify me," said Jesus). Yet it is through a close, inner relationship with the Spirit that this takes place. The Holy Spirit has become, in truth, Counselor, Comforter, Helper, Advocate. What a joy to know Him personally!

C. Distinct

The Holy Spirit, while being God, is also distinct. Even as Christ was both God and with God,[73] so the Holy Spirit is both God and from Him.

Genesis opens with God in action: "In the beginning God created the heavens and the earth" (1:1), and thereafter a further action: "The Spirit of God was moving over the face of the waters" (v. 2). Thus both God and the Spirit of God are deity: the one God. Yet they are not identical: there is a distinction—not a separation—between them.

The Spirit comes from God. Many verses in the Old Testament declare that "the Spirit of the LORD came upon

---

[70] Or "with groanings" (KJV, NASB, similarly NIV, NEB). The Greek word is *stenagmois*. Cf. Acts 7:34: the "groaning" of the Israelites in Egypt.

[71] Matthew 4:1 has "led up by the Spirit." Mark 1:12 says "The Spirit sent him out into the desert" (NIV).

[72] The Greek word is *koinōnia*.

[73] "In the beginning was the Word, and the Word was with God, and the Word was God" (John 1:1).

[someone]."[74] Sometimes the Spirit is said to be "sent forth": "Thou dost send forth Thy Spirit, they are created" (Ps. 104:30 NASB). Furthermore, God will one day "pour out" His Spirit (Isa. 44:3). All such statements point to a movement of the Spirit from God but without the Spirit's ceasing to be God.

Turning again to the words of Jesus about the Paraclete, we note that Jesus talked about the "sending" of the Holy Spirit. He spoke of "the Paraclete, the Holy Spirit," whom the Father would send in His name (John 14:26). Again, Jesus spoke of "the Paraclete" whom he would send to them from the Father, "even the Spirit of truth" (15:26). Similarly, He says concerning the Paraclete, "If I go, I will send him to you" (16:7). So the Holy Spirit was to be "sent" by both Father and Son. On the Day of Pentecost after the event had occurred, Peter declared that Jesus "being therefore exalted at the right hand of God, and having received from the Father the promise of the Holy Spirit . . . has poured out this which you see and hear" (Acts 2:33). In summary, on the basis of both John and Acts, we may say that while the Paraclete, or Holy Spirit, is sent by both Father and Son, He is sent by the Father through the Son.

But now a further matter needs to be recognized, namely, that the Holy Spirit proceeds from the Father. This is made clear in the additional words of John 15:26: "who proceeds[75] from the Father." While the sending of the Holy Spirit is from both Father and Son in the sense that He is sent by the Father through the Son, the Spirit proceeds only from the Father.[76]

We may properly speak of this as an eternal procession. While Jesus referred to an imminent event when the Holy Spirit would be sent, His statement that the Spirit "proceeds"— present tense—points to an ongoing, thus eternal, reality. Hence, we may say that in the mystery of the Godhead the Father is the eternal source of the Holy Spirit (even as He is the eternal begetter of the Son): the Spirit proceeds or, perhaps emanates, not outwardly but inwardly. There is dynamic movement within the Divine Being. This is not a movement by the Father's will, as is the sending of the Spirit, but belongs to His inward being; hence it occurs by nature, not by volition.

Thus the Holy Spirit is not only God and a person, but He also has His own distinct reality.[77] He is not simply the personal God acting in a certain manner. Rather here is a paradox: the Holy Spirit is God—not some Spirit other than or lower than God; yet He is not simply identical with God—He is the Spirit of God. Since this is also true of

---

[74]This is mentioned especially in Judges and 1 Samuel (see chap. 7, "The Enabling Spirit").

[75]The Greek word is *ekporeuetai* and literally means "goes out" (so NIV). The NEB translates it as "issues from."

[76]This is the affirmation of the Constantinopolitan Creed of A.D. 381 (popularly known as the Nicene Creed): "We believe . . . in the Holy Spirit, the Lord and life-giver, Who proceeds from the Father . . . ." In the West at the Council of Toledo in A.D. 589 "and the Son" (*filioque*) was added, with the result that the "filioque" addition has come to be generally accepted as a part of the creed in Roman Catholicism and Protestantism (though not so in Greek Orthodoxy). A modification of the Toledo statement was sought at the Council of Florence in A.D. 1439, namely, that the Holy Spirit proceeds *from* the Father *through* the Son. This, I believe, is a more adequate statement than either that of Constantinople or Toledo.

[77]The technical term is "subsistence" or "hypostasis" (see discussion in vol. 1, chap. 4, "The Holy Trinity"). I have used "distinct reality" above; but this must not be viewed as "distinct being," which would signify a separate deity.

the Word of God, the eternal Son, we are brought into the mystery of the Triune Godhead or the Trinity: one God in three persons—Father, Son, and Holy Spirit.

Now to return to the event of the sending[78] of the Holy Spirit: the procession is the same, but the sending involves both Father and Son. Since the Holy Spirit in this sense comes after the Incarnation and His coming is based on the action of Father and Son, He is often described as the "Third Person" of the Trinity. However, this does not mean any subordination of the Holy Spirit, for He equally shares the eternal being of the Godhead. The important matter is to affirm the eternal distinctiveness of the Holy Spirit.

This subject, described biblically and theologically, is confirmed by Christian experience. That the Holy Spirit is the one God, that He is a person, and that His person is a distinct reality—all of this transcending intellectual comprehension—is the universal affirmation of those who have experienced the mystery of His sending and coming. We know that He is wholly God and that He is profoundly personal. He is not the Father or the Son but is deeply experienced through their activity. He is, to be sure, the Spirit of both (such has been confirmed again and again); however, He is identical with neither. Thus the Christian faith can rejoice in singing the Doxology, "Praise Father, Son, *and* Holy Ghost!"

---

[78]"Procession" technically refers to the eternal movement within the Godhead; "sending" to the occurrence which takes place in time.

7

The Enabling Spirit

Let us now consider the activity of the Holy Spirit within the community of faith.[1] The Holy Spirit imparts capability for the execution of various tasks and functions. For such accomplishments there is the Holy Spirit's endowment of wisdom and strength for the fulfilling of God's purpose.

I. SPECIAL TASKS AND FUNCTIONS

In the community of the Old Covenant numerous tasks and functions are shown to be activated by the Spirit of God. The Holy Spirit is depicted as illuminator, energizer, and enabler.

A. Designing of Tabernacle and Temple

The first Old Testament reference to an enablement by the Holy Spirit is that of an artisan for the designing and building of the tabernacle. The man was Bezalel, and concerning him God spoke

through Moses: "I have filled him with the Spirit of God, with ability and intelligence, with knowledge and all craftsmanship, to devise artistic designs, to work in gold, silver, and bronze, in cutting stones for setting, and in carving wood, for work in every craft" (Exod. 31:3–5). The main point of this account was not Bezalel's natural capacity but his being illuminated and enabled by the Spirit so that a building of God's own design could become a reality. God expressed His approval of the finished project when "the cloud covered the tent of meeting, and the glory of the Lord filled the tabernacle" (Exod. 40:34).

Later, for the building of the temple, God gave David himself the pattern and design to pass on to his son Solomon. According to Scripture, "he [David] gave him [Solomon] the plans of all that the Spirit[2] had put in his mind for the courts of the temple of the Lord and all

---

[1] In previous chapters of *Renewal Theology* I have discussed the activity of the Holy Spirit in such other areas as creation and providence, the Incarnation, calling, regeneration, and sanctification. As we move on in this chapter (7) and several chapters to come (8–14), our focus will be on the community of faith.

[2] ". . . the pattern of all that he had by the spirit" (KJV). The key phrase in Hebrew, *hāyāh bārûah immô*, literally means "was by the Spirit [who was] with him."

155

the surrounding rooms, for the treasuries of the temple of God and for the treasuries for the dedicated things" (1 Chron. 28:12 NIV). Neither David's plan nor anyone else's became the design of God's house; rather, the pattern was given him by the illumination of the Spirit of God. When the work on the temple was finished by Solomon, "the house of the LORD was filled with a cloud, so that the priests could not stand to minister because of the cloud; for the glory of the LORD filled the house of God" (2 Chron. 5:13–14). The temple, like the tabernacle, was given in plan and pattern by God's own Spirit and was climactically filled with the glory of God.

B. Leading the People

During Israel's journey in the wilderness Moses found the task of leading the Israelites increasingly wearisome. To relieve Moses, God told him to gather seventy of the elders of Israel, saying, "I will take of the Spirit who is upon you, and will put Him upon them; and they shall bear the burden of the people with you" (Num. 11:17 NASB). Thus both Moses and the chosen elders are pictured as endowed with the Spirit for leadership over the Israelites. By the Spirit of God Moses and the elders shared in meeting the problems, handling disputes, and generally dealing with the innumerable concerns of thousands of people over a lengthy period of their wilderness journey.

Many years later when Moses was told by God that he could not lead Israel into the land of Canaan, Moses prayed, " 'May the LORD, the God of the spirits of all flesh, appoint a man over the congregation, who will . . . lead them out and bring them in.' . . . So the LORD said to Moses, 'Take Joshua the son of Nun, a man in whom is the Spirit, and

lay your hand on him . . . and commission him in their sight' " (Num. 27:16–19 NASB). The important matter is that Joshua was "a man in whom [was] the Spirit" and that by this Spirit he would lead the people. As a result: "Joshua the son of Nun was filled with the spirit of wisdom, for Moses had laid his hands on him; and the sons of Israel listened to him and did as the LORD had commanded Moses" (Deut. 34:9 NASB).

The Spirit in these cases endowed men for leadership. God gave Moses, the elders, and Joshua special wisdom and strength for both the wilderness journey and entrance into the Promised Land.

C. Judging

After Joshua's death Israel continued her struggle with the enemies who still remained in the Promised Land of Canaan. Then God raised up individuals called "judges" who were energized and enabled by His Spirit to fight against their enemies, render judgment, and variously rule over Israel. The Book of Judges frequently portrays the Spirit coming upon such persons. Othniel was the first of these judges: "The Spirit of the LORD came upon him, and he judged Israel; he went out to war, and the LORD gave . . . [the] king of Mesopotamia into his hand" (Judg. 3:10). Upon Gideon the Spirit came forcefully: "The Spirit of the LORD took possession of[3] Gideon; and he sounded the trumpet" (6:34). Gideon, henceforward, was invested with the presence and power of the Lord. It is said of Jephthah, like Othniel, that "the Spirit of the LORD came upon" him (11:29). Finally, we should take note of Samson, for even as a youth "the Spirit of the LORD began to stir him" (13:25). Thereafter on three different occasions "the

---

[3]The Hebrew word is lāḇᵉšâ and literally means "clothed itself with" (BDB).

Spirit of the LORD came mightily upon[4] him" (14:6, 19; 15:14), so that he tore apart a lion with his bare hands, slew thirty men of Ashkelon, and, snapping the ropes that bound him, killed a thousand Philistines with the jawbone of an ass.

These accounts in the Book of Judges depict diverse people who acted not out of their own resources but from the divine investment of strength and wisdom.

D. Ruling

After the judges, kings ruled in Israel. The first two kings, Saul and David, likewise had the Spirit come upon them. Saul, as a recently anointed king, heard the Ammonite threats of atrocity, and "the Spirit of God came upon Saul mightily" (1 Sam. 11:6 NASB). As a result he mobilized the men of Israel and Judea to fight against the enemy.

Concerning David, Saul's successor, the text reads: "Samuel [the prophet] took the horn of oil, and anointed him in the midst of his brothers; and the Spirit of the LORD came mightily upon David from that day forward" (1 Sam. 16:13). Of particular significance in David's case was the permanence of the endowment of the Spirit—"from that day forward." Regardless of what happened, either good or evil,[5] he remained until his death the Spirit-anointed ruler over Israel. Quite the opposite was Saul's case, for in the next verse we read, "The Spirit of the LORD departed from Saul, and an evil spirit from the LORD tormented him" (1 Sam. 16:14).

After David there are no scriptural references to a spiritual anointing of the kings. One king followed another in dynastic succession or, with the division of the kingdom, by the overthrow of the then-reigning monarch. In regard to hereditary succession, I might add, there is no assurance of a spiritual anointing; for in such succession the throne is occupied by natural heirs rather than by those whom the Spirit endows.[6]

E. Prophesying

There are several references in the Old Testament to prophetic utterances coming from the Spirit of God. Prophecy broke out momentarily among the seventy elders of Israel whom Moses had selected. Moses took them out of the camp to the tabernacle (also called "the tent of meeting"), and "it came about that when the Spirit rested upon them, they prophesied. But they did not do it again" (Num. 11:25 NASB). While this prophesying clearly happened only once on the occasion of their appointment by Moses, it is significant that it did happen.

Two other men, Eldad and Medad, who had remained in the camp, also prophesied: "The Spirit rested upon them . . . and they prophesied" (v. 26 NASB). Joshua was quite disturbed and cried out to Moses, "Moses, my lord, restrain them." To this Moses replied, "Are you jealous for my sake? Would that all the LORD's people were prophets, that the LORD would put His Spirit upon them!" (vv. 28–29 NASB).

---

[4]The Hebrew word is *wattislah* and literally means "and rushed upon" (BDB).

[5]In Psalm 51 David, who had committed adultery with Bathsheba, prayed earnestly to God: "Cast me not away from thy presence, and take not thy holy Spirit from me" (v. 11). These words point to David's continually being endowed by the Spirit and his deep concern not to lose what God had given. David was forgiven, and the endowment remained.

[6]". . . from the time of Solomon the spirit is never again mentioned in relation to a reigning monarch nor is a king's successor ever designated by the gift of the spirit. As soon as the monarchy became a dynastic institution, its successive rulers could no longer be charismatically designated. It had forfeited the gift of the spirit" (L. Neve, *The Spirit of God in the Old Testament,* 38–39). I am inclined to agree with this statement.

This passage about Eldad and Medad is very interesting because it shows that the Spirit of God could not be limited to a particular place (or occasion). The Spirit blows where and when He wills!

Perhaps the most striking example of the freedom of the Spirit occurred when a Mesopotamian, Balaam, gave oracles by the Spirit of God. "And Balaam lifted up his eyes, and saw Israel encamping tribe by tribe. And the Spirit of God came upon him, and he took up his discourse . . . 'Blessed be every one who blesses you, and cursed be every one who curses you'" (Num. 24:2–3, 9). However, even in this unique incident of a non-Israelite prophesying, the prophecy was directly related to Israel. Thus, it was an operation of the Spirit in connection with the community of faith.

I have already mentioned that the Spirit of God "came mightily" upon Saul. Thus he was endowed with special power for overcoming Israel's enemies. Also Saul was on occasion enabled by the Spirit to prophesy. Immediately after his anointing as king, Saul was told by Samuel (who had anointed him), "You will meet a band of prophets. . . .Then the Spirit of the LORD will come mightily upon you, and you shall prophesy with them and be turned into another man" (1 Sam. 10:5–6). Samuel's prediction was fulfilled shortly after, and many began to say, "Is Saul also among the prophets?" (v. 12). On a later occasion Saul sent messengers to capture David, but "when they saw the company of the prophets prophesying, and Samuel standing as head over them, the Spirit of God came upon the messengers of Saul, and they also prophesied" (1 Sam. 19:20). This happened likewise with a second and third group of messengers, so that finally Saul himself went. "And the Spirit of God came upon him also, and as he went he prophesied[7] . . . . He too stripped off his clothes, and he too prophesied before Samuel, and lay naked all that day and all that night" (vv. 23–24).

Several points may be made here. First, Saul was never really designated a prophet, and yet he prophesied more than once; this was also true of Saul's messengers. Second, Samuel and his company of prophets were so anointed by God that they mightily affected those who came near them. Third, nothing is said about the content of the prophesying on the part of Saul, the band of prophets, or Saul's messengers,[8] though the rather bizarre action of divesting themselves of their clothes is depicted. All of this signifies again that limits cannot be placed on the Spirit of God.

In this same connection consider David. We have noted that with his anointing as king the Spirit of God came on him mightily "from that day forward." This also included a prophetic anointing. In 2 Samuel 23:1–2 is this climactic statement, "Now these are the last words of David . . . the anointed of the God of Jacob, and the sweet psalmist of Israel, 'The Spirit of the LORD spoke by me, and His word was upon my tongue'" (NASB).

Let us briefly note other Scriptures that connect prophesying with the Spirit. It is said of Amasai, chief of thirty men, who joined David in his struggle against Saul: "Then the Spirit came upon Amasai . . . and he said, 'We are yours, O David'" (1 Chron. 12:18). In

---

[7]Or "he went along prophesying continually" (NASB). The NEB translation, "in a rapture as he went," is quite misleading.

[8]It would be too hasty a judgment, however, to term these prophetic utterances purely ecstatic, that is, devoid of intelligible content. To be sure, no content is mentioned, and there are unusual external phenomena. But there is no suggestion that the utterances were emotional, irrational outbursts (especially in 1 Sam. 10). Further, it was in this context of prophesying that Saul was "turned into another man."

subsequent years a false prophet named Zedekiah angrily struck the prophet Micaiah and said, "How did the Spirit of the LORD go from me to speak to you?" (1 Kings 22:24; cf. 2 Chron. 18:23). Micaiah had declared a "lying spirit" to be in the mouth of Zedekiah and the other prophets who had falsely prophesied victory in a battle of Israel against the Syrians. In the time of King Jehoshaphat when Judah was under severe attack, "the Spirit of the LORD came upon Jahaziel . . . a Levite," who cried out, "Fear not, and be not dismayed at this great multitude; for the battle is not yours but God's" (2 Chron. 20:14–15). The result was that the Lord wrought a great victory without Judah engaging in battle. Later in the time of King Joash, "the Spirit of God took possession of⁹ Zechariah the son of Jehoiada the priest; and he stood above the people, and said to them . . . 'Because you have forsaken the LORD, he has forsaken you'" (2 Chron. 24:20). Prophecy, again, is by no means linked only with those recognized as prophets, for Amasai was a warrior, and both Jahaziel and Zechariah belonged to priestly lines.

Little is said that directly connects the utterances of Israel's later writing prophets with the Spirit. The most frequent formula is "The word of the LORD came to . . ."¹⁰ without reference to the Spirit's inspiration. Micah, however, has a direct reference, for he compared his ministry with that of the prophets who falsely cried "Peace": "But as for me, I am filled with power, with the Spirit of the LORD, and with justice and might, to declare to Jacob his transgression and to Israel his sin"

(Mic. 3:8). Moreover, still later, Zechariah, a prophet after the exile, spoke reflectively of "the words which the LORD of hosts had sent by his Spirit through the former prophets" (Zech. 7:12). He thus affirmed that the words of prophets before him had been given by God's Spirit.¹¹ In sum: the word of the Lord came by the enabling of God's Holy Spirit.¹²

F. Empowering

Occasionally in the Old Testament there are references to the Spirit of God as a dynamic, empowering force. The most significant is the angel's address to Zerubbabel, governor of Judah: "This is the word of the LORD to Zerubbabel: 'Not by might, nor by power, but by my Spirit, says the LORD of hosts. What are you, O great mountain? Before Zerubbabel you shall become a plain; and he shall bring forward the top stone amid shouts of 'Grace, grace to it!' '" (Zech. 4:6–7). These remarkable words addressed to Zerubbabel concerning the postexilic rebuilding of the temple attest that it was only by the Spirit's empowering—not by human effort—that the "mountain" of obstacles and difficulties would be leveled and the task completed. The Spirit of power is also the Spirit of grace: God Himself would accomplish the work. Regarding the rebuilding of the temple, Haggai spoke similar words about the Spirit of God: "Yet now take courage, O Zerubbabel . . . take courage, O Joshua, son of Jehozadak, the high priest; take courage, all you people of the land . . . My Spirit abides among you; fear not . . . I will shake all nations, so that the treasures of all nations shall come in,

---

⁹The RSV margin reads "clothed itself with"; the Hebrew word again is lāb⁽ᵉ⁾šâ.

¹⁰E.g., Hosea, Joel, Micah, Zephaniah, and similarly many other prophets.

¹¹Similarly Ezra the priest, at the rebuilding of the temple and reading of the law, prayed to the Lord: "Many years thou didst bear with them [Israel], and didst warn them by thy Spirit through thy prophets; yet they would not give ear" (Neh. 9:30).

¹²See also New Testament reflections re the Holy Spirit and the prophets, e.g., Acts 28:5; Hebrews 3:7; 10:15; 1 Peter 1:11.

and I will fill this house with splendor, says the LORD of hosts" (2:4–7). Again, this will happen by the power of God's Spirit.

The preceding texts declare the power of the Holy Spirit to accomplish temple construction. There are other, quite different references to the Spirit as a moving force. Obadiah, an emissary of King Ahab, said to Elijah the prophet: "As soon as I have gone from you, the Spirit of the LORD will carry you whither I know not" (1 Kings 18:12). After Elijah had gone up by a whirlwind into heaven, the "sons of the prophets," not having seen it occur, surmised, "It may be that the Spirit of the LORD has caught him up and cast him upon some mountain or into some valley" (2 Kings 2:16). Ezekiel the prophet spoke several times of how "the Spirit of the LORD lifted [him] up" (3:12, 14; 8:3; 11:1, 24; 43:5). The prophet was taken to the exiles, or up between heaven and earth, or carried in visions from Chaldea to the temple in Jerusalem. The Spirit thus is not a blind, purposeless force but is the power of God to enable the prophet to behold and declare God's intention.

The Holy Spirit is truly the Spirit of power.

CONCLUDING SUMMARY AND REMARKS:

As we look back over these Old Testament accounts several comments are in order:

First, it is evident that the Spirit of God is largely depicted as the Spirit of enablement. The Spirit's activity was that of endowing an artisan, a judge, a king, a prophet, or a priest to perform certain functions or tasks. Whatever the individual's natural abilities and capacities, the endowment of the Spirit is shown to be something additional, hence supernatural. And it is by virtue of this special endowment that the person involved was enabled to fulfill a certain task or vocation.

Second, this activity of the Spirit is shown generally to be temporary and occasional. For example, in the case of Samson, the Spirit was said to come at various times upon Samson to enable him to perform mighty deeds. And even though from his early days the Spirit "began to stir" him, there was throughout his life a sporadic coming of the Spirit. In regard to Saul, the Spirit "came mightily" upon him that he might rally his fellow countrymen against the enemy. But later the Spirit of the Lord departed from him. In the case of prophets from Moses' elders onward, the Spirit was not a permanent possession to be used at will but came upon persons at the moment of their prophesying. It was God's endowment for the occasion of uttering His word of truth. In summary, the Spirit was able to "take possession" but was not possessed; the Spirit could "clothe" someone but, like clothing, was not a permanent vestment. Thus the endowment of the Spirit was largely transitory: for an occasion, for a task, or for an utterance. It was not an abiding reality.[13]

Third, it is apparent that this activity of the Holy Spirit relates in various

[13]David, as we have noted, was an exception. The Spirit came upon him "from that day forward." Moses also had such an anointing of the Spirit that God could say, "I will take of the Spirit who is upon you, and will put Him upon them [the elders]"; hence there was more than a merely transient Spirit upon Moses. However, there is no direct biblical reference to this being a permanent endowment. Joshua could also be an exception, for when he took the mantle of authority from Moses to lead the Israelites into Canaan, he was spoken of as a man "in whom is the Spirit" and also as one "filled with the spirit of wisdom." Again there is no specific biblical affirmation of Joshua's endowment as permanent.

ways to the life of the community of faith—the people of God. The Spirit "came upon," "took possession of," was "put upon"—all such expressions refer to an action of the Spirit wherein certain of God's people were enabled to serve His cause and kingdom.[14] The Spirit in this enabling activity had nothing as such to do with God's creative or redemptive work, nor with any divine action whereby the people of God were formed. Rather, the whole thrust of the Spirit of God presupposes the fact and existence of Israel as God's people. Thus the Spirit came to give direction, strength, and empowerment for their life and mission.

II. THE MESSIANIC VOCATION

We come now to the great and paramount task—namely, that of equipping the Messiah, the Anointed One.[15] The Messiah is described in both the Old and New Testaments as fitted by the Holy Spirit[16] for the exercise of His vocation.

A. The Coming One

In several passages the prophet Isaiah declares the coming and activity of One who would be endowed with the Spirit of the Lord. He would fulfill His mission under the Spirit's anointing.

We being with this striking prophecy: "There shall come forth a shoot from the stump of Jesse, and a branch shall grow out of his roots. And the Spirit of the LORD shall rest upon him, the spirit of wisdom and understanding, the spirit of counsel and might, the spirit of knowledge and the fear of the LORD" (Isa. 11:1–2). We should note several things. First, the One to come would be from the line of David (the son of Jesse). And, like David, who was continuously anointed with the Spirit, the Spirit was to "rest"—that is, remain— on the Messiah. Second, it would be an abundant endowment of the Spirit, containing the sixfold aspects mentioned;[17] hence, the Messiah would receive of the Spirit far more bountifully than any who had preceded him. And, third, the Messiah would have from the Spirit the ideal qualities—intellectual (wisdom and understanding), practical (counsel and might), and religious (knowledge and the fear of the Lord) for rule and judgment. Therefore it is said, "He shall not judge by what his eyes see, or decide by what his ears hear. . . . Righteousness shall be the girdle of his waist, and faithfulness the girdle of his loins" (vv. 3, 5). Peace will also abound:

---

[14]The only seeming exception to this is Balaam, a non-Israelite; however, even he was used by the Spirit to serve the cause of God's people as he prophesied divine blessings upon Israel.

[15]The title "messiah," meaning an "anointed one," occurs many times in the Old Testament and usually designates the king of Israel or Judah; however, reference is also occasionally made to priests and prophets. Of course, "the Messiah" refers to the *coming* Anointed One, who in the New Testament is "*the* Christ." *Christos* is the Greek equivalent of the Hebrew word *māšîah.*

[16]This, to be sure, is only one aspect of the way whereby the work of the Messiah or Christ is to be carried out. See vol. 1, chapter 13, "The Incarnation," for the full picture of Christ as "The Son of God" and "The Son of Man."

[17]The phrase "the sevenfold Spirit" comes from the LXX and Vulgate readings that add "piety" (see JB footnote; cf. Rev. 1:4; 3:1). The sevenfold Spirit in church tradition is reflected in the ninth-century hymn *Veni Creator:* "Come, Holy Ghost, our souls inspire, and lighten with celestial fire; Thou the anointing Spirit art, who dost Thy sevenfold gifts impart." Incidentally, the "sevenfold gifts" of the Spirit are not to be confused with the nine gifts of the Spirit in 1 Corinthians 12:8–10, though there is some overlapping (see chapter 13, "The Gifts of the Holy Spirit").

"They shall not hurt or destroy in all my holy mountain; for the earth shall be full of the knowledge of the LORD as the waters cover the sea" (v. 9). Such are to be the glorious results of the coming of Him on whom the Spirit of God will rest.

Next we observe one of the "servant" passages that points to the Coming One.

> Behold my servant, whom I uphold, my chosen, in whom my soul delights; I have put my Spirit upon him, he will bring forth justice to the nations. He will not cry or lift up his voice, or make it heard in the street; a bruised reed he will not break, and a dimly burning wick he will not quench; he will faithfully bring forth justice. He will not fail[18] or be discouraged till he has established justice in the earth (Isa. 42:1–4).

These words, quoted in the New Testament (Matt. 12:18–21) after Jesus compassionately healed many people, again depict the Messiah as One who is endowed with the Holy Spirit. As a result justice, humility, tenderness, steadfastness, and patience will mark His way.

One other passage, and surely the most remarkable because it is quoted in part by Jesus as referring to Himself, is the following:

> The Spirit of the Lord GOD[19] is upon me, because the LORD has anointed me to bring good tidings to the afflicted; he has sent me to bind up the brokenhearted, to proclaim liberty to the captives, and the opening of the prison to those who are bound; to proclaim the year of the LORD's favor, and the day of vengeance of our God; to comfort all who mourn . . . [to give them] the mantle of praise instead of a faint spirit; that they may be called oaks of righteousness, the planting of the LORD, that he may be glorified (Isa. 61:1–3).

It is in this passage that the Spirit and the anointing are most clearly connected: the Coming One will carry out His mission through the anointing of the Holy Spirit.

These passages in Isaiah depict the Coming One as being endowed with the Spirit so that He would be able to fulfill His unique vocation. This vocation included various aspects of the endowment given to leaders and judges, kings and prophets. However, the Messiah would surpass all others in the manifoldness of His anointing, the breadth of His calling, and the results to be achieved. Under the continuing enablement of the Holy Spirit He would carry forward His total ministry.

B. Forerunners

Just prior to the coming of the Messiah and in connection with His birth and infancy, several persons in the New Testament are depicted as being enabled by the Holy Spirit to fulfill various roles. The Gospel of Luke sets forth their story.

The first reference is to John the Baptist: "He will be filled with the Holy Spirit, even from his mother's womb. And he will turn many of the sons of Israel to the Lord their God, and he will go before him in the spirit and power[20] of Elijah to turn the hearts of the fathers to the children . . . to make ready for the Lord a people prepared" (Luke 1:15–17). John, therefore, was a climactic representative of the Old Testa-

---

[18]Or "falter" (NIV); the Hebrew word is yikheh. Isaiah suggests a metaphor of a lamp or fire that does not grow dim.

[19]The Hebrew word translated "GOD" is actually YHWH, which is ordinarily rendered in English translations as "LORD." "Lord LORD" would, of course, be an awkward sounding translation. The NIV has "Sovereign LORD" rather than Lord GOD," thus retaining "YHWH" as "LORD."

[20]The Greek phrase is *en pneumati kai dynamei.*

ment prophetic line—going before the Lord in the spirit and power of Elijah. The last two verses of the Old Testament in the Book of Malachi record, "Behold, I will send you Elijah the prophet before the great and terrible day of the Lord comes. And he will turn the hearts of fathers to their children" (4:5–6).[21] John, accordingly, is to be understood as Elijah, not literally, of course, but spiritually, as one who moved in his "spirit and power."[22]

In terms of the Spirit John the Baptist stands out above any Old Testament figure, for he was "filled with the Holy Spirit, even from[23] his mother's womb" (Luke 1:15). As we observed, it was said of David and his being anointed as king that "from that day forward" the Spirit of the Lord was upon him. But not of David or any other is there a suggestion that the Spirit was either upon him or filled him from his birth. John thus was an extraordinary figure with an unusual endowment, and, of course, with a unique role—that of preparing the way for the coming of the Lord.

The latter point is especially important: the purpose of John's endowment with the Spirit was totally directed beyond himself. It had nothing to do with his own salvation or edification, but everything to do with his mission, namely, that of making ready "for the Lord a people prepared." For so great a task John was fitted as none other; he was filled with God's Spirit from his birth onward.

We next note Mary, the mother of Jesus. Mary truly is the supreme human example of the enabling power of the Holy Spirit: "The Holy Spirit will come upon you, and the power[24] of the Most High will overshadow you" (Luke 1:35). No human father, accordingly, was to be involved in the birth; it was to be the work of the Holy Spirit,[25] the *dynamis* from above.

We observe again that this enabling and energizing action of the Holy Spirit was totally related to Mary's becoming the mother of the Lord. It had no relation to her salvation or sanctification.[26] The activity of the Spirit was for a particular purpose, and there is no suggestion in the Gospels that after Jesus' birth the Spirit remained upon her. Like others, she was to wait for the effusion of the Spirit at Pentecost.[27]

Not long after the announcement of the holy birth, Mary cried out in the presence of her kinswoman Elizabeth: "My soul magnifies the Lord, and my spirit rejoices in God my Savior" (Luke 1:46–47). Such praise and rejoicing,[28] though not specified as being from the Holy Spirit, strongly suggests an anointing of the Spirit similar to Eliza-

---

[21] Note the almost identical words about fathers and children in Malachi and Luke.

[22] Jesus Himself also identified John with the Elijah to come: "If you are willing to accept it, he is Elijah who is to come" (Matt. 11:14; cf. Matt. 17:12–13; Mark 9:13).

[23] Or "while yet in" (NASB); the Greek phrase is *eti ek koilias*. The KJV reading is the same as RSV above (likewise margins of NASB and NIV).

[24] The Greek word is *dynamis*.

[25] See vol. 1, chapter 13, "The Incarnation," III.B.1.

[26] The New Testament nowhere speaks of a special action of the Holy Spirit making Mary holy from birth, a so-called "immaculate conception." The action of the Spirit regarding Mary is rather enabling her womb to conceive and bear the Messiah, hence producing a "virgin birth." (For fuller discussion see vol. 1, chapter 13, "The Incarnation," III.B.2.)

[27] See Acts 1:14.

[28] The Greek word for rejoicing in this passage is *agalliaō,* to "exult," "rejoice exceedingly" (Thayer). It is used later in Luke where it is written that Jesus "rejoiced in the Holy Spirit" (10:21). Thus it is hardly too much to suggest that Mary's rejoicing here was likewise "in the Holy Spirit."

beth's (see next paragraph) for the prophetic utterance that fell from her lips. Again this is not depicted in the Gospel as a continuing endowment of the Spirit.

Next let us observe the activity of the Spirit in relation to Elizabeth, the mother-to-be of John the Baptist. In the sixth month of her pregnancy she was visited by Mary. When Mary greeted her, "the babe leaped in her womb; and Elizabeth was filled with the Holy Spirit and exclaimed with a loud cry, 'Blessed are you among women, and blessed is the fruit of your womb!' " (Luke 1:41–42). These words of blessing by Elizabeth preceded Mary's joyful exultation and are said to have resulted from her being "filled with the Holy Spirit."

It is quite significant that the occasion of Elizabeth's being thus spiritually "filled" was Mary's arrival, for Mary carried in her own womb the promised Son of God. On Elizabeth's part it was thus a responsive action to the presence of the coming Lord, so that by the Holy Spirit she broke forth into joy and blessing. However, this filling with the Spirit, for all of its profound character, was momentary, happening in a situation of extraordinary spiritual significance.

Concerning Zechariah, the husband of Elizabeth and father-to-be of John the Baptist, Luke writes, "And his [John's] father Zechariah was filled with the Holy Spirit, and prophesied, saying, 'Blessed be the Lord God of Israel, for he has visited and redeemed his people, and has raised up a horn of salvation for us. . . . And you, child, will be called the prophet of the Most High; for you will go before the Lord to prepare his way' " (1:67–68, 76). Thus Zechariah was enabled by the Holy Spirit to prophesy concerning both the Messiah to be born and the role of his own son, John.

The background of Zechariah's utterance in the Spirit is significant. There was a deep struggle between faith and doubt: first, difficulty in believing that a son could be born to him and Elizabeth since both were advanced in years, and, second, hesitation in regard to the name "John"—not a family name—which the angel had specified. Indeed, because of his doubt and hesitation Zechariah's speech was taken from him until after the boy was born (Luke 1:18–22). Later when he wrote on a tablet, "His name is John," and thereby submitted to God's purpose and designation, "immediately his mouth was opened and his tongue loosed, and he spoke, blessing God" (1:63–64). Then Zechariah was "filled with the Holy Spirit," and under that powerful anointing he blessed God yet further, unfolding the panorama of the coming ministries of both Jesus and John. It was against the background of revived faith and fresh obedience that Zechariah thus spoke by the Spirit.

The last in this series of accounts with reference to the Holy Spirit concerns Simeon, a man "righteous and devout, looking for the consolation of Israel" (Luke 2:25). There are in this account three distinct references concerning the Holy Spirit. "The Holy Spirit was upon him. And it had been revealed to him by the Holy Spirit that he would not see death before he had seen the Lord's Christ. And he came in the Spirit into the temple" (vv. 25–27 NASB).

Thus Simeon was prepared for the imminent arrival of Joseph and Mary with their infant child. He then took the child Jesus into his arms, blessed God, and rejoiced: "Mine eyes have seen thy salvation which thou hast prepared in the presence of all peoples, a light for revelation to the Gentiles, and for glory to thy people Israel" (vv. 30–32). To a man richly endowed[29] with the Spirit came this extraordinary disclosure of God's salvation, which was to include both Gentile and Jew. Here is recorded one of the greatest prophetic utterances in the Scriptures concerning the universality of God's purpose in providing a salvation available to all.

Following this, Simeon blessed both parents and then proclaimed that the child Jesus in His role as Savior would be "set for the fall and rising of many in Israel" and indeed that Mary herself would have a sword pierce through her own soul (vv. 34–35). Thus Simeon by the Spirit was enabled to discern both the joy and the pain that was soon to come.

We may summarize the preceding accounts as follows. First, there is the *strong religious character* of all who were activated by the Holy Spirit. Of Zechariah and Elizabeth the Scripture says that "they were both righteous before God, walking in all the commandments and ordinances of the Lord blameless" (Luke 1:6). Mary is depicted as one who "found favor[30] with God" (v. 30) and who humbly said, "I am the handmaid of the Lord" (1:38). Simeon was a man "righteous and devout" (2:25). John, son of righteous Zechariah and Elizabeth, was to be "great before the Lord" (1:15). All five persons represent the highest integrity of character, in many ways the finest flower of the Old Testament dispensation as transition is made into the New. Their righteousness, humility, and devoutness are the background for the Spirit's activity.

Second, everything about the Holy Spirit in these several narratives *focuses on Jesus Christ*. It is obvious that

the narratives are found in the beginning chapters of the Good News of Jesus Christ. But what is relevant to our concern is that all references to the Holy Spirit point directly to the coming of Jesus. John was filled with the Spirit to prepare a people for the advent of Christ; Mary was visited by the power of the Holy Spirit to bring forth the Son of God; Elizabeth was filled with the Spirit as the babe in her womb leaped for joy at the presence of Mary, who had just conceived Jesus; Zechariah prophesied under the anointing of the Spirit concerning "the horn of salvation" God had raised up; and Simeon took the child Jesus under the Spirit's leading and blessed God for His coming salvation. The Holy Spirit is witness throughout to Jesus Christ.

Third, each instance of the Holy Spirit's activity is that of *supernatural enablement for a particular purpose*. In several instances the Holy Spirit was unmistakably the Spirit of prophetic utterance: Elizabeth, Zechariah, and Simeon all spoke prophetically under the anointing of the Holy Spirit. It was not words of their own devising, but they made their declarations by the enabling of the Holy Spirit. John was to be filled with the Spirit from his mother's womb so that his total life and ministry would be suffused with the spiritual power necessary to prepare the way for Christ. The Holy Spirit came upon Mary for the one purpose of enabling her womb to conceive the Son of God. Supernatural enablement, whether for uttering the word of God, preparing the way of Christ, or bringing forth the Son of God, is the activity of the Holy Spirit in these varied accounts.

Fourth, in all instances except that of

---

[29]Note the three prepositions regarding the Holy Spirit in Luke 2:25–27: "upon" (*epi*) "by" (*hypo*) and "in" (*en*).

[30]"Favor" here signifies a life or demeanor pleasing to God. It is later said of Jesus Himself that He "increased . . . in favor with God and man" (Luke 2:52).

John, these actions of the Spirit are *temporary and occasional*. For Elizabeth and Zechariah, both of whom were said to be "filled with the Holy Spirit," blessing and prophecy immediately followed. There is no suggestion in the narrative that this was a permanent endowment of the Spirit; rather it was one given at the moment to make possible a prophetic message. In the case of Mary, the Holy Spirit came upon her for the one great moment of divine conception; hence this was temporary and for the single occasion. The Spirit was "upon" Simeon as one "looking for the consolation of Israel" (Luke 2:25); he was "in" the Spirit when he met Joseph and Mary and blessed the Christ child. Only in the case of John—forerunner of Jesus, hence with a mission unparalleled among men—was the Spirit to be a continuing endowment from infancy to the end of his ministry.

Fifth, the context for the activity of the Holy Spirit is that of *faith, expectancy, and obedience*. I earlier called attention to the strong religious character of all the persons; here we note the importance of their openness to God's word and promise. Zechariah, for all his righteous and unblemished character, had to move to the place where he could accept in complete faith and obedience the word from the Lord. The step from "You will be silent and unable to speak until the day that these things come to pass, because you did not believe my words" (Luke 1:20) to "His name is John" (v. 63) is a critical one requiring faith and obedience. Only then was Zechariah filled with the Spirit and only then did he begin to prophesy. Mary, on the contrary, readily believed: "Let it be to me according to your word" (v. 38). Elizabeth pronounced a blessing on her: "Blessed is she who

believed that there would be a fulfillment of what was spoken to her from the Lord" (v. 45). Simeon never wavered from the divine revelation that he would not die before he should see the Christ; and his faith and expectancy were abundantly rewarded.

Sixth, the atmosphere surrounding the activity of the Holy Spirit was permeated with *joy and blessing*. As the babe "leaped for joy" (1:44) in Elizabeth's womb, she was filled with the Holy Spirit and cried out with a loud voice blessing after blessing (vv. 41–45). Mary replied, "My soul magnifies the Lord, and my spirit rejoices in God my Savior" (vv. 46–47). Zechariah's tongue was loosed and he spoke, "blessing God" (v. 64). Later, filled with the Spirit, he cried forth, "Blessed be the Lord God of Israel" (v. 68). Simeon in the Spirit came into the temple and took the infant Jesus into his arms; he "blessed God" and thereafter blessed both Joseph and Mary (2:27– 28, 34). The Holy Spirit through all of this was active within an atmosphere of joy and blessing—even exultation.

Seventh, and finally, all this activity of the Holy Spirit is among those who are *people of God*. Zechariah was a priest "of the division of Abijah," and Elizabeth, his wife, was one "of the daughters of Aaron" (Luke 1:5)— hence a doubly strong priestly line. And, of course, from that line John himself came. Mary was betrothed to Joseph "of the house of David" (v. 27), and Simeon was obviously a devout Jew, one "looking for the consolation of Israel" (2:25). Mary spoke of "God [her] Savior" (1:47). Thus, all had a vital faith in the God of Israel and were in some sense already sharers in God's redemptive activity. Without being participants yet in the new covenant and the kingdom[31] to be fulfilled in Christ,

---

[31] Later concerning John, Jesus said, "I tell you, among those born of women none is greater than John; yet he who is least in the kingdom of God is greater than he" (Luke 7:28).

these five persons represent the highest and noblest fruition of people moving in the Spirit just prior to the coming of Jesus Christ.

C. The Ministry of Jesus

We are now ready to view the ministry of Jesus as it relates to the Holy Spirit. Having noted the various Old Testament references to the Coming One and having considered the various forerunners in the immediate New Testament spiritual background, we are better prepared to consider the operation of the Holy Spirit in Jesus' own ministry.

1. The Background of Ministry

The ministry of Jesus began just after His baptism by John and the descent of the Holy Spirit upon Him: "In those days Jesus came from Nazareth of Galilee and was baptized by John in the Jordan. And when he came up out of the water, immediately he saw the heavens opened[32] and the Spirit descending upon him like a dove; and a voice came from heaven, "Thou art my beloved Son; with thee I am well pleased' " (Mark 1:9–11).[33] All four gospels record this event as the background for Jesus' ministry. Luke specifically records that following the descent of the Spirit (3:22) "Jesus . . . began his ministry" (v. 23).[34]

It is therefore apparent that the coming of the Spirit upon Jesus was for the whole of His ministry. It was not for a particular or limited work and surely not for a special utterance or activity, but for the total vocation He fulfilled. With the coming of the Spirit He became the "anointed One" and therefore "the Messiah" or "the Christ." With that anointing He carried out His ministry and mission.

The coming of the Spirit upon Him was also a permanent endowment. According to the words of John the Baptist, "I have beheld the Spirit descending as a dove out of heaven; and He remained upon Him" (John 1:32 NASB). The word "remained" affirms the continuing character of the Spirit's anointing of Jesus. In this there is likeness to David on whom the Spirit came "from that day forward."

Also there was no limit or measure of the Spirit. As John's Gospel later records: "He whom God has sent utters the words of God, for it is not by measure that he gives the Spirit [to him]" (3:34). In this first reference to the measureless giving of the Spirit, it is clear that Jesus received the Spirit in abundance.

It is particularly important to recognize that this was a second operation of the Holy Spirit in the life of Jesus. The primary operation, of course, was the activity of the Spirit in His birth. He was conceived by the power of the Holy Spirit and so was born as the holy One, the Son of God.[36] At His baptism the second operation occurred in which Jesus was anointed by the Spirit for His entire life and ministry. Jesus was the divine and holy One at birth; He be-

---

[32] The Greek word is *skizomenous* and literally means "be divided," "split," "torn apart" (BAGD); cf. Luke 23:45; Matt. 27:51. The NEB and NIV read "torn open."

[33] See also Matthew 3:13–17; Luke 3:21–22; John 1:32–33.

[34] The Greek phrase is *kai autos ēn Iēsous archomenos* and literally means, "And Jesus Himself was beginning . . . . " The word "ministry" is implied

[35] The KJV puts these words in italics because they are not in the original text. I believe the primary reference is to Jesus, but it also is true that whenever and to whomever God gives the Spirit, it is "not by measure."

[36] Recall these words to Mary: "The Holy Spirit will come upon you, and the power of the Most High will overshadow you; therefore the child to be born will be called holy, the Son of God" (Luke 1:35).

came the anointed One at His baptism. By no means, I would add, is this characterization of Jesus as a Spirit-endowed person a deemphasis of His divine Sonship; that is presupposed. He did not become the Son of God at baptism,[37] though surely at that event He was recognized as such: "Thou art my beloved Son." But He did become the Spirit-anointed Son, in the sense of the Messiah, as the Spirit descended upon Him.

There is something unmistakably unique about the coming of the Holy Spirit upon Jesus. The Spirit had come upon others before, but there is a difference with Him. The imagery of the dove in relation to the descent of the Spirit is new and suggests fresh aspects of the kind of ministry Jesus would be fulfilling.[38] Also, the statement that the heavens were "opened," even "split" or "torn apart"[39] as the Spirit came down, points to an unprecedented irruption of the Spirit from the heavenly sphere into the earthly. The Spirit broke through with more intensity and character than before. This could also relate to what was previously noted, namely, that Jesus received the Spirit without measure: it was the limitless gift of the Holy Spirit from "opened" heavens.

The extraordinary Trinitarian character of the event of Jesus' baptism is also apparent. While our focus is on the Holy Spirit and His anointing of Jesus, surely we would err not to emphasize also how both the Father and the Son are involved. The voice that spoke from heaven was, of course, that of God the Father who addressed Jesus as "Son": "Thou art my beloved Son." Thus in one unique moment at Jesus' baptism, Father, Son, and Holy Spirit were all represented. There is no other scene in the New Testament that more vividly depicts the Triune Godhead in personal interaction.

It is also apparent that in this event of the Spirit's coming upon Jesus, God the Father was thereby affirming Jesus' divine Sonship and setting His seal of approval on Him: "Thou art my beloved Son, with thee I am well pleased." As the Fourth Gospel later says, "On him has God the Father set his seal" (John 6:27). By this sealing there was the heavenly approval and confirmation of Jesus, both for who He was and for the vocation to which the Father had called him.

Now a further word about the relationship between Jesus' baptism and the descent of the Spirit upon Him. John came proclaiming the necessity of "repentance for the forgiveness of sins" (Mark 1:4). Jesus, having no sins to repent of, and over John's protests,[40] insisted on John's baptizing Him, for, said Jesus, "thus it is fitting for us to fulfill all righteousness" (Matt. 3:15). By His baptism Jesus vicariously identified Himself with sinful humanity and man's necessity for repentance and forgiveness. It was this act of identification by Jesus that was the background for the coming of the Holy Spirit and the commencement of Jesus' ministry.

This does not mean, however, that the descent of the Spirit automatically followed Jesus' baptism. It was not the corollary—as if to say that the descent represented the "righteousness" Jesus came "to fulfill." No, that righteousness was already fulfilled through Jesus' vicarious identification with humanity in the waters of baptism. Something

---

[37] As Adoptionism affirms (see vol. 1, chap. 13, "The Incarnation," nn. 43 and 46).
[38] Recall the previous discussion of the symbol of the dove and its significance.
[39] See footnote 32.
[40] "John would have prevented him, saying, 'I need to be baptized by you, and do you come to me?'" (Matt. 3:14).

else, therefore, was happening in the descent of the Holy Spirit, which, though occurring in conjunction with Jesus' water baptism, was not its "spiritual side."[41] They are not two sides of the same event; nor does the former (the water baptism) bring about the latter (the descent of the Spirit). The water baptism with all it represents was preparation and background but not the cause of the descent of the Spirit.

According to the Gospel of Mark, the descent of the Spirit occurred "immediately" (1:10) after Jesus' baptism. Luke adds a further important statement that it happened in a separate distinct moment as Jesus was praying: "When Jesus also had been baptized and was praying, the heaven was opened, and the Holy Spirit descended upon him . . ." (3:21–22). It was at the moment of prayer, as Jesus looked toward the opening heavens, that the Spirit, like a dove, began His descent.

The point then is that the coming of the Holy Spirit upon Jesus was for an entirely different purpose from His baptism. Baptism was the essential background for identifying Himself with the need of all people for repentance and righteousness. Now that this had been done, Jesus was prepared for the descent of the Spirit by which He would be anointed with power for the ministry that lay ahead. As Peter later said to the Gentiles at Caesarea, "God anointed Jesus of Nazareth with the Holy Spirit and with power" (Acts 10:38). It was for this, and this alone, that the Holy Spirit came upon Jesus following His baptism: to enable Him to fulfill His ministry and mission.[42]

There is another significant matter to consider. Following these words of John the Baptist, "I have beheld the Spirit descending as a dove out of heaven, and He remained upon Him," John added, "And I did not recognize Him, but He who sent me to baptize in[43] water said to me, 'He upon whom you see the Spirit descending and remaining . . . this is the one who baptizes in[43] the Holy Spirit' " (John 1:32–33 NASB).[44] Thus a close connection is drawn between the event of the Holy Spirit's coming and remaining on Jesus and of Jesus' baptizing others in the same Holy Spirit. This suggests that through both the Spirit's coming and His remaining on Jesus, He would also endow others with the same abiding Spirit of power for the ministry of the gospel.

It is also noteworthy that in the Fourth Gospel prior to John the Baptist's words about Jesus as the One who baptizes in the Holy Spirit, John had declared about Jesus, "Behold, the Lamb of God, who takes away the sin of the world" (John 1:29). The Fourth Gospel does not, like the three Synoptics, actually describe Jesus' water baptism. Rather where it might have been expected, John the Baptist affirmed

---

[41] As if, so to speak, water were the "natural" or "physical" aspect and the Holy Spirit were the "spiritual." No, the "spiritual side" of water baptism was the "righteousness" about which Jesus spoke.

[42] "It was the spiritual, invisible, but effectual anointing of the Christ *with Holy Spirit and power* for His unique work: not for the Ministry only but for the whole term of the Messianic office." (H. B. Swete, *The Holy Spirit in the New Testament,* 47).

[43] The KJV, RSV, and NIV read "with." The NEB, like NASB, reads "in." Either is a possible translation of the Greek preposition *en* (also "by" is frequently the translation elsewhere). My preference here is "in" because of the basic meaning of the word "baptism." The Greek word for "baptize," *baptizō*, signifies " 'dip,' 'immerse' " (BAGD), "submerge" (Thayer). Hence "in" is the most suitable preposition.

[44] For the Gospel parallels about Jesus' baptizing in the Holy Spirit see Matthew 3:11; Mark 1:8; and Luke 3:16. Matthew and Luke read, ". . . in the Holy Spirit and fire."

Jesus' saving work, and in so doing declared the inner significance of His baptism. Thus Jesus is portrayed, first, as the Lamb of God who saves and, second, as the One who baptizes in the Holy Spirit.[45]

Finally, to return to the earlier point of departure: the ministry of Jesus is set against the background of His baptism by John and the descent of the Spirit upon Him. This means that He who was already the Son of God is henceforward also the Spirit-anointed man. Thus verily is He the Messiah, Jesus the Christ.

2. The Commencement of Jesus' Ministry

The Holy Spirit is also shown to be active in the beginning of Jesus' ministry. According to Luke's Gospel, "Jesus, full of the Holy Spirit, returned from the Jordan" (4:1). The word "full"[46] further emphasizes that the Spirit without measure had descended upon Jesus following His baptism. Moreover, the word "full" further portrays the internal abundance of the Spirit. Jesus is both He *on whom* the Spirit came in totality and He *in whom* the Spirit was fully at work.

First, after Jesus returned from the Jordan, He was "led by the Spirit for forty days in the wilderness, tempted by the devil" (Luke 4:1–2).[47] This was the first thing that happened after the Spirit came upon Jesus. According to the Gospel of Mark, "immediately the Spirit impelled[48] him to go out" (1:12 NASB). Jesus was to be tempted by Satan as He began His ministry, and—of utmost importance—He had to overcome every ruse and device that Satan could use against Him. Jesus emerged victori-

ous, and "when the devil had ended every temptation, he departed from him until an opportune time" (Luke 4:13).

Second, at the conclusion of the temptations, "Jesus returned in the power of the Spirit into Galilee, and a report concerning him went out through all the surrounding country. And he taught in their synagogues, being glorified by all" (Luke 4:14–15). The implication is clear: Jesus, anointed by the Spirit and victor over every temptation the devil could conjure up, now returned in triumphant power. The devil—or Satan—was by no means yet defeated. But for the time he was out of the way, and Jesus now began to minister in great power. The "power of the Spirit" that Jesus had received at His baptism was already a power that had begun to overcome the wiles of Satan and bring about the establishment of a new order. As soon as Jesus returned to Galilee, and before there is any mention of His teaching or any other activity, a "news report" began to spread about Him. Doubtless there was something in Jesus' own presence and demeanor under the Spirit's anointing that made a great impression on people everywhere. Even more, as He began to teach, His praises were sung by one and all.

Third, Jesus came to His hometown of Nazareth and in the synagogue read from the Book of Isaiah: "The Spirit of the Lord is upon me, because he has anointed me to preach good news to the poor. He has sent me to proclaim release to the captives and recovering of sight to the blind, to set at liberty those who are oppressed, to proclaim the acceptable year of the Lord (Luke 4:18–19). At the conclusion Jesus an-

---

[45] The purpose of this baptism in the Holy Spirit I will discuss later.

[46] The Greek word is *plērēs*.

[47] The meaning is "*to be* tempted by the devil," as the Gospel of Matthew makes clear (4:1).

[48] The Greek verb, translated "impelled," *ekballei,* has the forceful sense of "drive out, expel, throw out more or less forcibly" (BAGD).

nounced the fulfillment of this prophecy: "Today this scripture has been fulfilled in your hearing" (v. 21). He thereby declared His own anointing with the Holy Spirit for the purpose of carrying out His total ministry of preaching and teaching, healing and deliverance.[49]

Thus the ministry of Jesus had begun—and at every point we see the activity of the Holy Spirit. Jesus was *full* of the Spirit, *led* by the Spirit, *empowered* by the Spirit, and *anointed* with the Spirit. He clearly is the apex and transcendence of all people of the Spirit who have preceded Him.

3. The Continuation of Ministry

As Jesus carried forward His ministry through both word and deed, He did so in the power of the Holy Spirit. In regard to His teaching, this fact is implicit in such a statement as this: "They were astonished at his teaching, for he taught them as one who had authority, and not as the scribes" (Mark 1:22).[50] In another situation Jesus said, "The words I have spoken to you are spirit and life" (John 6:63). Whenever He spoke or taught, His words were Spirit-anointed and life-giving.[51]

Jesus' works of healing and deliverance are also on occasion said to have occurred through this special power that was upon and with Him. The Scripture says that before Jesus healed a paralyzed man, "the power of the Lord was with him to heal" (Luke 5:17). Hence, this healing and others that followed were performed by the power [*dynamis*] of the Lord. In a case of deliverance later, Jesus made it unmistakably clear that the source of His power was the Holy Spirit. After casting a demon out of a blind and dumb man and thereby healing him, Jesus said, "If it is by the Spirit[52] of God that I cast out demons, then the kingdom of God has come upon you" (Matt. 12:28). This is not a conditional "if" but a factual statement:[53] Jesus emphasized that He exercised this ministry of deliverance by none other than the Holy Spirit. Although there are no other direct references in the Gospels to Jesus' healing people and exorcising demons by the power of the Holy Spirit, the implication is clear: these deeds were done by "the power of the Lord," "by the Spirit of God"—that same Spirit that came upon Him at the Jordan and remained on Him. After Peter's statement "God anointed Jesus of Nazareth with the Holy Spirit and power" are these words: "He went about doing good and healing all that were oppressed[54] by the devil, for God was with him" (Acts 10:38). Simon Peter had been with Jesus throughout His ministry and could certify that Jesus' acts of healing and deliverance proceeded from His having been anointed by the Spirit of God.

---

[49] "As the mission on which he is sent goes deeper into the heart of things than that of the Old Testament priest or prophet, so the anointing he has received is no mere formal appointment to an office, or even a special gift of prophetic power, but the flooding of his whole humanity with the light and power of the Divine Spirit" (H. Swete, *The Holy Spirit in the New Testament,* 116).

[50] Cf. Matthew 7:28; Luke 4:32.

[51] "Whether He taught the multitudes in parables, or delivered the new law of liberty to His disciples, or gave commandment to His chosen Apostles, the Spirit of God, it was plain, spoke by His lips" (H. Swete, *The Holy Spirit in the New Testament,* 58).

[52] Luke 11:20 reads "finger of God." "Finger" represents power (e.g., note Exod. 8:19; 3:18; Deut. 9:10; Ps. 8:3), but even more the Spirit of God (cf. Ps. 8:3 with 33:6b).

[53] Over against the Pharisees who were saying, "It is only by Beelzebul, the prince of demons, that this man casts out demons" (Matt. 12:24).

[54] The Greek word is a form of *katadynasteuō*—"oppress, exploit, dominate" (BAGD).

It is important to recognize that the ministry of Jesus empowered by the Holy Spirit was an ongoing attack against the forces of evil that bound mankind. First, He had to withstand the assault against Himself and thus be fortified to help others. We have briefly noted Jesus' temptations by Satan and how He rebuffed the devil at every turn. With Satan's departure for a time, Jesus was able to return victorious in the power of the Spirit to begin His ministry of teaching and healing. Second, we observe that following the words "If it is by the Spirit of God I cast out demons" Jesus said: "How can one enter a strong man's house and plunder his goods, unless he first binds the strong man? Then indeed he may plunder his house" (Matt. 12:29). The "strong man" is, of course, Satan; the plundering of his house in this particular case was the liberation of a deaf and dumb person from Satan's bondage. The binding of the "strong man" refers to Jesus' so circumscribing and limiting Satan by the power of the Spirit as to render him incapable of holding on to his "demonized" captives. This binding surely began with Jesus' initial defeat of Satan in the wilderness so that He was able to return to Galilee and "plunder" Satan's house, with the result that in one place after another people were set free.[55] All of this occurred by the power of the Spirit, who rested upon and pervaded Jesus in an ongoing, liberating assault against the forces of the devil.

One of the most dramatic incidents in the ministry of Jesus occurred when He appointed seventy[56] persons to go forth ministering the word and healing the sick, and "the seventy returned with joy, saying, 'Lord, even the demons are subject to us in your name!' " (Luke 10:17). Then Jesus replied in vivid language: "I saw Satan fall like lightning from heaven. Behold, I have given you authority to tread upon serpents and scorpions, and over all the power of the enemy" (vv. 18–19). Hence the seventy, while themselves not anointed by the Holy Spirit, were delegated authority by Jesus to "tread upon" Satan and his minions and thereby to cast out demons. When this happened, Jesus beheld as in a vision Satan suddenly falling from heaven![57] The imagery, while different from that of Satan as a strong man being bound in his house, is nonetheless clear: he falls precipitously from heaven as the seventy heal and cast out demons. Thus by delegated spiritual authority, the disciples of Jesus shared in His ministry to those bound by Satan.

The presence of the Holy Spirit on this occasion is shown by the following extraordinary statement about Jesus: "At that very time He rejoiced greatly[58] in the Holy Spirit" (Luke 10:21 NASB). This is the only reference in the Gospels to Jesus' exulting in the Holy Spirit.

---

[55]The repulsing of Satan in the wilderness did not yet represent a full victory. There Satan was strongly rebuffed; hence Jesus in His ministry continued to plunder his house. But it was not until Jesus went to the cross that Satan was actually dispossessed. Jesus later said on the eve of His death, "Now shall the ruler of this world be cast out" (John 12:31). After that Satan no longer had control over the world nor did he possess it as his "house."

[56]Or "seventy-two." The early Greek manuscripts vary.

[57]"In a moment of ecstatic vision (during the absence of the missioners?) Jesus had seen Satan defeated and cast from heaven (cf. the imagery of Isa. 14:12, Rev. 12:7–9). Here, and in the saying in 11:20 ["if it is by the finger (Spirit) of God that I cast out demons . . ."], Jesus interprets successful exorcism as evidence that the forces of evil are dethroned and the new age has begun" (IB, 8:189).

[58]The Greek word here is *ēgalliasato* and is translated "exulted" (NEB) and "full of joy" (NIV). It was a rejoicing of a quality and character beyond anything ordinary, for it was "*in* the Holy Spirit."

Significantly, the occasion was the sharing of His ministry with His disciples. Satan was despoiled and his captives set free.

To summarize: The ministry of Jesus in word and deed was carried forward in the power of the Holy Spirit. In everything He did, Jesus knew in Himself a mighty force working that was beyond Himself. Accordingly, wherever Jesus was present, He could declare the Holy Spirit to be present also. Thus Jesus said on one occasion to His disciples: "He [the Spirit] dwells with you" (John 14:17). Jesus lived and moved in the presence and power of the Holy Spirit.

III. THE SPIRIT TO COME

During the earthly ministry of Jesus, the Spirit had not yet come. Jesus in His teaching made many references to the Spirit's impending arrival. Our attention will be focused on the relevant Scriptures.[59]

A. The Paraclete

First, we turn briefly to some of the Paraclete passages in the Fourth Gospel. Three such passages were earlier considered in our discussion of "the Spirit of truth"[60]—John 14:16–17; 14:26; and 15:26. Now I add a fourth— John 16:7: "It is to your advantage that I go away, for if I do not go away, the Counselor ["Paraclete"] will not come

to you; but if I go, I will send him to you." The Paraclete is the Holy Spirit who would come to Jesus' disciples, indeed, who was to be sent to them by Jesus. Moreover, Jesus added, "He, when He comes, will convict the world concerning sin, and righteousness, and judgment" (v. 8 NASB). Thus Jesus' disciples would be enabled to minister the word with convicting power that leads to salvation. So they were to carry forward the ministry and mission of Jesus.

We should particularly note that the Holy Spirit would not come until Jesus went away. This means, of course, Jesus' departure to the Father; then Jesus would send the Spirit. He would come after Jesus had returned to heaven, and from there the Holy Spirit was to be sent forth to enable the disciples of Jesus to proclaim the gospel. Peter, who was the first to proclaim the message (Acts 2), later wrote of "those who preached the good news . . . through the Holy Spirit sent from heaven" (1 Peter 1:12). Only after Jesus went "away"—and only then— was the Holy Spirit able and willing to come.[61]

Here we readily observe a parallel between Jesus and His disciples. In His case, as we have noted, "the heaven was opened, and the Holy Spirit descended." Thus was Jesus the forerunner of those who later "preached the

---

[59]There are a number of Old Testament references to the coming Spirit—e.g., Isaiah 44:2–3; Ezekiel 39:29; and especially Joel 2:28–29. Here, however, it is my intention to follow closely upon what has just been written in the previous section, "The Messianic Vocation." The Old Testament references will be noted in the next chapter, "The Coming of the Holy Spirit," III. A.

[60]Chapter 6, II.A.1.

[61]Thus the coming of the Spirit that Jesus promised is not to be confused with Jesus breathing on the disciples and saying, "Receive the Holy Spirit" (John 20:22). This insufflation of the Spirit occurred on the day of Jesus' resurrection; Jesus had not yet gone "away." Recall from our previous discussion (in chap. 2, "Regeneration") that the resurrected Lord breathed the Holy Spirit into the disciples for the restoration of life— regeneration. Thereby the Holy Spirit came to dwell within them. Thus on their behalf Jesus' words were fulfilled: "He dwells with you, and will be in you" (John 14:17). But the Holy Spirit had not yet come from the ascended Lord for ministering the gospel. Indeed, the disciples did no ministering until fifty days later when the Holy Spirit came at Pentecost.

good news through the Holy Spirit sent from heaven." The same Spirit from heaven anointed both Jesus and His disciples at the beginning of their ministry.

Another parallel—perhaps less obvious but highly significant—is that in both cases the Holy Spirit came upon those who were "born" of the Spirit. Jesus Himself was born of the Spirit in the womb of the Virgin Mary; the disciples were born of the Spirit in the room where Jesus breathed upon them and said, "Receive the Holy Spirit" (John 20:22). In Jesus' case, of course, it was generation; in the disciples' it was regeneration.[62] But for both, being born of the Spirit preceded the coming of the Spirit.

Before proceeding further, it is important to emphasize that the Holy Spirit would later come to the disciples as a newborn community of believers. To some extent the disciples had been believers for about three years; they had followed Him and even did miracles in His name. But it was not until the resurrection of Jesus that faith was firmly established. *All* had forsaken Him—"they all forsook him, and fled" (Mark 14:50)—on the night of His be-

trayal. *None* believed He would rise from the dead. Even when the report came of His resurrection, "they did not believe [it]" (Luke 24:11). It was only the appearance of the resurrected Jesus (as all the Gospels report) that changed their disbelief to faith. It was on Easter evening that disbelief and doubt were at last completely dispersed: the Spirit was breathed into them, and they became a community of living faith. As such a community—reborn, regenerate, redeemed[63] from abject disbelief and despair—they would later experience the coming of the Holy Spirit.

Now let us look at the connection between the coming of the Holy Spirit and Jesus' "glorification." Jesus said: "If any man is thirsty, let him come to Me and drink. He who believes in Me, as the Scripture said, 'From his innermost being[64] shall flow rivers of living water'" (John 7:37–38 NASB). Then the Scripture continues: "But this He spoke of the Spirit, whom those who believed in Him were to receive; for the Spirit was not yet given, because Jesus was not yet glorified" (v. 39 NASB). The glorification of Jesus accordingly had to take place before the Spirit could be given. Only after Jesus returned to

---

[62]Of course, not all who were later to receive the Holy Spirit at Pentecost were in the room. Possibly only ten disciples were present, as Judas was dead and Thomas was absent. However, it seems likely that the account in John 20:22 represents the sequence of regeneration preceding the later coming of the Holy Spirit.

[63]The word *converted* could also be used. Jesus had said to Peter shortly before his denial: "I have prayed for you that your faith may not fail; and when you have turned again [Gr. *epistrepsas*], strengthen your brethren" (Luke 22:32). This "turning again" or "turning around" or "conversion" (KJV translates: "when thou art converted") occurred on the day of Jesus' resurrection. Incidentally, the words of Jesus about Peter's faith not failing were true in the sense that neither he nor the other disciples, despite their forsaking of Jesus and disbelieving the reports of His resurrection, ever completely lost faith. On Easter all disbelief was driven out and a firm and unshakable faith was established. This "turning again" was so total in nature that it brought a lasting conversion. Furthermore, Peter later used the same expression "turn again" to refer to the conversion of others: "Repent therefore, and turn again [Gr. *epistrepsate*], that your sins may be blotted out" (Acts 3:19). Likewise the sins of Peter and the other disciples had been blotted out by the risen Lord so that new life began on Easter day!

[64]The Greek word is *koilias* and means "the hidden, innermost recesses of the human body" (BAGD). The KJV has "belly," RSV "heart"; NIV simply says "within him." NASB, I believe, best catches the meaning of *koilia* in this context.

heaven would this occur.[65] Once again, this will happen to those who are believers in Jesus.

In the words of John 7 we also observe that there is both a drinking and an outflowing of water. In relation to the former, Jesus had earlier spoken of drinking "living water" which would "become . . . a spring of water welling up to eternal life" (John 4:10, 14). Thus comparing these two passages (John 4 and 7), it is apparent that drinking means coming to Jesus in faith and receiving from Him the water of eternal life. In the case of the latter, there is an outflowing, indeed an abundance— "rivers of living water"—from those who believe. This occurred through the Holy Spirit after Jesus' final glorification. Thus living water is represented as both welling up to eternal life through faith in Jesus and flowing out for blessing through the activity of the Holy Spirit.

The latter point highlights the fact that the Spirit to come (or to be given) will be a source of blessing to others. Entrance into eternal life is, of course, the first and primary thing, without which there can be no ministry. But it cannot, and must not, end there. There should flow out of the believer such ministry—rivers of living water—as to be a blessing to all mankind.

One other matter calls for brief comment. In Jesus' first reference to the Paraclete, the Spirit to come, He spoke of Him as "the Spirit of truth, whom the world cannot receive, because it neither sees him nor knows him" (John 14:17). This further emphasizes the point that the Holy Spirit is available only to those who are *not* of the world; hence He may be received only by those who believe.

B. The Gift of the Holy Spirit

Leaving the Paraclete passages and turning to the Gospel of Luke, we now reflect on an important Scripture dealing with the Spirit to be given. We have already noted that the Spirit to come would be a gift,[66] hence the gift of the Spirit. So we come to Jesus' words: "If you then, who are evil, know how to give good gifts to your children, how much more will the heavenly Father[67] give the Holy Spirit[68] to those who ask him!" (Luke 11:13). Although these words of Jesus do not directly speak (as

---

[65]The theme of "glorification" in the fourth Gospel is a complex one. According to John 13:31, just after Judas had gone out to betray Him, Jesus said, "Now is the Son of man glorified, and in him God is glorified; if God is glorified in him, God will also glorify him in himself, and glorify him at once." Three moments in glorification are given: present ("is glorified"), future ("will glorify"), immediate future ("glorify at once"). Earlier Jesus had said, "It is my Father who glorifies me" (8:54)—hence, at whatever the moment. Jesus, prior to Judas' departure from the meeting of the disciples, said, "The hour has come for the Son of man to be glorified" (12:23)—thus immediate future. Still later, after Judas had left, Jesus prayed, "And now, Father, glorify thou me in thy own presence with the glory which I had with thee before the world was made" (17:5). Although the word "now" is used, it is evident that this full glorification "in thy own presence" could not occur until Jesus had returned to heaven. This would be the climactic glorification and doubtless the glorification referred to in John 7:39 above. (Also see John 12:16: "When Jesus was glorified . . . ." The perspective here is that of the final glorification; cf. Acts 3:13: "The God . . . of our fathers, glorified his servant Jesus, whom you delivered up and denied," a statement that points to Jesus' resurrection and exaltation [cf. Acts 2:32–33].)

[66]E.g., John 7:39: "The Spirit was not yet given" (NASB).

[67]The Greek phrase is *ho patēr ho ex ouranou* and literally means "the Father out of, or from, heaven" (see NASB mg). Note how this accords with the Spirit coming from heaven upon Jesus.

[68]The parallel text in Matthew 7:11 reads "good things" (Gr. *agatha*).

in the Fourth Gospel) of the Spirit as yet to come, a study of the larger context makes this clear.

Jesus recounts a situation (vv. 5–12) in which a man needed bread to give to a late-arriving visitor. He goes to a friend's house at midnight, saying, "Friend, lend me three loaves." Despite the fact that the hour is late and he is in bed, the friend finally gets up because of the persistence of his neighbor and gives him the bread. Jesus thereupon adds: "Ask . . . seek . . . knock," concluding with the words about the heavenly Father giving the Holy Spirit to those who ask Him. The purpose of the gift manifestly is that one may minister to the need of another, in this case to provide bread.

The still larger background of this passage on the giving of the Spirit is that of the Lord's Prayer. Jesus, after praying, was asked by one of His disciples, "Lord teach us to pray . . ." (Luke 11:1). Then Jesus gave some instructions: "When you pray, say: 'Father, hallowed be thy name. Thy kingdom come.[69] Give us each day our daily[70] bread . . .'" (vv. 2–3). Hence, the request for loaves of bread in the story that follows, which is later connected with the Holy Spirit, seemingly relates to the petition for bread[71] in the prayer Jesus taught His disciples. This whole matter of prayer concerning the Holy Spirit may then be grounded in both the prayer life of Jesus and the prayer He taught His disciples.

Concerning Jesus' instructions about the Father giving the Holy Spirit "to those who ask him," what finally is of critical importance is His encouragement to His disciples to ask—yes, even to seek and knock. Through such persistence His followers might receive this best of all good[72] gifts, namely, the Holy Spirit. The Father delights to give good gifts to His children, far more than any earthly father does. Such a precious gift as the Holy Spirit will not be given indiscriminately to seekers and non-seekers alike, but to those who earnestly desire it. God is not a reluctant or grudging giver who must be badgered into giving His favors. Hence, the persistence in prayer that is called for is not to overcome His unwillingness, but rather to demonstrate the wholeheartedness of those asking and thus to prepare the way for the extraordinary gift to be received.

Note carefully, this gift is the Holy Spirit Himself. The gift of the Holy Spirit is not some gift He makes or brings, but His own personal reality. To be sure, the purpose is to provide the resources for ministry; in this biblical story it was bread for another's needs. However, that purpose can be fulfilled only by one who has been visited by the presence and power of the Spirit of the living God. Only when and where the

---

[69] It is interesting that a variant reading of "Thy kingdom come" is "Thy Holy Spirit come upon us and cleanse us." According to IB, "there is some support in minuscule MSS and in the fathers" for this latter rendering, so that some scholars "have maintained that this is the original Lukan reading" (Luke 11:2b in loco). Swete, while stating that it is "clearly a gloss," adds: "But it expresses the great truth that the Kingdom of God as an inward power is identical with the working of the Spirit of God, and it is valuable as an ancient interpretation of the clause" (*The Holy Spirit in the New Testament,* 121).

[70] The Greek word translated "daily," *epiousion,* may be rendered in a number of ways (e.g., RSV margin has "for the morrow"). BAGD mentions, as one possibility among many, that it may refer "to the coming kingdom and its feast." This possible translation would closely relate to the preceding variant ("Thy Holy Spirit come . . .") and to "the coming kingdom."

[71] The Greek word for "bread" and "loaf" is the same: *artos.*

[72] The *agatha* of Matthew 7:11 comes to a focus surely in the Holy Spirit Himself.

Spirit is so experienced can there be an outreach of powerful ministry.

One further word: the Holy Spirit is given to those who are God's children. It is "the heavenly Father," the One who can be addressed as "Father" (Luke 11:2), who makes this amazing gift. Or, as the account also puts it, the gift is given to one who can address God as "Friend" (v. 5). Thus it is from within the context of a close relationship between God and man that the Holy Spirit is given and received.

C. Final Words of Jesus

Third, we turn to the final words of Jesus about the Spirit to come. Let us observe the relevant scriptures in the Book of Acts and the Gospel of Luke.

It was during the forty days after His resurrection, according to Acts, that Jesus delivered a charge to His disciples "not to depart from Jerusalem, but to wait for the promise of the Father, which, he [Jesus] said, 'you heard from me, for John baptized in[73] water, but before many days you shall be baptized in the Holy Spirit'" (Acts 1:4–5). The coming of the Spirit was at hand—"before many days." Note three things about this: (1) there was "the promise of the Father," which can be none other than the Holy Spirit;[74] (2) Jesus said they had heard this promise from His lips; and (3) this had to do with being "baptized in the Holy Spirit."

This "promise of the Father" was previously mentioned in Luke's Gospel. Following Jesus' injunction that "repentance and forgiveness of sins should be preached in his name to all nations" (24:47) and that the disciples were "witnesses of these things"

(v. 48), He said, "Behold, I send the promise of my Father upon you; but stay in the city, until you are clothed with power from on high" (v. 49). We observe several things: first, the message of the Gospel—repentance and forgiveness of sins; second, the disciples were to be witnesses; third, they would receive power from on high to carry forward their ministry. Although the Holy Spirit as such is not mentioned, there can be no question but that this power is to come from Him.

All of this presupposes that the disciples had themselves come to repentance and received forgiveness and hence had entered into a new life through Jesus Christ. As such a community of the "newborn," they were told by Jesus to remain in the city until they were endowed with power from on high (Luke), or until they were "baptized in the Holy Spirit" (Acts). Then, and only then, would they be truly ready to bear witness.

With this background, we may now review the earlier texts in the Synoptic Gospels where John the Baptist spoke first of his own activity of baptizing in water and then of Jesus' role of baptizing in the Holy Spirit. "I have baptized you in water; but he will baptize you in the Holy Spirit" (Mark 1:8); "I baptize you in water; but he who is mightier than I . . . will baptize you in the Holy Spirit and fire" (Luke 3:16); "I baptize you in water for repentance, but he who is coming after me is mightier than I . . . he will baptize you in the Holy Spirit and in fire" (Matt. 3:11).

John's baptizing in water, according to Matthew, was "for repentance." Indeed, as Mark and Luke earlier re-

---

[73] The Greek preposition is *en*. As I earlier stated (see n. 43), the connection with baptism suggests that "in" is the best translation. So I am substituting "in" for "with" ("with" is found in KJV, RSV, NIV, NASB, and NEB) in this verse and in similar contexts on the succeeding pages.

[74] This is further confirmed in Peter's words on the Day of Pentecost about Jesus: "[He] received from the Father the promise of the Holy Spirit" (Acts 2:33).

corded it, John came "preaching a baptism of repentance for the forgiveness of sins" (Mark 1:4; Luke 3:3). John's baptizing in water, however, was not the primary thing: first was the call to repentance. Before Matthew makes any mention of baptism, he records that John came preaching, "Repent, for the kingdom of heaven is at hand" (3:2). After this, multitudes of people "were baptized by him in the river Jordan, confessing their sins" (v. 6). In this manner John came "preaching a baptism of repentance for the forgiveness of sins." Hence, John's baptizing in water was in relation to repentance and forgiveness, which, as we noted, are the heart of the Gospel; they are needed for salvation.

This does not mean that John's call for repentance with its accompaniment of water baptism actually brought about salvation, but it prepared the way for Jesus and His work.[75] It pointed to Jesus as "the Lamb of God, who takes away the sin of the world" (John 1:29).[76] John adds a few words later: "For this I came baptizing with water, that he might be revealed to Israel" (v. 31). Hence John's baptizing in water for repentance was the preparation for, even the outward form of, the actual "taking away"—the washing away, the removal—of sin that would be effected through being baptized in the name of Jesus Christ. John came preaching, "Repent," and then he baptized people "for the forgiveness of

their sins." This foreshadowed Peter's preaching on the Day of Pentecost: "Repent, and be baptized every one of you in the name of the Jesus Christ for the forgiveness of your sins" (Acts 2:38). The *only* difference (but *the* critical difference that makes for salvation) was the statement "in the name of Jesus Christ"—the very One John had proclaimed as "the Lamb of God who takes away the sin of the world." The call for repentance was still there and the method of water baptism was still utilized. But now baptism could be done in the name of Jesus Christ who had taken away the sin of the world, making salvation possible. John's preparation was over; the reality was here!

Since John's baptizing in water was fulfilled through salvation in Jesus, we may better appreciate the fact that John spoke of a separate matter when he said about Jesus: "He will baptize you in the Holy Spirit." What the latter meant, however, could not be understood, or indeed could not happen, until Jesus had completed His work of redemption by taking away the sin of the world. After this initial proclamation by John the Baptist that Jesus would baptize in the Holy Spirit, nothing further is directly said[77] on this matter in any of the four Gospels. The expression is not used again until the Book of Acts when Jesus Himself said, "Before many days you shall be baptized in the Holy Spirit" (1:5). This, however, was *after* Jesus through His death and resurrec-

---

[75] Recall the words of the angel to Zechariah about John: "He will turn many of the sons of Israel to the Lord their God . . . to make ready for the Lord a people prepared" (Luke 1:16–17). Zechariah later prophesied, "And you, child, will be called the prophet of the Most High, for you will go before the Lord to prepare his ways, to give knowledge of salvation to his people in the forgiveness of their sins" (vv. 76–77). Although John the Baptist did not himself bring salvation, he gave "knowledge of salvation" and so prepared the way for the One who actually brought it.

[76] It is quite significant that in the Fourth Gospel just after mention is made of John's baptizing, the following verse reads, "The next day he saw Jesus coming toward him, and said, "Behold, the Lamb of God. . . .'" (1:28–29).

[77] Luke 24:49 is the closest approximation. Of course, these words also occur after Jesus finished His work of redemption.

tion had wrought mankind's redemption and His disciples had received it. Only then could the significance of this baptism in the Spirit become manifest: it will be *an immersion in the Spirit as total as John's immersion in water.*[78] Its purpose will be witness and ministry in the name of Christ. Those who bear witness will do so with such power and effectiveness that their words will be as fire[79] to purge away sin and evil, to bring forth good, and to gather people into the household of God.[80]

But the order of this is urgently important: there must first be the taking away of sin before this baptism in the Holy Spirit can occur. There cannot be the latter without the former, and the former is incomplete without the latter. The disciples were not allowed to enjoy their new life in Christ and forget the world outside; rather they needed a baptism in the Spirit that would empower their witness so that others might likewise enter into life and salvation.

This leads to the last words of Jesus to His disciples about the coming of the Holy Spirit. The forty days together had drawn to a close, and before He left them, Jesus said, "You shall receive power when the Holy Spirit has come upon you; and you shall be my witnesses in Jerusalem and in all Judea and Samaria and to the end[81] of the earth" (Acts 1:8). The Spirit would come to bring power—*dynamis*—and in that power they were to bear witness to all the world.

Here we must end our discussion concerning the Spirit to come. For the next word is that He did come at Pentecost—and comes again and again. This extraordinary event must be reserved for a comprehensive discussion in the pages that follow.

---

[78]As mentioned in footnote 43, the word "baptize" in Greek (*baptizō*) basically means "immersion."

[79]Recall the words of John the Baptist about Jesus: "He will baptize you with the Holy Spirit and fire." Then he added, "His winnowing fork is in His hand, and He will thoroughly clear His threshing floor; and He will gather His wheat into the barn, but He will burn up the chaff with unquenchable fire" (Matt. 3:11–12 NASB; cf. Luke 3:16–17). Baptism in the Spirit, accordingly, will make for a ministry of fire—fire in manner and utterance (cf. Acts 2:3–4)—that will both purge and consume, yet also make for salvation. (See the earlier discussion of the Holy Spirit as fire, chap. 6, II.B.2.)

[80]A further word about "baptism in the Holy Spirit": The meaning of this expression is best understood in the light of Jesus' own use of it: "John baptized in water, but before many days you shall be baptized in the Holy Spirit" (Acts 1:5). If we had only the earlier words of John the Baptist, baptism in the Spirit might seem to refer to regeneration, namely, that John's baptism in water was the outward preparation in water for the inner experience of new life, or regeneration, that Jesus' act of baptizing in the Spirit brings. Similarly Calvin, in commenting on Matthew 3:11, says, "Christ alone bestows all the grace which is figuratively represented by outward baptism . . . and bestows the Spirit of regeneration" (*Commentaries, Harmony of Matthew, Mark, and Luke,* 1:199, Beveridge trans.). The point is that, however John the Baptist may have understood the words, there is nothing further said about them in any of the Gospels. *Jesus' words in Acts therefore are decisive* (whether viewed as interpretation or reinterpretation). And, as we have already noted, they must refer especially to His action in the Spirit for the enablement of ministry (see chap. 10, "The Mission of the Holy Spirit," for further elaboration). Incidentally, Calvin in his *Institutes* speaks of baptism in the Spirit as "the visible graces [or gifts] of the Holy Spirit given through the laying on of hands" and adds, "It is nothing new to signify these graces by the word 'baptism' " (4.15.18, Battles trans.). In this statement Calvin goes beyond the view that identifies Spirit baptism with regeneration. In so doing he is much closer to the picture in Acts.

[81]The Greek word is *eschatou;* "the uttermost part" (KJV), "the remotest part" (NASB). Thayer suggests "the last in time or place," hence the last place, however distant or small.

8

The Coming of the Holy Spirit

I. INTRODUCTION

We will now consider one of the most stupendous and mighty acts of God—the coming of the Holy Spirit. Let us consider this event as set forth primarily in the Book of Acts. Although we will note relevant references in the Gospels and Epistles, our primary concern will be the narratives in Acts that variously depict this coming. The Gospels, as we have seen, point forward to it, and, as will be noted, the Epistles presuppose it. Hence, although consideration will also be given to the Epistles, the focus of our attention will be on the narratives in Acts.

Before proceeding further, let me emphasize that the coming of the Holy Spirit is a gracious act of God. It is a gift, or, to be specific, it is the gift of the Holy Spirit. As the Fourth Gospel puts it, "As yet the Spirit had not been given, because Jesus was not yet glorified" (7:39). As we have seen, there are also several allusions to the coming of the Holy Spirit in the same Gospel: "When the Spirit of truth comes . . ." (16:13; cf. 15:26; 16:7). The word "com-

ing" expresses the idea of event, happening, action; the word "gift" indicates that this coming is an act of God's grace. God gives the Holy Spirit.

Since the Spirit's coming is a gracious gift from God, the proper human response is that of reception. It is a gift to be received. Thus when the word "receive" is used in connection with the Holy Spirit, it refers to the gift of the Holy Spirit. This is important to recognize because words such as "giving" and "receiving" in association with the Holy Spirit refer to the event of the Spirit's coming.

We shall later note a variety of linguistic expressions in Acts for the coming of the Holy Spirit.[1] But first let us observe a number of passages primarily in Acts but also in the Epistles where giving or receiving the Holy Spirit is stated or implied.

First, of course, is the Day of Pentecost in Jerusalem (Acts 2). It was there that the waiting disciples of Jesus received the promised Holy Spirit (vv. 1–4). Although the word "received" is not used in this account, Peter years later declared of the Gentiles in Caesarea:

---

[1] See III, below.

"[They] have received the Holy Spirit just as we have" (Acts 10:47). "Just as we have" refers to the event of Pentecost. The second recorded instance of receiving the Holy Spirit is in Samaria (Acts 8). Peter and John went down from Jerusalem to Samaria and ministered to the Samaritans, and as a result the Samaritans "received the Holy Spirit" (v. 17). The third instance relates to Saul of Tarsus (Acts 9). Ananias went to Saul's lodging in Damascus and prayed for him that he might be "filled with the Holy Spirit" (v. 17). Although the word "received" is not used in this case, the term "filling" implies that Saul received the Holy Spirit.[2] The fourth narrative specifically relating to the reception of the Holy Spirit concerns the Caesareans (Acts 10)—the Roman centurion Cornelius, his household, and friends. Luke, in describing the event, refers both to "the gift of the Holy Spirit" (v. 45) and the fact that they had "received the Holy Spirit" (v. 47). The fifth recorded instance of the reception of the Holy Spirit concerns some twelve disciples in Ephesus (Acts 19). When Paul found them, he asked, "Did you receive the Holy Spirit when you believed?" (v. 2) and shortly thereafter ministered the Holy Spirit to them.

As I have said before, we will focus primarily on these passages in Acts because they alone depict the event of the Holy Spirit's coming.[3] In these five narratives various perspectives on the coming of the Holy Spirit will be observed; hence what is stated in them will be our main concern. This is by no means to suggest that the passages shortly to be quoted from some of the Epistles are of less importance. However, they are generally quite brief and compact; moreover, they refer to something that had *already* happened and thus give little or no detail. Hence, a better and fuller understanding will often call for a return to the events recorded in Acts.[4]

Several passages in the Epistles speak of a giving or receiving of the Holy Spirit. In Romans Paul writes that "the love of God has been poured out within our hearts through the Holy Spirit who was given to us" (5:5 NASB). Later in the same letter Paul says, "Ye have not received the spirit of bondage again to fear; but ye have received the

---

[2] This will be apparent later when we observe that the word *filled* is one of the terms used in Acts to describe what happened when the Holy Spirit came.

[3] Hence, I do not include at this juncture the account in Acts 2:42–47 describing the enlarged community of believers. The actual event of the Spirit's coming is not described as in Acts 2:1–4 and the other passages in Acts mentioned above.

[4] A proper methodology entails, wherever possible, giving priority to the narrational and descriptive over the didactic. For example, in regard to the study of the Incarnation, it is better to begin with the narratives in the Gospels before proceeding to the briefer references and interpretation in the Epistles. This is likewise true about the coming of the Holy Spirit. Since Acts is the actual record of this event, its narration is the primary place to gain perspective and understanding. Not all agree on that, I recognize. For example, John R. W. Stott writes that the "revelation of the purpose of God in Scripture should be sought primarily in its *didactic* rather than its *descriptive* parts. More precisely, we should look for it . . . in the sermons and writings of the apostles, rather than in the purely narrative portions of the Acts. What is described as having happened to others is not necessarily intended for us" (*Baptism and Fullness*, 15). Such an approach, I submit, reverses the proper order of understanding. Actually, it is a combination of the two, the narrational or descriptive *and* the didactic, with the former having priority, that is the best hermeneutical procedure. (For a helpful critique of the position represented by Stott, see Roger Stronstad, *The Charismatic Theology of St. Luke*, 5–9.)

Spirit[5] of adoption, whereby we cry, *Abba,* Father" (8:15 KJV). In 1 Corinthians Paul declares, "We have received, not the spirit of the world, but the Spirit who is from God, that we might know the things freely given to us by God" (2:12 NASB). In 2 Corinthians there are several references: "Now He who establishes us with you in Christ and anointed us is God, who also sealed us and gave us the Spirit in our heart as a pledge"[6] (1:21–22 NASB); "Now He who prepared us for this very purpose is God, who gave to us the Spirit as a pledge" (5:5 NASB); and "If you receive a different spirit from the one you received,[7] or if you accept a different gospel from the one you accepted, you submit to it readily enough" (11:4). In Galatians Paul asks, "Did you receive the Spirit by the works of the law, or by hearing with faith?" (3:2 NASB) and later speaks about "the blessing of Abraham" coming "to the Gentiles, so that we might receive the promise of the Spirit through faith" (v. 14 NASB). In Ephesians Paul writes about "the Holy Spirit of promise, who is given as a pledge of our inheritance" (1:13–14 NASB). In 1 Thessalonians Paul declares, "He who rejects this instruction does not reject man but God, who gives you his Holy Spirit" (4:8 NIV). Finally, in 1 John are these statements: "We know by this that He abides in us, by the Spirit whom He has given us" (3:24 NASB) and "By this we know that we abide in Him and He in us, because He has given us of His Spirit" (4:13 NASB).

It is apparent that the coming of the Holy Spirit, particularly expressed in terms of giving and receiving, is both described in its occurrence in a number of passages in Acts and declared as an accomplished fact in many Epistles. As we proceed in our study, we will look first to the paradigmatic record in Acts and trust that this will cast further light on the whole of the New Testament. Beyond that, our concern will be to elaborate connections with the spiritual renewal of the twentieth century.

One more prefatory remark: Since the first and, in many ways, the decisive coming of the Holy Spirit was on the Day of Pentecost in Jerusalem, we will give much attention to this initial event. By no means will we end there, but its significance for what follows cannot be exaggerated.

II. BACKGROUND

As we move ahead, we need to bear in mind certain factors that prepared the way for the coming of the Holy Spirit. Our discussion will be, in part, a review of some things previously said; however, because of the importance of this background, further reflection is in order.

A. The Promise of the Father

There are many promises of God in the Bible, but "the promise of the Father" uniquely relates to the coming of the Holy Spirit. First, there are the words of Jesus to His disciples as recorded in the Gospel of Luke and the Book of Acts: "Behold, I send the promise of my Father upon you" (Luke 24:49) and "While staying with them he charged them not to depart from Jerusalem, but to wait for the promise of the Father" (Acts 1:4). That this promise of the Father is the coming of the Holy Spirit is apparent from both contexts.[8]

---

[5] RSV and NASB have "spirit." However, as John Murray writes, "The spirit of adoption whereby we cry, 'Abba, Father,' is the Holy Spirit" (*Epistle to the Romans*, NICNT, 296).

[6] Or "earnest" (KJV); "guarantee" (RSV); "deposit" (NIV). The Greek word is *arrabōn*.

[7] "The one you received" was, of course, the Holy Spirit.

[8] In Luke 24:49 Jesus continued by saying, "But stay in the city, until you are clothed with power from on high." According to Acts 1:5, Jesus declared, "Before many days you shall

Next, the Book of Acts records the words of Peter in his sermon on the Day of Pentecost: "Having received from the Father the promise of the Holy Spirit, he [Jesus] has poured out this which you see and hear" (2:33). Peter was thereby referring to the coming of the Spirit that he and many others had just experienced (see vv. 1–4). The Spirit had come, and Peter related this occurrence to the promise "from the Father," which is "the promise of the Holy Spirit." Accordingly, the promise of the Father stood as background for the coming of the Holy Spirit on the Day of Pentecost.

Likewise, on the same day the promise was extended to Peter's audience, to their children, and to people of distant times and places. So Peter declared: "You shall receive the gift of the Holy Spirit. For the promise is for you and your children, and for all who are far off, as many as the Lord our God shall call to Himself" (Acts 2:38–39 NASB). Although the word "Father" was not directly mentioned, this is doubtless the same promise of the Father that Peter had mentioned a short time before.[9]

It is apparent that the coming of the Holy Spirit is to be a continuing occurrence. The promise of the gift of the Spirit was fulfilled at Pentecost, but the promise was by no means to be limited to the original company of disciples. Unlike the coming of Christ in the Incarnation, which was a once-for-all event, the coming of the Holy Spirit would occur an unlimited number of times.[10]

In the accounts that follow Pentecost in Acts, no further reference is directly made to the promise of the Father, i.e., the promise of the Holy Spirit. The closest reference is the Caesarean account in Acts 10, where, as we have noted, the event is described, in part, as a receiving of "the gift of the Holy Spirit." Since Peter's words at Pentecost stated clearly that the promise of the Father is the gift of the Holy Spirit, the centurion and his company surely experienced the fulfillment of that promise. The same thing is doubtless the case for all the other narratives in Acts that tell of the giving and receiving of the Holy Spirit.

References are made in two of the Epistles to the promise of the Holy Spirit. Both scriptures were quoted previously but without attention called to the word "promise": Paul speaks in Galatians 3:14 about receiving "the promise of the Spirit" and in Ephesians 1:13 about "the Holy Spirit of promise" (NASB). The Galatians had received the Holy Spirit, and the Ephesians (to add the context) were "sealed in Him [Christ] with the Holy Spirit of promise." Thus it is clear that in Galatia and Ephesus the promise of the Father, the Holy Spirit, was specifically fulfilled. By implication all references to the giving or receiving of the Holy Spirit in the other Epistles were instances of the fulfillment of the promise of the Father.

We may, accordingly, affirm that the same promise of the Father continues through the ages. The words of Jesus as recorded in both Luke and Acts, the message of Peter that the promise is for generations to come, the various incidents thereafter in Acts, and the many

---

be baptized with [or "in"] the Holy Spirit." (Recall our brief discussion in the preceding chapter.)

[9]So F. F. Bruce says, "The free gift which is promised . . . to those who repent and are baptized is the Holy Spirit Himself" (*The Book of the Acts,* NICNT, 77). I will discuss the priority of repentance and baptism in section C. below.

[10]This is not to deny the distinctiveness of the coming of the Spirit at Pentecost. That event was indeed a new and mighty act of God, but it was still the first in an unlimited number that came later.

references in the Epistles—all these are evidence of a continuing promise.

B. The Exaltation of Jesus

The second background factor for the coming of the Holy Spirit is the exaltation of Jesus. After His resurrection and ascension Jesus was seated at the right hand of the Father, and from that place of exaltation He sent forth the Holy Spirit.

On the Day of Pentecost Peter made clear that what had happened to the disciples in Jerusalem came from the exalted Jesus. He said, "Being therefore exalted at the right hand of God . . . he [Jesus] has poured out this. . ." (Acts 2:33). These words of Peter were similar to those of Jesus (already quoted): "Behold, I send the promise of my Father upon you." They emphasize that the fulfillment of the promise came only after Jesus had returned to heaven. From there He poured forth the Holy Spirit.

John wrote, "As yet the Spirit had not been given,[11] because Jesus was not yet glorified" (John 7:39). Since the word "glorified" in John's Gospel signifies exalted,[12] this statement shows that the exaltation of Jesus must precede the giving, i.e., the coming of the Holy Spirit.

The Gospel of John has several further references by Jesus Himself to the future sending, or giving, of the Holy Spirit. The first two of Jesus' statements point to the Father as the One who would be the primary agent: "I will pray the Father, and he will give you another Paraclete"[13] (14:16) and "The

Paraclete, the Holy Spirit, whom the Father will send in my name . . ." (14:26). In the succeeding two references Jesus points to Himself: "When the Paraclete comes, whom I shall send to you from the Father, even the Spirit of truth, who proceeds from the Father . . ." (15:26) and "It is to your advantage that I go away, for if I do not go away, the Paraclete will not come to you; but if I go, I will send him to you" (16:7).

The sequence above is quite illuminating. Following the scripture from John 14:16 to John 16:7, we see this picture: (1) The Father will give the Spirit at the request of Jesus, (2) the Father will send the Spirit in Jesus' name, (3) Jesus will send the Spirit from the Father, and (4) Jesus will send the Spirit.

Thus as Jesus unfolds the wonder of the sending of the Holy Spirit, there is a progression from the Father to the Son. Since the Father is primary in all activity, He ultimately gives, or sends, the Holy Spirit,[14] as the first two Johannine passages disclose. However, even in these two passages the Son is intimately involved, for it is at His request that the Father sends the Spirit, and He does so in the Son's name. But once it has been clarified that the Father's role is primary, Jesus moves on to state that it is through Himself that the Spirit comes. Then follows the transition in the third passage where Jesus says that He (not the Father) will send the Spirit but that the Spirit is "from the Father." Here the extraordinary balance is shown. While it is Jesus finally who sends the

---

[11] The preponderance of Greek manuscripts omit the word "given"; hence the text could be read simply, "The Spirit was not yet." However, English translations usually provide the word "given." This appears to be the intended meaning of the text.

[12] See prior discussion in chapter 7, III.A. about the use of the word "glorification" in the Fourth Gospel. The climactic glorification is that of Jesus to the right hand of the Father.

[13] Instead of "Counselor." See earlier discussion under "The Spirit of Truth," chapter 6, II.A. Also recall chapter 7, III.A., "The Paraclete."

[14] Even as He gives, or sends, the Son. "God so loved the world that he *gave* his only Son. . . . For God *sent* the Son into the world" (John 3:16–17).

Spirit, the Spirit, nonetheless, is from God the Father. Only after these three passages, which discuss the relationship between the Spirit and the Father, does Jesus finally say—with no reference to the Father—that the Son will send the Holy Spirit.

One additional point from John's Gospel is that Jesus speaks of the Spirit as proceeding from the Father: "The Spirit of truth . . . proceeds from the Father" (15:26). Thus not only is the Father the primary agent in the sending of the Spirit, but He is also the source of the Holy Spirit: the Holy Spirit "proceeds" from Him. Thus the Holy Spirit originates from the eternal source of all things. The Holy Spirit is from God the Father, and is therefore Himself also God. Hence when the Holy Spirit is sent to the world, nothing less than the eternal God Himself comes.

In regard to the sending of the Holy Spirit, we may say that both the Father and Son send the Holy Spirit in the sense that the Father sends the Spirit *through* the Son. There is no sending of the Holy Spirit by the Father except through the Son. Therefore the Holy Spirit, who is sent by the Father, is received only through the mediation of Jesus Christ. Thus, in the ultimate sense, the Holy Spirit is sent from the Father, but in a proximate sense He comes from the Son.

We return in our reflection to the exalted Jesus. For the Son through whom the Holy Spirit comes is the One at the Father's right hand. He who has been exalted by the Father to the place of honor and majesty sends forth the Holy Spirit. The Holy Spirit thus comes from heaven to earth, even from the Lord Jesus.

The coming of the Holy Spirit, accordingly, is not a divine event to which Jesus is only peripherally related, but a coming in which He is the essential channel. The Holy Spirit, though distinct from Jesus, is the Spirit issuing from Jesus. He is sent by Jesus. Thus it is not as if the exalted Jesus were one force among many from whom the Spirit might come. "All authority in heaven and on earth" (Matt. 28:18) has been given the exalted Lord, and from Him alone does the Holy Spirit go forth.

Now to return to the record in Acts, we recognize that every coming of the Holy Spirit recorded in Acts was from the exalted Lord Jesus. Although Jesus is not specifically said to be the channel after the Jerusalem Pentecost, this is clearly implied. For example, in the Caesarean account the Scripture states that "the gift of the Holy Spirit had been poured out upon the Gentiles also" (Acts 10:45 NASB). Since Peter had said it was Jesus who poured out the Spirit in Jerusalem, He was doubtless the One responsible again. Saul of Tarsus was confronted on the road to Damascus by the exalted Lord Jesus (Acts 9:3–5) and three days later was filled with the Holy Spirit. The Holy Spirit surely came from the exalted Lord. The same thing must also have been true of the giving of the Spirit in Samaria and Ephesus.

It follows that at any time thereafter when the Holy Spirit comes—in the Epistles or in later history—He comes from the exalted Lord. Christ today is at the right hand of the Father and from there the Holy Spirit is sent forth.

C. The Occurrence of Salvation

The final background factor for the coming of the Holy Spirit is the occurrence of salvation. Those who turn to Christ in true faith and thereby enter into a new life in His name may receive the gift of the Holy Spirit. Against the background of salvation, however worded,[15] the Holy Spirit is given.

---

[15]I have previously discussed salvation under the headings of calling (effectual),

We have earlier observed that the original disciples who received the promise of the Holy Spirit had entered into a new life in Christ. They had come to a vital faith in Christ as He who had lived, died, and risen again. As a community redeemed from their old life, they were told to wait for the Holy Spirit to come. Hence when the extraordinary event did occur, it happened to those who had already repented and now truly believed in Jesus Christ.

On the Day of Pentecost after the Holy Spirit had come to the waiting disciples, Peter affirmed that the same gift of the Holy Spirit was promised to all who likewise repented and believed. Just prior to the promise of the gift of the Holy Spirit Peter declared, "Repent, and be baptized every one of you in the name of Jesus Christ for the forgiveness of your sins" (Acts 2:38). By such repentance and faith there would be salvation;[16] and to such persons the Holy Spirit was promised.

The Samaritans' reception of the Holy Spirit through the ministry of Peter and John has already been noted (Acts 8:14–17). Some time before this occurred Philip had "proclaimed to them the Christ" (v. 5), and as a result the Samaritans came to faith and were baptized. The Scripture reads, "When they believed Philip as he preached the good news about the kingdom of God and the name of Jesus Christ, they were baptized, both men and women" (v. 12). Their baptism betokened repentance and faith,[17] through which they entered into salvation. Their conversion[18] to Christ, accordingly, was the background for their later reception of the Holy Spirit.

Now we turn to Saul of Tarsus. Saul's being "filled with the Holy Spirit" at the hands of Ananias was preceded by the encounter with Christ on the road to Damascus. In this encounter Saul was radically changed. Jesus became Saul's Lord—" 'What shall I do, Lord?' And the Lord said to me, 'Rise, and go into Damascus, and there you will be told . . .' " (Acts 22:10).[19] Saul

---

regeneration, justification, and (initial) sanctification (chaps. 1–4). Through repentance and faith this salvation occurs.

[16]Peter later adds the words, "Be saved from this perverse generation!" (v. 40 NASB).

[17]James D. G. Dunn in his book *Baptism in the Holy Spirit* says that the Samaritans' faith was "simply an assent of the mind to the acceptability of what Philip was saying" (p. 65). It was a matter of believing Philip—"they believed Philip"—but did not truly believe in Christ. Dunn's interpretation, I submit, is quite inadequate. Believing Philip surely means believing "the good news" that Philip proclaimed; and undoubtedly Philip understood it that way, for he thereupon baptized the Samaritans. Would Philip have done this on the basis of "simply an assent of the mind"? Or was Philip perhaps misled? The question scarcely merits an answer. It is true that Simon the magician also "believed" and was "baptized" (v. 13) and later was called to further repentance by Peter (vv. 20–22). But the text does not suggest that Simon's earlier faith and baptism were not genuine (indeed, he said to Peter, "Pray for me to the *Lord*" [v. 24]). The record in Acts also confirms the authenticity of the Samaritans' faith in v. 14: "Now when the apostles at Jerusalem heard that Samaria had received the word of God . . . ," "received the word of God" can hardly mean anything less than true and genuine faith (cf. Acts 11:1 where the same expression "received the word of God" is used concerning the Caesareans' faith, the genuineness of which is beyond dispute).

[18]"Conversion" is another term that may be used to refer to the occurrence of salvation. See earlier discussion in chapter 2, "Regeneration," IV.C.

[19]This is Paul's later recounting of his experience. In the first account in Acts 9 Saul simply says, "Who are you, Lord?" (v. 5), which could possibly be translated as "Sir" (as in Acts 16:30, "Sirs" [NASB]) because Saul did not yet know the identity of the speaker. According to I. H. Marshall, " 'Sir' . . . is the reverential address one would expect to be

(Paul) later wrote to the Corinthians, "Have I not seen Jesus our Lord?" (1 Cor. 9:1). It was at the moment of the vision vouchsafed to Paul on the road to Damascus that he became a new man in Christ. As one converted, saved, made new—whatever the language—Paul later received the Holy Spirit.[20]

In Caesarea, as we have noted, the centurion and his household received the Holy Spirit. Peter had preached the gospel, saying, "To him [Christ] all the prophets bear witness that every one who believes in him receives forgiveness of sins through his name" (Acts 10:43). So it was that these Gentiles repented and believed, for in later words regarding this incident the apostles and brethren in Jerusalem declared, "Then to the Gentiles also God has granted repentance unto life" (Acts 11:18). Against the background of their repentance and faith (to return to the event in Caesarea), the Holy Spirit came: "While Peter was still saying this [the words about belief and forgiveness], the Holy Spirit fell on all who heard the word" (Acts 10:44). That this was the occasion of the Caesareans' receiving the gift of the Holy Spirit is further attested by Peter's later reference to them as "the people who have received the Holy Spirit just as we have" (v. 47). But the relevant point here is that it was the Gentiles' "repentance unto life," i.e., their salvation,

that was background for the reception of the Holy Spirit.

Finally, in the case of the Ephesians who received the Holy Spirit through the ministry of Paul, it is apparent that they had come to faith in Christ. As we noted, Paul asked them, "Did you receive the Holy Spirit when you believed?" (Acts 19:2). It turned out that these Ephesians were only disciples of John the Baptist and knew nothing about the Holy Spirit: "No, we have never even heard that there is a Holy Spirit" (v. 2). Thereafter Paul characterized John's message as " 'telling the people to believe in the one who was to come after him, that is, Jesus.' On hearing this, they were baptized in the name of the Lord Jesus" (vv. 4–5). This was clearly the hearing of faith through which they received salvation, else Paul would not have baptized them. Following this, "when Paul had laid his hands upon them, the Holy Spirit came on them" (v. 6). Thus, once again, the occurrence of salvation was background for their receiving the Holy Spirit.

It is unmistakable that in all these accounts of the coming—the gift—of the Holy Spirit in Acts the occurrence of salvation was also essential background. Indeed, this was the subjective factor preparatory to the reception of the Holy Spirit. The other two background factors, the promise of the Father and the exaltation of Christ,

used in replying to any heavenly figure [10:4]" (*The Acts of the Apostles*, TNTC, 169). However, it is apparent from the account in Acts 22:10, where "Lord" is twice used, that this word signified a new relationship to Jesus Christ. William Neil puts it well: "In Paul's own account [Acts 22], after Jesus has disclosed his identity he [Saul] calls him *Lord*, with the full significance of the term" (*The Acts of the Apostles*, NCBC, 129). Hence, on the road to Damascus Saul gave himself totally over to Christ. In the words of A. T. Robertson, "Saul surrendered instantly. This . . . was the conversion of Saul" (*Word Pictures in the New Testament*, 3:117).

[20] In Paul's account of his experience in Acts 22 he speaks of Ananias saying to him, "Rise and be baptized, and wash away your sins, calling on his name" (v. 16). This could suggest that Paul's conversion did not occur until Ananias baptized him. However, it is clear from the initial account in Acts 9 that Paul had been converted and filled with the Spirit before baptism occurred (see vv. 17–18). Paul's baptism is better viewed as an outward sign of an inward washing that had already occurred.

were totally objective (though totally essential). Salvation, on the other hand, was deeply experiential; people repented and believed. Only when this occurred could the Holy Spirit be received.

Let me add a word concerning Peter's statement on the Day of Pentecost that the promise of the Holy Spirit was to "as many as the Lord our God shall call to Himself" (Acts 2:39 NASB). This calling of God "to Himself" may be spoken of as "effectual calling"— namely, the calling of God that results in salvation.[21] This call of God includes repentance and faith (as v. 38 states). Hence, the critical point again is that those effectually called—those who truly repent and believe—are promised the gift of the Holy Spirit.

In the Epistles all the aforementioned passages that speak of the giving or receiving of the Holy Spirit likewise presuppose salvation. To put it another way, in none of these scriptures is the giving of the Spirit said to be for salvation, nor is the receiving of the Holy Spirit a receiving for salvation. Romans 5:5, which speaks of "the Holy Spirit who was given to us" (NASB), is set against the background of justification and its effects (vv. 1–5); and

Romans 8:15, which refers to having "received the Spirit of adoption" (KJV), means the reception of the Spirit consequent to our adoption as sons.[22] First Corinthians 2:12 speaks of receiving the Holy Spirit, not for salvation but "that we might know the things freely given to us by God" (NASB). In 2 Corinthians those whom God has established and anointed are also "sealed" and given "the Spirit in [their] hearts as a pledge" (1:22 NASB). In 2 Corinthians 5:5 the Holy Spirit again is a pledge, in this case of God's future purpose for those who belong to Christ.[23] In Galatians 3:14 the Holy Spirit is promised to those who have experienced the blessing of Abraham, namely, justification (see vv. 6–9) or, through Christ, redemption (see v. 13). In Ephesians the background for "the Holy Spirit of promise" is again salvation, for the Scripture reads, "In Him [Christ], you also, after listening to the message of truth, the gospel of your salvation— having also believed, you were sealed in Him with the Holy Spirit of promise" (1:13 NASB).[24] First Thessalonians 4:8 speaks of "God, who gives his Holy Spirit to you" but does not specify prior salvation. However, nothing is stated in the immediate context (see vv. 1–7)

---

[21] See chapter 1, "Calling." F. F. Bruce writes in regard to this verse of "those whom the Lord Himself has called—and called effectually" (*The Book of the Acts*, NICNT, 78).

[22] This is particularly apparent in Galatians 4:5–6 where Paul first speaks of our "adoption as sons." Then he adds, "And because you are sons, God has sent the Spirit of his Son into our hearts." (See also my earlier discussion of "The Spirit of Adoption" in chapter 6, II.A.4.) John Murray writes that the Holy Spirit "is called 'The Spirit of adoption,' not because he is the agent of adoption but because it is he who creates in the children of God the filial love and confidence by which they are able to cry, 'Abba, Father' " (*The Epistle to the Romans*, NICNT, 296).

[23] Second Corinthians 11:4 (earlier quoted) is a somewhat different passage. In consecutive verses Paul speaks of receiving "a different spirit" and accepting "a different gospel." Paul does not say how one relates to the other. However, the very fact that both are mentioned shows that accepting the gospel (i.e., salvation) and receiving the Spirit are not the same thing. Moreover, the preceding phrase, "if some one comes and preaches another Jesus than the one we preached," suggests the priority of the gospel of salvation through Christ over receiving the Holy Spirit.

[24] A parallel with the account of Paul's ministry to the Ephesians in Acts 19 is apparent. Both in Acts 19 and Ephesians 1 salvation is the background for the reception of the Holy Spirit.

that suggests that the gift of the Spirit is for salvation. Finally, according to 1 John, it is "by the Spirit which He has given" that "we [believers] know . . . that He [Christ] abides in us"[25] (3:24 NASB). The gift of the Spirit was not for salvation but for assurance of Christ's continued abiding.

In summary, it is apparent also from the Epistles that the giving or receiving of the Holy Spirit is set against the background of salvation. It is those who truly believe—whom God has justified, adopted as children, and established in faith—that receive the Holy Spirit. Nothing is stated in the Epistles as to how this reception occurred. For that we must look back to the Book of Acts. But it is clear that both share a common background of salvation.

To round out the picture, we must return to the Gospels and recall some words in the Gospels of Luke and John. In the former Gospel Jesus speaks of the gift of the Spirit thus: "If you then, who are evil, know how to give good gifts to your children, how much more will the heavenly Father give the Holy Spirit to those who ask him!" (Luke 11:13). It is apparent that those who are already God's children,[26] children of the heavenly Father, may ask for and receive the gift of the Holy Spirit. According to the Fourth Gospel, Jesus declared, "If any man is thirsty, let him come to Me and drink. He who believes in Me, as the Scripture said, 'From his innermost being shall flow rivers of living water.'" Then John adds, "By this He spoke of the Spirit, whom those who believed in Him were to receive" (7:38–39 NASB). Believing, again, precedes receiving.[27]

The Gospels, Acts, and the Epistles agree in affirming that the coming of the Spirit presupposes the occurrence of salvation. But, to repeat, it is only in the Book of Acts that various narratives depict the actual coming—the giving and the receiving—of the Holy Spirit. Let us observe some of the descriptive language for this event.

III. DESCRIPTION

We arrive at a consideration of the actual coming of the Holy Spirit. The Holy Spirit promised by the Father and sent by the Son now comes into our time and history. God gives His Holy Spirit to human beings in various places and situations. It will be our procedure to observe the several terms[28] used to describe these occurrences and thus to reflect on the significance of the Spirit's coming.

A. Outpouring

Peter described the coming of the Holy Spirit to the waiting disciples on the Day of Pentecost as the *outpouring* of the Holy Spirit: "He [Jesus] has

[25]Cf. 1 John 4:13.

[26]According to Paul, as noted, we are God's sons, i.e., children by adoption into His family. All people are, of course, God's creatures, but only those whose status has been changed through faith are His children. So the Fourth Gospel puts it: "To all who received him, those who believed in his name, he gave the right to become children of God" (1:12 NIV).

[27]According to John 7:39, neither had the disciples come to full faith nor had the Spirit yet been given (the words continue: "for the Spirit was not yet given, because Jesus was not yet glorified"). Nonetheless, the sequence is clear: coming to Jesus and drinking, hence believing in Him, results in salvation, or eternal life (cf. John 4:10–14). Such believing is the background and basis for the outflow of living water that occurs through the receiving of the Holy Spirit.

[28]Some of these terms have appeared in previous quotations, but I have called no particular attention to them. We will now consider them in some detail.

poured out[29] this . . ." (Acts 2:33). Peter was referring to the mighty coming of the Holy Spirit that he and other disciples of Jesus had experienced a short time before.

Peter had earlier used the concept of "outpouring" when he quoted from the prophecy of Joel: "This is what was spoken by the prophet Joel: 'And in the last days it shall be, God declares, that I will pour out my Spirit upon all flesh, and your sons and your daughters shall prophesy, and your young men shall see visions, and your old men shall dream dreams; yea, and on my menservants and my maidservants in those days I will pour out my Spirit' " (2:16–18). "All flesh" meant both male and female, both young and old, both masters and servants. No longer would God's Spirit come only to a few (such as rulers, priests, and prophets),[30] but He would be poured out even on the lowliest of servants.

It is quite possible that those who had awaited the coming of the Holy Spirit— "in all about a hundred and twenty" (Acts 1:15)—included this wide range of persons mentioned in Joel's prophecy. The initial group gathered in the Upper Room contained the eleven apostles, several unnamed women,[31] Mary the mother of Jesus, and Jesus' brothers (v. 14)—hence already a var-

ied group of people. With the number of believers increasing to some one hundred and twenty the range would surely be even wider. It is not difficult to visualize the prophecy of Joel being thus fulfilled when the Holy Spirit was poured out at Pentecost.[32]

However, the "all flesh" on the Day of Pentecost, despite the diversity, was represented by Jews only. This, to be sure, was no small thing, for Israel had never before known such a visitation of the Spirit. Other Old Testament prophets had also spoken of a day when the Spirit would be poured out specifically on Israel. Isaiah declared, "Thus says the LORD . . . . Fear not, O Jacob my servant, Jeshurun whom I have chosen . . . I will pour my Spirit upon your descendants, and my blessing on your offspring" (Isa. 44:2–3). Ezekiel similarly spoke for the Lord: "I will not hide my face any more from them, when I pour out my Spirit upon the house of Israel, says the LORD God" (Ezek. 39:29). The Spirit of God would some day be poured out on Jacob's house, the house of Israel.

On another occasion after Pentecost the Spirit was said to have been poured out, this time on Gentiles. This occurred when Peter preached the gospel to the Roman centurion Cornelius and his household in Caesarea. Luke writes,

---

[29] Or "poured forth" (NASB), "shed forth" (KJV). The Greek word is *execheen* (from *ekcheō*). and has the basic meaning of outpouring.

[30] Recall my earlier discussion in chapter 7, I., under "Special Tasks and Functions."

[31] Luke, the author of Acts, in his Gospel account of the resurrection of Jesus had spoken of "Mary Magdalene and Joanna and Mary the mother of James and the other women" (Luke 24:10) as those who, first informed by the angels about Jesus' rising from the dead, then reported the Resurrection to the apostles. Probably they were all in the room also awaiting the coming of the Holy Spirit.

[32] From the reading of Acts 2 alone one could possibly believe that the coming of the Holy Spirit was to the eleven apostles only. According to verse 1, "they were all together in one place." Verse 14, which later refers to "Peter, standing with the eleven," might suggest that the Pentecostal outpouring was only upon the apostles. However, Acts 1 so definitely points to the one hundred and twenty that there can be little doubt that the larger group was included. As I. H. Marshall says, "The whole group of 120 people is doubtless meant, and not just the . . . apostles" (*The Acts of the Apostles*, TNTC, 68). Ernst Haenchen similarly writes, "At the dawning of the day of Pentecost, the Christians, i.e., the one hundred and twenty persons of 1:15, were all gathered together" (*The Acts of the Apostles*, 167).

"All the circumcised [i.e., Jewish] believers who had come with Peter were amazed, because the gift of the Holy Spirit had been poured out[33] upon the Gentiles also" (Acts 10:45 NASB). The astonishment of the Jewish believers who came with Peter is quite noticeable. They themselves had doubtless experienced the Spirit's outpouring, but for all its extraordinary range—not limited to any sex, age, or class—the Jewish believers were scarcely prepared for this extension to the Gentile world. The "all flesh" prophesied by Joel actually, and amazingly, also came to include Gentile flesh!

From the reading of these two accounts concerning the Jewish disciples in Jerusalem and the Gentiles in Caesarea, it is apparent that the outpouring of the Spirit occurred on both occasions.[34] There is no suggestion that the coming of the Spirit in Jerusalem was a once-for-all matter, or that somehow what happened in Caesarea was secondary or subordinate. The word "outpouring" is used in connection with both occasions, and the word "also" points to the equivalence of the two outpourings. Furthermore, some additional words of Peter underscore this point; for shortly

after the Holy Spirit had been poured out, Peter asked rhetorically: "Can any one forbid water for baptizing these people who have received the Holy Spirit just as we have?" (Acts 10:47). *"Just as we have,"* Peter said; in other words, there was no real difference.[35] When Peter later described his Gentile mission, he emphasized how "God gave the same gift to them as he gave to us. . ." (Acts 11:17). *"The same gift"*: the outpouring of the Holy Spirit in Caesarea was identical in essence with that in Jerusalem.

The other accounts in Acts of the coming of the Holy Spirit do not include the word "outpouring." However, another Scripture passage in the Epistles may be noted. Paul declares in Titus 3:5–6 that Christ "saved us . . . by the washing of regeneration and renewing by the Holy Spirit, whom He poured out[36] upon us richly through Jesus Christ our Savior, that being justified by His grace we might be made heirs according to the hope of eternal life" (NASB). If Paul is here speaking of the same outpouring of the Spirit as is found in Acts,[37] it is apparent that this

---

[33] The Greek word is *ekkechutai* (likewise from *ekcheō*).

[34] This serves to demonstrate, as earlier noted, that the coming of the Holy Spirit is a continuing event.

[35] There were additional sound and light effects (see Acts 2:2–3) preceding the first outpouring of the Spirit in Jerusalem; however, the reception of the Spirit was identical (including speaking in tongues; see the next chapter).

[36] The Greek word for "poured out," *execheen*, in Titus 3 is a form of the same word *ekcheō* found in Acts 2 and 10.

[37] Charles L. Holman writes that "the language and context of Spirit reception in these two verses point back quite distinctly to the pentecostal outpourings described by Luke in Acts, and especially to the initial outpourings on the day of Pentecost" ("Titus 3:5–6: A Window on Worldwide Pentecost," in *Probing Pentecostalism*, 55). I agree with this statement. The problem, as Holman also sees it, is "whether such an outpouring was considered integral to one's salvation experience." "However," Holman adds, "Titus 3:6 is quite parenthetical in the train of thought in 3:5–7 and is thus somewhat dissociated from a *necessary* connection with the 'salvation' of verse 5, which does include a work of the Spirit" (67, italics his). If that is the case, I would add—in line with a hermeneutic that gives primary importance to the narration in Acts—that the outpouring of the Spirit, while surely presupposed, is *not* integral to the salvation experience.

outpouring extended beyond Acts into the life of the early church.[38]

In this connection it is interesting to observe that reference was made in two early noncanonical writings to outpourings of the Holy Spirit. In his first letter (ca. A.D. 96) to the church in Corinth, Clement of Rome wrote, "A profound and abundant peace was given to you all, and ye had an insatiable desire for doing good, while a full outpouring of the Holy Spirit was upon you all."[39] The Epistle of Barnabas (not later than A.D.130) begins: "All hail, ye sons and daughters, in the name of our Lord Jesus Christ. . . . I rejoice exceedingly and above measure in your happy and honoured spirits, because ye have with such effect [or "so greatly"[40]] received the engrafted spiritual gift. . . . I truly perceive in you the Spirit poured forth from the rich Lord of love."[41] *A full outpouring of the Holy Spirit* (Clement) and *the Spirit poured forth from the rich Lord of love* (Barnabas): both statements clearly attest to an abundant outpouring of the Holy Spirit in at least certain areas of the early church. The word "abundant" is surely to be connected with the outpouring of the Holy Spirit. When God gives, He does not hold back. According to the Gospel of John, "it is not by measure that he gives the Spirit" (3:34).[42] The gift of the Holy Spirit is one of plenitude and boundlessness.

Finally, it is important to emphasize several things. First, there had been no outpouring of the Spirit prior to Pentecost.[43] We have observed certain Old Testament prophecies that pointed to a future outpouring, particularly the prophecy of Joel that Peter declared to be fulfilled at Pentecost: "*This* is what was spoken by the prophet Joel."

Second, since the Holy Spirit came from the exalted Lord Jesus (recall Acts 2:33), crucified and risen from the dead, it could not have happened at any time prior to His exaltation. It was only *after* Christ had completed the work of redemption that the Holy Spirit was poured out.

Third, accordingly, the outpouring of the Holy Spirit was an event in which Christ was the essential channel. The promise was from the Father, and in that sense He was the initiator. But the

---

[38] Another passage that associates the Holy Spirit and outpouring is Romans 5:5 (earlier quoted) where Paul writes, "The love of God has been poured out *[ekkechutai]* within our hearts through the Holy Spirit who was given to us" (NASB). Paul is speaking here of a *result* of the Spirit's being given, namely, God's love "poured out." Still the same Greek word is used for "poured out," and in the larger context of Romans 5:1–5 it may refer to an ensuing experience of the Holy Spirit.

[39] *The First Epistle of Clement to the Corinthians*, 2:2, *Ante-Nicene Fathers*, 1:5. The Greek phrase for "full outpouring of the Holy Spirit" is *plērēs pneumatos hagiou ekchusis*. *Exchusis* is likewise from the root *ekcheō*.

[40] The Greek word is *outos*.

[41] *The Epistle of Barnabas, Ante-Nicene Fathers*, 1:137. The Greek word for "poured forth" is *ekkechumenon*.

[42] It is unclear in this text whether the one giving is the Father or the Son. In either case, it is a divine giving. Incidentally, KJV adds "unto him" (in italics, signifying that the words are not in the Greek). But this, I believe, misses the important note that to *whomever* God gives His Spirit, it is without measure. (See also chap. 7, note 35.)

[43] There were occasional endowments of the Spirit under the old covenant, but none could rightly be called an *outpouring* of the Spirit. Keil and Delitzsch, commenting on Joel's prophecy, say it well: "Even if the way was opened and prepared for by the prophetic endowment of particular members of the old covenant, these sporadic communications of the Spirit of God in the Old Testament times cannot be regarded as the first steps in the *outpourings* of the Spirit of God" (*Commentary on the Old Testament, Minor Prophets*, 10:216–17).

Spirit came only *through* Jesus.[44] Even as Christ was the mediator in redemption, so was He the channel in the outpouring of the Holy Spirit.

Fourth, the outpouring of the Holy Spirit was not a once-for-all event. The Incarnation, to be sure, happened only once, but Christ thereafter from the Father's right hand poured forth the Spirit at least in both Jerusalem and Caesarea. The coming of the Spirit, accordingly, was a repeated event.[45] He came and came again.

Fifth, the outpouring of the Holy Spirit stands as a continuing promise for all future generations. To all who will come to repentance and faith in Christ[46]—all whom the Lord effectually calls—the promise is given: "You will receive the gift of the Holy Spirit."

It is the conviction of those in the contemporary Pentecostal/charismatic renewal that this renewal is an outpouring of God's Holy Spirit.[47] Since the beginning of the twentieth century there have been three major Pentecostal/charismatic movements: (1) the classical Pentecostal (beginning in 1901) now represented by a number of Pente-costal denominations, (2) the neo-Pentecostal/charismatic (beginning about mid-century) within the traditional Protestant churches, and (3) the Catholic charismatic (beginning in 1967) within the Roman Catholic Church. These three movements, according to Vinson Synan, Pentecostal historian, are three streams that basically constitute one outpouring of the Holy Spirit. Synan writes, "There is only one outpouring of the Holy Spirit in the latter days, although the streams flow through channels known as 'classical Pentecostalism,' Protestant 'neo-Pentecostalism,' and the 'Catholic charismatic renewal.' In the end it adds up to one great historical phenomenon which has had a profound effect on Christianity around the world."[48] That there are three streams but essentially one latter-day outpouring is the general testimony of the worldwide Pentecostal/charismatic renewal.[49]

B. Falling On

A second descriptive term used for the coming of the Holy Spirit is *falling on*. This language occurs in both the Samaritan and the Caesarean accounts.

---

[44]Recall my earlier discussion of this.

[45]This needs continual emphasis because of the erroneous teaching that the Holy Spirit was *given* to the church at Pentecost. As a case in point, the Roman Catholic Church officially views the original Pentecostal event as a permanent gift of the Holy Spirit wherein the Holy Spirit became "the soul" of the church.

[46]Eduard Schweizer writes that, according to Luke, "the outpouring of the Spirit can be repeated wherever men come to faith" (TDNT, 6:411). Hence, I would add, this applies to people of any time and place.

[47]I have been careful to say "*an* outpouring of God's Holy Spirit." Hence what follows about the Pentecostal/charismatic renewal by no means is intended to rule out other outpourings—or claims to such outpourings—since New Testament times. I will, however, be dealing basically with the Pentecostal/charismatic renewal in what follows. *Renewal Theology* (both volumes 1 and 2) is particularly related to this renewal.

[48]*In the Latter Days: The Outpouring of the Holy Spirit in the Twentieth Century*, ix.

[49]Synan, on the size of the renewal, quotes from David Barratt's *World Christian Encyclopedia* (1980) thus: "All persons professing or claiming to be Pentecostal-charismatics [number] over 100,000,000 world-wide" (Ibid, p. 18). It is interesting that Barratt himself, at the North American Conference "The Holy Spirit and World Evangelization" held in 1987, declared that "the worldwide charismatic movement has tripled in the past 10 years to total 277 million adherents worldwide" ("The Holy Spirit and World Evangelization," *Christianity Today* [Sept. 4, 1987], 45).

Let us begin with the event in Caesarea, for prior to the use of the word "outpouring" the term "falling on" is used. Luke writes, "While Peter was still saying this [his sermon to the Gentiles], the Holy Spirit fell on[50] all who heard the word" (Acts 10:44). Later Peter, rehearsing the event, stated: "As I began to speak, the Holy Spirit fell on[51] them just as[52] on us at the beginning" (11:15). Unquestionably, the Holy Spirit had fallen on the centurion and his company.

We note with interest that in both Luke's description and Peter's later account there is a note of *suddenness:* "While Peter was still saying" and "As I began to speak" both suggest an unexpected occurrence. There was a divine interruption of Peter's speaking activity; the Holy Spirit suddenly fell.

This matter of suddenness may also be observed in the account of the Pentecostal event in Jerusalem. On the Day of Pentecost the Jewish disciples were all gathered together when "suddenly a sound came from heaven like the rush of a mighty wind" (Acts 2:2). This was unmistakably the coming of the Holy Spirit and happened suddenly with no advance notice.[53]

Immediately we should add the word *forcefully.* For the coming of the Holy Spirit at Pentecost "like the rush of a mighty wind" was forcible,[54] strong, and driving. There was nothing quiet or hidden about it; it made an impact on all. The expression "fell on" suggests the same note of forcefulness; for when something—or someone—falls upon a person or a group, the effects are doubt-

less felt! We are dealing here, of course, with the Holy Spirit, not a thing or impersonal force; His coming was with far more memorable impact.

In all of this the *sovereignty* of God is much to be emphasized. The word "falling" connotes an action from above, from heaven to earth and therefore wholly initiated by God. This did not eliminate the human factors involved (which will be discussed later);[55] however, in both Jerusalem and Caesarea God moved in a sovereign manner to send down the Holy Spirit.

Next we observe that the word "falling" was used indirectly in another account often described as the "Samaritan Pentecost." Philip had preached the gospel to the Samaritans, and as a result they came to faith in Christ: "They believed Philip as he preached good news about the kingdom of God and the name of Jesus Christ" (Acts 8:12). However, in regard to the Holy Spirit, the narrative states that He "had not yet fallen on any of them" (v. 16). After that Peter and John came down from Jerusalem and "laid their hands on them [the Samaritans], and they received the Holy Spirit" (v. 17). Hence, by implication the Holy Spirit fell on them also, and as a result the Samaritans received the gift of the Holy Spirit.

We should observe that the apostles Peter and John laid hands on the Samaritans prior to their receiving the Holy Spirit. The laying on of hands did not happen later in Caesarea (nor earlier in Jerusalem), but the result was the same. The Holy Spirit fell on all those assem-

---

[50]The Greek word is *epepesen,* from *epipiptō* (*epi*—"upon," *piptō*—"fall").

[51]Again the Greek word is *epepesen.*

[52]Recall Peter's "just as" in the prior discussion of "outpouring."

[53]Jesus, to be sure, had told His disciples to "wait for the promise of the Father" (Acts 1:4). But He had by no means told them just when the promise would be fulfilled.

[54]The Greek word translated "mighty" is *biaias,* meaning "violent" or "forcible" (BAGD).

[55]See chapter 11.

bled.[56] Hence, in both Samaria and Caesarea the promise of the Holy Spirit was truly fulfilled.

In the twentieth-century Pentecostal/charismatic renewal, there is frequent testimony to a "falling" of the Holy Spirit. This is said sometimes to occur through the laying on of hands (as in Samaria),[57] sometimes without hands (as in Jerusalem and Caesarea).[58] In any event this "falling" is viewed as a sovereign act of God whether or not mediated through a human instrument.

C. Coming On

The primary term for the coming of the Holy Spirit is simply *coming on*. Jesus had said to His disciples shortly before Pentecost: "You will receive power when the Holy Spirit comes on[59] you" (Acts 1:8 NIV). Accordingly, Acts 2:1–4 describes the Holy Spirit's coming on them. The expression "coming on" is not, as such, used in the Pentecostal narrative; however, the fact that "there appeared to them tongues as of fire, distributed and resting *on* each one of them" (v. 3) depicts the "on-ness" of the Holy Spirit's coming.

Prior to Pentecost, it was not as if the Holy Spirit were absent from the disciples. The risen Jesus had breathed on a number of His disciples and said, "Receive the Holy Spirit" (John 20:22);[60] moreover during the forty days prior to His ascension Jesus had been giving "commandment through the Holy Spirit to the apostles" (Acts 1:2). But, still, the Holy Spirit had not yet come on them.

But had this not happened before? As we have earlier observed, there are a number of references in the Old Testament to the Spirit's coming upon various persons. For example, the Scripture says that the Spirit of the Lord "came upon," "clothed," or "came mightily upon" several of the judges. Much the same thing was said of Saul and David. However, this was largely temporary to enable a person to fulfill a certain role or function, such as judg-

---

[56] For further discussion of the laying on of hands, see chapter 11.

[57] The beginning of the Pentecostal renewal is generally dated to the first day of the twentieth century and to the experience of Agnes Ozman. She had asked Rev. Charles Parham to lay hands on her according to the example in Acts. She said, "It was as his hands were laid upon my head that the Holy Spirit fell upon me and I began to speak in tongues, glorifying God. . . . I had the added glory and joy my heart longed for and a depth of the presence of the Lord within that I had never known before, It was as if rivers of water were proceeding from my innermost being" (Klaude Kendrick, *The Promise Fulfilled*, 52–53). Note the words "The Holy Spirit *fell*. . . ."

[58] Rev. James Brown, one of the first Presbyterian ministers to become active in the "neo-Pentecostal" renewal, writes about an experience in his church: "There came a day when the Spirit of God invaded our small Saturday evening prayer group, where we met to pray for the Sunday worship service. Literally, the Spirit fell! He electrified everyone in the room! Immediately the gifts of the Spirit began to be distributed among us and we began to see signs, wonders, and miracles" (*Presbyterians and the Baptism in the Holy Spirit*, "Signs, Wonders and Miracles," 6–7). Again note that "the Spirit of God *invaded* . . . the Spirit *fell*. . . ."

[59] The Greek word is *epelthontos* ("coming upon") from *eperchomai*.

[60] See the earlier discussion of this in chapter 7, III.A. This was the occasion when Jesus breathed new life into the disciples. Thus they "received" His Spirit within themselves. This was not yet the giving and receiving of the Holy Spirit at Pentecost. Leon Morris writes, "It is false alike to the New Testament and to Christian experience to maintain that there is but one gift of the Spirit. . . . John tells us of one gift and Luke of another" (*The Gospel According to John*, NICNT, 847).

ing, ruling, or prophesying.[61] But with the outpouring of the Holy Spirit at Pentecost the situation was quite different, for the Holy Spirit came to remain.[62]

In regard to the Spirit's remaining, we may call to mind that when the Holy Spirit descended on Jesus, the Spirit remained. John the Baptist declared, "I have beheld the Spirit descending as a dove out of heaven, and He remained upon Him" (John 1:32 NASB). John added that God the Father said to him, "He upon whom you see the Spirit descending and remaining upon Him, this is the one who baptizes in the Holy Spirit" (v. 33 NASB); consequently, the Spirit will remain on all who receive Him through Jesus Christ.[63]

Before proceeding further we should observe one additional instance in the Book of Acts where the language of "coming on" is used. This is the later account of the apostle Paul ministering to the disciples in Ephesus. These Ephesians had come to faith in Christ and been baptized by Paul. Then the climactic moment occurred "when Paul laid his hands upon them, the Holy Spirit came on them" (19:6). In correspondence with the earlier significance in Acts, this coming on was a permanent one.

Now we may raise the question, What did this coming on and remaining mean? Perhaps the best answer is that it signified a *taking possession* by the Holy Spirit. Henceforward, the Holy Spirit was to be the controlling factor in their lives and ministry. It was not that the Jewish disciples or the Ephesians possessed the Holy Spirit after His coming; rather, it was that the Holy Spirit possessed them.

Here we quote some earlier words of Jesus: "Stay in the city, until you are clothed with power from on high" (Luke 24:49). The picture of being clothed, or endued, with the Holy Spirit contains the note of a continuing endowment. When the Holy Spirit comes and endues, not only will there be total possession but also activity after that will be vested with His presence and power.

"Coming on" and "being clothed with" are two aspects of the same operation of the Holy Spirit. The former terminology, in the active voice, expresses the divine side, namely, that the Holy Spirit thereby lays claim to or possesses people. The latter terminology, in the passive voice, expresses the human aspect, namely, that people are thereby invested with the Holy Spirit. A person does not himself put on the Holy Spirit; rather, the Holy Spirit clothes the person. Possession *by* the Holy Spirit and investment *with* the Holy Spirit: these are two aspects of God's gracious action.

In the contemporary spiritual renewal there is frequent testimony to the Holy Spirit's possession and investment. Whatever may have been the previous relation to God, many people sense a fresh and total claim on their lives. "I may have had the Spirit before, but now the Spirit has me"—such is a typical testimony of participants in the renewal. This points to a disposses-

---

[61] See my earlier discussion of this in chapter 7, I. Recall that David was the only expressed exception to the temporariness of the Spirit's coming: "The Spirit of the LORD came mightily upon David from that day forward" (1 Sam. 16:13).

[62] See the prophecy of Isaiah 59:21: "This is my covenant. . . . My Spirit, who is on you, and my words that I have put in your mouth will not depart from your mouth, or from the mouths of your children, or from the mouths of their descendants from this time on and forever" (NIV). This refers to believers under God's future covenant.

[63] The picture, mentioned earlier, of the Spirit's *resting* on the disciples at Pentecost suggests this remaining.

sion of the self so that one may be possessed by the Holy Spirit.[64]

Before going farther it is important to stress that the terminology thus far used in this chapter—"outpouring," "falling on," and "coming on"—points to a coming of the Holy Spirit from without and beyond. The experience of the Spirit thus depicted is not some kind of mystical participation in the immanent presence of God. Rather, the language suggests a profound experience of the transcendent God coming powerfully to people. In some ways it is a kind of spiritual invasion from the heights to the depths. But the coming from without and beyond is by no means to break down or destroy. It is rather (as we will discuss more fully later) a gracious act whereby human beings may better become participants in the purpose and activity of God.

D. Baptizing

Another term related to the coming of the Holy Spirit is *baptizing*. As we have earlier noted,[65] Jesus said to His disciples: "John baptized in[66] water, but before many days you shall be baptized in[66] the Holy Spirit" (Acts 1:5).

Accordingly, the event on the Day of Pentecost recorded in Acts 2:1–4 was the fulfillment of this promise; they were all baptized in the Holy Spirit. Although the expression is not used in Acts 2,[67] it undoubtedly applies. The phrase "baptized in the Holy Spirit" is found on one other occasion in Acts when Peter recounted what had happened to the Gentiles in Caesarea. We have previously noted that Peter said, "As I began to speak, the Holy Spirit fell on them just as on us at the beginning" (11:15). Then Peter continued, saying: "And I remembered the word of the Lord, how he said, 'John baptized in water, but you shall be baptized in the Holy Spirit'" (v. 16). Thus although the expression "baptized in the Holy Spirit" is not directly used in either account (Acts 2 or Acts 10), it is apparent that both occasions were baptisms[68] in the Holy Spirit.[69] By extension, since we have noted the use of such other terms as "outpouring," "falling on," and "coming on" associated with the coming of the Holy Spirit, we may properly speak of all these as occurrences of being baptized in the Holy Spirit.

---

[64] In the Roman Catholic spiritual renewal Leon Joseph Cardinal Suenens has played a leading part. He writes in his book *A New Pentecost?*: "We are not alone any more, we know we are guided by the Holy Spirit. As we dispossess ourselves, our being is possessed by God. The void is filled. . . . Those who allow themselves to be possessed by God resemble the log that little by little becomes white-hot. Their life, nourished by the fire of the Holy Spirit, becomes fire in turn. Is not this the fire of which Jesus spoke when he said: 'I have come to bring fire on the earth. . .' (Luke 12:49)? This is what it means to experience the Holy Spirit, who alone can renew the face of the earth!" (p. 70).

[65] Refer to chapter 7, III.C.

[66] I am continuing to substitute "in" for "with." Recall chapter 7, n. 43.

[67] The expression used in Acts 2:4 was "filled with the Holy Spirit" (see discussion of "filling" in next section). However, 2:1–4 was unmistakably the fulfillment of Jesus' promise.

[68] The noun *baptism* is not found in relation to the Holy Spirit. The coming of the Spirit is an event, a dynamic occurrence, a "being baptized." However, I do not think it improper to use the substantive form (similarly with "outpouring," which as such does not appear either; the text each time has "poured out") if one bears in mind its eventful quality.

[69] F. F. Bruce errs, I believe, in saying that "the baptism of the Spirit which it was our Lord's prerogative to bestow was, strictly speaking, something that took place once for all on the day of Pentecost" (*The Book of Acts*, NICNT, 76). Peter's own words in Caesarea contradict Bruce's statement.

It is important to emphasize that the expression cannot properly be rendered as "baptized by[70] the Holy Spirit." "By" would imply that the Holy Spirit is the agent. However, it is evident that Jesus is the agent, the baptizer, not the Holy Spirit. This is especially apparent when we recall the words of John the Baptist: "I have baptized you in water; but he [Jesus] will baptize you in the Holy Spirit."[71] Even as water is not the agent in water baptism, neither is the Spirit the agent in Spirit baptism. Water and Spirit are the elements in which baptism takes place.

One additional place (besides Acts and the Gospels) that possibly refers to being baptized in the Holy Spirit is 1 Corinthians 12:13. This text, however, reads in the Revised Standard Version: "By[72] one Spirit we were all baptized into one body—Jews or Greeks, slaves or free—and all were made to drink of one Spirit." It could be argued that Paul is dealing with a different matter here, namely, a baptism by the Holy Spirit, so that the Holy Spirit (unlike the cases in the Gospels and Acts) is the agent. However, since the Greek word trans-

lated "in" (en) is the same as that in the Gospels and Acts, it would seem preferable to translate it thus: "*In* one Spirit[73] we were all baptized. . . ." Accordingly, the Holy Spirit is again seen as element and not agent, and Christ (though not mentioned directly) is implied to be the agent.[74] That this is the more likely interpretation also follows from the second half of the verse: "all were made to drink of one Spirit." Incidentally, this latter statement may also be translated "all were imbued [or "saturated"][75] with one Spirit." Since the word "baptize" means to immerse, the best translation of the verse would then be "In one Spirit we were all immersed . . . and all were saturated with the Holy Spirit."[76] In any event it seems clear that Paul, like the Gospels and Acts, is also talking about a baptism *in* the Holy Spirit.

The significance of the expression "baptized in the Holy Spirit" now stands forth clearly. It depicts vividly the idea of being enveloped in the reality of the Holy Spirit. Since to be baptized in water means literally to be immersed in, plunged under, and even

---

[70] The Greek preposition *en* may, in some other contexts, be translated "by" ("in," "with," or "by"); it is inaccurate here (for the reasons stated above). Likewise, "of" is incorrect.

[71] Mark 1:8. Recall the parallels in Matthew 3:11; Luke 3:16; John 1:33.

[72] "By" is found also in KJV, NASB, and NIV.

[73] So reads the ASV.

[74] Gordon Fee says, "Nowhere else does this dative [*en*] with 'baptize' imply agency [i.e., that the Spirit does the baptizing], but it always refers to the element 'in which' one is baptized" (*The First Epistle to the Corinthians*, NICNT, 606). John R. W. Stott writes, "If 1 Corinthians 12:13 were different [from the Gospels and Acts passages] and in this verse the Holy Spirit were himself the baptizer, what would be the 'element' with which he baptizes? That there is no answer to this question is enough to overthrow this interpretation, since the baptism metaphor absolutely requires an element, or the baptism is no baptism. Therefore, the 'element' in the baptism of 1 Corinthians 12:13 must be the Holy Spirit, and (consistently with the other verses) we must supply Jesus Christ as the baptizer" (*Baptism and Fullness*, 27). This is well said. See also the helpful discussion in John Rea's book, *Layman's Commentary on the Holy Spirit*, 146–51, and the chart on 256.

[75] See the article on *potizō* in Thayer where "imbue" and "saturate" are given as possible translations.

[76] Similarly EGT, in loco, says that the Corinthians "were at once *immersed in* . . . and *saturated with* the Holy Spirit; the second figure supplements the first." In line with the second figure "baptism *with* the Holy Spirit" is a possible translation.

drenched or soaked with,[77] then to be baptized in the Holy Spirit can mean no less than that. In immersion no part of the body is left untouched; everything goes under. So with Spirit baptism the whole being of a person—body, soul, and spirit—is imbued with the Spirit of God. Likewise, the community of those who are so baptized is profoundly affected in its total life. Both individual and community are touched in every area by the presence and power of the living God.

Let us look again at the contemporary spiritual renewal.[78] There is no expression more commonly used for a decisive event in many lives than being "baptized in the Holy Spirit." For what has been said about the entire person being enveloped—immersed, imbued, saturated—in the reality of God is the testimony of countless numbers of people.[79] Many also declare that the experience of a Pentecostal baptism has at last cleared a way for God to operate in a more fruitful way in their lives.[80] Baptism in the Holy Spirit has been the gateway into a new dimension of the Holy Spirit's presence and power.[81]

---

[77] BAGD points out that in the non-Christian literature of the period the word *baptizō* often meant "plunge, sink, drench, overwhelm . . . soak." Such contemporary meanings certainly affected the New Testament usage of the word.

[78] Prior to the twentieth-century Pentecostal renewal, Charles Finney (1792–1875), an evangelist and later founder of Oberlin College, had used the expression "baptism of the Holy Ghost" about an early experience in his life. A few hours after what Finney described as a face-to-face encounter with Christ, the following occurred: "I received a mighty baptism of the Holy Ghost . . . without any recollection that I had ever heard the thing mentioned by any person in the world, the Holy Spirit descended upon me in a manner that seemed to go through me, body and soul. . . . Indeed it seemed to come in waves and waves of liquid love. . . . It seemed like the very breath of God . . . it seemed to fan me like immense wings. . . . I wept aloud with joy and love; and I do not know but I should say I literally bellowed out the unutterable gushings of my heart. These waves came over me and over me, one after the other, until I recollect I cried out, 'I shall die if these waves continue to pass over me' . . . yet I had no fear of death" (*Charles G. Finney: An Autobiography*, 20–21). Finney's experience of a "mighty baptism" is being variously attested in the twentieth century.

[79] "Talk about a baptism, it was just like I was being plunged down into a great sea of water, only the water was God, the water was the Holy Spirit" (*Catholic Pentecostals*, 16) This testimony of one of the first Roman Catholics in the renewal to his "baptism in the Spirit" is typical.

[80] One of the leaders of the Azusa Street revival in California that ushered in the world-wide twentieth-century Pentecostal renewal was Frank Bartleman. Bartleman wrote about His own Spirit-baptism several years later: "When my day of 'Pentecost' was fully come [in 1906] the channel was cleared. The living waters burst forth. The door of my service sprang open at the touch of the hand of a sovereign God. The Spirit began to operate within me in a new and mightier way. It was a distinct, fresh climax and development, an epochal experience for me." Then referring to the many who had come to Azusa Street, Bartleman added: "And for this we had been shut up as a company. The preparation was world-wide, among the saints of God. The results have already made history. In fact this has proven an epoch in the history of the church just as distinct and definite as the Spirit's action in the time of Luther and Wesley, and with far greater portent. And it is not yet all history. We are too close to it yet to understand and appreciate it fully. But we have made another step back in the way to the restoration of the church as in the beginning. We are completing the circle" (*Azusa Street* [originally entitled, *How Pentecost Came to Los Angeles*], 74–75).

[81] In accordance with this Martyn Lloyd-Jones writes that "the doctrine concerning baptism with the Holy Spirit [is] . . . the most urgent, vital and crucial matter for the

E. Filling

One final term used in connection with the coming of the Holy Spirit is *filling*. It is found particularly in the accounts concerning the disciples in Jerusalem and Saul of Tarsus in Damascus.

Interestingly, the first thing said concerning the disciples at Pentecost is that "they were all filled with[82] the Holy Spirit" (Acts 2:4). Peter later speaks of this as the "outpouring of the Holy Spirit" (as we have noted before), but primarily the narrative says that they were "filled."

Before the disciples were filled, the house was filled. The sound from heaven came "like the rush of a mighty wind" and "filled all the house where they were sitting" (2:2). The filling of the house suggests the presence of God in an intensive manner throughout the place of assembly. Those gathered knew themselves to be surrounded by and enveloped in the presence of the Holy Spirit. What was felt outwardly in fullness then became an inner total experience. They were all—as community and as persons—filled with the Spirit of God. Also, before the disciples were filled, "there appeared to them tongues as of fire, distributed and resting on each one of them" (2:3). Two comments: first, this calls to mind the words that Jesus would baptize with "the Holy Spirit *and with fire*" (Matt. 3:11; Luke 3:16); second, the tongues "resting on each" contains the imagery of the Holy Spirit descending on—as in the language of "pouring out on," "falling on," and "coming on"—so that the movement is from heaven to earth.

Hence, the disciples were filled from beyond themselves. It was not simply an intensification of an inward spiritual presence: it was a divine visitation in fullness.

Next we turn to the account of Saul of Tarsus and note how he was filled with the Spirit. Three days after Saul's encounter with the glorified Jesus, Ananias went to the blinded Saul: "So Ananias departed and entered the house. And, laying his hands on him, he said, 'Brother Saul, the Lord Jesus who appeared to you . . . has sent me that you may regain your sight and be filled with the Holy Spirit' " (Acts 9:17). So did Saul, later to be called Paul, receive the gift of the Holy Spirit.

Thus the experience of Saul of Tarsus was like that of the disciples at Jerusalem who were also filled with the Spirit. It came from the exalted Lord Jesus in each case and prepared both the disciples and Saul for the work that lay ahead. Indeed, it was the gift of the Holy Spirit promised by God to all He calls to Himself. Accordingly, being "filled with the Holy Spirit" in these two cases was clearly identical with the experience of the Samaritans, the people of Caesarea, and the disciples at Ephesus. It was the initial experience of receiving the gift of the Holy Spirit.

There is one other report in Acts of a being "filled with the Holy Spirit": "The disciples were filled with joy and with the Holy Spirit" (Acts 13:52). However, this text refers to those in Antioch of Pisidia who had been disciples for some time, and therefore probably refers to an ongoing filling.[83]

Other references in Acts to being "filled with the Spirit" concern persons

---

Christian church at the present time." (*Joy Unspeakable: Power and Renewal in the Holy Spirit*, 267).

[82] Or literally, "filled of the Holy Spirit"; the Greek phrase is *eplēsthēsan pneumatos hagiou*. The genitive case is also used in other passages we will note. According to BDF, this form "with verbs meaning 'to fill, be full of' is well preserved" (p. 95).

[83] The Greek word for "filled" here is *eplērounto*, the imperfect tense, and may be translated "were continually filled" (NASB) or "continued to be full" (PHILLIPS).

who had been filled earlier. Peter, when he later addressed the high council of Jews, was "filled with the Holy Spirit" and spoke to them (4:8). Afterward when Peter and the company of disciples prayed for boldness to speak the word, "they were all filled with the Holy Spirit" (4:31).[84] Saul of Tarsus, now called Paul, is described as "filled with the Holy Spirit" when he discerned the evil intentions of Elymas the magician and spoke against him (13:9). It would seem from these passages that, in addition to the initial experience of being filled, there may be subsequent fresh fillings with the Holy Spirit.

There is also reference to a condition of fullness: some persons are said to be "full of the Holy Spirit." Stephen and Barnabas are described as men "full[85] of the Holy Spirit" (6:5; 7:55; 11:24). The requirement for those elected to serve tables (including Stephen) was that they be men "full of the Spirit and of wisdom" (6:3). Indeed, it is also important for us to note that Jesus Himself, following His baptism by John, is described as being "full of the Holy Spirit": "And Jesus, full of the Holy Spirit, returned from the Jordan" (Luke 4:1). The language of spiritual fullness bespeaks God's overflowing gift of the Holy Spirit.

Thus, along with the initial reception of the gift of the Holy Spirit described as "filling" in the case of the first disciples and Saul of Tarsus, there are later repetitions of being filled as well as emphasis on continuing fullness. Such fillings in no way invalidated the initial filling but serve to show that the concept of filling is quite complex in richness and meaning.

In this connection we may note the words of Paul in Ephesians 5:18: "Be filled with the Spirit." These words might better be translated, "Be continuously filled [or "keep on being filled"][86] with the Spirit." This is the call to a dynamic Christian life in the ongoing filling by God's Holy Spirit.

What, then is the overall significance of being "filled" or "full"? It points to that dimension of the Spirit's bestowal that relates to interiority, that is to say, the whole community or person is inwardly pervaded by the Holy Spirit. Even as the sound of a mighty wind filled all the house (which signifies every room, nook, and corner), so for all persons who are filled, every aspect of individual and communal life is touched. The human situation is pervaded in a total way by the Spirit of the living God.

In the spiritual renewal of our time there are countless numbers of persons who testify to the reality of being filled with the Holy Spirit. There may have been a sense of emptiness for some time, and now God has come in His

---

[84]I. H. Marshall writes: "The story [in Acts 4:23–31] undoubtedly means that the disciples received a fresh filling with the Spirit. . ." (*The Acts of the Apostles*, TNTC, 107). F. F. Bruce likewise speaks of this as "a fresh filling of the Spirit" (*The Book of Acts*, NICNT, 107). Howard Ervin, contrariwise, denies that there can be repeated fillings with the Spirit and claims that Acts 4:31 refers to the disciples' initial and only filling (*Spirit-Baptism*, chap. 8, "One Baptism, One Filling"). I hold (in agreement with Marshall and Bruce) that this is "a fresh filling" since many in the narrative had doubtless been filled on the Day of Pentecost.

[85]The Greek word for "full" is *plērēs* and, according to Thayer, means "thoroughly permeated with." A form of this word is found in the references in Acts and Luke.

[86]The Greek verb is *plērousthe*, a present imperative passive. According to Francis Foulkes, "the Christian is to leave his life open to be filled constantly and repeatedly with the Holy Spirit" (*Ephesians*, TNTC, 152). So reads this text in Ephesians. According to Thayer (article on πληρόω), "Christians are said to be πληροῦσθαι . . . as those who are pervaded . . . with the gifts and power of the Holy Spirit."

fullness. There may have been an increasing yearning to glorify God in all that one is and does, and now God has flooded one's being with His presence. There may have been a deep desire to be used more effectively in sharing the good news of the grace received in Jesus Christ, and now God has filled one's life and speech with fresh power. Such testimony to being filled with the Holy Spirit points to a profoundly internal experience of the Spirit of God moving throughout like wind or fire until all barriers are breached and the Holy Spirit pervades everything.[87]

This is a totality of penetration with the Holy Spirit whereby, in a new way, all areas of one's being—body, soul, and spirit (the conscious and subconscious depths)—become sensitized to the divine presence and activity. Likewise, a community of people filled with the Holy Spirit finds that their relationship not only to God but also to one another becomes suffused with a profound sense of God's moving in and through whatever takes place. Further, the experience of being filled may occur afresh by God's sovereign action and in response to new situations. However, any renewed filling is against the background of the original breakthrough of God's Spirit when the Spirit moved throughout and all barriers were broken down. For the Holy Spirit is free to move again and again, as all of life becomes redolent with the presence and wonder of Almighty God.

Concluding Remarks

1. Our discussion of descriptive terms leads us to recognize that they depict various aspects of the Holy Spirit's coming. In one sense, this is an invasion from without (the Spirit poured out on, falling on, coming on); in another, it is an immersion (being baptized in); in still another sense, it is a penetration, a permeation (being filled with). The first expresses the movement of the Holy Spirit from "on high," coming from heaven to earth, powerfully coming on people; the second depicts the ensuing situation of people so affected that they are enveloped in the reality of the Holy Spirit; the third pictures the Holy Spirit moving within to activate persons in the entirety of their existence. These are all ways of expressing the extraordinary event of the coming of the Holy Spirit.

The coming of the Holy Spirit is thus expressed in many ways. Both individually and in their totality these expressions say much. But since they all relate to the coming of God Himself in the Holy Spirit, the event is far more than any words can contain.

2. What lies at the heart of the coming of the Holy Spirit—and what these terms variously express—is the event/experience of the *dynamic presence* of God in the Holy Spirit. The Holy Spirit is poured out on, falls on, comes on; hence there is movement, action. As a result people are baptized

---

[87] "How could a man think he was passing out the bread of life every Sunday and still remain so utterly hungry himself? I was empty, and I knew it. This was the end of the line." So writes Erwin Prange about his situation as a Lutheran pastor in his first parish. Then "all at once a voice seemed to come from nowhere and everywhere. . . . 'The gift is already yours. Reach out and take it.'" As Prange then stretched out his hands toward the altar, palms up, jaws tightening, and mouth open, "in an instant, there was a sudden shift of dimensions, and God became real. A spirit of pure love pervaded the church and drenched me like rain. He was beating in my heart, flowing through my blood, breathing in my lungs, and thinking in my brain. Every cell in my body, every nerve end, tingled with the fire of His presence." See Prange's autobiographical account, *The Gift Is Already Yours*, 52–53. Although the language does not precisely describe being "filled with the Holy Spirit," the experience was one of moving from emptiness to fullness, and such a fullness Prange vividly describes.

in and filled with the Holy Spirit. All this points to a momentous event and experience of the Holy Spirit.

We are to recognize this as the active presence of God. God, to be sure, is everywhere present; indeed, "in him we live and move and have our being" (Acts 17:28). However, omnipresence is not the same as dynamic presence, namely, His presence as event—dynamic event. The heart of Pentecost and its continuation is dynamic event: it may be expressed as "God has come." The "sound . . . from heaven" like "the rush of a mighty wind" on the Day of Pentecost and "tongues as of fire" resting on each person dramatizes the divine action and presence. It is the Spirit of the living God moving dynamically onto the human scene. Although the same imagery is not repeated in other accounts, the language of "coming on," "falling on," and "filling with" continues to emphasize this divine momentum and resulting presence.

3. Since it is God Himself in the person of the Holy Spirit who comes, His very coming is a manifestation of glory. For wherever God is present His glory shines forth.

We have already observed that on the Day of Pentecost the house was filled with a sound from heaven and immediately thereafter the gathered disciples were filled with the Holy Spirit. The Old Testament background is found in the accounts of the fillings of the tabernacle and temple with God's glory. After the tabernacle in the wilderness was completed, "the cloud covered the tent of meeting, and the glory of the LORD filled the tabernacle" (Exod. 40:34). Many years later, when the temple was made ready, "fire came down from heaven . . . and the glory of the LORD filled the temple" (2 Chron.

7:1). The presence of God's glory was so awesome that Moses could not enter the tabernacle (Exod. 40:35) nor could the priests go into the temple (2 Chron. 7:2; cf. 1 Kings 8:11). God's glory, in cloud and fire, was overwhelmingly present. But at Pentecost the far greater thing was not the filling of a tabernacle or temple (or even a house) but the fact that *people* were filled with God's glory. Truly the Holy Spirit is "the Spirit of glory."[88]

Hence every coming of the Holy Spirit is a manifestation of glory. Moreover, it centers in Jesus Christ. The Incarnation itself was a manifestation of Christ's glory. So the Gospel of John affirms, "We have beheld his glory, glory as of the only Son from the Father" (1:14). The Transfiguration was a manifestation of His glory. So Peter writes, "We were eyewitnesses of his majesty. For he received honor and glory from God the Father when the voice came to him from the Majestic Glory" (2 Peter 1:16–17 NIV). The death of Christ was a manifestation of His glory. So Jesus Himself said on the evening before His crucifixion: "The hour has come for the Son of man to be glorified" (John 12:23). Hence when the Holy Spirit came at Pentecost, Christ was again glorified, for Jesus had said, "He [the Holy Spirit] will glorify me" (John 16:14). This means that the glory manifested through the Holy Spirit was the glory of Christ, for in Him all the fullness of God's glory dwelt.

A further word of Jesus in the Gospel of John is quite relevant. In His prayer to the Father Jesus said, "The glory which thou hast given to me I have given to them" (17:22). This statement refers primarily to future believers,[89] and although the words might seem to refer to the past—"I have given"—

---

[88] Peter speaks of "the Spirit of glory" (1 Peter 4:14 NIV, NASB).

[89] After praying for His own disciples (vv. 6–19), Jesus said, "I do not pray for these only, but also for those who believe in me through their word" (v. 20).

they actually point to the future as an accomplished fact.[90] The glory of Jesus, therefore, will be given to those who believe in Him. Therefore when Christ gave the Holy Spirit on the Day of Pentecost[91] and later, He was giving the gift of His glory.

EXCURSUS: THE COMING OF THE HOLY SPIRIT AND SALVATION

It is important to reiterate that none of the New Testament accounts of the coming of the Holy Spirit are concerned with salvation. The occurrence of salvation was essential background for the gift of the Holy Spirit, but the Spirit was not given to bring about salvation.

I stress this because of a frequently expressed view that the gift of the Spirit was integral to salvation. From this perspective the gift of the Holy Spirit, for example, is viewed as the gift of saving grace;[92] or it is the means of inward cleansing;[93] or it is the application of Christ's "saving benefits."[94] The gift of the Holy Spirit, however, as we have observed goes *beyond* salvation;[95] it is promised to those who

---

[90] According to EGT, in loco, "the perfect tense is used, because the gift had already been determined."

[91] This is further evidenced by the fact that the words of John 17:22—"the glory which thou hast given me I have given them"—continue: "that they may be one even as we [Christ and the Father] are one." At Pentecost after the Holy Spirit came, one of the distinctive marks of the new community of believers was their unity: "All who believed were together and had all things in common" (Acts 2:44) and "The company of those who believed were of one heart and soul" (Acts 4:32). See further discussion in chapter 12, "Effects of the Coming of the Spirit."

[92] J. D. G. Dunn writes: "The gift of the Spirit . . . is the gift of saving grace by which one enters into Christian experience and life" (*Baptism in the Holy Spirit*, 226).

[93] I. H. Marshall states in connection with Acts 2:38 that "it is the Spirit who accomplishes the inner cleansing of which baptism is the outward symbol" (*The Acts of the Apostles*, TNTC, 81).

[94] F. F. Bruce writes, "The gift of the Spirit may comprehend a variety of gifts of the Spirit, but first and foremost 'the saving benefits of Christ's work as applied to the believer by the Spirit' " (Bruce quotes another source with which he expresses agreement). Though Bruce sees a possible connection ("may comprehend") elsewhere, he here gives primacy to the application of salvation.

[95] William Neil rightly sees the gift of the Spirit as the "gift of the new power which Peter's audience has seen at work in the Pentecostal experience of the Apostles and their associates" (*The Acts of the Apostles*, NCBC, 79). Neil does not connect this gift with salvation. Eduard Schweizer writes that in Acts "salvation . . . is never ascribed to the Spirit. According to Ac. 2:38 the Spirit is imparted to those who are already converted and baptised" (TDNT, 6:412). Hermann Gunkel similarly declares, "For Acts it is a commonplace that to be a believer and to be seized by the Spirit are separate events" (*The Influence of the Holy Spirit*, 17). Kirsopp Lake states that in the various Acts passages that deal with the gift of the Spirit "there is no suggestion of regeneration by the Spirit, or of the view that salvation depends on it" (*The Acts of the Apostles*, 5:109). Nor does Calvin, it is interesting to observe, attach salvation to the early gift of the Spirit (*Acts of the Apostles*, 1:120). He writes concerning Acts 2:38: "Remission of sins and newness of life were the principal things, and this [the gift of the Holy Spirit] was, as it were, *an addition* [italics mine]." The "addition," according to Calvin, was "that Christ should show forth unto them his power by some visible gift." Calvin thereafter adds that the Spirit is now given that "we may believe with the heart unto righteousness, that our tongues may be framed unto true confession . . . that we may pass from death to life" (p. 121) There is an obvious inconsistency in Calvin here, the gift of the Spirit meaning one thing in New Testament days and something else now. However, it is important to note that Calvin was on the right track about the biblical

repent and come to faith in Jesus Christ.

None of this concerning the gift of the Holy Spirit denies the prior operation of the Holy Spirit in salvation. There could be no repentance and faith without the work of the Holy Spirit making such possible. As Jesus said about the Holy Spirit, "He, when He comes, will convict the world concerning sin" (John 16:8 NASB). Hence, on the Day of Pentecost the conviction that resulted in repentance and faith was due to the Holy Spirit. The Holy Spirit, operating through Peter's preaching, produced conviction—and without such, salvation could not occur. But salvation itself was not the gift of the Spirit.

Accordingly, we may say that in all the Acts accounts of the gift of the Spirit being received there is the prior activity of the Holy Spirit in repentance and faith, or to use another term, in regeneration. While not explicitly stated after Pentecost, it is presupposed in the various accounts of the reception of the Holy Spirit.[96] All who believed did so by virtue of the Spirit's convicting power uniting them to Christ and bringing new life within.[97]

It should be added that Acts has little to say about the activity of the Holy Spirit in the occurrence of salvation because the focus of the book is on the role of the Spirit in the outreach of the gospel.[98] This is a marked difference, for example, from the letters of Paul in which much attention is given to the Holy Spirit in the Christian life.[99] The Book of Acts, on the other hand, deals almost wholly with the Holy Spirit in witness and in mission.[100]

THEOLOGICAL COMMENT

A final theological comment: In the history of the church's reflection on the Holy Spirit there has traditionally been the tendency to subordinate the work of

account in Acts, namely, that the gift of the Spirit was "an addition" to forgiveness of sins and new life.

[96] F. F. Bruce, in commenting on the account of the Samaritans receiving the gift of the Holy Spirit, writes, "The prior operation of the Spirit in regeneration and faith is not in view here" (*The Book of the Acts*, NICNT, 188, n.34). Bruce is on target this time!

[97] Calvin says of the Samaritans' reception of the Holy Spirit that "Luke speaketh not in this place of the common grace of the Spirit, whereby God doth regenerate us . . . the Samaritans were already endued with the Spirit of adoption" (*Acts*, 1:338–39). Their regeneration by the Spirit, their enduement of the Spirit of adoption preceded their reception of the Holy Spirit. R. C. H. Lenski says much the same thing: "They [the Samaritans] had been baptized as believers, they had received . . . the Holy Spirit in their hearts, and thus regeneration, conversion, justification, the power of a new life, in a word, salvation" (*The Acts of the Apostles*, 325). Later Lenski writes in connection with the Caesareans: "This falling of the Spirit upon people . . . is entirely separate from the Spirit's reception by faith for salvation" (Ibid., 431).

[98] I will discuss this in more detail later.

[99] E.g., Paul writes about the life-giving Spirit (Rom. 8:2), walking by the Spirit (Gal. 5:16), and being sanctified by the Spirit (2 Thess. 2:13), none of which is the concern of Luke in Acts. I should add that Paul, as we have seen, also speaks frequently of the giving and receiving of the Holy Spirit. Further, he has much to say about the gifts of the Spirit (as I will later discuss in detail). However, Paul's basic concern is the role of the Spirit in the Christian life.

[100] On this matter of mission H. B. Swete comments, "The purpose of the Son's mission was to give the rights of sonship; the purpose of the Spirit's mission, to give the power of using them. As the former was realized in human history at the moment of the Incarnation, so the latter connects itself historically with the moment of the Pentecostal coming" (*The Holy Spirit in the New Testament*, 204). This is an important distinction to maintain.

the Spirit to the work of Christ. Despite the orthodox formulation of the *ontological* equality[101] of the Spirit and the Son, there has tended to be a *functional* subordination. The role of the Holy Spirit in connection with Christ has been viewed largely as applying the benefits of Christ to the believer,[102] whereas His further work in the Pentecostal coming has been seriously neglected. With the emphasis on the former, the Holy Spirit's work has been functionally subordinated to that of Christ, hence a work of applicative instrumentality.[103] Accordingly, it has been insufficiently recognized that not only does the Spirit point to Christ but also Christ points to the Spirit, and that

beyond the Spirit's work in uniting to Christ (the area of salvation) is Christ's mediation of the Spirit to others. Indeed, this latter act of mediation, from the Father through the Son, is that climactic act of the sending of the Holy Spirit. This act, presupposing redemption, represents the coming of the Spirit to a redeemed humanity. The nature of this coming, its various aspects, its purpose, and its results have been given little attention.

We may be very grateful that in the contemporary spiritual renewal the Holy Spirit is being recognized for His unique and distinctive work. It is a challenging day to be alive both theologically and experientially!

---

[101] Equality in being: the Spirit of the same essence (*homoousios*) as the Son, both equally God. Such was the church's formulation in the Nicene Creed. See vol. 1, chapter 4, "The Holy Trinity," III.A.

[102] E.g., Calvin's *Institutes*, Book III, chapter 1 on the Holy Spirit is entitled, "The Benefits of Christ Made Available to Us by the Secret Operation of the Holy Spirit."

[103] On the matter of viewing the Holy Spirit as applicative and instrumental, I would especially call attention to Hendrikus Berkhof's *Doctrine of the Holy Spirit,* where he writes, "This is the main pneumatological trend in ecclesiastical theology. The Spirit is customarily treated in noetical, applicative, subjective terms. He is the power which directs our attention to Christ and opens our eyes to his work. The main result of his work is the awakening of faith in Christ. His work is merely instrumental. . . . So the Spirit is a second reality beside Christ, but entirely subordinate to him, serving in the application of his atoning work" (p. 23). Berkhof expresses dissatisfaction with this long tradition and urges that "the Spirit is far more than an instrumental entity, the subjective reverse at Christ's work." I gladly confess to having received helpful insight from what Berkhof has said in this connection.

9

The Phenomenon of Tongues

An extraordinary feature related to the coming of the Holy Spirit was the phenomenon of people's speaking in tongues. Let us examine this from various perspectives, first in the Book of Acts and later in the Epistles.

I. OCCASIONS

On several occasions in Acts when the Holy Spirit came, people spoke in tongues. The disciples who gathered on the Day of Pentecost "were all filled with the Holy Spirit and began to speak in other tongues,[1] as the Spirit gave them utterance" (2:4). This tongues-speaking preceded Peter's later address to the multitude (vv. 14–36). In Caesarea, where Peter first preached the gospel to the Gentiles, speaking in tongues occurred after the Holy Spirit was poured out. Luke writes, "The believers . . . who came with Peter were amazed, because the gift of the Holy Spirit had been poured out even on the Gentiles. For they heard them

speaking in tongues[2] and extolling God" (10:45–46). When Paul laid his hands on the Ephesians, "the Holy Spirit came on them; and they spoke with tongues[3] and prophesied" (19:6). Thus the coming of the Spirit in Jerusalem, Caesarea, and Ephesus was accompanied by speaking in tongues.

In the case of Samaria, speaking in tongues, while not specified, seems clearly to be implied. After the statement "they received the Holy Spirit" (8:17), the scripture reads, "Now when Simon [the magician] saw[4] that the Spirit was given through the laying on of the apostles' hands, he offered them [Peter and John] money, saying, "Give me also this power, that any one on whom I lay my hands may receive the Holy Spirit' " (vv. 18–19). What Simon saw, in all likelihood, was the Samaritans speaking in tongues, something extraordinary beyond his previous abilities in the realm of the occult. As a result he was willing to pay for the

---

[1] The Greek phrase for "to speak in other tongues" is *lalein heterais glōssais*. From *lalein glōssais* the word "glossolalia" is derived.

[2] The Greek phrase is *lalountōn glōssais*.

[3] The Greek phrase is *elaloun te*.

[4] Literally, "seeing," a participle. The Greek word is *idōn*.

power to lay hands on others for similar miraculous results. That the Samaritans spoke in tongues was the most logical reason for his request. Both the word structure in Acts 8:18–19 and the context imply that the Samaritans spoke in tongues.[5]

Concerning Saul of Tarsus and his being filled with the Holy Spirit, the Book of Acts is silent about his speaking in tongues. However, by Paul's own later testimony he spoke of his personal practice. In writing the Corinthians Paul says, "I thank God that I speak in tongues[6] more than you all" (1 Cor. 14:18). It is quite possible, though Luke does not say so specifically,[7] that Paul first spoke in tongues when he was filled with the Spirit.

To summarize: the record in Acts clearly states that in the majority of

cases—three out of five—those who received the gift of the Holy Spirit spoke in tongues; there is strong likelihood that this happened in four out of five; and it is possible in all five instances that people did so speak. The evidence in Acts does not allow us to draw an absolute conclusion that speaking in tongues invariably followed the reception of the Spirit; however, the texts much incline in that direction.[8]

It is of further significance that in the three accounts where tongues are explicitly mentioned, *all* of the people spoke in tongues. It was not the expression of one or two, or some, or many, but all. At Pentecost "they were *all* filled . . . and began to speak" (all 120 of them); at Caesarea "they heard *them* [the centurion and all his company] speaking in tongues; and at Ephesus

---

[5] Regarding word structure in this passage, A. T. Robertson states that the "participle [*idōn*] shows plainly that those who received the gift of the Holy Spirit spoke with tongues" (*Word Pictures in the New Testament*, 3:107). Concerning context, F. F. Bruce states that "the context leaves us in no doubt that their reception of the Spirit was attended by external manifestations such as had marked His descent on the earliest disciples at Pentecost" (*The Book of the Acts*, NICNT, 181). Johannes Munck writes that "Simon, who by virtue of his earlier life closely observed all wondrous faculties and powers, was struck by the apostles' ability to make the baptized prophesy and to speak in tongues by the laying on of hands" (*The Acts of the Apostles*, AB, 75). William Neil speaks of "an outburst of *glossolalia*" occurring among the Samaritans: "Simon sees the power of the Apostles to bring about an outburst of *glossolalia*" (*The Acts of the Apostles*, 123). There can be little doubt that the Samaritans spoke in tongues.

[6] The Greek phrase is *glōssais lalō*.

[7] Ananias was commanded by the Lord to lay his hands on Saul so that he might regain his sight (9:11–12). When Ananias laid his hands on Saul, it was for a twofold purpose: that Saul might regain his sight and that he might be filled with the Holy Spirit (v. 17). Luke states that Saul regained his sight (v. 18), and the reader is left to supply the fact that he was also filled with the Holy Spirit. Quite possibly, then, tongues-speaking is also implied. We have just observed the clear-cut statement in Acts 8 that the Samaritans did receive the Holy Spirit, with the strong implication that they spoke in tongues. Acts 9 strongly implies the reception of the Spirit by Saul and is silent about tongues—but Luke may be asking the reader to supply both. If both the reception of the Spirit and tongues were common knowledge and experience to Luke's readers (as I believe they were), he scarcely needs to say so each time. Incidentally, this same point may be made about belief in Christ and baptism in water. Often Luke specifically mentions water baptism in connection with faith in Jesus Christ (see Acts 2:38, 41; 8:12–13, 35–38; 9:18; 10:48; 16:14–15, 31–33; 18:8; 19:5); on other occasions he describes people coming to faith without reference to water baptism (see Acts 9:42; 11:21; 13:12, 48; 14:1; 17:12, 34). However, it is very likely that Luke would have the reader assume the occurrence of water baptism when it is not mentioned. Such baptism was doubtless common experience and practice in the early church.

[8] Ernst Haenchen puts it more directly: "The Spirit makes itself known in Acts by the gift of speaking in tongues" (*The Acts of the Apostles*, 304).

immediately following their speaking in tongues the Scripture adds, "There were about twelve of them in *all*" (19:7).[9] Speaking in tongues, wherever mentioned, was not the activity of some but of the whole body of newly Spirit-filled believers.[10]

II. PRIMARY ACTIVITY AND EVIDENCE

Next it is clear that the *primary activity* consequent to the reception of the Holy Spirit was that of speaking in tongues. We focus on the word "primary," because although other things were mentioned, speaking in tongues was first. The Jerusalem disciples spoke in other tongues (2:4–13) and thereafter Peter both explained what had happened (vv. 14–21) and proclaimed the gospel (vv. 22–36); the Caesareans were heard "speaking in tongues and extolling God" (10:46); and the Ephesians "spoke with tongues and prophesied" (19:6). Speaking in tongues, wherever mentioned, was primary.

It follows that speaking in tongues was clear evidence that the Holy Spirit had been given. Speaking in tongues was *the* evidence in Jerusalem. The multitude whom Peter later addressed assembled at the sound of the 120 speaking in tongues: "At this sound[11] the multitude came together, and they were bewildered, because each one heard them speaking in his own language" (2:6). Although the multitude was bewildered, this extraordinary speaking[12] was unmistakable evidence that something unusual had happened. Later, of course, Peter explained that this was the fulfillment of Joel's prophecy about the outpouring of the Spirit. But the point here is that the particular evidence was the speaking in tongues.

We have earlier noted that speaking in tongues, in all likelihood, followed also the Samaritans' reception of the Holy Spirit. Here I simply mention the evidential character of such speaking. Speaking in tongues, it seems apparent, was the extraordinary occurrence that lay behind Simon the magician's offer. Speaking in tongues was also *the* evidence of a power Simon wanted for himself so that he could produce in others the same phenomenal activity.

---

[9]There is no suggestion that, in addition to the twelve who spoke in tongues, there were others who did not so speak. The figure of twelve refers to the whole group (as the context shows).

[10]Sometimes the statement is made that the apostle Paul in his first letter to the Corinthians presents a different picture. In chapter 12 Paul describes tongues as one of several apportionments of the Holy Spirit—"to another [person] various kinds of tongues" (v. 10)—and later asks, "Do all speak with tongues?" (v. 30). The implied answer is "No, not all do." Does this contradict the accounts in Acts? Not at all, when one understands that Paul is dealing in the Corinthian letters with ministry in the church and how the Holy Spirit uses a diversity of gifts for building up the body. That all at Corinth were capable of speaking in tongues is evident from later words of Paul: "I want you all to speak in tongues" (1 Cor. 14:5). But when it is a matter of the edification of the body, if all so speak, it only causes confusion and disorder. The Holy Spirit therefore manifests Himself variously (see 1 Cor. 12:7): prophecy, tongues, healings, etc. Incidentally, prophecy is also listed as one of the several gifts apportioned; yet Paul makes it clear that prophecy is not limited to a few: "You can all prophesy one by one" (1 Cor. 14:31).

[11]The sound (*phōnē*) here refers to speaking in tongues and not to the earlier sound (*ēchos*), like "the rush of a mighty wind" (v. 2). The former sound (or "noise" [NASB, NEB]) preceded the disciples' being filled with the Holy Spirit and happened quickly. After this, they *began* to speak in tongues. Accordingly, it was this continued speaking that brought the crowd together. (So write Cadbury and Lake: "The sound mentioned here is φωνή, the voice of the inspired speakers rather than the ἠχος of the second verse" [*The Acts of the Apostles*, 4:18].)

[12]I will discuss the nature of the speaking later.

In the later accounts of the reception of the Holy Spirit in Caesarea and Ephesus, speaking in tongues may properly be called *initial evidence*. We have already observed that speaking in tongues is mentioned along with extolling God (in Caesarea) and prophesying (in Ephesus). In the former instance this combination is definitely mentioned as evidence that the Holy Spirit had been given to the Gentiles: "The believers . . . who came with Peter were amazed, because the gift of the Holy Spirit had been poured out even on the Gentiles. *For* they heard them speaking in tongues and extolling God" (10:45–46). Speaking in tongues was unmistakable evidence to Peter and those with him that the Caesareans had received the gift of the Holy Spirit. Therefore, when the Ephesians spoke in tongues and prophesied, it was also compelling evidence to Paul that they too had received the Holy Spirit.[13]

In summary, in all the accounts where speaking in tongues is specifically mentioned (in Jerusalem, Caesarea, and Ephesus) and clearly implied (in Samaria), we may properly say that speaking in tongues was the primary evidence of the people's receiving the Holy Spirit.[14]

III. NATURE AND CONTINUATION

From what has been thus far said it is apparent that speaking in tongues was the same phenomenon in all the cases recorded. For example, even as it was "the same gift"[15] of the Holy Spirit in Caesarea as in Jerusalem, so likewise the speaking in tongues must have been the same phenomenon in Jerusalem, Caesarea, and elsewhere. They were all

---

[13] Reviewing the evidence in Acts, Alan Richardson writes, "St Luke [the author of Acts] regards 'speaking with tongues' (glossolalia) as an unmistakable sign of the gift of the Spirit" (*An Introduction to the Theology of the New Testament,* 119). This, I believe, is a true statement.

[14] J. D. G. Dunn writes that if the Samaritan situation was marked by speaking in tongues (which he affirms to be "a fair assumption"), "then the fact is that *in every case* where Luke describes the giving of the Spirit it is accompanied and 'evidenced' by glossolalia. . . . Luke *intended* to portray 'speaking in tongues' as 'the initial physical evidence' of the outpouring of the Spirit [italics his]" (*Jesus and the Spirit,* 189–90). (Incidentally, Dunn used quotation marks for "evidenced" and "the initial physical evidence" as part of a quotation from a Pentecostal writer, J. R. Flower.) The Pentecostal movement from its historic beginning in 1901 has viewed speaking in tongues as the initial evidence of the gift of the Holy Spirit. In the previous chapter (n.57) I quoted the words of Agnes Ozman: "The Holy Spirit fell upon me and I began to speak in tongues." Rev. Charles Parham, head of the Bethel Bible college in Topeka, Kansas, had given his students, including Agnes, an assignment of "studying out diligently what was the Bible evidence of the baptism of the Holy Ghost" (*The Life of Charles F. Parham,* 52). To his surprise they all later reported that the evidence was speaking in other tongues. Hence when Parham laid hands on Agnes and prayed for her, it was with her expectation of receiving the Holy Spirit and giving evidence of it by speaking in tongues. According to Klaude Kendrick, "Although Agnes Ozman was not the first person in modern times to speak in 'tongues,' she was the first known person to have received such an experience as a result of specifically seeking a baptism in the Holy Spirit with the expectation of speaking in tongues. . . . For this reason the experience of Agnes Ozman is designated as the beginning of the Modern Pentecostal Revival" (*The Promise Fulfilled,* 52–53). Since that time, the term "initial evidence" is often used as official parlance in many Pentecostal bodies. It is contained in the statement of faith of the Pentecostal Fellowship of North America (an association of twenty-two large Pentecostal denominations): "We believe that the full gospel includes . . . baptism in the Holy Spirit with the initial evidence of speaking in other tongues as the Spirit gives utterance."

[15] Recall Acts 11:17.

cases of glossolalia.[16] Further, since according to Acts 2:4 they spoke in *other* tongues, it would follow that all occurrences of tongues were other than what the participants ordinarily spoke. And the key to the otherness of their speech doubtless lay in the fact that the Holy Spirit was providing the utterance. What happened at Pentecost, namely, that they "began to speak with other tongues, as the Spirit gave them utterance," must have been true in all other situations.

Hence, we may now refer to the nature of speaking in tongues as *spiritual utterance*—utterance or speech given by the Holy Spirit through the voices of people. This does not mean that the Holy Spirit did the speaking. Rather "they spoke," but the source was the Holy Spirit: *"as the Spirit* gave them utterance."[17] Accordingly, the speaking derived from the Holy Spirit was "other" than usual speech: it was spiritual, or pneumatic, utterance.

Before proceeding further, we should guard against three mistaken viewpoints. First, there is the view that speaking in tongues at Pentecost was *not* the same phenomenon that occurred later—that whereas at Pentecost foreign languages were spoken, in other situations they were "ecstatic or inspired" utterances.[18] This viewpoint actually distinguishes between two kinds of otherness: the otherness of foreign languages[19] and that of ecstatic[20] or inspired utterance. Such a distinction, however, brings inconsistency into the scriptural accounts and, for another thing, would have been wholly rejected by Peter, who made no differentiation between the tongues spoken at Caesarea and those spoken in Jerusalem.

A second view claims that all cases of glossolalia were basically emotional utterances. What occurred at Pentecost and after was an experience of great excitement in which noncognitive exclamations occurred. In relation to Pentecost, the apostles and others had been long awaiting the arrival of the promised Holy Spirit, so when the event occurred and they were "filled," they gave vent to their excitement in highly emotional, even frenzied utterance. The wildness of Pentecost (from this per-

---

[16]Recall footnotes 1–3. Philip Schaff in his *History of the Christian Church* puts it well: "The Pentecostal glossolalia was the same as that in the household of Cornelius in Caesarea after his conversion, which may be called a Gentile Pentecost, as that of the twelve disciples of John the Baptist at Ephesus, where it appears in connection with prophesying, and as that in the Christian congregation at Corinth" (1:230–31).

[17]The word translated "utterance" is *apophthengesthai,* literally "to speak out." *Apophthengesthai* is a term used of "the speech of the wise man [in Greek literature] . . . but also of the oracle-giver, diviner, prophet, exorcist, and other 'inspired' persons" (BAGD). This inspired speech is given by the Holy Spirit through the lips of men.

[18]Richard N. Longenecker refers to the speaking at Pentecost as "languages then current"; the tongues in Caesarea as "probably . . . ecstatic utterances" (*Acts of the Apostles,* EBC, 9:271, 394). Paton J. Gloag writes, "We are not . . . constrained to suppose that these Gentile converts spoke in foreign languages, as the converts on the day of Pentecost did; but the meaning may only be that they gave vent to inspired utterances, holy ejaculations" (*Acts of the Apostles,* 1:385). One may detect some hesitancy in both statements. The reason, I submit, is that both are out of accord with the biblical testimony.

[19]Tongues as presumably foreign languages is sometimes called *xenoglossolalia* (from *xeno* = foreign + *glossolalia*) and thus viewed differently from the later *glossolalia*. *Xenoglossolalia* is *not* a biblical term but an interpretation of what occurred at Pentecost.

[20]The NEB translates speaking in tongues at Caesarea and Ephesus as "tongues of ecstasy" (19:6). Since the NEB translates the tongues spoken in Jerusalem as "other tongues," there is the implication of foreign languages at Pentecost but ecstatic utterance after that.

spective) is demonstrated by the reaction of many in the multitude, who said, "They are filled with new wine" (Acts 2:13). Since this was the case at Pentecost, all later glossolalic utterance, even if to a lesser degree, demonstrated a high level of emotional excitement. Glossolalia thus signified the removal of psychological inhibitions and the breaking out in exuberant nonsensical speech.[21] To reply: This view founders quickly on the fact that the primary glossolalia narrative, the account of Pentecost, demonstrates intelligible content in these utterances. For before the scornful words about "new wine" were expressed, the Scripture reads that "each one heard them speaking in his own language" (v. 6; cf. v. 11). Hence although the disciples at Pentecost—and others later—may not have been speaking foreign languages,[22] there was intelligible content. Thus that this was mere emotional utterance is clearly an inadequate viewpoint.

Third, there is the view that speaking in tongues refers to speaking foreign languages. On the presumption that speaking in "other tongues" at Pentecost refers to speaking the languages of many peoples, those who hold this view believe that tongues spoken elsewhere were likewise foreign languages.[23] Although this position is a consistent one, namely, that tongues was the same phenomenon throughout, it makes little sense that the Caesareans and Ephesians were speaking foreign languages. At Caesarea the only people present to hear the tongues were Peter and the "believers from among the circumcised" (10:45) who came with him; at Ephesus the only other person present was Paul. It would have been pointless to speak foreign languages on these two occasions.

To return to the main point, speaking in tongues in all cases was spiritual utterance. People were speaking, but the source was the Holy Spirit. Accordingly, it was not the normal speech of everyday language; it was *transcendent* speech. If the word *ecstatic* is used (as many interpreters do),[24] this must mean

---

[21] Kirsopp Lake writes that "this kind of glossolalia [i.e., at Pentecost] is very common in history, and is merely the removal of inhibitions under the stress of great emotion." Again, "it was a deeply moving psychological experience" (*The Acts of the Apostles,* 5:117, 120).

[22] See below for further discussion of this matter.

[23] R. C. H. Lenski writes in his commentary *The Acts of the Apostles* that at Pentecost "the disciples spoke in foreign languages that were hitherto unknown to them" (61); in Caesarea "the miracle is the same, a sudden speaking in languages the speakers had never learned" (432); in Ephesus it was "the same speaking in foreign languages that occurred at the time of Pentecost" (784).

[24] F. F. Bruce describes tongues at Pentecost as "words spoken by the apostles in their divine ecstasy" (*The Book of the Acts,* NICNT, 17). EGT refers to the speaking at Caesarea as "jubilant ecstatic praise" (Acts 10:46 in loco). William Neil speaks of people in Jerusalem as "in the grip of . . . spiritual ecstasy"; at Caesarea there were "ecstatic cries of praise"; and the event at Ephesus was a "special manifestation of ecstatic utterance" (*The Acts of the Apostles,* NCBC, 73, 140, 203). I hesitate to use the word "ecstasy" because of the possible connotation of frenzied and uncontrolled behavior, speech that is an irrational, emotional utterance without intellectual content. For example, in the statement of Mark 3:21 "He is beside himself," the Greek word is *exestē,* a form of the verb *existēmi* and the noun *ekstasis.* Thus, though "ecstasy" may describe transport, joy, etc., it also tends to suggest unbalance, lack of control, and even madness. *Ekstasis* can also mean amazement, astonishment, or a state of confusion and bafflement. For example, the multitude, each person hearing speech in his own language, "were amazed [*existanto*] and wondered ["marveled" NASB], saying, 'Are not all these who are speaking Galileans?' " (Acts 2:7). Accordingly, it was the crowd hearing the tongues who were "ecstatic," not the disciples

ecstasy in the sense not of the irrational but of the suprarational. Unmistakably at Pentecost, as we have noted, there was intelligible content even if there was an outward character that could be interpreted as the speech of inebriation.

Here we note again that the tongues at Pentecost are spoken of as "other tongues." The word "other" suggests that glossolalia is both different and meaningful, hence it quite possibly refers to *another kind of speech*. "Other" can refer to a qualitative difference,[25] hence in this case not additional tongues but tongues of a different kind. If that is the meaning of "other" in this text, it underscores an amazing fact, namely, that the tongues being spoken were not like any other human tongues; indeed they were the Holy Spirit's own self-expression.

Let us look more closely. Some persons, as we have noted, view the tongues spoken at Pentecost as foreign languages. Earlier I have commented on the difficulty of harmonizing this with later instances of glossolalia. But now one may advance the argument that Pentecostal tongues must have been foreign languages because, according to Acts 2:6, "each one heard them speaking in his own language," and 2:11, "we hear them in our own tongues speaking of the mighty deeds of God" (NASB). What is said in these passages, however, is not the hearing *of* one's own language but the hearing *in* one's own language. Such being the case, at the same moment that "other tongues" were spoken through the Holy Spirit, they were immediately translated by the same Holy Spirit into the many languages of the multitude.[26] Closely related is the gift of interpretation that Paul describes in 1 Corinthians (12:10, 30; 14:5, 13). This gift follows a tongue and is given so that hearers can understand in their own language.[27] In any event the tongues spoken at Pentecost and thereafter were not foreign languages but pneumatic speech—the speaking by the Holy Spirit through the mouths of human beings.[28]

---

speaking them! On this point see also Larry Christenson, *Speaking in Tongues,* 24. Christenson is a Lutheran pastor and a leader in the contemporary renewal.

[25] The Greek word for "other" in Acts 2:4 is *heterais*. According to Thayer, *heteros* can refer to either *number* or *quality*. *Number* signifies additional, hence more than one; *quality* means difference in kind—"not of the same nature, form, class, kind." If *heteros* in this verse means number, then this would be the speaking of additional languages (Arabic, Greek, Chaldean, etc.); if quality, it would mean other languages of a different "nature, form, class, kind." The latter meaning seems correct in the context of Acts 2. A scripture that illustrates this sense is Mark 16:12: "After this he [Jesus] appeared in another (*heterā*) form to two of them." Christ's other form—His resurrection body—was certainly different from His physical body in form. It was now a spiritual body.

[26] Hence there is *both* a miracle of speech—other, different, spiritual tongues—*and* a miracle of understanding: each made possible by the Holy Spirit.

[27] Of course, Paul is depicting three parties involved: the one who speaks in tongues, the interpreter, and the one(s) to whom the interpretation is given. However, I am suggesting that in this first outburst of tongues the Holy Spirit provided His own interpretation. No interpretation is mentioned in the other Acts accounts.

[28] There is, however, the other viewpoint discussed earlier that speaking in tongues is the miraculous speaking of foreign languages (*xenoglossolalia*). For example, it was said of Saint Francis Xavier (1506–52), who went as a missionary to the Far East, that "God restored to St. Francis the gift of tongues; for he preached often to the Chinese merchants . . . in their mother-tongues, which he had never learned" (Alban Butler, *The Lives of the Fathers, Martyrs and Other Principal Saints,* 4:444). In the beginning of the twentieth-century Pentecostal movement there was a strong conviction that tongues were "missionary

One additional word may be added about the otherness of tongues. That this was a different kind of speech is further evidenced by the words of Mark 16:17: "And these signs will accompany those who believe: in my name they will cast out demons; they will speak in new tongues."[29] The very word *new* in the Greek[30] suggests a contrast with the old. It follows that tongues at Pentecost and thereafter were not additional languages but tongues that had never been spoken before.

The quotation from Mark 16 also suggests that speaking in tongues will be a *continuing experience*. There is no intimation that new tongues will be spoken only once, any more than casting out demons will be a one-time experience. In all cases Acts, to be sure, records tongues only in immediate connection with the coming of the Holy Spirit; however, there is no statement that tongues ceased thereafter. In regard to Acts 2, it is possible that the statement that the Jerusalem disciples *"began"* to speak with other tongues

---

tongues"—i.e., languages given for the preaching of the gospel in the native tongues of people everywhere. *The Apostolic Faith,* published by the Azusa Street Mission, stated in two early articles in 1906: "The gift of languages is given with the commission, 'Go ye into all the world and preach the Gospel to every creature.' The Lord has given languages to the unlearned, Greek, Latin, Hebrew, French, German, Italian, Chinese, Japanese, Zulu and the languages of Africa, Hindu and Bengali and dialects of India, Chippewa and other languages of the Indians, Esquimaux, the deaf mute language and, in fact, the Holy Ghost speaks in all the languages of the world through His children. . . . God is solving the missionary problem, sending out new-tongued missionaries" (*Apostolic Faith* [Sept. 1906], 1; [Nov. 1906], p. 2, quoted in *Azusa Street and Beyond,* L. Grant McClung, ed., 33–34). It was not long, however, before the missionary use of tongues was seriously questioned and the need for language study began to be stressed. This is good because there is no suggestion in Acts 2 that the tongues spoken were "missionary tongues." The tongues were addressed to God—declaring His "wonderful works" (v. 11)—and not to people. It was not until *after* tongues were spoken and explained (vv. 1–21) that Peter preached to the assembled multitude. Many Pentecostals, however, have continued to affirm that there are still occasions when foreign languages are spoken. See, e.g., Stanley H. Frodsham, *With Signs Following* (1946), chapter 12, and Ralph W. Harris, *Spoken by the Spirit: Documented Accounts of "Other Tongues" from Arabic to Zulu* (1973). Such accounts do indeed point to the occurrence of a miracle. However, with the account of Pentecost as our guide, the best way to describe such a happening is that it is not a foreign language that is being spoken but an "other" tongue, which through the Holy Spirit people hear in their own language. (Incidentally, in regard to documentation, tongues spoken have on occasion been recorded and later checked for language content. Evidence that they are a particular human language is totally lacking. This does not deny the miraculous character of tongues; indeed, quite the opposite, for by such documentation of questionable earthly content the way is left open that tongues may be spiritual utterance!) I might add that when tongues are understood in their basic content (see next section), the idea of tongues as human languages becomes wholly irrelevant.

[29] I recognize that Mark 16:17 is part of the "long ending" in Mark, viewed by many scholars as an interpolation added some time later in the second century. Whether this is true or not, the relevant matter is that "new tongues" are mentioned, which indicates an ongoing place in the early church. Dunn writes, "The significance of the reference is then that, with the Christian mission probably already a century old, speaking in tongues was regarded as a typical sign of the gospel's expression in the first century and perhaps also in the second" (*Jesus and the Spirit,* 246).

[30] The Greek word is *kainos.* According to Thayer, *kainos* "denotes the new primarily in reference to *quality*" (in comparison with *neos,* which denotes the new primarily in reference to *time*). *Kainos,* accordingly, is similar to *heteros* in the latter's qualitative meaning.

intimates continuation.[31] In any event Paul refers to his own experience of glossolalia as a present and ongoing fact: "I thank God that I speak in tongues . . ." (1 Cor. 14:18). He did not say, "I spoke," but "I speak."[32] Hence speaking in tongues, it seems completely clear, was a continuing experience beyond the initial reception of the Holy Spirit.

It is also apparent that speaking in tongues continued in the church at Corinth. The final words of 1 Corinthians 14:18 (quoted above) are "more than you all." This suggests that glossolalia was widespread in Corinth.[33] Indeed, speaking in tongues seems to have been practiced by everyone there; "more than you *all*" implies this. Also, Paul later wrote, "If . . . the whole church assembles and *all* speak in tongues . . . (v. 23).[34] All the Corinthian believers, it seems, spoke in tongues.[35] There needed to be regulation of the practice[36] but not its prohibition, for in the last words that Paul wrote on the subject he said, "Do not forbid speaking in tongues" (v. 39). Speaking in tongues, to summarize, clearly continued at Corinth as a common practice of the whole congregation.[37]

---

[31] It is interesting that the same word "began" in Acts 2:4 (*ērxanto*) is also used in Acts 1:1—"In the first book [the Gospel of Luke], O Theophilus, I have dealt with all that Jesus *began* [*ērxato*] to do and teach." What Jesus began, He continued to do; indeed the Book of Acts is a continuation beyond His lifetime on earth. Luke may have intended us to understand likewise that what began at Pentecost continued thereafter. Robert E. Tourville writes, "They 'began' . . . denotes a historical fact that they started, with a continuation but not stating the point at which it stopped." Then Tourville adds regarding Jesus, "What He began to do and teach we know continued through the disciples. . . . Then it is logical to think they continued to speak in other tongues" (*The Acts of the Apostles*, 27–28).

[32] The Greek word is *laleō,* a present indicative that signifies continuing action.

[33] It also suggests that Paul himself spoke *much* in tongues. To use the vernacular: Paul was the "champ" in this area—"more than you all"!

[34] Paul is by no means approving such churchwide utterance in tongues, for (as the verse continues) "if . . . outsiders or unbelievers enter, will they not say you are mad?" The relevant point here, however, is that the Corinthians could all speak in tongues.

[35] An earlier statement by Paul, "I want you all to speak in tongues" (v. 5), might suggest that some, but not all, spoke in tongues and that Paul wanted all others to do likewise. However, in light of what is said in verses 18 and 23 (as quoted above), it seems more likely that Paul is expressing approval of everyone's speaking in tongues. Paul does add (in v. 5), "but even more to prophesy." Evidently the Corinthians were so caught up with glossolalia that they were neglecting prophecy. (I will discuss the relative merits of tongues and prophecy in chapter 14.) However, at this juncture my only concern is to point out the universal practice of glossolalia in the church at Corinth.

[36] Paul later adds, "If any speak in a tongue, let there be only two or at most three, and each in turn" (v. 27). Evidently the Corinthians were so enthusiastic about their ability to speak in tongues that they needed some order. Paul sought to provide this.

[37] One final footnote about Corinth: Paul also speaks of glossolalia as a manifestation or gift of the Holy Spirit that not all possess. In describing the manifestations of the Spirit (12:8–10) Paul says, "to another various kinds of tongues" (v. 10). Toward the end of this chapter (vv. 28–30), Paul describes various appointments in the church, listing among them "speakers in various kinds of tongues" (v. 28), and adds rhetorically, "Do all speak with tongues?" (v. 30). To understand how these individualizing statements in chapter 12 relate to the generalizing ones quoted above in chapter 14, there is need to recognize that Paul first refers to diverse gifts for body ministry and later to the fact that the whole congregation could and did speak in tongues. It was the interplay between the individual gift of tongues for body ministry and the congregation-wide ability to speak in tongues that created some of the tensions in the Corinthian church. In 1 Corinthians 12–14 Paul is often dealing with the relationship between the particular gift (or manifestation) and the general practice. I will discuss this further in chapter 14, "The Ninefold Manifestation."

We should also note that Paul in this same letter identifies speaking in a tongue with praying in a tongue. After writing, "He who speaks in a tongue should pray for the power to interpret" (14:13),[38] Paul added, "For if I pray in a tongue, my spirit prays but my mind is unfruitful" (v. 14). Hence glossolalia was for Paul a vehicle of prayer. It was also spiritual prayer, not mental; thus praying in a tongue was utterance transcending the limits of human conceptualization. Obviously such prayer was not praying in a foreign language but praying as the Spirit gave Paul utterance. It is apparent that Paul's praying in a tongue was the same in essence as that which occurred in all the Acts narratives.

Two further points are significant. First, Paul does not discount tongues because in their expression the mind is unfruitful. Nor does he discount the mind because of his ability to pray in a tongue. For after asking the question, "What am I to do?" (v. 15), Paul replied, "I will pray with the spirit and I will pray with the mind also." He gives priority to praying with the spirit, i.e., in a tongue, but affirms both spiritual and mental prayer as important. Second, Paul then added, "I will sing with the spirit and I will sing with the mind also" (v. 15). In this context it is apparent that singing with the spirit refers to singing in tongues and that singing with the mind relates to singing with understanding.[39]

Paul's letter to the Ephesians may provide some parallels to the above statements. There is likely reference to singing in tongues in chapter 5, where Paul writes, "Be filled with the Spirit, addressing one another in psalms and hymns and spiritual songs"[40] (vv. 18–19). These "spiritual songs," or "Spirit-inspired songs,"[41] were in all likelihood songs uttered in tongues.[42] If so, Paul's words here parallel his references to singing "with the spirit" in 1 Corinthians 14.[43] Also in regard to praying "with the spirit" (in 1 Cor. 14), there is a likely parallel with Paul's words in Ephesians 6 where the apostle says, "Pray at all times in the Spirit" (v. 18).[44]

That such praying is glossolalic prayer is suggested not only by the similarity to the wording in 1 Corinthians 14 but also by the admonition "at all times." Since praying with the spirit, unlike praying with the mind, does not call for mental conceptualization, it can be carried on in the midst of other activities.

Now we may move on to observe

---

[38] For a discussion of interpretation see also chapter 14.

[39] The KJV translates, "I will sing with the understanding also."

[40] The Greek phrase for "spiritual songs" is ōdais pneumatikais. The same expression occurs in Colossians 3:16.

[41] So F. F. Bruce translates ōdais pneumatikais (Ephesians, NICNT, 380).

[42] Dunn says that "the word 'spiritual' . . . characterizes the song so described as one prompted by the Spirit and manifesting the Spirit" and refers to "spontaneous singing in tongues" (Jesus and the Spirit, 238–39). It is interesting that the Jerusalem Bible says in a note on Colossians 3:16 that "these 'inspired songs' could be charismatic improvisations suggested by the Holy Spirit during liturgical assembly."

[43] Also note the possible parallel between singing with the understanding and singing "psalms and hymns."

[44] Dunn, commenting on the verse, says, "In every specific situation hold yourself open to the prayer of the Spirit" (Jesus and the Spirit, 239). Prayer of the Spirit, I believe, is glossolalic prayer. Although Dunn immediately adds, "Cf. Eph. 5:18ff.," where, as noted, he speaks of "spontaneous singing in tongues," Dunn hesitates to draw quite the same conclusion about Ephesians 6:18. However, he includes Ephesians 6:18 among other "possible allusions to glossolalia" (245).

other possible allusions to glossolalia in the New Testament. Jude 20 may first be mentioned because the language is quite similar to that of Ephesians 6:18. Jude reads, "Pray in the Holy Spirit." The reference seems clearly to point to glossolalia.[45] Next we turn to Romans 8:26, where Paul writes that "the Spirit himself intercedes for us with groans[46] that words cannot express" (NIV).[47] Since the immediate background is that "we do not know what we ought to pray for" (also v. 26 NIV), the point of what follows is that the Holy Spirit intercedes on our behalf with deep articulations inexpressible in human words. Hence, these "groans" or "sighs" are not the activity of praying with the mind but with the spirit or, better, in the spirit. Indeed, this is the language of the Holy Spirit—glossolalic utterance.[48]

Paul in 1 Thessalonians 5:19 may also refer to speaking in tongues: "Do not quench the Spirit." The verse that follows reads, "Do not despise prophesying" (v. 20). Before examining these words in 1 Thessalonians, let us return for a moment to 1 Corinthians and note Paul's words in 14:39: "Earnestly desire to prophesy, and do not forbid speaking in tongues." In that letter prophecy and tongues are conjoined in an affirmative manner, with a strong injunction against forbidding tongues. In line with these words in 1 Corinthians 14 it seems quite likely that "Do not quench the Spirit" is another way of saying, "Do not forbid speaking in tongues" (even as "Do not despise prophesying" and "Earnestly desire to prophesy" are related). Moreover, the continuing conjunction of prophecy and tongues through 1 Corinthians 14 further suggests that tongues and prophecy are alluded to in 1 Thessalonians 5. In any event, to forbid speaking in tongues is surely a serious way of quenching the Spirit.[49]

---

[45] Richard J. Bauckham, in commenting on Jude 20, states that the language "indicates charismatic prayer in which the words are given by the Spirit" (*2 Peter and Jude*, WBC, 113). Dunn writes, "A reference to charismatic prayer, including glossolalic prayer, may . . . be presumed for Jude 20" (*Jesus and the Spirit*, 246).

[46] "Sighs" (RSV). The Greek word is from *stenagmos*—"sigh, groan, groaning" (BAGD).

[47] The Greek word is *alalētois*. The RSV and NASB read "too deep for words." The words are unutterable in ordinary speech.

[48] Hermann Gunkel in his classic work of 1888 entitled *Die Wirkungen des Heilige Geist*, now issued under the title *The Influence of the Holy Spirit*, writes, "There can be no doubt as to what Paul means by the Spirit's sighs that are too deep for words. They are uttered by the Christian in a condition in which he is no longer able clearly to express the feelings which powerfully seize him but pours these out in sighs, 'whose meaning words cannot express.' Now these sighs are conceived [by Paul] . . . as the sighs of the Spirit himself. *They are therefore glossolalic-ecstatic outbursts*" [italics mine] (80–81). F. F. Bruce says that "speaking to God in the Spirit with 'tongues' . . . may be included in this expression, but it covers those longings and aspirations which well up from the spiritual depths and cannot be confined within the confines of everyday words" (*The Epistle of Paul to the Romans*, TNTC, 175). I believe Bruce's statement is too weak; however, at least he recognizes the possible glossolalic connection in Paul's words. Gunkel, rightly, I think, saw much more. J. Behm writes that "the Spirit comes to aid him [the believer] in his weakness and represents him before God by the babbling [*sic!*] of glossolalia" (TDNT 5:813).

[49] Dunn refers to 1 Thessalonians 5:19 as one of several "possible allusions to glossolalia" (*Jesus and the Spirit*, 245). Incidentally, Dunn in this place also mentions Romans 8:26; Ephesians 5:19; 6:18; Colossians 3:16; "and possibly 1 Cor. 5:4." Leon Morris says that "the use of the Greek negative *mē* [in "do *not* quench the Spirit"] with the present imperative here denotes a command *to cease from doing something already in process*" (italics mine). Then Morris adds, "Most commentators take the injunction as referring to ecstatic gifts of the Spirit, such as speaking with tongues. . . . It is possible that this is what

From the New Testament references cited it is apparent that speaking in tongues continued into the New Testament church. What is recorded as happening in Acts several times and referred to in Mark 16 is an aspect of the life of the early church. As we have seen, this was the case not only in Corinth but also in other New Testament communities of faith.[50] Although there are possible differing interpretations of some of the Scriptures adduced, the overall picture comes through clearly: speaking in tongues was a common experience in New Testament times.

In regard to the Book of Acts we have observed that speaking in tongues was closely connected with the coming of the Holy Spirit. The Epistles make no such direct connection. Since, as earlier noted, many of the Epistles refer to the giving and receiving of the Holy Spirit, it seems likely that this is the general background for speaking in tongues.[51]

Before leaving this section I will make a few additional remarks about speaking in tongues, for, as is well known, speaking in tongues occupies a place of importance in the contemporary spiritual renewal. Furthermore, there is the testimony of countless numbers of people that their speaking in tongues was closely related to an original experience of receiving the gift of the Holy Spirit. Now with the biblical background in mind, I will make some comments.

---

1. The Holy Spirit provides the language

The human apparatus—mouth, tongue, vocal cords—is in full operation when tongues are spoken, but the words are not from the speaker; they are from and by the Holy Spirit. Human existence has been so penetrated by the Holy Spirit that words come forth in a new vein. A transposition thereby occurs so that human language becomes in an extraordinary way the vehicle of the Holy Spirit.[52]

---

is in Paul's mind, for the injunction to cease from quenching the Spirit is unusual." Morris, however, later expresses his doubt, for "the evidence cited cannot be said to be strong, and the words are very general" (*The Epistles of Paul to the Thessalonians,* TNTC, 104). I believe that the "most commentators" Morris mentioned are right and that Paul is referring to speaking in tongues. (Indeed, Morris's own statements seem to point to this direction until he finally states a contrary position.)

[50]To summarize the data thus far given, references directly stated or implied include Mark 16:17; Romans 8:26; 1 Corinthians 12–14 (*many* references in these three chapters); Ephesians 5:18–19; 6:18; Colossians 3:16; 1 Thessalonians 5:19; and Jude 20. Others could be added. For example, Gunkel also mentions the cry of "Abba! Father!" by us (Rom. 8:15) and by the Spirit (Gal. 4:6): "In Rom. 8:15 and Gal. 4:6 as well, glossolalic utterances are cited [by Paul] as words of the Holy Spirit" (*The Influence of the Holy Spirit,* 66).

[51]It may be significant that speaking in tongues is mentioned or implied, as we have noted, in Corinth, Rome, Ephesus, and Thessalonica. All those churches were said to have received the gift of the Spirit (recall section I, introduction). The letter of Jude, which also refers to (or implies) glossolalia, is the only exception. However, prior to his injunction "Pray in the Holy Spirit"Jude does make a cryptic reference to "worldly people, devoid of [literally, "not having"] the Spirit" (v. 19). This implies that those to whom Jude wrote were people "of the Spirit" and thus could "pray in the Holy Spirit."

[52]C. S. Lewis in his address entitled "Transposition" (in *Transposition and Other Addresses*) describes how a transposition occurs whenever a higher medium reproduces itself in a lower. If viewed merely from the perspective of the lower, the higher may be completely missed. Concerning glossolalia, "all non-Christian opinion would regard it as a

One speaks as the Holy Spirit gives him or her the ability to speak out.[53] There is no sense of compulsion or coercion. The Holy Spirit does not assume control, thereby forcing this speech to occur. There is no divine seizure. Rather, the person freely does the speaking, and the Holy Spirit graciously provides the language. Personal integrity is fully maintained even as individuals are able to speak forth in a way transcending anything they have ever before experienced.

The uniqueness of this speech is also related to the fact that the Holy Spirit is speaking through the human spirit. For the Spirit of God pervades the depths of the spirit of a person, and speech flows from that. The level is deeper or higher than the level of mind where speech is that of human conceptualization and articulation. The level is also more profound than that of human feelings where speech has largely an emotional content.[54] It is that level of the human spirit where the Spirit of God, speaking in and through the spirit of the human person, communicates with the transcendent God. To speak in tongues is to go beyond one's native speech into the realm of spiritual utterance.

2. Speaking in tongues has intelligible content

One of the most striking features about glossolalia is the fact that a new language is being spoken. It is a language totally unknown to the speaker, or it may be a variety of languages. Paul refers to one of the gifts of the Holy Spirit as "various kinds of tongues"[55] (1 Cor. 12:10); hence, any of these may be expressed as the Spirit wills. Whatever is spoken is the language of the Spirit.

Speaking in tongues, accordingly, is not irrational or nonsensical utterance, even though the mind is "unfruitful"[56] (1 Cor. 14:14) and there is no mental comprehension of what is being said. The very fact that interpretation may follow—or should follow in the church assembly[57]—is further evidence of intelligibility. When interpretation oc-

---

kind of hysteria, an involuntary discharge of nervous excitement" (p. 9). However, ". . . the very same phenomenon which is sometimes not only natural but even pathological is at other times . . . the organ of the Holy Ghost." (p. 10). "Those who spoke with tongues, as St. Paul did, can well understand how that holy phenomenon differed from the hysterical phenomenon—although . . . they were in a sense exactly the same phenomenon" (p. 17). Lewis later speaks about "the inevitableness of the error made about every transposition by one who approaches it from the lower medium only" (p. 19). "Transposition," accordingly, is an excellent term to express what happens when the Holy Spirit, the higher medium, is expressed in the lower, the human spirit. For the vehicle of expression, human language, becomes transposed into a new dimension of utterance.

[53] Recall footnote 17.

[54] Dennis Bennett, an Episcopal priest who is sometimes called the "spiritual father" of the neo-Pentecostal or charismatic renewal, writes in his book *Nine O'Clock in the Morning* about his initial experience of speaking in tongues: "The language was being given me from the central place in me where God was, far beyond the realm of my emotions. Speaking on and on, I became more and more aware of God *in* me. . . . God living in me was creating the language. I was speaking it—giving it voice, by my volition, and I was speaking it to God Who was above and beyond me. God the Holy Spirit was giving me the words to talk to God the Father, and it was all happening because of God the Son, Jesus Christ" (p. 23). Bennett's experience of baptism in the Spirit and speaking in tongues occurred in 1960 while he was rector of St. Mark's Church in Van Nuys, California.

[55] The Greek phrase is *genē glōssōn*, literally, "kinds of tongues."

[56] The Greek word is *akarpos*.

[57] See 1 Corinthians 14:12–13.

curs[58] and people hear and understand, this affirms that the original utterance contained meaning.

Speaking in tongues is suprarational utterance. It is totally beyond the capacity of a human to articulate. In 1 Corinthians 13:1 Paul may have been referring to this when he spoke of "the tongues of men and of angels," the latter possibly signifying glossolalia.[59] In any event speaking in tongues, while fully intelligible to God, is language beyond human capacity to speak or understand.

This is a far different picture from that of glossolalia as a kind of nonsensical speech or incoherent babbling.[60] Speaking in tongues is wholly the opposite: since the Holy Spirit is "the Spirit of truth," when He gives utterance through a person or persons, truth is being spoken. Such speech is far removed from nonsense and incoherence. Indeed, to speak "as the Spirit gives utterance" is the ultimate in intelligible expression.

3. Glossolalia is a new and peculiar sign

It is important to recognize the sign character of speaking in tongues. When the disciples of Jesus spoke in tongues on the Day of Pentecost, it was a *new* occurrence in biblical history. Although there may be intimations of glossolalia in the Old Testament[61] and although there is a prophecy of Isaiah that Paul connected with speaking in tongues,[62]

---

[58]Interpretation does not mean that the interpreter, any more than the glossolalist, understands what he is saying, for interpretation is also a suprarational utterance (see discussion in chapter 14, "The Ninefold Manifestation"). However, interpretation is in the known language.

[59]Gordon Fee says that "the Corinthians at least, and probably Paul, thought of tongues as the language(s) of angels" (*The First Epistle to the Corinthians*, NICNT, 630). Dunn writes that "Paul thought of glossolalia as speaking the language(s) of heaven" (*Jesus and the Spirit*, 244). It is possible that Paul was referring to the same thing when he wrote later in 2 Corinthians 12 about a man who "was caught up into Paradise, and heard inexpressible words [*arrēta rhēmata*]" (v. 4 NASB). He heard words beyond human expression, "something that cannot be expressed, since it is beyond human powers" (BAGD).

[60]I like the words of Peter Brunner on this: "This speech of tongues is not the babbling of babes, but it is a mode in which the inexpressible *verbal* form of the heavenly world [1 Cor. 12:3; 1 Cor. 13:1] breaks into this human world of ours" (*Worship in the Name of Jesus*, 270).

[61]E.g., in regard to Moses' seventy elders prophesying when the Spirit came upon them (recall my discussion in chap. 7, I.E.). Keil and Delitzsch speak of this prophesying "not as the foretelling of future things, but as speaking in an ecstatic and elevated state of mind, under the impulse and inspiration of the Spirit of God, just like the 'speaking in tongues,' which frequently followed the gift of the Holy Ghost in the days of the apostles" (*The Fourth Book of Moses, Commentary on the Old Testament*, 1:70). "Just like," I believe, is a good way of putting it, for though the elders' prophesying can hardly be called speaking in tongues, there is surely some kinship. George T. Montague speaks of this as "probably . . . prophetic ecstasy, as in I Sam. 10:5ff. and 19:20ff. [Saul and the band of prophets]" (*The Holy Spirit: Growth of a Biblical Tradition*, 111). Although, as previously stated, I have some difficulty with the use of the word "ecstasy," I believe that Keil and Delitzsch and Montague are pointing in the right direction.

[62]In one place Paul says, "In the law it is written, With men of other tongues [*"heteroglōssois"*] and other lips will I speak unto this people; and yet for all that will they not hear me, saith the Lord" (1 Cor. 14:21 KJV). Paul applies this free quotation from Isaiah 28:11–12 (referring to invading foreigners by whose "other tongues" God would speak to an unhearing Israel) to speaking in tongues (see the context in 1 Corinthians). Incidentally, the expression "other tongues," *heteroglōssois*, is quite similar to the "other tongues," *heterais glōssais*, in Acts 2:4.

when speaking in tongues first occurred on the Day of Pentecost, there was not a fully adequate way of relating it to the past.[63] Peter did draw on the words of Joel about prophesying—"Your sons and your daughters shall prophesy . . . my menservants and my maidservants . . . shall prophesy"—to seek to explain the disciples' speaking in tongues. Although Peter's words from Joel well bespoke this broad outpouring of the Spirit, it is obvious that the word "prophesy" cannot fully express the new phenomenon of glossolalia.

The point, then, is this: Pentecost was a new event in the history of God's mighty deeds. It was the event of the coming of the Holy Spirit, and as a new event it was accompanied by a *new* sign.[64] The new sign was not the sound from heaven ("like the rush of a mighty wind"), a thing that happened only once, but it was the sound of tongues that drew the huge crowd ("at this sound the multitude came together"). Speaking in tongues was *the* sign of a new and mighty act of God, both at Pentecost and later.[65]

Obviously, speaking in tongues was also a *peculiar* sign. When tongues were spoken on the Day of Pentecost, some observers mocked, saying, "They are filled with new wine" (Acts 2:13). For here were presumably normal men and women sounding forth like drunken people. Paul, underscoring the peculiarity of tongues, warned the Corinthians: "If, therefore, the whole church assembles and all speak in tongues, and outsiders or unbelievers enter, will they not say that you are mad?" (1 Cor. 14:23). Whether viewed as drunken babble or the antics of mad people, speaking in tongues obviously was to many observers a strange and peculiar activity.

The situation has remained much the same to this day. Glossolalia, to put it mildly, is not high on the list of proper and desirable activities. In popular perception, speaking in tongues is viewed as belonging to certain far-out sects given to emotion and frenzy; for some psychologists glossolalia represents emotional disturbance and dependent behavior;[66] and for some churchmen it

---

[63]It is sometimes suggested that Jesus spoke in tongues. This is usually based on Mark 7:34: "Looking up to heaven, he sighed, and said to him [a deaf mute], 'Ephphatha,' that is, 'Be opened.' " The Greek word for "sighed" is *estenaxen* similar to Romans 8:26 *"stenagmois alalētois,"* "sighs [or groans] unutterable," which could refer to glossolalia (see n. 48). However, I agree with Dunn who says: "Although Rom. 8:26 can be understood in terms of glossolalia with some justification . . . this is because the groans are described as 'unutterable, inarticulate, too deep for words' and ascribed to the Spirit; the use of στενάζειν by itself does not suggest glossolalia . . . [moreover] parallels break down, since in Mark 7:34 Jesus' word of healing was spoken in Aramaic, his native tongue" (*Jesus and the Spirit,* 86).

[64]Recall Mark 16:17: "They will speak in *new* tongues."

[65]A sign, however, is not identical with the reality to which it points. The gift of the Holy Spirit is the primary reality, and speaking in tongues is the sign that the gift has been received. So tongues are *not constitutive* of the gift of the Holy Spirit, that is, comprising the gift, *but declarative,* namely, that the gift has been received.

On this point it is a serious error to equate speaking in tongues with *the* gift (*dōrea*) of the Holy Spirit (although it surely is *a* gift (*charisma*) of the Spirit [1 Cor. 12:10]) or, even worse, to say that speaking in tongues is required for the Holy Spirit to be received. A sign is neither identical with nor prerequisite to the reality.

[66]John P. Kildahl states that glossolalia is a sign of "hypnotizability." "It is our thesis that hypnotizability constitutes the *sine qua non* of the glossolalia experience. If one can be hypnotized one can learn [*sic!*] to speak in tongues" (*The Psychology of Speaking in Tongues,* 54–55).

is still a taboo practice.[67] There have been, however, some changing attitudes, especially following the emergence of the neo-Pentecostal and Catholic charismatic movements in the 1960s.[68] However, speaking in tongues, even where officially recognized, is still largely viewed as undesirable behavior.

For those who speak in tongues the attitude is quite different. It may also be for them a peculiar activity (it is indeed strange to speak in tongues never learned or understood!), but it is also a special sign of something new and extraordinary in their lives. Those who have spoken in tongues bear in their own speech evidence of a miracle. They had never before so spoken, although there may have been many other spiritual experiences. Furthermore, they did not manufacture this speech;[69] rather, in all its peculiarity such speaking remains testimony to a special visitation of God and to His continuing

---

[67] The Southern Baptist Home Mission Board, according to a report in *Christianity Today* (Sept. 18, 1987), has developed a policy that "disqualifies missionary candidates who actively participate in, or promote the practice of speaking in tongues." Further, "any missions personnel already appointed, approved, or endorsed by the mission board who become involved in glossolalia will be counseled by a mission board representative. Continued participation in speaking in tongues would result in their dismissal." I may add, though it hardly needs saying, that the apostle Paul would be totally disqualified and rapidly dismissed! ("I thank God, I speak in tongues more than you all"!)

[68] Kilian McDonnell in his book *Charismatic Renewal and the Churches* shows some of the significant and positive changes in attitudes that have occurred in the social and behavioral sciences, particularly psychology, and in the official attitude of many of the historic churches. See especially chapter 3, "Enthusiasm and Institution: The Response of the Churches," and chapter 5, "The Move Toward Normality." For official statements of the churches worldwide, both Protestant and Roman Catholic, see McDonnell's edited work in three volumes: *Presence, Power, Praise: Documents on the Charismatic Renewal*. These volumes include 104 documents published between 1960 and 1980. On the whole, with some exceptions here and there, these documents show an increasingly open, though cautious, attitude officially toward glossolalia. Incidentally, the Southern Baptist negative attitude (previous footnote) was also evidenced in 1975 when certain Baptist churches in Dallas, Baton Rouge, and Cincinnati were "disfellowshiped" by the local association of Baptist churches for glossolalia and faith-healing practices. However, it is also important to observe that in June 1978 the Southern Baptist national convention voted down a motion to expel charismatic churches (see McDonnell's book, 73–75, and *Documents*, 2:114–16).
I should add that in neither McDonnell's book nor the edited volumes is tongues the main issue. The focus, as both titles suggest, is on the charismatic renewal. In his book McDonnell writes, "Any serious student of the Pentecostal-charismatic movement [whether the focus is on the classical, neo-Pentecostal, or Catholic charismatic expression], will immediately recognize that the issue is not tongues. The issue is, rather, totality of the gospel, life in Christ through the power of the Holy Spirit. . . . This is not to deny that tongues play a role, indeed is highly esteemed. But speaking in tongues is not what the Pentecostal-charismatic renewal is all about" (p. 11). I agree with McDonnell but have included reference to his books while discussing speaking in tongues because they contain valuable material that relates to glossolalia.

[69] William Samarin says, "Anybody can produce glossolalia if he is uninhibited and if he discovers what the 'trick' is" (*Tongues of Men and Angels,* 227–28), namely, the uninhibited expression of nonsense syllables. In reply I can confidently and emphatically say that anyone who has truly spoken in tongues knows that there is no possible comparison of it with human gibberish. As Simon Tugwell, a Dominican priest, succinctly says, "You cannot engineer tongues" (*Did You Receive the Spirit?* 63). This is not to say that within the parameters of the charismatic renewal there have been no counterfeit tongues—no mimicking of true glossolalia—in order to gain acceptance by others in the community.

presence and power. Tongues are—and continue to be—a special sign.[70]

IV. CONTENT

The content of speaking in tongues, according to Acts, was the *praise of God.* Here we draw basically on the Jerusalem and Caesarean accounts.

When the disciples spoke in tongues at Pentecost, they were praising God. This is apparent from Acts 2:11, which records the multitude's saying, "We do hear them speak in our tongues the wonderful works[71] of God" (KJV). We are not told for what "wonderful works" the disciples praised God. It is not hard, however, to imagine that since they had so recently lived through the events of Jesus' life, death, and resurrection, they were praising God for, among other things, having performed the great work of redemption. Also Christ had just now fulfilled the promise of the Father to pour forth the Holy Spirit.[72] They had much to praise God for.

It is important to add that when the disciples spoke in tongues, it was not for the purpose of communicating the gospel. Peter thereafter preached the gospel to the thousands assembled (Acts 2:14ff.). But prior to this, he and all the other disciples were praising God. The tongues therefore were not "missionary tongues" (as sometimes they have been designated),[73] equipping the disciples to go forth with a language given each to witness to a particular nation or people. Rather, their tongues were tongues praising God for all His wondrous deeds. Further, it is obvious from the comments of some who, "mocking, said, 'They are filled with new wine,' " that this was joyful, exuberant praise. Although this was deliberate mockery, the charge pointed to a certain rapturous joy[74] that has its counterpart in alcoholic inebriation. The point, however, was that the disciples were not filled with the wine of the grape but with the wine of the Spirit. They were praising God—*exceedingly.*

We may observe a parallel to this in Paul's words to the Ephesians in speaking against the drunkenness of wine and urging them instead to be filled with the

---

[70] Larry Christenson writes this about the objectivity of this sign: "To consummate one's experiences of the baptism with the Holy Spirit by speaking in tongues gives it an objectivity . . . regardless of feelings, that sign of the "new tongue" is there" (*Speaking in Tongues,* 55–56). Don Basham, describing his baptism in the Spirit and tongues, writes similarly, "This *was* God moving in my life more powerfully than ever before. . . . I had made entrance into a new and deeper spiritual dimension, clearly marked by praying in a language utterly unknown to me" (*Face Up With a Miracle,* 60). "Clearly marked" points up the significance of tongues as an objective and unforgettable sign.

[71] The Greek word is *megaleia,* meaning "magnificent, splendid, grand" (BAGD); "magnificent, excellent, splendid, wonderful" (Thayer). The RSV and NASB translations, respectively, as "mighty works" and "mighty deeds," do not fully capture the note of the magnificent and the wonderful. The NIV finely translates *megaleia* as "wonders."

[72] EGT, referring to *megaleia,* in loco, says that the word is "used here not only of the Resurrection of the Lord . . . but of all that the prophets had foretold, of all that Christ had done and the Holy Ghost had conferred."

[73] Recall note 28.

[74] G. C. Morgan writes, "These people were not preaching, they were praising; they were not indulging in set discourse, they were pouring out the rapture that filled their souls" (*Acts of the Apostles,* 38). Incidentally it would be a mistake to view the many languages spoken by the disciples as speech similar in unintelligibility to that of the gibberish of drunk persons. No, even the mockers understood what was being said ("each one heard them speaking in his own language" [v. 6]). The mockery, therefore, points rather to the disciples' joyous spiritual inspiration.

Holy Spirit. "Do not get drunk with wine, for that is debauchery; but be filled with the Spirit" (5:18). The result (as at Pentecost) will be joyful praise; for Paul continues, "addressing one another in psalms and hymns and spiritual songs, singing and making melody to the Lord with all your heart, always and for everything giving thanks in the name of our Lord Jesus Christ to God the Father'" (vv. 19–20). The exuberant praise of God with all one's heart flows out of being filled with God's Spirit.

Returning to Acts, we move on again to the situation of the centurion and his friends in Caesarea who were "speaking in tongues and extolling God" (10:46). Earlier I mentioned these two activities as if they were distinct. They may have been (the conjunction "and" suggests such);[75] however, it is more likely that the Caesareans were extolling God *through* speaking in tongues.[76] As we have observed, this was precisely what happened in the Jerusalem Pentecost: the disciples, while speaking in tongues, were declaring God's "wonderful works," in other words, extolling God.[77] Moreover, since Peter afterward spoke of the Caesareans as "people who have received the Holy Spirit *just as we have*" (v. 47), it seems altogether likely that just as on the Day of Pentecost the centurion and company through their speaking in tongues were extolling God.

The Book of Acts does not specify the content of the Caesareans' praise. However, since this was the original proclamation of the gospel to the Gentile world, it seems likely that the people in Caesarea were praising God for His great mercy in bringing them salvation. Peter, accompanied by his Jewish fellow believers, had preached the good news to the Gentile Cornelius and his Gentile family and friends. The Gentiles, who prior to this had "no hope and [were] without God in the world,"[78] had now heard the gospel, believed, and entered into salvation. Surely they had much to praise God for—a praise that came forth in the transcendent language of tongues.

Based on these accounts in Acts, speaking in tongues may be described as *transcendent praise:* praise that goes beyond ordinary capacity and experience. God had acted through Jesus Christ to bring about salvation and had poured out His Holy Spirit. So marvelous was this occurrence that nothing else could capture it but the transcendent praise of God. Such praise was not in an earthly language because no language of earth could begin to express the extraordinary depths and heights of the occasion. *Only* language uttered by the Holy Spirit on the lips of persons involved could be adequate. So they all praised God in the self-transcending language of other tongues.

Let us reflect for a moment on the praise of God in the worship of the church. In all true worship there is a

---

[75] See earlier discussion in section II.

[76] Gunkel speaks of this praise as "pneumatic in character . . . not the usual praise any Christian may give at any time but an ecstatic praise connected with glossolalia" (*The Influence of the Holy Spirit,* 18). EGT, in loco, calls this "jubilant ecstatic praise."

[77] Cadbury and Lake note "the Lucan tendency to vary the phrase while repeating the substance." Luke "changes λαλούντων . . . γλώσσαις τὰ μεγαλεῖα τοῦ θεοῦ ['speaking . . . in tongues the wonderful words of God'] into λαλούντων τῶν γλώσσαις καὶ μεγαλυνόντων τὸν θεόν ['speaking in tongues and extolling God']" (*The Acts of the Apostles,* 4:122). The substance, I agree, remains the same. The same Greek root is found in both Acts 2:11 and 10:46—*megal,* which connotes magnification. In both Jerusalem and Caesarea they "magnified" the "magnificent" works of God.

[78] This is Paul's language about the Gentiles in Ephesians 2:12.

desire to offer up worthy praise and adoration to Almighty God. And, according to the intensity of the sense of the Lord's presence, there is a yearning to find further ways of showing forth this praise. Ordinary language may seem to be inadequate, and perhaps some language of the past (Greek or Latin, for example) will be used in the desire for more worthy expression. There may be the use of praise language such as "Hallelujah!" or "Hosanna!" often repeated to voice an intensity of adoration. Or in the sensing of the wonder of God's grace, there may even be yearning for multiple tongues[79] as a means of declaring what is being deeply experienced. Such ways are examples that bespeak a growing concern to get beyond ordinary speech into another higher mode of worshiping God.

Here, of course, is where music occupies an important role. By moving into lyrical modes of expression, by adding melody to words, there may well be more satisfying worship of heart and soul. Thus human utterance is caught up to higher levels by the singing forth of God's praises. Yet music, even as ordinary speech, is ever seeking among ardent worshipers of God to find ways to reach still more sublime heights.

This brings us back to the praise of God in tongues. For ordinary language, even music, may be inadequate to declare the wonders of God, His deeds, and His presence. This is not to discount the various modes of human expression with all their possibilities to rise to greater heights. However, there may be a speech or language more suitable to the experience of the richness of God's dynamic presence. Humanly speaking, this is impossible, but, and herein is the marvel, God through His Spirit may go beyond what has been uttered or sung before and bring forth a new language![80]

Many of the things said above are reflected in the contemporary spiritual renewal. People have begun to praise God in tongues when under the impact of God's presence and activity in the Spirit they felt the intense desire to go beyond ordinary speech and offer Him worthy thanksgiving and praise. It was then that the Holy Spirit took over, and the praise of God in a new language broke forth.[81] Jerusalem, Caesarea, and now in the twentieth century, people extolled the wonderful works of God!

Here I would add a further word about "singing in the spirit." The ardent worshiper often goes beyond

---

[79] For example, the hymn of Charles Wesley beginning "O for a thousand tongues to sing my great Redeemer's praise" exhibits this intense yearning.

[80] This indeed is the answer to Wesley's yearning. Far better and greater than "a thousand tongues" is *one* tongue that can give full expression of praise.

[81] Larry Tomczak, a Roman Catholic layman, writes, "As thanksgiving and praise erupted from within, a profound sense of God's presence began to well up in me. I felt the rapturous and exultant joy of the Lord surging through me, and the more profuse my praise, the more intense became my desire to magnify the name of my Savior. I grew impatient with the inadequacy of the English language to fully express all that I was feeling, how much I loved God. Then, just at the right moment, new words began to flow from my heart. . . . I could not restrain my tongue, and my lips began to stammer, as a new language hopped, skipped and somersaulted from my mouth. The language was foreign to my ears, a heavenly language only God would understand. It was praise that had surged through my whole being to seek expression through the Holy Spirit in a new transcendence" (*Clap Your Hands!*, 112–13). Harald Bredesen, a Reformed pastor, succinctly states, "I tried to say, 'Thank You, Jesus, thank You, Jesus,' but I couldn't express the inexpressible. Then, to my great relief, the Holy Spirit did it for me. It was just as if a bottle was uncorked, and out of me poured a torrent of words in a language I had never studied before. Now everything I had ever wanted to say to God, I could say" (*Yes, Lord*, 59).

speech into a lyrical expression seeking to convey true worship and adoration of Almighty God. When tongues are given, this opens up in a fresh way the whole realm of spiritual singing. Such singing may not be in conjunction with the initial gift of the Spirit; indeed it often takes place later. However, it is an aspect of tongues, a singing in tongues,[82] but with the added factor of the melody also being provided by the Holy Spirit. This often happens in group worship and may be the climactic moment in the total experience of praise.[83]

Now a brief historical note: it is quite possible that out of the early praise of God in tongues has come some of the great music of the church. It has been suggested that Gregorian chant (plainsong) and certain musical parts of the liturgy emerged from the ancient practice of glossolalia.[84]

Another similar and fascinating activity in the history of the church has been *jubilation*. This may also be in some sense a continuation of glossolalia. To jubilate has been viewed as going beyond ordinary speech into a praise of God that even the most expressive words cannot convey. Thomas Aquinas (a thirteenth-century theologian) wrote, "Jubilation is an unspeakable joy, which one cannot keep silent; yet neither can it be expressed (in words) . . . it is beyond comprehension."[85] Jubilation represents various wordless outcries of joy and exaltation; hence, though it may not be identified as such with tongues (the emphasis being on wordless praise rather than praise in a new language), the connection is quite close. Each is motivated by the same intense yearning: to express the inexpressible and thus go beyond ordinary speech into the realm of transcendent praise.[86]

---

[82] Recall Paul's words in 1 Corinthians 14:14–15.

[83] "We were lifted out of ourselves in the worship of the Lord. There was a period of singing in tongues, and the variety in the sound was matched only by its harmony and the unanimity with which it began and ended, almost as if at the signal of a conductor; but there was no conductor—at least, not a human one." So writes Michael Green, an Anglican rector, about his visit to a church "full of the Holy Spirit" (*I Believe in the Holy Spirit,* 158–59). In an earlier book I described the experience of "singing in the Spirit" thus: "There may be long periods of joyful, lilting music, quite unplanned, moving back and forth through psalms, hymns, choruses, and the like—as the Spirit guides the meeting. But the climax is the moment when not only is the melody given by the Spirit but *also* the language, as words and music sung by the assembled worshipers blend into an unimaginable, humanly impossible, chorus of praise. Here is 'singing in the Spirit' at its zenith—the sublime utterance of the Holy Spirit through the human spirit to the glory of Almighty God" (*The Era of the Spirit,* 33).

[84] "The glossolalia of the early Eastern Church, as the original musical event, represents the germ cell or the original form of sung liturgical prayer. . . . In the sublime levitation and interweaving of the old Church tones, and even in Gregorian chant to some extent, we are greeted by an element that has its profound roots in glossolalia." (Words of Werner Meyer in *Der erste Korintherbrief: Prophezei,* 1945, II, 122 et seq., trans. Arnold Bittlinger; see also *Sounds of Wonder* by Eddie Ensley, 117.)

[85] Commentary on Psalm 46, as quoted in *Sounds of Wonder,* 53. Ensley gives many instances of jubilation in the history of the church and states that "indications are that jubilation is a continuation of the glossolalia of the New Testament" (115).

[86] Tongues are described as "a special language of jubilation" by Gerhard Delling in his book *Worship in the New Testament.* "The working of the Spirit brings about . . . an enthusiasm which expresses itself in a special language of jubilation, in a *praising of God which rises above the normal manner of speaking*" (italics his, 38). Incidentally, Delling's evaluation of glossolalia is also worth quoting: "It is an intimation [certainly an imperfect

We move on to Paul's description of speaking in tongues as uttering *mysteries*: "One who speaks in a tongue speaks not to men but to God; for no one understands him, but he utters mysteries in the Spirit" (1 Cor. 14:2).[87] This is an extraordinary statement about the content of speaking in tongues.

Now this could also be understood as praise, since in praise one "speaks not to men but to God." However, the emphasis here is not so much on tongues as an act of praise and worship that follows the primary experience of the visitation of the Holy Spirit, but on tongues in the continuing life of prayer. Speaking in tongues, or praying in the Spirit, has such a depth of communication between the person and God that what is said goes beyond ordinary speech into the utterance of divine mysteries. The profound reason: the Holy Spirit Himself pervades the human spirit and thereby communicates with God. Since this is an operation that transcends the human level, what is spoken likewise goes beyond the realm of ordinary knowledge and communication. This is the Spirit speaking through the human spirit the things of God.

The word "mysteries," as used by Paul, usually refers to those secret and hidden truths of God made known by special revelation. For example, Paul speaks of the mystery now made known to God's apostles and prophets that the Gentiles and Jews are "fellow heirs" in Christ (Eph. 3:4–6).[88] However, in the Corinthian context Paul is obviously not referring to those mysteries of God relating to decisive revelatory events in His dealing with mankind that are disclosed through the prophets and apostles. Rather Paul is here referring to the fact that speaking in tongues, by its very nature as spiritual utterance of the Holy Spirit, is transcendent speech, the content of which must be more than the mind can achieve.

Now we must quickly add, although the mysteries spoken in tongues are not ultimate mysteries, they are nonetheless "hidden things." One who speaks in tongues is involved in the extraordinary activity of communicating through the Holy Spirit things not achieved by the understanding. They are hidden from the highest reaches of human wisdom and knowledge.

First of all, these utterances carry the

---

and, in Paul's opinion at least, an inadequate one] of the praise and worship of God in the heavenly service; and thus at the same time an *anticipation of the future glory*. Men knew that they stood in the midst of the irruption of the coming age; they knew that in the gift of the Spirit they had received an earnest [$\dot{\alpha}\rho\rho\alpha\beta\dot{\omega}\nu$] of the consummation; furthermore the Spirit when bestowed did not remain simply a gift in the hidden chambers of the heart; it pressed for expression in special intimations in worship" (35).

[87] The KJV, NIV, and NASB have "spirit" (lowercase). Although this form is grammatically possible, it is hard to see how anyone could utter mysteries (as will be discussed above) with his own spirit. So Gordon Fee writes, "It does not seem remotely possible that in this context Paul would suddenly refer to speaking 'with one's own spirit,' rather than by the Holy Spirit" (*The First Epistle to the Corinthians*, NICNT, 656). I might add, however, that since Paul later speaks of praying in a tongue as praying with the spirit (here lowercase *s* because Paul compares such praying with the praying with the mind), such praying would also be praying in the *Spirit*.

[88] Paul uses the Greek word *mysterion* twenty-one times. He refers to a number of particular mysteries now revealed, such as the future of Israel (Rom. 11:25–26), what happens to believers at the Parousia (1 Cor. 15:51–52), the relationship between Christ and the church (Eph. 5:32), Christ in the believer (Col. 1:27), and the basic tenets of "our religion" (1 Tim. 3:16). Indeed, whatever is set forth in "the prophetic writings" (hence, Scripture in general) is "the revelation of the mystery which was kept secret for long ages" (Rom. 16:25).

speaker into the divine realm. The Holy Spirit, as Paul earlier said to the Corinthians, "searches all things, even the deep things of God" (1 Cor. 2:10 NIV). Since this is true, the speaker in tongues is primarily in communication about matters of transhuman profundity that the Holy Spirit searches out.[89] It is truly speaking "mysteries in the Spirit" concerning "the deep things of God."

Second, since the mysteries are hidden things, this may include things that relate to this life. Paul also says that "we have not received the spirit of the world but the Spirit who is from God, that we may understand what God has freely given us" (1 Cor. 2:12 NIV). Hence, one who speaks "by the Spirit who is from God" may also be opening up a deeper understanding of God's blessings. In that sense, though the speech is directed to God, it is not only about God (the "deep things of God") but about what He would have us to know about any given matter. Again, this is not knowledge derived from human reflection; rather, it originates in God's disclosure through the Holy Spirit. It is a mystery until God makes it known by the same Spirit.[90]

To utter mysteries in the Spirit lies at the heart of speaking in tongues.

Finally, speaking in tongues may also be the offering up of *prayers of supplication* to God. Herein the Holy Spirit enables the one who prays to reach a deeper and fuller level of praying.

Let us first note the words of Paul to the Ephesians about praying in the Spirit.[91] He writes, "Pray at all times in the Spirit, with all prayer and supplication. To that end keep alert with all perseverance, making supplication for all the saints" (6:18). According to Paul, prayer in the Spirit is a powerful vehicle of supplication;[92] it can occur "at all times";[93] it is comprehensive— "all prayer"; and it is far-reaching— "for all the saints." For when prayer is *in* the Spirit, it is *by* the Spirit; through Him the one who prays is offering up the Spirit's own prayers and supplications to God. There could be no richer and fuller praying than this.

Moreover, in doing this the Holy Spirit is actually helping us at a point of real difficulty, namely, not knowing what to pray for. There are always many subjects, many persons, and many needs for which we could pray. How do we know? What are we to do? Let us recall Paul's words in Romans 8:26: "The Spirit helps us in our weakness. We do not know what[94] we ought to pray for, but the Spirit himself intercedes for us with groans that words cannot express" (NIV).[95] Now let us add Paul's next words: "And he [God] who searches our hearts knows the mind of the Spirit, because the Spirit intercedes for the saints in accordance with God's

---

[89] Dunn writes that "Paul . . . characterizes the glossolalist as holding a secret conversation with God (he speaks to God—14.2); the subject matter is the eschatological secrets known only in heaven" (*Jesus and the Spirit,* 244).

[90] This calls for interpretation by the Holy Spirit. In chapter 14 I will discuss this important matter of interpretation as a gift of the Holy Spirit. At this juncture it would take us too far afield.

[91] Recall my discussion of such prayer as praying in tongues. See the previous section.

[92] The KJV puts this the clearest: "Praying always with all prayer and supplication in the Spirit." The close connection between praying in the Spirit and supplication is underscored.

[93] I will say more about "all times" in the next section.

[94] "What" is probably more accurate than "how" (as in RSV and NASB). On this matter see Everett F. Harrison, "Romans," EBC, 10:94.

[95] Recall our discussion of this in the preceding section (III) as glossolalic utterance.

will" (8:27 NIV).[96] Paul is saying that the Spirit we have received[97] makes intercession for us; the word "groans"[98] expresses the depth, even the burden, of His concern for all the world.[99] Moreover, His supplications through us are invariably in accordance with God's will, hence they cover everything for which we ought to pray.

Let me further elaborate the significance of these passages in Ephesians and Romans. All Christians have the responsibility of offering prayers and supplications, and surely this means to be as specific and comprehensive as possible. God calls upon us to pray for many persons with the mind and understanding. Paul wrote Timothy, "First of all, then, I urge that supplications, prayers, intercessions, and thanksgivings be made for all men, for kings and all who are in high positions" (1 Tim. 2:1–2). Hence, a primary place is to be given to intercession, and in that prayer we are to exercise diligence and perseverance. We need also to pray for other believers, for people who have not yet heard the gospel, and for the world and its needs: prevailing prayer is commanded of us. But still, no matter how long or inclusive are our prayers, we may ask, have we really done what we should? Moreover, how can such prayer be for "all the saints" and "for all men" when our prayers at best are so finite and so limited? This is precisely where praying in the Spirit comes in, because the Holy Spirit, and only

the Holy Spirit, knows what to pray for, for whom to pray, and how to reach out to all the world. "The mind of the Spirit" is an infinite mind.

Many believers are discovering this great help of the Holy Spirit in their prayers and supplications. Often after praying at length in one's own native tongue for many needs and many persons, it is a tremendous joy, indeed a relief, to be able to move into prayer in the Spirit. Praying with the mind is surely important; God expects it of us. But through the Holy Spirit He would like to bring our prayers to completion.

One further thought: in accordance with Paul's words, "I will pray with the spirit and I will pray with the mind also" (1 Cor. 14:15), a believer may want to begin prayers of supplication by praying first in tongues and thereafter with the mind. In so doing, the outreach of praying in the Spirit will by no means eliminate the need for praying with the understanding. Rather, it will enable a person to pray with greater specificity and assurance that God will hear his prayers because they originate in the mind of the Holy Spirit.

V. IMPORTANCE

The importance of speaking in tongues is doubtless apparent from what has already been said. However, I would like to make a few additional comments.

First, speaking in tongues is supremely *communication with God*. We

---

[96] Literally, "in accordance with God" (*kata theon*).

[97] Recalling verse 15: "Ye have received the Spirit of adoption" (KJV).

[98] In Romans 8:22–27 Paul speaks of *three* groanings: (1) the creation "groaning in travail together" (v. 22), a reference to the bondage of creation to decay and corruption; (2) "We ourselves, who have the first fruits of the Spirit, groan inwardly as we wait for . . . the redemption of our bodies" (v. 23); and (3) the groaning of the Holy Spirit. On the latter as glossolalic utterance see n. 48.

[99] According to R. W. Dale, "the whole passage illustrates in even a startling manner the truth and reality of the 'coming' of the Holy Ghost—the extent to which, if I may venture to say it, He has separated Himself—as Christ did at His Incarnation—from His eternal glory and blessedness, and entered into the life of man. . . . His intercession for us—so intimately does He share all the evils of our condition—is a kind of *agony*" (*Christian Doctrine*, 140f.).

have observed how the Jewish disciples in Jerusalem magnified God through tongues and how later in Caesarea the Gentiles similarly extolled God. The words of Paul that begin, "be filled with the Spirit, addressing one another in psalms and hymns and spiritual songs," continue with "singing and making melody to the Lord with all your heart" (Eph. 5:18–19). "Spiritual songs" (or "singing with the spirit"; recall again 1 Cor. 14:15) refer in a special way to melodic communication with God. Speaking in tongues is a way of transcending human resources and declaring in the Spirit the very mysteries of God. In all of this (and in other Scriptures mentioned) the very heart of speaking in tongues is communication with God.[100]

The importance of tongues in this connection can hardly be denied. There is surely a place for prayer and praise in one's own language (indeed, we often sorely lack here); however, since glossolalia is the language of the Holy Spirit, the communication with God through the Spirit takes on a note of extraordinary immediacy and directness.

Moreover, this is communication that the heart of the believer longs to express. Charles Wesley's words "O for a thousand tongues to sing my great Redeemer's praise"[101] is the yearning of the believer who has been deeply moved by what Christ has done. But earthly languages, even ten thousand of them, are not adequate to communicate this praise. Earthly tongues are far too limited—indeed far too soiled[102]—to express the deeds of the all-powerful, all-holy, and all-loving God. Someday, in the world to come, there will be language sufficient to express our joy and thanksgiving. But until then—or between now and then—God delights to bridge the gap between heaven and earth by granting us speech as the Spirit gives utterance. Thus He opens up in the depths of our spirits a line of communication that can more fully glorify Him. Then we can say and sing in a new way, "Bless the Lord, O my soul; and *all* that is within me, bless his holy name!" (Ps. 103:1).[103]

Again, speaking in tongues is important for *self-edification*. It is a valuable source for upbuilding the believer in his faith. Earlier we discussed how, according to Paul, "one who speaks in a tongue speaks not to men but to God; for no one understands him, but he utters mysteries in the Spirit" (1 Cor. 14:2). Shortly after, Paul adds that "he who speaks in a tongue edifies himself" (v. 4). While one is speaking through this new avenue of communication with

---

[100]I like Dunn's words about "effective communication": "*He who experiences glossolalia . . . experiences it as effective communication with God*" (italics his) (*Jesus and the Spirit,* 245).

[101]Earlier quoted in footnotes 79 and 80.

[102]According to the Book of James, "the tongue is a fire, a world of iniquity. . . . But the tongue can no man tame; it is an unruly evil, full of deadly poison. Therewith bless we God, even the Father; and therewith curse we men" (3:6, 8–9 KJV). James includes believers in his words (those who bless God the Father). How much we need *another* tongue that can purely and wholly bless God! As is sometimes said, in addition to our "mother tongue" we need a "Father tongue" that will *only* bless the Father and never do hurt to any other person.

[103]I inject here a personal word. It was shortly after saying these words of the psalmist a number of times with an intensity of desire to bless God with *all* my being that I first began to speak in tongues. I had already prayed to be filled with the Holy Spirit, and immediately thereafter God's presence became so real that I yearned to go beyond ordinary speech in blessing Him and giving thanks. To my amazement, but even more to my soul's joy and delight, God granted me this new language of the Spirit.

God, a reflexive action simultaneously occurs: the person is being edified spiritually.[104] Closely connected are the previously quoted words of Jude 20: "Pray in the Holy Spirit," which are preceded by the statement "Build yourselves up on your most holy faith." There is an upbuilding, an edification of the person through his or her praying in the Spirit.

We need to bear in mind that the spirit of a person is his deepest nature.[105] Although the mind is "unfruitful"[106] when praying in tongues, there is much inner edification.[107] The human spirit is being built up and, as a result, the whole of human nature is also being built up.

According to a well-known statement, "man's chief end is to glorify God and to enjoy Him forever."[108] This means simply that the more a person glorifies and enjoys God, the more he fulfills his true end. To glorify and enjoy God is the true end of human existence and the ultimate means of self-edification. Nothing else in all the world so edifies a person or so fulfills the purpose for which he was made as the glorification and enjoyment of God.

Now this can be done in many ways: for example, through worship, fellowship, service—indeed throughout a person's lifestyle. So we should not exaggerate the importance of speaking in tongues. Many people have glorified and enjoyed God—and will do so throughout eternity—who have never spoken in tongues. However, the relevant point here is simply that speaking or singing in tongues is the expression of highest praise and joy in the Lord, and in such expression there is great edification. The Day of Pentecost with its praise and exuberance in tongues is the paradigm of those fulfilling the "chief end" of human existence. In this glorifying of God and rejoicing in Him there was the rich edification of all. Such edification continues to this present day.

In our reflection upon speaking in tongues as speaking mysteries in the Spirit and as a profound way of intercessory prayer,[109] it is apparent that in this activity there is much self-edification. Through tongues as an avenue of uttering divine mysteries and receiving "hidden things" from God through His Spirit, one is continuously built up in faith and experience. And

---

[104]Paul's statement about edifying oneself is sometimes assumed to be a negative evaluation of tongues, i.e., that speaking in tongues is a selfish concern. E.g., John F. MacArthur, Jr., comments on this passage about speaking in tongues as "selfish ego building" (*The Charismatics,* 161). This negative viewpoint is thought to be reinforced by Paul's next words: "But he who prophesies edifies the church." However, to reply, Paul can hardly be negative here since he has just described tongues as address to God and the utterance of divine mysteries. Paul's concern in writing the Corinthians is primarily the upbuilding of the church, and tongues, *unless they are interpreted* (see v. 5), will not do that. Prophecy, needing no interpretation, can immediately edify. In this same verse Paul makes it clear that when the interpretation of tongues does occur, speaking in tongues and prophecy are equal in value.

[105]See vol. 1, chapter 9, "Man," II.B.

[106]Recall Paul's words in 1 Corinthians 14:14.

[107]Gordon Fee makes the perceptive comment that "contrary to the opinion of many, spiritual edification can take place in ways other than through the cortex of the brain" (*The First Epistle to the Corinthians,* NICNT, 657).

[108]These are the words of the answer in the Westminster Shorter Catechism to Question 1, "What is the chief end of man?" The answer given above is, I think, thoroughly in accord with Scripture. E.g., Paul writes: "Whether you eat or drink, or whatever you do, do all to the glory of God" (1 Cor. 10:31); and "Rejoice in the Lord always; again I will say, 'Rejoice' " (Phil. 4:4).

[109]See the preceding section (IV) regarding both.

the ability through the supplications of the Holy Spirit to reach far beyond one's own capacities and knowledge to the needs of many likewise results in much personal edification. Self-edification is by no means the primary concern; however, the more the focus of prayer is on God and others, the more there is personal blessing to the one who prays.[110]

To pray in the Spirit, to paraphrase Jude, is to be built up in our holy faith. Surely all believers need such edification.

Finally, speaking in tongues is an *eschatological sign*. We have earlier observed that speaking in tongues on the Day of Pentecost was both a new and a peculiar sign of the coming of the Holy Spirit. But now, and climactically, we may view this further as an eschatological sign—a sign of last things. Let us note this carefully.

Peter focused on the outpouring of the Holy Spirit and declared that this was an event signaling the end times: "In the last days[111] it shall be, God declares, that I will pour out my Spirit upon all flesh" (Acts 2:17). Peter also saw this outpouring as an event accompanied by certain signs of the end, for just after words about the outpouring of

the Spirit, Peter added, "And I will show wonders in the heaven above and signs[112] on the earth beneath, blood, and fire, and vapor of smoke." The "wonders" and "signs" probably refer both to the Day of Pentecost—the sound from heaven like a rushing wind and speaking in tongues—and to certain final events yet to come: "the sun shall be turned into darkness and the moon into blood, before the day of the Lord comes."[113] If "signs" includes speaking in tongues, which seems likely,[114] then it is quite possible that this was not only a sign of the Spirit's coming on the Day of Pentecost but also a sign to signal the final days.

Whatever the full understanding of Peter's words, it is clear that the whole event of Pentecost is seen as an occurrence in "the last days." Since the peculiar sign of Pentecost was the speaking in tongues, then such speaking, along with other signs, could well point to the final "day of the Lord."

We have previously noted reference to the Pentecostal/charismatic renewal of the twentieth century as a latter-day outpouring of the Holy Spirit.[115] If that is the case—and I believe it is—the particular sign of this renewal from 1901 forward has been generally recognized

---

[110]I will not discuss here the edification of the church that can also occur through speaking in tongues. I made brief mention of this in a previous note but will go into greater detail in chapter 14 on "The Ninefold Manifestation."

[111]In the prophecy of Joel, which Peter was quoting, the language was "It shall come to pass afterward, that I will pour out my Spirit on all flesh" (Joel 2:28). The "afterward" looks back to God's blessings received (vv. 18–27) and immediately forward to events of the last days (vv. 29–32). Hence Peter's words, though not a direct quotation, surely conveyed Joel's sense of this outpouring as an eschatological event.

[112]It is significant that Peter adds to Joel's words "signs." Joel simply reads "wonders in the heavens and on the earth, blood and fire and billows of smoke" (2:30 NIV).

[113]According to EGT, in loco, "Peter had already received a sign from heaven in the $\mathring{\eta}\chi o\varsigma$ ἐκ τοῦ οὐρανοῦ ["a sound from ḥeaven"], and a sign on the earth below in the λαλεῖν ἑτέραις γλῶσσαις ["speaking other tongues"]," but also Peter's thoughts "passed from the day of Pentecost to a period of grace and warning which should precede the Parousia."

[114]I. H. Marshall writes that "the signs are probably the gift of tongues and the various healing miracles which are shortly to be recorded" (*The Acts of the Apostles*, TNTC, 74).

[115]See the preceding chapter.

as speaking in tongues.[116] Despite almost unremitting opposition from without and occasional differences within,[117] tongues and Pentecostalism are almost inseparable in the public mind. At this juncture I regard this as a good thing because of the strong possibility of vital eschatological significance. Let me probe a bit.

Could it be that in this secular age God is sovereignly preparing His people through charismatic renewal for the consummation of history?[118] Is it possible that speaking in tongues is a sign of God's radical invasion of countless lives in preparation for the final outreach of the gospel?[119] Could speaking in tongues, despite all its strangeness, be preparation for uttering the word of God with new power?[120] If speaking in tongues signalizes the deep opening up

of a line of communication through the Holy Spirit between God and man, could this not result in better preparation to war against the powers of darkness that increasingly are pressing in upon us?[121]

I will not proceed further with such questions. However before closing this discussion of tongues as an eschatological sign, I would like to suggest that speaking in tongues is a harbinger of the coming kingdom. It has even been suggested that tongues represent "the approaching might of the kingdom of God."[122] In any event speaking in tongues, which is the sign of a divine-human immediacy, could represent the transitional phase into the future world where this immediacy will be wholly and completely realized. Now—that is, in our present flesh—there can be no

---

[116] In the words of Donald Gee, "It was the linking together of speaking with tongues and the baptism in the Holy Spirit that started off the Pentecost Revival" (quoted in Frederick D. Bruner, *A Theology of the Holy Spirit,* 48, n. 34).

[117] A few Pentecostal bodies view speaking in tongues as *one* of the evidences of the Holy Spirit rather than the *particular* sign. (See Bruner, 77, n.30.)

[118] G. Ernest Wright, an Old Testament scholar, writes, "In prophetic eschatology the consummation of the Kingdom of God is to be marked by a great revival of charismatic happenings. Both leaders and people will be Spirit-filled and Spirit-empowered on a scale hitherto unknown" (*The Rule of God,* 104). Is that what is happening now?

[119] See the next chapter for a discussion of the outreach of the gospel.

[120] I have often pondered the following extraordinary statement of Dietrich Bonhoeffer: "The day will come when men will be called again to utter the word of God with such power as will change and renew the world. It will be a new language, which will horrify men, and yet overwhelm them by its power. It will be the language of a new righteousness and truth, a language which proclaims the peace of God with men and the advent of his Kingdom" (*Prisoner for God: Letters and Papers from Prison,* 140–41). Bonhoeffer, I feel sure, did not view this "new language" as the language of tongues; however, his very wording—a language that "will horrify men, and yet overwhelm them by its power"—may well apply to the language of the Holy Spirit on the lips of people.

[121] Paul's reference to praying in the Spirit in Ephesians 6:18 is in the context of the believer's contending "against the world rulers of this present darkness, against the spiritual hosts of wickedness. . ." (v. 12). Along with "the sword of the Spirit, which is the word of God" (v. 17), praying in the Spirit is the way of withstanding the assaults of the evil one.

[122] These are Peter Brunner's words. I earlier quoted him as saying that the "speech of tongues is not the babbling of babes" (n. 60). In the same connection Brunner writes, "The New Testament shows that the verbal vessel of our language may disintegrate under the impact of the rushing new eon. This takes place in the language of tongues. . . . This rupture of speech into the speech of tongues shows us that the word will not remain unaffected by the approaching might of the kingdom of God. It, too, will be drawn symbolically into the future eschatological transformation of all things" (*Worship in the Name of Jesus,* 270).

more direct communication than through tongues: speaking to God as the Holy Spirit gives utterance. But even this will some day be transcended by the reality of seeing God face to face.[123] In the meantime we may rejoice that we are on the way to this final realization!

---

[123]Paul tells the Corinthians that some day tongues will cease: "As for prophecies, they will pass away; as for tongues, they will cease; as for knowledge, it will pass away" (1 Cor. 13:8). This will happen when we see God "face to face" (v. 12). In this present life we may be extremely grateful for what He has given us.

10

The Mission of the Holy Spirit

God the Father sends the Holy Spirit through Christ His Son. For what purpose does the Holy Spirit come? To answer this question, we will view the mission of the Spirit from several perspectives.

I. GUIDE INTO TRUTH

The Holy Spirit comes, first, to guide His disciples into all the truth. According to the Gospel of John Jesus declared, "When the Spirit of truth comes, he will guide you into all the truth" (16:13). It is noteworthy that the Holy Spirit is called the Spirit of truth,[1] for truth marks His character.[2] Hence when He comes, He will give knowledge of all the truth.

This truth is the truth that is found in Jesus Christ. Jesus had said earlier, "I am the way, and the truth, and the life" (John 14:6). Thus the Holy Spirit, who is Christ's representative[3] will speak only of the truth in Christ. Jesus explained in John 16, "He [the Spirit of truth] will glorify me, for he will take what is mine and declare it to you" (v. 14). Accordingly, "all the truth" refers not to truth in general but to the totality of truth that Christ embodies.

Thus when the Holy Spirit comes, He will be the guide to all the truth that is in Jesus Christ. The Holy Spirit will operate both from within and without. In Jesus' first statement about "the Spirit of truth," He said to His disciples, "I will pray the Father, and he will give you another Paraclete,[4] to be with[5] you for ever, even the Spirit of truth. . . . You know him, for he dwells with[6] you,

---

[1] Also in John 14:17 and 15:26. See the earlier discussion of this in chapter 6, "The Holy Spirit," II.A.1.

[2] In vol. 1, chapter 3, "God," I spoke of the character of God as holiness, love, and truth. The Holy Spirit as God accordingly has the character of truth.

[3] Jesus speaks of Him as the Holy Spirit, whom the Father would send in Jesus' name (John 14:26).

[4] For the translation of the Greek word *paraklētos* as "Paraclete," see chapter 7, III.A. *Paraklētos* literally means "called to one's side."

[5] The Greek word is *meth'*, from *meta*.

[6] The Greek word is *par'*, from *para*. "Beside" or "alongside" may be a more accurate translation than "with."

237

and will be[7] in you" (John 14:16–17). During Jesus' ministry the Spirit of truth was present "with" (or "beside") the disciples; later, on the day of Jesus' resurrection, He breathed "in" them the same Spirit (John 20:22); still later at Pentecost the Spirit of truth came to be "with" them forever. Regarding these last two stages, it is apparent that Christ's breathing into the disciples new life in the Spirit[8] was background for the Spirit's coming at Pentecost to guide them into all the truth.

It is significant that between these two events the disciples did not know the guidance of the Holy Spirit. The picture in John 21 (after Jesus breathed into them the Holy Spirit) is that of Peter and six other disciples going fishing (not for people, but for fish!), hence being very uncertain of themselves.[9] In Acts 1, although Jesus had spoken to the disciples for forty days about the kingdom of God (v. 3), they nonetheless asked, "Lord, will you at this time restore the kingdom to Israel?" (v. 6).[10] After Pentecost, how-

ever, with the Spirit guiding them into all the truth, the disciples never again referred to the kingdom as a restored Israel; the kingdom was invariably seen as a spiritual realm that may be entered by all.[11] Hence, this is further evidence that the Spirit of truth had come.

From chapter 2 onward the Book of Acts depicts persons moving in the Spirit of truth. Peter, a man filled with the Holy Spirit, proclaimed the gospel in its true and full dimensions on many occasions. Stephen, described as a person "full of the Spirit and of wisdom," showed this by his comprehensive declaration of biblical and gospel truth (Acts 7:2–53). Moreover, large numbers of believers who were forced to leave Jerusalem because of persecution "went about preaching the word" (8:4). In such accounts, which continue through Acts, the believers are clearly witnessing to the truth of the gospel.[12] The Spirit of truth was guiding them into all the truth.

Therefore, when the Holy Spirit came to various people, they now had

---

[7] Some early manuscripts have "is" (*estin*) rather than "will be" (*estai*). The weight of evidence points to the future tense.

[8] Recall the discussion of this in chapter 7, III.A.

[9] This uncertainty is also evidenced in what follows in John 21: the disciples' failure to recognize Jesus (v. 4); Peter's confusion in his conversation with Jesus (vv. 15–17); and Peter's question about John, a question for which Jesus rebuked him (vv. 20–22).

[10] According to F. F. Bruce, "the question in v. 6 appears to have been the last flicker of their former burning expectation of an imminent political theocracy with themselves as its chief executives" (*The Book of the Acts,* NICNT, 38). A. T. Robertson puts it well: "Surely here is proof that the eleven apostles needed the promise of the Father [the Holy Spirit] before they began to spread the message of the Risen Christ. They still yearn for a political kingdom for Israel. . . . They needed the enlightenment of the Holy Spirit (John 14–16) and the power of the Holy Spirit (Acts 1:4f.)" (*Word Pictures in the New Testament,* III, *Acts,* 9–10).

[11] See Acts 8:12; 14:22; 19:8; 20:25; 28:23, 31. The only other use of the word "restore" in Acts is found in Peter's words about Christ: "He must remain in heaven until the time comes for God to restore everything, as he promised long ago through his holy prophets" (Acts 3:21 NIV). This restoration obviously will go far beyond any idea of restoring the kingdom to Israel. According to F. F. Bruce, "the *apokatastasis* [restoration] here appears to be identical with the *palingenesia* [regeneration] of Matt. 19:28" (*The Book of the Acts,* NICNT, 91, n. 36).

[12] Philip the evangelist was able to open up the Old Testament Scriptures to the Ethiopian eunuch: "Beginning with this scripture [Isa. 53], he told him the good news about Jesus Christ" (Acts 8:35). Paul at the very beginning of his ministry "confounded the Jews who lived in Damascus by proving that Jesus was the Christ" (Acts 9:22).

the Guide "with"[13] them so that, following their Guide, they were able to lead others. Jesus had also said, "The Holy Spirit . . . will teach you all things" (John 14:26). Hence it was not simply a matter of immediate knowledge but also of continuing instruction. Nonetheless, from the moment the Spirit of truth came, the sure and certain knowledge of truth was essentially given to them and what they did not know would be progressively revealed to them.

It is important to recognize that the guidance of the Holy Spirit into all truth was not limited to the apostles[14] and other leaders in the early church. In the First Epistle of John (written probably toward the end of the first century), the author says, "Ye have an unction from the Holy One, and ye know all things" (2:20 KJV).[15] The unction, or anointing,[16] refers to the Holy Spirit, and the Holy One refers to Christ.[17] This special anointing had been received by those to whom the epistle was addressed, and they clearly were not apostles or other church leaders but ordinary believers. They too had received "the Spirit of truth"[18] and knew "all things." To reinforce this point John adds, a few statements later, "The anointing which you received from Him abides in you, and you have no need for any one to teach you. . . . His anointing teaches you about all things" (v. 27 NASB). This extraordinary statement does not rule out the need for teachers in the church,[19] but it does emphasize that the anointing of the Holy Spirit gives essential guidance and knowledge about all things relating to the Christian faith.[20]

A striking feature found elsewhere in the New Testament is the way in which this "all" knowledge among believers is often recognized as a given fact. Paul, near the end of his strong doctrinal

---

[13]Recalling Jesus' words in John 14:17 supra.

[14]The Johannine passages quoted thus far are sometimes assumed to be related only to Jesus' apostles, hence guidance into all truth is applicable only to them. In a primary sense this is the case because of their close relationship to Jesus, and thus such words as "the Holy Spirit . . . [will] bring to your remembrance all that I have said to you" (John 14:26). Therefore, whatever they say and teach has a foundational significance for believers after them. However, this does not mean that the words of Jesus in John 14–17 apply only to the apostles. (Would anyone think, for example, to limit Jesus' words in John 15 about His being the vine and His disciples the branches only to the apostles!) In a secondary sense they apply to all believers who receive the anointing of the Holy Spirit.

[15]"You all know" is the RSV and NASB translation (similarly NIV and NEB). The Greek manuscripts vary between *oidate panta*, "You know all things" and *oidate pantes* "You all know." However, in light of the later statement in 1 John 2:27, "His anointing teaches you about all things" (NASB, NIV), the translation of verse 20 as "you know all (things)" seems the more likely. This also better corresponds with John 14:26 and 16:23.

[16]The Greek word is *chrisma*. Jesus Himself was said to have been "anointed" by the Holy Spirit: "God anointed [*echrisen*] Jesus of Nazareth with the Holy Spirit and with power" (Acts 10:38; cf. Luke 4:18).

[17]Cf. John 6:69, Peter's words to Christ: "You are the Holy One of God." However, "the Holy One" could also mean God the Father (as in Acts 10:38, cf. n. 16). Ultimately it is God the Father through Christ; so either "God" or "Christ" may be "the Holy One."

[18]F. F. Bruce refers to the Gospel of John, saying, "They [those addressed in 1 John] have received 'the Spirit of truth' (John 14:17; 15:26; 16:13)" (*The Epistles of John,* 72).

[19]If that were the case, even John's letter would be ruled out, for it contains much teaching! John is particularly concerned with the false teachings of "many antichrists" (v. 18) and "those who would deceive you" (v. 26). Believers anointed by the Holy Spirit do not need such teachers.

[20]This is true regardless of false teachings that may circulate. The basic point is that the Spirit's anointing leads into all the truth.

letter to the Romans, wrote, "I myself am satisfied about you, my brethren, that you yourselves are full of goodness, filled with all knowledge, and able to instruct one another" (15:14). What Paul himself had written, he added, was written as a reminder: "But on some points I have written to you very boldly by way of reminder, because of the grace given me by God to be a minister of Christ Jesus to the Gentiles" (vv. 15–16). Paul therefore, despite all that he had written, did not claim to be imparting things unknown, for they were already "filled with all knowledge." His office as a minister of Jesus Christ was that of bold reminder. Consequently, Paul's declared role was to follow up on what the Romans already knew!

Peter also states in his second Epistle that his writing is by way of reminder. After detailing a number of things, Peter adds: "Therefore I intend always to remind you of these things, though you know them and are established in the truth that you have. I think it right, as long as I am in this body, to arouse you by way of reminder" (1:12–13). As with Paul, so Peter assumes a knowledge of the truth and writes to arouse his readers to remember. Nothing is said about the Holy Spirit in either of these passages; however, there is an obvious similarity between the way Paul and Peter speak of their readers being

"filled" and "established" in knowledge and John's words about his readers' knowing "all things" through the anointing of the Spirit.

It is significant that in these several cases the New Testament strikingly emphasizes the full complement of knowledge that believers possessed. I should add that this was also true in Corinth, despite the manifold sins in the congregation, for Paul wrote the church there, "I thank my God always concerning you, for the grace of God which was given you in Christ Jesus, that in everything[21] you were enriched in Him, in all speech and all knowledge" (1 Cor. 1:4–5 NASB). Could this have been due to anything less than the dynamic activity of the Holy Spirit?[22] It seems clear that "the Spirit of truth," whether mentioned directly or not, was actively guiding the early church to the full knowledge of truth.[23]

None of this means, however, that the believers had spiritually arrived. The apostolic writings of John, Paul, and Peter were, and are, highly important for clarification, reminder, and exhortation. Indeed, since the apostles had known Christ directly[24] and stood in the circle of His immediate revelation, what they said and wrote is not only full knowledge but also the touchstone and norm for all other Christian experience of the truth. Moreover, most persons, though they know the

---

[21] The Greek phrase is *en panti,* "in all things." Observe the similarity to John's *oidate panta,* "you know all things."

[22] Recall that 1 Clement spoke of a "full outpouring of the Holy Spirit" upon the Corinthians (chap. 8, III.A. supra). Also note Paul's own words in 1 Corinthians 2:12: "Now we have received not the spirit of the world, but the Spirit which is from God."

[23] This does not mean that there can be no increase in knowledge. Indeed, quite the contrary, the New Testament also emphasizes growing "in the grace and knowledge . . ." (so 2 Peter 3:18). Paul prays that God might give the Ephesians "a spirit . . . of revelation in the knowledge of him [Christ]" (1:17). However, this further knowledge, for all its importance, is *within the sphere of a knowledge already given.* Since this further knowledge is an aspect of the Christian walk, I will defer discussion of it until the last chapter, "Christian Living."

[24] John and Peter, of course, had been with Jesus through His ministry and had heard Him speak about "the Spirit of truth." Paul at his conversion was granted a direct, personal revelation of Christ.

truth, are quite immature in expressing it. Thus Paul wrote the Ephesians about the various Christ-given offices in the church, including those of pastor and teacher, to help believers grow up to "mature manhood . . . no longer . . . children, tossed to and fro and carried about with every wind of doctrine (4:13–14). *But*, as important and necessary as such teaching was, and is, its purpose is not to impart truth but to elicit and articulate the truth already received through the Spirit's activity. Earlier in his letter Paul spoke of the Ephesians as having "heard the word of truth" and being "sealed with the promised Holy Spirit" (1:13). Likewise (in the language of the Fourth Gospel) they had received "the Spirit of truth" and thus knew the essence of any future teaching.

We can also affirm that the coming of the Holy Spirit was to lead believers into a knowledge and understanding of God's manifold gifts. Paul declared, "We have received . . . the Spirit who is from God, that we might know the things freely given to us by God" (1 Cor. 2:12 NASB). Paul was speaking both for himself and the Corinthians—"we"; hence, the Spirit has been given to all of us. Thus to achieve full knowledge, all believers need the Guide. Then Paul continued with this significant statement: "And we impart[25] this in words not taught by human wisdom but taught by the Spirit, interpreting spiritual truths to those who possess the Spirit (v. 13 RSV)."[26] Those who "possess the Spirit," literally "pneumatics," are those filled with the Spirit.[27] They are capable of apprehending what Paul is saying because they are *already* Spirit-possessed people. To them the Spirit of truth has come; they only need an interpretation of what they have received.

EXCURSUS:
ON BIBLICAL EXEGESIS

It follows that true biblical interpretation calls for pneumatic understanding. The proper exegesis of Scripture is far more than linguistic analysis; it is most profoundly a matter of spiritual apprehension. Since Paul and the other biblical writers wrote words "taught by the Spirit," true understanding can occur only when one is existentially in accord with that same Spirit. When a person stands within the same pneumatic experience as the biblical writers did, he then has the spiritual capacity to receive what the Scripture teaches.[28]

---

[25] Literally, "speak"; the Greek word is *laloumen*.

[26] The latter part of the statement above reads similarly in the NEB: "We are interpreting spiritual truths to those who have the Spirit." The Greek phrase is *pneumatikois pneumatika synkrinontes*. The NIV reads, "expressing spiritual truths in spiritual words." The NASB reads similarly, "combining spiritual thoughts with spiritual words." The KJV has "comparing spiritual things with spiritual." I believe that the RSV (above) and NEB better express Paul's meaning (so likewise the NIV alternate reading: "interpreting spiritual truths to spiritual men") in light of the verses following about "the unspiritual man" (v. 14) and "the spiritual man," *ho pneumatikos* (v. 15). On this point see *I Corinthians*, ICC, in loco.

[27] Thayer, under πνευματικός, says "in reference to persons; one who is filled with and governed by the Spirit of God"; BAGD—"the one who possesses the Spirit . . . πνευματικοί (the) spirit-filled people."

[28] Howard M. Ervin speaks of a "pneumatic hermeneutic." He writes: "When one encounters the Holy Spirit in the same apostolic experience, with the same charismatic phenomenology accompanying it, one is then in a better position to come to terms with the apostolic witness in a truly existential manner. . . . One then stands in 'pneumatic'

Without such standing, biblical exegesis and interpretation fall far short of truth.

This is not to deny the need for a careful study of Scripture. We must hear what Peter, Paul, John, and the other writers are saying, which requires, at best, a knowledge of the language in which they wrote, the variations among manuscripts (since we do not have the original autographs), the purpose each had in writing, the historical and cultural setting, and so on. Each writer must also be heard for himself and then in conjunction with others, hence in both the unity and diversity of the Scriptures. All of this is quite important lest even the fullest spiritual understanding be confused and distorted by the failure to give adequate hearing to what the writers of Scripture say.

It is in the conjunction of pneumatic understanding and authentic hearing that the truth of Scripture breaks forth. How greatly we need this to take place!

Now we will quickly move to the spiritual renewal in our day. Insofar as people have received "the Spirit of truth," they are deeply grounded in spiritual truth. The Holy Spirit has come to bear witness of Christ and to guide believers into all the truth. In the experience of many there has come an intense awareness of the things of God. This does not mean a detailed knowledge of all aspects of Christian truth; indeed, there is often confusion and error in the attempts at expression and articulation. But a *deep resonance* with the truth exists whether, for example, it is the truth about God and the world, Christ and salvation, or the Holy Spirit and the gifts. They feel fully "at home" within the essential framework of Christian truth.[29]

Moreover, the Bible is gladly and fully accepted as God's word, not only because of its own claim to be true (e.g., 2 Tim. 3:16) but also because of its profoundly spiritual impact. As a result of the intense activity of the Holy Spirit in their lives—the same Holy Spirit who inspired Holy Scripture— many have found the Scriptures to take on new life and meaning. The Bible as an external norm for faith and as a historical witness to God's mighty deeds is unhesitatingly accepted. But the Bible has also become a fuller testimony to God's present activity. It is as if a door has been opened, and walking through the door they see spread out before them the extraordinary biblical world with its dimensions of angelic heights and demonic depths, of miracles and wonders, a world in which they now sense their own participation. The Bible has taken on new authority, not merely the authority of outward acceptance. It is the authority of inward confirmation, the Holy Spirit vividly confirming the words and deeds of Holy Scripture in contemporary experience.[30]

---

continuity with the faith community that birthed the Scriptures" ("Hermeneutics: A Pentecostal Option," in *Essays on Apostolic Themes,* Paul Elbert, ed., 33). I fully agree.

[29] Martyn Lloyd-Jones writes in his book *Joy Unspeakable: Power and Renewal in the Holy Spirit* that "when a man is baptized with the Spirit he knows the truth as he has never known it before" (110–11). Then Lloyd-Jones asks, "Would you know the Christian truth, would you know the Christian doctrine? Would you have a firm grasp and understanding of God's great and glorious purpose? The highway to that is the baptism with the Holy Spirit" (111). This fine book consists of sermons preached at Westminster Chapel, London, in 1964–65.

[30] I append here a word about biblical authority in light of some criticisms today that the charismatic renewal is based more on experience than on Scripture. To the contrary, I submit that people in the renewal often have a higher regard for the authority of God's

When the "Spirit of truth" comes, He indeed guides into all the truth!

II. POWER FOR MINISTRY

Second, the Holy Spirit comes to give power for ministry. The opening verse in the Book of Acts sets the stage: "In the first book [the Gospel of Luke], O Theophilus, I have dealt with all that Jesus *began* to do and teach." The implication is clear that Luke plans in his second book, Acts, to deal with what Jesus *continued* to do and teach. However, the exalted Lord will carry on this ministry through His disciples. For this they will need the power of the Holy Spirit.

The close connection between the coming of the Holy Spirit and power for ministry was earlier shown in Jesus Himself. All the Gospels record that at the baptism of Jesus in the Jordan the Holy Spirit "descended upon" (Luke 3:22)[31] Him; thereby He received the empowerment of the Holy Spirit. Afterward, "Jesus, full of the Holy Spirit, returned from the Jordan" (4:1). Following His wilderness temptation, He "returned in the power of the Spirit into Galilee" (v. 14) and there began His ministry.[32]

It is apparent from Acts that Jesus intended for the same Spirit of power that rested on Him to rest also on His disciples. Thus He declared, "You shall receive power when the Holy Spirit has come upon you" (Acts 1:8). Thereby His disciples would be able to move in the power of the Spirit for the ministry that lay ahead. It would not be in the energy that the Holy Spirit provided but in the power of the Spirit Himself.[33] The Holy Spirit would personally empower Jesus' disciples for the mission ahead.

Such an empowerment for ministry is described later in Acts when Saul of Tarsus was filled with the Holy Spirit. Ananias, the disciple who ministered to Saul, was told by the Lord, "Go, for he is a chosen instrument of mine to carry my name before the Gentiles and kings and the sons of Israel; for I will show him how much he must suffer for the sake of my name" (9:15–16). After Saul (Paul) was filled with the Spirit, he "grew more and more powerful" (v. 22 NIV). Much later, in writing to Timothy, Paul spoke about "the glorious gospel . . . with which I have been entrusted," adding, "I thank him who has given me strength[34] for this [ministry]" (1 Tim.

---

written word than many of their critics do. Because of the activity of the Holy Spirit moving so forcefully in people's lives—the same Holy Spirit who inspired Holy Scripture—they have found the Scriptures (as I remarked above) to take on new life and meaning. The Bible then is fully authoritative, not only as an accepted external norm but as a self-vindicating reality.

Actually, there are many critics of the renewal who, for all their talk, do not really accept the full authority of Scripture. For example, I have often observed that when some of them come to passages dealing with the outpouring of the Holy Spirit and the gifts of the Spirit, they subtly deny the force of what is said by relegating the passages to past history and in various other ways downplay their significance. Thus by their *lack* of experience they settle for a limited view of the Bible's full authority and normativity.

[31] See also Matthew 3:16; Mark 1:10; John 1:32. The Greek verb translated above as "descended upon" is *katabēnai*, from *katabainō*—"come down," "go down" (BAGD). Thus it parallels expressions previously noted: "come on" and "fall on."

[32] Recall my fuller discussion of the beginning of Jesus' ministry in chapter 7, II.C.2.

[33] Everett F. Harrison writes, "The power lay in the person of the Spirit rather than in some sort of spiritual energy He might release to them" (*Acts: The Expanding Church*, 39).

[34] The Greek word is *endynamōsanti*, literally, "strengthening, empowering." Thayer on the verb *endynamoō* reads: "to make strong," "endue with strength," "strengthen."

243

1:11–12). Paul, through the Holy Spirit who came from Christ, was given power to fulfill the ministry to which he had been called.

Hence when the Holy Spirit came at Pentecost and thereafter, He gave power that enabled the ministry of Christ to be carried forward. It was not power in a general sense, that is, an increment of supernatural strength that could have many uses, but power for ministry that flowed from the Father through the Son.

Power for ministry, then, is the central purpose for the Spirit's coming in the New Testament.[35] It must also remain the concern of the church in all ages, for without such power there can be no fully effective ministry.

Let us proceed to examine this power for ministry in terms of *effective witness* and *mighty works*,[36] or word and deeds.

A. Effective Witness

The ministry carried forward by Jesus' disciples was primarily *that of witness*. The power of the Holy Spirit enabled them to witness to Christ. Jesus said, "You shall receive power when the Holy Spirit has come upon you" and added: "You shall be my witnesses in Jerusalem and in all Judea and Samaria and to the end of the earth" (Acts 1:8). Thus when the Holy Spirit came, the disciples were empowered to bear witness to people of many lands and nations.

Let us review for a moment. When the Holy Spirit came upon the disciples in Jerusalem, they first praised God in other tongues (Acts 2:1–13). At that juncture the disciples' words were directed upward to God and not outward to people. The great crowd that assembled listened in on what was being said, but they were not yet the audience. It was only after the time of exuberant praise that the disciples addressed the assembled crowd.

Peter, "standing with the eleven,[37] lifted up his voice and addressed[38] them, 'Men of Judea and all who dwell in Jerusalem, let this be known to you, and give ear to my words'" (v. 14). Here Peter, an uneducated, common man[39]—a rough fisherman—spoke as he had never spoken before. He spoke to an assembly of devout Jews,[40] doing so with the authority, forcefulness, and penetration that could only come from the anointing of the Holy Spirit. No longer was it a matter of speaking in other tongues (as amazing as that was) but of speaking in the Jewish common

---

[35] I have earlier spoken of the coming of the Holy Spirit largely in terms of power for ministry (chap. 7, III, "The Spirit to Come"). However, in this chapter I am giving a more comprehensive picture of the mission of the Spirit (sections I, II, and III). Nevertheless, power for ministry is central and to this I now turn.

[36] "*Dynamis* [power] is expressed in proclamation on the one side . . . and miracles on the other" (W. Grundmann, article on δυναμις in TDNT, 2:311).

[37] Mention of "the eleven" other apostles standing with Peter signifies that through Peter as spokesman they were all bearing witness.

[38] Literally, "spoke out"; the Greek word is *apephthenxatō*, the same verb as in Acts 2:4 used there in connection with speaking in tongues: "They . . . began to speak in other tongues, as the Spirit gave them utterance [literally, 'to speak out,' *apophthengesthai*]." Hence, even as they spoke out in tongues to God under the inspiration of the Holy Spirit, so Peter spoke out to the people under the anointing of the same Spirit. I. H. Marshall writes that Peter's message "is regarded [by Luke] as being the work of a man filled with the Spirit" (*The Acts of the Apostles*, TNTC, 72–73).

[39] Peter and John are described as "uneducated, common men [or 'untrained laymen' (NEB); Gr. *agrammatoi . . . idiōtai*]" in Acts 4:13.

[40] "Now there were dwelling in Jerusalem Jews, devout men from every nation under heaven" (Acts 2:5). This was Peter's audience, enough to overwhelm almost any speaker!

language[41] with supernatural power and wisdom.

Peter's message that followed was twofold: first an explanation of the bewildering matter of tongues[42] (2:14–21), and second, the proclamation of Jesus' life, death, and resurrection, ending with the words "this Jesus whom you crucified" (vv. 22–36). Peter's words were simple and direct, but, of most importance, they were words set on fire by the Holy Spirit.[43] The fact that at the conclusion of Peter's message the assembled throng was pierced to the heart and cried out to Peter and the rest of the apostles, "Brethren, what shall we do?" (v. 37 NASB), showed that the message had brought deep conviction of sin. The way was thereby prepared for Peter to proclaim the good news of salvation: "Repent, and be baptized every one of you in the name of Jesus Christ for the forgiveness of your sins" (v. 38). The final result was that "those who received his word were baptized, and there were added that day about three thousand souls" (v. 41).

In summary: the coming of the Holy Spirit made possible a powerful and effective witness. Moreover, this witness occurred in an extremely difficult situation. Peter brought his message to an audience that came rushing together not to hear a sermon but because of the sound of some one hundred and twenty people speaking in tongues. Further, despite the amazing fact that everyone heard what the disciples were saying in his own language, many began to mock and accuse the disciples of drunkenness. Again Peter, who, so far as we know, had never before addressed even a small number of people, now confronted several thousand[44] and spoke in a Galilean accent(!).[45] Also the throng was not a multitude of woebegone sinners readily open to a message of salvation, but a crowd of devout Jews assembled for one of the great Jewish feast days in accordance with the Old Testament commandment. To cap it all, Peter was bold enough to say to them that *they* had crucified Jesus. His listeners might have responded by saying that they had not even been in Jerusalem at the time of the crucifixion,[46] or if they had been there, that they were not in the mob that cried, "Crucify Him," or that the responsibility was not theirs

---

[41] Since these were Jews whom Peter addressed, they all spoke, in addition to the languages of their own countries, the same Semitic language, Aramaic. Incidentally, "dwelling in Jerusalem" probably does not mean in this context permanent residents. Devout Jews from many countries came annually to Jerusalem for the feast of Pentecost and dwelt temporarily there.

[42] "They [the multitude] were bewildered, because each one heard them speaking in his own language" (2:6).

[43] The "tongues as of fire" that earlier rested on the disciples probably symbolized the powerful, penetrating witness possible from then on through the Holy Spirit. Calvin writes about the tongues of fire: "The Lord doth show that their voice shall be fiery, that it may inflame the hearts of men; that the vanity of the world being burnt and consumed, it may purge and renew all things" (*The Acts of the Apostles,* 1:76).

[44] The three thousand who were baptized were *not* the whole crowd; they were "those who received his word."

[45] Recall at the time of Peter's denial of Jesus what some of the bystanders in Jerusalem said to him: "Surely you are one of them, for your accent gives you away" (Matt. 26:73 NIV). His accent was Galilean (Bethsaida in Galilee was his home), an accent that was often derided by Jews in Judea and Jerusalem. R. T. France comments that the Galilean accent was "a matter of some ridicule in Judaean society" (*Matthew,* TNTC, 83). Doubtless at Pentecost, despite the power of the Holy Spirit, the accent was still there.

[46] This, of course, had occurred over fifty days earlier at the Feast of Passover.

but Pilate's, who gave the order, and so on. However, as the record reads, no excuses were given, no attempts at self-justification—only a cry, "Brethren, what shall we do?" Unquestionably, Peter's message was fully anointed by the Holy Spirit.

Surely what has just been recounted is indeed extraordinary. God enabled an ordinary human being in a humanly impossible situation to become a channel for the *radical transformation* of human existence! "Jews, devout men from every nation under heaven" (Acts 2:5) suddenly realized and accepted their awful guilt for the crucifixion of the Messiah God had sent. They were then baptized in that very name and through Him entered into a wholly new life by His grace. This almost incredible transformation could only have happened through the tremendous power of the Holy Spirit's anointing and making effective a human witness.

Let us look next at Philip the evangelist.[47] Philip was one of the seven men "full of the Spirit and of wisdom" (Acts 6:3), appointed by the apostles "to serve tables" (v. 2).[48] However, when persecution broke out against the church in Jerusalem, all the believers except the apostles were scattered throughout Judea and Samaria. Philip therefore was among them and went to a city of Samaria where he "proclaimed to them the Christ" (Acts 8:5).

The situation was again an extraordinary one. The original commission of Jesus to be His witnesses "in Jerusalem and in all Judea and Samaria and to the end of the earth" was given only to the apostles.[49] But here was Philip, a table server, initially bringing the gospel to the very Samaria Jesus had commanded the *apostles* to evangelize! In many ways it was an even more difficult situation than Peter had confronted in Jerusalem at Pentecost. Jews generally viewed Samaritans as half-breeds and sought altogether to avoid them, considering them to be totally outside God's promises.[50] The Samaritans were equally antagonistic against the Jews, especially those from Jerusalem.[51] Hence Philip had to reach across a wide cultural barrier to preach the gospel in Samaria. In addition, the problem was compounded because these Samaritans were devotees of the magician Simon and viewed him as the very power of Almighty God: "They all gave heed to him, from the least to the greatest, saying, 'This man is that power of God which is called Great'" (Acts 8:10). What a situation: Philip the table server from Jerusalem preaching the gospel to

---

[47] He is called "Philip the evangelist" in Acts 21:8. This Philip is not to be confused with Philip the apostle (mentioned in Acts 1:13). Nothing is said about the activities of Philip the apostle in the Book of Acts.

[48] These seven men are often viewed as the first deacons. "To serve tables" in the Greek is *diakonein trapezais,* literally, "to deacon tables." The purpose of this "deaconing" was to see that the widows of the Grecian Jewish believers ("the Hellenists") were not neglected in the daily distribution of food.

[49] Note Acts 1:2 in relation to Acts 1:8. It was only after the commission given by Jesus and after His ascension that the group was enlarged (see Acts 1:14 and 15).

[50] As John 4:9 puts it, "Jews have no dealings with Samaritans." Of course, the beauty of this passage in John's Gospel is that Jesus was ministering to a Samaritan (and a woman at that!).

[51] This Samaritan antagonism was especially shown on one occasion when Jesus sought to enter a village of Samaria, "but the people would not receive him, because his face was set toward Jerusalem" (Luke 9:53). In turn, the antipathy of two of Jesus' apostles was vividly demonstrated in that their response was the question to Jesus, "Lord, do you want us to bid fire come down from heaven and consume them?" (v. 54). There was no love lost between Samaritans and Jews.

hostile Samaritans who were also caught up in rampant idolatry! Humanly speaking, there was utterly no chance of success. Yet "they believed Philip as he preached good news" (v. 12). Truly he was Philip *the* evangelist!

But how could it have happened in Samaria? The answer again is that Philip bore witness to Jesus—he "proclaimed to them the Christ"—and did so in the power of the Holy Spirit, for he was a man "full of the Spirit and of wisdom." Through the anointing from "on high" (Luke 24:49) the miraculous salvation of the Samaritans took place. It was indeed an effective witness.

I have spent considerable time reviewing the accounts of the proclamation of the gospel in Jerusalem and Samaria because of their timeliness for today. The barriers to the task of bearing witness to Christ in our time are hardly less than what confronted Peter in Jerusalem and Philip in Samaria. Indeed, although the outreach of the gospel has in some sense now gone "to the end of the earth" so that believers are found around the world, the task that remains is extremely difficult. The rising tide of secularism in the West, the virulence of atheistic communism in Eastern Europe and in China, and the strong surge of Muslim extremism in the Middle East—just to mention a few things—stand rigorously opposed to the proclamation of the gospel. We

have many valuable missionary organizations and strategies; yet one critical factor must not be ignored: the evangelistic witness must be in the power of the Holy Spirit.[52] Hear these words: "If twentieth-century Christians could again know the Spirit that possessed the Christians in Acts, and add that to our present knowledge of organization, we could reach the world immediately."[53] This may be an overstatement—"reach the world immediately"—but the basic need is unmistakable: to "again know the Spirit that possessed the Christians in Acts."

Ultimately this is the concern of the Pentecostal/charismatic movement: to know the Holy Spirit and to move in His power in order to complete the task of worldwide evangelization. From the earliest twentieth-century beginnings, Pentecostals were fired with tremendous zeal to carry the gospel everywhere. There was at the outset "a veritable explosion of worldwide evangelistic activity"[54] as men and women went far and wide presenting the gospel. As a result Pentecostals in less than a century have evangelized over a hundred nations and have become the major form of Christianity in many Third World countries. With the vitalization of the charismatic renewal in many historic Protestant and Roman Catholic churches, there is fresh zeal for advancing with the task. One evidence of this was the North American Congress on

---

[52] John Wimber in his book *Power Evangelism*, after speaking of the increase of workers in domestic and foreign missions over the past fifteen years, adds, "Most evangelism practiced in the West lacks the power seen in New Testament evangelism" (38–39). Wimber holds that "programmatic evangelism" practiced by many evangelical bodies needs the reinforcement of "power evangelism" if we are to accomplish the job (see especially chap. 3, entitled "Power Evangelism").

[53] The words of C. E. Autry (*Evangelism in Acts*, 80).

[54] Words of L. Grant McClung, Jr., ed., *Azusa Street and Beyond*, 3. McClung also writes, "Early Pentecostal missionaries were a breed of men and women unlike any before them. They carried a burden for lost souls and were marked by the sacrificial self-giving of their predecessors. *But they were also the recipients of a new move of God in their time.* They saw their Pentecostal baptism with its resulting supernatural signs as evidence that the last days had come upon them and that God's hour of reaping was at hand" (p. 32, italics added).

World Evangelization held in New Orleans in the summer of 1987. Some 35,000 Pentecostals and charismatics committed themselves to the goal of bringing the majority of the human race to Jesus Christ by the end of the century.[55] It is not that Pentecostals and charismatics are alone in their concern for world evangelization; indeed it is estimated that there are some thirty to forty world-evangelization plans in force for this last decade. However, none of these affirms as emphatically as the Pentecostals and the charismatics the need of the power of the Spirit to accomplish the task.[56]

Let us return to the New Testament and observe next how Saul of Tarsus was also given the Holy Spirit for the purpose of witness. I earlier quoted the words of the Lord to Ananias concerning Saul: "He is a chosen instrument of mine to carry my name before the Gentiles and kings and the sons of Israel" (Acts 9:15). "To carry my name" refers to witness, a witness that would indeed be far-reaching. Many years later Paul recalled Ananias' words to him: "The God of our fathers has appointed you to know His will, and to see the Righteous One, and to hear an utterance from His mouth. For you will be a witness for Him to all men of what you have seen and heard"

(Acts 22:14–15 NASB). Not only would Paul's witness be far-reaching, but it would also spring from the Lord's own revelation to Paul: "what you have seen and heard." Once more in Acts Paul recounted his conversion experience, recalling Jesus' words to him on the road to Damascus: "Arise, and stand on your feet; for this purpose I have appeared to you, to appoint you a minister and a witness not only to the things which you have seen, but also to the things in which I will appear to you" (26:16 NASB). Again "witness" is used, but to what Paul would witness is even wider: "also to the things in which I will appear to you."

Unlike the witness of Peter and Philip, the witness of Paul was at first received negatively. After his conversion and filling with the Holy Spirit, "in the synagogues immediately he proclaimed Jesus, saying, 'He is the Son of God'" (Acts 9:20). Paul's witness in the power of the Spirit was so able that he "confounded the Jews who lived in Damascus by proving that Jesus was the Christ" (v. 22). Hence Paul's message got through to them; however, the result was not their turning to the Lord, for after several days "the Jews plotted to kill him" (v. 23). Paul escaped, to be sure, but without having had any outward success in his witness.[57]

---

[55]Sponsored by the North American Renewal Service Committee, the Congress was chaired by Vinson Synan. Looking back on the Congress, Synan wrote, "The body of Christ is about to arise and lead an evangelistic charge in the last decade of this century which will surpass any similar period in the history of the Church" (*AD 2000,* 1.6 [1987]: 5.

[56]A Southern Baptist missions researcher, speaking to a gathering of charismatic leaders in May 1987, said, "If the Great Commission is to be completed by A.D. 2000, you Charismatics must play a principal role. As I travel the world, I see Charismatics everywhere. You have a ready-made network of people with faith and vision, who operate in the supernatural. *You are the missing link to completing all the A.D. 2000 plans*" (italics added). These are the words of Rev. Jimmy Maloney as reported by Howard Foltz, "Moving Toward a Charismatic Theology of Missions," *Probing Pentecostalism,* the report of the Society for Pentecostal Studies, 17th Annual Meeting, 1987, CBN University, 73.

[57]In this, Paul was not unlike his Master. Shortly after Jesus was filled with the Holy Spirit, He returned to His own synagogue in Nazareth and there declared, "The Spirit of the Lord is upon me . . ." (Luke 4:18). At first the hearers "all spoke well of him" (v. 22) (as

The point, accordingly, is that witness in the power of the Spirit does not always lead to positive results. Nonetheless, it *is* effective, even if only to arouse opposition! People do not remain the same once a powerful witness has been made. The task of the Christian therefore is to witness—regardless. Further, there is no biblical promise that the witness "to the end of the earth" will bring all people to salvation. Indeed, there will be increasing resistance to the gospel; hence, despite the power of the witness, many will not receive it. The commission, however, is to proclaim the gospel in the power of the Spirit so that all may have an opportunity to hear and believe. Then the task will be done.[58]

I will not here pursue the accounts of Peter's successful witness in Caesarea and Paul's in Ephesus but rather remark on the purpose of receiving the Holy Spirit in the several situations. The point is simply this: since the central purpose of the gift of the Holy Spirit to the disciples at Pentecost and to Saul in Damascus was unmistakably for witness, it follows that the same thing was true in the other accounts. Nothing is directly said in the instances of the Samaritans, Caesareans, and Ephesians; however, this purpose is doubtless implied.[59]

For example, when Peter and John came down from Jerusalem to minister in the Holy Spirit, it was probably so that the Samaritans could also become a part of the witnessing community. Because of the long-standing schism between Jews and Samaritans, it was fitting that the Samaritans receive further ministry directly from Jerusalem and the chief apostles there. The result was that the people not only entered into salvation through Philip's ministry, but they also became a witnessing community through the ministry of Peter and John. Since Jesus had said to His disciples, "You shall be my witnesses in Jerusalem and in all Judea and Samaria and to the end of the earth," His reference to Samaria could well signify not only a people *to* whom witness is to be made but also *by* whom it is to be continued.

A principle logically follows that may now be enunciated vigorously: the Holy Spirit is a "missionary Spirit."[60] Wherever He comes upon people, they are charged with power to move beyond themselves and become a witness for Christ; they thereby become participants in the continuing outreach of the gospel to the end of the earth. Even as the Holy Spirit is a "proceeding" Spirit,[61] so those who are anointed by Him cannot possibly remain silent and confined in their faith but must "proceed" to tell the Good News everywhere.

In moving to the contemporary charismatic scene one finds a renewed emphasis on the gift of the Spirit and

possibly the Jews first did of Paul), but soon they were seeking to put Jesus to death: to "throw him down headlong" (v. 29) from a cliff.

[58]Cf. the words of Matthew 24:14: "This gospel of the kingdom shall be preached in the whole world for a witness to all the nations, and then the end shall come" (NASB).

[59]According to R. R. Williams, "throughout Acts, the Holy Spirit is thought of as the means whereby Christians receive power to witness to Christ and His resurrection" (*The Acts of the Apostles,* 36).

[60]For a forceful presentation of this theme see Roland Allen, *The Ministry of the Spirit,* especially chapter 1, Section II, "The Spirit Revealed as the Inspirer of Missionary Work." Also note Michael Green, *I Believe in the Holy Spirit,* chapter 5, "The Spirit in Mission."

[61]Recall the earlier discussion in chapter 8, II.B., regarding Jesus' reference in the Fourth Gospel to the Holy Spirit as He "who proceeds from the Father." This eternal procession becomes temporal in the gift of the Holy Spirit, and He continues to proceed from the lives of those to whom He is given.

power for witness[62] and on the Spirit as a "missionary Spirit." Persons who have received this gift thereby become Christ's witnesses in a fresh way; often their very being and manner is so filled with God's presence and power that others are profoundly affected. Also their words and actions are laden with new potency so that there is both wisdom and incisiveness in testifying to the gospel. In some cases people may have borne witness to Christ for years with varying degrees of success, but now there is a further breakthrough that brings about deep and abiding results.[63]

The "missionary spirit" is present—as many demonstrate in their daily work or as others carry the Good News both far and wide.

B. Mighty Works

Next let us note how the gift of the Holy Spirit enables believers to perform *mighty works*. The ministry of the gospel is not only that of word but also of deed wherein mighty works in the name of Christ are also performed.

It is apparent that not only did the early apostles speak about Jesus, but they also did extraordinary things. Such

---

[62] See, for example, the chapter entitled "Power to Witness" in *As the Spirit Leads Us* by Kevin and Dorothy Ranaghan. Here two spiritually renewed Roman Catholics describe how "it seems to be universally true that those who have come into this experience [i.e., baptism in the Holy Spirit] are taught not so much by one another but by the direct power of God, that every tongue (including theirs) is meant to proclaim that Jesus is Lord. . . . 'We cannot but speak the things we have seen and heard' " (103). Thus there is power for witness they never knew before.

[63] Dwight L. Moody, a nineteenth-century evangelist, after many years of preaching, related how two women would say to him regularly, "*You* need the power of the Holy Spirit." Moody reflected thereafter: "I need the power! Why, I thought I had power [because] I had the largest congregation in Chicago and there were many conversions. I was in a sense satisfied." Soon though, the two godly women were praying with Moody, and "they poured out their hearts in prayer that I might receive the filling of the Holy Spirit. There came a great hunger into my soul. . . . I began to cry out as I never did before. I really felt that I did not want to live if I could not have this power for service." Some time later Moody related this: "One day, in the city of New York—oh, what a day!—I cannot describe it, I seldom refer to it; it is almost too sacred an experience to name. Paul had an experience of which he never spoke for fourteen years. I can only say that God revealed Himself to me, and I had such an experience of His love that I had to ask Him to stay His hand. I went to preaching again. The sermons were not different; I did not present any new truths, and yet hundreds were converted. I would not now be placed back before that blessed experience if you should give me all the world" (W. R. Moody, *The Life of D. L. Moody*, 146–47, 149). Moody had witnessed to the gospel for many years and with some obvious effectiveness, but after being filled with the Spirit, there came an anointing he had never before experienced. Moody, while of course not a participant in the current spiritual renewal, is surely a precursor of those who likewise in our time are being filled with the Spirit and thereby finding a fresh power for witness.

I add here a word about Reuben A. Torrey, Moody's successor, and the first head of Moody Bible Institute (opening in 1899). Even more strongly than Moody he stressed the need to be filled, or baptized, with the Holy Spirit. For example, he wrote in his book *The Baptism with the Holy Spirit* (c. 1895 and 1897): "If a man has experienced the regenerating work of the Holy Spirit he is a saved man, but he is not fitted for service until in addition to this he has received the baptism with the Holy Spirit. . . . Any man who is in Christian work who has not received the baptism with the Holy Spirit ought to stop his work right where he is and not go on with it until he has been 'clothed with power from on high' " (pp. 17 and 31).

Neither Moody nor Torrey stood in the Holiness tradition with its stress on "entire sanctification." They both viewed baptism with the Holy Spirit as following upon regeneration and as empowerment for ministry. Torrey especially has had significant influence on the charismatic renewal.

deeds are first mentioned soon after Pentecost: "And fear came upon every soul; and many wonders and signs were done through the apostles" (Acts 2:43). Note first the multiplicity of extraordinary things ("many"); second, their description as "wonders and signs" suggests their character as miracles;[64] and third, these many wonders and signs were done "through" the apostles, the apostles being channels, not agents, of their occurrence. The whole atmosphere was charged with awe—"fear . . . upon every soul"—as the exalted Lord did His work through them.

Signs and wonders, I should quickly add, were done not only through the apostles but also through other disciples. On a later occasion Peter and John, after being warned to speak no more about Jesus, returned to the company of believers who then prayed for a common courage: "Grant to thy servants to speak thy word with all boldness, while thou stretchest out thy hand to heal, and signs and wonders are performed through the name of thy holy servant Jesus" (Acts 4:29–30). The immediate result was that "the place in which they were gathered together was shaken; and they were all filled with the Holy Spirit and spoke the word of God with boldness" (v. 31). Doubtless, the implication is not only that the prayer of the company for boldness of speech was answered, but also that they were all granted the ability to perform signs and wonders through the name of Jesus.

To further examine the above matter: though it is said more than once that the apostles did wonders and signs,[65] it is apparent that others such as Stephen the martyr and Philip the evangelist did likewise. "And Stephen, full of grace and power, did great wonders and signs among the people" (Acts 6:8). "And the multitudes with one accord gave heed to what was said by Philip, when they heard him and saw the signs which he did" (8:6). "Even Simon [the magician] himself believed, and after being baptized he continued with Philip. And seeing signs and great miracles performed, he was amazed" (v. 13). In addition, according to Mark 16:17–18, Jesus said, "And these signs will accompany those who believe: in my name they will cast out demons; they will speak in new tongues; they will pick up serpents; and if they drink any deadly thing, it will not hurt them; they will lay their hands on the sick, and they will recover." Similarly, "they went forth and preached everywhere, while the Lord worked with them and

---

[64] For a fuller discussion see vol. 1, chapter 7, "Miracles," III. Some of the things said in that section will be touched on here.

[65] In addition to Acts 2:43, supra, see 5:12: "Now many signs and wonders were done among the people by the hands of the apostles"; 14:3 regarding Paul and Barnabas: "So they remained for a long time [at Iconium], speaking boldly for the Lord, who bore witness to the word of his grace, granting signs and wonders to be done by their hands"; 15:12: "Barnabas and Paul . . . related what signs and wonders God had done through them among the Gentiles." Compare also Romans 15:18–19 where Paul says, "For I will not venture to speak of anything except what Christ has wrought through me to win obedience from the Gentiles, by word and deed, by the power of signs and wonders, by the power of the Holy Spirit." Paul also says, "The signs of a true apostle [literally, "truly the signs of the apostle"—*ta men sēmeia tou apostolou*] were performed among you in all patience, with signs and wonders and mighty works [or 'powerful deeds'—*dynamesin*]" (2 Cor. 12:12). This latter statement, incidentally, while again affirming that through Paul miracles took place, does not speak of them as solely apostolic certifications (hence, limited to apostles). The "signs of a true apostle," which Paul does not describe in this text, were performed with "all patience"; such "signs" (even certifications) were accompanied by "signs and wonders and mighty works."

confirmed the message by the signs that attended it" (v. 20).[66] Signs and wonders—extraordinary, miraculous deeds—were the practice of the whole Christian community.

It is abundantly clear that the performance of mighty works—signs, wonders, and miracles—belongs with the gospel proclamation. The early Christians testified *and* performed signs and wonders. The proclamation, therefore, is powerful word *and* miraculous deed (both by the Holy Spirit), which bear witness to the gospel. The deed is the confirmation of the word, the visible assurance of the message of salvation. Although the greatest wonder is new life, a new birth wrought by the word, such is invisible. Hence when a visible sign accompanies the word, there is undeniable attestation to the actuality of what has been inwardly wrought by the message of salvation.

Thus it is a serious error indeed to relegate miracles to the past.[67] It is sad to hear among some who vigorously affirm the message of salvation and the necessity of regeneration that miracles are not to be expected any longer. If through the proclamation of the word in the power of the Spirit the miracle of rebirth can and does occur, will not that same Spirit also work other "signs and wonders"? For surely other miracles, no matter how extraordinary,[68] are less significant than the miracle of new life and salvation.

Let me say further that it makes little practical difference whether one affirms that the miracles in Acts (and elsewhere) are simply legendary accretions to the record (and thus really did not happen) or that they did happen then but no longer occur in our time. Both views deny the reality of the living God, who is always free and able *in any time* to perform His extraordinary works through men. The "Bible believer" who affirms that miracles were for then but not for now is actually farther removed from a living faith than the "liberal" who has not locked the power of God into past history. Both persons, however, need to hear these words of Jesus: "Is not this why you are wrong, that you know neither the scriptures nor the power of God?" (Mark 12:25).

Fortunately the spiritual renewal of the twentieth century has recaptured the early church's belief in and practice of mighty works. Miracles are no longer believed to be past history or merely legendary additions to the biblical witness; they belong to the life of the believing community and to the proclamation of the gospel.[69] "Expect a mira-

---

[66] It is true that many ancient manuscripts of the Gospel of Mark do not include verses 9–20 in chapter 16. However, even if these verses are a later addition, the very fact that signs are ascribed to believers in general—"those who believed"—shows an early recognition that miracles are not limited to apostles or to deacons such as Stephen and Philip. (On Mark 16:17 see also my previous chapter, n. 29.)

[67] See vol. 1, chapter 7, Epilogue: "On the Cessation of Miracles."

[68] Even the raising of the physically dead (to which reference is made several times in the Scriptures) is less a "wonder" than the raising of the spiritually dead by the proclamation of the Good News. For the raising of the physically dead in Acts, see the accounts of Peter's raising of Tabitha (9:36–42) and Paul's restoring Eutychus to life (20:9–12).

[69] E.g., see *Nine O'Clock in the Morning* by Dennis Bennett, chapter 6, "More to the Package." Shortly after Bennett's baptism in the Spirit, he found miracles of many kinds beginning to happen. At the fellowship meeting he said, "Sometimes nearly everyone in the room had some kind of a report to give: not what God did years ago, or even last year, but what He did last week, yesterday, today!" (47). A further beautiful statement by Dorothy Ranaghan in *As the Spirit Leads Us* might be added: "The victorious life of Christ becomes known in the now. Healing, discernment, miracles, prophecy—all these signs, manifesta-

cle" is a commonly heard expression. Those who expect God to perform mighty works are not disappointed.

1. Healing

The performance of mighty works, made possible by the coming of the Holy Spirit, includes a wide range of extraordinary phenomena. We shall note two of these in particular, beginning with *healing*.[70]

In the ministry of Jesus next in importance to His preaching and teaching was His ministry of healing. For example, "He went about all Galilee, teaching in their synagogues and preaching the gospel of the kingdom and healing every disease and every infirmity among the people" (Matt. 4:23). Another text reads, "The power [*dynamis*] of the Lord was with him to heal" (Luke 5:17); and thereupon he healed a bedridden paralytic. This *dynamis* of God is precisely what Jesus promised His disciples through the gift of the Holy Spirit. And so it was—and is.

As we look again at the record in Acts, it is relevant that the first mighty work mentioned is healing. Following the coming of the Holy Spirit at Pentecost and the formation of the Christian community (Acts 2), there is the account of the healing of the lame beggar at the gate of the temple (3:1–10). Peter said to the man, "I have no silver and gold, but I give you what I have; in the name of Jesus Christ of Nazareth, walk" (v. 6). Thus it was the combination of the power of the Spirit ("what I have") and the name of Jesus Christ that led to the miraculous healing.

What followed is quite significant. Peter addressed the assembled crowd, who were amazed at the healing of one

they had seen many times begging at the gate, and told them that "the faith which is through Jesus has given the man this perfect health in the presence of you all" (v. 16). These words then led to the proclamation of the gospel to the crowd: "Repent therefore, and turn again, that your sins may be blotted out, that times of refreshing may come from the presence of the Lord" (v. 19). Later they were taken into custody by the temple authorities, who inquired, "By what power or by what name did you do this?" Peter, "filled with the Holy Spirit," replied, "Be it known to you all, and to all the people of Israel, that by the name of Jesus Christ of Nazareth, whom you crucified, whom God raised from the dead, by him this man is standing before you well" (4:7–8, 10). Peter concluded with the message of salvation: "And there is salvation in no one else, for there is no other name under heaven given among men by which we must be saved" (v. 12).

What is particularly important in this narrative of miraculous healing is the way in which it became the occasion for the proclamation of the gospel. As a result "many of those who heard the word believed; and the number of men came to about five thousand" (4:4). Thus it was similar to the Day of Pentecost, when miraculous speaking in tongues became the occasion for drawing a crowd together and the subsequent preaching of the gospel led to the salvation of some three thousand people (2:41). Miracles are shown again not only to be confirmations *of* the word (as we have seen) but also as occasions *for* the word. They set forth visibly, tangibly, and undeniably that an inexplicable power was present and at work, thereby making way for the message of salva-

---

tions or demonstrations of the Spirit cry out to men as they did in the New Testament times: 'Jesus is alive! Jesus works wonders! Jesus is the Lord!' " (14).

[70] I will discuss healing also in chapter 14, "The Ninefold Manifestation." However, the focus there will be on healing gifts within the Christian community.

tion. Healing, therefore, as well as other miracles, is not just supplemental, it is instrumental. It can become the avenue for the proclamation of salvation in Jesus Christ.[71]

The result is that people take notice when the church, the believing community, becomes the arena of God's supernatural activity. Wherever the gospel is proclaimed in the context of "signs and wonders"—whether they precede, accompany, or follow—it is obvious that something extraordinary is going on. In Jerusalem, at the speaking in tongues "all were amazed and perplexed, saying to one another, 'What does this mean?' " (Acts 2:12); at the healing of the lame man "they were filled with wonder and amazement" (3:10). Such amazement, perplexity, and wonderment betokens a startling sense of supernatural presence and prepares the way for the powerful ministry of the word of God.

It is significant to recall the prayer of the community of disciples following the prohibition of the council to testify about Jesus: "And now, Lord, look upon their threats, and grant to thy servants to speak thy word with all boldness, while thou stretchest out thy hand to heal, and signs and wonders are performed through the name of thy holy servant Jesus" (Acts 4:29–30). The prayer of the disciples was that they might speak the word with the accompaniment of healing signs and wonders.

Such visible demonstration of the supernatural activity of God would confirm the message and make many come to a living faith. Whether preceding, accompanying, or following, the occurrence of miracles underscores the reality of the proclaimed word as the power of God unto salvation.

The power of God to heal continued to be manifest in the early Christian community. The sick of Jerusalem were brought in great numbers to the disciples, many hoping for at least the shadow of Peter to fall on them (Acts 5:15). Also people began to come to Jerusalem from surrounding towns and villages, "bringing the sick and those afflicted with unclean spirits, and they were all healed" (v. 16). Likewise in the ministry of Philip at Samaria "the multitudes with one accord gave heed to what was said by Philip, when they heard him and saw the signs which he did. For unclean spirits came out of many who were possessed, crying with a loud voice; and many who were paralyzed or lame were healed" (8:6–7). At Lydda Peter later spoke to a man who was bedridden and paralyzed: " 'Aeneas, Jesus Christ heals you; rise and make your bed.' And immediately he rose. And all the residents of Lydda and Sharon saw him, and they turned to the Lord" (9:34–35). In the case of Paul who spent two years in Ephesus proclaiming the word, the Scripture adds,

---

[71] A vivid illustration of this is cited in the book by J. Herbert Kane, *Understanding Christian Missions*, about the preaching of French evangelist Jacques Girard in an Ivory Coast soccer stadium: "Morning and evening for six weeks thirty to thirty-five thousand people crowded into the stadium. During the first part of the crusade the evangelist emphasized the power of Christ to heal. Hundreds were healed, including some high government officials and their relatives. . . . During the second part of the crusade Mr. Girard emphasized the power of Christ to save. Having already witnessed the healing of the body, the people responded in droves" (424). Howard Foltz declares that "resistant groups, held in the clutches of Islam, Buddhism, Hinduism and animism can only be liberated by the signs and wonders that confirm the true preaching of the word" ("Mobilization Necessary for World Evangelization," *AD 2000*, 1.5 [1987]: 1). The proclamation of the gospel when *shown to work miracles* can break through the most resistant of forces and thus bring about salvation.

"And God did extraordinary miracles[72] by the hands of Paul, so that handkerchiefs or aprons were carried away from his body to the sick, and diseases left them and the evil spirits came out of them" (19:11–12). Paul ministered later at Malta to Publius' father, who "lay sick with fever and dysentery; and Paul visited him and prayed, and putting his hands on him healed him" (28:8). After this "the rest of the people on the island who had diseases also came and were cured" (v. 9). Such incidents demonstrate over and over that the power of the Spirit brought about manifold healings.

These instances of healing suggest a number of matters to reflect on. First, there is again the close connection between the proclamation of the word and healing. In one case (in Samaria), it was hearing the gospel in conjunction with seeing healings that led to the multitude heeding what was said; in another case (in Lydda), it was the peoples' seeing the healing that was itself the direct cause of their coming to faith. Second, in another situation (in Jerusalem), healing refers to curing the sick and delivering from "unclean spirits," thus both physical ailments and spiritual bondage. Third, there is evidently no limitation to the kinds of sicknesses of which people were healed, as if perhaps healing occurred to the psychosomatic but not the organic. The sick, whatever their infirmities, were healed. This calls to mind the fact that Jesus healed "every disease and every infirmity" (Matt. 4:23). The same was true for His Spirit-filled followers, who ministered in His name. Fourth, in two of the cases (in Jerusalem and in Malta) all were healed; in another (in Samaria) many[73] who were paralyzed and lame were healed.

On this last point let us consider further the totality of healing in two of the above situations and the partiality of healing in another. A significant and exciting aspect of the coming of the Spirit is that healing is now available to all. The statement "They were all healed"—the sick, the afflicted, the tormented—is a striking testimony to what the Holy Spirit can do through one like Peter who was an open channel and a willing instrument. It remains a testimony to this day that the power of God to heal is still present wherever His Spirit abounds. Even as salvation—the forgiveness of sins—is available to all, so also is the healing of all forms of physical, mental, and emotional ailments. There needs only to be, as in New Testament times, persons filled with God's Spirit, those who not only proclaim the gospel of new life in Christ but also minister healing in Jesus' name. Believing that God desires both salvation and health for all people, the Christian witness of our day needs to engage boldly in this total ministry. However, as we have observed, not all in Acts were healed in every situation— many, but not everyone. Why this was the case in Samaria is not specified;[74]

---

[72] Literally, "powers not the ordinary"; the Greek is *dynameis te ou tas tychousas.* *Dynameis* ("powers") is often best translated "miracles."

[73] "Many" can mean multiplicity rather than some out of all. However, it is apparent that in the Samaritan situation "many" refers to a large number but not all. In regard to the statement "unclean spirits came out of many who were possessed," the Greek reads literally, "many of the ones having unclean spirits. . . ." According to EGT, in loco, "πολλοὶ with the genitive, τῶν ἐχόντων (not πολλοὶ ἔχοντες), shows that not all the possessed were healed." The same follows for the paralyzed and lame.

[74] Before Philip healed the sick, "unclean spirits came out of many who were possessed"

however, the people "with one accord gave heed to what was said by Philip" (8:6), and of these many were healed. Earlier they "gave heed" (vv. 10–11) to Simon, and now they "believed Philip . . ." (v. 12). Healing, while available for the Samaritans, was not received by all.

Recall that in most situations Jesus healed all who were present. "He cast out the spirits with a word, and healed all who were sick" (Matt. 8:16); "many followed him, and he healed them all" (Matt. 12:15). Scriptures like these may be multiplied.[75] However, there were other times when Jesus did not heal everyone. On one occasion when Jesus came to His own home town, "he laid his hands upon a few sick people and healed them." It is clear that healing was restricted by the lack of receptivity and the unbelief of His townsfolk: "They took offense at him. . . . And he could do no mighty work there, except that he laid his hands upon a few sick people and healed them. And he marveled because of their unbelief" (Mark 6:3, 5–6). On still another occasion, at the sheep gate pool where "lay a multitude of invalids, blind, lame, paralyzed" (John 5:3), He healed only one,

a man who had been ill for some thirty-eight years. An atmosphere of unbelief does not here seem to be the reason that there was only one healing (although there is little suggestion that the sick multitude were expecting very much); rather, it was Jesus' own decision to help the one on whom He took special pity.

In sum, based on the record in Acts and in the Gospels, we may say that healing, while intended or available for everyone, may not be received by all. Such factors as a lack of receptivity or unbelief may be operative on the human side; on the divine side God may sovereignly decide to heal only one or a few. Thus it is quite erroneous and misleading to claim that all will be healed in every situation.

However, to conclude this discussion of healing affirmatively, it is highly important to recognize that the power of God's Spirit does make possible the healing of every kind of disease. Thus wherever people become channels of the divine power, extraordinary healings may be expected to occur.

In the spiritual renewal of our time, healing stands out as one of the most significant features.[76] The power of

---

[75] E.g., Matthew 14:14; Luke 4:40; 6:19 (". . . power came forth from him and healed them all").

[76] Since the beginning of the Pentecostal movement in the early twentieth century, healing has been viewed as a constituent part of the gospel message. Charles Parham wrote in 1902 (the year after Agnes Ozman's experience; see chap. 8, n. 57): "The healing of the sick is as much a part of the gospel as telling them of Heaven. . . . This is the great salvation that so many thousands are neglecting today, a salvation that heals the body as well as the soul" (*The Sermons of Charles F. Parham,* 46). Aimee Semple McPherson, Pentecostal founder of the International Church of the Foursquare Gospel (1927), summarized her basic "foursquare" message thus: "Jesus saves us according to John 3:16. He baptizes us with the Holy Spirit according to Acts 2:4. He heals our bodies according to James 5:14–15. And Jesus is coming again to receive us unto Himself according to 1 Thessalonians 4:16–17" (*The Four-Square Gospel,* 9). Stanley M. Horton, a contemporary theologian in the Assemblies of God (the largest Pentecostal denomination), similarly speaks of "four fundamental teachings—salvation, healing, the baptism in the Holy Spirit, and the second coming of Christ" (*Into All Truth,* 13). This is the "full gospel" (an expression common in Pentecostal circles), and healing is definitely a part of it. Independent Pentecostal evangelists such as Kathryn Kuhlman (see, e.g., her *I Believe in Miracles*) and Oral Roberts (see, e.g., his book *The Call: An Autobiography*) have in recent years focused on the ministry of healing. Contemporary

God to heal, resident within the gift of the Holy Spirit,[77] is being manifested on every hand. Since Jesus performed many healings and promised that His disciples would do even "greater works" (John 14:12) than He, and since He has sent the Spirit to carry forward His ministry, works of healing are to be expected. If they do not occur, therefore, it may be a negative sign, namely, that the gift of the Holy Spirit has not been received, or possibly that the Spirit has come, but people are failing to move out in faith and expectancy. However, the fact that healings of every kind are occurring so widely in the renewal of today[78] is one of the clearest evidences of the presence and power of the Lord in the Holy Spirit.

2. Deliverance

In the preceding paragraphs several references have been made to casting out demons or evil spirits. I earlier called attention to one case (at Jerusalem) where healing referred to both the curing of the sick and deliverance from evil spirits; however, in the other two instances (at Samaria and Ephesus) a distinction is made between healing the sick and the expulsion of demons. This distinction is also apparent in the aforementioned scripture,[79] which states that Jesus both cast out demons and healed the sick. It may also be pointed out that in Mark 16:17–18 a differentiation is made: "And these signs will accompany those who believe: in my name they will cast out demons. . . . They will lay their hands on the sick, and they will recover." Thus we may say that one of the mighty works made possible by the power of the Holy Spirit is *deliverance*.

Let us view this matter in more detail. We begin in the Book of Acts

---

leaders with international ministries of healing include charismatic Catholic Francis MacNutt (see his *Healing* and *The Power to Heal*) and Vineyard Christian Fellowship pastor John Wimber (see his *Power Healing*).

The emphasis on healing among Pentecostals and charismatics has its origins in the late nineteenth century. Healing was especially stressed in the Holiness movement, and this emphasis was carried over into the Pentecostal revival. (For a helpful study see Donald W. Dayton, *Theological Roots of Pentecostalism*, chap. 5, "The Rise of the Divine Healing Movement," especially 122–37.) However, the Holiness movement laid its main emphasis on holiness, or sanctification, as the basic source for healing; the Pentecostals (most of them from a Holiness background) came to stress the immediate source as the power of the Holy Spirit.

[77]Within the Pentecostal tradition there is occasional reference to healing as basically resident within the Atonement. Parham early affirmed this: "Healing is as certainly purchased in the atonement of Jesus Christ as salvation" (*Sermons*, 48). The Assemblies of God "Statement of Fundamental Truths" declares: "Deliverance from sickness is provided in the atonement, and is the privilege of all believers (Isa. 53.4–5; Matt. 8.16–17)." The Declaration of Faith of the Church of God (Cleveland, TN) states: "Divine healing is provided for all in the atonement." Other examples could be given. It is significant to note that this viewpoint (as with the Holiness) also goes back to the nineteenth century, with such advocates as A. J. Gordon, Baptist founder of Gordon College and Seminary, and A. B. Simpson, Presbyterian founder of the Christian and Missionary Alliance. See Gordon's *The Ministry of Healing* (1882) and Simpson's *The Gospel of Healing* (1885). E.g., in Simpson's book there is this statement: "If sickness be the result of the Fall, it must be included in the Atonement of Christ" (rev. ed. 1915, p. 34). Pentecostals, despite official statements as quoted, seldom stress this viewpoint because their stronger emphasis is on healing through God's special providence and the ministry of Christ in the Holy Spirit. (For my critique of healing in the Atonement see vol. 1, chapter 14, n. 36).

[78]For a description of the occurrence of such healings in many places see John Wimber, *Power Evangelism*, "Appendix B, Signs and Wonders in the Twentieth Century."

[79]Matthew 8:16. See above.

with one particular example of what casting out of evil spirits (deliverance) entails. As they went to the place of prayer in Philippi, Paul and his companions were followed daily by a slave girl who "had a spirit of divination."[80] She cried out for many days, "These men are bond-servants of the Most High God, who are proclaiming to you the way of salvation." Paul became increasingly annoyed and finally took action; he "turned and said to the spirit, 'I command you in the name of Jesus Christ to come out of her!'" The result was that "it came out at that very moment" (16:17–18 NASB).

This account is similar to various incidents recorded in the Gospels where people with demons frequently cried out in recognition of Jesus, and they were subsequently delivered. At the beginning of Jesus' ministry a man with an "unclean spirit" exclaimed: "What have you to do with us, Jesus of Nazareth? Have you come to destroy us? I know who you are, the Holy One of God." Jesus thereupon "rebuked him, saying, 'Be silent, and come out of him!' And the unclean spirit, convulsing him and crying with a loud voice, came out of him" (Mark 1:24–26). This incident made a profound impression on those who observed it: "What is this? A new teaching! With authority he commands even the unclean spirits" (v. 27).

It is significant that in the accounts of both Paul and Jesus, the spirit[81] in the person recognized the truth at hand ("these men . . . proclaim to you the way of salvation"; "you are the Holy One of God"). But occupying the human person was actually a foreign spirit, from which one needed deliverance. This foreign spirit was obviously supernatural, having instant recognition of the divine presence; in that sense it was a "spirit of divination." It was also an evil spirit, making the maiden a slave girl. The man with an "unclean spirit" was so bound that it convulsed him as it was cast out. In both instances the spirit could not withstand the person of Jesus or the name of Jesus (which Paul invoked) and immediately came out.[82]

The same spirits referred to elsewhere are frequently shown to both torment and disrupt. Hence they may be the deepest cause of physical or mental disability, even to the point of self-destruction.[83] Thus more is called for than healing, which is a matter of mending what is broken or diseased whether of body or mind. Demonic possession affects a still deeper area: it is a matter of the human spirit being

---

[80] Literally, "a spirit of a python" or a "python spirit" (*pneuma pythōna*). "Python" was the name of the Pythian serpent or dragon who was said to guard the Delphic oracle. Thus "a spirit of divination" has nothing to do with the Holy Spirit but stems from evil.

[81] The terms vary: "spirit," "unclean spirit," "evil spirit," "demon," and "spirit of an unclean demon" (Luke 4:33). A person with such a spirit is frequently described as "demon-possessed" (Mark 1:32 NASB), or as a "demoniac" (Mark 5:15). The Greek verb *daimonizomai* literally means "demonized," that is to say, "under the power of a demon."

[82] We should note that there was no protracted struggle with the spirit in either case. It came out immediately when commanded by Jesus Himself or by Paul in the name of Jesus. There is no example of a lengthy deliverance session in the New Testament.

[83] For example, there is the case of the Gerasene demoniac who could not be bound with chains; he constantly committed acts of self-violence: "Night and day among the tombs and on the mountains he was always crying out, and bruising himself with stones" (Mark 5:5). Incidentally, though the "unclean spirit" gave his name to Jesus: "My name is Legion; for we are many" (v. 9), Jesus had *already* commanded, "Come out of the man, you unclean spirit!" (v. 8). The important thing was to address the spirit, *not* the man, directly and command it to come out. Moreover, Jesus did not cast out one spirit after another, though they were "Legion . . . many." One command was sufficient for all.

taken into bondage by an alien power. Thus there is a pernicious force at work, often affecting mind and body[84] so disruptively that the only way to healing is through deliverance. Moreover, the only way deliverance from such evil can come is through the presence or name of the Holy One who has the power and authority to deliver from even the most vicious tormenting spirit.

Let me summarize a few points. First, such demonic possession comes to light in the presence of Jesus Christ. Whatever may or may not be the outward expression, the evil power that lurks deep within the human personality is aroused at the coming of the Holy One. Hence when one anointed with Christ's Spirit ministers in His name, there are occasions when this very ministry precipitates a crisis in one who is demon-possessed. Although such a person may have long turned away from truth and his inner spirit taken over by this alien spirit, now there is sudden, even startling recognition. For the dimension of perception has now become totally a spiritual one—spirit knowing Spirit—the evil spirit in the one possessed crying out in recognition of the Spirit of holiness. This may not be a verbal recognition—"I know who you are"—but usually some kind of an outcry or startled attitude betokening recognition of a divine presence. For

the inward spirit of evil knows when the Holy Spirit is at hand. Momentarily all the veils are dropped in the presence of the holy God.

Second, not only is there inward recognition but at the same time there may also be inward torment. The demonic spirit, now exposed, feels the awful impact of the Holy Spirit. No longer hidden within the human personality but exposed, it finds the divine presence almost unbearable. It seems as if the Spirit of holiness is bent on torturing the possessed person, thus eliciting some such response as mentioned earlier: "Have you come to destroy us?"[85] Of course, there is no intentional torment; it is simply that the Holy Spirit, like a hot flame of purity, burns into all that is evil.

Third, deliverance may now follow. The alien spirit that has long dominated a person is exposed; it feels the torment of the holy presence and is ready to be cast out. The evil spirit is now overcome by another spirit, the Holy Spirit, and is totally subject to the word that casts it out: "Come out of him, in the name of Jesus Christ." The departing spirit may so convulse a person that the person seems to be at death's door;[86] however, it is in truth the moment when that person experiences the marvel of deliverance into a new life.

This leads us back to the earlier point that this mighty work of deliverance

---

[84] There are several instances in Jesus' ministry when such bodily infirmities as blindness (Matt. 12:22), deafness (Mark 9:25), and dumbness (Matt. 9:32; 12:22; Mark 9:25) were cured when the demon-possessed person was delivered. In one case the evil spirit was addressed by Jesus thus: "You dumb and deaf spirit, I command you, come out of him, and never enter him again" (Mark 9:25). The spirit had caused violent seizures and convulsions (vv. 18, 20); so the problem in origin was deeper than deafness and dumbness. Clearly the physical disabilities were of demonic origin.

[85] Mark 1:24. See the comparable words of the Gerasene demoniac to Jesus in Mark 5:7: "I adjure you by God, do not torment me."

[86] In the deliverance recorded in Mark 9, after Jesus commanded, "Come out of him, and never enter him again," the text continues: "And after crying out and convulsing him terribly, it came out, and the boy was like a corpse; so that most of them said, 'He is dead.'" However, "Jesus took him by the hand and lifted him up, and he arose" (vv. 25–27).

continues through those who truly minister in Jesus' name[87] by the power of His Holy Spirit. During Jesus' lifetime when He was personally present with His disciples, He gave them power and authority over the evil spirits,[88] so that in His name they did exercise deliverance. Jesus Himself cast out demons by the power of the Holy Spirit,[89] and since He has completed His earthly ministry, this same power and authority devolves upon those who receive the gift of the Holy Spirit. They too are enabled to perform the mighty work of liberating people from demonic possession.[90]

It would be hard to overemphasize the value of this ministry of deliverance. For there are countless numbers of persons who desperately need such help. Their condition is not to be identified as sin (which needs forgiveness)[91] or disease (which calls for healing), but with possession, which cries out for

---

[87] The name of Jesus, however, is not some magical power that may be conjured up by anyone to bring about a deliverance. The later account in Acts 19:13–16 of the "itinerant Jewish exorcists" who "undertook to pronounce the name of the Lord Jesus over those who had evil spirits" is a vivid case in point. They tried to do this by saying, "I adjure you by the Jesus whom Paul preaches." The evil spirit, unaffected, answered, "Jesus I know, and Paul I know; but who are you?" Rather than being exorcised, "the man in whom the evil spirit was leaped on them, mastered all of them, and overpowered them, so that they fled out of that house naked and wounded." Conjuring up Jesus' name is ineffective, even dangerous, if not done by one who is truly ministering in Jesus' name.

[88] E.g., Luke 9:1–2: "And he called the twelve together and gave them power and authority [*dynamin kai exousian*] over all demons and to cure diseases, and he sent them out to preach the kingdom of God and to heal." (Note, incidentally, the threefold ministry of preaching, delivering, and healing.) But it was not just the Twelve who had such authority, for later Jesus sent out an additional seventy who "returned with joy, saying, 'Lord, even the demons are subject to us in your name!'" (Luke 10:17). It is important therefore to recognize that such authority in Jesus' day was not limited to the circles of apostles, nor is it limited to any particular "official" persons since that time. Recall Mark 16:17: "And these signs will accompany those who believe [hence, *all* believers]: in my name they will cast out demons. . . ." Incidentally, there is no special gift of deliverance; thus to say, as people sometimes do, that such and such a person has a "deliverance ministry" is in error. Truly there is the special gift of "discerning of spirits" (1 Cor. 12:10 KJV), but all believers are able in the name of Jesus through the power of His Spirit to cast out demons.

[89] On one occasion Jesus said, "If it is by the Spirit of God that I cast out demons, then the kingdom of God has come upon you" (Matt. 12:28). This was not a conditional "if" but a factual one. Even as Jesus healed by the power of God (recall Luke 5:17 supra), so likewise He cast out demons by the same spiritual power.

[90] The importance of prayer should also be noted. Just after the deliverance of the violent demon described in Mark 9, Jesus' disciples asked, "Why could we not cast it out?" Jesus replied, "This kind cannot be driven out by anything but prayer" (vv. 28–29). Shortly before Jesus had performed this exorcism, He had been in prayer on the mountain (vv. 2–4; also see Luke 9:28–36). Coming from the extended time of prayer, Jesus delivered this terrifyingly possessed man. To conclude, although the power of the Spirit is basic, much prayer is also needed for God to perform such a mighty work.

[91] Of course, the condition of every person outside of Christ is one of sin and guilt; thus forgiveness is always needed. The point here, however, is that a person may be so inwardly dominated by evil that unless this is broken he was no condition to hear the word of forgiveness (and reconciliation). It is by Christ that both occur: deliverance from the domination of Satan and forgiveness of sins. The commission that the risen Christ gave to Paul was that he go to Jew and Gentile alike. Jesus said, "I send you to open their eyes, that they may turn from darkness to light and from the power of Satan to God, that they may receive forgiveness of sins and a place among those who are sanctified by faith in me" (Acts 26:18). Turning from the power of Satan to God, therefore, may be essential background for receiving forgiveness of sins.

deliverance. Their inner spirit—the inmost centers of their personhood—have been claimed by an alien force; they are so demonized that they can scarcely hear the word concerning repentance and forgiveness. Their spirits are more than dead to the things of God; they have been *taken over* by another spirit. They may or may not give outward evidence of such possession. There may be an outward semblance of serenity or, contrariwise, that of distortion and violence,[92] but the only hope is the exposure of the deep inward condition and deliverance from it. If such a condition is not recognized and properly handled, there is much resulting confusion. Even the most faithful witness concerning the things of God or on the other hand attempts at healing (viewing such cases as emotional disorders) may leave that person still locked up in spiritual bondage and worse off than before. But when a situation bears the marks of demonic possession,[93] the only possible relief is deliverance by the power of the Holy Spirit.[94]

A further word may be added about the relationship between demonic possession and emotional disorders. Reference was just made to the misdiagnosis that can occur when possession is viewed as a treatable disorder. In such a case attempted healing, whether it be spiritual (through prayers, laying on of hands, etc.) or medical (through therapy and various other kinds of treatments), will fail because the situation is not understood *in depth*. If the situation involves possession, anything short of deliverance is inadequate and only further compounds the problem.

On the other hand, I must also emphasize that there are serious dangers in viewing what are actually emotional disorders as demonic possession. To seek to exorcise a person whose situation calls for other treatment—psychotherapy, medicine, or otherwise—can be a critical mistake and leave a person worse off than before.[95]

In all of this, there is need for much spiritual discernment, that is, discernment by the Holy Spirit, so that the one

---

[92] For example, compare the slave girl, who exhibited no obvious disturbance, with the Gerasene demoniac, who was patently in a condition of continual misery.

[93] From what has been said, the most evident marks are the sensitivity of a possessed person to the presence of holiness and at the same time a feeling of being tormented by that presence.

[94] See, for example, Michael Harper's *Spiritual Warfare,* Don Basham's *Deliver Us From Evil,* and *Deliverance From Evil Spirits* by Michael Scanlan and Randall J. Cirner. There has been extremism in certain sectors of the present renewal, with mass deliverance sessions held for Christians and non-Christians alike and with an exaggerated view that almost every vice is demonic and therefore needs deliverance. (For an effective counterbalance, see *The Dilemma: Deliverance or Discipline?* by W. Robert McAlister.) However, the importance, even urgency, of deliverance in many situations has come to be acutely recognized and is being responded to.

[95] In line with the previous footnote, it is a critical mistake also to seek to exorcise the sins of a believer. For the true believer, i.e., one in whose spirit the Holy Spirit dwells, the inner problem is not demonic possession but "the desires of the flesh." Paul writes that "the desires of the flesh are against the Spirit . . . these are opposed to each other" (Gal. 5:17). Hence what is called for is *not* casting out (deliverance, exorcism) but crucifixion (mortification, putting to death). For example, the first of "the desires of the flesh" that Paul mentions is (sexual) immorality (v. 20). It would be a serious mistake to seek to cast out a supposed "demon of immorality," since the situation calls rather for internal crucifixion by the power of the Spirit. Paul makes this clear in Colossians 3:5, saying, "Put to death ["mortify" KJV] therefore what is earthly in you: immorality. . . ." (Recall chap. 4, "Sanctification.") Immorality is to be put to death; it cannot be cast out. Indeed, let it be

who ministers may know how to proceed.[96] If there is not clear evidence of possession, it is better to proceed along other lines or leave the situation to those better qualified to help. On the other hand, if there is evidence of demon-possession, it is imperative that deliverance be ministered to those who are enduring the inward torments of such possession.

Finally, the ministry of deliverance is especially needed in these latter days because of the increase of diabolical activity. First, apostasy in the church causes the increase in such activity. Paul writes, "The Spirit clearly says that in later times some will abandon[97] the faith and follow deceiving spirits and things taught by demons" (1 Tim.

4:1 NIV). He refers here to believers who forsake the true faith and become captive to demons. Such persons may be beyond restoration; but if there is any hope of return, this will occur only through ministering deliverance.[98] Second, there is a vast increase outside the church in people participating in demonic activities: the occult, witchcraft, even the practice of Satanism.[99] Many have gone so far that a call to faith cannot be heard; they must first be delivered from demonic possession. Third, in many places today where the gospel is preached, there is such captivity to animism and spiritism that without a ministry of deliverance there can be only limited success. Missionaries who venture forth without the power of

---

emphasized: *You cannot cast out the flesh.* Such an attempt (calling the sin "a demon" and then seeking to exorcise it) may even be a cop-out from the arduous and often extended task involved in crucifixion. (Incidentally, the other side of the coin is also true: *One cannot crucify a demon;* it can only be cast out.)

An additional word about the believer: it is important to add that though he *cannot* be internally possessed by a demon, he nonetheless *will be* externally attacked again and again by the devil. The first thing that happened to Jesus after being filled with the Holy Spirit was His temptation by the devil: "Jesus, full of the Holy Spirit, returned from the Jordan, and was led by the Spirit for forty days in the wilderness, tempted by the devil" (Luke 4:1–2). Such assaults did not end there, for "when the devil had ended every temptation, he departed from him [Jesus] until an opportune time" (v. 13). If Satan thus attacked Jesus, how much more is this the case for a believer "full of the Holy Spirit." However, we have the assurance in 1 John 4:4 (NASB): "Greater is He who is in you than he who is in the world." How much we may thank God for this!

[96] Paul's response at Philippi to the slave girl's words, "These men are servants of the Most High God, who proclaim to you the way of salvation," is a good illustration of spiritual discernment. Outwardly such words might have seemed to be a confession of faith that would have pleased Paul; however, he recognized in them a "spirit of divination" that was not of God but evil. Rather than being deluded by her words or even proclaiming to her the word of salvation, Paul cast out the demonic spirit. Later that day Paul, along with Silas, was thrown into jail and after that told the Philippian jailer the good news of salvation, "Believe in the Lord Jesus, and you will be saved" (Acts 16:31). Paul did not in this case cast out an evil spirit, for he discerned there was none present. Rather, he led the jailer directly to faith in Christ. Thus through spiritual discernment Paul acted differently in the two situations. For a further discussion of spiritual discernment see chapter 14, "The Ninefold Manifestation."

[97] Literally, "apostasize from"; the Greek word is *apostēsontai* and is also translated "fall away from" (NASB), "depart from" (KJV, RSV), and "desert from" (NEB).

[98] A believer, as was said earlier, cannot be demon-possessed; however, if he departs from the faith, the Holy Spirit may also depart from him. Then an evil spirit can take over.

[99] Michael Green writes in his book *I Believe in Satan's Downfall:* "Satan worship, fascination with the occult, black and white magic, astrology and horoscopes, seances and tarot cards have become the rage. . . . Despite our professed sophistication, there is today in the West a greater interest in the practice *than for three centuries*" (9, italics added).

THE MISSION OF THE HOLY SPIRIT

the Holy Spirit cannot hope to deliver these captives from demonic spirits. All in all, as the time of the end draws near and Satan "knows that his time is short" (Rev. 12:12), there will be an intensified struggle for the souls of people. Surely all who minister the gospel will need every possible resource so that (in the words of Christ to Paul) "they may turn from darkness to light and from the power of Satan to God, that they may receive forgiveness of sins and a place among those who are sanctified by faith in [Christ]" (Acts 26:18).

In conclusion, it is evident that deliverance from demonic spirits (like healing) is one of the attestations of the gospel of salvation. When people are delivered, it is an extraordinary sign of God's power confirming the message of new life in Christ. Recall again the words of Mark 16: "These signs will accompany those who believe: in my name they will cast out demons . . ." with the result: "the Lord worked with them and confirmed the message by the signs that attended it" (vv. 17 and 20). Hence, casting out demons is one of the signs that shows forth the Good News about Christ. For when people behold the supernatural power of God to deliver the demon-possessed, they are vividly assured that the gospel must also be the power of God unto salvation.

III. CERTIFICATION— ATTESTATION, SEALING

Third, the Holy Spirit comes for the purpose of certification. By the coming of the Holy Spirit there is testimony to God's acceptance and approval of His people.

Let us begin with Jesus Himself. We have already mentioned the descent of the Holy Spirit from heaven upon Jesus and how this power enabled Him to begin His ministry. Now we observe that following Jesus' baptism when the Spirit descended as a dove, "a voice came from heaven, 'Thou art my beloved Son; with thee I am well pleased' " (Luke 3:22). The coming of the Spirit from heaven pointed to God's approval—"my beloved Son . . . well pleased." This was demonstrative testimony that Jesus was indeed God's Son, approved and pleasing in His sight.[100] In the Fourth Gospel are found these words about Jesus: "On him has God the Father set his seal" (6:27). The seal was undoubtedly the seal of the Father's approval given at the descent of the Holy Spirit.

We turn next to the account of the Caesareans and observe likewise that the coming of the Holy Spirit was certification of their acceptance and approval by God. When the Holy Spirit fell upon the centurion and his company, Peter himself was convinced that the Gentiles had been accepted by God, for he declared, "Can any one forbid water for baptizing these people who have received the Holy Spirit just as we have?" (Acts 10:47). Peter had no hesitation in proceeding to baptize these Gentiles because God had attested their salvation through the gift of the Spirit.[101] Some time later Peter rehearsed these events to the apostles and brethren in Jerusalem and described how the Holy Spirit fell on the Caesareans "just as on us at the beginning" (11:15). As a result, those in Jerusalem "glorified God, saying, 'Then to the Gentiles also

---

[100] N. Geldenhuys writes, "This opening of the heaven, the descent of the Holy Ghost in a visible shape, and the voice from heaven, were to Jesus the final assurance from God that He was indeed the Son and the anointed Messiah, and that God wholly approved of His assumption of the work of redemption" (*The Gospel of Luke,* NICNT, 147).

[101] As previously noted, the immediate evidence was the Caesareans' speaking in tongues and praising God, but, of course, this pointed back to the reason for these phenomena: they had received the gift of the Holy Spirit.

God has granted repentance unto life'" (v. 18). The fact that God had given the Holy Spirit to the Caesareans was certification to the apostles and brethren that the Gentiles had indeed received salvation.

But not only was the coming of the Holy Spirit certification to others of their salvation and acceptance; it was also God's witness to the Caesareans themselves. On a still later occasion Peter spoke to the apostles and elders how "God made choice among you, that by my mouth the Gentiles [at Caesarea] should hear the word of the gospel and believe" (Acts 15:7). Peter immediately added, "And God who knows the heart bore witness to them, giving them the Holy Spirit just as he did to us" (v. 8). God "bore witness to them" means "showed that he accepted them."[102] It was the Gentiles' own inner certification that they had truly heard and believed, and that God had "cleansed their hearts by faith" (v. 9)[103] They were now sons of God, attested by the Holy Spirit.[104]

To summarize the two accounts about the Caesareans: the coming of the Holy Spirit was both an external certification to others that they had indeed entered into salvation and a certification to themselves (hence internal) of their acceptance by God.

It is also likely that the gift of the Holy Spirit to the Samaritans and the Ephesians had the same dual certification. In addition to the fact that the Holy Spirit was given for enabling believers to witness to the world, His very coming at Samaria and Ephesus was also God's own attestation both to others and themselves that they had been accepted as His children. The Samaritans, particularly because the Jews viewed them as beyond the pale of God's concern, needed this certification. The far-distant Ephesians likewise by the gift of God's Spirit were shown to be fully accepted into God's family.

To move briefly to the contemporary scene: one of the striking features of the present spiritual renewal is the way in which people in many churches and denominations that have been long separated from and even antagonistic to one another have changed their attitude. For example, many Protestants who became involved in the renewal were ill-prepared to accept Roman Catholics because they (the Protestants) were not at all sure whether Catholics had experienced salvation. Then the Holy Spirit began to move among Catholics with the resulting dynamic presence of God, transcendent praise, and powerful witness to the gospel. All the Protestants could do (like the apostles and brethren in Jerusalem about the Caesareans) was to say, "Then to the Roman Catholics also God has granted repentance unto life!"

We return now to the New Testament and look further into this matter of inner certification by examining, first, some of Paul's words to the Romans. We have earlier noted this statement of

---

[102]The NIV translation.

[103]This suggests that the receipt of the earlier gift of the Holy Spirit promised at Pentecost likewise served as certification of salvation. J. H. E. Hull asks rhetorically, "When Peter told his congregation on the day of Pentecost that the gift of the Spirit could be theirs, did he not mean . . . that the receipt of the Spirit would, amongst other things, be proof of their salvation?" (*The Holy Spirit in the Acts of the Apostles*, 165–66).

[104]Obviously there is a great difference between the approval given to Jesus, who needed no salvation, and the Gentiles who had received it. However, the Gentiles had been accepted through faith in Jesus and by this faith had become sons of God. Hence, it was as if God were saying to them because of their salvation through Christ: "You are my beloved sons; with you I am well pleased."

his: "You have received the spirit of sonship. When we cry, 'Abba! Father!' it is the Spirit himself bearing witness with our spirit that we are children of God" (8:15–16). Thus through the reception of the Holy Spirit there is an inner testimony or certification that we are now God's children. Our very cry with great force and meaning[105] of "Abba! Father" [106] is the result of the Holy Spirit's inner testimony.

In regard to inner certification we should also note Paul's parallel language in Galatians: "To prove that[107] you are sons, God has sent into our hearts the Spirit of his Son, crying 'Abba! Father!' " (Gal. 4:6 NEB). This again is not a matter of external certification or proof, but a profoundly internal one, for the Spirit cries from within the heart.[108]

This inner certification may also be described as *assurance*. The fact that we are able to cry, "Abba! Father!" makes for a deep assurance of being God's children, hence heirs of salvation. In both Romans and Galatians the witness of the Spirit is not only to our sonship but also to our being heirs. Romans 8:17 says, ". . . if children, then heirs of God and fellow heirs with Christ" and Galatians 4:7, ". . . if a son then an heir." The Holy Spirit whom we have received is the assurance of our inheritance.

Let us pause a moment to reflect on the significance of this certification and assurance. Paul is *not* talking about the activity of the Holy Spirit in effecting sonship (salvation), *but* in certifying (bearing witness) to it. Without the work of the Holy Spirit there is, of

---

[105]The word for "cry," *krazō,* means to "cry out loudly." In Romans 8:15 *krazomen* ("we cry") "denotes the loud, irrepressible cry with which the consciousness of sonship breaks from the Christian heart" (EGT, in loco). Incidentally, it is possible that Paul is referring indirectly to glossolalic utterance in Romans 8:15 (see chap. 9, n. 50). "They . . . began to speak in other tongues, as the Spirit gave them utterance" (Acts 2:4) is quite similar to Paul's words "When we cry 'Abba! Father!' it is the Spirit himself bearing witness" (RSV). They (we) do the speaking, but it is the Spirit who gives the utterance (bears witness). Speaking with tongues and crying, "Abba! Father!" both signify a tremendous outbreak from deep within; both are cries that come from the activity of the Holy Spirit who has been given; both are addressed not to men but to God (recall 1 Cor. 14:2).

[106]The biblical expression is *"abba ho patēr." Abba* is an Aramaic word that expresses an intimate family relationship of child to father; *patēr* is the customary Greek term for father. Hence "abba" particularly displays this new relationship as God's child and through the Holy Spirit the cry breaks out with great power and heightened meaning. "Abba!" may, accordingly, be a borderline term between ordinary, yet intimate, speech and the transcendent speech of tongues. In that case Paul could be referring indirectly to glossolalia through the word "Abba" (see previous footnote). I will again interject a personal note. My first experience of speaking in tongues came at the very moment, when in the midst of God's visitation, I was saying "Ab-ba." Hardly had the second syllable been pronounced when I began speaking a new language! Truly the Father was being praised in language transcending even "Abba! Father!" Thereafter it has become a pattern of prayer to move from the transcendent language of the Spirit to the common language but with a heightened sense of God's intimate presence.

[107]The NEB translation of *hoti*. This translation, I believe, is preferable to "because" (in RSV, KJV, NIV, and NASB). Paul is speaking demonstratively—"to demonstrate that," as "proof of that," rather than causally. The *Cambridge Greek Testament*, in loco, reads, *"oti* is demonstrative 'But as a proof that,' rather than strictly causal."

[108]It is noteworthy that Romans 8:15–16 says that "we" cry out, whereas in Galatians 4:6 it is "the Spirit of his Son." Both, of course, are true: it is the one outcry in which we verbalize the speech and the Spirit provides the content.

course, no salvation;[109] however, this is *another* action of the Holy Spirit that, presupposing salvation, demonstrates God's certification and deepens our assurance. The significance of this for the Christian life is great because of the peace and joy it brings.

We may now look more closely into assurance. There is a sense in which every believer has an assurance of being a child of God. According to Hebrews 11:1, "faith is the assurance[110] of things hoped for, the conviction of things not seen." However, there is also a *"full assurance"*[111] that may lie ahead. Paul speaks of the full assurance of *understanding*; for he writes the Colossians of his concern for their "attaining to all the wealth that comes from the full assurance of understanding, resulting in a true knowledge of God's mystery, that is, Christ Himself" (2:2 NASB). In Hebrews there is concern expressed for the full assurance of *hope*: "We desire each one of you to show the same earnestness in realizing the full assurance of hope until the end" (6:11). Later in Hebrews there is an encouraging statement about full assurance of *faith*: "Let us draw near with a true heart in full assurance of faith" (10:22). Based on the three passages just quoted, there is the possibility of a full assurance of understanding, of hope, and of faith. This very possibility suggests that not all believers have such full assurance, but it is much to be desired and can be realized. From what has been previously said, it is apparent that the realization of this full assurance of understanding, hope, and faith is basically from and by the Holy Spirit.

In this connection it is interesting to note that the Westminster Confession of Faith (chapter XVIII, "Of the Assurance of Grace and Salvation") contains a statement about "an infallible assurance of faith." It speaks first about "true believers" who may "be certainly assured that they are in a state of grace." Then the Confession adds,

> This certainty is not a bare conjectural and probable persuasion, grounded upon a fallible hope; but *an infallible assurance of faith,* founded upon the divine truth of the promises of salvation, the inward evidence of those graces unto which these promises are made, *the testimony of the Spirit of adoption witnessing with our spirits that we are the children of God. . . .* This infallible assurance doth not so belong to the essence of faith, but that *a true believer may wait long, and conflict with many difficulties before he be partaker* of it. . ." (italics added).[112]

This statement adds to "full assurance" the concept of "infallible assurance." However, I believe the Confession is basically in accord with Scripture: not all believers have this assurance of faith and salvation, but it may come at a later time particularly through the inner witness or testimony of the Holy Spirit.

This full assurance means a great deal. For the individual there are many fruits—inner peace and calm, a continuing thanksgiving, and an increasing confidence in God.[113] This assurance also provides additional strength for Christian testimony, for there is nothing quite so convincing as the witness that stems out of complete certainty. Yet it is not one's own certainty but that which the Holy Spirit constantly rein-

---

[109] As I have described in prior chapters, especially "Calling," "Regeneration," and "Sanctification."

[110] The Greek word is *hypostasis.* The KJV and NEB translate it "substance."

[111] The Greek word is *plērophoria* and is used in the three cases that follow.

[112] Sections I–III.

[113] The Westminster Confession speaks of "the proper fruits of this assurance" namely, that the "heart may be in peace and joy in the Holy Ghost, in love and thankfulness to God, and in strength and cheerfulness in the duties of obedience. . ." (Sect. IV).

forces! This is the importance of full assurance in Christian faith and practice.[114]

In the contemporary spiritual renewal one of the striking notes is the inward assurance that is again and again attested. Many people are finding through the inward action of the Holy Spirit a deeper assurance of faith than they had ever known before. It is the same Holy Spirit who brought them to salvation, but the difference is quite marked.[115] "Full assurance" seems qualitatively beyond all previous experience. "Now I *know*" is the witness of many persons.

We will next consider a number of scriptures in First John that deal with *knowledge*. The purpose of this Epistle is stated near the conclusion: "I write this to you who believe in the name of the Son of God, that you may know that you have eternal life" (5:13).[116] John is concerned that faith become knowledge, assurance, certainty. How does such knowledge come about? I previously noted the words of 1 John 2:20, "You have been anointed by the Holy One, and you know all things," and then commented on the relevance of this statement for the knowledge of truth.[117] At this juncture we move on to

observe that this same anointing of the Spirit gives sure knowledge of our position in Christ. John focuses on abiding and declares two things: "We know by this that He abides in us, by the Spirit whom He has given us" (3:24 NASB) and "By this we know that we abide in Him and He in us, because He has given us of His Spirit" (4:13 NASB). In sum, by the gift—the anointing—of the Holy Spirit we know that Christ abides in us and we in Him, and that (in accordance with 5:13) we have eternal life.

At issue here is not the reality itself but the knowledge of the reality. It is not, for example, that by the anointing of the Holy Spirit Christ abides in us, but that through this gift we *know* He abides in us and we in Him. It is not by the gift of the Holy Spirit that we have eternal life, but that we *know* we have it. The Spirit brings inward certainty to all such spiritual matters.

Let us look at other Scriptures that speak of this inward certification as a *pledge* or *guarantee*. Two passages in 2 Corinthians contain this. First, "He [God] has put his seal upon us and given us his Spirit in our hearts as a guarantee" (1:22). This guarantee refers back to "all the promises of God" (v. 20), doubtless including eternal life.[118] Sec-

---

[114]Lest there be some confusion, let me add that I am *not* talking about "eternal security" (see chap. 5, "Perseverance") in the above paragraphs. Even the Westminster Confession, which does affirm eternal security (see the previous chap. XVII in the Confession entitled "Of the Perseverance of the Saints"), does not, as we noted, hold to a view of infallible assurance for all true believers. Whether one affirms or disaffirms eternal security, there is still the need for, and possibility of, "full assurance."

[115]In my first book related to the charismatic renewal, *The Era of the Spirit,* I wrote: "How different it is now! There is an assurance wrought by the Holy Spirit laden with surprising meaning and vitality . . . the fact is that the reality of grace and salvation has been fully confirmed by the inward testimony of the Holy Spirit. It is even possible to sing such a hymn as 'Blessed Assurance'—and to do so from the heart!" (p. 46).

[116]This may be compared with the Gospel of John where another purpose is likewise stated near the end: "These [things] are written that you may believe that Jesus is the Christ, the Son of God, and that believing you may have life in his name" (20:31). The purpose of the Gospel is that people may have faith and salvation; the purpose of the Epistle, written to those who have already experienced such, is that they may have knowledge and assurance.

[117]See section I.

[118]Philip E. Hughes speaks of this as "the authentic guarantee of the full inheritance of the glory yet to be revealed" (*The Second Epistle to the Corinthians,* NICNT, 43).

ond, "He who has prepared us for this very thing is God, who has given us the Spirit as a guarantee" (5:5). "This very thing" refers to the life to come—"a house not made with hands, eternal in the heavens" (v. 1). The guarantee, or pledge, of that future life is the gift of the Holy Spirit. Paul writes about this guarantee in a similar passage: "You . . . were sealed with the promised Holy Spirit, which is the guarantee of our inheritance until we acquire possession of it, to the praise of his glory" (Eph. 1:13–14). By the reception of the promised gift of the Spirit there is a sealing, which results in the guarantee of the future eternal inheritance.

Again, it is important to observe that the relevant matter is not the promises of God, the life to come, or the future inheritance, but the *guarantee* of these things. It is not by the gift of the Spirit that we have eternal life, but that we have the guarantee of it. The Spirit, who is given, guarantees the full possession of what is yet to come.[119]

One further thing needs to be added. The gift of the Spirit is by no means simply an outward pledge or guarantee of the future possession; it is profoundly an inward operation. The dynamic presence and power of the Holy Spirit makes for such spiritual intensity that the future in some sense is already present. This action of God's Spirit accordingly is a vital earnest,[120] or down payment, of the future inheritance.

To return to the present scene: one of

the highlights of the contemporary movement of the Holy Spirit is a strong eschatological awareness. There is, first, the sense of the presence of the future. The coming of the Spirit brings about a deepened knowledge that one has already passed from death into life and that while on the earth, one already has citizenship in heaven. This world seems less like a preparation for the next than an anticipation of what is to come. One of the common expressions is "Glory!"[121]—a word that conveys with extraordinary effectiveness the ineffable sense of the presence of the future consummation. Second, there is a heightened sense of expectation about the coming of the Lord. On almost every hand there is the renewed cry of "Maranatha"—"Our Lord, come" (1 Cor. 16:22). The cry does not come from a sense of His absence or distance, but from a sense of His powerful presence. It is the Lord, vividly known through the Holy Spirit, hence in His spiritual reality, whom His people yearn to behold in His glorious coming. It is the intense desire in the Spirit to see the Lord face to face.[122]

EXCURSUS: SANCTIFICATION

In this chapter we have dealt with the mission of the Holy Spirit in terms of guiding into truth, granting power for ministry, and certifying faith; however, nothing has been said about sanctification. This question may be put:

---

[119] According to Johannes Behm in TDNT (article on ἀρραβών), "the Spirit whom God has given them is for Christians the guarantee of their full future possession of salvation" (1:475).

[120] The word *arrabōn* ("pledge" or "guarantee") can also be translated "earnest" with the meaning found in the expression "earnest money."

[121] Peter speaks about being "a partaker in the glory that is to be revealed" (1 Peter 5:1).

[122] Emil Brunner, writing about the church, says it well: "The more powerfully life in the Spirit of God is present in it, the more urgent is its expectation of the Coming of Jesus Christ; so that *the fullness of the possession of the Spirit and the urgency of expectation are always found together* as they were in the primitive community" (*The Christian Doctrine of the Church, Faith, and the Consummation: Dogmatics* 3:400) (italics added).

Since it is the *Holy* Spirit who comes, would not another, perhaps even primary purpose be sanctification? Would not His mission above all be to bring about holiness?

In answer, it is apparent from the many scriptures quoted in the previous pages related to the mission of the Spirit that nothing is said in them about sanctification. This, however, is not because the Holy Spirit has no relation to sanctification (an impossible idea!) but because His coming, His mission, is *for a different purpose*. It is an action that presupposes the Spirit's sanctifying work that occurs in salvation. Recall the words of Paul in 2 Thessalonians 2:13, where he speaks of salvation "through sanctification by the Spirit." Hence, every believer has received this sanctification by the Holy Spirit.[123] Since the coming of the Holy Spirit presupposes salvation (as we have seen),[124] it presupposes the Spirit's fundamental and preparatory work in the operation of sanctification. Paul recalls, at one point, the words of Jesus to him about being "sanctified by faith in [Him]" (Acts 26:18).[125] This means that whenever people come to saving faith, they are essentially sanctified. Their hearts are "cleansed . . . by faith" (to use Peter's words in Acts 15:9), and cleansing is basically the work of the Holy Spirit.

Now we may add, *it is because this sanctification has occurred that a person is prepared for the coming of the*

Holy Spirit. The Holy Spirit comes only to those whose hearts and lives have been made ready. The Holy Spirit, accordingly, is given to those already sanctified by faith, hence to believers, for the purpose of mission.

At this juncture two misunderstandings must be guarded against. First, based on what has just been said, it is a mistake to identify the coming of the Holy Spirit (baptism in the Spirit, the gift of the Spirit, etc.) with sanctification. This confuses *the soteriological work of the Holy Spirit with His missiological work*. Clearly the first must precede the second but also *must not* be identified with it. Practically speaking, this mistake readily leads to the unfortunate assumption that every believer already—in his regeneration/sanctification—has experienced the coming of the Holy Spirit. Thus there is nothing further needed to equip him for the mission ahead. Such a view, often held in evangelical circles, effectively eliminates the entire dimension of the coming of the Holy Spirit with all that it brings about.

A second misunderstanding identifies *the coming of the Holy Spirit with "entire sanctification."*[126] This viewpoint recognizes that sanctification in salvation occurs, but that entire, or complete, sanctification is also possible through baptism in the Holy Spirit. Thus the Pentecostal experience, much to be desired, results in entire sanctification.[127] Here a double mistake

---

[123]See chapter 4, "Sanctification," for a fuller discussion of this subject. The sanctification referred to above is initial sanctification. There is also continuing, or progressive, sanctification.

[124]Recall chapter 8, "Concluding Remarks, no. 3.

[125]See also Acts 20:32. These are the only direct references to sanctification in the Book of Acts; both relate to salvation. Obviously neither of these references occurs in connection with earlier passages about the coming of the Holy Spirit.

[126]See chapter 4 "Sanctification," II.C., especially n. 37.

[127]In the Holiness movement of the late nineteenth century there was the frequent identification of "entire sanctification" with baptism in the Holy Spirit or Pentecost. For example, just one year prior to the Pentecostal outpouring in 1901, Charles J. Fowler, the president of the National Association for the Promotion of Holiness, wrote that he meant

occurs: first, that there is the possibility of entire sanctification in this life (this is neither biblically sound nor experientially valid) and, second, that such is to be identified with baptism in the Spirit. I might add, however, that the merit of this viewpoint is that there is the anticipation of a further work of the Holy Spirit beyond initial sanctification. Nonetheless, in addition to the double mistakes just mentioned, this viewpoint undermines (similar to some evangelical views) the great and challenging purpose in the coming of the Holy Spirit by misidentifying it with "entire sanctification."[128]

"by Pentecost what the New Testament means by it—what Methodism has always meant by it—we mean that work of grace one needs after his regeneration, and may have, and what is known in theology as ENTIRE SANCTIFICATION" (quoted by Donald W. Dayton in *Theological Roots of Pentecostalism,* 92). Incidentally, though John Wesley, the founder of Methodism, did teach "entire sanctification," he never identified this with the Pentecostal baptism in the Spirit. The Holiness movement, growing out of Methodism, widely made this identification (see further, Vinson Synan, *The Holiness-Pentecostal Movement,* 63).

[128]In the next chapter, "The Reception of the Holy Spirit," I will make reference to the view of complete sanctification held by some Pentecostal bodies. However, as will be noted, this sanctification is not identified with baptism in the Holy Spirit.

11

The Reception of the Holy Spirit

Let us now consider the reception of the Holy Spirit. The Holy Spirit is given, but a gift must be received. Here our concern will be with the basis of this reception, the matter of outward means, and the context in which the Holy Spirit is given and received. We will discuss these in turn.

I. THE BASIS: FAITH

The Holy Spirit comes to those who believe in Jesus Christ. From all that has been said about the Holy Spirit's being the Spirit of the exalted Lord, whose central purpose is to bear witness to Him, it is apparent that the gift of the Spirit is available only to those who believe in Him. Faith in Christ is the sole basis for the reception of the Holy Spirit.

A. The Essentiality of Faith

Thus we begin by emphasizing the *essentiality* of faith in Jesus Christ. This

faith is personally oriented. It is directed to Him as the One who lived, died, and rose again from the dead. Through a person's believing in Him forgiveness of sins becomes a glorious reality, and the way is prepared for the reception of the Holy Spirit. In the words of Peter on the Day of Pentecost: "Repent, and be baptized every one of you in the name of Jesus Christ for the forgiveness of your sins; and you shall receive the gift of the Holy Spirit. For the promise is to you . . ." (Acts 2:38–39). The promise of the Spirit is to those who have come to faith in Jesus Christ, and it is by that same faith that the Holy Spirit is received.[1]

In all the Acts narratives related to the coming of the Holy Spirit, faith in Christ is shown to be essential. Those who believe in Him receive the Holy Spirit. This is demonstrated most clearly in the accounts of the Caesareans, Samaritans, and Ephesians. Let us observe each.

---

[1]Michael Harper writes that "the benefits of the New Covenant include the gift of the Holy Spirit as well as the forgiveness of sins. From Pentecost onwards the Church faithfully proclaimed that Christ forgives *and* baptizes in the Holy Spirit. They taught that all who repent and believe are justified by faith, and that all who are justified by faith may receive the Holy Spirit by faith" (*Walk in the Spirit,* 13). It is faith—nothing else—faith in Christ, that is essential to receiving the Holy Spirit.

Peter proclaimed Jesus Christ and His life, death, and resurrection to the Caesareans—the Roman centurion and his household—and climaxed his message with these words: "To him all the prophets bear witness that every one who believes in him receives forgiveness of sins through his name" (Acts 10:43). Then follows this statement: "While Peter was still saying this, the Holy Spirit fell on all who heard the word" (v. 44). It was to those who believed in Christ, who "heard the word," setting forth Christ and calling for faith in Him, that the Holy Spirit was given.

Philip at Samaria "proclaimed to them the Christ" (Acts 8:5). As a result, the Samaritans came to faith and were baptized. "When they believed Philip as he preached the good news about the kingdom of God and the name of Jesus Christ, they were baptized, both men and women" (v. 12). Later Peter and John came down from Jerusalem and ministered to them the Holy Spirit (vv. 14–17). Again, the Holy Spirit came to those who believed in Jesus Christ.

Paul proclaimed Christ to the Ephesians before they received the gift of the Holy Spirit. He reminded them that "John baptized with the baptism of repentance, telling the people to believe in the one who was to come after him, that is, Jesus" (Acts 19:4). "On hearing this" the Ephesians "were baptized in the name of the Lord Jesus" (v. 5).

Later Paul laid hands on them, and they received the Holy Spirit (v. 6). Once again, to those who believed in Christ the Holy Spirit came.

We may also call to mind two relevant passages in Paul's epistles. In Galatians 3 Paul asks, "Did you receive the Spirit by works of the law, or by hearing with faith?" (v. 2). Since the implied answer is the latter, this further reinforces the point of the essentiality of faith. In Ephesians 1 Paul writes, "In him you also, who have heard the word of truth, the gospel of your salvation, and have believed in him, were sealed with the promised Holy Spirit" (v. 13). Hearing and believing, similar to "hearing with faith," is the basis for receiving the Holy Spirit.

It is apparent from both Acts and the Epistles that the Holy Spirit was received by those who believed in Christ. It was not a belief directed to the Holy Spirit[2] but to Jesus Christ, and in that same faith[3] the Holy Spirit was given.

B. The Dynamics of Faith

We now consider the dynamics of that faith in Christ wherein the Holy Spirit is received. At the outset it is important to recognize that faith is a dynamic, moving reality. Although its object, Jesus Christ, is the fixed focal point, faith may well be in process. It is not a static, once-for-all thing but may develop or increase under the impact of Jesus Christ. Indeed, all who believe

[2]It would be a mistake to say that faith has a second focus beyond Christ, namely, the Holy Spirit. Christian faith remains centered on Jesus Christ throughout. In Him is "every spiritual blessing" (Eph. 1:3), whether it be forgiveness of sins, the gift of the Holy Spirit, or anything else. However, while Christian faith must always keep the focus on Christ, it does also expect from Him the gift of the Holy Spirit. A failure to expect this is less than a Christ-centered faith.

[3]This whole matter of faith as the essential condition for receiving the Holy Spirit and also for the quality of life that follows is set forth well by Kevin and Dorothy Ranaghan: "If there is any one thing which most strikingly characterizes Catholic pentecostals it is not tongues or singing or prayer groups; it is that *they came to seek a renewal in the Spirit in simple faith*, and having received the answer to their prayer they begin to walk in a newness of faith. The people involved in the charismatic renewal are basically men and women of new, richer faith" (italics added) (*Catholic Pentecostals,* 144).

are called on to "grow in the grace and knowledge of our Lord and Savior Jesus Christ" (2 Peter 3:18); thus faith may be strengthened.[4]

This does not mean that the first moment of faith lacks genuineness or significance. Quite the contrary, for initial faith directed to Jesus is the moment of realizing the marvel of forgiveness of sins and new life in His name. Hence, entrance on the way of faith is far more important than anything that may happen afterward. This cannot be overemphasized.

Now we may proceed to speak of faith in movement, faith in process. This may be a matter of a deepening of faith through further repentance and commitment wherein God's resources of grace are all the more experienced. This may also lead to a point of spiritual breakthrough into fuller Christian life and witness.

Such an understanding of the dynamics of faith is essential to a proper consideration of the reception of the Holy Spirit. *There is a certain moment in faith, whether at the outset or somewhere along the way, when the Holy Spirit may be received.* This moment may or may not coincide with the moment of receiving forgiveness of sins. It may happen shortly after, or days, months, even years later. Whatever the case, faith in Jesus Christ is and remains the essential matter whenever the Holy Spirit is given.

Before going further, let us turn again to the record in the Book of Acts, for there is delineated in a vivid way the gift of the Holy Spirit in relation to faith.

Let us first reflect on the experience of Jesus' disciples. The coming of the Spirit to them on the Day of Pentecost was not at the commencement of their faith in Jesus. Some one hundred and twenty of them are described as "brethren" (note the language of Acts 1:15–16), brethren of one another through a relationship with Jesus Christ. It is they who awaited the promised gift of the Spirit. Of the one hundred and twenty, many had been with Jesus since the beginning of His ministry, the apostles as well as others, and had passed through a variety of experiences. There was the original call to discipleship, months and years of fellowship with Jesus, then a forsaking of Him at the time of His crucifixion and death, and after that a turning again ("conversion")[5] to Jesus in His risen presence. At that time according to the Fourth Gospel, the Holy Spirit was breathed into them (John 20:22). Some fifty days later at Pentecost (Acts 2:1 ff.) the Holy Spirit was poured out. Thus there was a period of some three or more years from the disciples' initial encounter with Jesus to the day of the coming of the Spirit.

How long had the first disciples been believers? This is not an easy question to answer. In one sense they had been believers for some time. They had long before given up everything to follow Jesus and had done mighty works in His name, including healing and the casting out of demons. Seventy of them were told by Jesus, "Do not rejoice in this, that the spirits are subject to you; but rejoice that your names are written in heaven" (Luke 10:20). This statement of Jesus suggests that their faith already

---

[4]Some of the Scriptures that depict faith as growing or increasing include Luke 17:5; 2 Corinthians 10:15; Philippians 1:25; and 2 Thessalonians 1:3.

[5]One thinks of the words of Jesus to Peter just prior to the Crucifixion: "Simon, Simon, behold, Satan demanded to have you, that he might sift you like wheat, but I have prayed for you that your faith may not fail; and when you have turned again, strengthen your brethren" (Luke 22:31–32).

was of eternal significance. According to John's Gospel, Jesus told His disciples shortly before His death, "You are already made clean by the word which I have spoken to you" (John 15:3). This also suggests that Jesus' presence and word had awakened such a response in the disciples that they had truly been made clean. Yet when Jesus spoke about His coming resurrection, there seemed to be little faith; it was only His risen presence that made their faith return. Their belief then took on a deeper and more living quality, and this kind of faith began with the Resurrection.[6]

Thus we may say that when the Pentecostal event occurred, it was to many who had long known Jesus. Despite numerous ups and downs, their faith had continued to grow. However we may evaluate the quality of their faith, it is an obvious fact that the gift of the Spirit occurred to those who were already believers. Indeed, Peter's later question to the apostles and brethren in Jerusalem concerning the gift of the Holy Spirit given to the Caesareans clearly implies this: "If then God gave the same gift to them as he gave to us believing[7] in the Lord Jesus Christ, who was I that I could withstand God?" (Acts 11:17). On the way of faith, believing, they received the gift of the Holy Spirit.

The experience of the first disciples points in the direction of what has been happening among many people in our day: the gift of the Spirit is being received by those who for some time have been walking the way of faith. Many who have long known Jesus and come to faith in Him are now receiving the Holy Spirit in fullness.[8] Thus in a striking manner this early Christian experience is recurring.[9]

---

[6] Recall our previous brief discussion of this as the disciples' day of regeneration (chap. 7, III.A. "The Paraclete").

[7] Here I do not follow the RSV, which has "when we believed." The RSV reading would suggest that it was only when the disciples came to faith that they received the gift of the Holy Spirit. However, the Greek word is *pisteusasin*, an aorist participle, which usually expresses action antecedent to the main verb, or, less frequently, simultaneous with it. If antecedent, the translation would be "having believed" or "after believing" (NASB); if simultaneous or coincident, the translation "when we believed" (RSV) would be more satisfactory. However, the participle could contain *both* ideas, and therefore the most adequate translation would be neither the RSV "when we believed" nor the NASB "after believing" but simply "believing." (The KJV and NIV reading as "who believed" does not sufficiently reflect the continuing quality of faith.) This would suggest that belief had been there for some time (antecedent aorist); but rather than being simply a past fact, it was also a continuing reality (simultaneous aorist). In other words, *on the way of faith* the Holy Spirit was poured out. F. D. Bruner in his *Theology of the Holy Spirit* quotes the RSV and adds, "The apostles considered *Pentecost* to be . . . the date of their conversion" (196). Unfortunately, Bruner does not go into the Greek text, which makes for other possible, and more likely, interpretations.

[8] It is sometimes said that it is improper to draw any parallel between the first disciples' experience of the Holy Spirit and Christian experience thereafter. For, unlike believers after them, they could not have received the Holy Spirit until a later time because the Spirit was not given until Jesus left them. In answer to this, I submit that while it is true that their experience was necessarily spread over a period of time, a rather extended way of faith, this should not rule out the possibility that many after them would follow a like pattern. *Unlike* the original disciples, we may receive the Holy Spirit at the initiation of faith; *like* the first disciples, we may and often do have to wait for an extended period.

[9] E.g., see the story of Russell Bixler in *It Can Happen to Anybody,* especially chapter 4, "The New Creation," and chapter 9, "The Power Flows." Several years of walking the way of faith as a Church of the Brethren pastor separate the two experiences. Incidentally,

As we survey various other narratives that refer to the reception of the Spirit, it is apparent that there are other parallels to the experience of receiving the Holy Spirit along the way of faith. In the first post-Pentecost account of the Holy Spirit being given—namely, to the Samaritans—this occurred some days after they first came to faith in Christ. We have already noted how Philip proclaimed the gospel and many believed. However, despite their new-found faith, they had not yet received the Holy Spirit. Several days later (at least four or five[10]) the apostles Peter and John came down from Jerusalem and "prayed for them that they might receive the Holy Spirit. . . . Then they laid their hands on them and they received the Holy Spirit" (Acts 8:15, 17). So it was along the way of faith that the Samaritans experienced the outpouring of the Holy Spirit.

The Samaritan story likewise has numerous parallels with the contemporary scene. Many, after coming to faith in Jesus Christ, have later had hands laid on them and have experienced the fullness of the Holy Spirit. As with the Samaritans, earnest prayer has often been the immediate background. Frequently, too, one person has been the evangelist (like Philip) to bring people to a commitment to Christ, and others have been used by the Lord in ministering the Holy Spirit.[11] Thus the two experiences have occurred over a period of time—from initial faith to the reception of the Holy Spirit.

We turn next to the account of Saul of Tarsus in Acts 9:1–19. There was likewise a delay of several days (in this case, three) between the time Saul first encountered Jesus and the moment he was filled with the Holy Spirit. As the narrative discloses, a voice from heaven said, "Saul, Saul, why do you persecute me?" (v. 4). Saul thereupon inquired, "Who are you, Lord?" and the voice replied, "I am Jesus, whom you are persecuting " (v. 5). After this encounter and the beginning of faith,[12] Saul fasted and prayed for three days in Damascus, after which Ananias came to him, and, "laying his hands on him, he said, 'Brother Saul,[13] the Lord Jesus

---

Dwight L. Moody's experience of being "filled with the Holy Spirit" (supra, chap. 10, n. 63) occurred fifteen years after his conversion.

[10] Samaria was about a two days' journey from Jerusalem. By the time word about the Samaritans' faith had reached Jerusalem, and Peter and John had traveled to Samaria for minstry, at least four days, possibly even a week, would have elapsed. The exact number of days, of course, is not important; clearly there was an intervening time, however.

[11] An illustration of this is the case of Dr. Charles Meisgeier, a university professor, who heard the evangelist Billy Graham at a Madison Square Garden meeting. Speaking afterward of his conversion, Meisgeier said, "Christ became my Lord and Saviour in a real and existential way." Years later, through the ministry of Dennis Bennett, an Episcopal priest, Meisgeier received the gift of the Holy Spirit. He describes the result: "It has been a new life for us all. There is a tremendous fulfillment in being baptized in the Holy Spirit; the Christian life goes on from there and gets better and better." See *The Acts of the Holy Spirit Among the Presbyterians Today,* 56–61.

[12] This was likewise the time of Saul's conversion (see previous discussion in chap. 8, II.C.). In a later parallel account (Acts 22:1–16), where Paul rehearsed this event, he stated that after Jesus had identified Himself ("I am Jesus . . . " [v. 8]), Saul asked, "What shall I do, Lord?" (v. 10). This suggests Saul had entered on the way of faith, acknowledging Jesus as Lord. I realize it can be argued that Saul is simply saying "Lord" (*kyrie*) in the sense of "Sir" or "Master," hence expressing little or no faith. However, the context, including the words from heaven, "I am Jesus," would seem to suggest more. Christian faith begins in a personal encounter with the living Christ; Saul's experience was hardly less than that!

[13] Ananias' greeting of Saul as "Brother" is another indication that Saul is already on the

... has sent me that you may regain your sight and be filled with the Holy Spirit' " (v. 17). Thus there was a period of time, though shorter than that of the Samaritans, between the inception of faith and the reception of the Holy Spirit.

What is important to recognize is that for the Samaritans and Saul there were two critical moments in their experience, although there is some diversity in details,[14] and that it was the second moment in which they received the Holy Spirit. This sequence of events is not unlike that experienced by many today who have "believed" (Samaritans), have called Jesus "Lord" (Saul), but who do not receive the fullness of the Spirit until later. Also, various persons may perform different functions in relation to the total experience. There may be someone who is especially the channel for initial faith (such as Philip, or the Lord Jesus Himself) and another—or others—becomes the channel for the reception of the Spirit (such as Peter and John, or Ananias). There is much diversity in the way

these moments on the way of faith occur.[15]

One further illustration of the reception of the Spirit occurring along the way of faith is that of the Ephesians in Acts 19:1–7. Paul encountered "some disciples" (v. 1) in Ephesus. He then asked them, "Did you receive the Holy Spirit, believing?" (v. 2).[16] After the Ephesians expressed their ignorance concerning the Holy Spirit, Paul led them step-by-step from "John's baptism," which they had experienced, into a faith in Christ accompanied by water baptism: "On hearing this [the word about Christ], they were baptized in the name of the Lord Jesus" (v. 5). The final step followed: "And when Paul had laid his hands upon them, the Holy Spirit came on them; and they spoke with tongues and prophesied" (v. 6). Here is a sequence of events, or moments, in which persons moved from a very limited faith to specific faith affirmed in water baptism, then to laying on of hands for the gift of the Holy Spirit. The temporal span between the first two may have covered many years;

---

way of faith before his filling with the Holy Spirit. Brother in the singular vocative in Acts (9:17; 21:20; 22:13) signifies "Christian brother."

[14] Such as the fact that the Samaritans were baptized in water at the inception of faith (8:12) and only received the Holy Spirit several days later (v. 17) whereas Saul's water baptism did not occur until after he was filled with the Holy Spirit (9:17–18).

[15] For a variety of testimonies in the early stages of the Roman Catholic renewal (in the late sixties), see *Catholic Pentecostals,* "Bearing Witness," 58–106; also *Catholics and the Baptism of the Holy Spirit.* For Protestant testimonies, see similar publications of the Full Gospel Business Men's Fellowship International on *Episcopalians* (or *Baptists, Methodists, Lutherans, Presbyterians,* etc.) *and the Baptism of the Holy Spirit.*

[16] Again (see n. 7), this is an instance of the aorist participle (as in Acts 11:17). The Greek word here is *pisteusantes,* translated in the KJV as "since ye believed" (antecedent aorist) while in the RSV and NASB as "when you believed" (coincident aorist). My preference again is simply "believing," which catches up both antecedence and coincidence as a continuing reality. What is important, however, is that regardless of the way the aorist participle is translated, there is the obvious implication that one believing may not yet have received the Holy Spirit. Initial faith is not necessarily accompanied by the gift of the Spirit. Even if it be argued that these "disciples" were not yet believers in a fully Christian sense because it turned out they were only disciples of John (see v. 3), the question still points up the possibility of believing without yet receiving. (E. Schweizer says, "In 19:1–7, Luke is telling about Christians who have not yet experienced the outpouring of the Holy Spirit" [TDNT, 6:413]. I think this overstates the situation, but at least Schweizer recognizes that, according to Luke, one may be a believer and not yet have experienced the Spirit's outpouring.)

the span between the second and third was quite brief. However viewed, there is a process of faith involved, a series of nonidentical events, with once again this basic fact: the gift of the Holy Spirit did not occur at the moment of initial faith.[17]

In regard to the events of Ephesus, it might be instructive to turn now to Ephesians 1:13, where the apostle is quite possibly rehearsing in similar language the event of their reception of the Holy Spirit:[18] "In him you also, who have heard the word of truth, the gospel of your salvation, and believing[19] in him, were sealed with the promised Holy Spirit." Unmistakably the Spirit promised is the same as that in Acts 2:39: "The promise is to you and to your children . . ." and the same received by the Ephesians in Acts 19:6. Further, the word "seal," while not used in Acts, is contained in the idea of consecration, dedication, and empowering[20] that operates all through the book. Accordingly, Acts 19 and Ephesians 1 seem to be parallel accounts, and—the point of particular relevance here—each portrays a reception of the Spirit after faith has begun. The Ephesians in both accounts received the promised Holy Spirit on the way of faith.

On the contemporary scene there are numerous parallels to the Ephesian narrative in Acts 19. Many persons today have long lived in a situation of quite limited faith. Their faith may have had a little more focus on Jesus than that of the Ephesians (maybe not); there may have been a little more knowledge about the Holy Spirit (maybe not), and they may have been viewed as disciples, or Christians, in some sense. But it was all rather nebulous. Many, in looking back, freely recognize how limited and inadequate their earlier faith had been. Then, much like Paul with the Ephesians, someone (or perhaps more than one) came along and led them into a faith focused clearly on Jesus, perhaps also into water baptism, and then through additional ministry into the reception of the Holy Spirit.[21]

Now that we have noted a number of accounts in Acts that depict the gift of the Spirit as occurring along the way of faith, another stands out particularly, because it describes the Holy Spirit's being given at the moment of initial faith. I make reference to the account of the Gentiles at Caesarea (Acts 10; 11:1–18). The apostle Peter came to the house of the God-fearing centurion Cornelius and preached the good news of Jesus Christ, that "every one who believes in him receives forgiveness of sins through his name." And "while Peter was still saying this, the Holy Spirit fell on all who heard the word"

---

[17] Whether one identifies the initial faith with the first or second moment, the reception of the Spirit occurred later (whether years later or in immediate succession). Schweizer, in looking back over the record in Acts, writes, "Days, and in exceptional cases, even weeks and years may pass before endowment with the Spirit follows faith" (TDNT, 6:412). Although I prefer to say "follows *initial* faith," I believe Schweizer is basically correct.

[18] Of course, I am not suggesting that Paul is simply addressing the original Ephesian disciples. My point is that Paul shows a similar pattern in Ephesians 1:13 to what happened in Acts 19:1–7.

[19] As in Acts 19:2, the same aorist participle *pisteusantes* is used. The RSV has "have believed" while the KJV translates it "after that ye believed" (similarly NIV and NASB). Again, I translate it simply as "believing." See previous footnotes 7 and 16.

[20] One of the uses of "seal" in the New Testament. ("Seal" sometimes means "endue with power from heaven" (BAGD, σφραγίζω, 2.b.).

[21] Again, see the testimonies in the books mentioned in footnote 15 supra. Many examples may be found. From the nebulous and limited to the clear and full is a transition that many are making in our time.

(10:43–44). The Spirit was given coincidentally with (cf. "while") the preaching of faith in Jesus Christ. The first moment of faith in Christ was also the very moment they received the Holy Spirit.

The parallel to contemporary experience is unmistakable. Many persons attest that there was no separation whatever in time between their initial faith in Jesus Christ and their reception of the Holy Spirit. Unlike others whose basic Christian experience occurred over a period of time, they simply came into it all at once.[22] This does not mean there has not been growth and development since that first moment, for there has been, but the basis for all to occur later took place at the beginning.

In reflecting on what has been said, one thing may be vigorously affirmed: it is impossible to press the operation of the Holy Spirit into a mold; accordingly, it is the same with the shaping of basic Christian experience. Moreover, contemporary Christians can testify to the variety of ways the Holy Spirit has been given, clearly echoing the witness of the church in its early formation. So it is that we find in the biblical record ample original testimony to what is again occurring in our time.[23]

II. OUTWARD MEANS

We turn now to a consideration of the reception of the Holy Spirit in relation to water baptism and the laying on of hands. Our concern at this point is the connection between these outward rites and the bestowal of the Spirit. How essential—or dispensable—are they? Is one or the other more closely associated with the gift of the Spirit?

It hardly needs saying that this has been an area of significant differences in the history of the church. This is evidenced by the fact, first, that both water baptism and the laying on (or imposition) of hands have been viewed as channels for the gift of the Holy Spirit. Some traditions have held the position that water baptism is sufficient: it is the means whereby the Holy Spirit is given. Accordingly, there is no need for the laying on of hands. Others have held that the laying on of hands is the critical matter; without it water baptism is incomplete, and there is no gift of the Holy Spirit. How are we to adjudicate between such critical differences?

That this is no small matter seems undeniable. If the gift of the Holy Spirit is what we have been describing—a veritable outpouring of God's presence and power—and if this gift is vitally related to an outward rite, then the identity of that rite and its proper execution are critical questions. If, on

---

[22] This is often the case for persons who have long been searching for reality—the "God-seekers" of the world, who, upon clearly hearing for the first time the call to a personal faith in Jesus Christ, not only receive forgiveness of sins but also the empowering of the Holy Spirit. I think, for example, of the recent "Jesus people," many of whom had been involved with drugs (representing an illusory search for reality) and were actually bearing witness to illusion. Many of these young people had a total experience of turning to Christ and at the same time of receiving the Holy Spirit. (As an example of this see Pat King, *The Jesus People Are Coming,* the testimony of Michael Mates, "Now I'm Free," 73–92.) It was estimated that at the peak of the "Jesus movement" over 90 percent of the persons involved were charismatic, not usually by virtue of a later charismatic experience, but because they became such in the initial breakthrough of Christian faith. At the very moment of their conversion they also became "turned on" witnesses for Jesus in the power of the Spirit.

[23] One sometimes hears it said that the Book of Acts presents so much confusing, even inconsistent, data about the reception of the Holy Spirit that the record is of dubious value for our contemporary situation. The truth of the matter, however, is that the varied descriptions give firm basis and example for what is happening in our time.

the other hand, there is no vital connection between the gift of the Holy Spirit and an outward rite, this ought also to be clarified so that we are not burdened by unnecessary concerns. That there needs to be serious reflection in this area is apparent; we can scarcely afford to be uncertain or confused in so important a matter.

Once again we look to the Book of Acts as the basic historical narrative that depicts the coming of the Holy Spirit and now consider its relationship to water baptism and the laying on of hands. There will be some reference also to the Gospels and the Epistles; however, as has been the case in previous chapters, Acts must be primary because it is the only New Testament book that shows the interrelationship between the gift of the Spirit, the occurrence of water baptism, and the laying on of hands.

A. Water Baptism

Let us begin with the relation of water baptism to the gift of the Holy Spirit. We are concerned, of course, with water baptism as a Christian rite and only incidentally with "the baptism of John" (which is transitional in Acts to Christian baptism).[24] How does the rite of Christian baptism relate to the gift of the Spirit? By way of reply, I will set forth a number of declaratory statements and seek to demonstrate these in the five basic narratives that describe the reception of the Holy Spirit.

Before proceeding further, we find that water baptism, wherever described in Acts, is performed in the name of Jesus only. There are four passages that mention His name in relation to baptism: Acts 2:38; 8:16; 10:48; and 19:5 with the slight variation between "the name of Jesus Christ" (2:38 and 10:48) and "the name of the Lord Jesus" (8:16 and 19:5).[25] What is important is that water baptism is done in the name of Jesus[26] (not the variation in the name) and how this Christian baptism relates to the gift of the Holy Spirit.

1. Water Baptism[27] May **Precede** the Gift of the Holy Spirit

We begin by observing that Peter, following his sermon on the Day of Pentecost, asserted, "Repent, and be baptized every one of you in the name of Jesus Christ for the forgiveness of your sins; and you shall receive the gift of the Holy Spirit" (Acts 2:38). Water baptism is obviously depicted as preceding the gift of the Spirit. It is not altogether clear from these words, however, whether a logical or a chronological priority is envisioned. Peter's words "and you shall receive the gift of the Holy Spirit" could mean either that the gift of the Spirit follows logically and therefore immediately upon water baptism, or that it may happen at some future time. Shortly after Peter's sermon, "those who received his word were baptized, and there were added that day about three thousand souls" (v. 41). Nothing is directly said about their receiving the Holy Spirit; however, that such followed water baptism

---

[24] This will be noted later, especially in connection with Acts 19.

[25] Three prepositions are used: *epi* (Acts 2:38), *eis* (8:16 and 19:5), and *en* (10:48). They could be translated "upon," "into," and "in." For all three, "in the name" is the usual English translation. This seems proper, since the Greek words do not, I believe, connote a difference.

[26] The formula in Acts, therefore, is obviously divergent from the triune emphasis of Matthew 28:19. I will return to this later.

[27] As I use the term "water baptism" from now on, I will ordinarily be referring to baptism in the name of Jesus Christ.

seems evident in light of the ensuing account (vv. 42–47).[28]

Let us turn next to the Samaritan account, in which water baptism is definitely shown to precede the gift of the Spirit. In this instance it is clear that there was an intervening period of several days. The Samaritans "were baptized, both men and women" (Acts 8:12). Later Peter and John "came down and prayed for them that they might receive the Holy Spirit; for it had not yet fallen on any of them, but they had only been baptized in the name of the Lord Jesus" (vv. 15–16). So prayer was offered and the laying on of hands was administered, with the result that the Samaritans received the Holy Spirit. Hence, there was an unmistakable separation in time between water baptism and the reception of the Holy Spirit.

This passage is quite important in demonstrating that the reception of the Holy Spirit is not bound to the moment of water baptism. The Samaritans clearly did not receive the Holy Spirit when they were baptized, thus leaving open the possibility that this could happen in other instances.[29]

That there may be such a delay is found in the experience of large numbers in the contemporary movement of the Spirit. There is abundant testimony to a reception of the Holy Spirit that frequently takes place later than baptism in water; rather than an exception, it is evident that this quite often occurs.[30] The Samaritan happening is a continuing reality.

One other account in Acts likewise specifically shows water baptism preceding the gift of the Holy Spirit, namely, the account of Paul and the Ephesian Christians. We have noted that the Ephesians had earlier been baptized "into John's baptism," but they had not received Christian baptism. After Paul's presentation of the gospel, the Ephesians "were baptized in the name of the Lord Jesus. And when Paul had laid his hands upon them, the Holy Spirit came on them" (Acts 19:5–6). Unlike the situation in Samaria, there was not a delay of several days between the Ephesians' Christian baptism and their receiving the Holy Spirit. Still there was some chronological separation, however brief, between the rite of water baptism and the reception of the Holy Spirit. Once again, as in the case of Peter's message to the Jerusalem multitude with baptism following and as in the case of the Samaritans, the administration of baptism preceded the gift of the Holy Spirit.[31]

---

[28]These verses, depicting a community of people devoted to the apostles' teaching, fellowship, sharing, and, climactically, "praising God and having favor with all the people" (v. 47), strongly suggest participation in the gift of the Holy Spirit.

[29]F. D. Bruner has this peculiar statement: "The Spirit is temporarily suspended from baptism here 'only' and precisely to teach the Church at its most prejudiced juncture, and in its strategic initial missionary move beyond Jerusalem, that *suspension cannot occur*" (italics his) (*A Theology of Holy Spirit,* 178). I should think that the passage teaches exactly the opposite: that *suspension may occur.* Bruner's interpretation is not actually based on the text but on a prior view (shown many times in his book) of the inseparability of water baptism and the gift of the Spirit.

[30]Of course, that is also true in many cases of conversion, particularly of those who received water baptism as infants. Years later they came to a life-changing experience with the Lord.

[31]We may also refer to the account of Philip and the Ethiopian eunuch (Acts 8:28–39). The eunuch came to faith, was baptized by Philip, and "when they came up out of the water, the Spirit of the Lord caught up Philip" (v. 39). According to some early manuscripts, the text reads, "And when they came up out of the water, the Holy Spirit fell upon the eunuch and an angel of the Lord caught up Philip." The point of this reading is undoubtedly to

2. Water Baptism May *Follow* the Gift of the Holy Spirit

This may seem surprising in light of the aforementioned incidents and especially in view of Peter's words at Pentecost, which show an order of repentance, baptism in the name of Christ, and the reception of the Holy Spirit. However, it is apparent that the previous instances were by no means definitive, nor are Peter's words a prescription of the way things must always happen. We will observe this in two other accounts.

The first is the narrative of Peter's ministry at Caesarea. As we have seen earlier, while Peter was still delivering his message, the Holy Spirit suddenly fell on the centurion and those gathered together with him (Acts 10:44). Obviously no water baptism of any kind had occurred. However, it was not disregarded, for shortly after that Peter declared, "Can any one forbid water for baptizing these people who have received the Holy Spirit just as we have?" Acting on his own declaration, Peter "commanded them to be baptized in the name of Jesus Christ" (vv. 47–48). Thus water baptism in this case unmistakably followed the reception of the gift of the Holy Spirit.

The other incident concerns Ananias' ministry to Saul of Tarsus. Ananias laid hands on Saul that he might be filled with the Holy Spirit (Acts 9:17). The next verse reads, "And immediately something like scales fell from his eyes and he regained his sight. Then he rose and was baptized." Hence subsequent to Saul's receiving the Holy Spirit he was baptized in water by Ananias.

What has been described about water baptism following the gift of the Holy Spirit is not unusual in our time. Many persons who have come to a living faith in Christ and received the Holy Spirit have afterward been baptized in water.[32] Often this stems from an intense desire to "go all the way with Christ," to participate corporally in His death and resurrection, to be wholly united to Him. Moreover, such baptism is seldom viewed as optional. Christ instituted it,[33] and Peter commanded it; thus it belongs to Christian initiation and discipleship. So when command is added to desire, if such persons have not been baptized in water before, it is quite likely to follow.[34]

We may properly raise a question about the one hundred twenty who were filled with the Holy Spirit at Pentecost. What about their water bap-

---

emphasize that, as with the Samaritans, the eunuch's baptism was followed by the gift of the Holy Spirit. (See F. F. Bruce's statement to this effect in his commentary, *The Acts of the Apostles*, 195.) Thus, in addition to the accounts in Acts that specify the gift of the Spirit as following water baptism, this may be implied in Acts 8:39.

[32] Donald L. Gelpi, S.J., suggests the case of a "Robert Z." who "a week before his sacramental baptism, while attending a prayer meeting . . . , receives Spirit-baptism and immediately begins praying in tongues" (*Pentecostalism: A Theological Viewpoint*, 178). Probably Father Gelpi had witnessed this, for he refers to this as "concretely possible." The problem, I might add, for Catholic theology is how does one relate such an experience to the traditional view that the Holy Spirit is received in baptism or confirmation? (See below for further discussion.)

[33] According to Matthew 28:19.

[34] There are many instances in the contemporary spiritual renewal of persons who had received baptism as infants and were baptized again as adults. In some cases such adult baptism is sought because of a growing conviction of the invalidity of infant baptism; in other cases adult baptism is viewed as not denying the validity of infant baptism, but as its fulfillment through personal, believing participation. I am referring, however, in the text above to those who have had no prior experience of baptism now becoming participants.

tism? This is not an easy question to answer. Though doubtless many[35] (like the later Ephesians) had participated in John's baptism, it is obvious they had not been baptized in Jesus' name before the event of Pentecost. Hence, the one hundred twenty appear to fall into the same category as Saul of Tarsus and the Caesareans, who without Christian baptism, received the Holy Spirit. Unlike the narratives of Saul and the Caesareans, however, that of the one hundred twenty does not specify that after they had been filled with the Spirit they were baptized in the name of the Christ. Quite possibly they were so baptized along with the three thousand later that day, but there is no clear-cut statement to that effect. It may have been, on the other hand, that because of their unique position as original disciples, who existentially were participants in Christ's death and resurrection (living through Good Friday and Easter) and recipients of His life-bestowing forgiveness, they needed no further tangible rite. For in a certain sense, even more intensely than others after them, they had been baptized into Jesus' reality. In any event, whether or not the original one hundred twenty later received water baptism in Jesus' name, they were similar to Saul of Tarsus and the Caesareans in that they received the Holy Spirit prior to any possible Christian water baptism.

3. Water Baptism Is Neither a Precondition nor a Channel for the Gift of the Holy Spirit

It is surely clear by now that water baptism is not a precondition. The very fact that Saul of Tarsus and the Caesareans received the Holy Spirit before they were water baptized rules out the idea of any precondition. Hence Peter's words "Repent, and be baptized . . . and you shall receive the gift of the Holy Spirit" cannot be viewed as a rule that water baptism must occur before the reception of the Spirit. His statement, while pointing to what may have been the usual pattern, did not establish water baptism as a precondition. Furthermore, if Peter's words were the rule, the rule had just been broken in his case! For as one of the one hundred twenty he had received the Holy Spirit with no prior water baptism in Jesus' name.

Many people in the spiritual renewal of our day bear testimony to receiving the gift of the Holy Spirit without a prior Christian baptism. This is especially the case for those who, like the Caesareans, received the Holy Spirit at the very inception of faith. Everything happened so quickly and powerfully that there was no opportunity for any ritual action! The one precondition (as we have earlier noted) for receiving the Holy Spirit is faith. Baptism, for all its importance, cannot function as a precondition or prerequisite for the reception of the Holy Spirit.[36]

Next we observe that neither is water baptism a channel for the gift of the Holy Spirit. None of the narratives in Acts represent the Holy Spirit as being given through water baptism. Though there may have been a close approximation of water baptism to the gift of the Spirit, there is no suggestion that such baptism is the medium or channel. Even less is water baptism portrayed as conferring the gift of the Spirit. The Holy Spirit comes from the exalted Lord who Himself confers the gift and surely does not relegate such to a rite conducted by man.

---

[35] Possibly all, the Scriptures give no certain information.

[36] Faith alone prepares the way. So E. Schweizer writes (in specific response to the Caesarean account as interpreted by Peter in Acts 15:8–9): "Faith, not baptism, purifies for reception of the Spirit . . ." (TDNT, 6:414).

Accordingly, there is no essential connection between water baptism and the gift of the Holy Spirit. It might be supposed, however, that, although water baptism is not a precondition for the gift of the Holy Spirit, whenever such baptism occurs, it is the outward form for the occurrence of the inward spiritual reality. From such a perspective it is not that water baptism conveys or confers the gift of the Spirit but that the two are related—the outward to the inward. Thus water baptism and the gift of the Spirit, or Spirit baptism, make one united whole. According to this view, wherever there is water baptism, there is also Spirit baptism: the visible action and the spiritual grace are essentially one.[37] However, in answer I must emphasize strongly that there is *no*

essential connection between water baptism and Spirit baptism,[38] no relation of one to the other as outward to inward. The reason is that they deal with two closely related but nonetheless different spiritual realities. Water baptism is for a purpose other than the reception of the Holy Spirit, and unless that is clearly seen there will be continuing confusion.[39] We now turn to this matter.

4. Water Baptism Is Connected With the Forgiveness of Sins

Here we arrive at the important point that water baptism is related primarily to the forgiveness of sins. To use the language of Peter at Pentecost: it is "for" the forgiveness of sins. "Repent, and be baptized . . . in the name of

---

[37] So F. D. Bruner writes, "Baptism and the reception of the Spirit are so synonymous as to be identical. Christian baptism is spiritual baptism" (*A Theology of the Holy Spirit*, 190). Bruner's sacramentalism, i.e., identifying the rite of water baptism with spiritual baptism, is not uncommon in sacramental church traditions. This is even true for charismatic Lutheran Arnold Bittlinger, who states that "Christian baptism is always a baptism with water and with Spirit" (*The Baptism in the Holy Spirit as an Ecumenical Problem*, 6). Similarly Kilian McDonnell, a Roman Catholic scholar, says, "By the sacrament of baptism one becomes a member of the body of Christ because in baptism one receives the Spirit" (*Statement of the Theological Basis of the Catholic Charismatic Renewal*, 4). I believe, on the contrary, that Dunn is correct in saying that "Spirit-baptism and water baptism remain distinct and even antithetical" (*Baptism in the Holy Spirit*, 227).

[38] Schweizer in his analysis of the Spirit in Acts writes: "The Spirit is not tied to baptism. Once He comes on men before baptism (10:44), once without it (2:1–4), once on a disciple who knew only John's baptism (18:25)" (TDNT, 6:414).

[39] Before moving on, I should add that positive interpreters of the charismatic renewal within a sacramental context, such as Bittlinger and McDonnell, go beyond the claimed reception of the Spirit in baptism. Bittlinger, for example, later adds: "What God has given in baptism must be ACTUALIZED in the life of the individual" (op. cit., 11). It is this actualization that lies at the heart of the charismatic experience of Spirit baptism. McDonnell makes use of such an expression as "manifestation of baptism whereby the hidden grace given in baptism breaks through the conscious experience" to describe "what is happening in the charismatic renewal" (*Baptism in the Holy Spirit*, 8). However, such attempts by Bittlinger and McDonnell, who intend respectively to maintain a Lutheran and Roman Catholic framework, unfortunately result both in binding the gift of the Holy Spirit to a particular sacramental action (What if the Spirit is *not* given in water baptism?) and to reducing the extraordinary charismatic experience to a secondary level of "actualization" and "manifestation" (or some other similar expression). Incidentally, McDonnell does not always associate the gift of the Spirit with water baptism; he also speaks more broadly of "the rites of initiation," which, in addition to baptism, include confirmation (see below on confirmation). From that perspective the charismatic experience could be described more broadly, for example as "reviviscence of the sacraments of initiation" (ibid.). I would still say that even such broader language likewise falls far short of the truly biblical and experiential meaning of the gift of the Holy Spirit.

Jesus Christ for the forgiveness of your sins." The climactic spiritual reality Peter attests to is the gift of the Spirit, but there is also the reality of forgiveness of sins, which is first mentioned. It is with this spiritual reality that water baptism is directly connected.

What then is the connection? We turn again to the statement of Peter in Acts 2:38 that baptism in Jesus' name is "for the forgiveness of your sins." The Greek word *eis,* here translated "for," could suggest "for the purpose of," "in order to obtain," thus a requirement for forgiveness to be received. However, *eis* may also be translated "concerning," "with respect to," "with reference to," "with regard to,"[40] and thus designates baptism as related to forgiveness but not necessarily for the purpose of obtaining it. Either translation is possible, although the latter seems most likely because there is no suggestion elsewhere in Acts that water baptism of itself obtains forgiveness. The point then of Acts 2:38 is not to specify water baptism as a requirement for forgiveness of sins; because forgiveness of sins comes by faith, not by baptism. But when baptism does occur, it is specifically related to that forgiveness.

What then is the nature of the relationship? I would answer that while water baptism does not of itself obtain forgiveness—hence is not required for that purpose—it does serve as a *means.* Forgiveness comes from faith in the exalted Lord; thus it is He who grants forgiveness; it can be obtained in no other way. Nonetheless, the ordinary channel or means for this forgiveness to be received is water baptism. This doubtless was the case for the three thousand who responded affirmatively to Peter's message: "Repent and be baptized, every one of you for the forgiveness of your sins." Baptism for each one of them was a visible, tangible expression of faith and repentance, an outward cleansing through which forgiveness was mediated. Thus water baptism was the means of receiving the grace of forgiveness and new life.

It would be a mistake, however, to view this as baptismal regeneration in the sense that the water itself, or the act of baptism, brought about forgiveness and new birth. On a later occasion Peter said, "God exalted him at his right hand as Leader and Savior, to give repentance to Israel and forgiveness of sins" (Acts 5:31). Although Peter again referred to repentance and forgiveness here, no mention was made of water baptism but only of the exalted Lord who gives repentance, forgiveness, and therefore new birth. Hence, when (as in Acts 2:38) water baptism is specified, it is obvious that such a rite does not, and cannot, bring about forgiveness and regeneration. But—and this is important—whenever water baptism is administered in the context of genuine faith and repentance, it does serve as the medium for forgiveness to be received.

A second answer to the relationship of water baptism to forgiveness is that it serves as a *sign* and *seal.* On the one hand, water baptism is a vivid portrayal of the cleansing that forgiveness brings about and thus signifies becoming a new creation. It is a public demonstration of the totality of the divine forgiveness[41]

---

[40] For example, note the earlier use of *eis* in the same chapter, verse 25, where Peter prefaces a quotation from a Davidic psalm thus: "For David says concerning him [the Christ]. . . ." The word translated "concerning" (RSV and KJV) is *eis. Eis* here clearly means "regarding," "in reference to," etc. For other similar translations of *eis* cf. Romans 4:20 ("concerning" [RSV], "with respect to" [NASB]); Ephesians 5:32 ("concerning" KJV], "with reference to" [NASB]); and 1 Thessalonians 5:18 ("concerning" [KJV]).

[41] Water baptism as immersion (the whole body covered) best symbolizes this. However,

and the complete cleansing and renewal that Christ accomplishes. Such baptism, since it is in Christ's name, testifies that in and with Him there is death and burial of the self and resurrection into newness of life.[42] Forgiveness is the remission of sins, and remission is nothing less than a total release from the past and the beginning of the wholly new. Water baptism thus is peculiarly the sign of the forgiveness of sins.

On the other hand, water baptism functions as a seal of faith and forgiveness. It is a tangible impression and certification of the reality of the remission of sins. In the waters of baptism there is "brought home" to a person the wonder of God's total cleansing: the spiritual reality of complete forgiveness being mediated and confirmed in the totality of the baptismal experience. In the combination of the divine gift and the corporal action the two are sealed: what is received in faith is confirmed in the waters of baptism. One who is so baptized in faith is a marked person—cleansed, forgiven, made new in Jesus Christ.[43]

Now we return to our original point, namely, that water baptism is directly connected with the forgiveness of sins. The specific nature of that relationship (which we have just been discussing) is less important for our concern than the fact of the connection. The reason for emphasizing this point is that frequently this connection is not seen and water baptism is mistakenly viewed as directly related to the gift of the Holy

Spirit. It is quite important to define this matter, or there will be continuing confusion in a vital area.

Before leaving the subject of water baptism, it is important to add that baptism, though not directly connected with the gift of the Holy Spirit, is still related. For where there is faith and forgiveness mediated through water baptism, the Holy Spirit is undoubtedly at work. It is the Holy Spirit who empowers the word of witness, convicts of sin, and thus brings about repentance. By the Holy Spirit is the origin of faith that leads to the forgiveness of sins and baptism in the name of Christ. All of this is apparent, for example, in Acts 2:22–38 where the outpoured Spirit is the agent in each of these matters. Thus the Holy Spirit is very much involved in the entire process of salvation. Since this process may include water baptism, it is the Holy Spirit who gives spiritual significance to the act of baptism; otherwise it is nothing but an empty rite. It is clear then that water baptism is closely connected with the activity of the Holy Spirit.

However—and here is the critical matter—this just-described activity of the Holy Spirit is by no means the gift of the Holy Spirit. The gift ordinarily follows upon forgiveness and baptism, like a promise attached to it: "Repent, and be baptized every one of you in the name of Jesus Christ for the forgiveness of your sins; and you shall receive the gift of the Holy Spirit. For the promise

---

the pouring of water over the person may likewise represent this totality. Sprinkling (in accordance with Ezek. 36:25, "I will sprinkle clean water upon you, and you shall be clean from all you uncleannesses") is a third possibility.

[42] E.g., see Romans 6:4: "We are buried therefore with him by baptism into death, so that as Christ was raised from the dead . . . we too might walk in newness of life" (cf. Gal. 3:27; Col. 2:12). Water baptism by immersion most vividly demonstrates burial and resurrection.

[43] This matter of baptism as a sign and seal relates to what Paul says concerning how Abraham "received the sign of circumcision, a seal of the righteousness that he had by faith while he was still uncircumcised" (Rom. 4:11 NIV). Water baptism is clearly the New Testament parallel, and thus, like circumcision, does not bring about righteousness or forgiveness, but is a sign and seal of it.

is to you and to your children and to all that are far off, every one whom the Lord our God calls to him" (Acts 2:38–39). The gift does not have to do with forgiveness, but with what is promised to those who repent and are baptized for forgiveness.[44] It is a promise to all whom God calls to Himself (such calling implemented through the working of the Holy Spirit) that they will receive the gift of the Holy Spirit.

Another matter that calls for some discussion relates to the difference in formulas for water baptism as set forth in Matthew 28:19 and in the Book of Acts. We earlier observed that water baptism is invariably depicted in Acts as being in the name of Jesus only, but we did not actually deal with the fact that in Matthew the formula is a triune one:[45] "Go therefore and make disciples of all nations, baptizing them in the name of the Father and of the Son and of the Holy Spirit. . . ."

Although there is no simple solution to the difference, a few comments relevant to our concerns may be made. First, the longer Matthean statement suggests that water baptism represents entrance into[46] a new relationship to God as Father, Son, and Holy Spirit.

Second, the shorter Lukan formula (in Acts) specifies that at the heart of this relationship is the forgiveness of sins that comes in the name of Jesus Christ (the Son). Third, since Jesus is "the fullness of the Godhead,"[47] baptism in His name only (as in Acts) is actually in relation to the fullness of the divine reality: it is also, by implication, in the name of the Father and Holy Spirit. Thus there is no essential difference between the Matthean and Lukan formulas: the former highlights the fullness of the relationship into which one enters at baptism, the latter specifies the purpose of the baptism.[48]

I would also suggest that the reference to the Holy Spirit in Matthew's baptismal formula—"in the name . . . of the Holy Spirit"—emphasizes that Christian initiation is also entrance into the sphere of the Holy Spirit's reality and activity. At the heart of such initiation is the forgiveness of sins (to which baptism in the name of Jesus, or the Son, points), but at the same time it is the beginning of a new relationship to the Holy Spirit (to which baptism in the name of the Holy Spirit points).[49] By this is meant not only that the Holy Spirit is active in bringing about forgiveness, as we have noted, but that hence-

---

[44] As earlier noted, water baptism is not so integral a part of forgiveness that it may not occur later. Particularly recall the account of the Caesareans in Acts 10:43–48. However, ordinarily the sequence is that of Acts 2:38–39.

[45] Mention was made of this formula in n. 26 above, but there was no elaboration of its significance.

[46] The Greek word for "in" ("baptizing them in") is *eis*, which though it may simply mean "in" (see n. 25), may also be translated "into." As I have earlier noted, *eis* may also signify "with reference to," hence "in relation to."

[47] "For in him dwelleth all the fulness of the Godhead bodily [Gr. *to plērōma tēs theoētos*]" (Col. 2:9 KJV).

[48] Hence either formula is suitable for use in water baptism. Within classical Pentecostalism the "Jesus only" churches (a minority group) insist that water baptism *must be only* in the name of Jesus. This is as equally one-sided as the insistence of some historic denominations that the formula of baptism *must* be in the Triune name. (For a description of the "Jesus only" movement see Vinson Synan, *The Holiness-Pentecostal Movement*, 153–54; also see the chapter by David Reed entitled "Aspects of the Origins of Oneness Pentecostalism" in *Aspects of Pentecostal-Charismatic Origins*, ed. Vinson Synan).

[49] The same thing is true about the Father—a new relationship to Him: by adoption one becomes a son of God and is able to address God as "Father" (cf. Rom. 8:15; Gal. 4:5–6).

forward life is to be lived in the sphere of the dynamism of the Holy Spirit.[50]

B. The Laying on of Hands

Let us now consider the relationship between the laying on of hands and the gift of the Holy Spirit. We will again be reflecting primarily on the five basic passages in Acts. What part does the laying on (or imposition) of hands play in the reception of the Holy Spirit?[51]

1. The Holy Spirit May Be Given Without the Laying on of Hands

In two of five cases, namely those regarding the gift of the Spirit in Jerusalem and at the centurion's household in Caesarea, there was no laying on of hands.

Concerning the Jerusalem narrative two observations may be made: First, it is obvious that there could have been no laying on of hands on the one hundred twenty. As the first disciples they had to receive the Holy Spirit before ministering to anyone else. Second, although the three thousand later that day were baptized, there is no reference to the laying on of hands. Peter said, "Repent, and be baptized . . . and you shall receive the gift of the Holy Spirit" (Acts 2:38); but there was no mention of imposition of hands for this gift to be received. Indeed, it is quite probable that Peter, having just experienced the bestowal of the Spirit

as a sovereign, unmediated action by the exalted Lord, expected all to receive the gift the same way the one hundred twenty had. Whatever his expectation, it seems that the three thousand also received the Holy Spirit without the laying on of hands.

In the Caesarean situation things happened so fast—"While Peter was still saying this [i.e., still preaching his message], the Holy Spirit fell on all who heard the word" (Acts 10:44)—that there was no time to lay on hands if anybody had been so minded! Incidentally, Peter might have expected this time to lay hands on the new believers because of the intervening incident when he and John had placed hands on the Samaritans for the reception of the Holy Spirit (Acts 8:14–17). However, as in Jerusalem, God sovereignly moved and poured out His Holy Spirit on all who heard.

What we have been describing is by no means an uncommon occurrence in the contemporary spiritual renewal. The Holy Spirit is frequently received with no human mediation of any kind. This may happen at the end of a period of time, as at Jerusalem, or with the suddenness of a Caesarea, but in neither case has there been the imposition of hands. This extraordinary, unmediated event is for many a source of continuing amazement and wonder.[52]

---

[50] In my book *The Pentecostal Reality* (chap. 6, "The Holy Trinity") I wrote: "The purpose of that part of the Great Commission, 'Go therefore . . . baptizing' is not to make learners out of people in regard to God, but to introduce them into life lived in the reality of God as Father, Son, and Holy Spirit" (p. 102). On the matter of the Holy Spirit, my later words are "This means life claimed by God through Jesus Christ in a total kind of way, the Spirit of the living God probing the depths of the conscious and the unconscious, releasing . . . new powers to praise God, to witness compellingly in His name, to do mighty works that only He can do. Do we know this?" (p. 107).

[51] There are other instances in Acts of the imposition of hands that are not directly concerned with the gift of the Holy Spirit: 6:5–6—the dedication of seven "deacons"; 13:3—the commissioning of Barnabas and Saul; and 28:8—the healing of Publius' father. While such instances of the laying on of hands are not for the gift of the Spirit, they obviously represent Spirit-inspired activities.

[52] The earliest testimonies in *Catholic Pentecostals* ("Bearing Witness," 24–37) of

It is apparent from the biblical record and contemporary experience that the laying on of hands is not essential for the Holy Spirit to be received. Moreover, there is no suggestion in Acts that following such a reception hands were later placed on believers as a kind of confirmation of what has already happened. Any idea of hands as being necessary or confirmatory is ruled out by the evidence.

These things are most important to emphasize in relation to church traditions that variously seek to canalize the gift of the Holy Spirit. There are those who hold that the Holy Spirit may be received *only* through the laying on of hands;[53] thus without personal ministry the Holy Spirit may not be given. Over against such a binding of the Holy Spirit to an outward action we need to stress the sovereignty of the Holy Spirit to move as He wills.

2. The Holy Spirit May Be Given With the Laying on of Hands

Returning to the Acts record, we observe that in three of the five accounts of the Holy Spirit's being received, this occurred in connection with the laying on of hands. Peter and John, ministering to the Samaritans, "laid their hands on them and they received the Holy Spirit"[54] (Acts 8:17). At Damascus, Ananias, "laying his hands on him he said, 'Brother Saul, the Lord Jesus who appeared to you on the road

by which you came, has sent me that you may regain your sight and be filled with the Holy Spirit' " (9:17). And Paul when he "had laid his hands upon them [the Ephesians], the Holy Spirit came on them . . ." (19:6). There is obviously a close connection between the laying on of hands and the gift of the Holy Spirit.

It is apparent once again that water baptism is not placed in an immediate conjunction with the gift of the Holy Spirit. Water baptism, as earlier mentioned, is related to forgiveness of sins, whereas the laying on of hands is connected with the gift of the Holy Spirit. The symbolism is unmistakable: water baptism vividly portrays the cleansing from sin in forgiveness; the laying on of hands, the external bestowal of the Spirit. Each of the outward acts is congruent with the spiritual reality to be received.

Looking more closely in the Acts narrative at this conjunction of the Holy Spirit and the imposition of hands, we observe that the Holy Spirit may be given *through* the laying on of hands. Thus it is not only a temporal conjunction, so that the gift of the Holy Spirit coincides with, or follows immediately upon, the laying on of hands. It is also an instrumental conjunction; that is, the imposition of hands may serve as the channel or means for the gift of the Spirit. Following the words quoted above about the Samaritans, the text

---

students who were baptized in the Holy Spirit at the "Duquesne weekend" especially depict an unmediated happening. One participant testifies, "There were three other students with me when all of a sudden I became filled with the Holy Spirit and realized that 'God is real.'. . . The professors then laid hands on some of the students, but most of us received the 'baptism in the Spirit' while kneeling before the blessed sacrament in prayer" (34–35). *The Acts of the Holy Spirit among the Presbyterians, Baptists, Methodists, etc.* contains many testimonies of the Holy Spirit being given without the laying on of hands.

[53] Or, as we have noted, through water baptism. Sometimes people entertain the view that there may be *two* gifts of the Holy Spirit: one at water baptism and the other with the imposition of hands.

[54] Literally, they "were laying [*epetithesan*—imperfect tense] the hands on them and they were receiving [*elambanon*—also imperfect] the Holy Spirit." The Greek tense suggests an action over a period of time, possibly indicating that the Samaritans one by one received the Holy Spirit.

reads, "Now when Simon saw that the Spirit was given through the laying on of the apostles' hands . . ." (Acts 8:18).[55] The word "through" (*dia*) specifies the instrumentality of hands in the reception of the gift of the Holy Spirit. The laying on of hands is thus the means of grace whereby the Holy Spirit may be received.

The laying on of hands for the gift of the Holy Spirit has continued variously in the history of the church. The practice belongs particularly to the Western tradition of Christianity,[56] but with diverse understanding of what is conveyed in the gift. Sometimes it is assumed that through the laying on of hands there is the completing or perfecting of what was given earlier in water baptism;[57] or again, it is held that water baptism needs no completion or perfection, so that what happens through the imposition of hands is rather a confirming or strengthening of the person for the Christian walk.[58] However, there is seldom in the traditional churches any expectation that through the laying on of hands an extraordinary spiritual event will take place, namely, the veritable outpouring of God's presence and power.

Here again is where the contemporary spiritual renewal is recapturing the biblical witness. Through the laying on of hands, people are receiving the gift of the Holy Spirit, not in the sense of completion or strengthening (though the gift may include elements of both), but in the sense of a divine visitation so overwhelming as to release extraordinary praise and channels of powerful ministry. There is the exciting expectation that when hands are laid on a person, the Holy Spirit Himself will be received.[59]

---

[55] The text continues with the recitation of Simon the magician's vain and sordid attempt to buy the power to confer the gift of the Spirit through his own hands. However, despite his perfidy, there is no question in the text that Simon correctly perceived it to be through the laying on of Peter's and John's hands that the Holy Spirit was given.

[56] The *Apostolic Tradition*, compiled by Hippolytus (2nd century A.D.) in regard to the Roman liturgy of initiation prescribes that following the candidates' baptism and anointing with oil, "the Bishop shall lay his hands upon them invoking and saying: 'O Lord God who hast counted these thy servants worthy of deserving the forgiveness of sins and the laver of regeneration, make them worthy to be filled with thy Holy Spirit. . .'" (chap. 22). Even though only the bishop was allowed to do this, it is important to note that the practice begun in Acts of laying on hands for the infilling of the Spirit continued in the early church.

[57] Cyprian (3rd century A.D. bishop of Carthage) wrote of how "they who are baptized in the Church are brought to the prelates of the Church, and by our prayers and the imposition of hands obtain the Holy Spirit, and are perfected with the Lord's seal" (*The Evpistles of Cyprian*, 72:9; *Ante-Nicene Fathers* 5:381). The Council of Elvira (A.D. 306) spoke of the role of the Bishop "to lay hands on the newly baptized, to perfect [complete] him" (canon 38).

[58] The word "confirmation" appeared for the first time in the canons of the Council of Orange (A.D. 441). This was later (by the twelfth century) to become a sacrament in the Roman Catholic Church, the sacrament of strengthening the believer, usually totally separated in time from earlier baptism. The purpose of the sacrament of confirmation has been recently reaffirmed by Pope Paul VI in the *Apostolic Constitution on the Sacrament of Confirmation*: "Through the sacrament of confirmation, those who have been born anew in baptism receive the inexpressible Gift, the Holy Spirit himself, by which they are endowed . . . with special strength." In churches growing out of the Reformation, confirmation, where retained, usually signifies a believer's confirmation of earlier baptismal vows taken on his behalf. It is viewed, not as a sacrament, but as a kind of "rite of passage" to full church membership. There is no thought of this rite as conferring the Holy Spirit. (The Episcopal/Anglican Church has retained more of the sacramental idea.)

[59] Recall that in the beginning of the twentieth-century Pentecostal renewal hands were laid on Agnes Ozman at her request by Rev. Charles Parham. She explains the result: "It

Here two points need emphasis: First, as we have already observed, there is no necessity for hands to be laid on persons for them to receive the Holy Spirit. The exalted Lord may dispense with ordinary means and sovereignly pour forth the Holy Spirit. Second, although the Holy Spirit may also be given through the laying on of hands, it would be a mistake to assume that this happens invariably, i.e., by virtue of the objective action.[60] We have earlier commented that faith (believing) is the essential element in the reception of the Holy Spirit; thus in all the biblical incidents of the laying on of hands it is on believers that hands are laid. For only those who believe in Jesus Christ may receive from Him the blessed gift of the Holy Spirit.

What then is the importance of the laying on of hands? If, on the one side, there is no necessity, and if, on the other, there is no guarantee, why not dispense with it? The answer seems clear: The laying on of hands is a divinely instituted means of *enabling* persons to receive the gift of the Holy Spirit. Hands signify contact, community, sharing—a human channel for the divine gift; the laying on of hands represents, as seen earlier, the coming of the Holy Spirit upon someone.[61] Although a person may receive the gift of the Holy Spirit without human mediation, the imposition of hands may greatly facilitate this reception.[62]

3. The Laying on of Hands for the Gift of the Holy Spirit Is *Not Limited* to the Apostles

As we have noted, the apostles Peter and John did minister the Spirit to the

---

was as his hands were laid upon my head that the Holy Spirit fell upon me and I began to speak in tongues glorifying God" (quotation in K. Kendrick, *The Promise Fulfilled,* 52–53). Also see the second set of testimonies in *Catholic Pentecostals,* "Bearing Witness," 58–106, having to do with events later at Notre Dame. Most cases of baptism in the Spirit occurred through the laying on of hands. (It might be suggested that the Duquesne experience was more like the first unmediated biblical outpourings on Jews and Gentiles at Jerusalem and Caesarea, Notre Dame more like the secondary outpourings on Samaria and Ephesus.)

[60] E.g., the traditional Roman Catholic view of the sacraments (baptism, confirmation) is that they are efficacious "*ex opere operato*"—"by the work performed." McDonnell, while holding that "the fullness of the Spirit is given during the celebration of initiation," speaks of "the scholastic doctrine of *ex opere operantis* [wherein] we receive in the measure of our openness." Thus, though there is an objective, and in that sense invariable, gift of the Spirit in "the celebration of initiation," there is no receiving without subjective appropriation (*One in Christ,* 10.2 [1974]: 117–18). McDonnell's view approximates my comments regarding the need for faith (see above) in the reception of the Holy Spirit. Some words of Calvin are quite relevant: "But what is a sacrament received apart from faith but the most certain ruin of the church?" (*Institutes* 4.14.14. Battles trans.).

[61] Edward O'Connor writes, "The gesture [of laying on of hands] does symbolize graphically the fact that God's grace is often mediated to a person through others, and especially through the community. God seems to bless the faith from which this prayerful gesture proceeds: again and again people find that they have been helped in a powerful and manifest way by it . . . the baptism in the Spirit is usually received thus" (*The Pentecostal Movement in the Catholic Church,* 117).

[62] A further word on the sacramental question: I believe it is far better to dissociate the charismatic experience from any sacramental action. Donald Gelpi, as I see it, is on the right track in saying that "Spirit-baptism is *not* a sacrament," but is the result of "full docility to the Spirit of Christ" (italics his) (*Pentecostalism: A Theological Viewpoint,* 182–83). Francis A. Sullivan, S. J., in his book *Charisms and Charismatic Renewal,* while affirming the traditional Catholic view of the objectivity of the sacraments, does *not* locate Spirit baptism within that framework. Rather, " 'baptism in the Spirit' means coming into some new experience of the power of the Spirit in one's life" (74).

Samaritans and the apostle Paul did the same for the Ephesians. However, it was a Christian brother, Ananias, with no claim to apostolic authority,[63] who was the minister of the Holy Spirit to Saul of Tarsus. Thus it would be a mistake to interpret the words of Acts 8:18 ". . . the Spirit was given through the laying on of the apostles' [Peter and John's] hands . . . " as the only way it could happen. Since Ananias, a lay brother, could minister the Holy Spirit to Saul, there is no inherent reason why Philip, the deacon-evangelist, could not have done the same for the Samaritans.[64]

Although little is said about Ananias in his ministry to Saul, a few things stand out. First, he was a man of faith and prayer. "The Lord said to him in a vision, 'Ananias.' And he said, "Here I am, Lord'" (Acts 9:10). Second, he was a man of obedience, for although he hesitated at the command of Christ to "rise and go" (9:11) because of Saul's evil reputation, he nonetheless went. Third, Ananias, as later described by Paul, was "a devout man according to the law, well spoken of by all . . ." (22:12). Hence he was a man of strong character and perhaps peculiarly prepared through his devotion to the law to minister to Saul the Pharisee. Such a combination of factors thus made Ana-nias an effective minister of the Holy Spirit, particularly suited to exercise the role of ministering to Saul's need.

It seems apparent that the basic qualification for the laying on of hands is not apostolic office but other more important matters. And so it continues into our own day and generation. Countless numbers of people are receiving the gift of the Holy Spirit through the ministry of laypeople. To be sure, many "official" clergy are likewise ministering the Holy Spirit with great effectiveness.[65] However, what really counts is not office (not even "apostolic succession") but attributes such as faithfulness, prayer, readiness, obedience, devoutness, and boldness. The ministering of the Spirit, which includes the laying on of hands, is happening through many such Christian people everywhere. Indeed, this ministry belongs to the whole people of God.

APPENDIX: HEBREWS 6:1-2

Related to the discussion about water baptism and the laying on of hands is an additional Scripture, Hebrews 6:1-2, which reads: "Let us leave the elementary teachings about Christ and go on to maturity, not laying again the foundation of repentance from acts that lead to death, and of faith in God, instruction about baptisms,[66] the laying on of

---

[63] Ananias is simply described in Acts 9:10 as "a disciple at Damascus."

[64] It is interesting that when Philip later proclaimed the gospel to the Ethiopian eunuch and baptized him (Acts 8:38), the next words according to the Western text (see footnote 31) are "And when they came up out of the water, the Spirit of the Lord fell upon the eunuch. . . ." Although this is likely a later textual addition, it does reflect some early church understanding that Philip was by no means dependent on apostolic help for the Holy Spirit to be given.

[65] In my book, *The Era of the Spirit,* I summarized the laying on of hands thus: "Wherever this laying on of hands occurs, it is not, as such, a sacramental action. It is rather the simple ministry by one or more persons who themselves are channels of the Holy Spirit to others not yet so blessed. The 'ministers' may be clergy or laity; it makes no difference. . . . Obviously God is doing a mighty work today bound neither by office nor by rank" (64).

[66] The Greek word is *baptismōn*. It is also translated as "baptisms" in KJV. The RSV has "ablutions"; NASB, "washings"; NEB, "cleansing rites." According to Oepke, " Βαπτισμῶν διδαχή denotes instruction on the difference between Jewish (and pagan?) 'washings' (including John's baptism?) and Christian baptism" (TDNT, 1:545). Similarly Beasley-

hands, the resurrection of the dead, and eternal judgment" (NIV). Here the text speaks of six "elementary" areas, at the center of which are baptisms and the laying on of hands.

The first two of these, repentance and faith, are obviously the most basic because it is by repentance and faith that one comes to salvation. The last two are climactic—the resurrection of the dead and eternal judgment. In between are instruction about baptisms and the laying on of hands. Let us examine these two, especially their connection with the foundations of repentance and faith.

"Instructions about baptisms" could refer to (1) the difference between various Jewish lustrations and Christian baptism, (2) the difference between John's baptism and Christian baptism,[67] or (3) the difference between baptism in water and baptism in the Spirit. The laying on of hands very likely refers to

the impartation of the gift of the Spirit through the imposition of hands.[68] If (2) above is the best understanding,[69] it is quite interesting that the sequence of faith in Christ (which includes repentance), baptisms (both John's and Christian), and the laying on of hands is the same as that in Acts 19:1–6.[70] Faith and repentance are followed by baptisms, but these are not the only rites; there is also the laying on of hands for the reception of the Spirit. This clearly implies both salvation and the gift of the Holy Spirit.[71]

In regard to these "elementary teachings" in Hebrews, we should note that the word "instruction" precedes baptisms and the laying on of hands (this is not the case in relation to repentance and faith). Is it too much to suggest that this is the area where instruction is particularly needed in our time? Of repentance and faith much is said, especially in evangelical ranks, but what of

---

Murray states, "In Heb. 6:2 'instruction about washings' . . . appears to concern the contrast between Christian baptism and all other religious washings" (NIDNTT, 1:149). F. F. Bruce, contrariwise, says, "It is very doubtful whether Christian baptism is directly in view here at all" (*The Epistle to the Hebrews,* NICNT, 114). I agree with Oepke and Beasley-Murray that the connection is here. Why would Hebrews speak of this matter as foundational if the reference is only, for example, to "Jewish ceremonial washings" (Bruce's words)?

[67] See previous footnote in relation to (1) and (2).

[68] Here I agree with F. F. Bruce, who relates this statement in Hebrews to "an early Christian practice, associated especially with the impartation of the Holy Spirit," adding that "it is most probably its significance here" (ibid., 116). Leon Morris writes similarly: "It is Christian beginnings, perhaps with the thought of God's gift of the Spirit, that is in mind here" (EBC, 12:53).

[69] The third suggestion is also quite possible, especially since the laying on of hands correlative to baptism in the Spirit is next mentioned. The sequence as described above remains the same.

[70] It is also similar to the Samaritan account in Acts 8: repentance (turning from previous domination by Simon the magician) and faith in Christ, baptism (not baptism*s*, though the Samaritans may have received instruction about multiple baptisms), and the laying on of hands to receive the gift of the Holy Spirit.

[71] Hebrews 6:4 also suggests salvation and the reception of the Spirit. Reference is made in this verse to those who have "once been enlightened, who have tasted the heavenly gift, and have become partakers [or "sharers"] of the Holy Spirit." "Once been enlightened" doubtless refers to salvation (cf. Heb. 10:32; also 2 Cor. 4:6), "tasted the heavenly gift" probably refers to enjoying the graciousness of the Lord (cf. 1 Peter 2:3, esp. KJV), and "partakers of the Holy Spirit" definitely implies participating in the Spirit's presence and power. Note that one step follows on another.

baptisms (in the plural)[72] and the laying on of hands?

What was so elementary to the writer of Hebrews and presumably to his readers, that he could say at the outset, "Let us leave the elementary teachings about Christ and go on to maturity," calls for serious reflection today. We must, almost as school children, go back to the ABCs and relearn some very elementary things. By no means are we ready to "go on to maturity" if we have not mastered and put into practice the rudimentary matters. "Repentance" and "faith" perhaps we understand (the first grade level), but "baptisms" and "hands" (second grade, shall we say) many of us have hardly mastered at all. How then are we ready for the mature, the headier stuff of doctrine and practice when we have not gotten beyond the most elementary?

We may be grateful that the spiritual renewal in our time has helped to recover some of this long-overlooked heritage.

III. CONTEXT

I have already emphasized that the Holy Spirit comes to those who believe in Jesus Christ; thus faith is essential. Now let us note the context, the situation or atmosphere, in which the Holy Spirit is given.

A. God's Sovereign Disposition

The divine context of God's will and intention is altogether basic. From within the pattern of God's purpose, by which He works all things according to the counsel of His sovereign will, God gives His Holy Spirit. Thus whatever may be and must be said on the human side about the situation, context, and atmosphere is altogether secondary to God's sovereign action. In this sense, God gives when He wills, not according to the human condition, but according to His overall design and purpose. Therefore, there is a continuing mystery and, humanly speaking, an unpredictability about the giving of the Holy Spirit.

This was surely true of the first Pentecost in Jerusalem. God had long purposed (and promised) the outpouring of His Spirit; and when the divinely planned time had arrived, the Holy Spirit was given. The opening words of Acts 2:1 suggest this: "When the day of Pentecost had come . . ." or better, "had been fulfilled . . . ."[73] So when the day was fulfilled, the Holy Spirit was given. This was God's timetable, not man's. It dealt with God's overarching plan in history. It was an event of "the last days" (v. 17) according to the divine promise.

Likewise, it is important to emphasize that the movements of the Holy Spirit throughout history to the present day are grounded in the sovereign pur-

---

[72] Of course, John's baptism is no longer a relevant issue. However, instruction about baptisms might legitimately include both baptism in water and in the Spirit (see [3] above), especially the relationship of the latter to the laying on of hands. Also the matter of "one Lord, one faith, one baptism" (Eph. 4:5) could call for consideration. F. F. Bruce makes the comment regarding "one baptism" that "it is beside the point to ask whether it is baptism in water or baptism of the Holy Spirit: it is Christian baptism—baptism 'into the name of the Lord Jesus' . . . which indeed involved the application of water, as John's baptism had done, but . . . was closely associated with the gift of the Spirit" (*The Epistles to the Colossians, to Philemon, and to the Ephesians*, NICNT, 336–37).

[73] The verb is *symplērousthai*, "to be fulfilled." According to TDNT, this means "fulfilled according to God's plan. . . . The verb itself points to the fulfillment of God's saving will in the event which takes place" (6:308). The KJV is closer to the Greek text than RSV (and many other versions) in translating *symplērousthai* as "was fully come."

pose of God.[74] The fact that in our present century there has been a crescendo of the Spirit's outpouring and that the movement has not become worldwide points basically to the divine intention. God is doing it again—and with such a universality ("upon all flesh") that we may surmise that "the last days" are being fulfilled and that history is reaching its consummation. However that may be, the critical point to underscore is the fact of divine sovereignty.

This divine context needs first to be emphasized, lest we too quickly come to the human situation. *Primarily* it is not a matter of human concern but God's concern. Like the original disciples who participated in the coming of God's Spirit because it was God's time, so do we participate in our own day. We are privileged to be alive in what may be the climactic outpouring of the Spirit at the end of the age. Our concern is not unimportant, neither is our readiness to participate in what God is doing, but the basic matter again is God's sovereign purpose.

Further, since it is a matter of the *gift* of the Holy Spirit, there is nothing anyone can do to earn it. By definition a gift is freely bestowed; it cannot be worked for or bought. It would be a serious mistake to think that while forgiveness is by grace, the gift of the Holy Spirit is by works. Here some of Paul's rhetorical questions are most apropos: "Did you receive the Spirit by works of the law, or by hearing with faith? . . . Does he who supplies the Spirit to you and works miracles among you do so by works of the law, or by hearing with faith?" (Gal. 3:2, 5). On the matter of being bought, the words of Peter to Simon the magician, who offered money for the power to confer the Holy Spirit, are vividly relevant: "Your silver perish with you, because you thought you could obtain the gift of God with money!" (Acts 8:20). The gift of the Holy Spirit cannot be earned, no matter how great the effort, nor can it be purchased no matter how large the amount.

Having said these various things about divine sovereignty and the Holy Spirit as a gift, we are ready to consider further the human context or situation. As we have earlier noted, on the human side, it is through faith that the Holy Spirit is received. Hence, however true it is that God sovereignly grants His Holy Spirit, it is to those believing in Jesus Christ, those who are on the way of faith.[75] Thus as we move on to observe the context in which the Spirit is given, we continue to stand within the sphere of faith. We do not add one iota to faith, as if it were faith plus something else. Rather, are we now dealing with various expressions *within* faith—constituents of faith, in a sense—so that the context[76] is not extraneous to faith but is its vital demonstration.

---

[74]I have sought to delineate some of these movements in my book *The Pentecostal Reality,* chapter 3, "A New Era in History."

[75]Refer to Section I.B for an elaboration of this matter.

[76]I speak of *context* rather than *conditions* for receiving the Holy Spirit. Charles W. Conn writes that "there are definite, stated conditions to be met; conditions that had to be met by the disciples, conditions that must be met by all who receive the Holy Ghost today" (*Pillars of Pentecost,* 96). The word "conditions" may however suggest something beyond faith, a kind of faith plus works; hence it should be avoided. F. D. Bruner expresses strong opposition to Pentecostalism because of what he calls their "doctrine of the conditions for the baptism in the Holy Spirit" (*A Theology of the Holy Spirit,* 87–111). Although Bruner's criticisms are exaggerated, his point concerning the use of the word, or idea, of conditions is well taken.

B. Prayer

Prayer is, of course, an essential element in the totality of Christian living—in its many aspects of praise, thanksgiving, confession, supplication, and dedication. But in a special way it is the context or atmosphere in which the Holy Spirit is given.

This may be seen first in Jesus' own experience and teaching. We are told that following His baptism in water by John, the Holy Spirit came upon Him. In that sense Jesus is the precursor of those whose water baptism is followed by the gift of the Holy Spirit.[77] It is quite relevant that Luke records that prayer was the context of the Spirit's coming upon Jesus: "Now when all the people were baptized, and when Jesus also had been baptized and was pray- ing, the heaven was opened, and the Holy Spirit descended upon him in bodily form, as a dove. . ." (3:21–22).[78] We should note here that, though the coming of the Spirit followed directly upon Jesus' baptism, the state- ment about prayer links the two events together. Although water baptism pre- pared the way[79] for the gift of the Spirit, it occurred to Him when He was in an attitude of prayer.

The importance of prayer in connec- tion with the gift of the Holy Spirit is further underscored in Luke's Gospel by these words of Jesus: "If you then, who are evil, know how to give good gifts to your children, how much more will the heavenly Father give the Holy Spirit to those who ask him!" (11:13).[80]

---

[77] See again Acts 2:38; 8:12–17; 19:5–6.

[78] That this was Jesus' own baptism in the Spirit is apparent in many ways: (1) Although the imagery of the dove differs, e.g., from the wind and fire of Pentecost, the picture is clearly of a coming of the Spirit from without; (2) Immediately after, that Jesus was "full of the Holy Spirit' " (Luke 4:1), thus a parallel to the disciples being "filled with the Holy Spirit" (Acts 2:4); (3) the Holy Spirit came at the Jordan to inaugurate Jesus' ministry even as at Pentecost to initiate the disciples'; (4) the Spirit who came is the Spirit of power: afterward it was said that Jesus moved "in the power [*dynamis*] of the Spirit" (Luke 4:14); likewise the promise was given to the disciples that they would receive power (*dynamis*) (Acts 1:8) when the Holy Spirit came upon them; (5) in the parallel passage in John's Gospel the descent of the Spirit upon Jesus is tied to Jesus' baptism of others in the Holy Spirit: "I myself [John the Baptist] did not know him; but he who sent me to baptize with water said to me, 'He on whom you see the Spirit descend and remain, this is he who baptizes in the Holy Spirit' " (John 1:33).

[79] The water baptism in Jesus' case, unlike that of others, was not "for the forgiveness of sins" (cf. Acts 2:38). When John the Baptist remonstrated against baptizing Jesus ("I need to be baptized by you, and do you come to me?"), Jesus replied, "Let it be so now; for thus it is fitting for us to fulfil all righteousness" (Matt. 3:14–15). Although Jesus was not a sinner needing baptism and forgiveness, baptism did represent identification with God's righteous purpose signified therein. Thus—and of relevance to our concerns—Jesus' water baptism, which fulfilled God's righteousness before the Spirit was given, illustrates the faith- righteousness that precedes the gift of the Holy Spirit.

[80] In the parallel Matthean account (7:11), instead of "the Holy Spirit" the expression is "good things" (*agatha*). Of all "good things," the gift of the Holy Spirit cannot be excelled. So EGT comments on Luke 11:13: "The Holy Spirit is mentioned here as the *summum bonum*, and the supreme object of desire for all true disciples." EGT also notes that "in some forms of the Lord's Prayer (Marcion, Greg[ory of] Nys[sa]) a petition for the gift of the Holy Spirit took the place of the first or second petition." Since Luke 11 begins with the Lord's Prayer and is the background for all that follows about prayer, climaxing with prayer for the gift of the Spirit, it is at least conceivable that the whole passage (vv. 1–13) is an elaboration of the petition for the Holy Spirit and what is involved in such petition. (For a previous discussion of the passage in Luke, see chapter 7, III.B., "The Gift of the Holy Spirit.")

This asking is earlier set forth in the story of a man who, having no bread to share with a visitor, goes to a friend's house at midnight. Although the friend is in bed with his children, the man continues to call out, knocking again and again. Jesus adds: " . . . though he will not get up and give him anything because he is his friend, yet because of his importunity[81] he will rise and give him whatever he needs. And I tell you, Ask, and it will be given you; seek, and you will find; knock, and it will be opened to you" (11:8–9). Hence importunate, persistent, unrelenting prayer is the context for the gift of the Holy Spirit. It would be pushing the story too far to suggest that God only grudgingly gives His Spirit; for the climax describes how God goes far beyond earthly fathers in His generosity. The point, however, is that God is pleased to give to those who earnestly desire something, otherwise the gift may mean very little. But where there is intense desire, the fulfillment of the prayer is all the more full of joy and thanksgiving.[82] Prayer to the heavenly Father is the channel for God's blessed gift of the Holy Spirit.

But now let us move on to the Book of Acts, where again the atmosphere of prayer is shown in several instances to surround the coming of the Holy Spirit. First, this is especially apparent in the account of Acts 1, which leads up to Pentecost. Jesus had charged the apostles to stay in Jerusalem and to await the promised Holy Spirit. Thus after Jesus' ascension the apostles returned to the city. Joined by various women who had been with Jesus, including Mary and Jesus' brothers, they gave themselves to prayer: "All these with one accord devoted themselves to prayer" (Acts 1:14).[83] Thus it was not simply an idle waiting, but a waiting in prayer; and it was not simply occasional prayer, but that to which they devoted themselves. Later the number of those waiting grew to about 120 persons (v. 15). On one occasion the company selected an apostle to succeed Judas (vv. 16–26), but the atmosphere continued to be that of prayer. On the Day of Pentecost it was to a group gathered in an attitude of prayer that the Holy Spirit was given.[84]

It should be pointed out that the disciples did not know exactly when the Holy Spirit would be poured out. They were not told by Jesus to wait for a given number of days, nor did they set aside a certain number of days for prayer after which they would turn to something else. No, they simply gave themselves to unlimited prayer, prayer doubtless in connection with the promised gift of the Holy Spirit, and God at the proper time[85] sent forth His Spirit.

[81] The Greek word is *anaideian,* literally, "shamelessness," hence a persistence or importunity that is almost indecent!

[82] Here I would like to testify personally how true this is. After I had spent some three days of continual prayer specifically for the gift of the Holy Spirit, God marvelously granted my request. It seemed many times that God (like the man in bed at midnight) would never answer, but because of my deep desire, importunate praying continued. At last when the answer came, it was all the more a thing of wonder and praise.

[83] Or "were continuing steadfastly in prayer" (*ēsan proskarterountes . . . tē proseuchē*). This more literal Greek reading points to the fact of their continuous devotion.

[84] The account in Acts 2:1–4 of the coming of the Spirit does not directly say that the disciples were praying when this happened. However, it is clearly implied both from the words of 1:14 (suggesting a continuing devotion to prayer) and the setting of 2:1–4 where they were "all together in one place" (v. 1) (suggesting a unity in prayer) and their "sitting" (v. 2) (suggesting an attitude of prayerful waiting) when the Holy Spirit came.

[85] We have already spoken of God's sovereign purpose—His own timetable—being fulfilled on the Day of Pentecost. However, this is not to be understood as making irrelevant

Thus if one brings together Luke 11 and Acts 1 (both written by Luke), it is apparent that much stress is laid on the need for prayer in the reception of the Holy Spirit. Even though the promise of the gift is clearly present in both cases, there is a call for continuing, persisting prayer. Just as this was true for the disciples prior to Pentecost in Jerusalem (Acts 1), so it is for God's other children who know their need (Luke 11). God delights to give His Spirit to those who earnestly ask Him.[86]

The importance of prayer in the reception of the Holy Spirit is, second, to be found in the account of Saul's being filled with the Holy Spirit. After his encounter with the risen Lord, Saul was led by the hand into Damascus and "for three days he was without sight, and neither ate nor drank" (Acts 9:9). This time of fasting was also a time of praying. When Ananias was told in a vision to go and help Saul, the Lord said of Saul, "Behold, he is praying" (v. 11). This expression connotes a continuing in prayer, a waiting on the Lord, during which time, as the Scripture records, Saul likewise had a vision of Ananias coming to lay hands on him. Both men had visions: Paul prayed, fasted, and waited. In that context God gave the Holy Spirit.

Third, much prayer was the environment and background for the coming of the Holy Spirit on the Gentiles at Caesarea. At the outset, Cornelius is described as "a devout man who feared God with all his household, gave alms liberally to the people, and prayed constantly to God" (Acts 10:2). In that atmosphere Cornelius had a vision in which he was told that his prayers and alms had "ascended as a memorial before God" (v. 4). He was instructed to send for Simon Peter in the town of Joppa. After that Peter was also in prayer (he "went up on the housetop to pray" [v. 9]) and likewise had a vision that resulted in his willingness to go to a Gentile home and proclaim the gospel. Then the Holy Spirit fell upon Cornelius and his household. The whole situation, much like that at Damascus, was one of continuing prayer, visions, and waiting on the Lord.

Finally, in the narratives concerning the Samaritans and Ephesians there is no indication (unlike the previous instances) that those who received the Holy Spirit had been in prayer. However, the Scripture does record that prior to the Samaritans' reception of the Holy Spirit, Peter and John prayed for them: They "came down [from Jerusalem] and prayed for them that they might receive the Holy Spirit" (Acts 8:15). After such intercession, the apostles laid their hands on the Samaritans for the reception of the Spirit.[87] While it

---

the human context of prayer. God fulfills His purpose through those who prayerfully await His action.

[86] The point is sometimes made that the account of the disciples waiting and praying prior to Pentecost cannot afford an example for others, since the Holy Spirit had not yet been given. For in the words of John, "the Spirit had not been given, because Jesus was not yet glorified" (7:39). Hence, there could be no reception of the Spirit prior to Jesus' glorification. However, Jesus *had* been glorified (i.e., returned to the Father's presence as Acts 1:9–11 records) before Pentecost, and yet they waited some ten days. When this fact is realized, and such a scripture as Luke 11:1–13, which seems clearly applicable to God's children at any time, is also considered, it is apparent that earnest prayer continues to be the context for the gift of the Holy Spirit.

[87] It is important to emphasize that there was no automatic reception of the Holy Spirit through the laying on of hands by Peter and John. Although hands were the medium, the gift came only to those who believed in Jesus. We now are noting a further point, namely, that it was not simply a matter of laying hands (apostolic or otherwise) on believers. Rather, prior to hands, and still more basic (as an expression of faith in operation), was prayer.

may be surmised that the Samaritans were in an attitude of prayer also, the emphasis rests on the prayers of Peter and John. In any event, it was against the background and in the context of believing prayer that the Holy Spirit was received.

Looking back at these several accounts, it is apparent that prayer lies close to the gift of the Holy Spirit. Such prayer was shown variously to be earnest, even importunate (Luke 11), a matter of steadfastness and devotion (Acts 2), of day-by-day continuation (Act 9), of intercession (Acts 8), and of constancy (Acts 10). There is no suggestion that prayer was a condition for securing the Holy Spirit, but over and over prayer is shown to be the background, the context, the atmosphere wherein God delights to grant His Holy Spirit to those who believe.[88]

In the contemporary situation this proves to be the case wherever spiritual renewal is occurring. The testimonies vary—some had been praying for some time, some only for a short period, some were prayed for by others, some had expressed little overt prayer—but it was in a prayerful atmosphere of waiting before God that the Holy Spirit was poured out.[89]

C. Obedience

The Holy Spirit is given within the context of obedience to those who obey God's command. In this regard one verse in the Book of Acts stands out: "And we are witnesses to these things, and so is the Holy Spirit whom God has given to those who obey him" (5:32).[90] This is obedience occurring within the area of faith, the obedience that suffuses the atmosphere surrounding those who become recipients of the gift of the Holy Spirit. It is indeed the obedience

---

[88] One of the questions in the Heidelberg Catechism (Q. 116) is, "Why is prayer necessary for Christians?" Then follows the striking answer: "Because it is the chief part of the gratitude which God requires of us, and because *God will give his grace and Holy Spirit only to those who sincerely beseech him in prayer without ceasing,* and who thank him for these gifts" (italics added).

[89] Prayer as the context for the outpouring of the Spirit has been evidenced since the early twentieth century. The usual date for the beginning of the Pentecostal/charismatic renewal is New Year's Day, 1901, in Topeka, Kansas. At Charles Parham's Bible School, a devout prayer service had been held on New Year's Eve, and all New Year's Day God's presence was felt "stilling hearts to wait upon greater things to come" (Klaude Kendrick, *The Promise Fulfilled,* 52). About 11:00 P.M. Agnes Ozman, one of the students, was prayed for to receive the gift of the Holy Spirit, and the Holy Spirit "fell" (recall chapter 8, n. 57). The second outburst occurred in Los Angeles on April 9, 1906, among a group of people, whites and blacks, who had prayed and fasted for ten days, asking God to send His Spirit. On the tenth day a young black man spoke in tongues, followed shortly by six others. Such early twentieth-century beginnings are repeated variously in our time. For example, it was at a prayer meeting that Dennis Bennett had his experience, and it was in prayer that the gift of the Spirit came. A friend prayed over him, and then Bennett "prayed out loud for about twenty minutes" before he began "to speak in a new language" (*Nine O'Clock in the Morning,* 20). Examples could be multiplied.

[90] Literally, "the Holy Spirit whom God gave to the ones obeying him" (Gr. *to pneuma to hagion ho edōken ho theos tois peitharchousin autō*). F. D. Bruner errs in saying that "the obedience spoken of in Acts 5:32 rather than being a condition is the result of the gift of the Holy Spirit" (*A Theology of the Holy Spirit,* 172). There is no suggestion here of obedience as a result; it is rather that God gives the Spirit to those obeying. E. Schweizer is correct in writing that "obedience must also precede the reception of the Spirit according to [Acts] 5:32" (TDNT, 6: 412). Also see John Rea, *Layman's Commentary on the Holy Spirit,* 74–78, entitled "Acts 5:32—Obedience and the Gift of the Holy Spirit."

of faith.[91] God grants His Spirit to those who in faith obey His command.

The above quotation from Acts 5:32 is taken from Peter's words before the Jewish council. He spoke for all the apostles (as the passage shows) and accordingly refers to their obedience as the context wherein the Holy Spirit was given. This then leads us back to the situation prior to Pentecost and to the important matter of the nature of their obedience. The Book of Acts begins with the words "In the first book, O Theophilus, I have dealt with all that Jesus began to do and teach, until the day when he was taken up, after he had given commandment[s][92] through the Holy Spirit to the apostles whom he had chosen" (1:1–2). Thus as men of faith they were under obedience to Christ's commands as transmitted through the Holy Spirit.[93] The apostles, accordingly, gave themselves to obedience as men under orders. After that came the specific commandment "not to depart from Jerusalem,[94] but to wait for the promise of the Father [the gift of the Holy Spirit]" (v. 4). What followed over a period of ten days was the obedient act of waiting for the fulfillment of the promise. As men under orders, with others joining them until the number came to be about one hundred twenty (v. 15), they awaited the promised gift of the Holy Spirit.

A like obedience of faith was demonstrated in the case of Saul of Tarsus who, following his encounter with the risen Christ, was commanded by Him: "Rise and enter the city [of Damascus], and you will be told what you are to do" (Acts 9:6). Saul obeyed and after three days was visited by Ananias, who likewise acted in obedience to a vision and a command of Christ (vv. 10–11). Saul thereafter was filled with the Holy Spirit. The atmosphere, the context, for the gift of the Holy Spirit was obedience by both parties: Ananias who ministered and Saul who received.

Quite similar is the story of the Roman centurion Cornelius at Caesarea, who, along with his kinsfolk and friends, received the outpoured gift of the Holy Spirit. Cornelius was commanded by the Lord in a vision: "And now send men to Joppa, and bring one Simon who is called Peter" (Acts 10:5). Peter, who likewise had a vision, was sent for by Cornelius, for Peter had been told by the Spirit: "Rise and go down, and accompany them [the servants of Cornelius] without hesitation. . ." (10:20). Then, in an atmosphere of the obedience of faith,[95] they received the Holy Spirit.

---

[91] The expression "the obedience of faith" is used by Paul in Romans 1:5: "Through whom [Christ] we have received grace and apostleship to bring about the obedience of faith [*eis hypakoēn pisteōs*] for the sake of his name among all the nations. . . ." Also see Romans 16:26 for the same expression. BAGD (under ὑπακοή) suggests that *eis hypakoēn pisteōs* be translated "*with a view to (promoting) obedience that springs from faith.*" Obedience that springs from faith is an excellent way of describing the obedience that is the context for the gift of the Holy Spirit.

[92] The RSV has the singular: "commandment"; however, the Greek word *enteilamenos* is plural.

[93] Although the Holy Spirit Himself had not yet been given, He was already present as the medium for Jesus' words. This prior presence of the Holy Spirit illustrates a point earlier made, namely, that the gift of the Holy Spirit by no means rules out the previous presence and activity of the Holy Spirit among people of faith.

[94] According to the Gospel of Luke (the "first book" referred to in Acts 1:1), the words are "stay [Gr. *kathisate*, literally, 'sit'; 'tarry' KJV] in the city" (24:49).

[95] At the moment of the Lord's command to the centurion, Cornelius was not yet a

These were all acts of specific obedience[96] that relate directly to the gift of the Holy Spirit. They call to mind again the words of Jesus, earlier quoted: "Ask . . . seek . . . knock" (Luke 11:9). These words, I now emphasize, are a strong, threefold command that relates altogether to the gift of the Holy Spirit. There may or may not be a direct word from Christ (as with the apostles, Saul, and the Roman centurion), but that is not necessary. The words of Christ are inscribed for all to read and obey: Ask, seek, and knock.[97] For the Holy Spirit, as Peter said, is given "to those who obey him."

Lest this be viewed only as a matter of obedience to a particular command "to wait," "to ask," etc., we should also recall the words of Jesus in the Fourth Gospel: "If you love me, you will keep my commandments. And I will pray the Father, and he will give you another Counselor. . ." (John 14:15–16). The Holy Spirit—the "Counselor" (Paraclete)—will be given to those who obey Christ's commandments. Before Jesus gave the specific command to the apostles to wait in Jerusalem, He gave "commandments through the Holy Spirit" (supra). Thus, willing obedience to *whatever* Christ commands and has commanded (as set forth for us in the gospels) is background and context for the Holy Spirit to be given.

This suggests that those who seek faithfully to walk in the way of Christ are living in an atmosphere conducive to the reception of the Holy Spirit. Such a walk in obedience, not done grudgingly or seeking a reward, is an expression of a heart right before God. There may and will be failures, but the essential intention and direction is that of obedience to the word of the Lord. Already in some sense walking in the way of obedience, such persons are in a position for further implementation of obedient living by the Holy Spirit. The way of obedience wherein God's word is gladly honored and heeded is the context for receiving the gift of the Holy Spirit.[98]

---

believer. However, he did become a believer, at which moment the Holy Spirit was poured out (10:43–44). Hence his obedience was caught up in faith. To such a one the Spirit is given.

[96]This has been noted in three instances, involving the original disciples in Jerusalem, Saul of Tarsus, and the Caesareans. As far as the Samaritans are concerned, the situation is less clear. It may be that one of the reasons for the delay of several days in their receiving the gift of the Holy Spirit was their need for more time after the beginning of faith for obedience to develop. The Samaritans had long been caught up in idolatrous adulation of Simon the magician—"They all gave heed to him, from the least to the greatest, saying, 'This man is that power of God which is called Great' " (Acts 8:10)—and were "amazed" by his magical practices (v. 11). Although the Samaritans had entered the way of faith, they may have needed more time for commitment—and obedience—to Christ to replace their deep-seated idolatry in regard to Simon. In the case of the Ephesians, we read nothing directly about obedience. However, the atmosphere is that of readiness to do what John the Baptist had commanded, and after that to follow Paul's injunctions (see Acts 19:4–6).

[97]This does not necessarily mean a long "tarrying" period for the Holy Spirit to be given. But, however short or long, the words do call for a *determination* to obey—to keep on asking, seeking, and knocking—until the answer comes. For many people, I would add, there was never such a time of overt seeking and asking; however, their hearts and lives were set on obedience (see next paragraph in the text), and to them God gave His Holy Spirit.

[98]Here I make reference to a nineteenth-century book by Andrew Murray, *The Spirit of Christ,* in the section subtitled, "The Spirit Given to the Obedient," 69–77. Murray writes, *"The obedient must and may look for the fullness of the Spirit"* (italics his). He speaks of

This means, on the other hand, that one of the barriers to the reception of the Holy Spirit may be disobedience. If a person is not walking in the way of faithful obedience to Christ's commandments—for example, the injunctions of the Sermon on the Mount (Matt. 5–7); if he is harboring anger, lust, or bitterness in his heart; if his love has grown cold and holiness is aggrieved, such a person is hardly in a position to receive God's *Holy* Spirit.[99] This does not mean that one must be without sin to receive the Holy Spirit. If that were the case, no one would be a recipient of Him. What is important is not the attainment of perfection, but ever seeking (regardless of many a failure) to walk in the way of obedience. For obedience lies at the heart of faith, and it is by faith alone that the Holy Spirit is received.

So to conclude this section: Obedience in general to the command of Christ, His word, His teaching, His direction, and specifically to the directive to "wait for the promise" is one aspect of the context for receiving the Holy Spirit. There may be no waiting, as in the case of the centurion whose prior obedience[100] was caught up into

---

this as "the promise of the conscious, active indwelling of the Spirit" and adds, "A living obedience is indispensable to the full experience of the indwelling. . . . Let each of us even now say to our Lord that we do love Him and keep His commandments. In however much feebleness and failure it be, still let us speak it out to Him. . . ." Murray, a Dutch Reformed pastor in South Africa, was one of the predecessors of the twentieth-century spiritual renewal. On the contemporary scene John Rea puts it well: "Christian obedience is a product of the inner heart, not of outward duty. It springs from gratitude for grace already received (Rom. 12:1–8) not from desire to gain merit" (*Layman's Commentary on the Holy Spirit,* 77). It is *this* obedience, which is not a work, that is context for the gift of the Spirit to be received.

[99] Many Pentecostals, accordingly, affirm the necessity of complete holiness or entire sanctification for the reception of the Holy Spirit. They do not identify complete sanctification with baptism in the Spirit (as did the late-nineteenth-century Wesleyan-Holiness movement; recall chap. 10, Excursus, n. 127), but they do retain the Holiness emphasis on entire sanctification as necessary to baptism in the Spirit. For example, the Church of God (Cleveland, Tenn.), one of the earliest Pentecostal denominations, declares, "We believe . . . in sanctification subsequent to the new birth . . . and in the baptism of the Holy Ghost subsequent to a clean heart." A similar view is held by such major Pentecostal bodies as the Pentecostal Holiness Church and the Church of God in Christ. Many other Pentecostal denominations such as the Assemblies of God, the Elim Pentecostal Church, and the International Church of the Foursquare Gospel do not affirm entire sanctification as "a second work of grace" (a common expression for "entire sanctification") prior to Spirit baptism. The charismatic movement has generally held this latter viewpoint. With its adherents largely in non-Wesleyan churches (e.g., Episcopal, Lutheran, Presbyterian, Roman Catholic), there has been little, if any, recognition of an intervening stage of complete sanctification between regeneration and the reception of the Holy Spirit.

My comment is that although holiness is surely important, it is difficult to deduce from the Book of Acts (or elsewhere in the New Testament) a second stage of entire sanctification between salvation and the gift of the Holy Spirit. Moreover, it is really asking the impossible—"entire sanctification"—and places too great a burden on people seeking the gift of the Holy Spirit. What rather needs to be said is that sanctification (not "entire sanctification") is essential to receiving the Holy Spirit, and that either at the time of initial sanctification or during its progress (see chap. 4, II.A.B, on the beginning and continuation of sanctification) the Holy Spirit may be given. To use my language in the text above, the gift of the Spirit is received on the way of obedience.

[100] As mentioned before, the centurion is described as a God-fearing man: "a devout man who feared God with all his household" (Acts 10:2); he was also a man who "does what is right" (v. 35). Thus against a broad background of devoutness of life and righteous concerns, Cornelius' obedience to the command of the Lord stands out vividly.

the obedience of faith. Immediately the Spirit was poured out at the commencement of his faith. But in every instance the Holy Spirit is given in the context of obedient faith.

D. Yielding

In an atmosphere of surrender to the lordship of Jesus Christ the Holy Spirit is given. When persons are ready to give up everything for the sake of Christ and the gospel and lay themselves completely at His disposal, God vouchsafes the abundance of His Spirit. One may also speak of emptiness before the Lord, and to this comes the answer of His divine fullness. When self is broken of all prideful claim, a new power is released—the power and anointing of God's Holy Spirit.

In the New Testament accounts concerning the original disciples of Jesus, Pentecost stands forth as the climax of a movement toward the all-sufficiency of Jesus Christ. Peter himself is a vivid illustration of this. Responding to the word of Jesus that the Twelve would deny Him, he had boastfully replied, "Even though they all fall away, I will not" (Mark 14:29). It was a quite different Peter after Pentecost. No longer did he look to himself but wholly to Christ, for he said to a cripple: "In the name of Jesus Christ of Nazareth, walk" (Acts 3:6), and then to the spectators astounded at what had happened he asked, "Men of Israel, why do you wonder at this, or why do you stare at us, as

though by our own power or piety we had made him walk?" (v. 12). Something had happened to Peter between the time of his self-affirmation and ensuing denial of Jesus and the time of his total Christ-affirmation. A transformation had occurred. The groundwork was the postresurrection encounters by which Jesus ministered new faith, new life, and a new commission,[101] but it actually occurred only after a period of waiting that culminated in Pentecost. This was the final time of preparation and of transition from self-dependency to complete dependence on Christ. The ten days in the Upper Room were surely days of yielding more and more of self until the final barrier was breached, the self was emptied of all vain striving, and the Holy Spirit rushed in to fill the vacuum with the presence and power of God. Thereafter for Peter and the other disciples it was to be life lived in the fullness of the Holy Spirit.

Essentially the same thing must have happened with Saul of Tarsus over a three-day period. Although Saul had been set on a new course by the risen Jesus—180 degrees opposite from his former direction—and now believed in the One he formerly persecuted, doubtless there was much still needed by way of yielding and surrender to his new Lord before he would be able to receive the commission from Ananias to preach Christ. Saul of Tarsus had been extremely self-reliant, proud, and defiant;[102] and although he had now

---

[101] In the Gospel of John the resurrected Jesus appeared to the disciples in a closed room and said, " 'Peace be with you. As the Father has sent me, even so I send you.' And when he had said this, he breathed on them, and said to them, 'Receive the Holy Spirit' " (20:21–22). Further evidence of this ministration of new life and new commission is found later in the Gospel of John where Jesus fed several of the disciples bread and fish and then three times commissioned Peter to feed His sheep and lambs (21:15–17). Likewise, in the Gospel of Luke there was the ministry of faith and life through Jesus' unmistakable resurrection presence (Luke 24:36–43) and the declaration of a new commission (24:46–48). This was prior to Pentecost, as Luke specifies in the Book of Acts, and thus it points to a further period of instruction, waiting, and yielding to the Lord.

[102] A Roman citizen, of the tribe of Benjamin, graduate of the school at Tarsus, Pharisee

received new life and direction, it would take these days of blindness and prayer and fasting for the full surrender to occur, so that all his strength henceforward would be from the Spirit of Christ, the Holy Spirit. The words of Paul to the Romans at a later time are quite apropos: "Yield yourselves to God as men who have been brought from death to life" (Rom. 6:13). There is a new life after death, and then a yielding of the total self to God!

Yielding makes for total availability; by this one becomes an instrument wholly devoted to the Master's service. It is not only to know Jesus as Savior but also to be "sold out" to Him. Yielding is not sanctification but servanthood[103] wherein the whole of life is placed at the disposal of Christ. Thereby the Spirit of the Lord possesses a person in totality—body, mind, and spirit—and all of life becomes a "living sacrifice"[104] to God.

Such yielding means no longer doing one's own will but the will of God: "not my will, but thine be done." It is to have "the mind of Christ," which means to humble oneself and become obedient unto death.[105] It means to surrender the tongue—"an unrighteous world among our members, staining the whole body . . . set on fire by hell. . . . With it we bless the Lord and Father, and with it we curse men. . . ."[106] Thus it becomes attuned only to the praise of God. *All* is to be yielded to Him.[107]

Yielding may also signify not only

---

of the Pharisees, master of legal righteousness, fierce foe of the church (see, e.g., Phil. 3:4–7): This was the Saul whom Jesus encountered on the road to Damascus.

[103] According to Paul in Romans 6, the "fruit" of such yielding is "unto holiness," but the yielding itself is that by which one becomes a servant, or slave, of God. "But now being made free from sin, and become servants [or "slaves"] to God, ye have your fruit unto holiness, and the end everlasting life" (v. 22 KJV).

[104] This is the language of Romans 12:1 where again Paul calls for a life of total commitment. All of life is to be poured out on the altar of complete self-giving.

[105] See Philippians 2:5–8.

[106] See James 3:6–10. The importance of surrender of the tongue—the "unrighteous world among our members"—can scarcely be exaggerated. It desperately needs control and direction by the Holy Spirit. As I have earlier noted, when the disciples at Pentecost—and many others later—were filled with the Holy Spirit, they "began to speak in other tongues as the Spirit gave them utterance" (Acts 2:4). In their total yielding, which included the tongue, the Spirit gave them this new utterance, which was to the praise and magnifying of God. So it continues to be in the contemporary movement of the Holy Spirit where speaking in tongues, among other things, is a sign of complete yielding to God. The tongue no longer "set on fire by hell" is aflame with the glory of God!

[107] Frank Bartleman, a leader in the Azusa Street revival of 1906, wrote tellingly of his own experience of yielding. He said, "My mind, the last fortress of man to yield, was taken possession of by the Holy Spirit. The waters that had been gradually accumulating went over my head. I was possessed of Him fully. The utterance in 'tongues' was without human mixture, as 'the Spirit gave utterance.'. . . Oh, the thrill of being fully yielded to Him! . . . In the experience of 'speaking in tongues' I had reached the climax in abandonment. This opened the channel for a new ministry of the Spirit in service. From that time the Spirit began to flow through me in a new way. . . . The Pentecostal baptism spells complete abandonment, possession by the Holy Ghost, of the whole man, with a spirit of instant obedience. I had much of the power of God for service for many years before this, but I now realized a sensitiveness for the Spirit, a yieldedness, that made it possible for God to possess and work in new ways and channels, with far more powerful direct results" (*Azusa Street*, 72–73). A few words further he wrote about his experience: "There was no strain or contortions. No struggle in an effort to get the 'baptism.' With me it was simply a matter of yielding. . . . I wanted to be fully yielded to God . . . I wanted more of Him, that was all" (ibid., 74).

submission to God but also submission to other persons. In four of the Acts accounts relating to the gift of the Holy Spirit the persons receiving the gift did so through the ministry of others. It was through the ministry of Peter and John that the Samaritans received the Holy Spirit, through the ministry of Ananias that Saul of Tarsus was filled with the Spirit, through the ministry of Peter that the Caesareans were blessed, and through the ministry of Paul that the Ephesians received the gift. In three of these instances the Holy Spirit was given through the imposition of hands of a fellow Christian. The very willingness to have hands laid on the head signifies an act of submission and a readiness to receive from other brethren what God has to give. This submission to the ministry of others, it should be added, is frequently the best antidote to a kind of religious pride that desires to deal only with God directly (as in private prayer). However, the Lord often makes use of human (and sometimes quite humble) vessels for His blessing. It is not always easy for a prominent Saul to submit to an unknown Ananias, but this may be the Lord's way of working.

One of the things that has been learned in the contemporary movement of the Holy Spirit is the importance of this ministry of fellow Christians. Although in many cases God sovereignly pours out His Spirit without human mediation, most often people receive God's gift through the laying on of hands. And the hands may be those of a cleric or a layman (as in the Book of Acts), whomever God chooses. This calls for submission and a degree of yielding that may not have been experienced before.[108]

It would be difficult to overemphasize this whole matter of yielding. Yielding is at the heart of receiving the gift of God's Holy Spirit. For it is only when a person lays himself totally at the disposal of God and holds back nothing that the Spirit moves in to take full possession. There are no shortcuts, no simplistic formulas, no outward manifestations that can bring this about. The Spirit is given only to those who let everything go, who are empty before the Lord, who thereby may be filled with His fullness. This yielding may mean the willingness to give up earthly reputation, security, and ambition so that God may be glorified. It is absolute and irrevocable surrender.[109]

Yielding is an act of faith. It is not something beyond faith, but it is faith in its profoundest expression. Whether such yielding occurs at the inception of faith or somewhere along the way of faith, it represents that total surrender

---

[108] In my own case it was not easy to be prayed for by an ordained minister from another denomination. It seemed a bit humiliating to one also ordained (and a theologian at that!). But God blessed this act of submission, and the gift of the Spirit was thereafter received.

[109] John Rea writes this about yielding: "The individual seeking to be baptized and filled with the Spirit must be willing to yield control of every part of his being to the Holy Spirit. You should yield yourself completely unto Jesus, as one who is alive from the dead, and also every member and faculty of your body as an instrument of righteousness. . . . Yield your will so that your motives are pure. . . . Yield your members, especially your tongues as the organ of expression of the Holy Spirit through you" (*Layman's Commentary on the Holy Spirit*, 65). Donald Gelpi (as was earlier noted) speaks of praying for "full docility to the Spirit of Christ." He adds, "[This] is in effect to express one's willingness to do whatever God may be calling one to do, no matter what the personal sacrifice or suffering that call might entail. The person who cannot pray such a prayer and mean it is not yet ready for 'Spirit-baptism' " (*Pentecostalism: A Theological Viewpoint*, 183). Yielding, "full docility"—indeed total surrender—is essential for the reception of the fullness of God's Spirit. What Rea and Gelpi speak about is illustrated countless times in the contemporary renewal.

wherein the Spirit of the living God comes to have complete sway.

E. Expectancy

Finally, expectancy is a context for the gift of the Holy Spirit. Although the word is not used in any of the Acts accounts, there is unquestionably an atmosphere of expectancy throughout. People who look for something to happen are particularly candidates for the reception of the Holy Spirit.

This was obviously true of the disciples waiting before Pentecost. I have remarked on their steadfastness in prayer, obedience, and total yielding; now we note the further important matter that they were all expecting something to happen. They had not only received a command to wait; they had also received a promise that the Spirit would be given. Thus their praying was expectant praying, a looking toward the coming of the Holy Spirit.

The atmosphere of expectancy may be sensed in other accounts. Peter and John prayed for the Samaritans to receive the Holy Spirit. Doubtless by praying with them, they built up expectation before the laying on of hands occurred. Ananias, as he was laying hands on Saul, spoke about his being filled with the Holy Spirit and thus created anticipation. Paul's question to the Ephesians "Did you receive the Holy Spirit, believing?" may well have brought about an expectation for what later was to happen.

Surely of significance in creating expectation were the words of Peter to the multitude in Jerusalem: "You shall receive the gift of the Holy Spirit. For the promise is to you. . ." (Acts 2:38–39).

Earlier the crowd had participated in the extraordinary event of everyone's hearing in his own language what the disciples were saying. Then they were told by Peter that this had happened through the outpouring of the Holy Spirit. Now he added that (following repentance and baptism in the name of Christ) they would also receive the same gift. Against the background of their own participation in an amazing event and now Peter's promise of their likewise receiving the gift, their expectation must have been very great.[110] Thus the atmosphere wherein the gift was received was laden with intense expectation.

Now to carry the role of expectancy forward, even to the present day, Peter said the promise of the gift of the Spirit was not only to his immediate audience but, he added, also "to your children and to all that are far off, every one whom the Lord our God calls to him" (Acts 2:39). "Far off"[111] suggests distance in both space and time, thus people of all places and ages, and particularly Gentiles (cf. Acts 22:21), for Peter had already included later Jewish generations in the expression "to your children." Hence the promise of the Spirit continues to our day. For those who truly hear the promise, desire it, and believe it, expectancy is once again the atmosphere for its fulfillment.

So it has been with countless people around the world in our time—people who, upon hearing about the gift of the Holy Spirit, have demonstrated a growing expectancy, even excitement, that the promise may be fulfilled on their behalf. Nor have they found this expec-

---

[110]In the words of Peter: "Repent, and be baptized every one of you in the name of Jesus Christ for the forgiveness of your sins; and you shall receive the gift of the Holy Spirit" (Acts 2:38). The multitude was promised two things: forgiveness of sins and the gift of the Spirit. Thus one could speak of a twofold expectation. It is important to emphasize again, however, that the latter is based on the former, for without the forgiveness of sins expectation of the gift of the Spirit is in vain.

[111]The Greek phrase is *eis makran.*

tation to be a delusion, for God has generously poured out his Spirit.[112] Contrariwise, when people have expected little and expressed satisfaction with their present spiritual situation, they have received little, if anything. But those who wait to receive everything God has to give, those who desire great things from God, those who stand on tiptoes of expectation—it is they whom God delights to bless. Expect a miracle, and miracles begin to happen!

[112]"The presupposition of the charismatic renewal today . . . is an expectant faith, a faith that expects God to do what he said." So writes Stephen B. Clark in an article "Charismatic Renewal in the Church" (*As the Spirit Leads Us,* 22). Jim Cavnar spoke about his own experience thus: "I knew that the baptism in the Spirit was received in faith by asking the Father for the outpouring of the Spirit promised by his Son. I felt that the most important thing was to ask in faith, with confidence in God and full of expectation . . ." (*Catholic Pentecostals,* 63). This note of expectant faith is found throughout the contemporary renewal.

12

The Effects of the Coming of the Spirit

Let us now briefly consider the effects or results of the coming of the Holy Spirit. Our concern is with both the immediate and extended effects of the giving of the Spirit. A number of these effects may be noted.

I. THE REALITY OF GOD'S PRESENCE

The coming of the Holy Spirit is the coming of God Himself. He comes to those whose sins have been forgiven and whose lives have been made new. He comes from the exalted Christ to be dynamically present in and among His people. Those to whom He comes are thereby more deeply aware of the presence and reality of God.

It is apparent that in the Book of Acts a strong sense of God's presence was the paramount fact in everything that occurred. When the Spirit was given at Pentecost, the company immediately began to declare the marvelous works of God. It did not matter that thousands were gathered around them, for so full were they of God's Spirit that they went right on praising Him. The reality of God's presence had gripped them both as a community and as individuals, and

in such fashion that in all that followed they sensed God moving in their midst.

In the case of Peter's ministry the reality of God's presence pervaded everything. In his message to the large Jewish audience in Jerusalem (Acts 2:14–39) he spoke of God with authority, of Jesus Christ with the assurance of personal knowledge, and of the Holy Spirit with the certainty of profound experience. He later pronounced healing in the name of Jesus Christ as one who was powerfully and personally present (3:6–7), and, "filled with the Holy Spirit," he did not hesitate to proclaim salvation even to the rulers, elders, and high priests (4:8–12). So real was the presence of God in the community of believers that Peter declared that to lie about a certain matter was to lie against God: "You have not lied to men but to God" (5:4). Further, the witness of Peter and the other apostles about Jesus was known by them to be a co-witness with the Holy Spirit: "We are witnesses to these things, and so is the Holy Spirit whom God has given . . ." (5:32). Also the Holy Spirit, prior to Peter's trip to Caesarea, spoke directly and personally to him: "The Spirit said to him, 'Behold, three men are looking for you. Rise and go down, and accompany them without hesitation; for I have sent them'" (10:19–20).

Likewise, from the outset of Paul's ministry there was a compelling sense of God's reality. The personal self-disclosure of the risen and exalted Lord to Saul of Tarsus—"I am Jesus . . ." (Acts 9:5)—and the ensuing experience of being "filled with the Holy Spirit" (v. 17) made Saul a man whose life and activity thereafter were dominated by the reality of God's living presence. "Immediately he proclaimed Jesus, saying, 'He is the Son of God'" (v. 20); this proclamation, like all else Paul did after this, stemmed from the certainty of God's pervading presence and action. One telling illustration of the dynamic presence of God in Paul's missionary activity is that in which the apostle, with Timothy, was led by the Holy Spirit to cross over from Asia Minor into Europe. First, Paul was "forbidden by the Holy Spirit to speak the word in Asia," and, second, when he purposed to go in another direction, "the Spirit of Jesus did not allow them" (16:6–7). This is unmistakable testimony to the reality of the divine presence and direction in whatever Paul did. Throughout Paul's ministry there is a continuing sense of the activity of the Holy Spirit.[1]

The Book of Acts is the record of a church intensely aware of the presence of God. When the prophets and teachers of the church at Antioch met together, the Holy Spirit was markedly present: "While they were worshiping the Lord and fasting, the Holy Spirit said, 'Set apart for me Barnabas and Saul for the work to which I have called them'" (Acts 13:2). When the apostles and elders of the church in Jerusalem convened to make a decision about the matter of Gentile circumcision, they sent a letter that included these words: "It has seemed good to the Holy Spirit and to us" (15:28). Whether in Jerusalem, Antioch, or Macedonia, the church was moving and acting in the reality of God's spiritual presence.

The Book of Acts, accordingly, is far more than the acts of men or the "Acts of the Apostles."[2] For though people were everywhere involved, it was basically the acts of God, of Jesus Christ, of the Holy Spirit that stood forth. God was present in a compelling manner and the sense of His presence and action was strikingly known and experienced. All that happened found its source and direction from Him. That God is real was the basic fact in the life of the early Christian community.[3]

---

[1] E.g., Acts 19:21: "Paul resolved in the Spirit to pass through Macedonia and Achaia and go to Jerusalem . . ."; Acts 20:22–23: "I am going to Jerusalem, bound in the Spirit . . . the Holy Spirit testifies to me in every city that imprisonment and afflictions await me."

[2] "Acts of the Apostles" is a title frequently given to the book. The title is doubly misleading. First, the Book of Acts, while mostly narratives about apostolic activity, also relates the acts of "deacons" such as Stephen (Acts 6–7) and Philip (Acts 8); of churches such as Antioch and Jerusalem (see above); of teachers such as Apollos, Priscilla, and Aquila (Acts 18:24–28); and of prophets such as Agabus (Acts 11:28; 21:10–11); second, the focus of the title is off center, for the main feature is not the acts of the apostles or any other believers but the acts of the Holy Spirit, or the acts of the exalted Lord through the Holy Spirit, the continuation of "all that Jesus began to do and teach" (Acts 1:1) in His earthly life.

[3] J. B. Phillips, in the introduction to his translation of Acts, writes, "We cannot help feeling disturbed as well as moved, for this surely is the Church as it was meant to be. . . . They were open on the God-ward side in a way that is almost unknown to us today" (*The*

What has been said about the experienced presence of God in the early church is again being confirmed in the contemporary movement of the Holy Spirit. A spiritual breakthrough is occurring whereby people are being made vividly aware of the divine presence. Through the outpoured gift of the Holy Spirit, God in His divine reality is manifesting Himself. That God is *real* is being affirmed by countless thousands, not as simply an affirmation of distant faith, but of vivid, undeniable experience.

In a day of the "absence" of God, the "eclipse" of God, even the "death" of God,[4] this spiritual breakthrough is a tremendous fact.[5] For the unreality of God has become the actual situation for vast numbers of people. This is the case not only for the secular world but quite often for people inside the church. It is a matter of the Real Absence rather than the Real Presence. Often, even when the gospel is preached, the Bible fully accepted as the Word of God, and the sacraments regularly shared in, there is little spiritual vitality. This may be the case also for churches that lay much stress on evangelistic and missionary activity; there is little excitement about the presence of the living God in the midst of His people. But now through the outpouring of God's Spirit, this is changing for many persons: There is spiritual rejuvenation, renewal, and a profound sense of the divine presence.[6] It is as if, after many years of occasionally sensing His presence (but usually only in a fleeting fashion), the full reality has broken through.

The fellowship of believers, accordingly, becomes the recognized arena of God's living presence. People do not just assemble to hear what God said and did thousands of years ago. They also gather, based on what did occur long ago, to experience His presence, to hear His contemporary word, and to witness His continuing deeds, such as acts of healing and miracles. For in the Spirit the present fellowship is the continuing arena of God's vital presence and activity.

That God is real and present is the primary testimony of the contemporary spiritual renewal.

II. FULLNESS OF JOY

Wherever the Holy Spirit is received, there is a great upsurge of joy. Some-

---

Young Church in Action, vii). "Almost unknown to us today"? *Perhaps*, unless one is aware of what is happening in the contemporary spiritual renewal!

[4]"Death of God" terminology was used by Nietzsche and taken up in the mid-sixties by so-called "death of God" theologians. This says far more about the human than the divine condition. For all practical purposes God is dead when there is no sense of His living presence.

[5]"In an era that cries, 'God is dead,' and questions whether 'Christianity' has a future, the charismatic renewal comes as a vigorous affirmation that God is indeed a living God, and that *Jesus Christ* is active in the world with sovereign power." So begins *Pentecost in the Modern World* by Edward D. O'Connor, C.S.C.

[6]In his autobiography, *Nine O'Clock in the Morning*, Dennis Bennett describes the sense of God's presence that came to him just following his receiving the gift of the Holy Spirit: "The Presence of God that I had so clearly seen in earlier days to be the real reason for living suddenly enveloped me again after the many, many years of dryness. Never had I experienced God's presence in such reality as now. It might have frightened me, except that I recognized that this was the same Presence of the Lord that I had sensed when I first accepted Jesus . . . only the intensity and reality of my present experience was far greater than anything I had believed possible. If those earlier experiences were like flashbulbs, this was as if someone had suddenly turned on the floodlights! The reality of God was something that I felt all the way through . . ." (24). Here, verily, is *the* answer to "the death of God"!

times the joy is so great as to be almost uncontainable. There is a holy exuberance in the Lord.

It is apparent that on the Day of Pentecost there was great rejoicing in the Lord. As we have noted, the Spirit-filled disciples immediately began to speak forth the "wonderful works of God." They did so in such fashion that many mockingly declared them to be "filled with new wine." However, it was not fruit of the vine but fruit of the Spirit, not an artificial joy soon to fade but a genuine joy that was thenceforth to penetrate their whole existence.

Indeed, this deep joy is again demonstrated in entirely different circumstances. The apostles were jailed for their witness, and after being beaten they were charged by the Jewish high council not to speak further in the name of Jesus. "Then they left the presence of the council, rejoicing that they were counted worthy to suffer dishonor for the name" (Acts 5:41). Hence, the joy that they along with many others had experienced on the Day of Pentecost was not only a joy related to favorable circumstances, but also one that continued in the midst of persecution and disrepute. It was the joy that Jesus spoke about when He told His disciples, "Blessed are you when men hate you . . . and revile you . . . on account of the Son of man! Rejoice in that day,

and leap for joy" (Luke 6:22–23). Truly this is fullness of joy!

This fullness of joy, promised to His disciples, was mentioned by Jesus in the Gospel of John several times on the night of His betrayal. The words are found first in 15:11: "These things I have spoken to you, that my joy may be in you, and that your joy may be full."[7] Note that the joy comes from Jesus ("my joy")[8] and that the promise is twofold: the joy is to be "in" His disciples and their joy is to be "full." Hence it is not only a promise of indwelling joy but also a promise of being filled with joy. Looking ahead, we can say that the Resurrection was the coming of joy, even great joy,[9] but only at Pentecost and thereafter did the disciples know the fullness of that joy.[10]

In the Book of Acts, again, there are several other accounts in which joy, or rejoicing, is mentioned. First, after the baptism of the Ethiopian eunuch by Philip, the Scripture declares, "When they came up out of the water, the Spirit of the Lord caught up Philip; and the eunuch saw him no more, and went on his way rejoicing" (8:39). Second, at Iconium "the disciples were filled with joy and with the Holy Spirit" (13:52). Third, the Philippian jailer, who had come to faith in the Lord Jesus and was then baptized, "rejoiced greatly,[11] having believed in God with his whole

---

[7]Cf. also John 16:24: "Ask, and you will receive, that your joy may be full," and John 17:13: "These things I speak . . . that they may have my joy fulfilled in themselves."

[8]The joy of Jesus may be observed, for example, upon the return of seventy disciples from a successful missionary journey: "In that same hour he rejoiced ["rejoiced greatly" or "exulted," Gr. ēgalliasato] in the Holy Spirit" (Luke 10:21). Here is fullness of joy in (or "by") the Holy Spirit that the disciples also were to experience later.

[9]E.g., the women, told that Jesus was risen, "departed quickly from the tomb with fear and great joy [Gr. charas megalēs]" (Matt. 28:8). Later Jesus appeared to the larger group who experienced "joy and . . . marveling [Gr. charas kai thaumazontōn]" (Luke 24:41 NASB). After the ascension of Jesus the disciples "returned to Jerusalem with great joy, and were continually in the temple blessing God" (Luke 24:52–53).

[10]The relationship between Resurrection and Pentecost continues for believers ever since then. Through the experience of the Resurrection there is the joy of entering into a new life or regeneration (see chap. 2. V. C., "A New Life"); with the experience of Pentecost there is fullness of joy.

[11]The Greek word is ēgalliasto, the same as in Luke 10:21 (supra).

household'' (16:34 NASB). In all of these accounts, joy is closely connected with the Holy Spirit, quite possibly as an immediate effect of the gift of the Holy Spirit.[12]

Beyond Acts we may also observe, first, how Paul writes to the Thessalonians that they "received the word in much affliction, with joy inspired by the Holy Spirit" (1 Thess. 1:6). That the Thessalonians had received the gift of the Holy Spirit is apparent from Paul's prior words: "Our gospel came to you not only in word, but also in power and in the Holy Spirit and with full conviction" (v. 5). Hence, the "joy inspired by the Holy Spirit" came out of the fullness of their experience of the Holy Spirit, a joy that broke forth even amid "much affliction." The result, Paul adds, is "that you became an example to all the believers in Macedonia and in Achaia" (v. 7). Second, Paul writes the Romans, praying, "May the God of hope fill you with all joy and peace in believing, so that by the power of the Holy Spirit you may abound in hope" (Rom. 15:13). "All joy" comes out of God's "filling," out of "the power of the Holy Spirit."

The fullness of joy expressed by these various scriptures is being exemplified across the world in the contemporary outpouring of the Holy Spirit. Many who have received the gift of the Spirit attest that one of the immediate effects is an intensity of joy. Often the experience is that of an inner movement of the Holy Spirit wherein the whole being is flooded with joy.[13] Something about this joy is quite different from ordinary joy or happiness; it is the joy of the Lord. In one popular chorus, based on 1 Peter 1:8, the wording goes: "It is joy unspeakable and full of glory, and the half has never yet been told!"

This joy, regardless of the ups and downs in the life of faith, continues as a wellspring ever bubbling up and overflowing. Jesus said about this joy that He promised His disciples: "No one will take your joy from you" (John 16:22). Since this joy is fulfilled through the gift of the Holy Spirit and this joy is the Lord's own joy, nothing can take it away. It is joy everlasting. Surely the words of Isaiah are appropriate: "And the ransomed of the LORD shall return, and come to Zion with singing; everlasting joy shall be upon their heads" (Isa. 51:11).

III. BOLDNESS IN SPEECH AND ACTION

We have earlier noted that the central purpose of the giving of the Spirit is for

---

[12]We may recall (see chap. 11, n. 31) that the Acts 8:39 passage in a number of early manuscripts reads: "And when they came up out of the water, the Holy Spirit fell upon the eunuch and an angel of the Lord caught up Philip." The point of this reading, as we before observed, is to emphasize that the eunuch's believing and baptism were followed by the gift of the Spirit. Accordingly, the rejoicing of the eunuch springs out of his experience of the Holy Spirit. In regard to Acts 16:34, nothing is directly said about the Holy Spirit. However, since once again the rejoicing (or great rejoicing) is closely connected with faith and baptism, the implication of the text is quite likely that the jailer had received the gift of the Holy Spirit.

[13]Earlier I quoted the words of Larry Tomczak about his baptism in the Holy Spirit: "I felt the rapturous and exultant joy of the Lord surging through me. . . . Then, just at the right moment, new words began to flow from my heart" (chap. 9, n. 81). Then Tomczak adds, "At the same time, like a mountain stream—pure, sparkling, cool, crystal clear—living joy began to flow upward and outward through my entire being." His concluding words are "Jesus Christ touched me that night, and, oh, the joy that filled my soul. . . . I opened the door and seemed to float through it. Looking up at the cool, crisp, early morning sky, I grinned foolishly, drunk for joy" (*Clap Your Hands!* 112–13). Also see the moving life story by Sister Mary Bernard, *I Leap for Joy.*

that enabling power by which the witness to Jesus can be carried forward in both word and deed. The gift of this power brings about extraordinary boldness and courage.

It is apparent in the Book of Acts that an immediate effect of the coming of the Holy Spirit was decisiveness and confidence of speech, courage in the face of all opposition, and readiness to lay down one's life for the sake of Christ. We may start with Peter's sermon at Pentecost, shortly after the disciples had been "filled with the Holy Spirit," and observe the confidence and directness of his words: "Men of Judea and all who dwell in Jerusalem, let this be known to you, and give ear to my words" (2:14). Thus Peter began, and the note of confidence[14] is apparent throughout. Nor in the climax did he mince words, proclaiming, "God has made him both Lord and Christ, this Jesus *whom you crucified*" (v. 36). A like confidence and boldness was demonstrated even more on a later day when Peter and John, after the healing of a cripple, were brought before the Jewish council (the same one that had called for Jesus' death) and were asked, " 'By what power or by what name did you do this?' Then Peter, filled with the Holy Spirit, said to them . . . 'Be it known to you all, and to all the people of Israel, that by the name of Jesus Christ of Nazareth, whom you crucified . . . this man is standing before you well' " (Acts 4:7–8, 10). Then Peter added that "there is no other name under heaven given among men by which we must be saved" (v. 12). The next verse begins: "Now when they saw the boldness of Peter and John. . . ." Here were boldness and courage indeed!

On another occasion, despite threats against them, the company of disciples prayed, "And now, Lord, look upon their threats, and grant to thy servants to speak thy word with all boldness" (Acts 4:29). The result was that "when they had prayed, the place in which they were gathered together was shaken; and they were all filled with the Holy Spirit and spoke the word of God with boldness" (v. 31).

The close connection between being "filled with the Holy Spirit" and boldness is evident in each of three preceding accounts. The immediate effect was a boldness, a confidence, and a courage of extraordinary character.

We note next the example of Stephen. Stephen, like the other men chosen to serve tables, was "full of the Spirit" (Acts 6:3).[15] After Stephen had performed signs among the people, a number of Jews began to oppose him, but they "could not withstand the wisdom and the Spirit with which he spoke" (6:10). However, through secret instigation and false witnesses, Stephen was brought before the Jewish council. When asked by the high priest to answer the charges, Stephen proceeded with total courage and boldness, not hesitating at the climax of his testimony to say to the council: "You stiff-necked people, uncircumcised in heart and ears, you always resist the Holy Spirit," and "the Righteous One . . . you have now betrayed and murdered" (7:51–52). The result was that members of the council were enraged and gnashed their teeth against him; but he did not stop. Rather, Stephen "full of the Holy Spirit, gazed into heaven and . . . said, 'Behold, I see the heavens opened, and the Son of man standing at the right hand of God" (vv. 55–56).

---

[14]E.g., "Brethren, I may say to you confidently . . ." (Acts 2:29). The Greek word translated "confidently" is *parrēsia* (*meta parrēsias*, "with confidence"), the same word that is often translated "boldly" (see below).

[15]Specifically, Stephen is called "a man full of faith and of the Holy Spirit" (Acts 6:5).

Such was the boldness of Stephen to speak against the evil of his audience and to proclaim to them the glorified Lord. He had a boldness and courage that withheld nothing. Thereupon they stoned him to death, but he never flinched to the very end.

This account of the extraordinary and indomitable courage of Stephen's witness is set in the context of the fullness of the Spirit. Laden with the presence and power of God, Stephen spoke with total fearlessness, even to his martyrdom.

In the narrative about Saul of Tarsus we observe once more the connection between the gift of the Spirit and boldness of witness. Saul was "filled with the Holy Spirit" (Acts 9:17) and immediately was boldly proclaiming in the synagogues that Jesus was the Son of God. When the Jews tried to kill him, Saul managed to escape their plots and went to Jerusalem. There Barnabas, bringing him to the apostles, spoke of Saul's conversion and how at Damascus he (Saul) had "preached boldly in the name of Jesus" (v. 27). Soon Saul "went in and out among them at Jerusalem, preaching boldly in the name of the Lord" (vv. 28–29). Because of Saul's zeal, his life was soon again at stake. To save him the brethren in Jerusalem took him down to Caesarea and sent him off to his home city of Tarsus.

From then on in all of Paul's missionary travels the same boldness marked everything he did. Journeying with Barnabas, Paul encountered a magician at Cyprus who tried to block the Roman proconsul from hearing the gospel message. Then "Paul, filled with the Holy Spirit, looked intently at him [the magician] and said, 'You son of the devil, you enemy of all righteousness, full of all deceit and villainy, will you not stop making crooked the straight paths of the Lord?'" (Acts 13:9–10). Then Paul boldly pronounced that the magician would become temporarily blind, and it happened. The result of Paul's bold word and action was that "the proconsul believed" (13:12). Other examples of such boldness are shown upon his visit to Antioch of Pisidia where, despite much Jewish reviling and opposition, "Paul and Barnabas[16] spoke out boldly, saying, 'Since you . . . judge yourselves unworthy of eternal life, behold, we turn to the Gentiles'" (13:46). And immediately thereafter, despite persecution and expulsion, Paul and Barnabas went on to Iconium, where "they remained for a long time, speaking boldly for the Lord" (14:3). Other examples could be added, but these should suffice to demonstrate again the marked connection between being filled with the Holy Spirit and being bold of speech and action.

Once again, to leave the scriptural record and to turn to the contemporary scene, we find much the same thing being exemplified. People who have received the gift of the Holy Spirit often demonstrate extraordinary boldness in the Lord. Particularly is this true immediately after the experience of being filled with the Spirit, when little hesitation is shown in proclaiming the word about Jesus anywhere and everywhere, and despite all opposition.[17] Sometimes

---

[16] Barnabas, like Paul, was a man filled with the Holy Spirit. Recall the earlier description in Acts 11:24: "He was a good man, full of the Holy Spirit and of faith." Hence, Barnabas' boldness came out of the same fullness of God's presence and power.

[17] One instance I recall among many involved a professor at a secular university who was newly filled with the Holy Spirit. Shortly afterward he witnessed boldly about Jesus on his own campus to students and faculty alike, indeed to all who would hear. Ridicule, opposition, and finally expulsion from his professorship resulted. But like Paul, he continued to carry on. Another example: Spirit-filled students at the university where I teach are often

this bold witness fades, but wherever there is earnest prayer for its renewal at whatever cost, there is a fresh filling with the Spirit and a new boldness in speaking the word.[18] This contemporary boldness is often not only of word but also of deed, as people do not hesitate to minister healing, deliverance, and other blessings in the name of the Lord.

We might do well also to mention the words of Paul to young Timothy, his son in the faith: "Hence I remind you to rekindle the gift of God[19] that is within you through the laying on of my hands, for God did not give us a spirit of timidity but a spirit of power and love and self-control" (2 Tim. 1:6–7). Boldness is the opposite of timidity, and boldness—along with power, love, and self-control—is given by God for witness to the gospel.

The boldness brought about by the Holy Spirit is a boldness unto death. It is a boldness and a courage that, removing all shame and hesitation, can cause a person to say with the apostle Paul: "It is my eager expectation and hope that I shall not be at all ashamed, but that with full courage[20] now as always Christ will be honored in my body, whether by life or by death" (Phil. 1:20). It is a boldness that does not exclude martyrdom as a very real possibility.

IV. DEEPENING OF FELLOWSHIP

When the Spirit is given, the individual is so filled and the group is so profoundly united as to create a fellowship of great love, sharing, and community. There is a remarkable deepening of fellowship.

In reviewing the account of the events in the early church, there is an unmistakable stress on community. Before the Day of Pentecost, as we have noted, the disciples were "with one accord" (Acts 1:14) in prayer, and when the day arrived, they were "all together in one place" (2:1). The sense of unity was obviously intensified with the coming of the Holy Spirit, as "they were all filled with the Holy Spirit" (v. 4). Later when Peter delivered his sermon, it was not simply as an individual spokesman, but "standing with the eleven" (v. 14), he addressed the crowd. A new and transcending unity had been brought about by the Holy Spirit.

Next, after some three thousand persons received Peter's word and were baptized, the text immediately reads: "And they were continually devoting themselves to the apostles' teaching and to fellowship [koinonia],[21] to the breaking of bread and to prayer" (Acts 2:42 NASB). Here was a tremendous sense of togetherness—in study, breaking bread, prayer—which the Holy

---

on the streets, in the parks, and on the beaches boldly and publicly testifying of the Lord. Opposition, when it occurs, only seems to make them all the more eager to witness!

[18]This parallels the case of the disciples in Acts 4:29–31 who prayed for boldness and again (as at Pentecost) were "filled with the Holy Spirit." Immediately they "spoke the word of God with boldness."

[19]The Greek phrase is *to charisma tou theou*. *Charisma* ordinarily refers to a *particular* gift (cf. Rom. 12:6; 1 Cor. 12:4, and elsewhere), not *the* gift of the Spirit Himself. "Gift" in that case, as in Acts 2:38, is *dorea*. (For further discussion of gift as *charisma* see chap. 13, "The Gifts of the Holy Spirit.")

[20]The Greek for "full courage" is *pasē parrēsia*, literally, "all boldness" (as in KJV and NASB).

[21]The Greek word *koinōnia* denotes "fellowship," "participation," and "sharing." Because of the richness of meaning in the Greek word, a single translation often seems inadequate. Thus many today simply use the Greek term.

Spirit had brought about.[22] One of the key terms is "fellowship" or "koinonia"; and the fact that they devoted themselves to koinonia signifies their profound new commitment to one another.

This commitment to one another is shown concretely in what follows: "And all those who had believed were together, and had all things in common; and they began selling their property and possessions, and were sharing them with all, as anyone might have[23] need" (2:44–45 NASB). This extraordinary spirit of sharing and fellowship is shown also in the next statement: "And day by day continuing with one mind in the temple, and breaking bread from house to house, they were taking their meals together" (v. 46 NASB). They sold property and possessions wherever there was need; they also opened their homes to one another; thus they held all things in common.[24]

While the number of disciples increased to about five thousand (Acts 4:4), the spirit of unity only deepened. Two examples follow: First, after Peter and John reported to the company the threats of the Jewish council, the disciples "lifted up their voice to God with one accord" (v. 24 KJV). With one voice[25] and with complete unanimity— one accord[26]—they prayed to God for boldness to continue to witness while the Lord healed and performed signs and wonders. Second, following this prayer in which they were "filled with the Holy Spirit" (v. 31), their unity is powerfully described in this way: "Now the company of those who believed were of one heart and soul, and no one said that any of the things which he possessed was his own, but they had everything in common" (v. 32). Again the commonality of possessions is expressed, but this time against the background of an intense unity of spirit: one heart and soul. It would be hard to imagine a more graphic or amazing statement of unity, because many thousands of people were involved.

A beautiful expression follows: "Great grace was upon them all" (Acts 4:33). And this great grace was further demonstrated: "There was not a needy person among them, for all who were owners of lands or houses would sell them and bring the proceeds of the sales, and lay them at the apostles' feet; and they would be distributed to each, as any had need" (vv. 34–35 NASB). While the language here does not state that people sold everything they had (only lands and houses are mentioned), it does suggest a readiness to commit their most valuable possessions.[27] Nor was there a profligate selling of proper-

---

[22] For reference to their receiving the Spirit, see chapter 11, n. 28.

[23] The imperfect tense is used for all three verbs (selling, sharing, having); thus they "were selling" and "were sharing" as anyone "was having" need. According to EGT, "this tense may express an action which is done often and continuously without being done universally or extending to a complete accomplishment" (in loco). Thus it would be a mistake to assume that all sold their property and shared. Rather, the point is that selling and sharing were constant, in relation to any who had need.

[24] It would be a mistake to view this as "Christian" communism. No one was forced to give up anything; indeed, there was voluntary sharing as the Spirit led and as there was need. There was no collective ownership of goods but a recognition through the Spirit that what each had was for the good of all.

[25] The Greek word is the singular *phōnēn* (hence, not "voices" as in RSV, NASB, and NIV).

[26] The Greek word is *homothumadon.* "With one accord" is a better translation than "together" (as in RSV and NIV).

[27] Barnabas is also mentioned as one who sold a field and brought the money to the apostles (Acts 4:36–37).

ties, as if there were some special virtue in getting rid of earthly things.[28] Rather, the selling was for the purpose of bringing the proceeds to the apostles,[29] that every need might be met.

It is evident, then, that the community of over five thousand was truly a koinonia of the Holy Spirit. It was a community united in prayer, in witness, and in fellowship. When any potential source of disruption entered, such as the dishonesty of Ananias and Sapphira (Acts 5:1–10) and the complaints of certain Hellenists (6:1–6),[30] the matter was promptly dealt with, and the koinonia maintained. The result was that "the word of God increased; and the number of the disciples multiplied greatly in Jerusalem, and a great many of the priests were obedient to the faith" (v. 7).

Now let me try to summarize a few things. Although the disciples were all Jews or converts to Judaism[31] at this stage, they represented the Mediterranean and Middle Eastern world,[32] they were Greek-speaking and Aramaic-speaking, they were men and women, they were laity and priests, and they were apostles and brethren in general from an immense variety of backgrounds and former loyalties, *but* now all were in one accord. They studied together, prayed together, broke bread together. They went to the temple unitedly, and also from house to house. Their commitment to one another was so intense that they no longer claimed any possessions as their own, but sold them, sharing wherever there was need. They were of one heart and one soul, and great grace was manifest in all they did. In every way it was the koinonia of the Holy Spirit.

But along with this came the growth of opposition from the religious leaders and ever-increasing threats and persecution. Finally, with the killing of Stephen a "great persecution" (Acts 8:1) began, and all the disciples, except the apostles, were scattered throughout Judea and Samaria. No longer could they

---

[28] There is no suggestion that ownership of goods is wrong and thus does not belong in the Spirit-filled community. No particular virtue is ascribed here to selling what one has and perhaps entering upon a life of poverty (as is frequently the case in monastic communities). The point rather is that under the impact of the fullness of the Spirit (4:31) there was such "great grace" upon them that they gladly shared everything, giving anything that might help those in need.

[29] Another evidence that the believers were not required to sell their property and bring the money to the apostles is found in the account of Ananias and his wife Sapphira that follows. They sold a piece of property and kept back some of the proceeds but pretended to give the whole amount (Acts 5:1–10). Peter spoke sternly to Ananias, "Ananias, why has Satan filled your heart to lie to the Holy Spirit?" (v. 3). Then Peter made clear that the sin was neither in owning the property nor in selling it as Ananias might choose: "While it remained unsold, did it not remain your own?" (v. 4). The sin—a great one directed against the Holy Spirit who pervaded the community—was the pretense of giving all. (Incidentally, this first recorded sin in the koinonia of the Holy Spirit brought sudden physical death to both Ananias and Sapphira [Acts 5:5, 10] even as the first sin in Eden brought spiritual death to Adam and Eve.)

[30] On the matter of Ananias and Sapphira, see the preceding footnote. The Hellenists were Greek-speaking Jews who had become Christians. They complained because their widows were neglected in the daily serving of food. The problem was rectified by the appointment of seven men (including Stephen and Philip) to have charge of this duty.

[31] One of the deacons appointed with Philip and Stephen was Nicolaus, "a proselyte of Antioch" (Acts 6:5).

[32] Recall that the thousands to whom Peter preached on the Day of Pentecost were "from every nation under heaven" (Acts 2:5). Later many nations and languages are mentioned, from Mesopotamia to Libya, from Asia (Minor) to Rome (vv. 9–11).

attend the temple together and participate in corporate worship. Still, wherever they went and whatever the opposition, they continued to be one in Christ, the koinonia of the Holy Spirit.

It would be an overstatement to say that there was invariable harmony or unity after that. For with the distance from Jerusalem, the absence of the apostles, and perhaps the dimming of intensity of the Spirit's presence, some disharmony and disunity were sure to appear. Factions and party spirit appeared in churches here and there. However, insofar as this happened, they were no longer really "spiritual people,"[33] no longer flowing in the Spirit of Christ, no longer what the Lord intended. Still, if they could remember who they were and be renewed in Spirit, once more they would be truly the koinonia of the Holy Spirit.

Along this line Paul wrote to the Ephesians that they should be "eager to maintain the unity of the Spirit in the bond of peace" (4:3). He concluded his second letter to the Corinthians with this prayer: "The grace of the Lord Jesus Christ and the love of God and the fellowship [koinonia] of the Holy Spirit be with you all" (13:14). This unity that comes from the Spirit, this koinonia, is to be zealously maintained and earnestly prayed for. These words of Paul agree with the great concern of Jesus expressed in His prayer for believers "that they may all be one . . . I in them and thou in me, that they may become perfectly one" (John 17:21, 23). It is in the unity of the Spirit that such oneness is a reality.

It is now time to return to the contemporary situation. What we have seen in our own day in the movement of the Holy Spirit is the renewal of deep Christian fellowship. People have found themselves drawn together in a profound unity of worship, community, study, and witness: the koinonia of the Holy Spirit. Such fellowship goes so much deeper than anything they had known before that they marvel at what God has done.

Through the gift of the Holy Spirit there has been a personal renewal of unmistakable quality, but at the same time it has been a community renewal of extraordinary character. People have been brought by the Spirit into such a mutual relationship that they know they belong to one another. It is not as if there was no sense of community before, but this has a richer quality. Now with a fresh enthusiasm and joy in the Lord they have an intense desire to be together, to enjoy one another's company, to hear what God has to say through a brother or a sister, to minister to one another, or to share whenever there is need. So full of the Lord's presence is the gathering of the community that nothing else is comparable to it, and the time spent with one another seems as no time at all. Frequency of gathering together, often extended hours of meeting, going from house to house for prayer and fellowship: all are a part of the present renewal.

Further, people caught up in the renewal of the Spirit come from a multiplicity of backgrounds. Nations around the world, denominations from across Christendom, people of many races, ages, and cultures—all are represented in the present renewal. While some fellowships are more limited culturally, denominationally, racially, etc.,

---

[33] For example, Paul later wrote to the Christian disciples in Corinth that he was not really able to speak to them as "spiritual men" (*pneumatikois*), but as "men of the flesh" (*sarkinois*), because there was "jealousy and strife" among them (1 Cor. 3:1, 3). Party spirit—"I belong to Paul," or "Peter," or "Apollos"—was replacing the unity of the Spirit with which they had first begun (1 Cor. 1:10–13).

the genius of the movement is clearly the way it essentially transcends all ordinary groupings. It is not unusual to find Protestants of many kinds, Roman Catholics,[34] possibly Eastern Orthodox, and people of no church background all together in the same koinonia of the Holy Spirit. This, however, is not a unity based on the lowest common denominator of religious belief, but on the fact that all have been brought by the Spirit into a profound and transforming relationship with one another.

As a result of this, prayer and praise fellowships, renewal communities, and transdenominational Christian centers have developed in many parts of the world. Some are communities of shared goods and properties, of a daily common life together. Some fellowships exist within more traditional church structures and seek to exercise renewing influence; others exist alongside these structures (para-congregational) or function totally separate from them. But wherever such communities are found, it is essentially in the same spirit of praise, fellowship, witness, and concern.[35]

The reaction from outside observers is often either one of attraction or opposition. Some find themselves strongly moved by the sight of people praising the Lord, meeting together in lively prayer and expectation, and showing great concern for one another. They have yearned for such a deeper fellowship and want to become a part. Many have grown weary with tradi-

tional forms and seemingly lifeless patterns of religious activity, and here they sense life, power, vitality. Thus persons in the renewal often find favor (cf. Acts 2:47) with people around, and many are added to their number. But others manifest opposition to the movement. Sometimes this comes from the secular world, which has little use for anything deeply religious and spiritual; but more often it comes from within the established church order. The renewal, in this case, is viewed with suspicion, even as a threat to some, and attitudes vary from cautious tolerance to strong opposition. These differing reactions, from attraction to repulsion, suggest that something is occurring in the fellowship of the Spirit of unusual significance for the whole church.

It seems quite possible that this renewal in the Spirit is the most profound ecumenical development of the twentieth century. This century, now moving to a climax, has witnessed many attempts to bring churches together, to get beyond the scandal of division, and to recover the oneness that the church at least verbally affirms. And there have been varying degrees of success: formations of councils, mergers of denominations, and surely many prayers for unity. Indeed, there is a growing sense that division is intolerable, that it is a huge obstacle to faith, and that Jesus' prayer that "they may all be one . . . so that the world may believe" (John 17:21) must somehow find an answer. Such is the growing ecumenical con-

---

[34] "The oneness in the Spirit which the Lord has created among Catholics and Protestants through the baptism in the Spirit is a precious miracle of grace in our day. I do not believe we have begun to grasp the significance of this breakthrough in the unfolding of God's plan for his people. The sharing of a faith common to us all, the growth in mutual trust and understanding in areas of cultural and doctrinal differences, the growing ability to pray and worship together genuinely while maintaining our integrity—all this is creating a new, strong, bold, witness to the reality and saving power of the Gospel of Jesus Christ." So writes Kevin Ranaghan in *As the Spirit Leads Us,* "Catholics and Pentecostals Meet in the Spirit," 144.

[35] For a good study of Christian community, see Stephen B. Clark, *Building Christian Communities: Strategy for Renewing the Church.*

cern, and its solution is to be found only in and through the renewal of the Holy Spirit.[36] As people, as churches, and as individuals are profoundly renewed by the Holy Spirit, the whole situation is transformed from a search after unity to its realization.

Surely hazards mark the way. For example, people renewed in the Spirit may allow a party spirit to set in and thus draw back into denominational enclaves or groups that no longer fellowship with others. They may begin to emphasize minor doctrinal points to such a degree that the unity of the Spirit is increasingly broken. Sometimes spiritually renewed groups set themselves apart from other groups and follow a particular leader or teaching, no longer recognizing the unity the Spirit has brought about. Indeed, there are hazards and situations that need repentance and correction. However, the overarching fact is that through the renewal of the Spirit there is a new and profound gift of unity that alone can bring into fulfillment the genuine oneness of the body of Christ. When this is realized afresh and is acted on accordingly, the prayer of the Lord will find its ultimate fulfillment.

It is appropriate to conclude this section with the words of Paul: "The love of God has been poured out within our hearts through the Holy Spirit who was given to us" (Rom. 5:5 NASB).

When through the gift of the Holy Spirit the love of God is truly shed abroad in the hearts of all, there is then a deep creation of fellowship, sharing, and unity with one another. Through such God-given love we become the koinonia of the Holy Spirit.

V. THE CONTINUING PRAISE OF GOD

Finally, the coming of the Holy Spirit results in the continuing praise of God. Those who are filled with God's Spirit are people of praise.

We have earlier observed that on the Day of Pentecost the immediate effect of the outpouring of the Spirit was the magnifying of God. This they did in tongues, but in this very speech they were declaring "the wonderful works of God" (Acts 2:11). Years later in Caesarea, as we have noted, a similar thing occurred among the Gentiles. The Spirit came on the centurion and his household, resulting in their "speaking in tongues and extolling God" (10:46). Hence from the beginning, the coming of the Spirit has been accompanied by the praise[37] of God.

This follows from the fact that when the reality of God breaks in on people, the only appropriate response is the offering of praise. In the Old Testament precursor of Pentecost the glory of God filled the temple: "When all the children of Israel saw the fire come down and

---

[36]John A. Mackay, former president of Princeton Theological Seminary, put it forcefully: "What is known as the charismatic movement—a movement marked by spiritual enthusiasm and special gifts and which crosses all boundaries of culture, race, age, and church tradition—is profoundly significant. . . . Because 'no heart is pure that is not passionate and no virtue is safe that is not enthusiastic,' the charismatic movement of today is the chief hope of the ecumenical tomorrow" ("Oneness in the Body—Focus for the Future," *World Vision Magazine* [April 1970]). James W. Jones, an Episcopal clergyman, analyzes it thus: "Structural ecumenism which does not grow out of a genuine ecumenical life will produce only empty wineskins, just as patterns of renewal that do not grow out of a renewed life will themselves have no vitality. The charismatic movement is *the* ecumenical movement, not because it is creating structural alignment (it isn't), but because it is bringing into being a new sense of the common life of the people of God" (*Filled With New Wine: The Charismatic Renewal of the Church*, 135).

[37]I am not now referring only to the praise of God in tongues (which I earlier called "transcendent praise" in chap. 9, IV.) but to the praise of God however offered.

the glory of the LORD upon the temple, they bowed down with their faces to the earth on the pavement, and worshiped and gave thanks to God" (2 Chron. 7:3).[38] Worship and praise were the immediate response. When the Pentecostal event occurs, the glory, the reality, the presence of God is far more intense—not just a temple but people filled with God's glory. Praise and worship of God is far richer and fuller and, indeed, far more enduring.

In the Book of Acts on the Day of Pentecost it was first the 120 who praised God, but later in the day it was the whole community of more than 3000 people. We have earlier observed how the newly formed fellowship of believers shared with one another. Now we note that their community life was one of constant praise to God; they were "praising God and having favor with all the people" (Acts 2:47). This was being done "in the temple" and "from house to house" (v. 46 KJV). Everywhere the believers went, praise continually erupted from their lips and hearts.

Here I turn to the present spiritual renewal because it is essentially a renewal of praise. There is, to be sure, an extraordinary unity of love of believers for one another, but overarching all else is the constant praise and glorification of God. This overflowing praise happens whether at church (the "temple") or in people's various homes ("from house to house"). "Praise the Lord," uttered through many a song and prayer and testimony, is the hallmark of the contemporary renewal.

The continuing praise of God is marked by the *adoration* of God. The adoration of God has always been a part of the church's worship, so in a sense there is nothing new or different in the renewal. However, there is both an intensity and an intimacy in this adoration that goes beyond usual worship. When people sing such a chorus as "We exalt thee, O God," it is with mounting zeal and fervor. Hands are often upraised. Frequently after the chorus is finished, there is the further movement of praise into "singing in the Spirit." The intensity of worship at such a point almost defies description. To illustrate the matter of intimacy, there is a chorus whose stanzas begin, "Father, I adore you," "Jesus, I adore you," and "Spirit, I adore you." This suggests a deeply personal sense of the presence of the Father who has created and provides, of the Son who has redeemed and is alive, and of the Holy Spirit who has sanctified and is dynamically present. Such a personal, intimate, and thankful adoration of God lies at the heart of the contemporary spiritual renewal.

There is also the distinguishing mark of *spontaneity*. We may recall Paul's words "Be filled with the Spirit, addressing one another in psalms and hymns and spiritual songs, singing and making melody to the Lord with all your heart" (Eph. 5:18–19). Such praise of God finds a rich fulfillment in spiritual fellowship as people freely move back and forth between singing "psalms and hymns" in their own language as well as "spiritual songs" inspired by the Holy Spirit. Through it all there is spontaneity: no set order, no set liturgy. Frequently under the impact of the Spirit, new songs and new choruses are given.

A final mark of this continuing praise is *anticipation*. There is the sense that the more truly and fully praise to God is offered, the more closely one approaches the glories of the world beyond. According to the Book of Revelation, John was "in the Spirit" (4:2) and beheld the throne of God (4:2 ff.) and

---

[38]Recall my previous mention of this in chapter 8, "Concluding Remarks," no. 3.

the Lamb near the throne (5:1 ff.). The scene depicts total praise, climaxing with the words "And I heard every creature in heaven and on earth and under the earth and in the sea, and all therein, saying, 'To him who sits upon the throne and to the Lamb be blessing and honor and glory and might for ever and ever!' And the four living creatures said, 'Amen!' and the elders fell down and worshiped" (5:13–14). When the people of God are moving "in the Spirit," they sense that their praise is the earthly counterpart to the worship that never ceases in heaven and is a glorious anticipation of the perfect worship that is to be known in the age to come. Truly life can have no higher fulfillment than the continuing praise of God.

13

The Gifts of the Holy Spirit

Now we arrive at the important consideration of the gifts of the Holy Spirit. For the Holy Spirit who is given bestows gifts in turn. It is these gifts of the Spirit that here become the focus of our attention.

I. INTRODUCTION

The primary New Testament delineation of the gifts of the Holy Spirit is in 1 Corinthians 12:8–10:

For to one is given the word of wisdom through the Spirit, and to another the word of knowledge according to the same Spirit; to another faith by the same Spirit, and to another gifts of healing by the one Spirit, and to another the effecting of miracles, and to another prophecy, and to another the distinguishing of spirits, to another various kinds of tongues, and to another the interpretation of tongues" (NASB).

A few verses earlier Paul declared, "Now there are varieties of gifts, but the same Spirit" (v. 4). The word for "gifts" in this text is *charismata*;[1] hence, we may speak of the *charismata*[2] of the Spirit. Thus we are dealing with Spiritual[3] gifts, spiritual *charismata*. After listing these nine gifts Paul adds, "But one and the same Spirit works all these things, distributing[4] to each one individually just as He wills" (v. 11 NASB). The spiritual gifts, accordingly, are distributions[5] of the Holy Spirit.

---

[1] The Greek word *charismata* (*charisma*—sing.) means "gifts of grace." Thayer states that "in the technical Pauline sense *charismata* . . . denote extraordinary powers, distinguishing certain Christians and enabling them to serve the church of Christ, the reception of which is due to the power of divine grace operating in their souls by the Holy Spirit." (See excursus, pp. 345–46, for a more detailed study of the word *charisma*.)

[2] Some prefer to speak of "charisms," hence the "charisms" of the Spirit.

[3] If the capital "S" is reduced to a lowercase "s" as is usually done, it is to be borne in mind that the Holy Spirit is being referred to, not the human (or some other kind of) spirit.

[4] The Greek word is *diairoun* and is translated "dividing" (KJV), "apportions" (RSV), and "gives" (NIV). The NEB, like NASB, has "distributing."

[5] In Hebrews there is also reference to "distributions" of the Holy Spirit (2:4). The word there, however, is from *merismos*. The passage is concerned with the message of salvation:

Before proceeding further, we should observe that although gifts are referred to elsewhere, they are not described as gifts of the Holy Spirit. In Romans 12:6 Paul wrote about our having "gifts [*charismata*] that differ according to the grace given to us," and then he briefly described seven of these (vv. 6–9). Here the source of the gifts is not directly specified, though God seems to be implied (see v. 3). Further, this list overlaps with 1 Corinthians 12:8–10 at only one point: prophecy. "Gifts" are also described in Ephesians 4; however, there they are not called *charismata* but *domata*. Shortly after quoting Psalm 68:18 "he gave gifts [*domata*] to men" (v. 8), Paul listed five such gifts (v. 11). Here it is clearly stated that the source of the gifts is Christ (see v. 7). Again the only overlap with 1 Corinthians 12:8–10 is in the area of prophecy.[6] In sum, the gifts of the Spirit are specifically dealt with in 1 Corinthians 12 alone.[7] We will now turn our attention to these.[8]

In considering these gifts, we are moving into a critically important area of the contemporary spiritual renewal that is often termed "charismatic." For it is true that these nine gifts, or *charismata*, particularly occupy the attention of "charismatics."[9] However, since the *charismata* represent a wider range than 1 Corinthians 12:8–10 (Romans 12 also, as we have observed),[10] properly speaking the charismatic renewal signifies an embracing of all these gifts. The focal point, nonetheless, is the *charismata* of the Holy Spirit. Since these are spiritual, or pneumatic, gifts, it is peculiarly a "pneumatic renewal."[11]

"It was declared at first by the Lord, and it was attested to us by those who heard him, while God also bore witness by signs and wonders and various miracles and by gifts of the Holy Spirit distributed according to his own will" (vv. 3–4). The latter portion literally reads, "by distributions [*merismois*] of the Holy Spirit." Thus there is no direct mention of gifts or *charismata*, though obviously it is the same Holy Spirit who "distributes." The word "gifts" is supplied in RSV (also KJV, NIV, NASB, and NEB), for it is clearly implied.

6However, in Ephesians 4 the gift of Christ is specified as "prophets." We will later discuss the distinction between the *charisma* of prophecy and the *doma* of prophet (see chap. 14, "The Ninefold Manifestation," VI).

7It is quite common to list all the gifts in Romans 12, Ephesians 4, and 1 Corinthians 12 as "gifts of the Spirit." To be sure, the Holy Spirit is involved in the gifts of God (Rom. 12) and the gifts of Christ (Eph. 4), even as God the Father and Christ are involved in the gifts of the Spirit, for God is one. However, He is also three persons, each operating particular spheres. And as the Holy Spirit He operates the spiritual gifts: "*One and the same Spirit* works all these things," namely, the *charismata* recorded in 1 Corinthians 12:8–10.

8The gifts in Romans 12 and Ephesians 4 (also in 1 Peter—mentioned hereafter) are omitted from consideration, not because of any idea of their lesser importance. Far from that! All these gifts are essential to a total picture of the life of the church and call for a study that goes beyond the confines of *Renewal Theology*, volume 2. Since our focus at this place is on the Holy Spirit and His gifts, I will not go into a broader study of the other gifts.

9In a certain sense all Christians are "charismatic," because all have received the gift or *charisma* of eternal life. Paul writes in Romans 6:23: "The wages of sin is death, but the gift [*charisma*] of God is eternal life in Christ Jesus our Lord" (NIV). (Also compare Paul's words in Romans 5:15–16, where *charisma* twice occurs in regard to justification.) However, the term has come to be used today for those who participate in the "charismatic renewal" of our time.

10See also 1 Peter 4:10, where the singular, *charisma*, is used: "As each has received a gift [*charisma*], employ it for one another . . . ." Peter goes on to describe two expressions of this *charisma* (v. 11).

11"Charismatic renewal" is nonetheless a proper designation, as participants do not

Looking at 1 Corinthians 12, we note from the outset that Paul is writing about *pneumatika*. The opening verse begins, "Now concerning spiritual gifts . . . ."[12] Thereafter Paul uses the terminology of *charismata*; hence he will deal peculiarly with those charismatic expressions that are pneumatic, thus of the Spirit. In regard to these *pneumatika* Paul did not want the Corinthians to be "uninformed" (v. 1).[13] If this were the need for those to whom Paul wrote, it is hardly less so in our time. But first let us note the context within which the presentation of the gifts is elaborated.

II. CONTEXT

It is significant that Paul was not writing to the Corinthians about what they had *not* experienced but what they *had* experienced. This is the context of 1 Corinthians 12:8–10. Their being "uninformed" had nothing to do with their being inexperienced. Rather, it was to give instruction in the proper exercise of what they had experienced in abundance. For this we turn back to the opening of Paul's letter where he wrote, "In every way[14] you were enriched in him [Christ] with all speech and all knowledge—even as the testimony to Christ was confirmed among you[15] —so that you are not lacking in any spiritual gift [*charismati*]" (1:5–7). The Corinthians were abundantly "enriched"; they were not lacking in any of the spiritual *charismata*. Hence, when he wrote about the gifts of the Spirit, Paul addressed a church that already fully exercised them.[16] It was a wholly pneumatic community.

Their full participation in the gifts of the Spirit further implied a dynamic experience of the Spirit Himself. In this connection it is significant that shortly after delineating the spiritual gifts and how the Holy Spirit distributes them, Paul wrote, "For by[17] one Spirit we

---

intend to exclude the *charismata* of Romans 12 (or 1 Peter 4), whereas they *do* include 1 Corinthians (over against many who seek to exclude them all or in part, as will be noted later). However, the word "pneumatic" does highlight the embracing of the spiritual (or pneumatic) gifts of 1 Corinthians 12:8–10.

[12] The Greek phrase is *peri de tōn pneumatikōn*, literally, "now concerning spirituals." This could signify "spiritual matters" or even "spiritual persons" (cf. 1 Cor. 14:37, where *pneumatikos* refers to a spiritual person). However, almost all translations supply the word "gifts" in light of what follows in 1 Corinthians 12 (cf. also 1 Cor. 14:1).

[13] After the words "Now concerning spiritual gifts," Paul adds, "I do not want you to be uninformed" (*agnoien*). *Agnoien* is translated "ignorant" in KJV, NIV, and NEB; "unaware" in NASB. I prefer "uninformed." Gordon Fee writes, "Paul almost certainly does not intend to give new information, but an additional slant, or a corrective, to their understanding of 'the things of the Spirit' " (*The First Epistle to the Corinthians*, NICNT, 576). "Ignorant" or "unaware" does not convey that idea as well as "uninformed."

[14] Or "in every thing" (KJV, NASB); the Greek phrase is *en panti*.

[15] It is likely that Paul here refers to the gift of the Holy Spirit as the confirmation of the testimony. A parallel to this would be Peter's words that the gift of the Holy Spirit to the Gentiles in Caesarea had been a confirming testimony by God Himself: "God who knows the heart bore witness [or "testimony"] to them, giving them the Holy Spirit just as he did to us" (Acts 15:8). These words suggest a like "testimony to Christ" (or "of Christ," *tou Christou*) being confirmed to the Corinthians by the gift of the Spirit. (See also my earlier n. 5 relating to Heb. 2:3–4.)

[16] Indeed it becomes clear, as Paul's letter unfolds, that their problem was not the need for more gifts but the proper regulation of what they had!

[17] Or "in" (see NASB mg). The Greek preposition is *en*, which is usually translated "in" or "with," although "by" is possible. "In" or "with" (NIV mg has both) seems preferable, especially if we understand that it is not the Spirit who baptizes but Christ (see my fuller discussion of this in chap. 8, III.D.)

were all baptized into one body—Jew or Greeks . . .—and all were made to drink of one Spirit" (1 Cor. 12:13). The latter part of the verse may also be translated "that one Holy Spirit was poured out for all of us to drink" (NEB), or "we were all imbued (or saturated) with[18] that one Spirit." Hence, whatever the translation, there was an abundant outpouring of the Spirit that all had shared.[19] As a result of this, the people were abounding in spiritual gifts.

It is important, then, to emphasize that the context for the gifts of the Spirit was the experience of the Spirit's outpouring. Without this there would not have been vitality and power sufficient for the gifts to be manifested and multiplied. The Corinthians were "not lacking in any spiritual gift" because the testimony to Christ had been "confirmed"[20] among them; they had been "saturated with" the Spirit. Whatever may have been their faults—and they were manifold (as Paul depicts them in chapter after chapter)—they knew the fullness of the Spirit and His multiple gifts.[21]

The charismatic renewal of our day is in basic accord with the Corinthian situation. The background for the believers' claims to the operation of the gifts of the Holy Spirit is their experience of the outpouring[22] of the Spirit. At some time, in some situation, there has been a distinctive—even "saturating"—experience of the Holy Spirit's presence and power. This has been, it is claimed, the dynamic source of all the spiritual gifts that have followed.

This brings us back to the matter of the spiritual gifts themselves and to participation in them. Against the background of sharing in the Holy Spirit and the consequent gifts of the Holy Spirit,[23] information, instruction, and teaching concerning them becomes relevant. A fundamental thesis may here be set forth: *Any vital information concerning the gifts of the Spirit, the pneumatic charismata, presupposes a participation in them.* Without such participation, whatever is said about the gifts may only result in confusion and error. A primary example of the latter is the

---

[18]The relevant Greek word is *epotisthēmen*. Thayer (article on ποτίζω) suggests "imbued" or "saturated" as the translation of this word (again see chap. 8, III.D).

[19]It is significant (as I mentioned in chap. 8, III.A) that in an early noncanonical letter, written from the church at Rome, Clement addressed the church at Corinth as one that had experienced "a full outpouring of the Holy Spirit" (1 Clement 2:2). Clement had just spoken of the Corinthian church as one long known for its hospitality, humility, and consecration to Christ. Then he added, "Thus a profound and abundant peace was given to you all, and ye had an insatiable desire for doing good, while a full outpouring of the Holy Spirit was upon you all." Thereafter Clement (like Paul in his letter) chastised the Corinthians for boasting and rivalry. But this did not vitiate the fact that, in Clement's eyes, the Corinthians had experienced a rich outpouring of the Holy Spirit. This accords with Paul's words in 1 Corinthians 12:13.

[20]See my earlier note 15 how this confirmation was likely that of the gift of the Holy Spirit.

[21]"The strong assurance with which the Corinthians embraced the Gospel was followed by a shower of spiritual energies, of which they had a lively sense. . . . No church excelled the Corinthians in the variety of its endowments and the satisfaction felt in them" (EGT, 2: 760).

[22]The word "baptism," which suggests immersion or saturation, is commonly used: "baptized in [or "with"] the Holy Spirit." (For a fuller discussion of this term and similar ones, see chap. 8, III.)

[23]Incidentally, note the sequential reference in Hebrews to those who have "shared in the Holy Spirit" and "tasted . . . the powers of the coming age" (6:4–5 NIV). These "powers" (*dynameis*) may well refer to manifestations of the Holy Spirit consequent to sharing in that same Spirit.

statement sometimes made that the spiritual gifts, either all or in part, are "not for today." Whatever the attempted exegetical and historical interpretations made to justify such a view (and they are numerous), the truth of the matter is that a lack of significant experience of the pneumatic *charismata* results in the efforts of some people to distance themselves from the gifts because of not really knowing how to cope with them. Accordingly, despite the obvious Pauline teaching of their relevance for the church throughout the ages,[24] such people seek to confine the gifts to the New Testament period.[25] The spiritual damage in such subterfuge (whether recognized as such or not) is great, for it is precisely through these spiritual gifts that the Holy Spirit manifests Himself in power and vitality.

Here in our own day, as represented by the charismatic renewal, is the reemergence of the early church's dynamism,[26] with the gifts signifying a fresh breaking forth of that primitive power. How tragic, then, that some try to seal the lid over the past when there is such

vast need for everything the Holy Spirit has to give! One could hope that those who deny scriptural relevancy of the gifts for the church of today[27] (often while claiming that the Bible is inspired throughout!) and therefore eviscerate the word of God of its power would humble themselves, admit their need, and allow the Lord to do a new work in their lives.

Let it be firmly said that the church cannot be fully or freely the church without the presence and operation of the gifts of the Holy Spirit. What is depicted therefore in 1 Corinthians— and recurring in our day[28]—is in no sense a peripheral matter but is crucial to the life of the church. For the recurrence of the *charismata* of the Holy Spirit signals the church's recovery of its spiritual roots and its emergence in the twentieth century with fresh power and vitality.

III. BACKGROUND

We now move on to a consideration of the background for the gifts of the Holy Spirit. Paul deals with a number of

---

[24] Surely what Paul says in the preceding verses about the Lord's Supper (11:17–34) is relevant for the whole age of the church. How then can one possibly deny the continuing relevance of the immediately succeeding verses in 1 Corinthians 12 about the gifts?

[25] A prime example of this is the faulty exegesis of some commentators in relation to 1 Corinthians 13:8–13. I will describe this later.

[26] The Corinthian church for all its faults knew that dynamism. In reading the passage in 1 Corinthians 12:8–10 one is carried back into primordial spiritual depths, to the church described by one exegete as in its "rudimentary and protoplasmic state" in which its "substratum and vital tissue" are manifest (EGT, 2:733). Without this "substratum and vital tissue" the church cannot truly survive. F. L. Godet writes about 1 Corinthians 12–14 thus: "These chapters are to us like a revelation of the power of that spiritual movement which went forth from Pentecost, and of the wonderful spiritual efflorescence which at the outset signalized the new creation due to the power of the gospel" (*Commentary on the First Epistle of Paul to the Corinthians*, 600).

[27] Sometimes the attempt is made to divide the spiritual gifts into "permanent" and "temporary" and then to label most of the gifts of 1 Corinthians 12:8–10 as temporary, i.e., belonging only to the apostolic age (see, e.g., John Walvoord, *The Holy Spirit*, chap. 19, "Permanent Spiritual Gifts" and chap. 20, "Temporary Spiritual Gifts"). Such juggling with Scripture has even less to commend it than a forthright dismissal of all the spiritual gifts. (Walvoord actually comes close to such dismissal; under the heading "Permanent Spiritual Gifts" he admits only one of the nine [faith] and wrongly categorizes two others as "works of the Spirit" rather than "gifts" ["word of knowledge" and "word of wisdom"].)

[28] Of course, this is not admitted by anticharismatic zealots who in confusion categorize contemporary manifestations as "psychological," "spurious," or even "demonic."

important matters in 1 Corinthians 12:2–7. These background matters relate to the lordship of Christ, the activity of the Triune God, and the manifestation of the Holy Spirit.

A. The Lordship of Christ

Behind the operation of the spiritual gifts is the lordship of Jesus Christ. Although the *charismata* are pneumatic, hence operations of the Spirit, they are all derived from Jesus the exalted Lord. It is through His lordship, recognized and affirmed, that the spiritual gifts become a reality.

Continuing with Paul in 1 Corinthians 12, we observe in verses 2 and 3 that after reference to the Corinthians' pagan past when they were "led astray to dumb [voiceless] idols," and after words concerning others who proclaim an anathema on Jesus, Paul adds, "No one can say 'Jesus is Lord' except by [or "in"][29] the Holy Spirit." It is obvious that this statement about Jesus is far more than a verbal affirmation that anyone could utter. Paul, rather, is emphasizing that Jesus' lordship can be genuinely recognized and affirmed only in the Spirit, hence by those moving in the sphere of the Holy Spirit. It is Jesus the exalted Lord who pours forth the Holy Spirit; thus only in and by that Spirit whom He has given can His lordship be truly acclaimed.[30]

Significantly, in relation to the spiritual *charismata* Paul speaks of the lordship of Jesus prior to the delineation of the gifts. This serves to underscore the important fact that those who affirm and continue to affirm in the Spirit that "Jesus is Lord" are those to whom the Spirit distributes the gifts. The focus of the community is *not* the Spirit but the exalted Lord. A truly charismatic community, therefore, is not Spirit-centered but Christ-centered. It does not look to itself, nor even to the Holy Spirit moving in its midst, but to Jesus, who is exalted above all.

The important point at this juncture is that in the continuing recognition that Jesus *is* Lord (hence *now*) and acclaiming Him as such, He acts in His Spirit to multiply the gifts. Hence, as people come together in the Spirit to worship Jesus as Lord, to acknowledge His total sovereignty over their lives, and to offer themselves in trust and obedience, He moves in their midst. Through the pneumatic gifts He makes known depths of wisdom and knowledge, performs mighty deeds of healing and deliverance, indeed works miracles of many kinds.

A community of people proclaiming "Jesus is Lord" in the Holy Spirit is an extraordinary gathering. There are, to be sure, expressions of Jesus in many other ways than through the spiritual gifts; however, it is in and through them peculiarly that extraordinary, even supernatural, demonstrations of His power are made manifest. When this is realized and the community of people are expectant and the Lord begins to move, there is no place so full of

---

[29] The Greek preposition is *en*. The ASV translates it as "in" (likewise NASB mg). Although "by" is possible (as also in KJV, NASB, NIV), "in" is probably the better translation in this context. The meaning is not, as "by" suggests, that the Holy Spirit makes the declaration, "Jesus is Lord," but that those "in" the Spirit so declare. The NEB puts it well: "No one can say 'Jesus is Lord!' except under the influence of the Holy Spirit."

[30] J. D. G. Dunn writes, "The confession of Jesus' Lordship . . . is a charismatic conviction born of inspiration and expressed in words given from beyond. It is thus a direct and immediate manifestation of Spirit" (*The Spirit of Jesus,* 319). F. W. Grosheide writes, "That confession nobody can make except he be in the Spirit of God. . . . In this context these words are not to be taken of the ordinary confession of the believer but of the confession in glossolalia" (*First Epistle to the Corinthians,* NICNT, 281).

anticipation and excitement as that in which the Lord Jesus is glorified.

The lordship of Christ, affirmed in the Spirit, is the primary background for the operation of the spiritual gifts.

B. The Triune God

Before coming to a discussion of the spiritual *charismata*, it is important next to recognize the activity of the Triune God. We proceed with Paul: "Now there are varieties of gifts, but the same Spirit; and there are varieties of ministries,[31] but the same Lord, and there are varieties of operations,[31] but it is the same God who operates[32] them all in every one" (1 Cor. 12:4–6).

Here we note several things: (1) Whatever the diversity of gifts, of ministries, of operations, it is the same Holy Spirit, the same Lord Jesus, the same God at work in each: there is diversity but at the same time unity. Separation, division, factionalism—any playing off of one activity against another—cannot be of God. (2) There is no simple identification of the gifts of the Holy Spirit with the ministries of the Lord Jesus or the operations of God. In a peculiar sense the Spirit is at work in the gifts, Christ in various ministries, and God in a wide range of operations.[33] (3) Whatever are gifts of the Holy Spirit are also ministries of the exalted Lord Jesus and likewise operations of God the Father. Although there

is no simple identification of gifts, ministries, and operations,[34] the Triune God is at work in and through all of them. There is no gift that is not a ministry, no ministry that is not an operation or working, and the same God—Father, Son, and Holy Spirit—is in them all. (4) Finally, there seems to be a kind of ascending movement. Paul begins with the gifts of the Spirit within the community, next speaks of ministries of the exalted Lord, then culminates with the overall operations of God.[35] The Spirit, as always, leads us back to the Son, and the Son in turn points us back to the Father. This is the way of the blessed Trinity.

In all of this it is important to bear in mind that behind the spiritual gifts stands the Triune God. Although the gifts are primarily expressions of the Holy Spirit, they have behind them the full weight of the Godhead: Father, Son, and Holy Spirit.

It follows that a truly charismatic community, moving in the pneumatic gifts, is Trinitarian in its fundamental operation and lifestyle. While it is a fact that through the pneumatic *charismata* the Holy Spirit manifests Himself (see next section) and, accordingly, there is a heightened sense of His person and presence, it is not as if the Holy Spirit is alone recognized. Just as the focus is not the Holy Spirit but Christ (previous section), so the total operation is not

---

[31] The RSV has "service" and "working." Since the Greek text has *diakoniōn* and *energēmatōn*, plurals for words that may more adequately be translated "ministries" (NASB) and "operations" (KJV), I have substituted these words.

[32] The Greek word is *energōn*, hence "operating" or "working."

[33] Accordingly, there may be some justification for viewing 1 Corinthians 12:8–10 as particularly referring to the gifts of the Spirit; Ephesians 4:7–11 as the ministries of Christ; and Romans 12:3–8 as the operations of God. (See my earlier brief comments on these three passages in the Introduction.)

[34] "What is a χάρισμα in respect of its quality and ground, is a διακονία in view of its usefulness, and an ἐνέργημα in virtue of the power operative therein" (EGT, 2:887).

[35] I like the statement of H. A. W. Meyer: "The divine Trinity is here indicated in an ascending climax, in such a way that we pass from the Spirit who bestows the gifts to the Lord [Christ] who is served by means of them, and finally to God, who as the absolute first cause and possessor of all Christian powers works the entire sum of charismatic gifts in all who are gifted" (*Commentary on the New Testament, First Corinthians*, in loco).

the Holy Spirit but the Triune God. To be truly pneumatic is to be both thoroughly Christocentric and Trinitarian.

C. The Manifestation of the Holy Spirit

The final and most immediate background to our discussion of the spiritual gifts is that the gifts are "the manifestation of the Spirit" (1 Cor. 12:7).[36] It is just after these words that Paul moves into his delineation of the gifts of the Spirit.

Through the pneumatic *charismata* the Holy Spirit shines forth and openly shows Himself. The Spirit who is invisible now manifests Himself visibly[37] and audibly. When the Holy Spirit was given at Pentecost, thousands of people were drawn to the place where they beheld and heard the Spirit-filled disciples speaking in "other tongues." Peter in his explanation of the event said, "Being therefore exalted at the right hand of God, and having received from the Father the promise of the Holy Spirit, he [Jesus] has poured out this which you see and hear" (Acts 2:33). Thus what the crowd saw and heard was the manifestation, or showing forth, of the Holy Spirit. In that sense the disciples' "other" speech was such a manifestation. However, all the spiritual *charismata*, not just glossolalia, are the Spirit's self-manifestation.

It is important, then, to emphasize that whenever and wherever the pneumatic *charismata* occur, the Holy Spirit is thereby manifesting Himself. The nine gifts listed by Paul in the next three verses (8–10), therefore, are various exhibitions of this. To use an analogy, the gifts may be thought of as lights that turn on from a hidden electrical current. The current cannot be seen, but when the lights come on, they are vivid evidence and demonstration of its presence and power. So it is that in and through the spiritual *charismata* the invisible Holy Spirit shines forth.

The gifts of the Spirit, I might add, are clearly to be differentiated from the fruit of the Spirit. Paul elsewhere writes, "The fruit of the Spirit is love, joy, peace, patience, kindness, goodness, faithfulness, gentleness, self-control" (Gal. 5:22–23). Thus there is both a ninefold manifestation (the gifts) and a ninefold fruit. Although the same in number, the gifts and the fruit are totally different in character. Even the most cursory comparison of 1 Corinthians 12:8–10 and Galatians 5:22 discloses this.[38] Moreover, the gifts of the Spirit are the immediate self-expression of the Spirit occurring through instruments open to His presence and power. The fruit of the Spirit, on the other hand (like fruit in general), takes a length of time to develop and is found only among those who are maturing in their Christian lives. In the case of the gifts

---

[36]The phrase is *phanerōsis tou pneumatos*. That this is a subjective genitive, i.e., the Spirit manifesting Himself, seems probable from the larger context. According to TDNT, "the gen. τοῦ πνεύματος is to be taken as a subj. gen., for only in 12:8ff. are the different operations named and v. 11 expressly repeats that the Spirit is the subject at work (in different ways)" (9:6). BAGD, however, says that "the syntax . . . cannot be determined with certainty," but then adds, "Whether the genitive is subj. or obj. the expr. means the same thing as χάρισμα." I am inclined to the subjective genitive and agree with James Dunn that the important thing is that "*The Spirit reveals Himself* in the charismata" (*Jesus and the Spirit,* 212). The NEB translation points this direction: "the Spirit is manifested."

[37]Arnold Bittlinger writes, "The Spirit is not just given in an 'invisible way.' He wants to manifest Himself visibly" (*Gifts and Graces,* 24).

[38]I have earlier commented on the overall difference between the *charismata* of 1 Corinthians 12 and those of Romans 12 (also 1 Peter 4). However, the difference lies in the varieties of gifts. Galatians 5 is totally different in that Paul is not speaking of gifts of any kind.

even very young and immature believers may manifest them (as did the Corinthians), but with the fruit there must be a lengthy process of growth and maturation. Both gifts and fruit are valuable for very different reasons. But they are by no means the same.[39]

What is of particular significance about the spiritual gifts is that through their expression there is *dynamic manifestation*. By the gift of the Holy Spirit there is entrance into the dynamic dimension; by the gifts of the Spirit there is the occurrence of dynamic manifestation. Hence, when we are dealing with the spiritual gifts, their importance is neither little nor secondary, but fundamental. For through the gifts the Holy Spirit Himself is "on the scene" in dynamic self-manifestation.

A word again about the charismatic renewal. Criticism is sometimes made that participants are preoccupied with "the sensational." Rather than being satisfied with their salvation and a "normal" Christian walk, they are caught up in such things as tongues, prophecies, healings, and the like. Moreover, the criticism sometimes continues, charismatics exhibit a lot of carnality and therefore would do well to leave the gifts and be more concerned with holiness and righteousness. To reply to the latter: modern-day charismatics may, and sometimes do, show forth carnality and insufficient devotion to holy living. In that sense they are not unlike the Corinthians to whom Paul wrote. There is undoubted need today for many of Paul's admonitions throughout the letter. *But* the answer cannot be to forget the spiritual gifts, for they and they alone are *the* manifestation of the Spirit. In regard to the first charge that charismatics are caught up in the sensational, it may also be true that some do overestimate certain of the gifts and make too much of their exercise. However, what seems like the sensational to one not familiar with the gifts could actually be the mighty power of God in operation. The word "sensational" (or a similar term) may indeed be used in an effort to avoid coming to terms with the Holy Spirit. Incidentally, these very critics may be among the "unlearned"[40] about whom Paul later writes, and consequently need humbly to learn and experience more of the Holy Spirit and His manifestations. Disregard in this matter is sad indeed.

One can only conclude that a people, a church, or believers in general— whatever their salvation and sanctification, their dedication and service—who disregard[41] the spiritual gifts are missing out on the dynamic reality of the Spirit's own self-manifestation. This surely is no minor thing, for it is not simply a matter of gifts (as important as they are) but *God* Himself in the Holy Spirit declaring Himself, of *Christ* the Lord ministering now through the *Spirit*. How desperately does everyone need to be alerted to what is at issue in the gifts and to be open to God's visitation!

It should be finally noted that the manifestation of the Spirit is *through people*. From Paul's statement that "to each one is given the manifestion of the Spirit" (1 Cor. 12:7 NASB), it is clear that the Spirit's self-manifestation is through individuals. This means, accordingly,

---

[39] For further discussion of the fruit of the Spirit see chapter 15, "Christian Living."

[40] See 1 Corinthians 14:16, 23–24. In these verses Paul makes reference to one who is an *idiōtēs* (or plural, *idiōtai*), translated in KJV as "unlearned." More specifically this may refer to "him that is without gifts" (RSV mg). The NASB translates the word as "ungifted," suggesting in the margin of 1 Corinthians 14:16 "unversed in spiritual gifts."

[41] This disregard may be deliberate (i.e., by relegating them, wholly or in part, to the past) or in ignorance (not knowing what they are all about). It may also stem from the previously described opposition to the "sensationalism" of charismatics.

the extraordinary fact that human beings, finite creatures, become the channel of the Spirit's manifestation. It happens by virtue of the gifts the Spirit imparts; and, as they operate in and through human beings, the Spirit thereby discloses Himself. To be permitted to have some share in this is beyond comprehension, and in this experience there is great rejoicing and glorifying of God.

IV. PROFILE

Before coming to a specific consideration of the gifts of the Holy Spirit, I will give an overview of their nature and expression. In so doing a number of Paul's statements in 1 Corinthians 12–14 will be examined. Let us turn now to a profile of the spiritual gifts.

A. Divine and Human Activity

In all the gifts there is both a divine and a human activity. On the one hand, each gift is a manifestation of the Spirit; on the other hand, the gifts are expressed through human beings. The gifts are primarily distributions of the Holy Spirit—the Spirit "apportions" or "distributes"—but the gifts operate in and through persons: He "apportions to each one" (1 Cor. 12:11). In the operation of the spiritual gifts the Holy Spirit expresses Himself in and through human activity.

It is important to stress, first, the *divine side*. Since we are dealing with a manifestation of the Holy Spirit, thus a spiritual gift, the divine aspect is primary. In that sense all the gifts are supernatural[42] or extraordinary. This is the case for those seemingly ordinary as well as those seemingly extraordinary gifts. For example, a "word of wisdom" is just as much a supernatural manifestation as "working of miracles," a "word of knowledge" as "speaking in tongues." All are extraordinary, all basically supernatural.[43]

Gifts of the Holy Spirit, accordingly, are not latent natural talents or trained abilities brought to heightened expression. The spiritual gifts are by no means more of what is already present, no matter how elevated. They are not simply an added spiritual injection that causes talents and abilities to function with greater effectiveness or transposes them to a higher level. They are gifts of the Spirit, endowments, not enhancements[44]—apportionments of the Holy Spirit.

Indeed, a manifestation of the Spirit may occur with someone regardless of background, experience, or education. Thus a word of wisdom, prophetic utterance, gifts of healing, and so on, may operate through those from whom they are least expected. The highly trained intellectual is not always the one

---

[42]I have some hesitancy in using the word *supernatural* because of a possible connotation of the "otherworldy" or even the "ghostly." Also "supernatural" may suggest something totally beyond the human, or even in contradiction to it. However, on the positive side the word does imply a dimension more than human and guards against a reduction of the spiritual gifts to the purely natural level.

[43]Hence, any attempted separation of the spiritual gifts into supernatural/natural, extraordinary/ordinary, or even miraculous/nonmiraculous is in error. As an example of the latter, see M. E. Unger, *The Baptism and Gifts of the Holy Spirit*, 138–40, where the author lists four of the gifts as "temporary, miraculous sign-gifts," thus relegating the other gifts to a nonmiraculous category. (It is noteworthy that the idea of "temporary" goes along with "miraculous," hence not for today.)

[44]Bittlinger writes contrariwise that "a gift is manifested when being set free by the Holy Spirit, natural talents blossom forth glorifying Christ and building up His church" (*Gifts and Graces,* 72). Bittlinger errs, I believe, in failing to recognize that spiritual gifts are *not* "natural talents" that "blossom forth" (i.e., enhancements). Rather, they are essentially endowments of the Spirit.

to express the wisdom of God, the talented orator the one to speak prophetically, the physician with much training and experience to exhibit gifts of healing. Quite the contrary: these very attainments may even block the way to an openness to the gifts of the Holy Spirit. The Spirit is free to use— and often does use—the uneducated and unpracticed[45] layman to bring about extraordinary results.

Second, there is also *human activity* involved. The statement that "to each one is given the manifestation of the Spirit" signifies that a person, an individual, is the recipient of the Spirit's manifestation. Thus, in the operation of the gift it is the human person, not the Holy Spirit, who acts. Accordingly, when the Holy Spirit apportions a *charisma* such as a word of wisdom or knowledge, tongue or prophecy, it is a human being who speaks. On the Day of Pentecost "*they . . . began to speak in other tongues as the Spirit gave them utterance*" (Acts 2:4). The Holy Spirit "gave" them to "speak out,"[46] thus the words that they were to say. But He Himself did not do the speaking. Each person present spoke forth in his human integrity; nothing was automatic or forced. Thus in the functioning of any spiritual gift the recipient with the totality of his background, ability, training,

and experience is involved. The human element is fully present.[47]

Next, I need to emphasize that the various distributions of the Spirit may also use those who are positively prepared through study, practice, and experiences of many kinds.[48] For example, a word of knowledge,[49] though supernaturally inspired with its origin not of man but of God, may be given to one who is quite knowledgeable and already a well-trained communicator. Indeed, spiritual communication ordinarily calls for the best possible use of all means available so that the message will come through with maximum effectiveness. The same could be true, for example, of another spiritual gift, "distinguishing of spirits."[50] While the gift is wholly of God, thereby enabling one to have profound insight into the spiritual situation of people, that very insight may be further clarified and applied through the knowledge of human nature in its various aspects. What then is *basic* is the gift of the Spirit, but what is *instrumental* is the totality of the human situation.

Since in all charismatic activity there is a human aspect, this is open to analysis and description. Scientific study (physiological, linguistic, psychological) has its proper place and importance. For example, linguistic and psychological analysis of a tongue spoken,

---

[45] Prime examples of this are Peter and John, used mightily by the Holy Spirit in witness and healing, who were perceived by the Jewish high council as "uneducated and untrained men" (Acts 4:13 NASB).

[46] The Greek word translated "utterance" is *apophthengesthai,* to "*speak out, declare boldly or loudly*" (BAGD). Also the word suggests speaking under divine inspiration (see chap. 8, n. 17).

[47] Donald Gee writes that we should "value . . . the precious quality of divine inspiration in all the gifts of the Spirit, while at the same time we recognize the inescapable human element in them" (*Spiritual Gifts in the Work of the Ministry Today,* 35). This "inescapable human element" must not be overlooked.

[48] We have earlier observed how God mightily used the uneducated and untrained Peter and John. But also—my present point—He made great use of the highly educated and trained Paul. Paul's "great learning" (Acts 26:24) was placed at the disposal of many operations of the Holy Spirit.

[49] In chapter 14 this gift will be discussed in more detail.

[50] This gift also will be more fully discussed in chapter 14.

empirical investigation of a miracle worked, medical testing of a healing performed—all such can have value.[51] However, the limitation—a critical one—is that no human science is able fully to comprehend or encompass that which is essentially spiritual.[52]

This last statement calls for an emphasis on the limitation of the natural in the realm of things spiritual. The natural man, whether the most capable psychologist, scientist, or linguist, or one who is untrained in any of these areas, is in no way capable of comprehending spiritual realities. Thus Paul writes earlier in 1 Corinthians: "A natural[53] man does not accept the things[54] of the Spirit of God; for they are foolishness to him, and he cannot understand them, because they are spiritually appraised" (2:14 NASB). Hence, to say that a spiritual gift has a perfectly natural explanation or that a particular manifestation is nonsense may be a declaration of spiritual blindness. It is the Spirit alone who gives the eyes and ears and heart that can make for true recognition.

Third, *the nature of the divine and human relationship* in the spiritual gifts needs to be recognized. It is important to affirm now that since all the gifts are the manifestation of the Spirit, He is free to operate "just as He wills" (1 Cor. 12:11 NASB). The spiritual gifts, accordingly, are not so set in place that the Holy Spirit may not operate differently in another situation. The spiritual gifts are not offices[55] or appointments,[56] for even though they are distributed individually and may function on some occasion through a particular person, they are by no means so limited. This may be illustrated by the fact that though prophecy is listed as one of the nine spiritual gifts, Paul later said, "You can all prophesy one by one" (14:31 RSV). Also he wrote, "When you assemble, each one has a psalm, has a teaching, has a revelation, has a tongue, has an interpretation" (14:26 NASB).

---

[51] E.g., linguistic analysis of a tongue spoken can prove or disprove the validity of the claim that it is a particular known language.

[52] It would, for example, be a grievous error to seek to comprehend a tongue spoken as wholly a natural phenomenon, hence subject totally to the science of linguistic analysis. William Samarin, a linguist by profession, overreaches his skills when he says, "Glossolalia is fundamentally *not* language. . . . Glossolalia is not a supernatural phenomenon" (*Tongues of Men and Angels,* 225). The linguist can demonstrate that tongues is not a particular language (see preceding note) or even that it does not conform to any language patterns with which he is familiar, but he cannot rule out the possibility that glossolalia has an origin, forms, and meaning completely beyond his competence to analyze.

[53] The Greek word is *psychikos*; RSV and NEB read "unspiritual"; NIV, "without the Spirit"; KJV, like NASB, "natural." *Psychikos* denotes "the life of the natural world and whatever belongs to it, in contrast to the supernatural world, which is characterized by πνεῦμα" (BAGD).

[54] RSV translates as "gifts," which in light of 1 Corinthians 12 may be Paul's meaning. The Greek word is simply *ta,* "the things."

[55] The *domata* of Ephesians 4 represent offices. They include "prophets" ("He gave some . . . as prophets" [v. 11 NASB]) who hold a continuing office in the church. Prophecy in 1 Corinthians 12:10 is an activity not limited to the office.

[56] Appointments are mentioned later by Paul in 1 Corinthians 12:28: "God has appointed in the church . . . ." Again prophets are included; but also, in relation to the spiritual gifts, Paul speaks of "miracles," gifts of healings" (NASB), and "various kinds of tongues." But in no case are these activities but rather placements. (The word "appointed" might better be translated as "placed" or "set" [as in KJV].) God has, for example, set in the church "miracles"; they occupy a continuing place therein. But it is the Holy Spirit that, so to speak, activates the placement by the gift of "workings of miracles." The latter is by no means limited to a particular person.

The point then is that the manifestation of the Spirit may vary considerably. Spiritual gifts, therefore, are different from other gifts (such as those of Romans 12 and 1 Peter 4). Since they are not continuing possessions, the Spirit moves freely in and through His manifestations, apportioning variously as He wills. A person may, for example, manifest a word of knowledge on one occasion and prophecy on another (or any other combination). It is also significant to note that the expression "is given"[57] (12:7) clearly refers to the present. Thus it is not a past gift, which one, so to speak, carries with himself; rather, it is to be received and expressed only when people gather in worship and fellowship.[58]

A proper understanding of this makes for a vital sense of the *contemporaneity* of the Spirit's activity. The focus is not on the past but the present; hence when people assemble, there is a lively expectation of fresh, perhaps different, manifestations of the Holy Spirit. Also, since one may not know ahead of time what gift the Spirit will impart, each person may come with keen anticipation, even excitement, about what the Spirit will do through him. All this means that the gathered community becomes the arena of God's mighty and wondrous activity in the Holy Spirit.

B. Ministry in the Community

We next observe that the gifts of the Holy Spirit are for ministry in the body of believers: "To each one is given the manifestation of the Spirit for the common good" (1 Cor. 12:7 NASB). The importance of the spiritual gifts is thus in their role of *common ministry*.

The orientation of the gifts is, first, "for the common good";[59] that is, the good of the community. Thus each of the spiritual gifts named, from "word of wisdom" to "interpretation of tongues," is for the profit of all. Accordingly, when the Holy Spirit manifests Himself in a gift to an individual, it is not for the sake of the individual but for the good or profit of the whole body. The spiritual *charismata*, therefore, have a horizontal reference, for whereas they are given to individuals, they are wholly for "the common good," the community of believers.

To be more specific: the gifts of the Holy Spirit, not unlike the gift, are the means whereby the exalted Lord carries forward His ministry through persons.[60] Through the *gift (dōrea)* of the Holy Spirit the Lord invests people with the power to witness mightily in word and deed; through the *gifts (charismata)* He enables them to minister effectively to one another. The ministry may be to one person, to several, or to the whole body, as the Lord knows and

---

[57]The Greek word is *didotai*. This may be compared with the *edōken* ("gave") of Ephesians 4:11 and the *etheto* ("placed") of 1 Corinthians 12:28. The latter two are in the aorist tense and signify completed action whereas the former (a present tense) points to an ongoing activity; "*didotai* . . . indicates continuous bestowment" (EGT, 2:287).

[58]This is not to deny that certain persons may more regularly express certain manifestations of the Spirit. Thus, for example, some may be said to have a *charisma* of prophecy (even called "prophets" in 1 Cor. 14:29–32). Still, whenever the gift occurs, it is a present manifestation of the Spirit.

[59]The Greek phrase is *pros to sympheron* and means "to the profit" or "advantage" (BAGD), hence "for the profit." It is apparent from what follows that "the profit" has to do with the community, thus the KJV rendering "to profit withal." "For the common good" (RSV, NIV) suggests this community ideal.

[60]It will be recalled that after Paul speaks of "varieties of gifts, but the same Spirit," he adds, "varieties of ministries, but the same Lord." Hence the spiritual *charismata*, in all their variety, are also "ministries" of the Lord. (See earlier discussion in III.B.)

meets the needs. As each person exercises a gift, the body is built up for its ministry in the gospel.

The spiritual gifts, accordingly, are for the *upbuilding* of the community. We have earlier noted the statement "When you assemble, each one has a psalm . . . a teaching . . . a revelation . . . a tongue . . . an interpretation." Paul adds immediately: "Let all things be done for edification" (1 Cor. 14:26 NASB). Whatever the manifestation of the Spirit, its one purpose is the edification, the building up, of the body of believers. It is the intention of the Lord that His people be strengthened as a community. So when a word of wisdom or a prophecy is spoken, a word of knowledge or a tongue expressed, a healing or a miracle wrought, it is for one purpose: edification.

It follows that any exercise of a gift of the Spirit that does not result in edification of the body is inappropriate and out of order. As a prime example, speaking in tongues is later discouraged by Paul if there is not also interpretation. The apostle by no means negates the importance or validity of the gift; indeed, quite the contrary, for he states that through a tongue there is direct address to God and the utterance of "mysteries in the Spirit" (1 Cor. 14:2). How could there be a higher expression than this? However—and this is the basic point—since "tongues" is speaking "not to men but to God" (v. 2), there can be no group edification unless someone interprets. When that happens, the church is edified (vv. 4–19). If interpretation is not also exercised, the manifestation of tongues is out of order. Paul's words to the Corinthians, in the context of discussing speaking in tongues, are unmistakable: "Since you are eager for manifestations of the Spirit, strive to excel in building up the church" (v. 12). That is to say, the overriding concern should not be the spiritual gifts themselves (as important as they are and as eager as one may be for their occurrence) but the edification of the body. Any expression of a spiritual gift that does not build up is contrary to the Lord's intention. In summary, the validity of an exercise of a gift of the Spirit is its aid in the edification, or building up, of the community in Christ.

Now to return to the matter of the overall purpose of the gifts of the Spirit: It is apparent that concern for these gifts is by no means a self-oriented preoccupation. The spiritual gifts are not for private benefit but wholly for the edification of others. Moreover, this is not a matter of upbuilding "in the natural realm" by human words and acts of kindness, but "in the Spirit" through persons open to His ministrations. Thus there is ministry to one another in far greater depth and quality.

In connection with this common ministry, second, *each person has a distinctive role to fulfill.* That is to say, not only are the spiritual gifts for the sake of the community but also each member is a participant: "to each one is given . . . ." The common good is the orientation of the gifts, and to that end each person is involved.

Now let us focus on the "each one."[61] Each and every person in the community is given a manifestation of the Spirit. It is not a matter of certain individuals, perhaps leaders or officeholders, who are so gifted. No one is left out. Even as the spiritual gifts are for the whole body, so everyone in the

---

[61] The Greek word in 1 Corinthians 12:11 is *hekastō*; "to each" (RSV), "to every man" (KJV). "To each one" (NASB, NIV) better expresses the individual direction of the manifestation of the Spirit. "Every" suggests the all-inclusiveness of the Spirit's distribution. Both ideas are contained in the Greek word *hekastos*.

body is equally involved in the ministry of edification.

Accordingly, in a Spirit-gifted community people do not look to one person or a few to minister to the assembly. Rather they look to the Lord, expecting Him to minister by the Spirit through each one present. In this sense pulpit and altar become secondary, for the spiritual ministry is not through preacher or priest, but through each and every individual. Each person is equally a participant in the worship and fellowship by virtue of the Spirit's anointing. Every person in the assembly is to be actively involved, for the Holy Spirit wishes to manifest Himself not through a few but through all.

This calls for further emphasis in light of the fact that the involvement of each person as a vehicle for the Spirit's manifestation has been greatly neglected in church tradition.[62] Especially is this true in liturgical churches where worship is ritualistic, and the congregation is little more than spectators. Even when the assembly is expected to join in prayers, singing, and responses, there is rarely the expectation that any individual, much less all, will be the channel for a manifestation of the Spirit.

We may be grateful that this long neglect is finding significant remedy in the contemporary spiritual renewal in which people frequently come together in expectation of the manifestation of the gifts of the Spirit. Whenever this occurs, there is an extraordinary sense of community participation and expectation for what the Lord may do through any and all.[63]

Paul's instruction in 1 Corinthians concerning individual participation suggests a gathering of believers of such size that this can more readily happen. A larger assembly may surely be in order for a time of preaching, teaching, or public worship, but it is scarcely suitable for the ministry of the spiritual gifts. Clearly, something like the "house church"[64] is needed, not to replace the "temple church"[65] but to supplement it. In such a smaller gathering there is better opportunity and often more freedom for the spiritual gifts to operate.

All of this calls for individual responsibility of a high order. For however true it is that the Spirit gives to each and apportions as He wills, it happens to individuals who are, in turn, responsible for the ensuing expression of the gift. This means, for one thing, to follow closely the leading and prompting of the Holy Spirit, and whenever He imparts a gift not to hold back. It is not that everyone must speak or act,[66] but

---

[62] This is true despite the recovery during the Reformation of the biblical truth of the priesthood of all believers. Unfortunately, the pragmatics of church polity has virtually nullified the outworking of this doctrine in much congregational ministry.

[63] There is always the danger that a church leader, particularly a pastor, will so assume direction of the assembly as to allow little participation on the part of the people. The pastor, to be sure, has a highly important function to fulfill, but it is *not* to monopolize or dictate the meeting of believers. The manifestation of the gifts does call for order, but orchestration of the gifts is entirely in the hands of the Lord through His Spirit.

[64] Frequent reference is made in the New Testament to the "church in . . . [someone's] house." See Romans 16:5; 1 Corinthians 16:19; Colossians 4:15; Philemon 1:2.

[65] The earliest Christians in Jerusalem are described as "continuing daily with one accord in the temple, and breaking bread from house to house" (Acts 2:46 KJV). There was *both* temple and house. The latter was also a place of worship; the "breaking bread" suggests the Eucharist and fellowship in the Lord.

[66] On the matter of speaking in tongues and prophesying Paul counsels that there be only

each person is responsible that what has been given be used in the edification of the community.[67]

This leads to the further recognition of the importance of all the gifts for the proper and full functioning of the body. Since "in[68] one Spirit we were all baptized into[69] one body" (as we noted before), and as Paul proceeds to say, "The body does not consist of one member but of many" (1 Cor. 12:14), then all members are necessary.

Paul uses the imagery of the physical body with its various parts—foot, ear, eye, hand, head, even "unpresentable parts"[70] (1 Cor. 12:15–26)—stating that all equally belong and that all are necessary to the body. It is utter nonsense for one part to speak up and say, "I have no need of you" (v. 21). Hence by implication each member in the spiritual body of Christ expressing his spiritual gift is essential to the whole body. The body cannot function as well without it; all gifts are needed. Moreover, to look down on or despise the

manifestation of another gift is totally unwarranted.

This is particularly relevant to situations where some of the *charismata* of the Spirit may be disregarded or even unwelcomed. I have earlier commented on those who claim that these gifts in whole or in part have no contemporary relevance. What they are really saying is that these spiritual gifts are not needed, or that only certain ones are: word of wisdom, yes; gifts of healing, no; word of knowledge, yes; working of miracles, no; faith, yes; prophecy, no; etc. In other words: foot, yes; ear, no; eye, yes; hand, no; head, yes; "unpresentable parts," no. It is hard to describe a more devastating dismemberment of the body if or when such an attitude prevails.

In this connection let me add a word about the difficulty some people have with one spiritual gift in particular—that of tongues. This manifestation is often not only unwelcome but even despised. Tongues are not only viewed as "unpresentable parts" to be cov-

---

"two or three" (1 Cor. 14:27, 29). The implication is that others similarly gifted by the Spirit need not speak.

[67] It is obvious that with basically nine gifts of the Spirit, even a fairly small group (ten or more) must share in a number of the manifestations. Although each person need not experience more than one gift, he or she is responsible that its expression occur at some time before the assembly concludes.

[68] Translating this time (see note 17) en as "in."

[69] "Unto" or "in relation to" is also possible. The Greek preposition is *eis*. For the meaning of "unto" (or "for") see, e.g., Matthew 10:10; Luke 14:35; Acts 2:38, 11:18; 2 Corinthians 5:5, 9:8. For "in relation to" (or "with respect to," "concerning") see, e.g., Acts 2:25; Romans 4:20; Ephesians 5:32; 1 Thessalonians 5:18 in various translations. Commenting on 1 Corinthians 12:13, EGT states: "*en* defines the element and ruling influence of the baptism [i.e., the Holy Spirit], *eis* the relationship to which it introduces [i.e., one body]" (2: 890). This would mean that baptism in the Spirit is *not* into one body (the usual translation) but "unto" or "in relation to," namely, that there might be oneness or unity in the body. John Rea writes: "In v. 13 he [Paul] is explaining the *relation,* the unity or common bond, which pertains in the one-and-the-same Spirit for all who are already believers . . . . The baptism in the Spirit is the great unifying factor in a body of such diverse members" (*Layman's Commentary on the Holy Spirit,* 146–47).

[70] Verse 23, "unseemly members" (NASB); the Greek word is *aschēmona,* "the unpresentable, i.e. private, parts" (BAGD). Gordon Fee writes: "Paul is undoubtedly referring to the sexual organs, on which we bestow greater honor, and which therefore have greater decorum, because we cover them" (*The First Epistle to the Corinthians,* NICNT, 613–14).

ered, but in some cases forbidden to function at all![71] And yet if it is true, as Paul later says, that when speaking in tongues one "utters mysteries in the Spirit" (1 Cor. 14:2), what could more edify the body than having these mysteries interpreted?

It is urgent that no gift of the Holy Spirit be denigrated, despised,[72] suppressed, or set aside. All gifts have their proper and essential place in the full functioning of the body of Christ. Even if one gift, one member, is missing or not functioning, the body is sorely handicapped. When each performs his Spirit-given part, then verily the body is both able to function normally and to be built up in faith and ministry.

One further word concerning the meaning of "to each one is given." Since each spiritual *charisma* is a gift, any legitimate ground of boasting is nonexistent. Each *charisma* is a gift of grace, and therefore boasting concerning spiritual gifts is ruled out.[73] This does not mean that boasting never occurs, for the sin of pride can slip in and lay claim to the *charismata* as human accomplishments. This evidently happened in the Corinthian church, for Paul earlier wrote, "What have you that you did not receive? If then you received it, why do you boast as if it were not a gift?" (1 Cor. 4:7). Such boasting then or now can only occur by failing to recognize the totally gift nature of the *charismata*. All are manifestations of the Holy Spirit, and God alone is to be glorified.

Actually, in the experience of the contemporary spiritual renewal, the manifestations of spiritual gifts seldom lead to boasting. Most persons, especially those new to charismatic experience, rejoice all the more in the Lord whenever a manifestation occurs. There is usually a joy that it is He who is moving and acting, that anything truly said or done is from Him, and that every operation is a blessing from God. This may be the case, for example, when those who are wise and knowledgeable by natural ability or training recognize that they have no claim on such gifts as "word of wisdom" and "word of knowledge." In fact, those "naturally" wise often come to recognize that worldly wisdom is simply *not* the wisdom of God, and that one must "become a fool" to apprehend and express God's true wisdom. "If any one among you thinks that he is wise in this age, let him become a fool that he may become wise. For the wisdom of this world is folly with God" (1 Cor. 3:18–19). When there is such a recognition, ministry in the spiritual gifts is totally different from the exercise of natural capacities, and God, not man, receives all the praise and glory.[74]

C. Spiritual Gifts and Love

Because of their great value in building up the body of Christ, the spiritual (pneumatic) *charismata* are much to be desired; however, they need to function in an attitude of love. Here we observe

---

[71]It surely is not without significance that Paul in his discussion of the "unpresentable parts" speaks about the "greater modesty" with which we treat them, but adds that "God has so adjusted the body, giving the greater honor to the inferior part" (1 Cor. 12:23, 24). If this is possibly a reference to the sometimes lowly esteemed (even "indecent" to some) gift of tongues, it only shows that God's evaluation is quite a bit different than ours!

[72]Paul warns against the despising of another gift, namely, prophecy: "Do not despise prophesying" (1 Thess. 5:20). It is apparent that despising spiritual gifts has been around since Paul's own time.

[73]This obviously is the opposite extreme from despising a gift or gifts.

[74]"Ministry on the line of the natural gifts . . . often draws attention to the brilliance of the individual and glorifies man. But true ministry of the spiritual gifts leaves man in the background and glorifies God" (Donald Gee, *Concerning Spiritual Gifts*, 16).

the later words of Paul in 1 Corinthians 14:1: "Follow the way of love and eagerly desire[75] spiritual gifts[76] . . ." (NIV).

Let us first consider the matter of *eager desire for the spiritual gifts*. This injunction of Paul may, on first reflection, seem contrary to his earlier words that the Holy Spirit distributes "to each one individually just as He wills" (1 Cor. 12:11 NASB). If the spiritual gifts are His sovereign action, His apportionments, or distributions, what difference does anyone's desire make? The answer, first, is the same as in regard to the gift of the Spirit; for though the gift is God's sovereign bestowal, it is given (according to Luke 11:9–13) to those who ask, seek, and knock—that is, to those who earnestly desire it.[77] God delights to "give good things to those who ask him" (Matt. 7:11), and so it is with the "good things," [78] the "good gifts" of the Holy Spirit. He will not waste His gifts on those who do not desire them. Second, God is still in control. For all our asking and desiring, the Holy Spirit distributes "as He wills." We are to eagerly seek the gifts, but God is still in charge. He knows far better than we the gift that at any time will be the best channel for his ministration through us.

In accordance with Paul's injunction to eagerly desire spiritual gifts, it is proper for the Christian community to be zealous in this regard.[79] There should be an intense desire for all the gifts of the Holy Spirit to be manifest— not just a few, but all of them. Through their variety and totality the body of Christ fully functions, multiple needs are met, and the whole community is thereby edified.

A word of admonition: no Christian fellowship should be satisfied with only a few of the gifts. Unfortunately, even in some groups of "charismatically renewed" believers there seems to be satisfaction if only two or three of the gifts (perhaps prophecy, tongues, and interpretation) are manifest. One may be grateful for the activity of any spiritual gift, especially in light of the dearth in many churches. However, the body cannot be properly built up without the full complement of pneumatic gifts in operation. Hence, the admonition or counsel: pray for, earnestly desire, seek after the gifts; do not be satisfied until all frequently occur. A physical body with only certain members functioning is handicapped; even more so a spiritual body, a body of believers. It is beautiful to behold a community of Christians that begins to move in all the spiritual gifts. Truly then there is maximum edification, and God is all the more glorified.

Concern for the spiritual gifts—as I earlier emphasized—is in no sense a self-concern; hence, to desire them eagerly is not a self-centered desire. Zeal for the gifts is anything but a preoccu-

---

[75] The Greek word is *zēloute*; "strive, desire, exert oneself earnestly" (BAGD). RSV and NASB read "earnestly" rather than "eagerly."

[76] The Greek term is *ta pneumatika*, "the spirituals." "Gifts" is supplied in almost every translation (see previous n. 12).

[77] See chapter 7, III.B. "The Gift of the Holy Spirit"; also chapter 11, III.B. "Prayer."

[78] According to Luke 11:13, God gives "the Holy Spirit to those who ask him"; according to Matthew 7:11, God gives "good things [also described as "good gifts" in the same verse] to those who ask him." The parallel is unmistakable.

[79] Indeed, the Corinthian church was exactly that, for Paul later said to them, "You are zealous [literally, "zealots," *zēlōtai*] of spiritual gifts" (1 Cor. 14:12 NASB). One might ask: That being the case, why does Paul urge them to be zealous? The answer is that Paul in 1 Corinthians 14:1 sets the injunction to eagerly desire, hence to be zealous, in the context of following love: "Follow the way of love and eagerly desire . . ." (NIV).

pation with "my needs, my wishes, my pleasures," etc. The concern is essentially altruistic, that is, for other persons. Then Christ, the glorified Lord, may in His Spirit minister through the gifts for the blessing of many. To be sure, there is mutual edification—God intended it to be—but the intention of each and every spiritual gift is not one's own blessing but ministry to the body of believers.

Let us now notice that Paul even earlier wrote, "But eagerly desire[80] the greater gifts"[81] (1 Cor. 12:31 NIV). This injunction suggests a hierarchy of gifts, or at least that some of the *charismata* occupy a higher rank than others. This may seem unusual in light of the fact that Paul later (as we have noted) says simply, "Eagerly desire the spiritual gifts" rather than "the greater gifts." How are we to understand this? Also, since all are gifts of the Holy Spirit, how can one gift be "greater" than another? If such is possible, we may also ask, what are those gifts that are "greater" than others? If such is possible, we may also ask, what are the "greater gifts" that the church is exhorted to strive after?

First, in understanding the relationship between desiring "the greater gifts" (12:31) and desiring "the spiritual gifts" (14:1), we may be sure there is no basic difference. The Christian fellowship is to desire *all* the gifts, whether greater or lesser. Paul probably adds the words in 1 Corinthians 14:1 lest there be some misunderstanding about 1 Corinthians 12:31, namely, that we are to eagerly desire only the greater gifts. We need every spiritual gift that God will give.

Second, one spiritual gift may be greater than another because of its capacity to edify. All are equally gifts of the Holy Spirit and thus have intrinsically the same value. But since the gifts are community oriented and "for the common good," whatever gifts most build up the community are most greatly to be desired. Paul states this clearly in 1 Corinthians 14:12: "Since you are eager to have spiritual gifts,[82] try to excel[83] in gifts that build up the church" (NIV). The greater gifts are clearly those that most edify the community of believers.

Third, Paul does not specify in 1 Corinthians 12:31 what "the greater gifts" are; however, in 1 Corinthians 14:1 after "eagerly desire spiritual gifts," he

---

[80] The Greek word again is *zēloute*. Linguistically this can be either imperative (as above) or indicative: "But you are eagerly desiring" (cf. NIV mg). Bittlinger (*Gifts and Graces,* 73) holds that the indicative is correct in light of 1 Corinthians 14:12 (q.v.). However, by looking further to 1 Corinthians 14:1 where *zēloute* is unquestionably imperative, the imperative translation (as found in KJV, RSV, NASB, NIV, and NEB) seems correct. (For further discussion and confirmation of this, see D. A. Carson, *Showing the Spirit: A Theological Exposition of 1 Corinthians 12–14,* 53–58, and Gordon Fee, *The First Epistle to the Corinthians,* NICNT, 623–35, 654–55).

[81] RSV and NEB have the "higher gifts"; KJV has the "best gifts." The Greek expression is *ta charismata ta meizona. Meizona* is from *megas,* usually translated as "large" or "great." Hence I have followed the NIV (also NASB).

[82] The Greek word is *pneumatōn,* literally "spirits." The word is a bit surprising since Paul up to this point had spoken of *pneumatika* (1 Cor. 12:1; 14:1). Leon Morris suggests that " 'spirits' stresses a little more the 'spirit' character of the gifts" (*1 Corinthians,* TNTC, 190). The RSV translation, "manifestations of the spirit," catches this idea.

[83] Or "seek to abound" (NASB). The Greek phrase is *zēteite hina perisseuēte.* "Try to excel" should not be understood to mean competition with one another for the gifts but rather for all to seek to abound or overflow in edifying gifts.

continues, "especially[84] the gift of prophecy"[85] (NIV). Accordingly, it follows that prophecy is one of "the greater gifts." What else a greater gift might be, Paul does not immediately say. However, it is readily apparent that prophecy belongs in this high category. Thus we can proceed to 1 Corinthians 14:12 and fill in the word "prophecy": "Since you are eager to have spiritual gifts, try to excel in prophecy." For truly prophecy excels in building up the church.[86]

To summarize this section: we are called upon to eagerly desire the spiritual gifts—all of them. Among those gifts are certain excelling ones, including prophecy, that we are especially urged to seek after. None of them are for self-aggrandizement. Even if one receives the gift of prophecy, there is no reason to boast, because the gift is wholly from God and is for the edification of the body and must work in harmony with the other gifts. The important thing is to pray for, seek after, and be zealous for the spiritual gifts that the Lord may move mightily in the midst of His people.

Now it is time to turn our attention, second, to the *relationship between love and the spiritual gifts*. Let us hear again the words of Paul: "Follow the way of [or pursue][87] love and eagerly desire spiritual gifts" (1 Cor. 14:1 NIV). Love should be the way of the gifts: they are to function closely together.

To examine this in more detail, let us again return to 1 Corinthians 12. At the conclusion of this chapter are these words: "But eagerly desire the greater gifts. And now I will show you the most excellent way" (v. 31 NIV). Here as well as later in 1 Corinthians 14:1, the gifts and love are set in close relationship except that "the greater gifts" in 1 Corinthians 12:31 are mentioned before love. Then follows chapter 13, also on the gifts and love, as the connecting

---

[84]The Greek expression is *mallon de* (repeated in v. 5). The KJV translates it "but rather," which gives an adversative sense. Although *mallon de* sometimes carries that connotation (e.g., see Eph. 4:28), it may also have an intensive and supplementary force. Thayer says that it "does not do away with that with which it is in opposition, but marks what has the preference: more willingly, more readily, sooner." Hence, "especially" or "but especially" (NASB). The RSV (like the NIV above) omits the adversative altogether, simply translating it "especially" ("above all" NEB).

[85]Literally, "that you may prophesy" (RSV and NASB).

[86]One further word on Paul's injunction in 1 Corinthians 12:31 to "eagerly desire the greater gifts": It is surely a mistake to look back in chapter 12 and try to discover Paul's meaning. Some persons have tried to identify "the greater gifts" with the first two of the nine *charismata* listed, i.e., "word of wisdom" and "word of knowledge" (v. 8). To be sure, these are gifts, but prophecy is far down the list in sixth place! Paul is clearly *not* setting forth a hierarchy of gifts in verses 8–10; rather, it is the "varieties" (v. 4) of gifts that he is describing. Again, others have attempted identification of "the greater gifts" with "apostles" and "prophets," perhaps also "teachers" (v. 28). This might seem more likely, for, first, Paul had just been talking about apostles, prophets, teachers, etc. (28–30), prior to his statement about desiring the greater gifts (v. 31) and, second, this (unlike vv. 8–10) is definitely a listing according to priorities: "first apostles, second prophets, third teachers, then workers of miracles . . . ." However, Paul cannot be referring to this list for two reasons: first, he speaks of these not as *charismata* but as *appointments*: "God has *appointed* in the church first apostles . . . ," and, second, it is quite foreign to Paul's writing, indeed to the New Testament, to view the offices, or appointments, of apostles, prophets, and teachers as something to be eagerly desired. In the language of Ephesians 4 they are divine *domata*, not charismata, and the sovereign Lord gives these as He wills. Eager desire has *nothing to do* with becoming an apostle or prophet or teacher.

[87]The Greek word is *diōkete*; "run after," "pursue" (BAGD).

link between 1 Corinthians 12:31 and 14:1.

Regarding 1 Corinthians 12:31 it is important to stress, first, that in the following chapter Paul describes the way—"the most excellent way"—wherein all the spiritual gifts are to be exercised. Immediately we must guard against any idea that Paul intends to describe a way better than desiring the *charismata*. Unfortunately, many translations suggest that the way of love is a better way; for example, the Revised Standard Version reads: "I will show you a still more excellent way."[88] The implication in such a translation is that Paul will show a way far better than the spiritual gifts. Incidentally, if such were the case, then the whole question of what are "the greater gifts" becomes moot in light of there being a "still more excellent way" than zeal for the greater gifts. However, a more precise rendering of the Greek text, if nothing else, points in a quite different direction, for it literally reads, "And I now show you *a way beyond measure*."[89] Thus Paul is *not* setting forth here an alternative to desiring the gifts; he does not intend to show something better. Rather, Paul is declaring that he will show a super-excellent way—"a way beyond measure"—wherein the gifts, including "the greater," are to be exercised.[90]

With this understanding of Paul's words, what he has to say in 1 Corinthians 13, the "love" chapter, falls into proper perspective. Verse after verse, from 1 through 13 (the last), Paul describes the way beyond measure of love. All the gifts—tongues (v. 1); prophecy, knowledge, faith (v. 2)—must be exercised in love; else they are noisy, abrasive, and virtually worthless. Hence, the importance of love cannot be exaggerated. Moreover, "love never ends"[91] (v. 8), whereas the gifts will pass away when "the perfect" has come: "as for prophecies, they will pass away; as for tongues, they will cease; as for knowledge,[92] it will pass away. But when the perfect comes, the partial[93] will pass away" (vv. 8, 10). "The perfect"[94] refers to

---

[88] Similarly the NASB has "I show you a still more excellent way"; the KJV reads, "Yet shew I unto you a more excellent way."

[89] The Greek phrase is *kath hyperbolēn hodon*, "beyond measure [or "comparison"] a way." See, e.g., Galatians 1:13—"beyond measure" (KJV, NASB); 2 Corinthians 4:17—"beyond all comparison" (also NASB). Thus the translations "a still more excellent way" and "a more excellent way" are quite misleading. According to EGT, "*kath hyperbolēn* is superlative, not comparative; Paul is not pointing out 'a more excellent way' than that of seeking and using the charisms of chapter xii . . . but 'a super-excellent way' to win them" (2:896). Although I might differ on the last phrase "to win them," EGT is surely right to disregard the comparative idea. BAGD, under κατα, translates *kath hyperbolēn* as "beyond measure," "beyond comparison."

[90] The NIV translation, earlier quoted, "I will show you the most excellent way," avoids the comparative idea. However, the more literal rendering, "a way beyond measure," is preferable.

[91] The Greek word is *piptei*, literally "falls." (See chap. 15, n. 122, for a fuller discussion.)

[92] The knowledge that will pass away is the gift of the "word of knowledge." According to F. F. Bruce, this knowledge is "a manifestation of the Spirit designed for the present requirements of church life" (*1 and 2 Corinthians*, NCBC, 127). Knowledge in a broad sense will, of course, continue. Paul later adds in reference to the future: "Then I shall know fully, even as I am fully known" (v. 12 NIV).

[93] "Partial" is the NASB reading. The Greek phrase is *ek merous*, "in part" (BAGD, under μέρος).

[94] The Greek phrase is *to teleion*. Incidentally, I hardly need to comment on the attempt of

the perfection of the glory to come, for Paul shortly added, "Now we see in a mirror dimly, but then face to face" (v. 12). When we are "face to face" with the majestic glory, tongues, prophecy, and knowledge—indeed all the charismata[95] —will fall away, for they belong to the present age, and will be utterly transcended in the vision of God. So it is that in the glory to come (as Paul reaches his climax), "faith, hope, love abide, these three; but the greatest of these is love" (v. 13).

But to return to our earlier point, Paul is by no means saying that love is a better way than the charismata, hence to be earnestly desired rather than the gifts. To be sure the gifts will some day be no more. But while they are available in our present life, they are much to be desired. However, they *must* be exercised in love if there is to be genuine edification. Thus, it is not at all proper to say that the concern for gifts should be transcended by the pursuit of love. Indeed, as Paul makes his transition into chapter 14 after saying, "the greatest of these is love," he writes (as we have noted): "Follow the way of love and eagerly desire spiritual gifts"

(NIV). It is not either/or but both/and, with love as the way, the way beyond measure, wherein the gifts find their truly meaningful expression.

Again, in regard to chapter 13, we need to mention an additional error sometimes made: that of viewing the greatest of the gifts as love. We have reflected on the mistake of considering love as a way superior to the gifts; but we need also to recognize that love is in no sense the greatest—or "the greater"—of the gifts. Paul does indeed say that "the greatest [literally, "the greater"][96] of these is love"; however, it is apparent that he is not talking about the greatest among the charismata, but the greatest among the triad of faith, hope, and love. Paul is speaking of eternal verities: those realities of faith, hope, and love that "abide" or "remain."[96] He is not referring to gifts that, for all their greatness, pass away in eternity.[98] It should be added that neither here nor elsewhere in the Scriptures is love depicted as a gift, or charism. Rather, it is a *fruit* of the Spirit (Gal. 5:22—the first-mentioned fruit). It is an *effect* of the Holy Spirit's inner presence: "The love of God has been poured out within

---

some biblical interpreters to identify *to teleion* with the completion of the canon of Scripture. Merrill Unger, translating *to teleion* as "the complete," writes, "This passage, by strict adherence to the context, necessitates interpreting the complete thing as the New Testament Scriptures" (*The Baptism and Gifts of the Spirit,* 141–42); Walter Chantry similarly declares, "Tongues will vanish away, knowledge will cease at the time that the New Testament is finished" (*Signs of the Apostles,* 51). See also Douglas Judisch, *An Evaluation of Claims to the Charismatic Gifts,* chapter 4, "The Explicit Testimony of Paul." Such an attempt, which actually is only a device to seek invalidation of any continuation of gifts in the church, is utterly futile. For a good refutation of this view and other related ones, see D. A. Carson, *Showing the Spirit,* 68–72; also note Gordon Fee, *The First Epistle to the Corinthians,* NICNT, 644–45, especially note 23, which includes the words "It is an impossible view, of course, since Paul himself could not have articulated it" [!]).

[95] In 1 Corinthians 13 Paul mentions only prophecies, tongues, and knowledge (i.e., word of knowledge). These are doubtless illustrative of all the spiritual charismata mentioned in 1 Corinthians 12:8–10.

[96] The Greek word is *meizōn*.

[97] The NEB translates the clause as follows: "There are three things that last for ever: faith, hope, and love . . . ."

[98] Faith (*pistis*) uniquely functions both as a gift of the Spirit (see 1 Cor. 12:9) and as one of the eternal verities. Faith as a charism is a special faith for healing, working of miracles, etc. (see the next chapter). The faith that "abides" is eternal faith and trust in the living God.

our hearts through the Holy Spirit who was given to us" (Rom. 5:5 NASB). But love is not a charism. Since love is not a gift, it cannot be one of the "greater gifts" about which Paul wrote.

Incidentally, it is not always recognized that this classic chapter[99] on love is set in the midst of a discussion of the spiritual gifts. Paul writes to those who know the gifts and who are experiencing them. He urges them to earnestly desire the "greater gifts (1 Cor. 12), indeed "spiritual gifts" in general (1 Cor. 14). Chapter 13 is not basically a dissertation by Paul on the Christian life at large, the way of love, and so forth.[100] It is mainly a discourse on the way the gifts are to be exercised. Paul's words, as is apparent from the still larger context, were written to people who did not lack in any spiritual gift but obviously lacked much in love.[101] Hence, the apostle's words are surely applicable to believers today who need to be encouraged to seek after the *charismata* and in their every expression to exhibit the spirit of love.

The message, then, is unmistakable and needs to be heard again and again by those who participate in the spiritual gifts. We can, and should, be grateful that these gifts are reappearing in our time, but with their reappearance there is all the more need to exercise them in love. Otherwise, as with the Corinthians, division, pride, jealousy,[102] and much else can settle in. If—and only

if—the Christian community pursues love, in which such ills may be overcome, will the exercise of gifts prove salutary and zeal for the gifts make for the edification of the body.

EXCURSUS ON THE WORD *CHARISMA*

The word "charismatic" is derived from the Greek word *charisma* (χάρισμα) meaning "a gift of grace" (*charis*—χάρις). The plural form is *charismata* (χαρίσματα), "gifts of grace."

The word, in its singular and plural forms, is found seventeen times in the New Testament. It is almost wholly a Pauline term (the one exception being in 1 Peter) and is largely found in Romans (six times) and 1 Corinthians (seven times). In addition *charisma* occurs one time each in 2 Corinthians and 1 and 2 Timothy.

The word *charisma* or *charismata* is used in reference to:[103]
1. The gift of salvation
   a. Justification: Romans 5:15–16: "The *gift* is not like the trespass . . . the *gift* followed many trespasses and brought justification" (NIV).
   b. Eternal life: Romans 6:23: "The wages of sin is death, but the *gift* of God is eternal life in Christ Jesus our Lord" (NIV).

---

[99] Of course, there is no chapter in the original letter. Unfortunately, the chapter division can easily lead to isolation from the overall context.

[100] This is not to say that the chapter has no relevance to the general Christian walk. Quite the contrary, there is much of great edification (note especially vv. 4–7), regardless of the gifts. But the chapter both begins specifically with the gifts (vv. 1–3) and later continues with them (vv. 8–10). Thus it is clear that however much Paul goes beyond the gifts as he speaks of love, the context is the spiritual *charismata*. Hence, the chapter was written primarily, even directly, to believers who are experiencing the gifts of the Holy Spirit.

[101] See especially 1 Corinthians 1. Whereas Paul expresses his thanksgiving to God that the Corinthians were "not lacking in any gift [*charisma*]" (v. 7), he also later mentions the "quarreling" (v. 11) and divisions among them.

[102] Love is the counter to all such, according to 1 Corinthians 13:4–7.

[103] Each use of the word "gift" or "gifts" below is a form of *charisma* or *charismata*.

2. The gift of particular blessings

a. Israel's special privileges: Romans 11:29: "The *gifts* and the calling of God [to Israel] are irrevocable" (NASB).

b. Marriage and single life: 1 Corinthians 7:7: in discussing the matter of sexual self-control Paul said, "Each man has his own *gift* from God" (NASB).

c. Rescue from mortal danger: 2 Corinthians 1:11: Paul, after speaking of his deliverance by God from physical death, refers to this as a "*gift* bestowed upon us . . ." (KJV).

3. Gifts in reference to the service of others in the community

a. Romans 12:6–8: "We have different *gifts,* according to the grace given us" (NIV). Paul then lists in sequence prophesying, serving, teaching, encouraging (or exhorting), contributing (or liberality), leadership, and showing mercy (NIV and NASB). Also see Romans 1:11.

b. 1 Corinthians 12:4–10: "There are varieties of *gifts,* but the same Spirit" (v. 4). Then Paul lists the gifts of the word of wisdom, the word of knowledge, faith, *gifts* of healing, miracles, prophecy, the distinguishing of spirits, tongues, and the interpretation of tongues (vv. 8–10). Also see verses 28, 30–31.

c. 1 Timothy 4:14 and 2 Timothy 1:6: "Do not neglect the *gift* you have, which was given you by prophetic utterance when the council of elders laid their hands upon you. . . . I remind you to rekindle the *gift* of God that is within you through the laying on of my hands."

d. 1 Peter 4:10–11: "As each has received a *gift,* employ it for one another, as good stewards of God's varied grace: whoever speaks, as one who utters oracles of God; whoever renders service . . . by the strength which God supplies."

It is obvious from this summary that the word *charisma* is used to refer to a wide range of gifts. However, in all their variety each gift represents God's gracious bestowal. Thayer defines χάρισμα as "a gift of grace; a favor which one receives without any merit of his own." The gifts are, and remain, gifts of God's grace.

14

The Ninefold Manifestation

The ninefold manifestation of the Spirit is expressed in nine spiritual gifts. With reference to 1 Corinthians 12:7 ("To each is given the manifestation of the Spirit for the common good") and the gifts listed in 1 Corinthians 12:8–10, we will examine each gift in turn.[1]

It is noteworthy that the first two, word of wisdom and word of knowl-edge, and the last two, various kinds of tongues and the interpretation of tongues, are closely connected. The first two are word (*logos*) gifts; the last two deal with tongues. In between are five other gifts. The two-five-two group-ings quite likely represent different ca-tegories of gifts.[2] We will follow them in sequence.[3]

---

[1] Paul does not say that the nine gifts he lists are the *only* gifts of the Holy Spirit. It is quite possible that the Holy Spirit manifests Himself through other gifts. Thus the list may be exemplary rather than inclusive. However, since Paul speaks of the gifts as "*the* manifestation of the Spirit" and, after listing the gifts, says, "one and the same Spirit works all these things, distributing to each one individually just as He wills" (v. 11 NASB), I will operate within the confines of the nine gifts.

[2] The two-five-two groupings are connected by the Greek word *heteros*, "another." Thus the text reads, "to another [*heterō*] faith," "to another [*heterō*] various kinds of tongues." Between all the other gifts the word *allos* with *de* is found, e.g., between word of wisdom and word of knowledge—"and to another [*allō de*] the word of knowledge," between faith and gifts of healing—"and to another [*allō de*] gifts of healing," etc. Because the word *heteros* is used to connect the two-five-two groupings, this may be Paul's way of suggesting a transition to a different category of gifts. As EGT, in loco, puts it, "The third (faith) and eighth (tongues) . . . indicate points of transition . . . from one sort of endowment to another." (It could be argued that *heteros* and *allos* refer more directly to persons than to gifts; however, gifts may be implied since Paul's concern here is primarily with the various manifestations, or gifts, of the Holy Spirit.) ICC states, "The change to ἑτέρῳ may be made merely to break the intolerable monotony of ἄλλῳ eight times in succession," but then adds: "Nevertheless, if we take each as marking a new division, we get an intelligible result . . ." (*1 Corinthians*, 265). The result will be discussed later. Godet (*Commentary on First Corinthians*, 622) and Lenski (*Interpretation of First and Second Corinthians*, 499) write similarly. Conzelmann (*1 Corinthians*, 209) briefly speaks of the same things.

[3] Quite commonly, particularly in Pentecostal and charismatic expositions, Paul's sequence is somewhat altered by organizing groups of three: to word of wisdom and word of

INTRODUCTION: WORD OF WISDOM AND WORD OF KNOWLEDGE

"For to one is given the word of wisdom [*logos sophias*] through the Spirit, and to another the word of knowledge [*logos gnōseōs*] according to the same Spirit" (1 Cor. 12:8 NASB).

Since the Holy Spirit is "the Spirit of truth" (John 14:17; 15:26; 16:13), both "word of wisdom" and "word of knowledge" are expressions of the truth made known through Him.

Word of wisdom and word of knowledge manifested by the Holy Spirit draw on the treasure that is to be found in Jesus Christ, "in whom are hid all the treasures of wisdom and knowledge" (Col. 2:3).

Ultimately, both word of wisdom and word of knowledge are from God Himself.[4] They are not the expression of ordinary wisdom and knowledge (as will be shown later), even of the most enlightened kind, but emanate from a higher source. Both are the result of divine illumination;[5] neither is attainable by the human mind. They originate beyond all human capacity.

Word of wisdom and word of knowledge involve the mind. Although both gifts stem from divine illumination, the mind is not bypassed. In word of wisdom and word of knowledge the mind is fully functioning.[6]

The two gifts are gifts of speaking. *Logos* may be translated as "utterance,"[7] hence, utterance of wisdom and utterance of knowledge. The gifts are not wisdom and knowledge, but speaking or uttering wisdom and knowledge. Wisdom and knowledge are the contents of the gift; however, the gift itself is not wisdom or knowledge, but the declaration thereof.[8] In that case, the gift may be called oracular utterance.[9]

---

knowledge is added distinguishing of spirits; prophecy is added to tongues and interpretation of tongues; faith, gifts of healing, and effecting of miracles are retained in that order. Such groupings are done perhaps for symmetry (three-three-three is neater than two-five-two!) but also because of the way in which some of the gifts are viewed. I will comment on this later. It seems better to me to follow Paul's own order rather than some other pattern. Ray Hubbard puts it bluntly: "The arrangement on which to work is the two, five, two, division, given by the Spirit" (*Gifts of Grace*, 41). In any event, I believe that as we proceed the advantage of viewing the gifts seriatim will become increasingly clear.

[4] According to Proverbs 2:6, "the LORD gives wisdom; from his mouth come knowledge and understanding."

[5] "We are not speaking of a wisdom or knowledge attained gradually by practice and faith but of a condition proceeding from higher illumination" (Hermann Olshausen, *First and Second Corinthians*, 195).

[6] This is unlike the gifts of prophecy, tongues, and interpretation. See later discussion.

[7] As in RSV; NIV has "message." According to Thayer, *logos* may refer to speaking or thinking. He adds in regard to speaking that it is "a word, yet not in the grammatical sense . . . but language, *vox*, i.e. a word which, uttered by the living voice, embodies a conception or idea."

[8] "It is the discourse, not the wisdom or knowledge that is behind it, that is the spiritual gift" (C. K. Barrett, *The First Epistle to the Corinthians*, HNTC, 284–85). "The *word* of wisdom is the gift of speaking or communicating wisdom; and the *word* of knowledge is the gift of speaking or communicating knowledge" (C. H. Hodge, *An Exposition of the First Epistle to the Corinthians*, 245).

[9] Peter writes, "As each has received a gift [*charisma*], employ it for one another, as good stewards of God's varied grace: whoever speaks, as one who utters oracles [*logia*] of God" (1 Peter 4:10–11). "Oracles" (also the KJV translation of *logia*) refers to divine utterances given through a charismatic gift. BAGD describes *logia* in 1 Peter 4 as "the utterances of

Finally, since "word" in both cases is without the definite article, reference is made to a particular disclosure of wisdom or knowledge. It is an utterance of some aspect of divine truth in a given situation.

I. WORD OF WISDOM

"Word of wisdom" is listed first in the two *logos* gifts, for the utterance of wisdom is of fundamental importance to ministry in the body. Wisdom operates on the level of deep understanding; hence, its utterance can bring much edification to others.

Earlier in his letter to the Corinthians Paul has much to say about the utterance of wisdom.[10] For example, he declares that Christ sent him "to preach the gospel—not with words of human wisdom,[11] lest the cross of Christ be emptied of its power" (1 Cor. 1:17 NIV). The clear implication is that the words in his preaching were not derived from his own wisdom but came from another source, namely the Holy Spirit. Paul says much the same thing about his proclamation to the Corinthians: "When I came to you, brethren, I did not come proclaiming to you the testimony of God in lofty words[12] of wisdom. For I decided to know nothing among you except Jesus Christ and him crucified" (2:1–2). Hence Paul, in proclaiming the gospel, spoke words of

spiritual wisdom without high-flown eloquence.

We may next observe that Paul denies any attempt on his part to use persuasion in his speech: "My message [*logos*] and my preaching were not in persuasive words of wisdom, but in demonstration of the Spirit and of power"[13] (1 Cor. 2:4 NASB). They were "words of wisdom" that did not issue from a human attempt to persuade. Rather, they came from the Holy Spirit—His "demonstration" or "making manifest."[14] They were the manifestation of the Holy Spirit.

Thus when Paul elaborates the gifts, or the manifestation of the Spirit, in 1 Corinthians 12, he is declaring that such spiritual utterance is one of the distributions of the Holy Spirit. There is no suggestion that only Paul himself spoke such a word of wisdom; rather, "to *one* [without specification] is given through the Spirit the utterance of wisdom." A person who so speaks will, like Paul, not depend on human wisdom, eloquence, or persuasiveness but wholly on the inspiration of the Holy Spirit.

Next we note that although the gift itself lies in the utterance of wisdom, it is not to be supposed that such wisdom belongs to the present order of things. Paul had earlier declared, "Has not God made foolish the wisdom of the world?" (1 Cor. 1:20). God's wisdom,

---

those Christians gifted w. the charisma of the word." TDNT speaks of these *logia* as "the words and statements spoken by the charismatic" (4:139).

[10]Notice especially chapters 1–3, where the word "wisdom" (or "wise," "wiser") occurs twenty-five times. Quite often it is the utterance of wisdom that Paul has in mind. Incidentally, it is important to turn to Paul's own writing, especially 1 Corinthians, to discover what he means by "word of wisdom." There can be much wasted, even misdirected, energy in beginning elsewhere.

[11]Literally, "in wisdom of speech," *en sophia logou*.

[12]Literally, "in excellence of speech," *hyperochēn logou*.

[13]Donald Gee, after quoting Paul's words about "demonstration of the Spirit and power," comments: "Note carefully that he is not saying that his preaching was *accompanied* by such demonstrations; it was in itself just such a demonstration. It manifested the Spirit of God in action through the speaker" (*Spiritual Gifts in the Work of the Ministry Today*, 23).

[14]The Greek word is *apodeixei*; in addition to "demonstration" it also contains the meaning of "a making manifest, showing forth" (Thayer).

Paul adds, which is folly to the world, is "Christ crucified, a stumbling block to Jews and folly to Gentiles" (v. 23). Paul later says, "We do impart [or "speak" NIV, NASB] wisdom, although it is not a wisdom of this age or of the rulers of this age. . . . But we impart a secret and hidden wisdom of God, which God decreed before the ages for our glorification" (1 Cor. 2:6–7).

Such declarations of Paul underscore the point that the wisdom referred to is not a wisdom of this world/age, but a hidden wisdom that focuses essentially on Jesus Christ, the crucified Lord.

Hence, a word of wisdom is in some way an explication of the mystery of God that centers in Jesus Christ. Paul also speaks of Christ Himself as our wisdom: ". . . Christ Jesus, whom God made our wisdom" (1 Cor. 1:30). Accordingly, that which speaks of Christ, particularly the wonder of the cross, is an utterance or word of wisdom. Such a word is spoken out of the mystery of God and glorifies Jesus Christ.

Now we take the next step and observe that the wisdom uttered is itself a result of revelation from the Holy Spirit. Paul proceeds to say: " 'What no eye has seen, nor ear heard, nor the heart of man conceived . . .' God has revealed to us through the Spirit" (1 Cor. 2:9–10). Although the "to us" refers primarily to Paul, it may also include other believers.[15] In other words, although the primary and authoritative revelation of God's mystery was given to the apostle Paul, other believers through the Holy Spirit may likewise receive revelation[16] and out of such revelation declare the truth of God. Such an utterance, accordingly, is a word of wisdom.

It is also of interest and significance that immediately following his statement in 1 Corinthians 2:9–10, Paul adds, "For the Spirit searches everything, even the depths of God" (v. 10). The Holy Spirit plumbs "the deep things"[17] of God, searches out profound mysteries, and through revelation makes these available to believers.[18] Hence, those who so receive them will be able, as the Holy Spirit wills, to proclaim them to others.

We may now turn to Paul's letter to the Ephesians where the apostle prays, ". . . that the God of our Lord Jesus Christ, the Father of glory, may give you a spirit of wisdom and of revelation in the knowledge of him" (1:17).[19]

---

[15] Leon Morris, commenting on "to us" (KJV—"unto us") of verse 10, says: "*Unto us*, believers, great things have been revealed" (italics his) (*The First Epistle of Paul to the Corinthians*, TNTC, 57). Similarly, F. W. Grosheide writes that "in this verse Paul states . . . what God has given to believers" (*The First Epistle to the Corinthians*, NICNT, 67). However, the primary revelation was surely to Paul.

[16] Paul speaks later about such revelation in 1 Corinthians 14:26: "What then, brethren? When you come together, each one has a hymn, a lesson [or "a teaching" NASB], a revelation, a tongue, or an interpretation." Cf. Philippians 3:15: "God will reveal that also to you."

[17] The Greek word *bathē* may be translated either as "depths" or "deep things" (Thayer).

[18] According to Robertson and Plummer, "the *logos sophias* ["word of wisdom"] is discourse which expounds the mysteries of God's counsels and makes known the way of salvation" (*I Corinthians*, ICC, 265).

[19] Paul wrote these words to people who had been "sealed with the promised Holy Spirit" (v. 13)—hence had received the Holy Spirit, the "Spirit of truth"—that they might be further gifted with "a spirit of wisdom and revelation" in the knowledge of God. According to EGT, in loco: "What Paul prays for on behalf of these Ephesian converts is that God might continue to bestow upon them the gift of His Holy Spirit already imparted to them, and that to the effect both of making them wise to understand the things of His grace and of disclosing to them more of the mysteries of His kingdom."

Paul's prayer implies that the believer does not automatically receive spiritual wisdom and revelation; such is a gift of God. This additionally suggests that the primary matter in a word of wisdom is not the utterance itself, but openness and receptivity to the wisdom God gives. Out of such revealed wisdom (and only where there is that wisdom) can there be a true word of wisdom.

Hence, we need to stress that he who speaks a word of wisdom is, first of all, one who is operating under the revelation of the Holy Spirit. This means more than a knowledge of Scripture; more than a knowledge of the facts of Christ's life, death, and resurrection; even more than a personal experience of salvation. It means, in addition to all that has been mentioned, that the Holy Spirit who has now come searches the divine depths and increasingly makes known those depths. Paul, immediately following his words about "a spirit of wisdom and revelation in the knowledge of Him," adds, "having the eyes of your hearts ["inward eyes" NEB] enlightened" (Eph. 1:18). It is this illumination of the inmost self to the level of depth understanding[20] that the Holy Spirit, the Searcher of the depths of the Godhead, brings about the wisdom of God. It is *this* wisdom, or some aspect of it, that when spoken forth is the charismatic gift of the Holy Spirit.

Such wisdom is primarily and most profoundly Jesus Christ in whom are hid all the treasures of wisdom and knowledge, for it is "Christ Jesus whom God made our wisdom." The more that is revealed to us by the Spirit about Christ, especially relating to the central mystery of the cross, the more wisdom

we will have to speak to others as the Spirit wills.

Now a further word in regard to the Scriptures: first, since they record the life of Jesus Christ, one who speaks a word of wisdom will be grounded in them. Since the Scriptures testify of Christ,[21] whatever is said in an utterance of wisdom will be in total accord with the written testimony. Second, the one who speaks will do so under the illumination of the Holy Spirit. Since the Scriptures are inspired ("God-breathed")[22] by the Holy Spirit, it is that same Spirit who alone is able to convey proper understanding. Hence a word of wisdom under the Spirit's illumination can bring a true apprehension of the scriptural meaning. Third, a word of wisdom may also go beyond the illumination of scriptural words into a particular revelation of the One to whom Scriptures bear witness. In this case it will be a word from the Holy Spirit that will provide some specific insight into the truth of God, of Christ. It will not add any supposedly new truth beyond Scripture and surely will contradict nothing contained in Scripture, but because of the plenitude of the Spirit's operation it will provide a fuller or deeper apprehension of some truth to which Scripture bears witness. A word of wisdom, accordingly, will be spoken by one who, in Paul's words, has been granted "a spirit of wisdom and revelation." The Holy Spirit illuminates "the eyes of the heart," out of which enlightenment and depth of understanding may break forth in the word of wisdom.

I need also to emphasize that the revelation that stands behind a word of wisdom is altogether secondary to the revelation that Paul, for example, re-

---

[20]The Greek word translated "hearts," *kardias,* may also be rendered "understanding" (so KJV).

[21]". . . the scriptures . . . bear witness to me" (John 5:39).

[22]According to 2 Timothy 3:16, "All scripture is inspired by God . . . ," literally, "God-breathed" (*theopneustos*).

ceived. Paul as an apostle occupied the position (with other apostles and prophets) of receiving the primary revelation concerning many mysteries of the gospel. Paul spoke of a mystery concerning the hardening of Israel (Rom. 11:25–26); he declared that he and other apostles were "stewards of the mysteries of God" (1 Cor. 4:1); he affirmed vigorously, "Lo! I tell you a mystery!" in regard to the translation and resurrection of believers (1 Cor. 15:51). And he stated that a mystery was made known to him personally: "the mystery was made known to me by revelation" being also "revealed to his holy apostles and prophets by the Spirit," namely, that "the Gentiles are fellow heirs" (Eph. 3:3, 5–6).[23] The primary revelation was given to Paul and the other apostles and prophets; all other subsequent revelation is subordinate[24] to it.

But having emphasized this primacy of apostolic revelation, we note again that others may receive revelation. I have already mentioned 1 Corinthians 14:26 and Ephesians 1:17 (also 1 Cor. 2:10 is a possible example). Paul spoke further in Colossians 1:26 of "the mystery hidden for ages and generations but now made manifest to his saints."[25] Behind this manifestation to believers stands the office of Paul "to make the word of God fully known" (v. 25, hence again the priority is with the apostle), but there is also manifestation[26] to the saints. Then in Colossians 2:2–3 Paul expressed earnest desire for

both Colossians and Laodiceans that "their hearts may be encouraged as they are knit together in love, to have all the riches of assured understanding and the knowledge of God's mystery, of Christ, in whom are hid all the treasures of wisdom and knowledge." The Colossians and Laodiceans did not already have this assured understanding and knowledge of "God's mystery"; rather, Paul's prayer is that they might get it. To have such would be to know God's mystery and this means revelation.[27]

Our discussion brings us to the point that a word or utterance of wisdom, as a "manifestation of the Spirit" (1 Cor. 12:7), is based on revelation. There is first of all the apprehension of some aspect of God's mystery in Jesus Christ; this occurs through the revelation of the Spirit. Then there is the speaking forth of that revelation in which the mystery is made manifest. By this the Holy Spirit, who is the revealer of mystery, manifests Himself through the spoken word. This, accordingly, is a word of wisdom.

It is apparent that the word of wisdom occupies a high place among the manifestations of the Spirit. For it signifies the speaking forth of a revealing word that centers in Jesus Christ. While it is a mental operation, it is more than a merely rational utterance because it involves deep things that only spiritual eyes and hearts can apprehend. Also it adds nothing to Scripture but exposes some depth or height of what Scripture attests. But when such a word is spoken

---

[23] Later in Ephesians Paul also speaks of the mystery concerning Christ and His church (5:32). For the subject of mystery primarily related to Paul's ministry, also see 1 Corinthians 2:7; Ephesians 1:9; 3:9; 6:19; and Colossians 4:3.

[24] For a brief discussion of "subordinate revelation" see vol. 1, chapter 2, 43–44.

[25] "Saints," of course, refers to believers ("God's people" NEB).

[26] The Greek word for "made manifest" (above) is *ephanerōthē*, the verbal form of *phanerōsis* used by Paul in relation to "the manifestation of the Spirit" in 1 Corinthians 12:7.

[27] A mystery can be disclosed only by revelation. E.g., recall Paul's words in Ephesians 3:3: "The mystery was made known to me by revelation." (Also see vol. 1, chapter 2, 32–33.)

through the Spirit, the Spirit certainly manifests Himself and all who hear this word are truly blessed.

Finally, a few other comments: A word of wisdom does not depend on one's being either a wise person or a persuasive speaker. Concerning the former, in the same letter where Paul spoke of someone uttering a word of wisdom (1 Cor. 12:8), he earlier said, "Not many of you were wise according to worldly standards" (1 Cor. 1:26). "Not many" implies that some were wise, but whether one is naturally wise or not is basically irrelevant. For, as Paul adds shortly after that, it is Christ Jesus "whom God made our wisdom" (v. 30).

Hence, to be grounded in Christ as a person, to truly know "Christ and him crucified, " to be given "a spirit of wisdom and revelation in the knowledge of him"—these are the things that really count. A naturally wise person may actually be blocked from this true wisdom because of pride in his or her own wisdom and utilization of worldly insight and judgment in approaching things of faith. On the other hand, a naturally wise person or one who has grown in wisdom through much study and experience may also receive this wisdom in a "mystery" if humbly open to it. In the latter case, God may mightily use him (as He did Paul the scholar); but he can also use the uneducated, the "common person" (as represented by Peter).

In regard to being a persuasive speaker, a word of wisdom clearly does not depend on this either. As we have observed, Paul vigorously emphasized that his speech was "not in persuasive words of wisdom." Paul made no claim to being an orator; moreover, there were those who found his speech "contemptible."[28] The important thing, however, was not persuasive oratory, which could have stood in the way of truly spiritual utterance, but words spoken through the enabling of the Holy Spirit. The persuasion thereby was totally from the Spirit of God and not from human eloquence. So it remains to this day. The speech may be far more "contemptible"[29] than that of Paul; but if the words are inspired by the Holy Spirit, they may verily proclaim the wisdom of God.

A final comment: "Word of wisdom" is particularly needed in the preaching ministry of the church. We may here recall Paul's statement that he was sent by Christ "to preach the gospel—not with words of human wisdom" (1 Cor. 1:17 NIV). Preaching, or proclamation, that sets forth Christ under the anointing of the Spirit is the utterance of spiritual wisdom. We may think particularly of the pastoral function of ministering the word in a local congregation, where preaching may indeed be the occasion for a word of wisdom. The fact that much preaching is little more than an exercise in human wisdom and oratorical skill ought not to derogate from the fact that preaching can also be and often is so anointed by the Holy Spirit that wisdom from God is proclaimed.[30]

---

[28] Paul quotes others as saying about him: "His letters are weighty and strong, but his personal presence is unimpressive, and his speech contemptible" (2 Cor. 10:10 NASB).

[29] We should not make too much of the word "contemptible" in relation to Paul's speech. For, as is elsewhere shown, he could stand before an Athenian audience that included philosophers and draw careful attention (Acts 17:22–34). We may recall also that Festus and King Agrippa (Acts 26) were impressed with Paul's "great learning" (v. 24) and persuasive ability (v. 28).

[30] See Donald Gee, *Spiritual Gifts in the Work of the Ministry Today,* chapter 2, "Spiritual Gifts for Preaching and Teaching," where, for example, Gee says, "At the heart of such

The important matter concerning word of wisdom is that both the wisdom and the utterance come from the Holy Spirit. Whether in a more formal preaching situation or simply in a gathering of believers for mutual edification, the Holy Spirit may so move upon a person as to impart depth-understanding to a truth of the gospel. As He speaks this forth, a word of wisdom is truly being exercised.[31]

II. WORD OF KNOWLEDGE

"Word of knowledge" is listed second in the two *logos* gifts and in close conjunction with word of wisdom. Paul elsewhere links wisdom and knowledge, and in the same order. In this connection we may again recall Paul's words in regard to Christ as One "in whom are hid all the treasures of wisdom and knowledge" (Col. 2:3). Also

Paul says in Romans: "O the depth of the riches and wisdom and knowledge of God!" (11:33). Wisdom *and* knowledge—and in that order. Further, each is a gift of the Holy Spirit: a word of wisdom "*through* the Spirit," a word of knowledge "*according to* the same Spirit" (1 Cor. 12:8).

In regard to the speaking or utterance—hence, word—of knowledge, we turn again to 1 Corinthians 2. Paul writes, "Now we have received, not the spirit of the world, but the Spirit who is from God, that we might know the things freely given to us by God, which things we also speak, not in words taught by human wisdom, but in those taught by the Spirit" (vv. 12–13 NASB). Three things are said here: first, there is the background of the reception of the Spirit;[32] second, thereby are known the

---

ministries there can sometimes be a supernatural operation of the Spirit that adds something that lifts them to a truly Pentecostal level" (37–38),

[31] Some Pentecostals and charismatics see other aspects in "word of wisdom." Arnold Bittlinger, a Lutheran charismatic, begins his presentation of "the word of wisdom" thus: "In a difficult or dangerous situation a word of wisdom may be given which resolves the difficulty or silences the opponent" (*Gifts and Graces,* 28). As an illustration of the former, Bittlinger discusses first Solomon's word to two women, each of whom claimed a certain living child as her own (1 Kings 3:16–28) and, in regard to the second, the words of Jesus to a trick question about tribute to Caesar (Luke 20:20–26). Bittlinger then adds a third category to word of wisdom, namely, a word spoken by a Christian in an adversarial situation (e.g., Luke 12:11–12). My reply is that I do not question that such situations represent the expression of supernatural wisdom; however, they hardly seem to represent what Paul was talking about nor the community context for a word of wisdom. The late Pentecostal teacher Harold Horton takes a still more extreme position: "The Word of Wisdom is the revelation of the Purpose of God concerning people, things or events in the *future* or looking to the future" (*The Gifts of the Spirit,* 57). Horton misses both the point that a word of wisdom is a gift of utterance stemming *from* revelation (indeed he adds, "it is not a gift of utterance but of revelation" [58]) and that the word basically relates to Jesus Christ. It is unfortunate that Bittlinger and Horton, among some others, have not first turned to Paul for insight into what he means.

At the other extreme is the quite limited view that word of wisdom is something like advice or practical instruction. In the popular Living Bible 1 Corinthians 12:8a is paraphrased, "To one person the Spirit gives the ability to give wise advice." C. K. Barrett, speaking from an Old Testament perspective, suggests that word of wisdom is possibly "a practical discourse, consisting mainly of ethical instruction and exhortation" (*The First Epistle to the Corinthians,* 285). Such views, whether in popular paraphrase or scholarly language, scarcely do justice to the basic biblical meaning.

Truly in both charismatic and noncharismatic circles there is often need for a more perceptive biblical understanding in this regard.

[32] Grosheide writes in regard to the reception of the Spirit: "The reference is here to

things God has given; and third, these things are spoken in words the Spirit teaches. Hence, they will be "according to," that is, in accordance with, the Spirit's teaching. This clearly is Paul's own example of a word of knowledge.

Let us examine Paul's statement more closely. First of all, for a word of knowledge to occur there must be the prior reception of the Holy Spirit. This, of course, is true of all the gifts of the Holy Spirit; the gift of the Spirit precedes the gifts. Second, Paul deals here in the realm of knowledge of "the things" God has graciously given. Accordingly, reference is made to knowledge of the wide range of blessings[33] that God has bestowed on us in Jesus Christ. Third, out of the knowledge of these things, and in words taught by the Holy Spirit, we then speak.[34] It is this third stage that, strictly speaking, is a word of knowledge. Not until the speaking occurs is the gift of a word of knowledge made manifest.

Now looking specifically at the occurrence of a word of knowledge: the words are those taught by the Holy Spirit. This further suggests that the message comes forth in the form of

teaching. So Paul continues by saying, ". . . interpreting spiritual truths to those who possess the Spirit" (1 Cor. 2:13 RSV),[35] i.e., truths about God's blessings in Spirit-taught words.

The matter of knowledge is critical because the gift is a word of *knowledge*. Here we recall Paul's words about "having the eyes of your hearts enlightened." After making this statement Paul adds, "that you may know what is the hope to which he has called you, what are the riches of his glorious inheritance in the saints, and what is the immeasurable greatness of his power in[36] us who believe" (Eph. 1:18–19). This describes believers'[37] knowledge of both future and present blessings. To know such hope, such riches, such power surely provides abundant background for their declaration to others. Hence, we may say that the more fully such blessings are known, the more opportunity there is for a word of knowledge to be spoken.

The knowledge just referred to is the knowledge of an enlightened mind: "that you may know . . . ." It is more than a knowledge to be gained from even the most thorough biblical study;

Pentecost. . . . What is meant is not the perpetual indwelling of the Spirit in the congregation but the historical fact of his coming" (*First Epistle to the Corinthians,* NICNT, 70).

[33]RSV translates "the things" as "the gifts." However, the Greek word is simply *ta*, literally, "the things." "Gifts" as a translation might suggest only spiritual gifts (*charismata*). Paul, rather, is thinking of the manifold things, hence blessings, we have in Christ. NEB vividly translates: ". . . all that God of his own grace has given us."

[34]J. D. G. Dunn writes that against the background of 1 Corinthians 2:12 this denotes "some charismatic insight into 'the things given us by God' . . . that is, some understanding of the relationship of God to the believer(s), some recognition of the charismatic dimension . . . to the believer's life individually or as a community" (*Jesus and the Spirit,* 219). In chapter 10, "The Mission of the Holy Spirit," I dealt with the words about speaking (v. 13) in terms of Paul himself. However, it is also the case (as I am now saying) that the phrase "which things we also speak" refers to others who have likewise received the Holy Spirit ("we have received . . . the Spirit" includes both Paul and others). Paul's word (the apostolic word) is alway primary and normative for our speaking but by no means eliminates our own utterance (or word) of knowledge.

[35]Or "combining spiritual thoughts with spiritual words" (NASB). See chapter 10, n. 26.

[36]Or "toward" (NASB). The Greek word is *eis*.

[37]For a valuable discussion of this, see *The Gifts of the Holy Spirit* by C. R. Vaughan, chapter 2, entitled "Gift of Peculiar Knowledge or Intuition to Believers."

it is a deeper knowledge, which, while based on such study, is brought directly to the human mind by the Holy Spirit.[38] A word of knowledge, accordingly, is an utterance stemming from this spiritual illumination.

It is interesting that Paul speaks of the Corinthians as a people abundantly blessed: "In every way you were enriched in him [Christ] with all speech [or utterance] and all knowledge" (1 Cor. 1:5). Their knowledge was not limited nor was there any limitation on its expression; a word of knowledge could therefore readily occur. This does not mean that the Corinthians were a profoundly spiritual church, for they were not.[39] But insofar as knowledge and utterance were concerned, they were amply equipped. A word of knowledge could be spoken at any time through the Spirit in the gathered assembly of believers.

Paul speaks similarly of the Romans. They were a people "full of goodness, filled with all knowledge" and, he adds, "able to instruct one another" (Rom. 15:14).[40] People so abundantly endowed with knowledge are thus qualified to teach one another.[41] Such teaching is an utterance, a word of knowledge.

Hence, a word of knowledge is essentially an inspired word of teaching or instruction that occurs within the context of the gathered community. To be sure, there are also those who hold the office of teacher and thus have a unique place in giving instruction. However, the gift of a word of knowledge is that which is expressed from within the community itself. Perhaps nowhere is this put more vividly than in Paul's words to the Colossians: "Let the word of Christ dwell in you richly, as you teach and admonish [or "instruct"[42]] one another in all wisdom" (3:16). It is apparent that Paul here refers to mutual teaching and admonishment. The background is not the office of teacher but the word of Christ indwelling "richly."[43] With the word of Christ so indwelling believers, there can be beneficial teaching of one another.[44]

Yet, I must immediately add, this gift is not just mutual teaching. It is, in addition, a special impartation of teaching that is given by the Holy Spirit through a particular person. It is the speaking of inspired knowledge, an articulation of truth, that in its very utterance edifies the gathered body of believers. The Holy Spirit enables the one who so speaks to declare truth in a

---

[38] Biblical study is essential, for through such study the Holy Spirit may bring this deeper knowledge. My point is that the study of Scripture in itself without the activity of the Spirit can bring no true enlightenment.

[39] As Paul says later, "I, brethren, could not address you as spiritual men, but as men of the flesh, as babes in Christ" (1 Cor. 3:1).

[40] I earlier quoted this verse with emphasis on the Romans' being "filled with all knowledge" (chap. 10, I, "Guide Into Truth"). Here I am stressing the second part of the verse: "able to instruct one another."

[41] This by no means eliminates the office of teacher (see, e.g., Eph. 4:11), or teaching as a particular charisma of God's grace (see, e.g., Rom. 12:7). Nonetheless all are "able to instruct one another."

[42] As in Romans 15:14. The same Greek word, *noutheteō*, is used in both Romans 15:14 and Colossians 3:16.

[43] The "word of Christ" indwelling "richly" is doubtless a parallel to the Spirit's infilling. In Ephesians 5:18 Paul writes, "Be filled with the Spirit" and shortly after adds in verses 19–20 many of the same, or similar, words to those found in Colossians 3:16–17.

[44] I. Howard Marshall writes in another context that "Christians possessed by the Spirit give one another mutual instruction, without which no single individual can appreciate the whole of God's truth" (*The Epistles of John,* NICNT, 163).

way totally beyond his own natural capacity or experience. The words, while being framed by the mind of the speaker, spring from a higher source. Accordingly, they are oracular utterances.[45]

Such a word of knowledge will often, as we have seen, relate to God's blessings. We may here again recall Paul's statement about "the things freely given to us by God." To know these and to express them in particular ways and at particular moments is truly the utterance of knowledge. However, the important matter is the conveyance of God's truth whatever its nature—the "things" of God in any aspect—in such a manner as to make them clearly known.[46]

How, we may finally inquire, do word of wisdom and word of knowledge relate to each other? Obviously they are closely connected as gifts of utterance and both have to do with the truth of God. The gifts, consequently, are sometimes difficult to distinguish. However, from what has been said it is apparent that word of wisdom has more to do with the speaking forth of the central mysteries of Christian faith. Such mysteries are disclosed to the enlightened mind and heart; hence there stems from it a depth of understanding and declaration. All of this occurs through the activity of the Holy Spirit. Word of knowledge likewise is concerned about the truth of God but operates more in terms of articulation. It is the knowledge of a spiritually enlightened mind that, in correspondence therewith, clearly sets forth the truth for others to understand. It is utterance stemming from inspired knowledge.

Again, word of wisdom refers to the essential truth of God wrought into man's inmost self: his heart, his spirit. The communication of that truth through the mind speaks profoundly to the hearts and spirits of those who hear. Word of knowledge may relate to the same truth or similar truths (such as God's varied blessings); but in it the truth is intellectually apprehended, objectified, and set forth. What occurs in a word of wisdom "*through* the Spirit" is expounded "*according to* the same Spirit" in a word of knowledge. Word of knowledge makes the things of God understandable to His people.

Both gifts are spiritual manifesta-

---

[45]Recall note 9 on 1 Peter 4:10–11.

[46]According to a popular understanding of "the word of knowledge," such "things of God" relate particularly to hidden facts within the human situation, for example, that someone has a certain disease, that a lost article may be found in such and such a place, etc. This would be supernaturally revealed information rather than teaching or instruction. The background for such information is often that of a vision or picture that is given the one who is to declare the information. In the Old Testament "the seer" (hence, a man of vision) might see into a situation as common as one in which animals are lost and he would know their location (e.g., the location of Saul's father's lost donkeys, which Samuel "the seer" perceived [1 Sam. 9:3–10:2]). In the New Testament, e.g., Jesus declared to the Samaritan woman, without her telling Him, that she had had five husbands and that the one she was then living with was not her husband (John 4:16–18). To this the woman replied, "Sir, I perceive that you are a prophet" (v. 19). Both of these examples (and many others could be added) demonstrate the activity of a seer/prophet who truly does perceive and declare hidden things. But they are not as such the speaking of a word of knowledge. Stanley Horton has put it well: "God did give knowledge of facts through visions and in various other ways, but there is absolutely no indication in the Bible that the gift of a word of knowledge is meant to bring revelation of where to find lost articles or of what disease or sin a person may be suffering with" (*What the Bible Says about the Holy Spirit*, 272–73). By no means do we discount the importance of such God-given knowledge of facts. The only point here is that to speak of that kind of knowledge as a "word of knowledge" is a mistake.

tions. Whereas the gift of a word of wisdom is more related to the preacher and a word of knowledge to the teacher, neither preaching nor teaching as such is the manifestation of the Spirit. Both depend on the anointing of the Holy Spirit through revelation and enlightenment. Moreover, the two gifts may be apportioned by the Spirit in a given situation to those who occupy neither an official preaching nor an official teaching position. The Holy Spirit distributes "as he wills" (1 Cor. 12:11); hence anyone in the assembly of believers may be used by God to declare His truth.

Finally, we rejoice that all gifts relate to Jesus Christ. Since in Him are "hid all the treasures of wisdom and knowledge," both word of wisdom and word of knowledge will exhibit some aspect of that treasure. Unto Him be all praise and glory!

III. FAITH

Faith is next listed as a manifestation or gift of the Holy Spirit—"to another faith [*pistis*]" (1 Cor. 12:9). It may be called "special faith."[47] Such faith is to be differentiated from both "saving faith" and "fruit faith," the former

referring to the faith through which a person comes to salvation,[48] and the latter to faith as a fruit of the Holy Spirit in the believer's life.[49] The gift of faith is rather a special impartation of faith by the Spirit that is for the good of others—"the common good." Moreover, it is granted to a particular individual: "to another [is given] faith."

Faith as a gift of the Spirit is the first of a series of gifts that operate in distinction from the mind.[50] These gifts—faith, gifts of healing, effecting of miracles, prophecy, and distinguishing of spirits—are particularly active ministry gifts.[51] They represent faith flowing out in action.

The gift of faith relates to the first two gifts, word of wisdom and word of knowledge, operating "by the same Spirit." Accordingly, though there is transition into a different area, it is the same Spirit who is at work in the gift of faith.

Moreover, the first two gifts may also prepare one for the exercise of the gift of faith. The very utterance of a word of wisdom or a word of knowledge wherein the things of God are spiritually declared may make for the creation of an atmosphere of faith. The statement

---

[47]Weymouth in his *New Testament in Modern Speech* so translates (even though the Greek word is simply *pistis,* "faith").

[48]"Saving faith" is referred to in Ephesians 2:8: "By grace you have been saved through faith." This salvation, by grace through faith, is a gift of God. Such faith through which salvation comes is prerequisite to faith—"special faith"—as a gift of the Spirit.

[49]"Fruit faith," a fruit of the Spirit, is delineated in Galatians 5:22: "the fruit of the Spirit is love, joy . . . faith [*pistis*]" (KJV). *Pistis* is translated "faithfulness" in RSV, NASB, and NIV, and "fidelity" in NEB. In these cases *pistis* does not so much signify faith toward God as faithfulness, trustworthiness, and dependability in relation to other persons. Whether the better translation is "faith," "faithfulness," or "fidelity," *pistis* in Galatians 5:22 refers to character; hence, like a fruit, it may take some time to mature.

[50]The first two, word of wisdom and word of knowledge, as we have observed, are basically mental gifts—the Holy Spirit working through the mind. The five gifts that follow are extramental. According to EGT, the first category "exhibits the πνεῦμα [Spirit] working through the νοῦς [mind]," the second in distinction from the νοῦ (2:888). As was previously noted, the Greek word *heteros* is the connective between these two categories.

[51]Godet uses the word "force" in connection with them: "The following five [after the word of wisdom and word of knowledge] proceed from a communication of *force,* in other words, from an influence of the Spirit, no longer specially on the understanding, but on the will" (*Commentary on First Corinthians,* 624).

that "faith comes from hearing" (Rom. 10:17 NASB)[52] also applies to the gift of faith; for against the background of hearing a spiritual utterance of the truth of God, faith may spring forth.

The gift of faith, in turn, may be the immediate background for the exercise of the two ministry gifts that follow: gifts of healing and effecting of miracles. Faith is the atmosphere in which healings occur;[53] it is likewise the basic precondition for the working of miracles.[54] For example, the gift of faith trusts for miracles, whereas (obviously) the working of miracles effects miracles. Faith, while seemingly passive, is the critical factor in these ensuing gifts.[55] It is a faith that has visible results.[56]

Before examining further the relation of the gift of faith to what follows, it is important to recognize that this gift has its own unique significance. Because it is listed as a separate gift from what follows, faith may operate in other spheres of ministry as well. For example, there may be a special God-given faith in some situation to strengthen the faith of others. An illustration of this is Paul's prophecy on board a violently storm-tossed ship; he said to others who had given up all hope: "Take heart, men, for I have faith in God that it will be exactly as I have been told" (Acts 27:25).[57] Although the men in the boat were not believers,[58] Paul's words doubtlessly much encouraged them not to despair.

Similarly, the gift of faith may occur in a situation today where someone is given a special trust in God that reassures others. Where faith is weak or wavering, words of encouragement or exhortation issuing from the gift of faith can be exactly what is needed. For example, one who has been given a strong faith in God's presence and purpose can be a catalytic agent to mightily affect those around him or her. Through the gift of faith the faith of others is thereby built up.[59] The situation may be one of crisis involving anxiety and fear; the gift of faith can bring courage. Or it may be in a gathering of believers that this gift will offer assurance that God is ready to speak and act if people will not hold back. God is ready to move; let us move with Him![60]

---

[52]Although the faith mentioned in Romans 10:17 relates more specifically to "saving faith," it is nonetheless true that the gift of faith may come the same way.

[53]See the discussion of this in section IV.

[54]See the discussion of this is section V.

[55]This could also include the other two ministry gifts, prophecy and distinguishing of spirits. EGT speaks of the gifts of healing and working of miracles as the "material" sphere, prophecy and distinguishing of spirits as the "spiritual" sphere—and that faith operates through both: "ἰάματα [healings] and δυνάμεις [miracles] are operations of such faith in the material sphere. . . . προφητεία [prophecy] and διακρίσις πνευμάτων [distinguishing of spirits] in the purely spiritual sphere" (2:888).

[56]Gordon Lindsay puts it well: "Although the gift of faith *appears* to be passive . . . in reality it sets forces in motion that are irresistible" (*Gifts of the Spirit,* 2:43).

[57]Paul had been assured by an angel that no life would be lost. Paul believed what he was told; hence, his words to the seamen may be viewed as an expression of the gift of faith.

[58]I say this in light of the fact that gifts of the Spirit are basically for the edification of believers. However, in this case the purpose of Paul's expression of faith was likewise to strengthen, hence edify, those around him.

[59]Arnold Bittlinger speaks of certain situations in which "the gift of faith is given, above all, to strengthen the weak faith of the people" (*Gifts and Graces,* 33).

[60]Dennis Bennett describes the gift of faith as "a sudden surge of faith, usually in a crisis,

In the Old Testament there are many illustrations of special faith. Elijah on Mount Carmel, believing that God would vindicate Himself before Israel, cried out for the fire to fall: "Answer me, O LORD. . . that this people may know that thou, O LORD, art God" (1 Kings 18:37). Concerning Daniel in the lion's den, the Scripture says, "No manner of hurt was found upon him, because he believed in his God"[61] (Dan. 6:23 KJV). Both stories depict extraordinary faith in God. The writer of Hebrews, looking back, said, "Time would fail me to tell of Gideon, Barak, Samson, Jephthah, of David and Samuel and the prophets—who through faith conquered kingdoms, enforced justice, received promises, stopped the mouths of lions . . ." (11:32–33). These and the others that follow are examples of heroic faith and better help in understanding the significance of the gift of faith.

Now to return to the New Testament: the gift of faith may appropriately be called "mountain-moving faith." In 1 Corinthians 13 Paul speaks about "all faith, so as to remove mountains" (v. 2).[62] This suggests that the gift of faith specified in 1 Corinthians 12:9 relates to the moving of "mountains." In this connection we may also turn to this statement of Jesus: "Have faith in God. Truly, I say to you, whoever says to this mountain, 'Be taken up and cast into the sea,' and does not doubt in his heart, but believes that what he says will come to pass, it will be done for him" (Mark 11:22–23).

What, we may inquire, is the nature of a "mountain" and how is it removed? Paul does not say what it is, but Jesus spoke against the background of the withering of a fig tree He had cursed (Mark 11:12–14, 20–21). The fig tree, withered to its roots, was totally removed—and surely by no human means. A mountain, accordingly, is that which cannot be overcome or accomplished by human effort. Its removal therefore requires the humanly impossible. In one Old Testament situation a "mountain" referred to a seemingly insurmountable task: "What are you, O great mountain? Before Zerubbabel you shall become a plain" (Zech. 4:7).[63] That this task was humanly impossible is disclosed in the prior statement to Zerubbabel: "Not by might, nor by

---

to confidently believe without a doubt, that as we act or speak in Jesus' Name it shall come to pass" (*The Holy Spirit and You*, 134). Dunn writes similarly: "Paul presumably has in mind that mysterious surge of confidence which sometimes arises within a man in a particular situation of need or challenge and which gives him an otherly certainty and assurance that God is about to act through a word or through an action (such as laying hands on someone sick)" (*Jesus and the Spirit*, 211). It is interesting that both Bennett and Dunn use the word "surge." Truly this well expresses what happens in the gift of faith: faith surges!

[61] Daniel himself is a good illustration of the faith that trusts for miracles (as previously discussed). Also in the Book of Daniel there is the amazing testimony of the three Hebrews facing the fiery furnace: "O Nebuchadnezzar. . . . If it be so, our God whom we serve is able to deliver us from the burning fiery furnace; and he will deliver us out of your hand, O king. But if not . . . we will not serve your gods or worship the golden image which you have set up" (3:16–18). Our God is able! Truly this is a vivid demonstration of a faith that believes, whether or not a miracle occurs.

[62] The stress in 1 Corinthians 13 is the necessity of love for the beneficial operation of the gifts. Regarding faith: "If I have all faith, so as to remove mountains, but have not love, I am nothing." Here, for all its importance, our concern is not with love but with Paul's amplification of the gift of faith.

[63] Reference is to the mountain of opposition that impeded Zerubbabel from completing the rebuilding of the temple.

power, but by my Spirit, says the LORD of hosts" (v. 6). In sum, a mountain and its removal goes far beyond any human capacity.

And the limits? According to Jesus, there are none, for in a parallel passage, after the words "it will move," He added, "nothing will be impossible to you" (Matt. 17:20). Truly, this is an astounding statement!

Now the critical matter is faith. According to Jesus, it does not have to be large—the size of a tiny mustard seed will do[64]—but it has to be there. The preface to Jesus' words concerning moving a mountain is faith: "Have faith in God" and "If you have faith . . . ."[65] Few things disturbed Jesus more than the lack of faith on the part of His disciples. This is markedly brought out on another occasion when a demonized boy was brought by his father to Jesus' disciples, who were unable to cope with the situation. When Jesus saw this, He cried out: "O unbelieving generation, how long shall I be with you? How long shall I put up with you?" (Mark 9:19 NASB). Having spoken these words, Jesus proceeded to cast out the demon.

It is important next to emphasize that the necessary faith is wholly related to God—"Have faith in God"! This means, for one thing, that this special faith is faith in God's power and ability to do wonders.[66] It is not faith in any word or action of one's own—for example, believing that by speaking to the mountain it will move. It is not faith in faith, as if by believing with sufficient strength and vigor the wonder will be accomplished.[67] It is faith in God—believing that He as the living God is able and ready to move mountains. Such faith rests wholly in God.[68]

Accordingly, this faith has its source in God: it is faith that comes from Him. It is, as I said at the outset, a gift of the Holy Spirit. Like all the other gifts, faith is apportioned according to His will.[69] He either gives it or there is no faith at all. It may be no larger than a mustard seed, but if the faith, the believing, is from God, it can accomplish far more than the greatest of human efforts to believe.[70] To say, "I believe, I believe" before praying for a healing is to substitute a mental activity for the grace of faith by which the work

---

[64] It is interesting that in Matthew 17:20 before Jesus declared the need for mustard seed faith to remove a mountain, He spoke of the "little faith [Gr. *oligopistia*]" of His disciples. This implies that their faith was less than that of a grain of mustard seed! Another interpretation of Jesus' words is that He was not actually dealing quantitatively with faith ("little faith" compared to "mustard seed" size might suggest a rather minute quantitative difference), but was referring to their faith as poor faith, a poverty of faith (see, e.g., EBC: "Despite the etymology of the word, it probably does not refer so much to the littleness of their faith as to its poverty" [8: 391]). In any event, a vital faith, though small as a mustard seed, is what Jesus calls for.

[65] "If you have faith" is found in Matthew 21:21. This is the parallel passage to Mark ("Have faith in God") concerning the fig tree and moving a mountain.

[66] Another name for this special faith, in addition to "mountain-moving," might be "wonder-working" faith! The Amplified Bible reads: "To another (wonder-working) faith."

[67] There is always the danger, even unknowingly, of replacing God with faith.

[68] The Greek words translated "Have faith in God" are *echete pistin theou*. This means, "Have a faith which rests on God" (so NBC, in loco). Incidentally, it is a mistake to read the genitive *theou* as a subjective genitive, hence "of God," as if the faith were God's faith (an impossible conception). Rather it is an objective genitive, thus "in God" (as all translations read).

[69] Recalling the words of 1 Corinthians 12:11: "All these [*charismata*] are inspired by one and the same Spirit, who apportions to each one individually as he wills."

[70] What is needed is not so much a *great faith* in God as faith in a *great God*!

is truly accomplished.[71] Faith comes only from God.

Still, we may, and should, ask for it. Like all the gifts of the Holy Spirit, this kind of faith may be earnestly desired[72] and prayed for. On one occasion Jesus' apostles said to Him, "Give us faith" (Luke 17:5 Weymouth).[73] It does not take much, for Jesus replied, "If you had faith as a grain of mustard seed, you could say to this sycamine tree, 'Be rooted up, and be planted in the sea,' and it would obey you" (v. 6). But even that much faith—a faith that can bring about amazing results—must come from the Lord. This the apostles knew, as their request demonstrated. Unmistakably, the same thing is true today. The Lord, the Spirit, apportions as He wills, but not without regard to the prayers and desires of His people.[74]

Another point: this faith cannot coexist with doubt. According to Matthew 21:21, Jesus said to His disciples, "If you have faith, and do not doubt, you shall not only do what was done to the fig tree, but even if you say to this mountain, 'Be taken up and cast into the sea,' it shall happen" (NASB). Doubt clearly abnegates faith; indeed, if it is present, there is no faith at all—and no results. The words might be spoken, "Be taken up . . . " (or any other "mountain-moving" words), yet the results would be nil.

But how, one may ask, is it possible not to doubt, especially in light of the things Jesus talked about—blighting fig trees, moving mountains, uprooting sycamines?[75] Am I to try with all my might not to doubt, saying, "I will not doubt, I will not doubt, I will not doubt . . ."?[76] Such efforts are surely in vain, for not only is such a mental exercise more likely to increase doubt than to dispel it, but also—and this is the real issue—doubt is most deeply a matter of the heart. In the parallel Markan account of the fig tree, Jesus said (as we have earlier quoted) that the true believer "does not doubt *in his heart*" (11:23). This means that no effort of mind and will can suffice.[77] It is only through the dispelling of doubt in the heart that faith can exist and bring about results.

---

[71]Charles S. Price writes, "To believe *in* healing is one thing; but to have faith *for* it is altogether something else . . . . We have made faith a condition of the mind, when it is a divinely imparted grace of the heart" (*The Real Faith,* 8–9). Truly said!

[72]To "make love your aim, and earnestly desire the spiritual gifts" (1 Cor. 14:1) surely includes the gift of faith.

[73]In most translations the wording is "Increase our faith" (so KJV, RSV, NASB, NIV, and NEB). That translation is surely possible, for the Greek word rendered "increase," *prostithēmi,* often means "add, put to" (BAGD, 719). However, a secondary meaning is "provide, give, grant," which results in the translation (as BAGD gives it) "grant us faith." TDNT concurs with this, translating Luke 17:5 as "Lord, confer faith on us" (8:168).

[74]According to Luke 11:13, the *gift* of the Holy Spirit comes to those who ask God. In this verse Jesus said, "If you then, who are evil, know how to give good gifts to your children, how much more will the heavenly Father give the Holy Spirit to those who ask him." Surely the *gifts* come the same way (cf. Matt. 7:11)—by asking.

[75]One might add to the list the ability to walk on water! We may recall the words of Jesus to Peter, who had ventured out to walk on the sea and began to sink: "O man of little faith, why did you doubt?" (Matt. 14:31).

[76]This obviously is the counterpart to "I believe, I believe" mentioned earlier.

[77]This is why the suggestion of some that the way to handle doubt is not to admit its existence misses the mark. Kenneth Hagin, for example, writes, "You don't have to doubt, because you are not a doubter: you are a believer. So keep on believing" (*How to Turn Your Faith Loose,* 28). Such a denial of doubt—"you are not a doubter"—may only compound the problem. If I *do* doubt in my heart, no matter how much I try with my mind to "keep on believing," I will only fail.

Here a word about the importance of prayer in relation to faith and doubt should be injected. According to the earlier incident in which Jesus cast the demon out of the boy, the disciples afterward asked Him, "Why could we not cast it out?" Jesus replied, "This kind cannot come out by anything but prayer" (Mark 9:29 NASB).[78] When we relate this to Jesus' previous words "O unbelieving generation . . . ," it is apparent that He is declaring the close connection between faith (or the lack of it) and prayer.[79] Mountain-moving, demon-exorcising faith, while truly from God, is given to those who in much prayer are open to receive it. Prayer, accordingly, is an antidote to doubt arising in the heart because in such prayer God is experienced as powerfully present and at work.

A further word about prayer and doubt: if one is given to prayer, there is also a greater sensitivity to God's purpose in a particular situation. A person will not be praying for every mountain to be removed or even seeking to exorcise every demon *unless* he senses it is God's intention and God's timing. Doubt may arise in the heart when one is *not* certain he is in God's will.[80] This may be all the more the case if the person is self-preoccupied and basically seeks his own good rather than that of others. Since the gift of faith is *wholly* oriented (as are all the spiritual gifts) to the good of other people, doubt is sure

to exist where self-concern dilutes faith's operation.

To not doubt and, consequently, to believe also applies to what one says. The words of Jesus in Mark 11:23 continue—after "does not doubt in his heart"—thus: ". . . but believes that what he says will come to pass, it will be done for him." Believing, therefore, relates not only to faith in God ("Have faith in God" [v. 22]) but also to the words spoken—"Sick man, be healed"; "Blind eyes, be opened"; "Evil spirit, come out"—and expects their fulfillment. It is not as if the words themselves have the power to accomplish such results,[81] for the power resides in God and the faith that issues from him. Simply to pronounce a healing or a miracle and assume that fulfillment will automatically follow is totally mistaken. However, if the words are spoken in the faith that comes from God without any doubt in the heart, then, according to Jesus, they will surely be fulfilled.

Here a statement needs to be added about the danger of presumption. Words and actions cannot be some kind of demand upon God. Jesus Himself was tempted by Satan to leap from the pinnacle of the temple—"Throw yourself down from here" (Luke 4:9)—by claiming God's Old Testament promises "He will give his angels charge of you, to guard you . . . . On their hands they will bear you up, lest you strike your

---

[78] Some manuscripts add "and fasting." EBC, in loco, speaks of the addition of "and fasting" as "probably an early scribal gloss." This seems likely.

[79] Prior to casting out the demon Jesus had been on a mountain (the Mount of Transfiguration) praying (Mark 9:2–8; cf. Luke 9:28: "He . . . went up on the mountain to pray").

[80] For example, a person may pray for a mountain literally (i.e., a geographical mountain) to be removed, and doubts will surely crowd in because one suspects such is not God's intention (even Jesus never removed an earthly mountain). Another example on a less grandiloquent scale is that of praying for a dying person to continue to live. If, however, it is God's time for the person to end his days on earth, doubts will surely enter, for the prayer is actually contrary to God's determination.

[81] Such a view is closer to magic than faith. See, e.g., Acts 19:13–16 where such a view backfired on the sons of Sceva.

foot against a stone" (vv. 10–11, quoting from Ps. 91:11–12). Jesus replied bluntly: "You are not to put the Lord your God to the test" (v. 12 NEB, quoting from Deut. 6:16). For Jesus to have thrown Himself down from the temple even on the basis of Scripture would not have been an act of faith but of presumption; it would actually have been an attempt to force God's hand.[82] Similarly, to say to a lame person, "Throw away your crutches" and God "will bear you up" may be no word of faith at all, but a demand upon God to intervene. The results, moreover, can be serious indeed—broken bones, emotional pain, and even diminished faith.[83] Jesus did indeed say that it is necessary to believe what one says, but such speaking must not presume upon God and seek to coerce His action. However, if the words and actions spring out of the faith that comes from God—a

faith that also is not alloyed with doubt—there can be no coercion, no presumption. For it is God Himself moving through that kind of faith, and the results are sure.

Let me conclude by emphasizing the importance of the gift of faith. Through that gift God often brings about healings, works miracles, and meets many human needs. This special faith recognizes the existence of problems, sickness, pain,[84] and the like, and confidently through God seeks to minister help in these situation. All believers, to be sure, have faith and all are called upon to minister;[85] however, there is also this special gift of faith uniquely apportioned within the body that can have extraordinary effects. Accordingly, this manifestation of the Holy Spirit, the gift of faith, needs earnestly to be sought, recognized, and utilized so that the community of believers may

---

[82] Charles Farah writes in his valuable book *From the Pinnacle of the Temple: Faith vs. Presumption* that "presumption is such a universal possibility that even our Lord was tempted by it" (p. 21). Farah thereafter paraphrases Jesus' words to Satan: "No one has the right . . . to put God to the test—*not even the Son of God*. No one has the right to force God's hand" (p.25).

[83] Far worse than the illustration above about crutches being discarded are instances in which medication has been dispensed with (insulin, for example, being laid aside), with sometimes fatal results. To be sure, God may heal in response to faith so that medicine becomes unnecessary, but to discard medicine prior to God's healing is presumptuous: this is again an attempt (whether realized or not) to force God's hand. The difference can be a matter of life and death. Incidentally, in the words of C. S. Price, "the act can be born of faith, not faith of the act" (*The Real Faith*, 27); that is to say, giving up crutches, medication, etc., *may* follow a word of true faith *but* to take some such action in an attempt to muster up faith is wholly mistaken and possibly calamitous.

[84] I earlier quoted Kenneth Hagin's words about doubt—"you are not a doubter." To confess doubt is a "negative confession," so likewise is it to confess sickness. "Confessions of lack and sickness shut God out of your life and let Satan in. Confession of disease and sickness gives sickness domain over you" (*Bible Faith Study Course,* 91). What is needed, therefore, is the recognition by the believer that these evils do not exist; instead, he will only confess prosperity (not "lack") and health (not "sickness"). This is "positive confession." From this perspective there is no need for the gift of faith by which life's negativities may be overcome; faith rather makes a "positive confession" that all is well. I submit that this viewpoint is basically unbiblical, renders unnecessary the gift of faith (also the next gift, healing), and is seriously ineffective in dealing with human problems. To confess healing, for example, in spite of continuing sickness may lead to disillusionment and despair because it leaves people *in* their situation rather than providing a way *out*. (See also the Excursus to follow.)

[85] According to Mark 16:17–18, "These signs will accompany those who believe: in my name they will cast out demons . . . they will lay their hands on the sick, and they will recover."

receive fuller ministry and God may be all the more fully glorified.

EXCURSUS: THE WORD-OF-FAITH TEACHING

Here I add a few comments about the "word of faith teaching"[86] and its relation to the gift of faith. Kenneth Hagin through his many writings has been the chief proponent of this faith teaching[87] and has had wide influence.

My first comments are positive. Hagin's life and ministry have surely been a testimony to him as a man of faith who has ever been willing to venture forth for God. Moreover, through his ministry large numbers of people have heard the gospel and particularly his teaching on such matters as total belief in God's Word, faith's priority over feelings, and the importance of a positive orientation to life. Kenneth Hagin will be remembered as one of the leading charismatic figures of the twentieth century.

I do, however, have serious reservations about Hagin's teaching at certain critical points. First, there is an exaggeration of the *role of faith*: it assumes almost godlike proportions. In Lesson 21 of his book *New Thresholds of Faith* entitled "The God Kind of Faith" Hagin speaks of God's creating the world through faith: "How did He do it? God believed that what He said would come to pass."[88] This statement clearly is contrary to the scriptures that *never* attribute faith to God; rather He created through the Word. In the subtitle of this lesson Hagin writes, "Central Truth: The kind of faith that spoke the universe into existence is dealt to our hearts."[89] This means that we have "the God kind of faith,"[90] the same faith as God the Creator has. As a result, says Hagin, we can put God to work for us: "I have learned how to put the Greater One to work for me."[91] Such an incredible statement actually places my faith in control of God: *He works "for me"!* Hagin entitled a later lesson, "How to Write Your Own Ticket with God."[92] This equally extraordinary statement shows what faith can do: *By it you can write your own ticket with God!* Hagin adds in the same lesson: "Too few people today know that they can write their own ticket with God."[93] Since "the God kind of faith" can do this, faith almost becomes divine, because it is not God but we who write the ticket. God's sovereignty is now overarched by man's control.

Second, there is a misapprehension of the *place of confession*. Hagin has much to say about confession; e.g., every chapter in *How to Turn Your Faith Loose* has to do with confession. Chapter 3, "A Positive Confession," climaxes with these words: "*You will never be a conqueror before you believe you are one. . . .* You have to *confess* it first to become one. *Faith's confessions create reality*" (all italics his). Confession, accordingly, because it is the

---

[86] Sometimes called simply "faith teaching."

[87] Kenneth Copeland is the other best-known "faith teacher."

[88] *New Thresholds of Faith,* 75.

[89] Ibid., 74.

[90] Hagin retranslates Mark 11:22, "Have faith in God" as "Have the God kind of faith." This, says Hagin, is how "Greek scholars tell us this [verse] should be translated" (ibid.). No Greek scholar, to my knowledge, gives such a translation (see also n. 68).

[91] Ibid., 80. Hagin uses the expression "the Greater One" in reference to 1 John 4:4: "Greater is he that is in you, than he that is in the world" (KJV).

[92] Lesson 23. "How to Write Your Own Ticket with God" is also the heading for a section in Hagin's *Bible Faith Study Course,* 103–10.

[93] Lesson 23 in *New Thresholds of Faith,* 84.

means of turning faith "loose," now occupies center stage: it—confession—*creates* reality! Thus what you confess is yours: you possess it. In his *Bible Faith Study Course*, a section entitled "Confession Brings Possession,"[94] Hagin writes, "To tell you the truth about it, what I confess—I possess. If you want to wait and possess it first, and then confess it, you're wrong. . . . You'll never get it that way."[95] Again, "My confession gives me possession. Faith is governed by our confession."[96] Surely this misconstrues confession, placing it over faith, and therefore leads to some dangerous conclusions. If what I confess is what I possess, then, for example, in the financial area the key to results is confessing prosperity.[97] Hagin speaks of a time when money was in short supply and many were confessing lack (a "negative confession"); then they shifted to "positive confession." The result: "We confessed plenty and we had plenty."[98] So it is that "our lips can make us millionaires or keep us paupers."[99] Since "faith's confessions create reality," how could it be otherwise?

Obviously there is something critically off-balance here. The area of prosperity alone is a far cry from the New Testament picture of Jesus, who confessed (negatively?) to not having even a place to lay His head (Luke 9:58), and Paul, who said, "I know how to be abased, and I know how to abound; in any and all circumstances I have learned the secret of facing plenty and hunger, abundance and want" (Phil. 4:12). Why did not Paul make a "positive confession of plenty" (recall Hagin: "We confessed plenty and we

had plenty") rather than a "negative confession" of hunger and want, and thus have all in abundance? Paul's position is far different, as his next statement reads: "I can do all things in him who strengthens me" (v. 13). Hagin's "positive confession" of plenty is light years distant from Paul's confession of Christ, who strengthens *regardless* of one's earthly condition. Positive-confession teaching, further, may result in anguish and pain: what if my confession of plenty is followed by nothing but more want? Paul's words on the other hand provide a way of peace and joy whether there is want or abundance.

The word-of-faith teaching, all in all, is man-centered and not God-centered. This has been evidenced in such errors as believing that we can put God to work for us and that our lips can make us paupers or millionaires. Both faith and confession tend to assume divine prerogatives; that is, they create realities. A positive confession is seen to be a sure ticket to health and prosperity because the confession itself brings about the possession. Such a viewpoint, prevalent also in much so-called positive thinking today, is basically self-oriented and ultimately makes our words (not God's Word) the power behind successful living.

One final word: "Faith teaching" has little to say about faith as a gift. The important matter in this teaching is the *release* of faith (so the title of Hagin's book, *How to Turn Your Faith Loose*). There is the valid recognition that faith is based on hearing and accepting God's Word, but then the important matter becomes the release of one's faith by confession. What is needed in this

---

[94] Pages 92–96.

[95] Ibid., 93.

[96] Ibid., 96.

[97] Hagin assures us in *How to Turn Your Faith Loose* that "God wants us to have material, financial, physical and spiritual prosperity" (141).

[98] *Bible Faith Study Course*, 96.

[99] Ibid., 91. Also in *New Thresholds*, 77.

teaching is a deeper stress on faith as God's gift—a gift of the Holy Spirit—and on the fact that He apportions faith as He wills. The truly basic matter is not the expression of my faith so that I possess what I confess, but faith as God's continuing gift by which He always remains in charge and my confession stems out of *His* will and purpose.[100]

IV. GIFTS OF HEALINGS[101]

The next manifestation of the Spirit, "gifts of healings," is also an individual distribution of the Spirit: "to another gifts of healings [*charismata iamatōn*] by the one Spirit" (1 Cor. 12:9). Paul refers to this again in his later rhetorical question: "All do not have gifts of healings, do they?" (v. 30 NASB).[102] "Gifts of healings" are undoubtedly individual appointments by the Holy Spirit within the community of believers.[103]

It is significant that this gift of the Spirit is not healings as such but *gifts* of healings. This is the only gift (*charisma*)

that is gifts (*charismata*);[104] hence the gift is not healings as such but gifts or *charismata* of healings. Thus the one who receives such gifts does not directly perform the healings; rather he simply transmits the gifts. He is a kind of "delivery boy" who brings the gifts to others. Hence such a person does not become a healer even for a moment: he or she only passes on the healings to others.[105]

Let us also observe that though the gifts of healings are many, the person is one. It is not that one person has a particular gift of healing and somebody else another; rather to the one person the *charismata* of healings are given. Even as the Spirit from whom the gifts come is one—"by the one Spirit"—so the person is one. To one person from the one Spirit come multiple gifts.

Now to return to the emphasis on multiple healings: this suggests that even as there are many sicknesses and diseases, the gifts relate to healings or cures of many disorders. Looking back into Jesus' ministry, we recall that He went about "preaching the gospel of the kingdom and healing every disease and

---

[100] For a further helpful evaluation of "faith teaching" or "positive confession," see the Assemblies of God brochure #34–4183, "The Believer and Positive Confession" (copies are available from the Gospel Publishing House, Springfield, MO 65802). Also see Bruce Barron, *The Health and Wealth Gospel* and D. R. McConnell, *A Different Gospel*.

[101] The KJV, RSV, NIV, NASB, and NEB all read "gifts of healing." I have here added the *s* (as in ASV and NKJV) because the Greek phrase is definitely plural: "*charismata hiamatōn.*" "Gifts of healing*s*" sounds a bit awkward; however, it is important to retain the double plural (see below).

[102] "Gifts of healings" is also mentioned by Paul shortly before he raises the above question. Paul had just spoken of various appointments in the church: "God has appointed in the church, first apostles, second prophets, third teachers, then miracles, then gifts of healings" (1 Cor. 12:28 NASB). (On the matter of "appointments" see discussion in preceding chap. 13, IV.A.n.56.)

[103] Paul is not dealing here with the fact that all believers may engage in healing especially in the proclamation of the gospel. Mark 16:18 reads, "They [believers] will lay their hands on the sick, and they will recover"—a statement that is set within a missionary context. Paul's concern is ministry *within* the body, where healing is particularized.

[104] Note that this is the only time that *charismata* appears in the list of nine gifts. The word "*charismata*" was earlier used by Paul to refer to "varieties of gifts" (v. 4) of the Spirit, namely, to all the gifts. But in regard to the area of healing, there are gifts.

[105] "Each individual healing is a gift of God's grace. The bearer of the gift has nothing in his hand; each cure is a new *charisma*" (Siegfried Grossman, *Charisma: The Gifts of the Spirit*, 42).

every infirmity among the people. . . . They brought him all the sick, those afflicted with various diseases and pains, demoniacs, epileptics, and paralytics, and he healed them'' (Matt. 4:23–24). Since it is the same Lord Jesus who by the Holy Spirit is at work in the gifts, there is no limit to the infirmities and diseases that He will heal through one to whom the gifts are given.

Gifts of healings are wholly supernatural endowments. They are not natural gifts, nor are they the result of developed skills. The word ''gifts,'' *charismata,* emphasizes their continuing divine origin and character. They come directly from the exalted Lord. Where He is recognized and received as Lord (''Jesus is Lord'' [1 Cor. 12:3]), He freely moves through a particular person to bring about healings.

Gifts of healings, however, may use natural means: a human touch and/or the use of various materials. One situation in Paul's own ministry involves the laying on of hands for healing: ''It happened that the father of Publius lay sick with fever and dysentery; and Paul visited him and prayed, and putting his hands on him healed him'' (Acts 28:8).[106] Paul's laying on of hands was not the cause of healing but did provide a tangible human contact. Similarly James writes, ''Is any among you sick? Let him call for the elders of the church, and let them pray over him, anointing him with oil in the name of the Lord'' (James 5:14).[107] The anointing with oil as such had no medicinal value but did represent the healing of the

Spirit. We note that in His ministry Jesus often used a human touch, for example, in curing people of leprosy (Matt. 8:3), fever (Matt. 8:15), blindness (Matt. 9:29), and deafness and dumbness (Mark 7:33–35). Jesus' disciples also ''anointed with oil many that were sick and healed them'' (Mark 6:13). In summary, natural means may be used; however, there is no suggestion that the natural or material means in themselves had any curative power.

To reinforce this last point: most instances of healing in the New Testament make no reference to any natural means. The opening statement in Matthew 4:23–24 about Jesus' healing ministry only says that ''he healed them.'' The same thing is true in many situations after that.[108] This was often the case in the early church; for example, ''The people also gathered from the towns around Jerusalem, bringing the sick and those afflicted with unclean spirits, and they were all healed'' (Acts 5:16). Nothing is said about human contact.

Now let us look again at Paul's words in 1 Corinthians 12:9 ''. . . to another gifts of healings by the one Spirit.'' What is said elsewhere about healing at large surely applies to healings in the body of believers. One who is gifted by the Spirit with gifts of healings may or may not use natural means. The laying on of hands, the use of oil, the touch of an affected area of the body—all may be used, but there is surely no requirement. The person bringing a gift of healing may simply pass it on verbally. A fine illustration of this is found in the

---

[106]The Scripture adds, ''And when this had taken place, the rest of the people on the island who had diseases also came and were cured'' (v. 9). This demonstrates ''gifts of healings'' for many people and many illnesses.

[107]This does not exactly parallel Paul's description of one person ministering the gifts of healings, for here elders (plural) minister. The words of James, however, should not be understood to rule out individual ministry. Individuals, whether elders or not, may be used in the ministry of healing.

[108]E.g., see Matthew 8:13, 16; 12:15; 14:14; 15:28, 30; 19:2; also accounts in the other Gospels.

words of Peter to the bedridden and paralyzed Aeneas: " 'Aeneas, Jesus Christ heals you; rise and make your bed.' And immediately he rose" (Acts 9:34). What counts is not the method of healing but the One who does it—Jesus Christ.

Before saying more, I call attention to the relationship between the gift of faith and the gifts of healings. They are separate distributions of the Holy Spirit, but they also operate in close connection with each other. We have observed this in the preceding section on the gift of faith, especially noting that faith is the background and energizing force for the gifts that follow, the most immediate one being gifts of healings. It is a faith *for* healings, then for miracles, and so on. Where the gift of faith is present there is an atmosphere conducive to healings.

We may briefly review the incident of Jesus' ministry to the demonized boy. The father declared, "I brought him to your disciples but they could not heal him." Then Jesus quickly exclaimed, "O unbelieving and perverse generation . . . how long shall I stay with you? How long shall I put up with you?" (Matt. 17:16–17 NIV). With those words Jesus passionately and painfully condemned His generation for its perverseness and lack of faith. Jesus then had the boy brought to Him, and He cast out the demon. The result was that "he was healed from that moment" (v. 18 NIV). When Jesus' disciples later asked Jesus privately why they could not cast out the demon, Jesus replied, "Because of your little faith" (v. 20 RSV). From

this narrative it would be hard to imagine a more vivid demonstration of the vital connection between faith and healing:[109] faith makes possible the healing of even the most desperate situation.

The change in Jesus' disciples after Pentecost was indeed extraordinary. For example, when Peter and John encountered a man lame from birth, Peter said to him, "I have no silver and gold, but I give you what I have; in the name of Jesus Christ of Nazareth, walk" (Acts 3:6). Here in the power of the Spirit was demonstrated an unwavering faith, and the man was immediately healed. Later when Peter was sharing the event with the gathered crowd, he said, "His name, by faith in his name, has made this man strong . . . and the faith which is through Jesus has given the man this perfect health in the presence of you all" (v. 16). Faith in the name of Jesus, first on the part of Peter and then on the part of the crippled man himself,[110] brought about total healing.

Now let us consider again the gift of faith and the gifts of healings. Although they are not the same gift, the vital connection between faith and healings is unmistakable. One may be apportioned the gift of faith, another gifts of healings, but the latter surely require faith for their operation. Moreover— we need now to stress—it is faith *totally directed away from oneself.* Shortly before Peter made the statement to the assembled crowd (quoted above), he said, "Men of Israel, why do you wonder at this, or why do you stare at us, as though by our own power or

---

[109] Although the account deals more directly with demon possession than a bodily ailment, there is unquestionably a healing involved (note the word "healing" twice used). In any event, whether there is need of healing or exorcism, unmistakably faith is critically needed to handle it.

[110] F. F. Bruce writes, "Was the faith theirs [John and Peter's] or his? Probably both" (*The Acts of the Apostles,* 110). EGT speaks of "the faith of the Apostles as of the man who was healed" (in loco). IB stresses more the apostles' faith: "The faith in question is either the lame man's or, perhaps more probably, the apostles' faith in Jesus which enables them to work miracles in his name" (in loco).

piety we had made him walk?" (Acts 3:12). Jesus alone is the healer, and only by faith in Him and in His name can a gift of healing be imparted to another. This cannot be emphasized too much.

But now having observed the close connection between the gifts of faith and healings, we must not simply merge the two. A person may be apportioned the gift of faith without that faith being directed to healing. As I have commented earlier, the gift of faith makes an impression on all the succeeding gifts; however it is a gift distinct from the others. Accordingly, as closely related as the gift of faith is to the gifts of healings, a person may function in the one without the other. Specifically, a person may be a channel for the *charismata* of healings without having the gift of faith. Of course, there has to be faith present in the one ministering if healing is to occur; he must surely be a believer.[111] But this does not, in and of itself, mean that he also has the *charisma* of faith—"special faith," "charismatic faith."[112] In another situation, perhaps on another occasion, the same person may that time operate in the gift of faith (or another gift), because the Holy Spirit is free to distribute all the gifts "as he wills" (1 Cor. 12:11). But my basic point here is that the two, the gift of faith and the gifts of healings, are distinctive apportionments of the Holy Spirit.

We may now raise the question, How does one receive the gifts of healings?[113] Two answers may be given. First, since the Holy Spirit is in charge,

it is He alone who makes the decision. Each and every gift is His sovereign disposition, thus He may give something entirely different from what a person expects. A doctor or nurse, for example, has no more claim on, or right to, gifts of healings than anyone else, even as desirable as such gifts would seem for those in a healing profession. Indeed there is the danger in such a case to view the gifts of healings as an auxiliary to what one already has (the knowledge and experience of healing gained over the years), and then to boast in both one's professional and spiritual competence. However, the Holy Spirit must—and will—remain Lord! Second, since we are also told to "eagerly desire the spiritual gifts," there is no reason anyone may not desire—ask for, seek after, pray for— the gifts of healings. Indeed, to put it more positively, the Lord welcomes our earnest requests so that if a person really and sincerely wants to be used in healings, He would encourage that individual (whether layman or professional) to seek after these gifts. When the earnest desire is for His glory—not ours—and to bless others, He all the more delights to answer our request.

Another question may follow: How does a person know whether he has received gifts of healings? Is there a word from the Lord, the Spirit, that this has happened? Such a word may indeed be spoken[114] but often is not. Is there perhaps a tingling or warm sensation in one's body of healing power going out to another that confirms that the gifts have been given? Sometimes this oc-

---

[111]Recall again the words of Mark 16:17 where "those who believe" will, among other things, "lay their hands on the sick, and they will recover" (v. 18).

[112]It may be possible that one person will have both gifts (or perhaps other additional ones); however, the stress in 1 Corinthians 12 is on the diversity of distributions *and* individuals.

[113]I have often heard it said, "If I could have any gift, I would prefer healing, because it would be such a blessing to others."

[114]Perhaps through a word of prophecy (see sec. VI, pp. 380–88).

curs,[115] but often does not. Usually the best way to know is to *venture forth*. If there is someone sick, and a person has any reason to believe that the Holy Spirit is anointing him with gifts of healings, then he should step out in faith![116] If a healing occurs, this confirms that the Spirit has singled out that person to bear a gift of healing to another person.[117]

Still another important question: If a healing does not occur, does this necessarily mean that the one ministering does not have gifts of healings? The answer, I submit, is no for several reasons. First, the persons prayed for may not have faith to receive the healing. As Mark records, even Jesus' healing power could be limited by unbelief: "He could do no mighty work there [in His home town], except that he laid his hands upon a few sick people and healed them. And he marveled because of their unbelief" (Mark 6:5–6). Jesus healed "a few," but many obviously were not healed, not because Jesus lacked the healing power but because they did not believe. Now of course a charismatic fellowship, unlike Jesus' home town, consists of believers. But believing is not simply a fixed condition; it is also an active trusting, accepting, receiving. Hence one may be moving fully in the gifts of healing; however, if there is not the response of faith, the healings cannot be received.[118]

Second, the one who is prayed for may have some sinful impediment that needs removal for healing to occur. An Old Testament illustration of this is the case of Miriam, Moses' sister, who was smitten with leprosy by God for condemning an action of Moses. Moses cried out, "Heal her, O God, I beseech thee" (Num. 12:13). Rather than granting Moses' request to heal her at the time, God shut Miriam outside the camp for seven days, and only then was she restored. Thus if sin or evil, especially of a blatant or persistent kind, stands in the way, healing will not

---

[115] Jesus on occasion recognized a healing power in Himself that moved through Him to energize and heal others. In relation to the woman with a hemorrhage who touched His garment, the Scripture reads, "At once Jesus realized that power had gone out from him" (Mark 5:30 NIV). Interestingly, Dunn writes concerning Mark 5:30: "This sort of experience is fairly common in cases of faith and spiritual healing" (*Jesus and the Spirit*, 401, n. 36). Then Dunn quotes from J. C. Peddie (*Forgotten Talent*, 123): "The person ministering is always conscious of the power passing through (provided he has developed sufficient spiritual sensitivity) and the patient is aware of its presence from the strange heat or coldness that develops."

[116] Frequently in charismatic groups everybody joins in prayers for healing (perhaps in a circle around the sick person, all laying on hands). This is not wrong surely, for all believers should pray for the sick. However, this group effort may actually frustrate the activity of the Holy Spirit in anointing *one* person (according to 1 Cor. 12) with gifts of healings. Thus it may be much better for the group to wait for such a person to step forward in ministry. More significant results may follow.

[117] Incidentally, to say a healing has occurred when there is no evidence of such is a serious breach of truth. In that situation, to say, for example, "You are healed; claim your healing in faith" is a disservice both to the one praying and the one prayed for. Sometimes a person prayed for will say, "I am healed though the symptoms still remain." This sounds pious enough and may for the moment make everyone feel good, but it may be a gross distortion. The Holy Spirit, the Spirit of truth, desires no hypocrisy.

[118] We may recall again the words about the healing of the lame man through Peter and John's ministry. There was faith on *both* sides. Also a later Scripture about Paul and another cripple reads: "Paul, looking intently at him and *seeing that he had faith to be made well*, said in a loud voice, 'Stand upright on your feet.' And he sprang up and walked" (Acts 14:9–10).

occur. In similar vein James wrote, "Therefore[119] confess your sins to one another, and pray for one another, that you may be healed" (James 5:16). For example, if someone in the fellowship asks for prayer for an illness brought on by a bitter and unforgiving spirit, a change in attitude is essential for the healing to occur. It is significant that in the Gospel of Mark after Jesus said, "I tell you, whatever you ask in prayer, believe that you receive it, and you will" (11:24), He added, "And whenever you stand praying, forgive, if you have anything against any one; so that your Father also who is in heaven may forgive you your trespasses" (v. 25). Hence if one asks for a healing, believing is urgent; and receiving will occur unless an unforgiving spirit stands in the way. The point is this: One may be truly operating in the gifts of healings, yet a person will not be healed if there is a sinful barrier.

Third, and this is the most difficult area, the illness may be dealt with in other ways than through ministry in the gifts. On one occasion in the Old Testament God promised healing to King Hezekiah through Isaiah the prophet: "I have heard your prayer and seen your tears; I will heal you" (2 Kings 20:5 NIV). Verse 7 reads, "Then Isaiah said, 'Prepare a poultice of figs.' They did so and applied it to the boil, and he recovered" (NIV). A supernatural sign was also given (see vv. 8–11); however, the relevant matter is that a medical means was used.[120] To apply this to today: it might be a serious misreading of God's intention to pray for the supernatural healing of a boil or any other physical ailment when there are natural means available.[121] The mistake sometimes made is to fail to see God at work in the natural as well as the supernatural, through physicians and nurses as well as the prayers of believers. Truly we should use whatever means God provides.[122]

---

[119]The word "therefore" refers to the preceding words about a sick person calling for the elders of the church to pray for him; then "let them pray over him, anointing him with oil in the name of the Lord; and the prayer of faith will save the sick man, and the Lord will raise him up; and if he has committed sins, he will be forgiven" (5:14–15). In those words the emphasis is on "the prayer of faith" (which I have also been stressing) and, secondarily, on the forgiveness of the sick man's sins. However, James 5:16 proceeds to point out an integral connection between confessing sins and being healed.

[120]A poultice of figs was commonly used for opening boils and abscesses of many kinds. Incidentally, in the noncanonical Book of Ecclesiasticus are these words: "The Lord created medicines from the earth, and a sensible man will not despise them" (38:4). It is interesting also that Ecclesiasticus combines prayer to God with the importance of a physician: "My son, when you are sick do not be negligent but pray to the Lord and he will heal you . . . and give the physician his place. . . . There is a time when success lies in the hands of physicians for they too will pray to the Lord that he should grant them success in diagnosis and in healing, for the sake of preserving life" (vv. 9, 12–14). Sometimes 2 Chronicles 16:12—which reads "[King] Asa was diseased in his feet, and his disease became severe; yet even in his disease he did not seek the LORD, but sought help from physicians"—is viewed as condemning turning to physicians. However, the words "*even* in his disease he did not seek the LORD" refer back to Asa's not seeking the Lord in a time of battle but relying instead on foreign help (v. 7). So now Asa totally relied on physicians. Keil and Delitzsch speak of Asa's "superstitious trust in physicians" and add, "Consequently it is not the mere inquiring of the physicians which is here censured, but only the godless manner in which Asa trusted in the physicians" (*Commentary on the Old Testament*, 3:370).

[121]I vividly recall the instance of a friend with a broken leg being prayed for and expecting a miracle. When the miracle did not occur, he very reluctantly went to the hospital where the fracture was mended. My friend felt that God had let him down.

[122]There has been some serious misunderstanding in this area. Harold Horton writes,

It is sometimes said that the New Testament changes all this. While it is true that the ministry of spiritual healing abounds, this does not deny all possibility of natural means or the role of the physician. Sometimes the verse is quoted about the woman with a serious hemorrhage, "who had suffered much under many physicians, and had spent all that she had, and was no better but rather grew worse" (Mark 5:26), as if this were a condemnation of physicians and medical help. However, in the narrative of healing that follows, Jesus did not condemn her actions (vv. 27–34). In another situation the Synoptic Gospels all report this statement of Jesus: "Those who are well have no need of a physician, but those who are sick" (Matt. 9:12; Mark 2:17; Luke 5:31). Although Jesus later applied these words to His own ministry, He clearly seemed to acknowledge the legitimate place of a physician in relation to the sick.[123] In reference to medical help, Jesus told the parable of the Samaritan who, after ministering to a man beaten by robbers, "bound up his wounds, pouring on oil and wine" (Luke 10:34). Paul wrote Timothy, "Stop drinking only water, and use a little wine because of your stomach and your frequent illnesses" (1 Tim. 5:23 NIV). Here, if anywhere, is an unmistakable affirmation of the use of natural means for even "frequent illnesses." Paul did *not* say, "I am praying for your healing" or "If you have sufficient faith, God will heal you" or "Do not confess to being sick, else you will continue that way."[124] No, since wine—a natural product of God's creation and of human production—was adequate, there was no need to look for supernatural healing.[125]

To return to the main point: ministry in the gifts, while truly a blessing of God, does not necessarily apply to

"Medicine and surgery is the world's way. God's way, the only way revealed in the Word, is healing by supernatural divine power. *These two ways are entirely opposed*" (italics added) (*Gifts of the Spirit,* 96). Horton even discounts medical healing as "second best": "Medical healing is not as some people declare, 'God's second best.' It is entirely of the educated world. God has no second best" (ibid.). This view has wrought havoc in some situations where people with medically controllable or curable ailments have spurned treatment, believing that God works only supernaturally. As a result, bodily deterioration and even death have sometimes ensued. For example, there is the tragic account of twelve-year-old diabetic Wesley Parker, who was taken off insulin by his parents because they believed God would heal him through prayer. (See the account in the book of Charles Farah, *From the Pinnacle of the Temple,* chap. 1).

[123] On one occasion Jesus applied to Himself the proverb "Physician, heal yourself" (Luke 4:23). Again, there is no suggestion of antagonism against the role of a physician.

[124] According to "faith teaching" (discussed in the previous section), it is the "negative confession" of sickness that closes the door to becoming well. Recall the quotation from Hagin (n. 83): "Confessions of lack and sickness shut God out of your life and let Satan in. Confession of disease and sickness gives Satan dominion over you." Paul's words "Stop drinking only water" would be radically altered by Hagin to "Stop confessing you are sick." Furthermore, Paul, by recognizing Timothy's "frequent illnesses," was from the "faith teaching" perspective clearly playing into Satan's hands—letting "Satan in." (It is obvious that the apostle was not aware of the dangers of "negative confession"!)

[125] Unfortunately in some groups today if a Timothy were to show up with a stomach problem, there would be much more readiness to pray for a supernatural healing than to give some down-to-earth Pauline advice! Such advice seems so much "less spiritual." The mistake obviously is to set the spiritual and natural into an antithesis. A good balance, I suggest, is to first pray for the physical ailment. If there is no spiritual healing, then encourage the person, as Paul did Timothy, to use the best natural means (doctor's help, medication, etc.) available.

every sickness. Thus one may genuinely be a channel for gifts of healings and yet a particular healing not be received. However, this should in no way lessen a ministry in these gifts, because the Holy Spirit through them often does mighty works of healing grace.

Now a further question may be raised about the nature of sickness for which ministry may be offered. It is sometimes said that the proper sphere for this ministry is the wide range of psychosomatic ailments—i.e., those of body and mind resulting from emotional stress, but not those that are organic or structural. However, in the New Testament no such limitation is apparent. The Gospels attest that Jesus healed every kind of disease—"healing every disease and every infirmity" (Matt. 4:23; 9:35).[126] On one occasion Jesus said about His ministry: "The blind receive their sight, the lame walk, lepers are cleansed, and the deaf hear, the dead are raised up" (Luke 7:22). This was clearly not limited to the psychosomatic;[127] whatever the ailment, Jesus healed it. Likewise, Jesus

sent out the apostles "to heal *every* disease and *every* infirmity" (Matt. 10:1). To the seventy He said, "Whenever you enter a town . . . heal the sick . . ." (Luke 10:8–9)—obviously no limitation. Believers, according to Mark 16:18, "will lay their hands on the sick, and they will recover"—again no limitation. It follows that in the ministry of the gifts through believers of all times including today, the Holy Spirit, the Spirit of the Lord, will heal every kind of disease. We *must* not place limitations on what God is willing and able to perform.

A final comment in the general area of healing: Although God's will is perfect health, this does not mean that human life will be free of all sickness. This is true of even the most dedicated Christian lives. We have just recalled the situation of Timothy who had "frequent ailments." Paul himself at least on one occasion had a severe bodily ailment. He wrote the Galatians, "You know it was because of a bodily ailment[128] that I preached the gospel to

---

[126] Also cf. Mark 1:34; 3:10; Luke 4:40; 6:17.

[127] Dunn writes contrariwise: "No doubt Jesus was responsible for curing mental illness, blindness, lameness and deafness; but these could all be hysterical disorders. Even the healing of leprosy and raising of the dead, which Jesus probably [*sic*!] claimed . . . may not take us beyond the range of psycho-somatic illnesses. . . . What is rather striking is that no instances of healing purely physical injuries or mending broken limbs are attributed to Jesus in the earliest stratum of tradition. . . . There is no instance of a healing miracle which falls clearly outside the general category of psycho-somatic illnesses" (*Jesus and the Spirit,* 71). It is hard to see how Jesus' healing the blind, lame, and deaf, the curing of lepers and the raising of the dead can possibly be reduced to the level of psychosomatic illnesses. Dunn's reductionism is an unfortunate reading of Jesus' full healing ministry.

[128] The Greek phrase is *astheneian tēs sarkos,* literally "illness of the body." The NEB and NASB translate this phrase as "bodily illness." This illness may have been of the eyes (based on Paul's further statement, "You would have plucked out your eyes and given them to me" [v. 15] and "See with what large letters I am writing to you with my own hand" [6:11]). EGT speaks of Paul's eyesight as possibly "imperilled by a virulent attack of ophthalmia" (3:178). Some have suggested also the possibility of a form of malaria prevalent in regions of Galatia (e.g., see EBC, 10:478; Alan Cole, *The Epistle of Paul to the Galatians,* TNTC, 121); however, there is no biblical evidence of that. Since the word *astheneia* may also be translated "weakness," or "infirmity" (KJV), others have suggested that Paul was not referring to a disease but to a bodily condition resulting from the many attacks against him in that region, including stoning (see Acts 14:19; cf. 2 Tim. 3:11). So Ridderbos writes, "We can think of this infirmity as the result of what Paul had suffered from his enemies" (*The Epistle of Paul to the Churches of Galatia,* NICNT, 166). However, as Cole says, "The

you at first" (4:13). Paul wrote to Timothy about a Christian brother named Trophimus: "Trophimus I left ill at Miletus" (2 Tim. 4:20). If Paul, Timothy, and Trophimus all had occasions of illness, then it can hardly be suggested that a truly dedicated, Spirit-filled believer will always experience perfect health. Truly God "heals all your diseases" (Ps. 103:3), but this is no guarantee of freedom from all disease.[129] Since God's will is health, when disease and sickness come upon us, He will again and again act as our Healer.

Thus we should not hesitate to move boldly in the area of gifts of healings. "Gifts of healings" have been permanently placed in the church ("God has *appointed* in the church . . . gifts of healings" [1 Cor. 12:28 NASB]).[130] To the degree we are open to such gifts, desire such gifts, and minister such gifts, God will be glorified and His people richly blessed. The living Lord Jesus through the Holy Spirit is ever ready to bring healing!

V. WORKINGS OF MIRACLES[131]

We come next in the list to "the workings of miracles"—"to another the workings of miracles [*energēmata dynameōn*]"(1 Cor. 12:10). Miracles or powers (*dynameis*) are again mentioned by Paul in 1 Corinthians 12:28—"then miracles" (NASB).[132] As with "gifts of healings" Paul thereafter asks rhetorically: "All are not workers of miracles, are they?" (v. 29 NASB). Thus, as with the others, this gift is an apportionment of the Spirit to a particular person.

Note again the plural words:[133] workin*gs* of miracle*s*. The person is one— "to another"—but the gift is multiple. Since the word "workings" is plural, a miracle may be wrought by many ways or methods. Since the word "miracles" is plural, many kinds of miracles may take place.

In a broad sense miracles as powers include all demonstrations of supernatural power. When on one occasion Jesus sent out the apostles, He said, "Preach as you go, saying, 'The kingdom of heaven is at hand.' Heal the sick, raise the dead, cleanse lepers, cast

---

stoning itself was not a 'bodily weakness' " (*The Epistle of Paul to the Galatians,* TNTC, 121). The language of Galatians 4:13, I submit, points clearly to a bodily, physical ailment.

[129]One will not be free of all ailment any more than one will be free of all sin. God in Christ does bring salvation from sin, yet sin remains in even the most holy life. Only in the world to come will we know perfect holiness. The same is true of perfect health. We have yet to receive what Paul called "the redemption of our bodies" (Rom. 8:23).

[130]Especially sad, then, is the view of some that such gifts are no longer operational. Ronald E. Baxter writes, "Does God heal today? Yes. Are 'the gifts of healing' for today? No. God always healed and always will, but the gifts of healing were temporary" (*Gifts of the Spirit,* 129). Such antiscriptural teaching is unconscionable and destructive. If God still heals, why will He not do so through healing gifts? Baxter gives this reason: "They [the gifts of healing] passed away as the need for authentication of both the message and the messengers of New Testament truth was swallowed up in the unspeakable power and grandeur of the perfect word of God" (*ibid.*). Tragically, Baxter's denial of that teaching of "the perfect word of God"—namely, that "to another [*is given*] gifts of healings by the one Spirit"—strips that very word of its living truth.

[131]NASB has "effecting of miracles" (as in my quotation from 1 Cor. 12:8–10 in the introduction to chap. 13); the RSV reads "working of miracles." However, the Greek word translated "effecting" and "working" is in the plural: *energēmata*. I am using the plural, despite its seeming awkwardness, for reasons I will shortly mention.

[132]In this verse "miracles" precedes "gifts of healings." Their order seems to have no particular significance.

[133]As with "gifts of healings."

out demons" (Matt. 10:7–8). Healing is here included along with other works of power.[134] The Gospel record thereafter and the Book of Acts show the apostles many times healing the sick, casting out demons (e.g., Mark 6:13; Luke 10:17), and both Peter and Paul raising the dead (Acts 9:36—41 and 20:7–12).[135] Thus the apostles accomplished many miracles.

In the Fourth Gospel Jesus spoke of what believers in Him may do: "Truly, truly, I say to you, he who believes in me will also do the works that I do; and greater works than these will he do, because I go to the Father" (14:12). The works that Jesus did, as reported in the Fourth Gospel, included turning water into wine (chap. 2), healing at a distance an official's dying son by speaking a word (chap. 4), healing a man crippled and helpless for thirty-eight years (chap. 5), feeding a multitude with five loaves and two fish (chap. 6), giving sight to a man born blind (chap. 9), and raising a man (Lazarus) from the dead (chap. 11). According to Jesus, one believing in Him will be able to do the same works—and even more: "Greater works than these will he do." These words are all clearly works of supernatural power. Even the healings go beyond the limits of many healings recorded in the other Gospels. For example, a blind man did not only have his sight restored by Jesus (similar to other Gospel accounts),[136] but he was one who had been born blind. The other works of Jesus clearly moved beyond healing into unmistakably miraculous deeds. All this—and more—one believing in Christ will be enabled to accomplish.[137]

Hence when we look at Paul's words again—"to another the workings of miracles"—much is to be expected. Paul as an apostle had healed the sick,[138] cast out demons,[139] and raised the dead.[140] Paul made no claim in 1 Corinthians 12 that he alone could do such works; rather, he included the company of believers. Indeed, in his letter to the Galatians, Paul also spoke of miracles done within the community. This comes out indirectly in a question: "Does he [God] who supplies the Spirit to you and works miracles among you do so by works of the law, or by hearing with faith?" (3:5). The working of miracles within the Galatian churches was a recognized fact. Could this not have been additional demonstration of Paul's phrase "to another . . . miracles"? Is it not also possible that many miracles relating to Jesus' words in John 14:16 were also being accomplished?

---

[134]I say this because, though healing is mentioned by Paul as a separate gift of the Spirit, it is likewise a work of supernatural power.

[135]No direct reference is made to the apostles' cleansing lepers; however, that activity is probably included in the general references to their "healing everywhere" (Luke 9:6).

[136]E.g., see Matthew 9:27–30; 12:22; 15:30–31; 20:30–34; Mark 8:22–26; 10:46–52; Luke 7:21–22; 18:35–43.

[137]See my prior discussion of John 14:12 in volume 1, chapter 7, "Miracles," 156–58. Incidentally, to view the promise of Christ to do His works and greater works as having only a spiritual meaning, i.e., the bringing of people into His kingdom, is to disregard the meaning of "works" in the Gospel of John and to limit Jesus' promise. Finis Dake puts it well: "To make this a promise of spiritual works only when he did material and spiritual works is a poor excuse for unbelief" (Dake's Annotated Reference Bible, The New Testament, 112, note r).

[138]According to Acts 19:11–12, "God did extraordinary miracles by the hands of Paul, so that handkerchiefs or aprons were carried away from his body to the sick, and diseases left them and the evil spirits came out of them." See also Acts 28:7–9 for other healings.

[139]Acts 16:18; cf. 19:12.

[140]As previously noted.

Now we need to examine the connection of miracles with faith. The gift of miracles is sovereignly distributed by the Holy Spirit but also is clearly given to one who believes. We have observed that the works of Jesus, including greater works, will be done by a believer ("he who believes"). Also we may recall the words of Mark 16:17–18 about believers in general: "These signs[141] will accompany those who believe: in my name they will cast out demons; they will speak in new tongues; they will pick up serpents, and if they drink any deadly thing, it will not hurt them;[142] they will lay their hands on the sick, and they will recover." Believing in Christ, from the human side, is the essential matter.

In relation to believing and miracles, two things need emphasis. First, believing is an ongoing *trust* in Christ. It is a continuing faith in Him as the living Lord who is active among His people. Such dynamic faith expects miracles now, because "Jesus Christ is the same yesterday *and today* and for ever" (Heb. 13:8). Even as He did many miracles "yesterday" in New Testament times, so He will do them today: Christ does not change. Hence in a gathering of believers where there is need for a miracle, we may expect a miracle to happen. Since Christ is one person, He will ordinarily move through one person to perform a mighty work; hence, "to another the workings of miracles." If we truly believe in Christ and His promises of mighty works, then the atmosphere becomes increasingly expectant for Him to move mightily.

Second, believing also means *acting*. Christ never performs a miracle among His people unless there is the readiness to step out for Him. A miracle does not happen by sitting back and waiting for it to occur. A person must step out in faith. One of the extraordinary miracles in the New Testament was Peter's walking on the sea (Matt. 14:28–32). It would never have happened unless Peter had courageously stepped out.[143] Moreover Jesus had said to him, "Come" (v. 29), so it was not a foolhardy or presumptuous action. *He stepped out at Jesus' bidding.* So in the occurrence of any miracle there must be movement only when one knows Jesus is calling for it and then acting without hesitation. One further thing about such action: it is essential to keep on believing for the miracle. Peter continued to walk on the water for a time; then he began to sink until Jesus reached out and saved him, saying, "O man of little faith, why did you doubt?" (v. 31).

---

[141]"Signs" is a word often used for miracles; the Greek word is *sēmeia*. See vol. 1, chapter 7, "Miracles," 149–53.

[142]References to picking up serpents and drinking poisons are protectional statements. Paul, for example, was protected from harm when a deadly viper was accidentally picked up and it "fastened on his hand" (Acts 28:3). This was such a miracle that the natives who saw it came to view him as "a god" (v. 6). The New Testament records no example of a person protected from the effects of drinking poison; however, Eusebius (*The History of the Church,* 151) states that this happened to Joseph Barsabbas (named in Acts 1:23). In any event, the deliberate picking up of snakes or the drinking of poison should not be understood as the demonstration of a miracle. Either would be testing God, and Jesus spoke against this kind of evil when He was tempted by Satan to throw himself down from the pinnacle of the temple: "Do not put the Lord your God to the test" (Matt. 4:7; Luke 4:12 NIV). Thus the activities of snake-handling cults should be viewed as presumptuous rather than miraculous.

[143]To be sure, Peter soon began to sink because of his "little faith" (v. 31), but this does not discount the miracle of his walking on water for a time.

Little faith mixed with doubt[144] spells the end of a miraculous event.

Thus we return to the gift of faith. We have observed that this is a special faith not given to everyone ("to another faith by the same Spirit"), yet this special faith stands in the list of the nine gifts prior to both gifts of healings and workings of miracles. Hence, though this faith has its own unique place without necessary connection to healings and miracles,[145] it surely prepares the way for them. Thus in regard to miracles this faith may be called "faith for miracles": a special Spirit-given faith that believes a miracle will happen. As was said earlier, the gift of faith trusts for miracles, the working of miracles effects miracles. Thus in a given situation the Spirit may apportion to one person this special faith that provides the atmosphere and background for another to perform a miracle.[146] It may be a simple statement in a community gathering such as "I have faith that the Lord is ready to move in miracles" that prepares the way for the gift of miracles to be set into operation. Faith of course, as we have observed, needs to be present in the person who performs the miracles; but special faith, the gift of faith, may provide an additional valuable stimulus.

Next we observe that there must be the need for a miracle to be performed. Miracles were never done in the New Testament by Jesus and His apostles simply as a display of power[147] but invariably because of a compelling need. The motive again and again was compassion. For example, preceding the miracle of feeding four thousand people with seven loaves and a few fish, Jesus declared, "I have compassion on the crowd, because they have been with me now three days, and have nothing to eat" (Matt. 15:32; Mark 8:2). Similarly, before the miracle of raising the son of a widow from the dead, the Scripture reads, "And when the Lord saw her, he had compassion on her . . . " (Luke 7:13).[148] The same compassion was shown by Jesus in healing a leper: "Moved with compassion, He stretched out His hand, and touched him" (Mark 1:41 NASB); likewise in giving sight to two blind men: "Moved with compassion, Jesus touched their eyes" (Matt. 20:34 NASB). When Peter raised Tabitha from the dead, he was responding to the tears of many widows (Acts 9:36–41). And when Paul brought the boy Eutychus back to life, he first "threw himself on the young man and put his arms around him" (Acts 20:10 NIV). In all these accounts there is striking evidence of compassion and of deep human need.

It follows that when believers work miracles, there likewise must be a real need that only a miracle can remedy and a genuine compassion on the part of the one ministering to the need. Since Jesus Himself through a human vessel

---

[144]Recall our earlier discussion of the problem of doubt in section III on "the gift of faith."

[145]Recall our earlier discussion of this.

[146]It is worth noting that the first miracle of Jesus, turning water into wine, came at the instigation of His mother Mary. At the wedding in Cana when the wine ran out, Mary said simply to Jesus, "They have no wine" (John 2:3). Regardless of the fact that Jesus responded to Mary rather abruptly, "O woman, what have you to do with me? My hour has not yet come," she turned to the servants and said, "Do whatever he tells you" (vv. 4–5). Mary had not the slightest doubt that Jesus could and would act. Thus her complete faith in Him set in motion actions that led to the miracle.

[147]While miracles are "powers" (*dynameis*), they are not wrought to display power.

[148]Likewise in raising Lazarus, the love of Jesus stood behind it: "Now Jesus loved Martha and her sister and Lazarus" (John 11:5).

is ultimately the One who does the miracle, there cannot possibly be anything less.

Since this area of miracles is one of high intensity and often results in confusion, I will summarize a number of additional points.

1. Miracles are *not magic*. Magic stems from psychic or demonic forces rather than from God. Aaron by the command of God cast down his rod in the court of Pharaoh and it became a serpent; the magicians of Egypt did the same "by their secret arts" (Exod. 7:10–12). The act seemed the same (rods becoming serpents) but only the act of Aaron was a true miracle because it came from God. Hence in our proper concern for the recurrence of miracles today we must guard against the pseudo-miracles that stem from other forces. Indeed, one of the marks of "the man of lawlessness" (2 Thess. 2:3) in the days shortly before the return of Christ is his performance of pseudo-miracles: "The coming of the lawless one will be in accordance with the work of Satan displayed in all kinds of counterfeit miracles, signs and wonders" (v. 9 NIV).[149] Hence not all that purports to be miracles is of God. So while we should desire miracles in our time, we must guard against magical practices abounding in the realm of the occult—witchcraft, spiritualism, Satanism, and the like.

2. Miracles are *not to be associated with exhibitionism*. We have already seen how Jesus was tempted by Satan to leap spectacularly from the temple and thus dazzle the crowds. By such an extraordinary feat Jesus could have possibly avoided the hard and sacrificial way of the cross and instantly been proclaimed Messiah and King. Something perilously close to this occurs today when an evangelist perhaps advertises, "Come, tonight, and see miracles happen!" "Come, claim your miracle," etc. The Pharisees wanted Jesus to perform a miracle,[150] but He would not go on exhibition for their satisfaction. Thus in a revival, a church meeting, or a prayer group the moment there emerges a desire to show off, *nothing* will happen (at least nothing from God). Miracles are not the display pieces of those seeking to demonstrate their own powers.

3. Miracles *cannot be programmed*. Although the Lord is a miracle-working God, He acts according to His own purpose. In a given situation one may genuinely be open to "the gifts of miracles," there may be a vital faith present, and the occasion may seem to call for a miracle,[151] but God does not

---

[149]The man of lawlessness will operate "in the temple of God" (v. 4). This could signify the church (cf. 1 Cor. 3:16). Actually the word translated "temple" is *naos*, the inner sanctuary, the Holy of Holies. Probably, Paul is saying metaphorically that "the man of sin" and deception will operate out of the very shrine of God's usual presence.

[150]"The Pharisees came . . . seeking from him a sign [*sēmeion*] from heaven, to test him" (Mark 8:11).

[151]E.g., the death of Stephen (the first martyr) might have been followed by the miracle of his resurrection. Stephen had been active as a deacon in the community of faith, and he himself had done "great wonders and miraculous signs among the people" (Acts 6:8 NIV). However, after Stephen was stoned to death (Acts 7:58), the only thing said about the action of the church was that "devout men buried Stephen, and made great lamentation over him" (Acts 8:2 RSV). Seemingly there was no prayer or other activity by the believing church for a miracle of Stephen's return to life (as, for example, when Peter prayed for Tabitha and she was restored). If the church (Peter or someone else) had prayed for Stephen's resurrection, it would doubtless *not* have happened because the Lord had other reasons for Stephen's death (see Acts 8:1 about Saul's consenting to Stephen's death: Saul's later conversion may

act in the way expected. He remains the sovereign Lord and is ever ready to work through gifts of miracles, but He may delay or choose another way. Indeed, the Lord may work a miracle even when there is little faith for it. Peter was thrown into prison by King Herod and "earnest prayer for him was made to God by the church" (Acts 12:5). Miraculously Peter's chains fell off, and the prison doors were opened. But when he went to one of the houses "where many were gathered together and were praying" (v. 12), no one at first believed it had happened. "You are mad," they said to the servant girl who announced that Peter was at the door (v. 15). God sovereignly wrought the miracle: it was His time, His programing. So it remains today: it is important that we seek to operate in the gifts of miracles, but God is free to move in surprising ways outside and beyond the gifts. For that we should indeed be grateful.

A final word: We may be in the beginning of a period of increased miracle activity.[152] If miracles may also be described as "powers of the age to come"[153] (Heb. 6:5) and if that age is drawing quite near, we may expect increasing miraculous activity. Miracles were in some sense signs of the inbreaking of the kingdom in Jesus' day; thus His words: "If it is by the Spirit of God that I cast out demons, then the kingdom of God has come upon you" (Matt.

12:28). Hence as the time draws near for the final coming of the kingdom, miracles may multiply as powers of the age to come breaking in upon the present age. The "man of lawlessness" is only a counterfeit of the real thing (as the magicians were of Aaron and Moses); hence we may hope and expect that far greater will be the genuine miracles that herald the coming of the kingdom in power and glory. To God be all praise!

VI. PROPHECY

Paul wrote, ". . . to another prophecy [*prophetēia*]" (1 Cor. 12:10). This is again the listing of an individual distribution of the Holy Spirit—the Spirit who "apportions to each one individually as he wills" (v. 11).

The importance of prophecy, as has been earlier noted, is highlighted in Paul's injunction "Earnestly desire the spiritual gifts, especially that you may prophesy" (1 Cor. 14:1). Also in the listing of *charismata* in Romans 12 Paul first mentions prophecy: "Having gifts that differ according to the grace given to us, let us use them: if prophecy, in proportion to our faith" (v. 6). No other gift can excel prophecy in importance for the body of Christ.

Although this gift is an individual distribution by the Holy Spirit, it is available to all. In Paul's discussion of prophecy he later begins a statement with these words: "If all proph-

---

have been affected by the way Stephen died. Also there is reference in the same verse to resulting persecution and scattering of the church, which led to a wider Christian witness). So today the situation from the human perspective may seem to warrant a miracle, but it may not be God's intention. (I recall quite vividly some years ago a group of us praying a long time over the body of a young child whose death was seemingly accidental. It was a believing, "Spirit-filled" group, including the parents, who prayed and reached out to the little body. Through prophecy a word finally came that God had honored our faith and obedience, but that He had sovereignly taken the child to Himself and was fulfilling His own good purpose.)

[152] See, e.g., John Wimber, *Power Evangelism* "Appendix B: Signs and Wonders in the Twentieth Century." Also see Pat Robertson, *Beyond Reason: How Miracles Can Change Your Life*.

[153] The Greek phrase is *dynameis te mellontos aiōnos*. BAGD speaks of *dynameis* in Hebrews 6:5 under the heading of "deed of power, miracle, wonder."

esy . . ." (1 Cor. 14:24) and shortly thereafter in another context says, "You can all prophesy one by one" (v. 31). Potentially, everyone in the assembly of believers can prophesy. Peter on the Day of Pentecost declared that the words of Joel were now fulfilled: "And in the last days it shall be, God declares, that I will pour out my Spirit upon all flesh, and your sons and your daughters shall prophesy . . . yea, and on my menservants and my maidservants . . . I will pour out my Spirit; and they shall prophesy" (Acts 2:17–18). Accordingly, wherever the Spirit is outpoured, the result is that people without distinction of sex or class are able to prophesy. In regard to gender it is worth noting that even before Paul begins his discussion of the gifts of the Spirit in 1 Corinthians 12–14 he had already spoken (in chap. 11) of both men and women prophesying— "any man who prays or prophesies . . . any woman who prays or prophesies . . ." (vv. 4–5). Thus at Corinth and in all Spirit-anointed assemblies, everyone may prophesy.

On the other hand, since prophecy is also an individual apportionment of the

Spirit, a certain person or persons will be singled out on a given occasion to speak forth in prophecy. This is the gift of prophecy to be eagerly desired; by no means do all persons assembled have it. Those who do may be designated "prophets." Paul's statement, already noted, beginning, "you can all prophesy one by one," continues a few words later, "and the spirits of prophets are subject to prophets" (1 Cor. 14:32). Thus those particularly gifted with prophecy function[154] as prophets whenever they are used by the Holy Spirit in this role. This does not mean that a person functioning as a prophet at a given time holds the office of a prophet. The New Testament clearly portrays others also called prophets who in association with the apostles laid the foundation of the church[155] or who were a special order in the early church.[156] However, in the context of 1 Corinthians 14:32 prophets are simply those who prophesy.[157] They are persons gifted individually by the Holy Spirit on a particular occasion to speak forth prophetically.

The background of prophecy is revelation. Paul wrote about two or three

---

[154] Wayne Grudem speaks of the functional use of the word "prophet" and adds that "Paul calls anyone who prophesies a προφήτης in 14.32" (*The Gift of Prophecy in 1 Corinthians,* 232, from the section entitled, "Informal Recognition: Those Who Prophesy Are Prophets," 231–34).

[155] Paul speaks in Ephesians 2:20 about the church as "built upon the foundation of the apostles and prophets" (cf. 3:5; 4:11; Rev. 18:20). In regard to the order of divine appointments he writes, "God has appointed in the church first apostles, second prophets . . ." (1 Cor. 12:28).

[156] See Acts 11:27–28: "In these days prophets came down from Jerusalem to Antioch. And one of them, named Agabus . . ."; 13:1: "In the church at Antioch there were prophets and teachers"; 15:32: "Judas and Silas, who were themselves prophets . . ."; 21:10: ". . . a prophet named Agabus came down from Judea." (Acts 21:9 speaks of Philip's daughters as those "who prophesied"; they are not designated "prophetesses" [as NASB translates the term]).

[157] This distinction between a prophet as one who occasionally prophesies and the prophets (foundational or special) is not always clear in the New Testament. G. W. H. Lampe says, "Within the New Testament period there seems to have been a definite, though to us obscure, distinction between occasional prophesying by 'ordinary' church members, on the one hand, and the exercise of a ministry by 'specialist' prophets on the other" (*Christ and Spirit in the New Testament,* 257). However obscure, this "definite" distinction needs to be carefully recognized.

prophets speaking (1 Cor. 14:29), immediately adding, "If a revelation is made to another [prophet] sitting by, let the first [prophet] be silent" (v. 30). Thus a person prophesies because God has revealed something to him, and through his mouth a message from God is declared. This obviously is not a prepared message, for the revelation immediately issues in the spoken prophecy. Spontaneity marks such an occasion and the words are divinely inspired.[158] Such revelation, I must immediately add, does not place the prophetic message on the same level as Scripture.[159] It is revelation that is subordinate[160] to what God has special-

ly revealed to apostles and prophets[161] and has been set forth in Scripture.[162] Nonetheless such subordinate revelation is directly from God and is spoken with divine authority.

Prophecy, accordingly, is an immediate communication from God in the common language. It is a "speaking for"[163] God by which a person's tongue is completely at the disposal of the Holy Spirit. The concepts and words do not derive from the speaker[164] but from a divine source. So God communicates in a given situation a special message to His people.

Thus the occurrence of prophecy is an extraordinary event. Perhaps the

---

[158]Dunn writes, "For Paul prophecy is a word of revelation. It does not denote the delivery of a previously prepared sermon; it is not a word that can be summoned up to order, or a skill that can be learned; it is a spontaneous utterance, a revelation given in words to the prophet to be delivered as it is given (14:30)" (*Jesus and the Spirit,* 228). George Montague writes that "the text of 14:30 suggests that the gift involves a sudden revelation at the moment" (*The Holy Spirit: Growth of a Biblical Tradition,*153). It is important to recognize this because prophecy has sometimes been identified with preaching. For example, Robertson and Plummer write that prophecy is "preaching the word with power. . . . This gift implies special insight into revealed truths and a great faculty for making them and their consequences known to others" (*1 Corinthians,* ICC, 266). Leon Morris distinguishes the two by saying that prophecy is "something like our preaching, but it is not identical with it. It is not the delivery of a carefully prepared sermon, but the uttering of words directly inspired by God" (*1 Corinthians,* TNTC, 187). Gordon Fee writes, "By prophecy . . . [Paul] does not mean a prepared sermon, but the spontaneous word given to God's people for the edification of the whole. *Most contemporary churches would have to be radically reconstructed in terms of their self-understanding for such to take place*" (*The First Epistle to the Corinthians,* NICNT, 660, italics added). Fee's statement is worth pondering.
[159]D. A. Carson writes, "When Paul presupposes in 1 Corinthians 14:30 that the gift of prophecy depends on revelation, we are not limited to a form of authoritative revelation that threatens the finality of the canon" (*Showing the Spirit,* 163).
[160]See vol. 1, chapter 2, B.3. "Subordinate Revelation."
[161]These are the apostles and prophets of Ephesians 2:20.
[162]The canon of Scripture contains this special revelation given to the apostles and prophets.
[163]"Prophecy" is from the Greek words *pro* ["for"] and *phēmi* ["speak"].
[164]Dunn, as earlier quoted, referred particularly to 1 Corinthians 14:30 as "a revelation given in words to the prophet *to be delivered as it is given*" (italics added). In this connection Dunn also quotes favorably words from J. Lindblom, *Prophecy:* " 'The prophet knows that his thoughts and words never come from himself; they are given him' " (*Jesus and the Spirit,* 418). Grudem in regard to the same passage (1 Cor. 14:30) denies a "divine authority of actual words" and speaks only of "a divine authority of general content" (*The Gift of Prophecy in 1 Corinthians,* 67). This statement says far too little. Of course, if a prophecy derives from God, it may be wondered why words often differ so much. Why, for example, do the words of God in Hosea sound quite different from those in Amos; or why, on the contemporary scene, does one person sometimes prophesy in King James English and another in more modern speech if the words in both cases are from the Lord? The answer surely is that *whatever the mode* God may speak His word through any human utterance.

fact that Paul lists it immediately after miracles is significant. Prophecy has been called "miracle in the form of speech,"[165] for while prophecy is in the common language, it is given by God. Even such a miracle as God's raising the dead bodily is not as extraordinary as God's speaking directly in human words to the minds and spirits of His gathered people. Prophecy, as Paul says in 1 Corinthians 13:9, is "in part,"[166] but that is due primarily to the fact of our finite situation. God speaks fully but within the limits of the human condition. Such is the amazing nature of prophecy.

Now let us look at the purpose of the gift of prophecy. According to Paul it is for upbuilding, exhortation, and consolation: "One who prophesies speaks to men for edification [upbuilding] and exhortation and consolation"[167] (1 Cor. 14:3 NASB). Prophecy is for the purpose of building up and strengthening people, exhorting and encouraging certain actions, and bringing consolation and comfort.[168] Hence prophecy, as a direct word from the Lord, serves first to build up people.[169] Prophecy, accordingly, is not destructive in tone or manner; it is for building up, not tearing down.[170] Prophecy is an edifying message, strengthening people in their faith and life. Second, prophecy may be a word of exhortation. In that sense prophecy may contain an admonition about certain activities[171] and an urging to move ahead in a proper manner.[172] Hence there is also a note of

---

[165]F. L. Godet (*Commentary on First Corinthians*, 626). In relation to another gift, healing, Godet adds that the result of prophecy "is in the spiritual domain an effect analogous to that which is produced on the sick man by the 'Rise and walk' pronounced by him who has the gift of healing" (ibid.).

[166]So reads KJV, NIV, NASB (NEB similarly has "partial"). The Greek phrase is *ek merous*, signifying *not* "imperfect" (as RSV translates) but partial. *Ek merous* is quantitative rather than qualitative. As Fee says, "It [prophecy] is 'partial' because it belongs only to this age" (*The First Epistle to the Corinthians*, NICNT, 645). The next verse (10), reading "when the perfect [*teleion*] comes, the partial will be done away" (NASB), is better translated by C. K. Barrett as "when totality comes, that which is partial shall be done away with" (*The First Epistle to the Corinthians*, HNTC, 306). Prophecy is "in part," not because of imperfection in it, but because the complete, the "totality," belongs to the future age.

[167]The Greek phrase is *oikodomēn kai paraklēsin kai paramuthian*. The RSV translates this phrase as "upbuilding and encouragement and consolation"; NIV, as "strengthening, encouragement and comfort."

[168]In Ellicott's vivid words, prophecy is for "building up, stirring up, cheering up!" (as quoted by Harold Horton in *The Gifts of the Spirit*, 170).

[169]Prophecy generally is directed to the whole assembly—"he who prophesies edifies the church" (1 Cor. 14:4); however, because (as quoted) the one prophesying "speaks to men," this could imply speaking to individuals as well. Experience today in the charismatic renewal points to both general and individual prophecy.

[170]Similarly Paul wrote later to the Corinthians about the authority given him as an apostle, "for building [them] up rather than pulling [them] down" (2 Cor. 10:8 NIV).

[171]Dunn speaks of prophecy meeting a "need in the assembly . . . for a word of challenge and rebuke to careless or slipshod or detrimental activities" (*Jesus and the Spirit*, 229). This is well said.

[172]The first use by Paul of *parakaleō* in 1 Corinthians is in 1:10, where Paul says, "I exhort [*parakalō*] you, brethren, by the name of our Lord Jesus Christ, that you all agree, and there be no divisions among you, but you be made complete in the same mind and in the same judgment" (NASB). (See also, e.g., Rom. 12:1; 15:30; 2 Cor. 10:1; Eph. 4:1; Phil. 4:2; 1 Thess. 4:1; 1 Tim. 2:1; note also the use of *parakalō* in 1 Peter 2:11; 5:1). An exhortation in the assembly by a believer might be similar to these admonitions by Paul and Peter.

encouragement.[173] Third, prophecy may serve for consolation and comfort. Where there is hurt and suffering[174] or need for a sympathetic word, a prophecy may speak an inspired message that brings comfort and consolation. Altogether the threefold purpose of prophecy—upbuilding, exhortation, and consolation—speaks to a wide range of needs in the gathered assembly.

Prophecy in the assembly, I now add, is not basically foretelling.[175] It is much more a "forthtelling" than a "foretelling." Prophecy speaks to the present situation of people within the congregation. Of course, a word of upbuilding, exhortation, or consolation may very well have a future aspect (for example, "God's grace will be sufficient for you in the days ahead"), but it is not primarily predictive (as in some such word as "If you go to this place, God will richly bless you"). A related re-

mark is that prophecy may confirm but never by itself direct (as in some such word as "God wants you to marry this person"). Directional prophecy can undermine a person's own relationship to God and also possibly lead to disastrous results. However, a prophecy may indeed be confirmational; for example, a person in the assembly already through Scripture reading, prayer, and the like, may have become convinced that God is leading in a certain direction. Then a prophecy occurs that confirms this leading and as a result the person is much blessed. Predictive prophecy—prophecy as essentially foretelling—is to be strongly guarded against.[176]

From what has been said, it is clear that prophecy is primarily for believers. So Paul later wrote, "Prophecy is not for unbelievers but for believers" (1 Cor. 14:22). However, a secondary

---

[173]The Greek word *paraklēsis* is often best translated "encouragement" (as in RSV and NIV here). Paul writes in 1 Thessalonians 5:11: "Therefore encourage [*parakaleite*] one another, and build up [*oikodomeite*] one another, just as you also are doing" (NASB). A further translation of *parakaleō* is "comfort" (especially see 2 Cor. 1:3–6, where a form of *parakaleō* is "comfort" (especially see 2 Cor. 1:3–6 where a form of *parakaleō* is used nine times; clearly "comfort" is the proper translation in these verses). However, in 1 Corinthians 14:3 either "edification" or "encouragement" is more likely (cf. 14:31, where "comfort" is even less likely than in v. 3). Also since Paul uses a third term, *paramythia* (see next above), which may also be translated "comfort," it is unlikely that *paraklēsis* should bear so similar a meaning.

[174]The use of *paramythia* in its verbal form is clearly shown in John 11:31 that speaks of "the Jews who were with her in the house, consoling [*paramythoumenoi*] her," namely, Mary who was mourning the death of her brother Lazarus. *Parakaleō* and *paramythomai* may also be seen together in 1 Thessalonians 2:11: "We exhorted and comforted . . . every one of you" (KJV). In 1 Corinthians 12 Paul writes, "If one member suffers, all suffer together" (v. 26). It may be to that particular situation that Paul writes in 14:3 about prophecy as consolation.

[175]One in the special order of prophets, namely Agabus, did predict the future. I earlier quoted words from Acts 11:27: "Now in these days prophets came down from Jerusalem to Antioch [hence reference to a special order of prophets]." Then the text continues, "And one of them named Agabus stood up and foretold by the Spirit that there would be a great famine over all the world; and this [famine] took place in the days of Claudius" (v. 28). (Also see Acts 21:11 for a further prediction by Agabus.) We should continue to bear in mind that in regard to the gifts of the Spirit Paul is not talking about a special order of prophets but of prophesying within the gathered community of believers. Agabus was an itinerant prophet (along with others who "came down" to a certain place) and as such did predict the future; prophesying in the local body is (as I have described it) basically nonpredictive.

[176]This is especially true today when astrology, fortunetelling, and horoscopes abound. Their claims to predict the future (and thereby possibly to control it) are a far cry from genuine prophecy.

function of prophecy is to convict unbelievers of sin so that they turn to God. Paul continues, "If all prophesy,[177] and an unbeliever or outsider[178] enters, he is convicted by all, he is called to account by all, the secrets of his heart are disclosed; and so, falling on his face, he will worship God and declare that God is really among you" (vv. 24–25). This extraordinary change occurs not through the proclamation of one person (as in preaching) but through the prophesying of many. That many believers are channels for God to speak directly brings such overwhelming conviction, judgment, and heart searching that the unbeliever or outsider can only fall on his face and worship God. Moreover, he will know for a certainty that God is truly present among His people. It is most noteworthy that this happens as prophecy goes forth *not* to the unbelievers and outsiders but to believers ("prophecy is . . . for believers"). The coming of unbelievers and outsiders to a vivid experience of the Lord is a *side effect* (but what a great one!) of proph-

ecy sounding forth in the believing community.

Because of the importance of prophecy, the words spoken need to be considered carefully. Paul writes, "Let two or three prophets speak, and let the others[179] weigh[180] what is said" (1 Cor. 14:29). The basic purpose of this weighing is to discern the significance and relevance of a given prophecy within the body of believers.[181] If God is truly speaking in prophecy, then it is important to weigh each word. This includes such matters as the import of the prophecy, the person(s) addressed, and the relation to other prophecies that may have been spoken. There should be no hurrying past a prophecy as if it were only a human word. The prophetic message, as God-given, needs careful weighing by all.

But the weighing may also include judging. In fact the admonition of Paul could be read thus: "Let two or three prophets speak, and let the others pass judgment" (NASB).[182] In another letter Paul wrote, "Do not despise prophesy-

---

[177]This is contrasted with everyone's speaking in tongues and the effect that that would have on unbelievers (v. 23). (See section VIII, "Kinds of Tongues," for a discussion of that matter.)

[178]The Greek word is *idiōtēs*. The KJV reads "one unlearned," NASB "an ungifted man," NIV "some who do not understand" (NIVmg "some inquirer"). According to BAGD, the "ιδιῶται and ἄπιστοι [unbelievers] together form a contrast to the Christian congregation. The ιδ. are neither similar to the ἄπιστοι . . . nor are they full-fledged Christians; obviously they stood betw. the two groups as a kind of proselytes or catechumens." Hence an *idiōtēs* may also be called an uninitiated person, one who is not yet a "full-fledged" Christian but is inquiring about, looking into, and perhaps being instructed in the faith. He is an "outsider," but as prophecy goes forth his position may quickly change.

[179]"The others" (*hoi alloi*) is best understood to refer to the others not prophesying, hence the rest of the assembled believers. If the reference were to a limited group of prophets, the Greek phrase would probably be *hoi loipoi*, "the rest" (i.e., of the prophets). In verse 31 Paul adds, "You can *all* prophesy one by one, so that *all* may learn and *all* be encouraged." Thus "the others" refers to "all" the rest (i.e., the entire assembly). (On this see especially Grudem, *The Gift of Prophecy in the New Testament and Today,* 70–74, and Fee, *The First Epistle to the Corinthians,* NICNT, 694.)

[180]The Greek word is *diakrinetōsan*; NIV (similar to RSV above) has "weigh carefully."

[181]F. F. Bruce, following the words "weigh what is said," has in parenthesis "(lit. 'discern' or 'distinguish' it [cf. 12.10], or, just possibly, 'discuss' it), so as to ascertain its direct relevance" (*1 and 2 Corinthians,* NCBC, 134).

[182]KJV reads "judge"; NEB has "exercise their judgment upon what is said."

ing, but test[183] everything; hold fast what is good" (1 Thess. 5:20–21). But why, one may ask, would prophecy, or prophesying, call for judging and testing? Is not prophecy (as earlier stated) God's speaking directly? The answer is yes—in all *true* prophesying. Let me clarify. There is always a possibility that a presumed prophecy is *not* from God. John writes, "Beloved, do not believe every spirit, but test the spirits to see whether they are of God; for many false prophets have gone out into the world" (1 John 4:1). A person may claim to speak in the name of God, and yet his spirit is not "of God"; hence the prophecy is a false one. Someone may enter the assembly and speak a "Thus says the Lord"[184] and yet the message be totally false.[185] In addition it is possible for someone in the assembly to claim to speak a prophetic word, but it may come from his own mind and spirit.[186] There is no guarantee that because one uses the language of prophecy he is truly prophesying. Thus the importance, the urgency, of testing prophecy cannot be overemphasized.

In summary, the weighing of prophecy consists of discerning both the significance and the source of what is uttered.[187] The latter is actually primary, for if the source is not of God, then it is pointless to consider the significance. However, ordinarily in a believing community where Jesus is recognized as Lord, the significance is the main concern. What, and perhaps to whom, is the Lord speaking through this prophecy?

Nonetheless, testing remains important because of the high-powered nature of prophecy. Because true prophecy is the very utterance of God, hence extremely important, it is urgent that any recognized false prophecy be cast aside. Let us, accordingly, look at a number of statements that will affirm the character and spirit of true prophecy and at the same time throw light on the dubious and the false.

1. True prophecy is an expression of the mind and Spirit of Christ. Prophets of old prophesied "by the Spirit of Christ within them" (1 Peter 1:11). This is true in even greater and fuller

---

183The Greek word is *dokimazete*; "to test, examine, prove, scrutinize (to see whether a thing be genuine or not), as metals" (Thayer).

184As Amos did in the Old Testament (Amos 1:3, 6, 9, 11, 13; 2:1, 4; 3:11; 5:4 KJV); similarly Agabus in the New Testament: "Thus says the Holy Spirit" (Acts 21:11).

185Jesus Himself said, "Beware of false prophets, who come to you in sheep's clothing . . ." (Matt. 7:15). Our gathering of believers some years ago had a jolting experience. A man entered the group and prophesied that God wanted all the people gathered to leave their "dead churches." After the immediate shock many in the group expressed their judgment that the Lord was not speaking in the man's word. The man, now shown to be a false prophet, left the meeting in anger, never to return.

186In the Old Testament God through Jeremiah denounced the false prophets. He said to the people, "Do not listen to the words of the prophets who prophesy to you, filling you with vain hopes; they speak visions of their own minds, not from the mouth of the LORD" (Jer. 23:16). Through Ezekiel God similarly spoke against "those who prophesy out of their own minds" (Ezek. 13:2). Such false prophesying is still possible.

187Dunn speaks of "*an evaluation, a testing, a weighing of the prophetic utterance* [italics his] by the rest . . . to determine both its source as to inspiration and its significance for the assembly" (*Jesus and the Spirit*, 234). This is well said. Grudem views the weighing as relating to the individual words spoken, "a process whereby every member of the congregation would listen carefully and evaluate each statement, distinguishing what he felt to be good from the less good . . . helpful from the unhelpful . . . true from the false" (*The Gift of Prophecy in 1 Corinthians*, 64–65). However, contra Grudem, there is no suggestion in Paul's words about "weighing" that he intends such piecemeal evaluation. A prophecy is either from God or not; if it is, then it is to be totally received.

measure since Christ has come in the flesh and has sent the Holy Spirit. Any prophecy, accordingly, that breathes a spirit foreign to Christ cannot be a true prophecy. This is the primary test of prophecy: namely, a valid representation of Christ.

2. True prophecy is harmonious with God's own word in Scripture. Because the Scriptures have the Holy Spirit as their ultimate Author and it is the same Spirit who speaks in prophecy, there can be no dissonance. Moreover, since the Scriptures are God's comprehensive word to which nothing substantial can be added, any utterance that goes beyond or adds to what is contained in Scripture cannot be true prophecy. Prophecy has its checkpoint in Holy Scripture.

3. True prophecy builds up the community: "He who prophesies edifies the church" (1 Cor. 14:4). Accordingly, any utterance that is basically judgmental or negative in word or manner is false prophecy. Prophecy is for building up, not tearing down. There may indeed be admonition and warning, even exhortation to desist from some evil, but the whole purpose is positive: the strengthening of faith and practice.

4. True prophecy finds consent and agreement in the minds and hearts of others in the community. Since the same Holy Spirit is at work in all, all are in a position to "pass judgment" on the validity of what is spoken. There should be a prevailing sense in the community that the prophecy was divinely inspired. The spirit of one prophesying and his or her words stand under the judgment of others.

5. True prophecy serves to glorify God, not man. Peter writes, "As each has received a gift [*charisma*], employ it

for one another, as good stewards of God's varied grace: whoever speaks, as one who utters oracles of God . . . that in everything God may be glorified through Jesus Christ" (1 Peter 4:10–11). Such oracular utterance surely includes prophecy. Hence if one prophesying seeks by that to elevate himself, if prophesying is basically self-serving, it cannot be from God. The end of true prophecy is the glorification of God.

Now I add a few miscellaneous remarks about prophecy. First, the act of prophesying has a vital connection with faith. As we have earlier observed, the gift of faith is related to the gifts that follow: healings, miracles, and now prophecy. Without faith, healings and miracles do not occur, nor does prophecy. Paul, writing to the Romans about the *charismata*, says, ". . . if prophecy, according to the proportion of his faith" (12:6 NASB). Prophecy, while coming from revelation, must find a correspondence in faith,[188] so that the person who prophesies does so out of a faith that God will speak through his words. Prophesying calls for the courage to launch out in speech, believing that God will supply the words. This is not always easy because the one prophesying usually knows nothing of what will be said beforehand and must rely totally on the Spirit of God.

Second, there is no set form for the language of prophecy. Since God is speaking through the words of true prophecy, the language is often in the first person, like the language of Acts 13:2: "The Holy Spirit said, 'Set apart for me Barnabas and Saul for the work to which I have called them.' "[189] Or the language may be more that of the third person, such as that of Agabus,

---

[188] EGT speaks of prophecy as "an ἀποκάλυψις [revelation] of hidden things of God realised through a peculiar clearness and intensity of faith" (2:888).

[189] The prior verse speaks of "prophets and teachers" (v. 1). The implication is that through one of the prophets present the words of the Holy Spirit came forth.

"Thus says the Holy Spirit, 'So shall the Jews at Jerusalem bind the man who owns this girdle . . .'" (Acts 21:11).[190] In either case, God is speaking through the lips of people.[191] True prophecy may be spoken a variety of ways as the Lord Himself wills it.

Third, prophesying should be done in an orderly manner. Paul wrote, "Let two or three prophets speak, and let the others weigh what is said. If a revelation is made to another [prophet] sitting by, let the first be silent" (1 Cor. 14:29-30). Orderliness calls for one person to prophesy at a time and a readiness on the part of that person to defer to another when he receives a revelation. Prophesying can and should be done "one by one" (v. 31). It is not a disorderly outburst—an "I *just had to* do it" sort of thing. Thus Paul adds, "The spirits of prophets are subject to prophets" (v. 32),[192] meaning that prophetic speech, though it is of God, is always under the control of the one prophesying. This implies that there is no justification at any time for one prophesying to interrupt what else is going on, for example, preaching and teaching. Disorderliness is not God's way, for, as Paul concludes at this point, "God is not a God of confusion but of peace" (v. 33).

We are just beginning again to appreciate the powerful gift of prophecy in the assembly of believers. There is little wonder that Paul said, "Eagerly desire the spiritual gifts, especially that you may prophesy." We are to desire this not for self-aggrandizement but that God's voice may be heard and His people thereby edified. May prophecy truly flourish in the church!

VII. DISTINGUISHINGS OF SPIRITS[193]

This next listed gift of the Holy Spirit again relates to an individual: "to another the distinguishings of spirits [*diakriseis pneumatōn*]" (1 Cor. 12:10 NASB). As with all the preceding gifts, this is a particular gift or manifestation of the Spirit for the common good.

The word "distinguishings" may also be translated as "discernings"[194] and refers to a "judging through,"[195] a piercing through what is outward to the inner reality. Since "distinguishings" is in the plural, more than one discerning in a given situation is implied. The individual to whom the gift is imparted will be enabled to accomplish more than one distinguishing or discerning.

This discerning is not just discernment in general[196] but relates to "spir-

---

[190] In both cases just described, the prophets were those recognized as such and not those who occasionally prophesied. However, whatever the variation between established and occasional prophets, there seems no reason to believe that the method of prophesying differs.

[191] Incidentally, this does not call for an unnatural voice. A loud, booming voice crying forth a "Thus saith the Lord" is no more divinely inspired than a quiet and natural voice declaring His word! (The unnatural voice, meant to impress, might even be that of a false prophet.)

[192] The NIV translates verse 32 thus: "The spirits of prophets are subject to the control of prophets."

[193] The Greek word translated "distinguishings" is in the plural. So again (as with the previous two gifts), despite the awkwardness in English, I am translating it as plural.

[194] KJV reads "discerning" (singular). I will frequently use the plural, "discernings," in what follows.

[195] The verbal form of *diakrisis* is *diakrinō*—literally, to "judge through" (*dia* + *krinō*). *Diakrinō* is the same verb used in 1 Corinthians 14:29: "Let the others weigh [or judge] what is said" (recall our discussion in sect. VI, "Prophecy").

[196] As Harold Horton says, "There is no such gift as the Gift of Discernment" (*The Gifts of the Spirit*, 70).

its." "Spirits," in turn, may refer to a wide range of the human, the demonic, even the angelic. All human beings are embodied spirits, the spirit being the inmost essence of human nature; demons are evil, unclean spirits; and angels are "ministering spirits" (Heb. 1:14). Hence, discernings of spirits can well relate to a whole range of spirits possibly operating in a given situation.[197] Accordingly, more than one discerning (thus the plural, "discernings" or "distinguishings") may be needed to deal with the complexity of spiritual forces that are at work.

Such distinguishings of spirits are possible only by another spirit, indeed by the Holy Spirit. It is by the illumination of *the* Spirit through the spirit of a particular individual that spirits are perceived. Since this manifestation of the Spirit is for the common good, it serves particularly to discern the Spirit at work in any expression or activity within the Christian community.

A. Human Spirits

First, there is the perception of human spirits. Paul speaks in 1 Corinthians 14:32 about "the spirits of prophets." Accordingly, one who is operating by the Holy Spirit in the gift of discernings of spirits is able to perceive the spirits of those prophesying. By extension, since all may prophesy[198] (1 Cor. 14:24), the discernings of spirits relates to each person who is present in the fellowship. By the sudden illumination of the Holy Spirit, hence a supernatural action, the spirits of those present may be discerned.

Jesus Himself had a total sensitivity to people in their inner nature. On first seeing Simon, Jesus declared, "You shall be called Cephas (which means Peter)," that is, "Rock" (John 1:42). Jesus looked deep into Simon's inner being and saw the making of solid character. Jesus, shortly thereafter, saw Nathanael and declared, "Behold, an Israelite indeed, in whom is no guile!" (v. 47); hence Jesus perceived in Nathanael a guileless spirit. According to John 2:25, Jesus "knew what was in man." This is demonstrated in accounts that follow—for example, Nicodemus (John 3) and the woman of Samaria (John 4). Another Gospel states that Jesus perceived "in his spirit" that some scribes "questioned within themselves" (Mark 2:8). Jesus is shown in these accounts, and many others, to be One who in His spirit sensed the nature and motivations of those whom He encountered. Since the Holy Spirit is the Spirit of Jesus, that same Spirit through the gift of discernings of spirits can reach deep into the spirits of people.

Through the gift of discernings of spirits, it follows that inner feelings and motivations are perceived. It again is the piercing through the outer surface to the inner spirit. People who gather in the fellowship represent a wide spiritual range. Some may be present with a heavy spirit or an anxious spirit; there may be a weak spirit or a proud spirit; some may come with a jealous spirit or a bitter spirit. Such spirits may not be apparent to others; indeed, the believers may not be fully aware of them among themselves. Yet such spiritual attitudes are likely to affect whatever happens in the dynamics of interrelationships. Hence, the gift of the discernings of spirit can be of signal importance, for by a supernatural action— that of the Holy Spirit—the spirits of people are disclosed.[199] When this oc-

---

[197] Bittlinger speaks of this gift as "the ability to distinguish between divine, human, and demonic powers" (*Gifts and Graces,* 45).

[198] Recall our discussion in section VI.

[199] In Hebrews 4:13 there is this statement: "Before him [God] no creature is hidden, but

curs, the area of need may become apparent and proper ministry rendered.

Some illustrations may help. For example, as the body of believers comes together, someone senses by the Spirit that a certain person has a spirit of heaviness and anxiety. This spirit is a block for him in group participation; for it is hard to speak a word of wisdom or knowledge, to minister in healings or miracles, to give a prophetic utterance when one is inwardly burdened. Furthermore, this person may not even be aware of his situation until someone in the Spirit says something like this: "I perceive in you, my brother, a heavy spirit of deep anxiety." When this spirit is recognized and ministry follows,[200] not only is the burdened person blessed but also the whole group may move ahead in the operation of the other gifts. A further example: someone in the gathering may come with a headache and ask for ministry through the gifts of healings. Another person who senses that the Holy Spirit will use him as a channel for healing is about ready to minister when still another individual now being gifted with discernings of spirits senses that the root of the headache is a bitter and unforgiving spirit. Until this is recognized and properly dealt with, healing is quite unlikely to occur. Thus the gift of discernings of spirits may clear the way for the healing to take place.

Through this gift the Holy Spirit provides depth perception of a spiritual problem that lies at the root of a human ailment. There are bodily ailments that physicians are competent to deal with; there are many difficulties in the human mind and emotions that psychologists can help to resolve. However, on the deepest level of the human spirit,[201] where many problems have their rootage, there can be no perception of what lies there except through the illumination of the Holy Spirit.

We must be circumspect here. The gift of discernings of spirits by which the human spirit is probed is not a problem-solving gift. Like X-ray, it provides in-depth illumination without which the inner person is shrouded in darkness. But the illumination itself does not resolve the problem. Nevertheless, the important thing is that the spiritual situation be discerned; after that other actions may follow (such as proceeding with the ministry of the gifts of healings, suggesting possible follow-up by qualified physicians, psychologists, and the like). Without the original illumination by the Holy Spirit there is likely to be uncertainty and confusion as to how to proceed.

But there is also another direction the gift of discernings of human spirits may take. Beyond focusing on problem situations, there may also be the perception of the positive. For example, a person may sense the Holy Spirit moving upon the spirit of someone to manifest Himself in a specific way, but that person is holding back. A word of encouragement may help him step out in the gift that he is being granted. For example, "I discern that the Spirit is anointing you to prophesy" may be all that is needed for someone to begin to speak forth. A gentle nudge by the Spirit can make a great difference!

Or it may be that through the Holy

---

all are open and laid bare to the eyes of him with whom we have to do." Accordingly, through the action of the Holy Spirit—the Spirit of God operating by the gift of discernings of spirits—human spirits are "open and laid bare."

[200]This is not necessarily done by the person operating in the gift. Someone else, or others, may now be used in providing that ministry.

[201]A person in totality is body, soul (including mind, emotions, and will), and spirit (see vol. 1, chap. 9, "Man," II.). Spirit is more than and deeper than soul or mind even when such is viewed in its subconscious dimension.

Spirit a person discerns, for example, love, joy, and peace in the spirits of many people. As the discerner calls attention to this, all in the gathering may thereby be edified. One line in a chorus expresses this beautifully: "There's a sweet, sweet Spirit in this place; and I know that it's the Spirit of the Lord." To discern that Spirit and share it with others is to bring a rich blessing.

B. Demonic Spirits

Second, the perception of demonic spirits is a critically important function of the gift of discernings of spirits. For where the Holy Spirit (the true supernatural) is at work, often the counterforce of evil spirits (the false supernatural) is also present. Hence, there is the urgency of a clear discerning of such demonic forces. Only then can they be adequately dealt with.

Jesus is frequently shown in the Gospels as One who discerned demonic spirits. To illustrate: He recognized immediately an "unclean spirit" torturing a man (Mark 1:23–25); He also saw behind many illnesses the presence of demonic forces, for example, a "deaf and dumb spirit" (Mark 9:25). He saw Satan at work in a seemingly loyal statement by Peter and responded vehemently, "Get behind me, Satan!" (Matt. 16:22–23). He "perceived" the "craftiness" of the Pharisees in an apparently open question about tribute to Caesar (Luke 20:23–25). Jesus often discerned behind the outward semblance an inner force of the demonic at work.

In the early church Peter demonstrated discernings of spirits when he perceived that Ananias and Sapphira had lied about the disposition of their property: "You have agreed together to tempt the Spirit of the Lord" (Acts 5:1–9). Earlier Peter had said to Ananias, "Why has Satan filled your heart to lie to the Holy Spirit?" (v. 3). Hence Peter perceived that Satan was at work. Paul likewise showed discernment of a demonic force as he "looked intently" at Elymas the magician and declared Elymas' opposition to the gospel to be satanic—"You son of the devil" (Acts 13:8–10). Later Paul recognized "a spirit of divination" in the slave girl who repeatedly declared that Paul and his companions were "bond-servants of the Most High God, who are proclaiming . . . the way of salvation"; Paul "greatly annoyed . . . turned and said to the spirit, 'I command you in the name of Jesus Christ to come out of her!' " (Acts 16:16–18 NASB).[202] Through such spiritual discernment of demonic spirits Peter and Paul gave leadership to the church in its formative period.

Now let us move into the local church setting. Insofar as the Holy Spirit is at work in the various gifts, it is important to recognize where evil may also be operative. This can be particularly true in the case of prophetic utterance. Significantly, Paul lists the gift of discernings of spirits immediately after prophecy as if to say that discernment is particularly needed when prophecies

---

[202]Three comments: (1) The gift of discernings of spirits is much needed before an exorcism occurs: it can be a serious mistake, often resulting in serious harm, if deliverance is attempted when no evil spirit is present. (2) The gift of discernings of spirits is *not* a gift of exorcism. When the discernment is correctly made, the way is prepared for any believer— of course, including the discerner—to engage in deliverance. (3) The gift of discernings of spirits does not ordinarily relate to exorcism within the Christian fellowship, since (as previously discussed) believers are not demon-possessed; however, there can be demonic attacks of many kinds that need to be perceived and properly dealt with.

occur.[203] We have previously noted that true prophecy finds consent and agreement with others in the community;[204] now we further observe that a particular individual through the discernings of spirits may perceive on occasion an evil force at work even when "good things" are proclaimed. So it was with Paul and the slave girl who spoke quite flattering, even true, words about Paul and his companions; yet Paul perceived that they came from a spirit of divination, not from the Holy Spirit. How particularly subtle such "religious" words, or similar ones, can be within the Christian community! And how important it is that they be recognized.

To follow up on this last point: pleasant and soothing words are not always from God. A prime example of this is found in the Old Testament narrative of some prophets who prophesied victory for the king of Israel: "Go up to Ramoth-gilead and triumph; the LORD will give it into the hand of the king" (1 Kings 22:12). However, this was a "lying spirit" (v. 23), and the king of Israel thereafter was killed in battle. The lesson here is that prophecies in the Christian community that speak only good things—which, of course, people generally like to hear—may not be from the true Spirit but from a lying spirit. For example, a prophetic word such as "All is well; go ahead; God will give you success in this undertaking" *might not* be a word from the Lord but from the adversary. The end could be anything but pleasant. Hence I stress the importance of the gift of discernings of spirits that may quickly perceive the

deception at work and alert others before dire results follow.[205]

The failure to discern an evil spirit can indeed be tragic. This was the terrible failure at the beginning of the human race that led to sin and the Fall. When the evil spirit, Satan himself, in the guise of a serpent, declared to the woman the heady words "You will be like God" (Gen. 3:5), she discerned no evil at all and, with her husband later concurring, took the fatal plunge by eating the forbidden fruit. If there had been a true discernment of spirit, Satan would have been repulsed and the man and the woman would have remained in fellowship with God. The failure to discern led to tragedy beyond measure.

The discernings of spirits is also important in dealing with certain cases of illness. Is a particular ailment only physical or mental, or is there perhaps some demonic power at work? It is quite significant that in His ministry Jesus dealt with two situations of deafness in radically different ways. In the one case there was a man who "was deaf and had an impediment of speech"; and in relation to the deafness Jesus placed His fingers in the man's ears saying, "Be opened," and the deaf man was healed (Mark 7:32–35). In the other case there was a convulsive boy who was deaf and dumb; Jesus helped him by saying, "You dumb and deaf spirit, I command you, come out of him, and never enter him again," and the boy was made whole (Mark 9:25–27). The first case of deafness was physical and dealt with by a healing touch; the latter was spiritual and handled by deliverance. *Jesus discerned*

---

[203]EGT states that " 'discernment of spirits' is the counterpart and safeguard of 'prophesying' " (2:888). Dunn writes, "Discerning of spirits is to be understood as *evaluation of prophetic utterances, an investigating and interpreting which throws light on their source and their significance*" (*Jesus and the Spirit,* 236, italics his).

[204]Section VI, 4.

[205]Dunn adds to the words quoted in n. 203: "The importance of this charisma as a regulative force within the charismatic community can hardly be overemphasized" (*Jesus and the Spirit,* 236).

the difference. Surely this is relevant today, for it is sometimes urgent to discern the root of a given illness and thus to know whether the ministry of healing or exorcising is called for.

Another important and somewhat similar function of the discernings of spirits is in relation to miracles. We have earlier discussed "the workings of miracles" as a gift, or manifestation, of the Holy Spirit. Now I emphasize that not all that seems to be a miracle is of God; for Satan can produce his counterfeits. Accordingly, there is critical need for discerning what forces are at work. From Pharaoh's court magicians who could also turn rods into serpents (Exod. 7:10–11)[206] and water into blood (vv. 21–22) to "the man of lawlessness," who will display "all kinds of counterfeit miracles, signs and wonders"[207] (2 Thess. 2:3–9 NIV), there is the continuing need to discern the source of supernatural deeds.[208] In our day, with the multiplication of occultism, witchcraft, spiritism, etc., and the demonic powers operating in them, there is all the more need for spiritual discernment. This is true even in the church, the fellowship of believers, because Satan most desires to penetrate there[209] and to perform his counterfeit miracles. So it is that in the body of believers, where miracles, along with other spiritual gifts, are much to be desired, there must be spiritual discernment of the nature and source of supernatural manifestations when they do occur.

Thus it is apparent that the gift of discernings of spirits is of much importance in relation to the preceding three gifts of healings, workings of miracles, and prophecy. For through this gift or manifestation of the Holy Spirit there is invaluable discernment as to whether healing or deliverance is called for, what spirit is at work in a supernatural demonstration of power, and what is the source of a prophetic utterance. Because of the possible penetration of evil forces in all these areas, the distinguishings, or discernings, of such demonic spirits is greatly needed. In this central area of active ministry gifts[210] the discernings of spirits is of critical importance.

C. Angelic Spirits

Third, there may be the perception of angelic spirits.[211] If evil, or demonic, spirits are perceptible by a special gift of the Holy Spirit, it surely follows that good, or angelic, spirits may likewise be recognized by that same Spirit.[212]

I have earlier mentioned the description of angels as "ministering spirits." The full text in Hebrews is "Are not all angels ministering spirits sent to serve those who will inherit salvation?" (1:14 NIV). If angelic spirits (angels) are sent

---

[206]Recall the earlier discussion in section V, "Workings of Miracles."

[207]Literally, "miracles, signs, and wonders of a lie [Gr. *pseudous*]."

[208]Not all that is supernatural is of God. Satan also operates in that realm.

[209]"The man of lawlessness," it is important to observe, "takes his seat in the temple of God" (2 Thess. 2:3–4). See n. 149 supra. Whether "the temple" refers to Jerusalem (many commentators) or the church (Calvin and others), the significant thing is that the force of evil is most satanic—subtle, blinding, misleading—when operating within God's holy precincts.

[210]To review: these five gifts are faith, gifts of healings, workings of miracles, prophecy, and discernings of spirits. Faith heads this list as essential basis for all that follows; discernment rounds out the list as illumination on all that has preceded. Thus ideally all these gifts work together in perfect harmony.

[211]For a helpful discussion of this see *Gifts of the Spirit* by Gordon Lindsay, volume 2, chapter 2, "The Discerning of Angelic Spirits."

[212]See also vol. 1, chapter 8, scetion V: "Human Experience of Angels."

to serve believers,[213] then we may expect to have some experience of their presence and activity. This could be all the more true for one who is gifted with the discerning of spirits.

An Old Testament illustration of angelic perception is found in a narrative relating to Elisha the prophet. Elisha was surrounded in a city by the horses and chariots of the king of Syria; however, the prophet, undisturbed, said to his servant, "Fear not, for those who are with us are more than those who are with them." Elisha then prayed, "O LORD . . . open his eyes that he may see." As a result the servant saw, and "behold, the mountain was full of horses and chariots of fire round about Elisha" (2 Kings 6:16–17). These were angelic forces that Elisha, and subsequently his servant, discerned. It all happened through spiritually opened eyes.[214]

Angels often are recognized in the New Testament. Among those who saw them were Joseph, Mary, Zechariah, certain shepherds, Mary Magdalene, Peter, Cornelius, Paul, and John. After Jesus' temptation experiences, "angels came and ministered to him" (Matt. 4:11; cf. Mark 1:13); also during His agony in Gethsemane "there appeared to him an angel from heaven, strengthening him" (Luke 22:43). The New Testament is laden with experiences of angels.

In regard to angels and the gathering of the Christian community, one of the most relevant passages is found in Hebrews 12. There the worship of believers is vividly depicted: "You have come to Mount Zion and to the city of the living God, the heavenly Jerusalem, and to innumerable angels in festal gathering . . ." (v. 22). Although this great company (literally, "myriads") of angels ordinarily is as invisible to us as "the heavenly Jerusalem," they surely may be spiritually experienced. Indeed, it is quite possible that someone gifted with the discernings of spirits may perceive God's presence and that of His angels. So a contemporary chorus testifies:

> Surely the presence of the Lord is in this place.
> I can feel His mighty power and His grace.
> I can hear the brush of angels' wings,
> I see glory on each face.
> Surely the presence of the Lord is in this place.[215]

To "hear the brush of angels' wings" (or however else the perception of angels may be understood) may well be the climactic experience in the discernings of spirits.

INTRODUCTION: KINDS OF TONGUES AND INTERPRETATION OF TONGUES

These final two gifts of the Holy Spirit—kinds of tongues[216] and interpretation of tongues—belong together. Even as the first two (word of wisdom and word of knowledge) relate to word or utterance so the last two (tongues and interpretation of tongues) relate to tongues. However, the relation between tongues and interpretation is more intimate, for one is not to function

---

[213]"Those who will inherit salvation" points to the believers' completion of salvation in the coming age.

[214]Elisha also had beheld "a chariot of fire and horses of fire" (2 Kings 2:11) when Elijah was taken up into heaven. Truly Elisha had a singular gift of perception.

[215]By Lanny Wolfe, used by permission, Lanny Wolfe Music Co. (ASCAP).

[216]RSV and NASB translate 1 Corinthians 12:10 as "various kinds of tongues"; NIV— "different kinds of tongues; KJV—"divers kinds of tongues." However, the Greek phrase is simply genē glōssōn, "kinds of tongues."

without the other.[217] Tongues and interpretation of tongues are twin gifts to be properly exercised together in the assembly of believers.

Both tongues and interpretation of tongues are unique in that, unlike the preceding seven gifts, they never occurred before the coming of the Holy Spirit at Pentecost. Hence, we cannot go back, as we can with the other seven gifts, to the Old Testament or even to the Gospels to find illustration. In connection with tongues Paul did quote a passage in Isaiah thus: "With men of other tongues[218] and other lips will I speak unto this people" (1 Cor. 14:21 KJV; Isa. 28:11 LXX). However, Paul does not apply this passage to a pre-Christian situation but to the Corinthian context (see 1 Cor. 14:20–22). The Gospels contain no incident of speaking in tongues with interpretation following.[219] Hence, these last two gifts occur only with the dawn of the Christian era.

In regard to the listing of the gifts, it is possible that tongues and interpretation of tongues are mentioned last because they were the last *charismata* to be given. They were the last to arrive on the scene.[220] Also these two gifts signify in a climactic way the Spirit's own self-expression—people speaking but the Holy Spirit giving the utterance and in turn giving the interpretation of what has been said. It is sometimes said that Paul lists these gifts last because they were least[221] or because they (especially tongues) were the problem in Corinth;[222] however, such viewpoints seem quite inadequate. I would far rather say—to repeat—that they are listed last because they were the last gifts given and in unique fashion highlight the Spirit's self-manifestation. Truly these two gifts point in singular fashion to a community of believers moving in the presence and power of the Holy Spirit.

One further word of introduction: These last two manifestations of the Holy Spirit form a distinctive category of gifts that operate *beyond* the mind. When Paul says, "If I pray in a tongue, my spirit prays but my mind is unfruitful ['my intellect lies fallow' NEB]" (1 Cor. 14:14), he is speaking of a category of gifts quite different from the first two (word of wisdom and word of knowledge, which are *mental* gifts) and the next five (which are *extramental* gifts).[223] Here in these climactic two

---

[217]Word of wisdom is not necessarily followed by word of knowledge whereas tongues must be followed by interpretation (see below for fuller discussion).

[218]The Greek for "other tongues" is *heteroglōssois* in 1 Corinthians; it is *glōssēs heteras* in the LXX. It will be recalled that "other tongues" in Acts 2:4 is *heterais glōssais*. (Also see chap. 9, n. 62.) I will discuss the Isaiah quotation later.

[219]In the Gospels there is frequently a word or words given in Aramaic then immediately translated into Greek (e.g., Matt. 27:33; Mark 5:41; 15:34; John 1:38, 41–42). Obviously, Aramaic is not spoken in tongues; nor is the translation an interpretation (see section IX).

[220]The other seven gifts are found earlier in the Old Testament and the Gospels.

[221]E.g., Bruce speaks of "nine forms of 'spiritual manifestation'" as "probably in descending order of value" (*1 and 2 Corinthians*, NCBC, 119), thus tongues and interpretation of tongues are the least in value. Incidentally, the idea of "last because least" hardly is in line with Paul's speaking in 1 Corinthians 13 about "faith, hope, love" (v. 13) in *that* order. "Love" is listed last, but it surely is not least, for Paul adds, "but the greatest of these is love"!

[222]Fee says that tongues "is listed last not because it is 'least,' but because it is the problem" (*First Epistle to the Corinthians*, NICNT, 572). Even if one were to affirm that the Corinthians overrated tongues (which is quite possible), it by no means follows that Paul's order relates to a problem.

[223]Recall footnote 50 regarding mental and extramental phenomena.

gifts the human mind is transcended[224] by the operation of the Holy Spirit through the human spirit to give both language and the interpretation: these are *supramental* gifts.[225] Tongues and interpretation of tongues operate on a level above and beyond the mind; they signify the climax in spiritual directness and intensity.

VIII. KINDS OF TONGUES

This is the gift of "kinds of tongues [*genē glōssōn*]" (1 Cor. 12:10). The word "kinds" suggests that the tongues referred to are not always of the same character, hence there may be a variety of tongues uttered. Since this is a manifestation of the Holy Spirit, there is no limitation on the languages spo-

ken: spiritual utterance is multiple in kind.[226]

Moreover, this gift is *not* "the ability"[227] to speak in tongues; *nor* is the gift that of "ecstatic utterance."[228] "Ability" implies some human capacity, whereas the gift is essentially the Spirit's doing; "ecstatic utterance" suggests irrational speech, whereas the gift is suprarational and profoundly spiritual. The only ability a person has is to make his tongues and lips available to the Holy Spirit for Him to give the utterance: the Spirit alone has the ability. Ecstasy is a term that at best connotes emotional delight. Although speaking in tongues surely is a joyous experience, there is always the content of communication; it is speech, not simply emotional expression.

---

[224] The quotation from EGT (in n. 50 referred to above), following the statement about the Holy Spirit working "through the *noûs* [mind]" (the first two gifts), and "in distinction from the *noûs*" (the next five gifts), continues with the words "in supersession of the *noûs*" (the last two gifts). The Greek word *heteros*, "another," as previously mentioned, separates these three categories.

[225] Prophecy might also seem to belong in this category. However, although the message is from the Holy Spirit, the words are in one's native tongue, so in that sense they could be called extramental rather than supramental. Interpretation of tongues to be sure is also in one's native speech (in that sense like prophecy); however, since the tongue interpreted is in the language of the Spirit, this belongs to the supramental category.

[226] It has been frequently suggested that Paul was referring to "kinds of tongues" when he wrote, "If I speak in the tongues of men and of angels . . . " (1 Cor. 13:1). Tongues from such a viewpoint would refer to a multiplicity of human languages (as possibly at Pentecost) and of angelic languages. In regard to human languages see my previous discussion (chap. 9, III.). Regarding languages of angels I have earlier called attention to Dunn's statement that "Paul thought of glossolalia as speaking the language(s) of heaven" (*Jesus and the Spirit*, 244). See likewise Fee, *First Epistle to the Corinthians*, NICNT, 630; Barrett, *First Epistle to the Corinthians*, HNTC, 299–300; Bruce (*1 and 2 Corinthians*, NCBC, 125). H. Conzelmann writes that "the wording does not in itself require the equating of angels' language and speaking with tongues," but then he adds, "Yet Paul is presumably after all thinking realistically of the language of angels" (*1 Corinthians*, 221). I have some difficulty in equating angelic languages with speaking in tongues since it is the Holy Spirit, the Spirit of God, who gives the utterance and therefore presumably would speak more than the language of angels. Ralph P. Martin perhaps put it best when he said that "the tongues of angels' " is "a Jewish phrase to denote a type of prayer-speech eminently suited to praising God" (*The Spirit and the Congregation*, 43). Thus the "tongues of angels" is another way of referring to spiritual utterance as being from heaven, even if it is not literally the speech of angels. (Cf. 2 Cor. 12:4, where a man [presumably Paul himself] was said to have been "caught up into paradise, and heard unspeakable words" [KJV].)

[227] As in the 1978 edition of the NIV: "to another the ability to speak in different kinds of tongues." In the 1983 revision the word "ability" is omitted, the reading being simply "to another speaking in different kinds of tongues." This is a fortunate alteration.

[228] As in the NEB translation: "another has the gift of ecstatic utterance of different kinds." (See chap. 9, n. 24, for my objection to the use of the word "ecstatic.")

Kinds of tongues is a particular gift, or manifestation, of the Holy Spirit: ". . . to another various kinds of tongues." As with the other spiritual gifts, it is a distribution of the Spirit "individually as he wills" (1 Cor. 12:11). Thus this is not a gift that everyone has. Paul emphasizes this in a later rhetorical question, "Do all speak with tongues"? (v. 30). The implied answer is no—"All do not speak with tongues, do they?"[229] The Holy Spirit sovereignly manifests Himself in tongues through an individual: it is a particular gift or manifestation of the Holy Spirit.

This gift of tongues belongs within the context of the gathered community. Like all other spiritual gifts, it is "for the common good" (1 Cor. 12:7). "Kinds of tongues" is a gift of the Spirit for the edification of the body. Tongues function as a necessary manifestation through one or more individual members of that body without which the community would be incomplete.

At this point we need to recognize that there is an important difference between tongues as an accompaniment of the coming of the Holy Spirit and tongues as an individual gift of the Spirit. As we have observed in some detail,[230] the accounts of speaking in tongues in Acts included all persons present: it was not limited to one or a few. In the Epistles, as we noted, speaking in tongues is frequently referred to or implied as a continuing experience in the lives of believers.

Tongues belong to the ongoing life of prayer and praise. There is no limitation: all believers thus may speak in tongues. Moreover, this New Testament truth has been confirmed countless times in the lives of Spirit-filled believers. However—and herein is the critical point—by no means do all who speak in tongues devotionally (i.e., in prayer and praise) also speak in tongues for the edification of the body of believers. Tongues in the latter case— "kinds of tongues"—are not spoken by all but only by those through whom the Holy Spirit chooses to act.

Since there often is confusion in this matter, we need to stress the difference between *devotional* tongues and *ministry* tongues. Devotional tongues, originating in the coming of the Spirit and continuing in the life of prayer and praise, have no limitation: *all* may speak in tongues. Indeed, Paul implies this later in 1 Corinthians 14:5, where he says, "I want[231] you *all* to speak in tongues." The apostle is obviously talking about something desirable and possible for all. Also Paul begins a later statement in this way: "If . . . the whole church assembles and *all* speak in tongues . . ." (v. 23). In this statement Paul goes even further by implying that all the Corinthians could speak in tongues. Clearly such speaking must refer to a different use of tongues than is described in 1 Corinthians 12, where Paul refers to tongues as an individual gift ("to another" [v. 10]) so that not all speak in tongues ("Not all speak

---

[229]This is the NASB translation, a good rendition of the Greek text, "*mē* [not] *pantes glōssais lalousin?*"

[230]See chapter 9, "The Phenomenon of Tongues."

[231]The Greek word for "I want" is *thelō*. According to TDNT, "θέλειν [*thelein*] denotes in Paul the weighty and authoritative discharge of office. In this form it always implies *resolute will*" (italics added) (3:49). Translations of 1 Corinthians 14:5 that read, "I wish that you all spoke in tongues" (NASB), "I would like every one of you to speak in tongues" (NIV), and "I would that ye all spake with tongues" (KJV) are far too weak. The RSV is correct; it is a matter of Paul's will: "I *want* you . . ." (Note the "I want" [*thelō*] likewise in 1 Cor. 10:1, 11:3, and 12:1; in these instances *thelō* is translated "I want" [or "do not want"] also in NIV and NASB.)

with tongues, do they?" [v. 30]). The difference is apparent: Paul in 1 Corinthians 12:10, 30 is dealing with speaking in tongues as a particular gift for ministry; in 1 Corinthians 14:5, 23 Paul is referring to the general practice of tongues in the devotional life of all in the community.

Hence, although it may be correct to say (as sometimes people do), "I do not speak in tongues because that is not my gift" in reference to body ministry, it is incorrect to add, "Therefore God does not want me to speak in tongues at all." Such an attitude may both prevent a person from experiencing the overflow in tongues that results from being filled with the Holy Spirit as well as the continuation of prayer and praise in the fullest dimension. It is *urgent* that we distinguish between tongues as a normal accompaniment of the Spirit-filled life and tongues as a gift (freely given, never possessed) of the Spirit when the community comes together. Both devotional tongues and tongues for ministry are urgently needed.

There is, however, no essential difference between devotional and ministry tongues. The differentiation is *not in essence but in practice*. For example, a person who speaks in tongues on an occasion of body ministry is one who *already* speaks in tongues in his prayer life. It is essentially the same speaking but now oriented to the upbuilding of the community.

Another point: a person may regularly speak in tongues, even sing in tongues,[232] but only rarely, if at all, experience the gift of tongues. The latter depends basically on the Holy Spirit, who distributes that gift as He wills.[233] It may be His decision to apportion another gift rather than tongues. However, the gift of tongues for ministry may, like all the other gifts, be earnestly desired and prayed for. Although such a desire does not determine what the Spirit does, it may prepare the way for God's sovereign action.

I will now summarize a few additional points about tongues.

1. The very expression "kinds of tongues" suggests a variety and multiplicity. The double plural is similar to that of gifts of healings, workings of miracles, and distinguishings of spirits. Although the person is one, he speaks various kinds of tongues in the community. This in itself is an extraordinary phenomenon because most people who speak in tongues speak only one tongue in ordinary speech. Now by the Holy Spirit a person is enabled to speak not only a new tongue but a variety of tongues.

We have earlier observed that the content of tongues at various times is at least threefold: praise to God, speaking His mysteries, and offering supplications.[234] Here is a variety of utterances in tongues (hence "kinds of tongues") that when offered in the community of believers edify much. Since speaking in tongues is primarily transcendent praise, and praise is the basic activity of a gathering of believers, it follows that tongues, whether spoken or sung,[235] may be the catalyst to bring forth further community praise. Traditional prayers and hymns, even choruses, though surely valuable, may after a time become somewhat routine, with little spiritual vitality in their utterance. Then someone speaks or sings in tongues, and often a spiritual breakthrough oc-

---

[232]Recall the previous discussion of this in chapter 9.

[233]To be sure, all tongues are given (one does not achieve such) including devotional tongues; however, tongues for ministry is a special *charisma* or gift of the Holy Spirit.

[234]See chapter 9, "The Phenomenon of Tongues," IV, "Content."

[235]As in 1 Corinthians 14:15.

curs. Again, since in tongues a person speaks forth mysteries, hidden things, the very declaration of these things of God can have profoundly significant effects in the community. We have earlier observed how word of wisdom and word of knowledge open up many vistas of truth; speaking in tongues reaches deep into the mysteries of God and thus can richly bless the community. Still again, since tongues may also at times be avenues of supplication and intercession, this can greatly enhance the outreach of the community in its prayerful concern for others.[236]

Now none of this means that only one person may be used by the Holy Spirit for such multiple ministry. One person *may* be, for the gift is kind*s* of tongues. However, Paul, in describing the community in action, later says, "If anyone speaks in a tongue, it should be by two or at the most three" (1 Cor. 14:27 NASB).[237] In any event, whether there be only one or two, or three, each person speaking can greatly edify the body of believers. "Kinds of tongues" are invaluable to full ministry.

2. Speaking in tongues, while a blessing for believers, is a sign to unbelievers. Paul writes, "So then tongues are for a sign, not to those who believe, but to unbelievers" (1 Cor. 14:22 NASB). The background of Paul's statement is his free quotation from the Book of Isaiah: "In the law it is written, With men of other tongues and other lips will I speak unto this people; and yet for all that they will not hear me, saith the Lord" (v. 21 KJV). The words "So then . . ." immediately follow. Although the "other tongues" in Isaiah refer to the language of a foreign nation through whom God spoke to an uncomprehending people,[238] Paul freely applies this to the language of glossolalia to which unbelievers turn a deaf ear. The very fact that God speaks through tongues and yet unbelievers spurn the words is a judgment on them: they are all the more confirmed in their disbelief.[239]

Let me apply this briefly to today. Speaking in tongues should be evidence to unbelievers of supernatural utterance. The very fact that the utterance cannot be satisfactorily explained as a language of man, moreover that millions of believers today speak in tongues *none* of whom claim that the language comes from themselves, ought to be striking evidence that a Higher Power is involved. The fact that unbelievers do not listen, indeed, often are very critical of glossolalia, only deepens their unbelief and hardness to the things of God.

This serves to confirm Paul's earlier words in 1 Corinthians: "A natural man[240] does not accept the things[241] of

---

[236]To be effective all of this calls for interpretation (see section IX).

[237]Paul is speaking of the regulation of tongues (see below); however, the relevant point here is that there may be more than one person who speaks in tongues.

[238]Isaiah 28:11, which reads in the RSV as "strange lips and with an alien tongue the LORD will speak to this people," refers to the speech of the Assyrians who invaded Judah in Isaiah and Hezekiah's day. Assyrian/Akkadian, while a cognate language to Hebrew, was different enough to be incomprehensible to the average Judean.

[239]Barrett puts it well: "When they are not met with faith (cf. Heb. iv. 2) tongues *serve* to harden and thus to condemn the unbeliever" (*The First Epistle to the Corinthians*, HNTC, 323).

[240]The Greek phrase is *psychikos anthrōpos*. The RSV reads "unspiritual man"; NIV has "man without the Spirit." These translations make it clear that "natural man" (NASB and KJV) is opposite of "spiritual man."

[241]The RSV reads "gifts." Although the Greek is simply *ta*, "things," the RSV correctly appreciates that Paul is dealing with spiritual gifts. The background of Paul's statement

the Spirit of God; for they are fool-ishness to him, and he cannot under-stand them, because they are spiritually appraised"[242] (2:14 NASB). The person who is an unbeliever, a "natural man," cannot "accept" speaking in tongues—one of "the things" of the Spirit of God. By not accepting tongues, even declaring them to be "foolishness," the natural man stands all the more under God's judgment. So it is that speaking in tongues is a sign not to those who believe,[243] for they spiritually discern the Spirit of God in operation, but it is a sign to those who are unbelievers. They are confirmed as "natural" persons. The situation has not changed in our own time.

But now, to turn in a different direc-tion, tongues may in some situations be a sign to unbelievers that prepares the way for faith. I refer particularly to the Pentecostal event of Acts 2 in which a multitude of unbelieving Jews heard the 120 speaking in tongues, and some 3000 hearers came to believe the gospel. All of the multitude gathered at the sound-ing forth of tongues—"at this sound[244] the multitude came together" (v. 6). It was speaking in tongues that first caught their attention. So in this case speaking in tongues was used by the Holy Spirit to bring a multitude of inquisitive unbelievers together, a num-ber of whom later came to salvation.

Speaking in tongues at Pentecost there-fore did not deepen the unbelief of all who heard; rather it was the primary attractive force that eventuated in sal-vation for many.[245]

We may draw some contemporary parallel in that speaking in tongues, because of its extraordinariness, can gain an unbeliever's positive attention. The hearing of tongues spoken or sung may have a kind of shock effect that leads to inquiry and sometimes open-ness to the message of the gospel.[246]

3. Tongues have a regular place in the ongoing ministry of the church. This is apparent from the fact that tongues is one of the manifestations of the Spirit for the common good: "to another kinds of tongues." In this connection we may observe an additional statement of Paul, relating particularly to worship: "When you assemble, each one has a psalm, has a teaching, has a revelation, has a tongue, has an interpretation" (1 Cor. 14:26 NASB). Moreover, it is not a matter of "*may have*" but "*has*." "Each one" does not mean that every-body has a tongue any more than every one has a psalm, a teaching, a revela-tion, and an interpretation. Paul means rather that one person has this, another person has that; hence each person is fully involved. And this unmistakably includes having "a tongue."

In this portrait of assembled believers

---

relates particularly to the gifts of "word of wisdom" and "word of knowledge" (see previous sections I and II).

[242] Or "discerned" (KJV, RSV, NIV). The Greek word is *anakrinetai*.

[243] In another sense, speaking in tongues is a positive sign for believers: a sign of God's spiritual presence and power. Paul, however, as we have observed, is speaking in 1 Corinthians 14:22 of a sign in terms of judgment, a sign "to" unbelievers.

[244] I.e., the sound of tongues. See chapter 9, n. 11.

[245] George Montague writes, "A sign is something that makes a person stop and think—and the gift of tongues at Pentecost did just that for the Jews of all languages living in Jerusalem. . . . It got their attention. In this sense it was a sign for those who did not believe, of whom some would come to believe, some not" (*The Holy Spirit: Growth of a Biblical Tradition,* 179).

[246] In my experience, singing in the Spirit (in tongues) may particularly have this effect. This is especially the case when a number of people sing together, both words and melody being spontaneously uttered. It is as if an unseen Director were leading the music. The impact on an unbeliever can be quite pronounced.

it is striking that none of the other spiritual gifts except interpretation is directly mentioned. A psalm or hymn is a song of praise,[247] a teaching is probably a spontaneous word of instruction,[248] and a revelation quite likely refers here to the background for a prophetic utterance.[249] But a tongue is unambiguously what Paul has been describing throughout.

If we view what Paul is describing in 1 Corinthians 14:26 as paradigmatic for a contemporaneous gathering of believers, then the gift of tongues clearly occupies a place of continuing importance. Unfortunately if Paul were to visit most churches in our time, he would have to say not "each one" but "no one" has a tongue. Indeed, if someone does have a tongue, often it is

discouraged or even forbidden. This leads us to some words of Paul about tongues: "Do not forbid speaking in tongues" (1 Cor. 14:39). There are many churches and church institutions that either overtly[250] or covertly[251] act counter to Paul's injunction. For the church at large in our day tongues simply have no place at all.

On the other hand we must guard against exaggerating the place of tongues. It seems that the Corinthians did precisely that. These words of Paul imply as much: "But now, brethren, if I come to you speaking in tongues, what shall I profit you, unless I speak to you either by way of revelation or of knowledge or of prophecy or of teaching?"[252] (1 Cor. 14:6 NASB).[253] Then follow a

---

[247]This psalm or hymn (RSV, NIV, NEB; the Greek word is *psalmon*) is probably a charismatic utterance in the Spirit. Barrett writes that *psalmon* refers to "a fresh, perhaps spontaneous, composition, not an Old Testament psalm" (*First Epistle to the Corinthians*, HNTC, 327).

[248]"A teaching" likely is a charismatic presentation (see Rom. 12:7 on the charisma of teaching) of a particular theme, hence spontaneous. Dunn writes in regard to this verse (also 1 Cor. 14:6) that "in Paul's view the activity of teaching . . . is also a charismatic act . . . in v. 26 both 'hymn' and 'teaching' are probably thought of as spontaneous utterances" (*Jesus and the Spirit,* 237).

[249]For a connection between revelation and prophecy recall 1 Corinthians 14:30: "If a revelation is made to another [prophet] sitting by, let the first [prophet] be silent." Revelation may also be the background for "word of wisdom" and "word of knowledge" (as discussed in sections I and II). In any event revelation itself is not a gift of the Spirit but background for gifts to follow.

[250]Recall my illustration in chapter 9, n. 67. I will now give another. An applicant for a particular church college must sign the following statement: "If I am offered admission to . . . and become enrolled, I will not speak in tongues publicly or privately and I will not promote the gift of tongues to fellow students, staff, or faculty." This is as flat a denial of Paul's words "Do not forbid . . ." as can be imagined.

[251]While I was teaching in a seminary some years ago, it became known that I spoke in tongues. For several years afterward there was a quiet but persistent attempt to silence me or else to get me to move on to another place. This covert action in my case has had many parallels elsewhere.

[252]Recall the discussion of teaching and revelation in prior footnotes 247 and 248. "Knowledge" probably refers to "word of knowledge" (1 Cor. 12:8). In this case revelation seems to be the immediate background, but prophecy may also be in view.

[253]Paul surely does not mean in this statement to minimize tongues or to state a preference for revelation, knowledge, prophecy, and teaching. It is rather a matter of an implied *also*—"unless I also." Further, it has been suggested that the speaking by way of revelation, knowledge, etc., is actually an interpretation of the tongue. Barrett mentions both possibilities, writing after "unless I speak to you" thus: "in addition, that is, or perhaps by an interpretation of the tongue" (*First Epistle to the Corinthians*, HNTC, 317). Howard

number of statements by Paul about the need for intelligibility in utterance (vv. 7–11), concluding with the words "So also you, since you are zealous of spiritual gifts, seek to abound for the edification of the church" (v. 12 NASB). There may have been so much elation among the Corinthians over their ability to speak in tongues that such speaking became the predominant feature in their assembly. Later Paul says, "If, therefore, the whole church assembles and all speak in tongues, and outsiders or unbelievers enter, will they not say that you are mad?" (v. 23 RSV). "*All*" seem to have been speaking in tongues, and this produced a negative effect on outsiders and unbelievers. Tongues have a proper but not all-important place.

This leads to a final word on speaking in tongues: there needs to be order. One of the last statements of Paul relating to tongues is this: "If any speak in a tongue, let there be only two or at most three, and each in turn" (1 Cor. 14:27). By this he speaks of both limitation, "two or at most three," and order, "each in turn." The Corinthians, abounding in tongues, doubtless needed that word—and so do some Pentecostal and charismatic groups in our day. Disorder brings neither edification to the body of believers nor attractiveness to outsiders who may be present. Another summary statement of Paul reads, "All things should be done decently[254] and in order" (v. 40). Propriety and fittingness are to be the hallmark of all

things in the assembly. The immediate context is tongues—"Do not forbid speaking in tongues" (v. 39)—and behind that are prophecy and other spiritual manifestations. Earlier Paul had written, "God is not a God of confusion but of peace" (v. 33). This is truly an important message to the church at Corinth and to the church of any time and place.

IX. INTERPRETATION OF TONGUES

The final gift of the Holy Spirit listed by Paul is "interpretation of tongues" [*hermēneia glōssōn*] (1 Cor. 12:10). This is likewise a gift to an individual: "to another the interpretation of tongues." Paul later asks rhetorically, "Do all interpret?" (v. 30),[255] implying that interpretation of tongues is an individual gift or manifestation of the Holy Spirit.

This gift is not interpretation in general but functions only in relation to tongues. All the other gifts, though closely related, are independent manifestations of the Holy Spirit.[256] However, there is no spiritual gift of interpretation as such; rather, the gift is only that of interpretation of tongues.

To be sure, there are other kinds of interpretation. For example, in the Scriptures there is the interpretation of dreams. Joseph and Daniel were both interpreters of dreams through which God spoke.[257] God Himself gave the

---

Ervin opts for the latter and writes that "tongues are the vehicle for conveying revelation, knowledge, prophecy, and teaching" (*Spirit Baptism*, 131). I have difficulty with this viewpoint because of the lack of biblical and experiential evidence for tongues and interpretation covering this wide a range.

[254]The Greek word is *euschēmonōs*. The NIV has "fitting" ("a fitting and orderly way"); NASB reads "properly." BAGD has "decently, becomingly."

[255]The NASB reads, "All do not interpret, do they?" This more literally follows the Greek *mē pantes diermēneuousin* ("not all interpret?").

[256]This is true even of the gift of faith. Although this gift is often the background and stimulus for such other gifts as healings and miracles, faith has its own unique contribution (see earlier discussion in section III).

[257]For Joseph, see especially Genesis 40–41; for Daniel, see Daniel 2–5, 7.

interpretation.[258] There is also the interpretation of the Scriptures themselves. Jesus, for example, "beginning with Moses and all the prophets, . . . interpreted[259] to them [the men on the road to Emmaus] in all the scriptures the things concerning himself" (Luke 24:27). Christ Himself continues to be the key to biblical interpretation, and through the Holy Spirit who inspired the writing of Scripture the truth is made known. The proper interpretation of Scripture[260] therefore is basic and normative for Christian faith and experience. But now we are focusing on neither the interpretation of dreams nor the interpretation of Scripture but on the interpretation of tongues.

The interpretation of tongues is a supramental[261] operation of the Holy Spirit. Interpretation of tongues is in a known language; however, there is no rational comprehension of what the prior tongues have declared. The one interpreting has no more knowledge than the glossolalist of what has been said; the interpreter simply speaks out and the Holy Spirit gives the interpretation. Unlike interpreting a foreign language into common speech, no human ability is required. Of course, as with speaking in tongues, there must be the utilization of mouth and lips and, as with prophecy, a person must begin to speak in his native language. However, what is said in interpretation is basically from a realm beyond the human mind. It is not that the interpreter understands what is said in the tongue and so makes its contents known; rather, the interpretation is solely and totally from the Holy Spirit.

By this gift there is the interpretation of what is spoken in a tongue. Interpretation can be translation, so that what is said in tongues is set forth word by word;[262] however, interpretation is directed more to the meaning of the prior utterance. Paul writes that the problem for the hearer of a foreign language is that he or she does not know "the meaning of the language" (1 Cor. 14:11); later, in relation to tongues, Paul discusses the need for interpretation (v. 13). To know the meaning of what is spoken in a foreign language usually calls for more than word-for-word translation. Skilled interpretation is needed to elucidate the meaning fully and accurately. Thus an interpretation, whether of an unknown foreign language or a tongue of the Spirit, may be lengthier, or sometimes it may even be shorter, than the incomprehensible utterance.[263]

The latter statement is quite pertinent to what often happens in a charismatic fellowship when a tongue is interpreted. The interpretation sometimes varies considerably in length from the tongue spoken, so much so that those present may wonder if the interpretation is actually of the tongue. It is possible that the words of a presumed interpretation are not given by the Holy Spirit (a parallel to a prophecy that is from the human spirit or even from a diabolical

---

[258] In the words of Joseph, "Do not interpretations belong to God?" (Gen. 40:8).

[259] The Greek word is *diermēneusen*.

[260] This is the area of *hermeneutics* (from *hermēneia*): principles of interpretation.

[261] See the previous references to this in the introduction to sections VIII and IX.

[262] An interesting Old Testament prefigurement is found in the narrative of Daniel and the handwriting on the wall of Nebuchadnezzar's palace—MENE, MENE, TEKEL, PARSIN, literally "Numbered, numbered, weighed, divided." Daniel took this cryptic message and then proceeded to interpret its fuller meaning (Dan. 5:25–28).

[263] In either case there is a dynamic equivalence. David Pytches speaks of interpretation as "the dynamic equivalent of that which was spoken in tongues" (*Spiritual Gifts in the Local Church*, 73).

spirit)[264] and need to be quickly refuted. Also it may be that the apparent interpretation is a prophecy, since the language of interpretation and prophecy are often much the same.[265] In that case there is need to recognize the prophecy and continue to look for an interpretation of the tongue.[266] But now that we have recognized these two other possibilities, it is also a fact that many a valid interpretation will be of a longer, occasionally shorter, duration than the tongues spoken.

The significance of interpretation of tongues is that it makes known the valuable content of what has been spoken in a tongue. For example, a tongue is often simply an offering of praise to God.[267] This was the case at Pentecost when the 120 Spirit-filled believers were speaking in "other tongues" (Acts 2:4) and declaring in those tongues the "wonderful works of God" (v. 11 KJV). Paul, after writing about praying "with

the spirit" (1 Cor. 14:15)—that is, praying "in a tongue" (v. 14)—proceeded to speak of blessing "with the spirit." He said, "If you bless ("are praising" NIV, NEB) with the spirit,[268] how can any one in the position of an outsider[269] say the 'Amen' to your thanksgiving when he does not know what you are saying?" (v. 16). Interpretation is needed if the content of the tongue spoken, namely blessing or praise, is to be made known to the outsider[270] and he can respond with an "Amen."[271]

A tongue, as we have earlier observed, may also be the speaking of mysteries: "One who speaks in a tongue . . . utters mysteries in the Spirit"[272] (1 Cor. 14:2). By "mysteries" Paul refers to hidden or secret things that are not achievable by human understanding and accordingly can be disclosed only by the Holy Spirit. These mysteries are not ultimate ones such as

[264]See the discussion of this in section VI.

[265]For a discussion of the difference see footnotes 276, 278, 290.

[266]This is quite irregular, although it does happen occasionally. Such disjunction is largely due to inexperience. Paul's prescription (about which more will be said later) is that interpretation should immediately follow (see 1 Cor. 14:13, 27).

[267]For a fuller discussion see chapter 9, IV; also see the brief reference in preceding section VIII.

[268]Fee translates this phrase as "by the Spirit" (*The First Epistle to the Corinthians,* NICNT, 667; also see his n. 3). Whether lowercase *s* or uppercase *S*, the meaning is the same: Paul is referring to tongues.

[269]The Greek word is *idiōtou*. See section VI, n. 178 on the *idiōtēs* as an uninitiated or inquiring person. An *idiōtēs* was not an unbeliever (1 Cor. 14:23–24 differentiates "outsiders" from "unbelievers"), but not yet a member of the church (as 1 Cor. 14:23 makes clear: "If, therefore, the whole church assembles . . . and outsiders or unbelievers enter . . .").

[270]In a sense this would likewise be the case for all believers present, since they also would not understand the language. However, because of their previous experience of blessing God "with the spirit," they could, regardless of interpretation, more readily say the "Amen" than one who as an uninitiated or inquiring person is still an "outsider."

[271]Often in charismatic fellowships singing in tongues occurs without interpretation following. Paul speaks in both Ephesians 5:19 and Colossians 3:16 about singing "psalms and hymns and spiritual songs." If spiritual songs are songs in tongues, as seems likely (recall my previous discussion in chap. 9, III.), there is no suggestion by Paul in this context of subsequent interpretation. Perhaps the reason is that such spiritual singing—a high occasion in worship, both words and melody coming from the Spirit—is in itself edification for all present, including the "outsider." It could be urged, however, that with interpretation following, there would be further benefit. Either way, the important matter is that all present may be fully able to enter into the worship of God.

[272]Again see chapter 9, IV., and preceding section VIII.

Paul himself occasionally received through special revelation;[273] however, they are hidden matters spoken in a tongue, perhaps about such matters as God's purpose, His blessings, and His direction, and these matters can have tremendous value. Hence there is the signal importance of interpretation, for through interpretation the hidden things are made known.

In both cases mentioned above, in which through tongues there is the offering of praise and the speaking of mysteries, it is apparent that a person is speaking directly to God and not to other people. Yet communication to others does take place because through interpretation there is understanding of what has been said in tongues of praise or in the speaking of mysteries. For example, although the 120 on the Day of Pentecost were speaking in tongues only to God of His "wonderful works," the very words were a communication to all who heard and understood. This doubtlessly later prepared the way for Peter's preaching the gospel. Again, when a person blesses God in tongues and interpretation follows, there is intellectual comprehension that further adds to the richness of worship. Or once more, when there is an utterance in a tongue of some "mystery" or hidden things followed by interpretation in intelligible speech, this very communication can have a powerful impact on mind and will.

Hence, through interpretation a *message* may be given. Interpretation, as we have observed, is usually more than literal translation: it is a setting forth of the meaning of an utterance in tongues. Now, we further note, the word interpretation also implies personal application. For example, Psalm 145 begins, "I will extol thee, my God and King, and bless thy name for ever and ever" and ends with the words "Let all flesh bless his holy name for ever and ever." The praise spoken includes a summons to praise; so likewise may a tongue of praise.

Similarly mysteries spoken in the Spirit, while addressed "not to men but to God" (1 Cor. 14:2), may contain a message to people when interpreted by that same Spirit. What is spoken to God about hidden things when interpreted can bring a powerful message to whomever it is especially addressed.[274] The same thing is true of tongues that speak forth supplication and intercession:[275] although they are addressed to God and not to people, such prayers obviously relate to people. Hence if interpretation occurs, there will be a message that significantly relates to others who are present. Tongues indeed can convey personal messages.

Accordingly, there is a distinctiveness about what is spoken through tongues and interpretation. It is sometimes said that tongues plus interpretation equals prophecy $(T + I = P)$.[276]

---

[273] For some of these mysteries see chapter 9, n. 88.

[274] It is sometimes said that since in a tongue one speaks not to men but to God, the interpretation following must likewise be addressed to God. Hence there can be no message to people. Thus if such a presumed interpretation is spoken, it is either another gift of the Spirit (for example, prophecy) or simply a false statement. This viewpoint, I submit, is mistaken. Harold Horton puts it well in writing, "Suppose that in other tongues one were saying to God, O Lord, thou lovest the humble and resistest the proud, would it not be a perfectly good and truthful interpretation on the lips of another: The Lord loveth the humble and resisteth the proud"? (*The Gifts of the Spirit,* 155).

[275] Again see chapter 9, IV, and preceding section VIII.

[276] If tongues plus interpretation equals prophecy, I submit, there would be no need for the former two. Why bother about those two gifts (with their complexity) when one gift will

However, although both may contain a message, this does not mean that the results are identical. Prophecy, as we have seen, is basically for the threefold purpose of edification, exhortation, and consolation (1 Cor. 14:3). Tongues relate essentially to the praise of God, uttering mysteries in the Spirit, and offering supplications. Thus the interpretation of tongues, while often including elements of edification,[277] exhortation, and consolation, operates out of a different context. The results accordingly are not the same.[278]

Now I will make a few comments about *order* in interpretation of tongues. The basic matter is that only *one* person is to interpret. Previously we have noted Paul's words ". . . to another the interpretation of tongues." Later Paul applies this singularly to a situation in which two or three people speak in tongues. As earlier quoted, Paul writes that "if any speak in a tongue, let there be only two or at most three, and each

in turn"; then he adds, "and let one interpret" (1 Cor. 14:27). This "one" does not necessarily mean one of the tongues speakers, though that is possible,[279] but simply some person. This suggests that since tongues are to be spoken "each in turn," interpretation will follow in turn after each utterance. Thus one person—and only one—who has the gift of interpretation of tongue*s* will be used in interpreting each tongue in sequence.[280] Hence, in summary, there may be two or three tongues spoken but *not* two or three interpreters: only one person will be gifted by the Holy Spirit to that end on that occasion.[281]

But there is also an earlier directive given by Paul that needs to be heard: "Let one who speaks in a tongue pray that he may interpret" (1 Cor. 14:13 NASB). Paul writes this because of the urgency of interpretation following a tongue[282] and because the speaker himself may be the one so anointed by the

---

do equally well? Remember, however, that both tongues and interpretation are as much distinct gifts of the Holy Spirit as prophecy. Would the Holy Spirit apportion tongues and interpretation when prophecy would suffice? Clearly there must be room, important room, for all three manifestations of the Holy Spirit.

[277]Definitely edification also occurs through interpretation (see 1 Cor. 14:5: "Some one interprets, so that the church may be edified").

[278]Many charismatic fellowships need to reflect more on this matter. The tendency often prevails to identify the interpretation of a tongue with a prophecy. Indeed, as earlier mentioned, though it is out of order, someone may prophesy following a tongue. If, however, an interpretation properly follows a tongue, the results will be different. The interpretation will be of the praise, mystery, or supplication uttered in a tongue; prophecy will be essentially edification, exhortation, or consolation. There is a difference, but it is not always readily recognized. It may take a while for the fellowship to perceive the difference, but the gain will be significant. To recognize and act on the different messages of the Holy Spirit coming forth through prophecy and interpretation is much to be desired.

[279]See next paragraph.

[280]Robertson and Plummer wrote: "One, and one only . . . was to interpret; there was to be no interpreting in turn, which might lead to profitless discussion. Moreover, this would be a security against two speaking with Tongues at the same time, for one interpreter could not attend to both" (*First Epistles of St. Paul to the Corinthians*, ICC, 321). This is an interesting observation!

[281]Often in Pentecostal churches one individual regularly speaks in tongues while another usually gives the interpretation. This is *not* what Paul is speaking about.

[282]I will discuss this in some detail later.

Holy Spirit.[283] It may be that there is no one else to interpret, and if such is the case the speaker in tongues must remain silent. Immediately after Paul said, "Let one interpret," he added, "If there is no interpreter,[284] the speaker should keep quiet in the church and speak to himself and God" (v. 28 NIV). Of course, if the speaker prayed for the gift of interpretation (as Paul earlier directed) and believed God had heard his request, he would not have to remain silent: he could boldly speak forth in tongues. Also, he would be able to interpret other tongues that might later be spoken.

This matter of order in regard to interpretation of tongues is important for all believers moving in the gifts of the Spirit. Sometimes the situation is quite confusing with more than one person seeking to interpret tongues. Accordingly, words may be spoken that are *not* interpretation,[285] and there is no edification of the body.

This brings us to another critical issue: the failure to have interpretation at all. In the Corinthian situation this seems to have been the basic problem: people were speaking in tongues with little or no concern for interpretation to follow. This is apparent from a number of things Paul says. In 1 Corinthians 14, following a word about interpretation ("greater is one who prophesies than one who speaks in tongues, unless he interprets, so that the church may receive edifying" [v. 5 NASB]), Paul devotes several statements to the inadequacy of simply speaking in tongues. We have already noted the statement "If I come to you speaking in tongues, what shall I profit you, unless I speak to you either by way of revelation or of knowledge or of prophecy or of teaching?" (v. 6 NASB). Later Paul talks about musical instruments that give indistinct sounds and tongues speech that either is not clear or is unknown to the hearer—all of which refers to tongues that are not interpreted (vv. 7–11).[286] This obviously relates to the Corinthians' practice of speaking in tongues without interpretation following.

Two other illustrations of the Corinthians' disregard for interpretation may be noted. First, there is the picture of the person who blesses "with the spirit" (v. 16) but does not interpret.[287] Second, there is the picture of the assembly where everybody is speaking

---

[283]This also demonstrates that though the gifts are individual impartations of the Spirit—"to one . . . to another . . . to another" (on through the list of the nine gifts)—the same person may be granted more than one gift.

[284]The Greek word is *diermēneutēs,* the only use of the noun in the New Testament. One should not, however, understand "interpreter" to be an office (i.e., an "official" interpreter), for no such office exists. "Interpreter" simply means "someone interpreting" (the RSV translation, "if there is no one to interpret," is a helpful paraphrase).

[285]As earlier noted, such words may be valid as another operation of the Spirit or invalid as coming from another spirit.

[286]Verse 13, already quoted, shows Paul's concern: "Therefore let one who speaks in a tongue pray that he may interpret" (NASB).

[287]See prior discussion. Also we may observe that Paul soon after adds, "I thank God, I speak in tongues more than you all; however, in the church I desire to speak five words with my mind, that I may instruct others also, rather than ten thousand words in a tongue" (vv. 18–19 NASB). Here Paul expresses both his own superabundant use of tongues and his personal desire to instruct people with his mind. To that end tongues, even "ten thousand," with interpretation are inadequate (none of the gifts of the Spirit rule out the need for solid teaching). Paul is by no means setting aside tongues and interpretation, but he "also" (a key word in Paul's statement) wants to instruct people: to that end ten thousand words in a tongue are of less value than five words with the mind.

407

in tongues but is obviously unconcerned about interpretation: "If, therefore, the whole church assembles and all speak in tongues, and outsiders or unbelievers enter, will they not say that you are mad?" (v. 23). Paul is by no means opposed to the Corinthians' speaking in tongues, even all of them;[288] but if everyone is involved at the same time, it will sound to outsiders and unbelievers like sheer madness. Without interpretation of what has been said—and interpretation is impossible when all the believers are speaking at once or even in sequence—the effect on others will be wholly negative. Indeed, Paul says later, two or three may make ready to speak in tongues, but "if there is no one to interpret, let each of them keep silence in church and speak to himself and to God" (v. 28). Interpretation of what is spoken is utterly essential.

Let it be stated strongly: the problem at Corinth was not their speaking in tongues but the failure to give an interpretation. *The problem was uninterpreted tongues.*[289] Although speaking in tongues is spiritual utterance, there is also need for rational comprehension. Intelligibility must follow if there is to be the edification of all who are present. *Tongues plus interpretation* make for the edifying of everyone.

Indeed, we may note that interpreted tongues are equal in value to prophecy.[290] Let us look again at the words of Paul, "Greater is one who prophesies than one who speaks in tongues, unless he interprets, so that the church may receive edifying" (1 Cor. 14:5 NASB). The first part of the statement without the second would place prophecy on a higher value scale than tongues with interpretation.[291] However, the second part definitely elevates interpreted tongues to the same level as prophecy.[292]

Furthermore, since prophecy is surely one of the "greater gifts" (1 Cor. 12:31) to be eagerly desired,[293] this places interpreted tongues among these gifts.[294] Strikingly, perhaps even surprisingly, rather than tongues with interpretation being the least of the gifts (as it is sometimes claimed), they are now seen to occupy, with prophecy, the very top echelon!

Finally, let me say a word concerning the importance of the gift of the interpretation of tongues. Without interpretation spiritual tongues must remain silent in the gathered community. From all that has been observed about the intrinsic value of tongues, such silence would indeed be a serious loss. Thus interpretation of tongues in itself is a gift of the Spirit to be earnestly desired. "Earnestly desire the spiritual gifts" (1 Cor. 14:1) means *all* of them, the last

---

[288]Recall that Paul said, "I want you all to speak in tongues" (v. 5).

[289]Accordingly, Fee writes about the Corinthians: "The real issue is not tongues per se, but *uninterpreted tongues*" (italics his) (*The First Epistle to the Corinthians*, NICNT, 653).

[290]Earlier I made the point that tongues plus interpretation do not equal prophecy in their *results*. Now I refer not to results but to *value*.

[291]Paul's prior words all the more seem to elevate prophecy: "I want you all to speak in tongues, but even more to prophesy" (also v. 5).

[292]So Grosheide writes, "Interpreted glossolalia has the same value as prophecy" (*The First Epistle to the Corinthians*, NICNT, 320). Similarly Montague: "Paul equates interpreted tongues with prophecy" (*The Holy Spirit: Growth of a Biblical Tradition*, 176). According to EGT, "The power to interpret superadded to the glossolalia . . . puts the mystic speaker on a level with the prophet: first, 'uttering mysteries'—and then making them plain to his hearers, he accomplishes in two acts what the prophet does in one" (2:903).

[293]Recall our discussion of this in chapter 13, IV.C.

[294]For a much more comprehensive discussion of this, see my article entitled "The Greater Gifts" in *Charismatic Experiences in History*, Cecil M. Robeck, Jr., editor.

of which (in 1 Corinthians 12:8–10) is interpretation of tongues. Perhaps this gift seems modest when compared with such gifts as healings and miracles (who would not desire them?); moreover, it is dependent on another gift, the gift of "kinds of tongues," even to function. *Yet*—and this is a large "yet"—the interpretation of tongues alone is the key that for the community unlocks the profundity of things that are uttered in the Spirit.

"To another the interpretation of tongues." The Holy Spirit apportions the gift as He wills. Are we eager to receive it?

15

Christian Living

In this final chapter we will deal with some basic elements of the Christian way of living. This will contain both a review of some things said previously and a consideration of new areas. The subject before us is the Christian lifestyle.

I. DOING THE WILL OF GOD

The primary concern in Christian living is that of doing the will of God. In the Sermon on the Mount Jesus taught His disciples to pray, "Thy will be done, on earth as it is in heaven" (Matt. 6:10). Paul speaks about "doing the will of God from the heart" (Eph. 6:6);[1] the writer of Hebrews prays, "The God of peace . . . equip you with everything good that you may do his will" (13:20–21); John writes that "the world passes away, and the lust of it; but he who does the will of God abides for ever" (1 John 2:17). The will of God should stand at the forefront of Christian living.

Before proceeding further, let us observe that the will of God is the cause of all that exists. The universe itself came into being because God willed it. In the Book of Revelation the elders around the throne of God sing forth, "You are worthy, our Lord and God, to receive glory and honor and power, for you created all things, and by your will they were created and have their being" (4:11 NIV). *By God's will all things exist.* Again, Christ gave Himself for our redemption according to God's will: "[He] gave himself for our sins to deliver us from the present evil age, according to the will of our God and Father" (Gal. 1:4). *By God's will Christ died for us.*

Also, according to Paul, our salvation is the result of God's will: "He predestined us to adoption as sons through Jesus Christ to Himself, according to the kind intention[2] of His will (Eph. 1:5 NASB). *By God's will we have been adopted as His sons.* Similarly, our sanctification has occurred: "By that will we have been sanctified through the offering of the body of Jesus Christ once for all" (Heb. 10:10). *By God's*

---

[1]This is said to Christian slaves (see vv. 5 and 8), but surely applies to all believers.
[2]The KJV reads "good pleasure." The Greek word is *eudokian*.

411

will we have been sanctified.[3] Further, God's will is all encompassing: He "works all things after the counsel of His will" (Eph. 1:11 NASB). *By God's will all things are accomplished.*[4] The will of God stands behind everything.

To do the will of God, therefore, is to be in accord with God's will. It is a harmonious flow between heaven and earth. In Christian living doing God's will should have priority over all else.

In His own life Jesus again and again demonstrated the absolute priority of the will of God. Several statements in the Gospel of John particularly show this. On one occasion Jesus said to His disciples, "My food is to do the will of him who sent me, and to accomplish his work" (4:34). The will of God was the basic subsistence of His life. Later Jesus declared, "I seek not my own will but the will of him who sent me" (5:30). Again Jesus said, "I have come down from heaven, not to do my own will, but the will of him who sent me" (6:38). Jesus completely placed His will at the disposal of God the Father. The Synoptic Gospels record Jesus' readiness to do God's will even in the midst of great anguish. He prayed in Gethsemane, "My Father, if it be possible, let this cup pass from me: nevertheless, not as I will, but as thou wilt" (Matt. 26:39; cf. Mark 14:36; Luke 22:42). He prayed similarly two more times, asking to avoid, if possible, the coming horror of crucifixion, but only if such were God's will. However, since God willed the cross for His Son, Jesus thereafter unhesitatingly accepted it. The will of God was supreme in Jesus' life.

It is apparent that for Jesus, doing God's will was neither automatic nor coercive. Since He was the Son of God, it might be assumed that He automatically did His Father's will. Although He came from heaven, as He said, to do the Father's will, Jesus still spoke about seeking the will of His Father. Even though He was the Son of God, Jesus was also human and, accordingly, had to seek God's will. Nor was the will of God a matter of coercion. Jesus' struggle in Gethsemane, if nothing else, makes it abundantly clear that whereas the Father willed the cross for His Son, He did not compel it. Jesus willingly went to His death on the cross.

This highlights two important facts. First, although God's will is supreme in the universe, so that by His will all things are accomplished, this did not rule out the freedom of Jesus' action in doing that will. Second, it follows that for those who belong to Jesus there is likewise freedom to do that same will. There is neither necessity nor compulsion.

Now let us observe the high importance Jesus likewise attached to His disciples doing the will of God. On one occasion Jesus was teaching in a house, and a man told Him that His mother and brothers were standing outside trying to speak to Him. Jesus replied to the man, "Who is My mother and who are My brothers?" Then, "stretching out His hand toward His disciples, He said, 'Behold, My mother and My brothers! For whoever does the will of My Father who is in heaven, he is My brother and sister and mother'" (Matt. 12:48–50 NASB). This doubtlessly shocked all who heard Jesus. His listeners must have been startled at such a seeming breach of the commandment, "Honor your father and your mother," as well as a denial of obvious family relationships. Mary and her sons must have felt a sharp anguish and the pain of exclusion as they remained outside. And Jesus' own disciples surely must have been

---

[3]This refers to our initial sanctification (there is also continuing sanctification). See chapter 4, "Sanctification."

[4]For detailed discussion see vol. 1, chapter 6, "Providence," 123–26.

amazed at hearing themselves described as His mother and brothers, indeed His family. The climax was like a lightning bolt: "*Whoever* does the will of My Father . . . is My brother and sister and mother."

This incident dramatically shows the importance of doing the will of God. Since Jesus Himself constantly did that will, all who do the same are His spiritual family: they are of kindred spirit. A person cannot, of course, do God's will if his will is still in bondage to sin and evil (there must be prior salvation); but if that bondage has been essentially broken (as with every true believer), then the person is able to do God's will. To do God's will faithfully is to be close to Jesus, so that among those doing His will an older woman may be called His mother, a younger woman His sister, and other men His brothers.[5] A higher stress on the importance of doing God's will would be hard to imagine.

Jesus also spoke in the Sermon on the Mount on the relationship of doing of God's will to entrance into the kingdom. "Not everyone who says to Me, 'Lord, Lord,' will enter the kingdom of heaven; but he who does the will of My Father who is in heaven" (Matt. 7:21 NASB). Then Jesus spoke of those who some day will say, "Lord, Lord, did we not prophesy in Your name, and in Your name cast out demons, and in Your name perform many miracles?" adding, "Then I will declare to them, I never knew you; DEPART FROM ME, YOU

WHO PRACTICE LAWLESSNESS"[6] (vv. 22–23 NASB). What is of striking relevance here, especially for the charismatic renewal in our time, is the fact that disciples may prophesy, exorcise demons, even perform miracles, *all in Jesus' name*, but not truly belong to Him.[7] Supernatural demonstrations as such do not prove citizenship in the kingdom of heaven. The final proof— above and beyond all mighty works—is the doing of God's will.

Let us leave the subject of false disciples and again stress the need for Jesus' true disciples to do the will of God. Bear in mind the ongoing example of Jesus who said, "I seek not my own will but the will of him who sent me" and "Whoever does the will of my Father . . . is my brother and sister and mother." We need to check often to see whether the will of God is foremost in our lives. There simply is no guarantee that because we are growing in holiness or because we are charismatically endowed that we are living according to God's will. Indeed, if the Father's will was not always easy for Jesus—*the* Holy One and *the* Charismatic One— how much more is it the case for us!

I will be quite blunt. Again and again today there are examples of Christians—many of them longtime believers—who have allowed concern for their own goals and ends to usurp the place of seeking God's will and purpose. This is often the most obvious among church leaders who become driven by a will to succeed, to receive

---

[5]None, however, could be called His father because Jesus had but one Father in heaven (cf. "My Father" in the quotation above).

[6]Capitalized in the NASB because it is a quotation from the Old Testament.

[7]Later in Jesus' ministry one of His disciples said to Him, "Teacher, we saw a man casting out demons in your name, and we forbade him, because he was not following us" (Mark 9:38). Hence the man did not truly belong to Jesus. Quite interestingly, Jesus replied, "Do not forbid him; for no one who does a mighty work [or "miracle"] in my name will be able soon after to speak evil of me" (v. 39). In the Book of Acts there is the account of "some . . . itinerant Jewish exorcists [who] undertook to pronounce the name of the Lord Jesus over those who had evil spirits" (19:13). (See also my earlier discussion of false prophets and counterfeit miracles [chap. 14, sections V and VI].)

the acclaim of others, to be a "kingdom builder." Once perhaps they were sincerely devoted to God's will, but self-will now drives them on. Thus no longer are they truly acting as brothers and sisters of Jesus, a part of His doing-God's-will family, although they may achieve worldly success. Moreover, even if they are so spiritually endowed as to prophesy mightily, to cast out demons, to work miracles, they are now existing in the camp of the false followers of Jesus who deserve only a "Depart from me. . . ." How much they need—indeed, how much all of us need—to say from the heart "Not my will, Lord, but thine be done."

But let us move from these higher echelons of church leadership to the practice of the average Christian. Here we need to ask ourselves, How much am I really concerned to do God's will? This pertains, first, to major decisions in life such as vocation and marriage. Is God's will primary for me as I consider a vocation or a vocational change? Is it what *I* want or what *He* wants? In a marriage consideration, there may be love, but is this the partner God intends for me? Likewise, am I the one for the other person? Then, second, there are the day-by-day decisions at home, school, business, and so on, to be made. Am I asking at every point, "Lord, is this what you want me to do?" James in his epistle speaks of businessmen who say, " 'Today or tomorrow we will go to this or that city, spend a year there, carry on business and make money' " (4:13 NIV). James then expostulates, "Why, you do not even know what will happen tomorrow. What is your life? You are a mist that appears for a little while and then vanishes. Instead, you ought to say, 'If it is the Lord's will, we will live and do this or that' " (vv. 14–15). *If it is the Lord's will:* this should be the concern of every Christian man and woman in every plan and decision.

It is unmistakable that the doing of God's will should be foremost. But now the important question follows: *How do we know God's will?* We cannot very well do it if we do not know it. In the matter of knowledge Paul prayed for the Colossians that they might be "filled with the knowledge of his [God's] will in all spiritual wisdom and understanding" (Col. 1:9). How can we be "filled" with such knowledge? Later in the same letter Paul speaks of being "mature and fully assured in all the will of God" (4:12).[8] How does such assurance come about? These are no small matters, for knowing the will of God in matters both great and small is of signal importance.

First, *we must be seekers.* Once again we hear the words of Jesus: "I seek not my own will but the will of him who sent me." "Seek" is the key word. It means to make the knowledge of God's will a dedicated concern. It is quite possible that a Christian may become so preoccupied with the things of the world—"the lust of the flesh and the lust of the eyes and the pride of life" (1 John 2:16)[9]—that any real desire to know God's will recedes into the far background.[10] Consequently, we do not really want to know God's will; we are even fearful that it might not be what we want. As a result nothing is revealed. It may even seem safer to pray, "Thy will be done on earth," than to

---

[8] Paul writes that this was the prayer of Epaphras, "one of yourselves" (also v. 12). Doubtless Paul concurred with it.

[9] These words precede the statement previously quoted, "The world passes away, and the lust of it; but he who does the will of God abides for ever" (v. 17).

[10] Earlier I stressed how ego interests may bring about a decreasing concern for God's will. Here the basic point is that lusting after things of the world can have the same result.

pray "Thy will be done in my own life," or in this particular matter. To seek is urgent[11]—and as we honestly, earnestly, and perpetually seek to know God's will, He will surely reveal it.

Second, *we need to pray much*. Again, our true guide is Jesus Himself. Not only did He teach His disciples to pray for God's will to be done, but He also demonstrated this in His own life. Many times in the Gospels Jesus is shown to be in prayer. One of the most significant was early in His ministry when He spent a whole night in prayer. The next morning He chose twelve to be His apostles. The Scripture reads, "He went out to the mountains to pray; and all night he continued in prayer to God. And when it was day, he called his disciples, and chose from them twelve, whom he named apostles" (Luke 6:12–13). Doubtless, these many hours of prayer were spent seeking His Father's will about the choice of apostles. This would be a momentous decision affecting the whole future of the church, so Jesus knew that He must be in perfect agreement with His Father's will. So He prayed hour after hour through the night. This extended praying of Jesus dramatically shows that the will of His Father, which He always did, was not received or understood except through persistent praying. It follows that if this was true of the Son of God, how much more do we need to pray, and sometimes at great length, to know what God's will is. The other outstanding occasion in Jesus' life, already mentioned, was in the Garden of Gethsemane, where He agonized long in prayer. He prayed once, twice, three times before he had the final assurance that all other possibilities were ruled out and

the Father willed that He continue to the cross. Thereafter, despite all the humiliation, pain, and suffering He went calmly to His death.

These accounts of Jesus refer to matters of huge consequences in which through prayer He sought the Father's will. Surely it needs to be the same with us when critical matters calling for decision are at hand. If Jesus did not say a quick prayer of "God's will be done" but prayed long and earnestly on many occasions, can we do less? It is also certain that in all matters, however large or small, we need constantly to know what God's will is. There is hardly a day when we will not profit from praying quietly, "O Lord, what is your will in this regard?" God will surely guide and bless those who so seek.

Third, *we must constantly hear God's word in Scripture*. The most direct answer to knowing God's will is that of listening to His written word. The psalmist declared, "Thy word is a lamp to my feet and a light to my path" (119:105). The more we are immersed in Scripture the more that lamplight illumines the way to go. For example, the Ten Commandments, the words of the prophets, and the teachings of Jesus and the apostles all give concrete instructions on what God wills. Since the Tenth Commandment says, "Thou shalt not covet," coveting the things of the world must not replace zeal for God's will and desire. We must keep that commandment always before us. The Lord spoke through Jeremiah, saying, "Let not the wise man glory in his wisdom, let not the mighty man glory in his might, let not the rich man glory in his riches; but let him who glories glory

---

[11] This is apparent also in the words of Jesus regarding the kingdom of God, "Seek first his kingdom and his righteousness" (Matt. 6:33); likewise in relation to the gift of the Holy Spirit: "Seek, and you will find" (Luke 11:9, 13). According to Hebrews, God "rewards those who earnestly seek him" (11:6 NIV).

in this, that he understands and knows me" (9:23–24). Thus, we must glory in only this; it is God's will. Since Jesus declared "If any man would come after me, let him deny himself and take up his cross daily and follow me" (Luke 9:23), we are not free as His disciples to seek our own self-fulfillment and personal ambition. We must apply Jesus' words continuously to all our projects. Many other scriptural injunctions, Old Testament and New, could be added; however, the important thing is to so live in God's word that we will increasingly know God's will in all matters.

Fourth, to know God's will *we often need the help of other believers*. It is important to listen to the word of God from a Christian brother or sister. Peter in his first epistle writes to "the exiles of the Dispersion" (1:1) that "it is God's will that by doing right you should put to silence the ignorance of foolish men" (2:15). This is a specific word about the will of God addressed to a large number of fellow Christians.[12] So it is today that God's will may be spoken through one of God's servants, perhaps a pastor, an evangelist, or a prophet. Through the Christian community a word spoken may serve to clarify or confirm God's intention. I have discussed at some length the gifts of the Holy Spirit,[13] all of which are for the edification of the assembled believers. This edification will, at times, include a word that enables a person to know God's will better.

The community cannot substitute for the personal seeking of God's will. However, because we are members of one another in Christ, we need never go it simply alone. Through the fellowship of others and by their words, we may often gain further insight into the will of God.

Fifth, *we need to have a personal ongoing renewal of the mind*. The will of God is clearest to those whose minds are continually being renewed. Here we focus on the words of Paul: "Do not be conformed to this world, but be transformed by the renewing of your mind, that you may prove [by testing][14] what the will of God is, that which is good and acceptable and perfect" (Rom. 12:2 NASB). In this extraordinary statement Paul declares that we may prove by testing and therefore truly discern God's will.[15] This implies that God's will can be proved and tested in any given situation. A person has many possibilities, but which of these is what God desires? Even the reading of Scripture does not always clarify. The answer of Paul is that we may prove, that is, be certain of, the will of God through the renewal of the mind. A person whose mind is regularly renewed can truly discern the will of God. Such a one can perceive God's intentions beyond the conflicting opportunities and possibilities. Indeed, a person with a renewed mind can test alternatives and know the certainty of God's will. Even more, "what is good and acceptable and perfect" will be known. This indeed is much to be desired!

Since such proof and knowledge come through the renewing of the mind, how does this process take place? Paul's words are clear: "Do not be conformed to this world, but be transformed. . . ." The less we are conformed to the world—its ways, values, goals—the more we can be transformed by the renewing of our minds and, as a result, prove out the will of God. Still,

---

[12] See context of 1 Peter 2:13–17 for what this "doing right" involves.

[13] In chapters 13 and 14.

[14] See chapter 4, n. 62.

[15] The NEB translates, "Then you will be able to discern the will of God."

nonconformity to the world is not an easy thing. How do we become nonconformers? Paul answers this in the prior verse: "I urge you therefore, brethren, by the mercies of God, to present your bodies[16] a living and holy sacrifice" (v. 1 NASB). This is not a once-for-all action; rather, we are continually to surrender our total selves to God. Such a surrender is the opposite of conformity to the world. Through this ongoing surrender the renewing of the mind occurs. In this renewal a transformation takes place whereby we can then prove God's will by testing it.

Accordingly, this is one aspect of the process of sanctification.[17] The more we surrender ourselves totally to God[18] the more we will know His will. By undergoing this transformation we can actually examine various possibilities and so prove (as one might prove metal) what is the good and acceptable and perfect will of God. It is no longer a matter of guesswork or of hoping we have chosen rightly: we *know* what is His will.

Our statements in this section about the renewing of the mind should not stand alone. We also continuously need to be seekers, to pray much, to hear God's word in Scripture; none of this can be overlooked. Without the continuous renewing of the mind, however, we lack that culminating proof of God's will. The decisions may still not be easy, but with a renewed mind we have a touchstone for examining what lies before us and for determining God's will from among all the options.

But let us remember this: the critical matter is the surrender of oneself. The more we offer ourselves as "living and holy" sacrifices—that is, die to ourselves—the more we are able to discern God's intention and purpose. If we are dying to self-will, no longer are we blocked from seeing and knowing God's will. Our minds, our thoughts, our plans no longer center in ourselves; they center in God. We then see, know, and, yes, prove God's will. The challenge is before us: let us die to self-will and live in the will of God!

We have spoken of *knowing* the will of God; now, as a final point, how do we go about *doing* it? Knowing, though obviously basic, is by no means enough; there must be the follow-up of doing the will of God.

First, there is need for *energetic action*. Few people disturbed Jesus more than those who heard God's word but did not do anything about it. We have earlier noted Jesus' statement that to say "Lord, Lord" is not enough; a person must do the will of the Father. Shortly after this, Jesus brought his Sermon on the Mount to a climax: "Every one then who hears these words of mine and does them will be like a wise man who built his house upon the rock. . . " (Matt. 7:24). Those who hear but do not act are "like a foolish man who built his house upon the sand" (v. 26). Although one must begin by hearing (and in that sense knowing), if there is no corresponding action his house is built on sand that will soon collapse.

Hence, as surely as we know God's will, we must act on that knowledge. If

---

[16]While "bodies" is the literal translation (the Greek word is *sōmata*), Paul doubtless intends the total self (so NEB translates: "your very selves"). Since in the Old Testament animals were killed and their dead bodies presented as sacrifices, Paul is saying that our bodies, hence our whole selves, should be presented not as dead but as living sacrifices. Paul J. Achtemeier writes, "Like the burnt offering given wholly to God, the Christian is to be a total sacrifice to God, and that sacrifice is to consist of the whole of life" (*Romans*, 195).

[17]See chapter 4, "Sanctification," III.B.2.a, "The Mind."

[18]I spoke in chapter 4 of "dying to sins" (IV.B.1).

God has revealed to me a certain course of action (perhaps in regard to vocation, marriage, or business, or some more mundane matter), I must forthwith act on it. Indeed, if I do not so act, I may become self-deceived, namely, as if to know God's will somehow suffices for doing it. James puts it bluntly: "Be doers of the word, and not hearers only, deceiving yourselves" (James 1:22). We must not fail to act on what God has revealed about His will.

This is not always easy. What God wills we may not like. The Bible is laden with accounts of persons, often leaders and prophets, who were bidden to do things that they would not ordinarily choose to do. God spoke to Moses, "I will send you to Pharaoh that you may bring forth my people . . . out of Egypt" (Exod. 3:10). Nothing could have suited Moses less; the will of God was not easy. Or consider God's commission to Isaiah, "Go. . . . Make the heart of this people fat, and their ears heavy, and shut their eyes" (Isa. 6:9–10). Who would naturally want this? Both Moses and Isaiah obeyed, and God used each of them mightily.

But, I repeat, action is urgent in small matters as well as large. I quote James again: "Whoever knows what is right to do and fails to do it, for him it is sin" (4:17). We may paraphrase this by saying, "Whoever knows what God wills in a given matter and fails to do it, for him it is sin." Our God is a God of action, Jesus was a man of action—a "doer of the word"—and as His disciples we must energetically do whatever God reveals to us.

Second, *there is need for endurance*. It is important to persevere in the action to which we commit ourselves. The way may seem difficult, the obstacles many, the results slow in working out; nonetheless, if we know we are on the path of God's will, we must endure. This is especially needed if our action results in travail and pain, perhaps persecution. The Book of Hebrews, after speaking about suffering and abuse, adds, "You have need of endurance, so that you may do the will of God and receive what is promised" (10:36). Yes, endurance is highly important. Sometimes persons begin on the path of doing God's will, but because of rough experiences they simply fall away. Truly we all have need of endurance.

The example of Paul's determination to get to Rome is especially noteworthy. In his letter to the Romans Paul twice refers to God's will in this connection. He first speaks of his own prayers "asking that somehow by God's will[19] I may now at last succeed in coming to you" (1:10), and later "that by God's will I may come to you with joy and be refreshed in your company" (15:32). Paul has no question about God's will in this matter or other matters,[20] for he himself had doubtless done what he urged the Romans to do about proving the will of God.[21] Timing was the only question, that is, exactly when it would occur. In any event Paul, knowing God willed that he go to Rome, remained steadfast through many trials, attempts on his life, and near death at sea (Acts 21–28). Even when he reached Rome, he became a prisoner there. But at last he was able to preach the gospel in Caesar's stronghold. In writing Timothy Paul later said, "This is my gospel, for which I am

[19]The will of God is much stressed by Paul. He uses the Greek word for "will," *thelēma*, twenty-four times in his letters.
[20]In one of the accounts of his conversion Paul declared that Ananias said to him, "The God of our fathers appointed you to know his will" (Acts 22:14).
[21]Recall our prior discussion of this.

suffering even to the point of being chained like a criminal. But God's word is not chained. Therefore I endure everything for the sake of the elect" (2 Tim. 2:8–10 NIV). "I *endure everything.*" Paul knew the will of God and endured all things to fulfill it. Then come the triumphant words of Paul in which he includes all true believers: "If we endure, we shall also reign with him [Jesus Christ]" (v. 12 NIV).

Endurance in doing the will of God is imperative. Again, this refers not only to large matters such as persevering in our life's calling, but also to any and every situation in which God has placed us. If we know what the will of God is, we are called upon to endure—to hold fast, to persevere regardless of what may come. Satan may attempt to frustrate our action, untoward circumstances may cause much difficulty, even friends may seek to lure us away (perhaps thinking they know better); through it all we must endure.

If endurance sounds grim and heavy, actually there can be joy in it. Jesus, far more than Paul, is the great example of endurance, indeed all the way to the cross. But there was joy even in that. Hebrews puts it like this: "[Christ] *for the joy set before Him* endured the cross, despising the shame, and has sat down at the right hand of the throne of God" (12:2 NASB). Accordingly, we are summoned to "run with endurance the race that is set before us, fixing our eyes on Jesus, the author and perfecter of faith" (vv. 1–2). Whatever may be God's will, by following Jesus' example we can endure with joy.

Third, and finally, we need *supernatural strength.* We are called to act energetically according to God's re-

vealed will and to endure throughout; however, we can do this only by looking for strength beyond ourselves. I have earlier called attention to Paul's statement about being "filled with the knowledge of his will in all spiritual wisdom and understanding" (Col. 1:9). A few words later Paul says, "May you be strengthened with all power, according to his glorious might, for all endurance and patience with joy" (v. 11). Note again, incidentally, the phrase "endurance with joy." But the critical matter is that we be "strengthened with all power" to carry out the will of God. We need the supernatural strength that comes from "his [God's] glorious might."

Luke records one of the most touching scenes in Gethsemane in his Gospel. Just after Jesus prayed, "Father, if thou art willing, remove this cup from me; nevertheless not my will, but thine, be done" (22:42), the narrative reads, "And there appeared to him an angel from heaven, strengthening him"[22] (v. 43). Even the Son of God in His humanity needed supernatural strength to follow the will of God to the very end. Also memorable are the words of Paul: "I can do all things through Him who strengthens me" (Phil. 4:13 NASB). Paul could not have endured all his trials without relying on the strength of the Lord.

In conclusion, doing the will of God simply cannot be carried out in our own strength. No matter how great our resolve—since it is *God's* will, not ours—we need His supernatural strengthening. Paraphrasing the words of Paul: "May we—you and I—be strengthened with *all* power . . . for *all* endurance." In His strength we can accomplish *all* His will. Praise God!

---

[22]This verse is omitted in some early manuscripts. Geldenhuys writes that "most probably the verses were omitted by later copyists because they had no idea of the Saviour's real humanity and could therefore not understand why an angel had to strengthen Him" (*The Gospel of Luke*, NICNT, 577).

II. WALKING IN THE LIGHT

A second concern in Christian living is walking in the light. Paul puts it in imperative form: "Walk as children of light" (Eph. 5:8). Let us consider what it means to walk in this light.

By way of background, we first observe how the Gospel of John especially sets forth Jesus Himself as the light. According to the prologue, "in him was life, and the life was the light of men. . . . The true light that enlightens every man was coming into the world" (John 1:4, 9). Later Jesus declared, "I am the light of the world" (8:12; also 9:5; cf. 12:46). As the true light Jesus always walked in the light. At one point He asked, "Which of you convicts me of sin?" (8:46). None could respond, for He was wholly light, with no trace of darkness in Him. He walked only in the light.

Second, believers are those who have become people of light. Jesus declared, "While you have the light, believe in the light, that you may become sons of light" (John 12:36). Paul describes believers as "sons of light": "You are all sons of light and sons of the day" (1 Thess. 5:5). Elsewhere Paul speaks of believers as "saints in light," for, he said, "He has delivered us from the domain of darkness . . . " (Col. 1:12–13 NASB). Peter, in similar fashion, writes about "the wonderful deeds of him who called [us] out of darkness into his marvelous light" (1 Peter 2:9). The New Testament bears striking witness that believers are people of light.

Surely our Christian experience confirms this. There was a time when each one of us was in darkness, lost in the shadows of sin and evil. The paths we trod may now and again have seemed to be light, but in the end they were swallowed up by darkness. Then the day came when the "light of the world" truly enlightened us, and we knew for the first time the wonder of becoming people of light. Paul can say to each one of us, "Once you were darkness, but now you are light in the Lord" (Eph. 5:8). Yes, praise God, we are light in Him!

This is tremendously important because the surrounding world is still in darkness. Paul speaks of "a crooked and perverse[23] generation, among whom you shine as lights in the world" (Phil. 2:15). Without the light of Christ shining through believers, deep darkness enshrouds all. The people of light are essential to a world still in darkness.

But now we come to a critical point: unfortunately we do not always show forth that light. Although we are people of light, we often allow the darkness to crowd in again. If this happens, the darkness can be vast indeed. In the Sermon on the Mount Jesus said to his disciples, "You are the light of the world,"[24] and then added: "Let your light so shine before men, that they may see your good works and give glory to your Father who is in heaven" (Matt. 5:14, 16). Later Jesus declared, "If then the light in you is darkness, how great is the darkness!"[25] (6:23).

Against this background the challenge is clear: we must indeed determine to walk in the light. It is immediately following his words "Now you are

---

[23] The Greek word *diestrammenēs* may also be rendered "depraved" (so NIV; cf. BAGD—"perverted in the moral sense, depraved").

[24] It is interesting to compare this with the words of Jesus in the Fourth Gospel, "I am the light of the world."

[25] Jesus had just spoken of the physical eye as "the light of the body" (6:22 KJV), which he applies metaphorically to spiritual light. Although the context of Matthew 5:14, 16 and 23 is different, the relevant point for our consideration is that though we are shining lights the light in us may become darkness. How great—tragically great—is that darkness!

light in the Lord" that Paul speaks the imperative: "Walk as children of light." Listen to the apostle's full statement in this regard:

> Walk as children of light (for the fruit of the light consists in all goodness and righteousness and truth), trying to learn what is pleasing to the Lord. And do not participate in the unfruitful deeds of darkness, but instead even expose them (Eph. 5:8–11 NASB).

Paul's words provide a helpful framework for this walk in the light.

A. The Character of This Walk

This walk must be "in all goodness and righteousness and truth" (Eph. 5:9 NASB)

This is "the fruit of the light," for walking in the light means walking in goodness, righteousness, and truth. To walk in the light is to be devoted to the good over against the evil, to the right or just over against the wrong, to the truth over against what is false. The walk is by no means an easy one because we likewise live in "a crooked and perverse generation"—indeed in a time when crookedness, perversity, and depravity seem greatly on the increase. But people of the light *must* not participate in any of this.

Shortly before Paul wrote about walking in the light he firmly declared: "Among you there must not be even a hint of sexual immorality, or of any kind of impurity, or of greed, because these are improper for God's holy people" (Eph. 5:3 NIV). "Not even a hint!"[26] These words are much needed

today, for sadly many "people of light" have become involved in sexual immorality, various kinds of impurity in life and speech,[27] and are following the world's way of greed and covetousness. However, not the slightest hint of such activity should be among us, for we are children of light, not children of darkness.

As I write these words, there are many scandals abroad in the land among God's people. "Hints" of immorality? Alas, far more: indulgence in sexual vices and greedy materialism have infected large numbers in both high places and low. This is not simply happening among lukewarm believers who are easily carried away by the corruption of our time, but also among many in positions of church leadership. In particular, I must painfully refer to some in the Pentecostal tradition who occupy places of high responsibility. They have succumbed to immorality and greed, giving in to sexual vice and allowing covetousness for the things of the world to pervert their ministries. This is a double tragedy: not only have they nearly destroyed themselves,[28] but they have also undermined the faith of many who had believed in them.

Let me speak quite plainly: There can be *no* substitute for goodness, righteousness, and truth, or, in a word, *holiness*. Preaching the gospel with great effectiveness, "soul-winning" on the streets and in the marketplace, abounding in charismatic gifts—all such admirable activity needs the deep undergirding of holy living. I will speak

---

[26]The Greek text more literally reads "not even be named among you" (as in RSV and NASB). However, the NIV vividly captures the meaning of these words.

[27]Paul adds, "Nor should there be obscenity, foolish talk or coarse joking" (v. 4 NIV).

[28]Paul explicitly adds, "For of this you can be sure: No immoral, impure, or greedy person—such a man is an idolater—has any inheritance in the kingdom of Christ and of God" (v. 5 NIV). It can be argued that Paul is now speaking of unbelievers; however, his words follow injunctions to "God's holy people" (v. 3). For them surely there is the possibility of repentance and forgiveness no matter how egregious the immorality and/or greed; however, the warning of Paul must not be minimized. Such sins are not insignificant: they are contrary to all that represents "the kingdom of Christ and of God."

here particularly of this in relationship to charismatic gifts. Previously I have devoted many pages to the gifts of the Holy Spirit—their importance, nature, function, etc. But now I must warn about accompanying immoralities.

Let us first look again at the Corinthian situation. As we have noted, Paul could say of the Corinthians that they abounded in spiritual gifts: "You are not lacking in any spiritual gift" (1 Cor. 1:7). In that sense they are an ideal over against today's church, which so often lacks in this area. However, the Corinthians lacked much in terms of holiness and righteousness. For example, there was the heinous sin of incest in their midst—"immorality," says Paul, "of a kind that is not found even among pagans; for a man is living with his father's wife" (5:1). Moreover, the Corinthians were doing nothing about the situation. Also, they were defrauding one another: "You yourselves wrong and defraud, and that even your own brethren" (6:8). In addition, they were also guilty of gluttony. When the Corinthians gathered for the Lord's Supper, described by Paul as "a participation in the blood of Christ" and "a participation in the body of Christ" (10:16), they were profaning the holy: "It is not the Lord's Supper that you eat. For in eating, each one goes ahead with his own meal, and one is hungry and another is drunk" (11:20–21). These are glaring examples of unrighteousness in a church that abounded in spiritual gifts!

Paul is very blunt: the charismatic Corinthians *must* mend their ways. We may particularly note Paul's strong words regarding the incestuous relationship: "Drive out the wicked person from among you" (1 Cor. 5:13).[29] Paul's intention was not to condemn the man forever but actually to save him,[30] *and* that thereby the church might be purged of its inner evil. Indeed Paul, in this same context, further tells the Corinthians, "You [are] not to associate with any one who bears the name of brother if he is guilty of [sexual] immorality or greed, or is an idolater, reviler, drunkard, or robber—not even to eat with such a one" (v. 11). Paul had made it clear that he was not referring to association with the immoral of the world: ". . . then you would need to go out of the world" (v. 10). In the church, however, the situation has to be entirely different, for in it toleration of sin and association with overt sinners must not exist. At one point Paul asks, "Do you not know that a little leaven leavens the whole lump?" (v. 6). Then the apostle adds, "Cleanse out the old leaven that you may be a new lump, as you really are unleavened" (v. 7). Later in his second letter to the Corinthians Paul urges, "Beloved, let us cleanse ourselves from all defilement of flesh and spirit, perfecting holiness in the fear of the Lord" (7:1 NASB). The emphasis of Paul is starkly clear: known sin is intolerable in the Christian community; it must not be dealt with lightly, for the Lord intends his people to be a holy people.[31]

---

[29] F. F. Bruce writes concerning this verse: "It is almost an exact quotation of the LXX version of Dt. 17:7b; 22:24 (cf. Dt. 13:5), where idolatry and adultery are to be purged out of the community by the most drastic means" (*1 and 2 Corinthians*, NCBC, 59).

[30] Paul had earlier said, "You are to deliver this man to Satan for the destruction of the flesh, that his spirit may be saved in the day of the Lord Jesus" (v. 5). Although the worldly ravages of Satan would be fierce indeed, repentance and thus salvation were the goal.

[31] Gordon Fee perceptively comments, "The Pauline principle is simple: Free association outside the church, precisely because God, not the church, judges those on the outside; but strict discipline within the church, because in its free association with the world it may not

I have dealt at some length with the Corinthian situation because of its only too obvious parallels with the contemporary church scene. Paul's words, to be sure, relate to any church, whether liberal, traditional, or evangelical—all need to hear these apostolic injunctions. But since the Corinthians were charismatics par excellence ("not lacking in any spiritual gift"), the words of Paul should send a strong message particularly to the charismatic renewal of our time. Simply put, charismatic gifts, even in multiplicity, cannot and must not be a substitute for goodness, righteousness, and truth. *A charismatic community, just because it is laden with so much spiritual power, must be all the more concerned that such power be allied with holiness.* From the leadership down to all in the community there needs to be a vital concern for integrity, righteousness, and holiness in every matter.

Moreover, the members of the community must not be tolerant of evil in their midst (for example, by quickly condoning or too lightly forgiving). God's people should not display harsh judgmentalism but should temper their mercy with an eye to God's justice.[32] There needs to be a strong, ongoing concern for purity and holiness.

Let it be said loudly and clearly: *a multiplicity of spiritual gifts cannot substitute for goodness, righteousness, and truth.* On the other hand—I must add—*a genuine concern for holiness ought never to be set over against the gifts of the Spirit.* How desperately the

church needs both: a holy and righteous walk on the one hand and an ongoing exercise of the gifts on the other. When and if that day comes, the blessings of God will surely abound.

B. The Motivation for the Walk

Our motivation for the Christian walk is "trying to learn[33] what is pleasing[34] to the Lord" (Eph. 5:10).

These words of Paul introduce an additional note, namely, that God's people of light should walk with a total desire to learn what pleases the Lord. The Christian walk, which is doing the good and the righteous and the true, is inspired by a continuing desire to learn and do what is pleasing to Christ.

The word "please" removes any possible idea that walking in the light is only a matter of doing the right thing. Such could become an impersonal legalism by which believers do the good, the righteous, and the true because it is commanded of them. But when the motivation and—I might add—the goal of walking in holiness is to please the living Lord, there is a great desire to learn what is pleasing in His eyes and to act accordingly.

Here we first have the example of Jesus Himself. In relation to God the Father Jesus declared, "I always do what is pleasing to him" (John 8:29). Note the word "always"—not just now and then but at every moment. Paul writes similarly, "We speak, not to please men, but to please God who tests our hearts" (1 Thess. 2:4), adding later, "You ought to walk and please God

---

take on the character of the world in which it freely lives" (*The First Epistle to the Corinthians*, NICNT, 227).

[32] Sin by God's people often has tragic consequences. David's adultery with Bathsheba resulted in the death of their son, despite David's repentance (2 Sam. 12:13–19).

[33] The Greek word is *dokimazontes*, translated in the KJV as "proving." Since *dokimazō* basically refers to proving or testing (e.g., precious metals), Paul's idea here is to try to learn through testing what pleases the Lord.

[34] The Greek word is *euareston*, translated in the KJV as "acceptable." Although this translation is possible, "pleasing" or "well pleasing" is the more likely translation in this context (see TDNT, 1:457).

(just as you actually do walk), that you may excel still more" (1 Thess. 4:1 NASB). Pleasing God is both the motivation and goal for the Christian walk. Paul's strongest personal statement in this regard relates to his discussion of being at home in the body (this life) or at home with the Lord (the life to come): "Whether we are at home [in the body] or away [with the Lord], we make it our aim to please him" (2 Cor. 5:9). The pleasing of the Lord: motivation and aim both now and in the life to come!

It is quite significant that immediately following Paul's prayer for the Colossians that they might be "filled with the knowledge of His will,"[35] Paul adds, "so that you may walk in a manner worthy of the Lord, to please Him in all respects" (1:9–10 NASB). Here is an additional striking idea: Since believers have a Lord, they should walk worthily of Him in every way, thus reflecting His own nature and character. To claim to be a Christian and *not* to walk in the way of Christ is surely a dishonor to Him and a disgrace before the world.

Finally, doing what pleases the Lord is also the strongest motivation to shun the things of evil and darkness. If one constantly seeks to please a living Lord who is the very embodiment of goodness, righteousness, and truth, there is an inner revulsion against walking in evil. Sin is intolerable, even a hint of it, in the presence of the holy Lord. To seek to please Him in all things is the surest way to walk in the light.

C. The Walk in Light and the Surrounding Darkness

The Christian has this directive: "Do not participate in the unfruitful deeds of darkness, but instead even expose them" (Eph. 5:11 NASB).

Paul at this point contrasts the blessedness of walking in the light with the hurtfulness and fruitlessness of walking in darkness. The apostle adds that "it is disgraceful even to speak of the things which are done by them in secret" (v. 12 NASB). Thus believers are not only to walk in the light by abstaining from all evil,[36] but also to expose the works of darkness—to "show them up for what they are."[37]

First, there is a strong sense in which the very walk of Christians in the light exposes surrounding evil and darkness. Light by its nature exposes darkness, so that everything hidden becomes visible. So Paul continues, "All things become visible when they are exposed by the light" (5:13 NASB). Things may have been in deep darkness, even hidden, but when the light shines, they are exposed. So when believers walk in the light, the deeds of darkness are made manifest. Jesus declared, "For nothing is hid that shall not be made manifest, nor anything secret that shall not be known and come to light" (Luke 8:17).[38] This occurs through His disciples, true believers who steadfastly walk in the light. The hidden, the secret, perhaps covered over and even tacitly approved, is exposed by the light.

Hence, from this perspective it is not so much what believers say but who they are that exposes the darkness. On occasion Jesus did not have to speak a word; His presence was sufficient to expose evil and darkness, which cried out in the anguish of exposure. Two demoniacs, seeing Jesus approaching, called out, "What have you to do with

---

[35] Recall our discussion of this in section I.

[36] As discussed in the previous section.

[37] The NEB translation of Ephesians 5:11.

[38] These words do not directly speak of Jesus' disciples as the light. However, the preceding verse (v. 16) about the lamp on a stand undoubtedly relates to His own followers (cf. Matt. 5:14–15).

us, O Son of God? Have you come here to torment us before the time?" (Matt. 8:29). Similarly the very presence of believers walking in the light can expose the darkness of the surrounding world.

This is not to say that a darkened world likes being exposed. We have just noted how the demons cried out in torment at the presence of Jesus. So it is that evil people hate the light. According to the Fourth Gospel, "every one who does evil hates the light, and does not come to the light, lest his deeds should be exposed" (3:20). Accordingly, believers who shine forth the light ought not to expect evil to delight in their presence. Indeed, as with Jesus, those in darkness will often do everything they can to extinguish the light so that they can continue their evil way.[39] This does not matter: we *must* allow the light to keep on shining forth as purely and brightly as possible so that evil may be exposed.

I hasten to add that the purpose of our light's shining is not simply to expose evil, but that people, whose evil is now unmistakably manifest, will come to the light. Jesus' very presence was like a brilliant light that exposed the deep and vast darkness of the human race. However, the Lord Jesus did not come to condemn but to save, so that when people recognize their darkness they may come into the light of salvation. Thus it must be for Christians: we are to shine as lights in a darkened world so that people may see their evil in all its dark and terrible dimensions, turn from it, and enter upon the way of eternal life.

Second, walking in the light also includes exposure of the surrounding evil and darkness by speaking to those who are evil. Although the primary exposure of evil is through the presence of the good and righteous and true, there are times when reproof is necessary. The word earlier translated "expose" ("even expose them") may also be rendered "reprove":[40] "even reprove them." One clear illustration of this is King Herod, who had taken his brother's wife and who was verbally "reproved"[41] (Luke 3:19) by John the Baptist for committing this sin. Jesus, the light of the world, many times reproved the evil that confronted Him. For example, He did not hesitate to reprove the scribes and Pharisees for their hypocrisy and evil, even calling them "serpents" and "a brood of vipers." He asked them, "How are you to escape being sentenced to hell?" (Matt. 23:33). Paul many times in his epistles reproved evil in the world. Addressing humanity in general, "O man," he declared, "by your hard and impenitent heart you are storing up wrath for yourself on the day of wrath . . . " (Rom. 2:3, 5). To Timothy Paul wrote, "I solemnly charge you in the presence of God and of Christ Jesus . . . preach the word; be ready in season and out of season; reprove,[42] rebuke, exhort, with great patience and instruction" (2 Tim. 4:1–2 NASB). A great number of other similar references could be cited.

---

[39] A striking passage is found in *The Wisdom of Solomon* (a noncanonical apocryphal book) in which evil men say, "Let us lie in wait for the righteous man . . . the very sight of him is a burden to us, because his manner of life is unlike that of others. . . . Let us condemn him to a shameful death" (2:12, 15, 20). Note the statement "The very sight of him is a burden . . . ."

[40] As in the KJV. The Greek word is *elenchete*. *Elenchō* is frequently best translated "reprove" (or perhaps "rebuke"). See, e.g., Luke 3:19; 1 Timothy 5:20; 2 Timothy 4:2; Titus 1:13; 2:15.

[41] The Greek word is *elenchomenos*, literally, "being reproved."

[42] The Greek word is *elenxon*.

The point, then, is this: walking in the light often also includes the reproof of evil wherever it exists. The example of believers as shining lights is in itself an exposure of evil; however, the exposure is intensified when words, like shafts of light, further penetrate the darkness. If words are *not* spoken—and sometimes action not taken—it may seem as if Christians are not really serious about sin and evil, indeed consenting to its practice. In a day when evil is so rampant in the world, can Christians, the people of the light, afford to be silent? Surely judgment begins "with the household of God" (1 Peter 4:17), and we must continue to do housecleaning of our own evil (as we earlier discussed). But this cannot relieve us of speaking against the evil in the world.

Christians should be the first to speak out against moral corruption in society. This should be done by the church at large wherever it sees God's moral laws being broken—for example, through killing, adultery, stealing, false witness, greed, the killing of the unborn, sexual perversions of multiple kinds (in addition to adultery), misuse of public funds (a form of stealing), lying in high places and low, covetousness of riches and power, and on and on.

Personally also—although this is often more difficult—there needs to be the reproof of evil, especially when it lies close at hand. If, for example, in the place of business, corruption is unmistakably going on, the Christian needs to bear witness against it. Primarily, of course, there should be the witness of one's own honesty and integrity; however, there may also need to be verbal reproof of corrupt practices. Or, if in the public school where one is teaching it becomes apparent that reference to God and moral values is being increasingly eliminated, the Christian teacher needs to continue to bear witness to the truth and possibly reprove corrupting forces. For where neither God nor morality is recognized, the door is wide open for the whole tide of evil (dishonesty, insubordination, drug abuse, covetousness, sexual license, etc.) to sweep in. Or again, if a Christian has responsibility for some aspect of the television medium and encounters an increasing tendency to portray violence and obscenity, he has the right and the obligation to speak out against such and, if necessary, to take appropriate action.

Many such examples could be added. The word of Paul—to repeat—is clear: "Do not participate in the unfruitful deeds of darkness, but instead even expose them" (Eph. 5:11 NASB). This is not an injunction to leave the world—e.g., the place of business—but a call to nonparticipation in the "deeds of darkness." To be sure, the Christian may finally, if there is no change, decide to leave—or he or she may be forced to leave (the world does not often take kindly to Christian reproof!). The hope, of course, is that positive change may occur. For the purpose of reproof and rebuke is never destructive, but they are offered in the hope and prayer that repentance and alteration may come about.

In this connection we may understand the climactic words of Paul: "Everything exposed by the light becomes visible, for it is light that makes everything visible. This is why it is said, "Wake up, O sleeper, rise from the dead, and Christ will shine on you'" (Eph. 5:13–14 NIV). The final intent of all exposure and reproof is that one who receives it (could this include an institution as well as an individual?) may awaken from deadly evil and corruption and thereby receive the light of Christ. Reproof can indeed lead to new life and salvation.[43]

I close this section, "The Walk in the Light and the Surrounding Darkness," with some memorable words from John: "If we walk in the light as He Himself is in the light, we have fellowship with one another, and the blood of Jesus His Son cleanses us from all sin" (1 John 1:7 NASB). Our concern now moves from our witness in the world to the life of Christians among themselves. The message is clear. First, walking truly in the light makes for genuine fellowship with other believers. The darkness of sin—self-assertion, jealousy, rivalry, pride, and the like—that enshrouds human relationships is now pervaded by light, so that believers can walk in an even richer and fuller harmony with one another. By walking in the light, Christians experience deep and abiding fellowship among themselves. Second, for those who walk in the light Jesus' blood is available to cleanse from all sin. This is good news indeed, for no matter how faithfully we seek to walk in the light, sinful elements often stand in the way. Christ our Savior, however, knowing that we seek to walk in His light, continues to cleanse us of every sin that mars our walk. For truly, as John later adds, "if we confess our sins, he is faithful and just, and will forgive our sins and cleanse us from all unrighteousness" (v. 9). Confessing our sins and receiving His cleansing forgiveness, we move ahead in the light.

To walk in the light stands at the center of Christian living.

III. FOLLOWING THE WAY OF LOVE

The final concern of Christian living is following the way of love. Paul writes, "Follow the way of love . . . "[44] (1 Cor. 14:1 NIV). To follow this way is the climax of the Christian lifestyle.

Jesus Himself was, of course, the supreme example of One who followed this way. The love of Christ—His compassion and His mercy—is shown throughout the Gospel narratives. In regard to Jesus' own disciples, the Fourth Gospel states, "Having loved his own who were in the world, he loved them to the end" (13:1). Later in this same chapter Jesus declared, "A new commandment I give to you, that you love one another; even as I have loved you, that you also love one another" (v. 34).[45] The new commandment is not love—such had been commanded before—but to love one another *even* as He had loved. Such love also goes beyond the love of Christians for one another: it includes all people whether believers or not, and beyond that even one's enemies. Jesus commanded, "Love your enemies and pray for those who persecute you" (Matt. 5:44). What Jesus commanded He also did. Even at the cross among His last words were these: "Father, forgive them; for they know not what they do" (Luke 23:34). Truly Christ loved to the very end.

So when Paul writes, "Follow the way of love," he means to follow the

---

[43] According to EGT, "the quotation ["Wake up, O sleeper . . . "] comes in relevantly, therefore, as a further reinforcement both of the need for the reproof which is enjoined, and of the good effects of such a reproof faithfully exercised" (3:360).

[44] The Greek phrase is *diōkete tēn agapēn*. According to BAGD, *diōkete* in this context means "pursue, strive for, seek after, aspire to." The KJV has "follow after charity," RSV, "make love your aim," NASB, "pursue love." The NIV reading, "Follow the way of love," seems appropriate in the light of Paul's previous description of the "way" of love in 1 Corinthians 13.

[45] See also John 15:12 and 17.

way of Christ. Indeed, the apostle puts it vividly elsewhere: "Walk in love, as Christ loved us and gave himself up for us, a fragrant offering and sacrifice to God" (Eph. 5:2). "As Christ loved us" parallels "even as I have loved you"; hence to walk in love is to follow the way of Christ, which He has made known to us. It is, further, to show forth this love to all people.

Here we turn again to 1 Corinthians 13,[46] for nowhere else does Paul spell out more comprehensively the way of love.[47] Furthermore, it is only after the description of love in this chapter that Paul proceeds to say, "Follow the way of love" (1 Cor. 14:1 NIV). As we have earlier observed, this chapter is immediately preceded by these words of Paul: "I will show you a way beyond measure"[48] (1 Cor. 12:31). Hence, 1 Corinthians 13 spells out this way of love that Paul urges us to pursue. While reference will be made to other scriptures, the focus of our attention will be this famous "love chapter."[49]

I will be dealing largely with 1 Corinthians 13:4–7, where Paul describes the way of this love. However, it is important to recall that before Paul arrives at his description of the way of love, he speaks of the urgency of all spiritual gifts being exercised in love (vv. 1–3). Indeed, says Paul, even the most extraordinary exercise of the gifts is profitless without love. The five "ifs" (in vv. 1–3) are an imposing array—"*If* I speak in the tongues of men and of angels . . . . *If* I have prophetic powers [or "prophesy"], and understand all mysteries and all knowledge[50] . . . . *If* I have all faith, so as to remove mountains . . . . *If* I give away all I have . . . . *If* I deliver my body to be burned . . . ." Hence, if I have not just one gift but several even to the maximum degree (note the repetition of the word "all"), plus sacrificially endure martyrdom,[51] but do not have love, the results are virtually nil. "I am," says Paul, "a noisy gong or a clanging cymbal . . . I am nothing . . . I gain nothing." The gifts are still valid—Paul does not question that—but the results are jarring and abrasive for the community, and

---

[46] Recall chapter 13 (pp. 343–45).

[47] The word *agapē* (love) is found 75 times in Paul's letters (eight of which are in this chapter). This is out of a total of 116 times in the New Testament.

[48] This is my translation, as in chapter 13, n. 89.

[49] In chapter 13 I dealt to some degree with 1 Corinthians 13 in discussing the gifts of the Spirit. My concern in that chapter was to emphasize in a cautionary manner that love not be viewed as the greatest of the spiritual gifts but as the "way beyond measure" of the gifts. I also stated that Paul in 1 Corinthians 13 is primarily addressing people who are exercising these gifts. However, as I further intimated there, Paul's words also refer to all Christians. Karl Barth puts it well in saying that love is "the way which Christians have always to tread whether or not they are endowed by the Spirit or however they are endowed" (*Church Dogmatics* 4,1, 825).

[50] Paul's reference to "all mysteries and all knowledge" probably has for background such gifts as word of wisdom and word of knowledge (see chap. 14, I and II). In the context of tongues and prophecy (also faith to be mentioned next), the gifts themselves are also doubtless in mind.

[51] Paul goes beyond the spiritual gifts in referring to giving away all one's possessions and laying down one's life. This is significant to note because although Paul is primarily demonstrating the need for the gifts to operate in love, he also includes sacrificial acts that could occur without genuine love. For example, a person might give away everything out of a sense of duty or even sacrifice his body to gain some hoped-for glory (perhaps a better reward in heaven). It is interesting that some early New Testament manuscripts, after the words "my body to be burned," add "that I may boast [or "glory"]." See margins of RSV, NIV, NASB, and NEB.

the person himself becomes nothing and gains nothing from such exercise.[52]

It may seem strange that people can move in the spiritual gifts to an unparalleled degree and yet not have love, but such is possible. The Corinthians themselves are sad illustrations. They were "not lacking in any spiritual gift" (1 Cor. 1:7)—quite an amazing statement by Paul about them. Yet in succeeding pages Paul speaks of such matters as their dissensions and quarrels (1:10–13), jealousy and strife (3:3–4), conceit and boasting (4:6–7; 5:2–6), grievances against one another (6:1–8), pride of knowledge and insensitivity (v. 8), and selfishness at the Lord's table (11:17–34).[53] The Corinthians who lacked nothing in spiritual gifts seemed to lack everything in terms of love.

The relevance of all this for the present-day charismatic renewal should not be missed. Many groups have been blessed with a multiplicity of spiritual gifts; others are hoping for and praying for a larger endowment of the gifts; but often there has not been a corresponding growth in love. Earlier I wrote that one of the effects of the renewal is a new sense of unity and community:[54] this has been all to the good. Yet too often divisions have arisen; petty jealousies and struggles pervade groups; pride and ambition so affect leaders as

to bring much opprobrium on the whole movement. The sad, even tragic, thing about some of those who are spiritually blessed in the charismatic renewal, is that through lack of love they have fallen so low as to become—in Paul's word—"nothing." Yes, such persons often still operate in the gifts, exhibit great faith, move in healings and miracles, speak in tongues, and prophesy. By doing so they often attract large numbers of people, but in the eyes of God they have become as nothing because of lack of love. God is love—and when there is no love, a terrible vacuum exists: "I am—we are—nothing."[55]

On the other hand, if love is truly present, a community moving in the gifts can be a tremendous place of God's power and presence. If, for example, what Paul speaks of in the opening three verses of 1 Corinthians 13 in terms of tongues, prophecy, knowledge, and faith is happening and is also suffused with love, then the community of believers is greatly blessed and is of untold blessing to others about them.[56]

Before going further we need to proceed with Paul's description of the way of love. This can serve as a kind of grid to be placed over the Corinthian lifestyle as well as our contemporary situation. Some of Paul's emphases seem particularly relevant to our day, and

---

[52] Dunn emphasizes thus: "*Even man at his religious best, at the limit of charismatic possibility, if in all that he lacks love, does neither himself any good (nor presumably his community)*" (*Jesus and the Spirit*, 294). Bruce writes, "The most lavish exercise of spiritual gifts cannot compensate for lack of love" (*1 and 2 Corinthians*, NCBC, 124).

[53] See below for a fuller description of some of these Corinthian failures.

[54] Chapter 12, section IV.

[55] Although I refer to charismatic renewal groups above, it hardly needs adding that the problem of lack of love is often to be found in many other sectors of the church. My point, however, is that the more that has been given, the more tragic is the default. As Barth says, "The more intensive the work of the Holy Spirit, the richer and the more powerful His gifts . . . the more urgent it is indeed to call them [Christians] back to this distinctive reality, which is love" (*Church Dogmatics* 4, 2, 826).

[56] Lenski writes, "While these three verses are negative in form they, nevertheless, imply a corresponding affirmative thought, namely that with love present in the heart all gifts and all works become the treasures which God intends them to be for their possessor" (*Interpretation of First and Second Corinthians*, 553–54).

these will be considered in more detail. Also I will be alluding to other scriptures, especially in Paul's writings, statements that deal with the relevance of love to the community of faith. Let us concentrate, however, on 1 Corinthians 13:4–7.

A. The Exercise of Love

Paul begins his description of the way of love with a twofold affirmation: "Love is patient, love is kind"[57] (v. 4 NIV, NASB). More literally, this reads, "Love exercises patience, love exercises kindness."[58] Hence patience and kindness are aspects of love in operation. Love is not an abstraction but is concretely shown in the exercise of patience and kindness.

This is demonstrated, first of all, by God Himself. In his letter to the Romans, Paul speaks of patience and kindness as attributes of God in relation to people who think they will escape His judgment: "Do you presume upon the riches of his *kindness* and forbearance and *patience*? Do you not know that God's kindness is meant to lead you to repentance?" (2:4).[59] Hence we can see that patience and kindness find their origin and pattern in the love of God that is extended generously to all people.

Jesus Himself in every way demonstrated patience and kindness. Indeed, Paul refers to the "perfect patience" of Christ. He describes himself as the "foremost of sinners" who "received mercy . . . that in me, as the foremost, Jesus Christ might display his perfect patience[60] for an example to those who were to believe in him for eternal life" (1 Tim. 1:15–16). Jesus' "perfect patience," His longsuffering, even when Paul persecuted Him,[61] is an example of the way He deals with others as they come to faith in Him. In regard to Jesus' kindness Peter wrote, "You have tasted the kindness of the Lord" (1 Peter 2:3). Indeed, throughout Jesus' whole ministry He showed kindness repeatedly to the weak, the poor, the outcasts of society, the brokenhearted, the little children. Many truly "tasted" Jesus' kindness.

It follows that God's people, believers in Christ, should likewise act with patience and kindness. This exercise of love is in one sense an action of the will. Paul makes this point in writing, "Put on then, as God's chosen ones, holy and beloved, compassion, *kindness*, lowliness, meekness, and *patience*" (Col. 3:12). Like clothing that a person puts on at the beginning of the day, so kindness and patience are to be worn by the believer in his contact with others. Patience and kindness are not so much virtues to be admired as actions to be fulfilled. Love puts on and exercises patience and kindness.

However, lest this seem too voluntaristic, it is important to recognize that the source of patience and kindness is the Holy Spirit. These qualities are designated by Paul as belonging to "the fruit of the Spirit": "The fruit of the Spirit is love, joy, peace, *patience*,

---

[57]The Greek words are *makrothymei* and *chrēsteuetai*.

[58]The Greek words are both verbs. The KJV catches the verbal note in regard to the first by translating "suffereth long."

[59]Cf. 2 Peter 3:9—"He is patient with you, not wanting anyone to perish, but everyone to come to repentance" (NIV). Also on God's patience see Romans 9:22; 1 Peter 3:20.

[60]Literally His "all-patience"; the Greek is *hapasan makrothymian*. The NIV reads "unlimited patience."

[61]Recall the words of the exalted Lord to Saul who was ravaging the church: "Saul, Saul, why do you persecute me?" (Acts 9:4).

kindness . . . " (Gal. 5:22).[62] The Christian virtues of patience and kindness stem from the Holy Spirit, the Spirit of God. Surely they are to be "put on," hence there is a continuing action of the will, but this can be done only in the strength of the Holy Spirit. Since the word "fruit" also suggests maturation (fruit does not mature overnight), this further points to the fact that the exercise of patience and kindness is a matter of growth and development. If this comes slowly, we must keep at it!

Patience and kindness—constantly demonstrated by God in Christ—represent the operation of love in relation to all people. Although in the context of 1 Corinthians 13 this particularly refers to the life of the community of faith, such love must reach far beyond.

1. Patience

Let us now examine *patience* more closely. The exercise of patience suggests, for one thing, a willingness to give people time to change their ways or to perform in some better manner. Paul writes, "We exhort you, brethren, admonish the idle, encourage the fainthearted, help the weak," completing his exhortation by saying, "Be patient with them all" (1 Thess. 5:14). Patience does not mean tolerating laziness or timidity or weakness but while exhorting toward positive improvement of action to be patient with results. For example, in the area of the gifts of the Spirit people may be reluctant to move out in boldness. Thus encouragement may be needed as well as patience with those who are slow to act. Patience in any situation means a willingness to wait so that people are given time to

move ahead. James writes that "the farmer waits for the precious fruit of the earth, being patient over it until it receives the early and the late rain" (James 5:7). Patience is needed if one is to see results happen in due time.

Patience also closely relates to *forbearance*. Patience is not always easily acquired because it may mean forbearing things in others we do not like. Paul writes the Ephesians, "I . . . beg you to lead a life worthy of the calling to which you have been called, with all lowliness and meekness, with *patience, forbearing*[63] one another in love" (4:1–2). Also following the word "patience" in Colossians 3:12 (quoted above), Paul adds, "forbearing one another" (v. 13). To forbear—to put up with—the attitudes and personality traits of some people is not easy. They may "rub" the wrong way; hence all the more patience is needed. This may particularly be the case in a small group of Christians where the faults and foibles of people become increasingly apparent to one another. Even the way some may operate in the spiritual gifts can seem offensive ("he [or she] is too loud in prophesying" or "too quick to lay hands on everybody," etc.). Forbearance can be quite difficult.

Further, forbearance may also mean *forgiveness*. This can be even harder. Paul continues in Colossians 3:13, "If one has a complaint against another, forgiving each other; as the Lord has forgiven you, so you also must forgive." Even in the closest-knit Christian communities complaints and grievances often occur. Rather than holding on to them, perhaps suppressing them, or even giving vent to them, the way of

---

[62] Paul here lists patience and kindness alongside love, whereas in 1 Corinthians 13 they are described as aspects of love in operation. However, since love is listed first among the fruit of the Spirit, it is possible to view love as having priority over patience and kindness. Surely love, though it may be viewed separately, *includes* patience and kindness.

[63] The Greek word is *anechomenoi*, from *anechō*, "endure, bear with, put up with" (BAGD). To "put up with" is a vivid, down-to-earth translation (see, e.g., 2 Cor. 11:1—"I hope you will put up with [*aneichesthe*] a little of my foolishness" [NIV]).

431

love is the way of forgiveness. By remembering that the Lord has forgiven far worse things in us than we can ever find in a brother or sister, we are able then to forgive.

Love—as patience, forbearance, forgiveness—is the beginning of the way of love.

2. Kindness

Love also is kind: it exercises kindness. Again this goes back to God Himself. In Jesus' words, "He is kind to the ungrateful and wicked" (Luke 6:35 NIV). Paul speaks of God's kindness in regard to our salvation: "When the kindness and love of God our Savior appeared, he saved us, not because of righteous things we had done, but because of his mercy" (Titus 3:4–5 NIV).[64] This kindness of "God our Savior" was exhibited in Christ throughout His earthly life. To walk in kindness is to walk in the way of Christ.

So it is that Paul says, "Be kind to one another" (Eph. 4:32). Love exercises kindness in that it always exhibits goodwill and benevolence to other persons. Kindness accordingly is quite the opposite of harshness and bitterness. Regardless of how unresponsive, even antagonistic, another person may be, love continues to reach out in kindness.

Kindness, accordingly, is a matter of the heart. Added to Paul's words "Be kind to one another" is the word "tenderhearted."[65] Peter similarly writes, "All of you, have unity of spirit, sympathy, love of the brethren, a tender heart and a humble mind" (1 Peter 3:8). The word "sympathy" also beautifully expresses a tenderness of heart, for

sympathy means to reach out to the other person, to enter into his situation, to share his feelings, even, if need be, to suffer with[66] him. Similar is our English word "compassion,"[67] which also expresses a loving outreach to others. Frequently Jesus is described as having compassion on people. For examples note the following statements: "He had compassion for them [the crowds], because they were harassed and helpless" (Matt. 9:36). "Moved with compassion, He stretched out His hand, and touched him [a leper], and said . . . 'Be cleansed' " (Mark 1:41 NASB). "When the Lord saw her [a widow whose only son had died], he had compassion on her" (Luke 7:13) and raised her son from death. Such compassion was deeply from the heart and issued in acts of kindness.

Being kind to one another is very much needed in the fellowship of believers. A kind word, a sympathetic touch, a compassionate deed—all from the heart and at the right moment—can do wonders in the lives of people. This is love in action; it is following the way of Jesus.

Showing *mercy* is another way of expressing kindness. Just after Jesus said, "He [God] is kind to the ungrateful and wicked," He added, "Be merciful, just as your Father is merciful" (Luke 6:36 NIV). Kindness moves into mercy when an action toward the other person goes beyond what he really deserves to receive. Mercy does not disregard what justice may call for, but reaches out to the undeserving in loving and compassionate concern. Mercy toward another person, who rightly

---

[64] Also see Romans 11:22—"God's kindness to you." Paul also speaks of "the severity of God . . . toward those who have fallen [away]." The kindness of God does not eliminate His severe judgment upon sin. However, kindness is the primary note in God's dealings with mankind.

[65] The KJV, NASB, and NEB also read "tenderhearted"; NIV has "compassionate." The Greek word is *eusplanchnoi*.

[66] The Greek word for sympathy is *sympathēs*, from *sympatheō*, literally "to suffer with."

[67] "Compassion" is from Latin: *com*—"with" and *pati*—"suffer."

stands under judgment for his own actions, often radically changes the person for the better. As James puts it, "Mercy triumphs over judgment" (2:13). Mercy truly can be the way to restoration and wholeness.

In connection with kindness we may likewise speak of *gentleness*. Paul also calls it a fruit of the Spirit. I believe this appropriately comes after kindness[68] because gentleness adds the note of careful, loving action. On one occasion Jesus declared, "Come to Me, all who are weary and heavy-laden . . . . I am gentle and humble in heart; and YOU SHALL FIND REST FOR YOUR SOULS" (Matt. 11:28–29 NASB). Jesus was One who would "not break a bruised reed or quench a smoldering wick" (Matt. 12:20).[69] He was gentle with broken spirits, with weary and torn people, with all who cried out for help. In relation to the Thessalonians Paul writes, "We were gentle among you, like a nurse taking care of her children" (1 Thess. 2:7). There again is the note of careful, loving action. In Ephesians Paul links gentleness with humility as an aspect of the Christian walk: "I . . .

entreat you to walk in a manner worthy of the calling with which you have been called, with all humility and gentleness" (4:1–2 NASB). Gentleness should mark our daily lives in every relationship,[70] and surely in our close relationships within the community of faith. Especially is the latter important when someone in the community has strayed from the path. Paul writes, "Brethren, if a man is overtaken in any trespass, you who are spiritual should restore him in a spirit of gentleness"[71] (Gal. 6:1). This, indeed, is not easy to do, but gentleness should mark all dealings that lead to restoration.

The way of love is the way of kindness, tenderheartedness, mercy, and gentleness. Those who walk this way are following the way of Christ.

B. The Opposites of Love

Paul continues his description of the way of love by setting forth a number of opposites. He speaks eight times of *what love is not* before proceeding again in a positive direction. By setting forth these opposites of love the way of love can be seen all the more clearly.

---

[68] Kindness, in Paul's statement about the fruit of the Spirit, is followed by "goodness," "faithfulness," then "gentleness" (Gal. 5:22–23). In another place gentleness is also mentioned after kindness: "kindness, humility, gentleness" (Col. 3:12 NIV).

[69] Matthew quotes here from the prophecy of Isaiah in which God declared, "A bruised reed he will not break, and a dimly burning wick he will not quench" (Isa. 42:3).

[70] Paul also speaks of gentleness in relation to opponents: "The Lord's servant must not be quarrelsome but kindly to every one . . . correcting his opponents with gentleness" (2 Tim. 2:24–25). Peter urges believers in relation to outsiders: "Always be prepared to make a defense to any one who calls you to account for the hope that is in you, yet do it with gentleness and reverence" (1 Peter 3:15). Gentleness should mark our way in relation to the outside world.

[71] Bruce writes in regard to this passage: "It is likely that Paul is not thinking of behaviour which so flagrantly flouts accepted standards that it brings the community into public disrepute (cf. 1 Cor. 5:5) or which can best be dealt with by a temporary withholding of social fellowship (Rom. 16:17; 1 Cor. 5:11)" (*Commentary on Galatians*, NIGTC, 260). In line with Bruce's statement I would especially urge that when a church leader flouts Christian standards and thereby also brings the church into public disrepute, procedures and actions mentioned in 1 Corinthians 5:5, 11 and Romans 16:17 are then in order. An early restoration, as in Galatians 6:1, even "in a spirit of gentleness," may deal far too lightly with the matter.

1. Jealousy

"Love is not jealous"[72] (1 Cor. 13:4).

The first problem in Corinth that Paul addressed was jealousy. Despite all their complement of spiritual gifts (1 Cor. 1:7), there was quarreling, strife, and divisions among them. Some of the people claimed to belong to Paul, some to Apollos, some to Peter, and some to Christ (vv. 11–12). Paul later refers to this as "jealousy and strife" and says, "For since there is jealousy and strife among you, are you not fleshly, and are you not walking like mere men?" (3:3 NASB).[73] In fact this jealousy was so serious a matter that Paul said, "I, brethren, could not speak to you as to spiritual men, but as to men of flesh" (v. 1). If love truly operated among them, this jealousy, strife, and rivalry would not exist.

Unfortunately the situation at Corinth is often repeated today. Far too often local churches become involved in petty quarrels that result in jealousy, strife, and rivalry among the people. Frequently divisions occur and the unity of Christ's body is further broken. Love is wholly eclipsed when jealousy brings forth such strife and division. Many charismatic churches and fellowships have likewise given in to jealousy and strife. Divisions often follow.

Jealousy also may occur among leaders in the church. One leader vies with another to win the adulation of the people and to gain their commitment to his views and enterprise. Sometimes a leader, intensely jealous of the seeming success of another church or group, will adopt almost any plan or program that will denigrate the other while elevating himself. Love is forgotten—as further ill will and separation occur.

A word needs to be added to those in charismatic fellowships. If jealousy among believers about the accomplishments or successes of others occurs, there is, regardless of the operation of the gifts, little or no edification. Jealousy, sadly, replaces love.

Jealousy indeed may be the primary evil to break down fellowship. In the words of Proverbs 27:4: "Wrath is cruel, anger is overwhelming; but who can stand before jealousy?" Wrath and anger are indeed cruel and overwhelming, but when jealousy begins to operate, *no one* can stand.

Love is the answer to jealousy. Love unites what jealousy divides; it rejoices in the success of another and is always glad to take second place.[74] Such is the way of love.

2. Boastfulness, Arrogance, Rudeness

"Love is not . . . boastful; it is not arrogant or rude" (1 Cor. 13:4–5).

These three terms may be grouped together because they all represent egocentric actions that are the opposite of love.[75] Moreover, each was occurring in the church at Corinth and frequently takes place in the church of our day.

---

[72]The Greek word is *zēloi*. The NIV reads "It [love] does not envy" (similarly KJV and NEB). Either "jealous" or "envy" is an adequate translation.

[73]Also see 2 Corinthians 12:20, where Paul speaks of his concern that there may still be "quarreling, jealousy . . . " among the Corinthians. In Galatians 5:20 Paul includes "strife, jealousy" among "the works of the flesh."

[74]As Lenski puts it, "Instead of being envious love is satisfied with its own portion and glad of another's greater portion" (*Interpretation of First and Second Corinthians*, 556).

[75]Also they are connected with the prior sin of jealousy. In regard to boasting and what precedes it, Godet writes, "With *envy* [or jealousy], which bears on the advantages of others, there is naturally connected *boasting* in regard to one's own" (*Commentary on First Corinthians*, 673).

Love does not boast.[76] This may initially refer to a whole community of believers who are given to boasting. The Corinthian church was indeed a boasting church, tending to forget that everything it had was a gift of grace. Paul writes, "What have you that you did not receive? If then you received it, why do you boast as if it were not a gift?" (1 Cor. 4:7). Doubtless the Corinthians boasted of their superior status because of the multiplicity of their spiritual gifts. Over against all boasting Paul early in his letter wrote, "God chose what is low and despised [i.e., even the Corinthians] . . . so that no human being might boast in the presence of God . . . as it is written, 'Let him who boasts, boast of the Lord' " (1 Cor. 1:28–29, 31).

Much harm is done today when boasting occurs: leaders who brag of their big churches, evangelists who boast of the numbers of souls saved in their meetings, charismatics who vaunt themselves as being on a higher spiritual plane than others. All such is the denial of love.

Love is not arrogant.[77] Arrogance is really another aspect of boastfulness. To boast about anything (except the Lord!) is a sign of arrogance, false pride, and conceit. Paul urges the Corinthians not to be "puffed up in favor of one against another" (1 Cor. 4:6). This statement of Paul immediately precedes his words about their boasting, and is again related to their party spirit[78]—how they became "puffed up" in their sectarian position. Also they were arrogant in spite of gross sexual immorality in their midst: "A man is living with his father's wife. And you are arrogant! Ought you not rather to mourn? Let him who has done this be removed from among you" (1 Cor. 5:1–2). Some of the Corinthians were so arrogant that they were not willing to submit to the apostle's teaching (1 Cor. 4:18).[79] Also there was the Corinthian way of allowing knowledge to eclipse love. Paul declared, "Knowledge puffs up, but love builds up" (1 Cor. 8:1 NIV).[80] Arrogance lay at the heart of many of the Corinthians' problems.

Unfortunately the same situation often prevails today. Party spirit in the church, prideful unwillingness to deal with gross sin, rebellion against God-given authority, haughtiness of those who claim to know but act without love—in various ways we see these ancient Corinthian attitudes everywhere around us. Moreover, all the spiritual gifts in operation, both then and now, are no guarantee against the destructive forces of arrogance. Love alone can change this; so "follow the way of love."

---

[76] The Greek word translated "boastful" in RSV is *perpereutai*, a verb, hence, "Love does not boast" (so in NIV; KJV reads, "vaunteth not itself"). BAGD gives for the verb *perpereuomai*, "behave as a πέρπερος ("braggart, windbag")." NASB translates, "Love does not brag."

[77] The Greek word is *physioutai* and is also translated "puffed up" KJV, "proud" NIV, "conceited" NEB. The verb *physioō* may also be translated "to inflate . . . to bear oneself loftily" (Thayer).

[78] See the beginning of verse 6, where Paul speaks of Apollos and himself.

[79] See verses 14–21. The word "arrogant" twice occurs.

[80] Chapter 8 begins, "Now concerning food offered to idols . . . ." Throughout the verses that follow Paul deals with the difficult question of whether Christians should eat food previously offered to idols and then sold in the marketplace. Knowledge says of course one may eat, for idols have no real existence; however, love says that if some weaker believer may stumble because one eats this food, forbearance is called for. The danger, however, is that knowledge will so "puff up" that the imperative of love will be completely disregarded. Knowledge pridefully claims the right to eat; love foregoes the claim.

Love is not rude.[81] Love does not act in an unbecoming or shameful manner. Love senses what is proper in any given situation.[82] Again the Corinthians were failing badly in this regard. Paul had earlier written about the situation of women in the church at Corinth who were not covering their heads when praying or prophesying (1 Cor. 11:2–16). The apostle said that by so doing a woman "disgraces her head" (v. 5 NASB) and disregards her proper relationship to men (vv. 7–9).[83] Such behavior, therefore, is rude and unseemly. Next Paul deals with another impropriety in the church (11:17–34), namely, the rude behavior of people when they came together in a fellowship meal to partake of the Lord's Supper. Actually, says Paul, "it is not the Lord's Supper you eat, for as you eat, each of you goes ahead without waiting for anybody else. One remains hungry, another gets drunk" (v. 20–21 NIV). Again, in relation to the operation of the gifts, unseemliness and disorder were doubtless occurring. This is clearly implied in Paul's language, for example, about all speaking in tongues (1 Cor. 14:23) and prophecies given without weighing (v. 29).[84] In all these situations there was rudeness, impropriety, and unseemly action. What love called for was sadly lacking.

The issue is not so much that of right and wrong, but of what is seemly and orderly. Hence, wherever in our churches and fellowships there is indecorous dress and behavior, rudeness with others on an occasion of coming together,[85] disorderliness in the practice of the gifts, and other similar improprieties, there is much need for correction. It is interesting that Paul concludes his discussion of prophecy and tongues by saying, "All things should be done decently[86] and in or-

---

[81]The Greek word is *aschēmonei*, a verb, hence "does not act rudely"; "unbecomingly" NASB; "doth not behave itself unseemly" KJV, "behave disgracefully, dishonorably, indecently" BAGD. I believe that NASB and KJV best capture the meaning of *aschēmonei*.

[82]Paul's only other use of the verb *aschēmoneō* is in 1 Corinthians 7:36, translated in NIV thus: "If anyone thinks he is acting improperly [*aschēmonein*] toward the virgin he is engaged to, and if she is getting along in years and he feels he ought to marry . . . they should get married." This suggests the impropriety of stirring up a young woman's affections but holding her off until she is past the blossom of youth. Marriage should take place. (1 Corinthians 7:36 is a difficult passage; so note other translations. Regardless of the varying renditions, the main point is the impropriety, the unseemliness, of a certain action.)

[83]Despite the commonly accepted custom in Paul's day of women being veiled in any public place, it is apparent that some Christian women in the Corinthian church were disregarding this practice, hence "disgracing" their heads. Paul also asserts that since a man properly prays with his head uncovered, for a woman to do the same is to disregard the distinction in sexes. Propriety and order call for the Christian woman praying or prophesying in the church to be veiled. The principle remains the same today, I would add, even though veiling is no longer a sign of modesty and sexual orderliness in Western countries. Women (and men) should dress modestly (I like the words of Robertson and Plummer: "Love is tactful, and does nothing that would raise a blush" [*1 Corinthians*, ICC, 293]).

[84]Just after discussing the exercise of tongues and prophecy Paul adds, "God is not a God of confusion but of peace" (1 Cor. 14:33). Obviously confusion existed.

[85]What happened in Corinth regarding people rudely rushing ahead to eat while leaving some hungry, also some even getting drunk, may seem little related to today. However, the Corinthian disregard for other persons at the fellowship meal, which led to unseemly behavior, surely can be repeated. Such behavior may not be as crude as that of the Corinthians, but who has not experienced the subtle temptation, for example, at a potluck supper to rush ahead of others to get the "choice" food? Sometimes the last in line finds little remaining! Such rude behavior is the opposite of love.

[86]The NASB reads "properly"; "in a fitting . . . way" NIV. The Greek word is

der" (1 Cor. 14:40). Such is the way of love.

3. Self-seeking

"Love . . . is not self-seeking"[87] (1 Cor. 13:5 NIV).

Here we arrive at the total opposite of love: self-seeking. This is not just self-seeking in general, which is always wrong, but self-seeking over against seeking the good of other persons. That this is the meaning is apparent from Paul's earlier words: "Let no one seek his own good, but the good of his neighbor"[88] (1 Cor. 10:24). Love is totally outgoing.

Surely this is first of all exemplified in Jesus Himself. As Paul puts it in his second Corinthian letter, "You know the grace of our Lord Jesus Christ, that though he was rich, yet for your sakes he became poor, so that you through his poverty might become rich" (8:9 NIV). "For your sakes"—surely not for His own did He forsake the riches of heaven and take on the poverty of an earthly existence. Likewise throughout His ministry on earth Jesus totally embodied a lifestyle of concern for other persons. In His own words: "The Son of man came to seek and to save the lost" (Luke 19:10). Even as Jesus sought only to do the Father's will,[89] so also He sought always to reach out to others: to teach, to heal, to bless, to save. Jesus walked the way of love.

Let us turn again to Paul. Shortly after urging that no one seek his own good but that of his neighbor,[90] Paul adds, "Give no offense to Jews or Greeks or to the church of God, just as I try to please all men in everything I do,[91] not seeking my own advantage, but that of many, that they may be saved" (1 Cor. 10:32–33). "Not seeking my own advantage" is the crux: it was the way of Christ, so that Paul can say in the next verse, "Be imitators of me, as I am of Christ" (11:1).[92] Paul, like His Master, constantly sought the good of others.

It is apparent that the Corinthians were little concerned about seeking the good of others. For one thing they filed lawsuits against one another. Rather than being concerned about the good of the other person, they were suing and being sued. Paul writes, "To have lawsuits at all with one another is defeat for you. Why not rather suffer wrong? Why not rather be defrauded? But you yourselves wrong and defraud, and that even your own brethren" (1 Cor. 6:7–8). Again, there was the matter of food offered to idols.[93] Some Corinthian believers evidently felt conscience-free to eat such food regardless of the fact that weaker brethren, seeing them, might be caused to stumble. Paul concludes, "If food is a cause of my brother's falling, I will never eat meat, lest I cause my brother to fall" (1 Cor. 8:13). Paul

---

euschēmonōs, the opposite of *aschēmonei* in 1 Corinthians 13:5. "Decently" is, I believe, a better translation to set over against the idea of the rude, the unseemly, the disgraceful.

[87] The Greek reads literally, "seeks not the things of itself" (*ou zētai ta heautēs*); similarly KJV and NASB. The RSV reading, "does not insist on its own way," is more of a paraphrase.

[88] Literally, "of the other." The Greek phrase is *to tou heterou*. The KJV reading "another's wealth" is quite misleading today.

[89] Recall our discussion in section I of this chapter.

[90] 1 Corinthians 10:24, supra.

[91] This is not the pleasing Paul speaks *against* in Galatians 1:10 and 1 Thessalonians 2:4, namely, a compromise of the gospel to curry people's favor. Paul in 1 Corinthians is talking about *no unnecessary* offense. See also 1 Corinthians 9:19–23, which begins, "For though I am free from all men, I have made myself a slave to all, that I might win the more."

[92] This is an unfortunate chapter division; 1 Corinthians 11:1 is the climax of Paul's preceding words.

[93] See note 80 for elaboration.

expands this elsewhere, saying, "It is good not to eat meat or to drink wine, or to do anything by which your brother stumbles" (Rom. 14:21 NASB). To return to the matter of lawsuits: one's rights are not nearly so important as the concern for the good of the other. If one is willing to suffer wrong, even to being defrauded, the brother may change by this show of love. This is what Paul describes as overcoming evil with good: "Do not be overcome by evil, but overcome evil with good (Rom. 12:21). One's rights are not the primary issue: indeed, one should gladly forswear these for the good of the brother.[94] The same thing is true about freedom. A strong Christian may be able freely to eat and drink with no compunction of conscience, but if what he eats and drinks causes another person to stumble, then love calls for abstention. For, as Paul says, "if your brother is being injured by what you eat [or drink],[95] you are no longer walking in love" (Rom. 14:15). The basic issue for one's walking in love can never be one's own rights or freedom, but always the good of other persons.

Love thus is not self-seeking. This does not mean that there are no legitimate self-concerns. We all have to eat and drink, clothe ourselves, work for a livelihood, carry out innumerable responsibilities, and indeed work faithfully to fulfill God's purpose in our lives. But still, the emphasis of love in whatever we do comes down to seeking the good of others. Paul wrote the Philippians, "Do not merely[96] look out for your own personal interests, but also for the interests of others" (2:4 NASB). Ultimately, whatever may be our own legitimate interests and concerns, the emphasis cannot rest there. We must ever be reaching beyond to other persons. Such is the heart of following the way of love.

4. Irritability, Resentfulness, Rejoicing at Wrong

"Love . . . is not irritable or resentful; it does not rejoice at wrong" (1 Cor. 13:5–6).

These three may be grouped together as unloving responses to other persons.[97] Let us examine each briefly.

Love is not irritable.[98] It is very easy for any person to become irritable or provoked at the attitude or behavior of others. This may have been the reason the Corinthians were going to the civil authorities about one another. In any event, other Christians can so get on our nerves that it is difficult not to become irritable and be provoked into

---

[94] C. K. Barrett puts it well: "Love not merely does not seek that which does not belong to it; it is prepared to give up for the sake of others even what it is entitled to" (*The First Epistle to the Corinthians*, 303).

[95] It is proper to include "drink" here as Paul speaks of drinking wine in verse 21.

[96] The word "merely" ("only" [RSV, NIV]) is not in the Greek text. Although it is justifiable to add "merely" because of the "but also" in the words that follow, it is apparent that the emphasis falls on "the interests of others." The succeeding words about Christ's total self-emptying (vv. 5–8) make this all the more apparent.

[97] Bittlinger speaks of these three as "the trial experienced by the Christian because of the darkness in others" (*Gifts and Graces*, 85). The prior five represent "the trial experienced by the Christian because of the darkness within himself" (ibid., 82).

[98] The Greek word is *paroxynetai*, a verb. The NASB translates "is not provoked"; KJV reads "is not easily provoked" (however, there is no "easily" in the Greek text); similarly NIV has "is not easily angered"; NEB reads "not quick to take offence." The only other New Testament usage of *paroxynō* is in Acts 17:16—Paul's "spirit was provoked [*parōxyneto*] within him as he saw that the city was full of idols." It is interesting that our English word "paroxysm," which refers to "a sudden violent emotion or action" (Webster), derives from the Greek substantive form *paroxysmos*.

some unloving response and action. Hence even though, for example, we and our fellow believers also may be used powerfully in the gifts, the atmosphere can become one of irritability, either overt or covert, and the spirit of love dissipated.

Prickly Christians, touchy Christians,[99] are not loving Christians. Being quick to react against the slightest offense (whether imagined or real), being easily upset if others do not agree with one's words or actions, becoming aggravated by another person's peculiarities of speech and manner: these are some of the ways in which irritability expresses itself. All such is the opposite of love.

Love is not resentful.[100] It cherishes no resentment. Again, as in the case of irritability, the actions of other persons may bring about increasing vexation and annoyance. As such actions continue, it is far too easy to become annoyed at every perceived offense and thus to build up resentment. Love, however, is quite the opposite. It takes no offense at a wrong suffered; it keeps no record of evils endured;[101] it is only concerned about the welfare of the other person.

Surely the most significant New Testament statement regarding this is found in the words of Paul concerning God's action in Christ: "God was in Christ reconciling the world to himself, not counting[102] their trespasses against them" (2 Cor. 5:19). Rather than maintain a vast ledger in which are entered all human debts, i.e., trespasses, God was concerned through Christ to reckon not a single sin against the human race. God harbored no resentment despite the countless evils He had endured; rather, He acted in love to save those who had sinned against Him.

Love is not vindictive. No matter what the vexation or evil that one experiences, love seeks to bless the offender. Love forgives—and forgets—and in its so acting, all things take on fresh life and meaning.

Love does not rejoice at wrong.[103] One who walks in love can take no delight in the wrongdoing of other persons. Whatever is wrong or unrighteous aggrieves one whose heart is full of love. Such a wrong may refer to acts of social or economic injustice, for example, abuse of the poor and downtrodden; or to acts of personal immorality—for example, adultery, theft, false witness. Love rejoices over none of these, because all such evils destroy human well-being.

Paul may also mean that love takes no delight in rejoicing over the wrongdoing of someone who has been a

---

[99] Barrett translates Paul's words thus: "Love is not touchy" (*The First Epistle to the Corinthians*, 303).

[100] The Greek expression is *ou logizetai to kakon*, literally, "does not reckon the evil." The NASB translates "does not take into account a wrong suffered"; NIV reads "it keeps no record of wrongs" (similarly NEB). The KJV reading, "thinketh no evil," misses the meaning, since it implies that the evil is given rather than received. (See BAGD on *logizomai*, sec. 1.)

[101] D. A. Carson puts it well: "Love 'keeps no record of wrongs,' a private file of personal grievances that can be consulted and nursed whenever there is possibility of some new slight" (*Showing the Spirit*, 62).

[102] The Greek word for "counting" is *logizomenos*, a form of the same word as in 1 Corinthians 13:5.

[103] The Greek phrase *ou chairei epi tē adikia* literally reads "does not rejoice over wrong [or "unrighteousness"]. The wrong, or unrighteousness, is not in oneself but in the other person: it is "over" wrong. The KJV, NIV, and NASB translations that variously read "in" are misleading. The NEB, while more of a paraphrase than the RSV, rightly reads "over": "does not gloat over other men's sins."

source of personal provocation and resentment.[104] It is quite possible, humanly speaking, to delight in the faults of another person, especially if these faults are getting him into trouble. Love cannot, and will not, rejoice in the wrong whether perpetrated against another or inflicted on oneself.

Over against this last negative Paul declares a positive: Love "rejoices with the truth" (NIV, NASB).[105] Wherever truth appears, love greatly rejoices. Paul in 2 Corinthians declares, "We cannot do anything against the truth, but only for the truth" (13:8). It is in that kind of attitude that love delights, for love can rejoice only where truth abounds.

Love's rejoicing with the truth occurs even if the truth adversely affects it. It is not easy to rejoice, for example, if the truth spoken against oneself is a word of discipline or rebuke. Still, if the word is true, genuine love takes no offense but rejoices at the word spoken. Love rejoices greatly whenever and wherever the truth is made manifest.

C. The Scope of Love

Now the climax is reached in the description of the scope of love. After Paul carefully delineates the opposites of love, he declares, "Love bears all things, believes all things, hopes all things, endures all things" (1 Cor. 13:7). The scope of love is indeed vast.

1. Love Bears All Things[106]

Love bears whatever may come. Paul had earlier written, "We put up with anything [literally, "all things"][107] rather than hinder the gospel of Christ" (1 Cor. 9:12 NIV). Now he proceeds to say that love does this in regard to all things: it bears, it puts up with, whatever may happen. Love can stand[108] under the most difficult of circumstances. Love bears all things without wavering.

To bear all things surely refers to many of Paul's previous statements about love. It is not easy for patience and kindness to continue when there is only a negative response. How long can one bear it when the recipients of patience and kindness show thank-

---

[104] As previously discussed.

[105] The Greek reads *syncharei . . . tē alētheia*. Note that this second rejoicing is more intensive. The word for the previous rejoicing concerning wrong is only *charei*, but in regard to truth it is *syncharei*. The NEB rendering of *syncharei* as "delights in" catches the note of this more intensive joy.

[106] The Greek phrase for "bears all things" is *panta stegei*. The NEB reads, "There is nothing love cannot face"; NIV has "It [love] always protects." This latter reading derives from another meaning of the verb *stegō*. For translations of *stegō* Thayer first mentions "protect" and "cover," adding that some view the meaning of *stegō* to be "hides and excuses the errors and faults of others; but it is more appropriately rendered . . . *beareth*." TDNT renders *stegō* as "covers" (7:587). Barrett translates it "supports" (*First Epistle to the Corinthians*, 304). Gordon Fee writes that the "range of meanings [for *stegō*] would allow 'protect . . . cover . . . supports' "; however, he opts for "puts up with," similar to "bears" (*First Epistle to the Corinthians*, NICNT, 640, n. 24). I believe Thayer and Fee are correct, so I am retaining the more traditional translation (as in KJV, RSV, and NASB). Paul's use of *stegō* elsewhere (as we will see in later discussion) gives further support to the translation "bears" (note "puts up with," "stands," in what follows).

[107] The Greek phrase for "we put up with all things" is *panta stegomen*, hence basically the same as in 1 Corinthians 13:7.

[108] The same Greek word *stegō* is used by Paul in 1 Thessalonians 3:1: "So when we could stand [*stegontes*, literally, "standing" or "bearing"] it no longer . . . "(NIV). Also verse 5 reads, "When I could stand [*stegōn*] it no longer, I sent to find out about your faith" (NIV).

lessness, indifference, or—far worse—become even more hardened and unresponsive? How long can one continue to seek the good of others rather than one's own good when those being helped become antagonistic and belligerent? How long can one endure provocation and avoid resentfulness when others seem determined to irritate and offend? The simple but profound answer is that love bears all things.

Jesus Himself was the perfect demonstration of this love. He bore with the multitudes around Him who pressed Him on every side; He put up with His own disciples in their slowness to learn and ultimately even in their forsaking Him; He received the attacks of His enemies, never protesting or crying out under their mockery and persecution. Jesus, the Incarnation of love, bore all things.

That love bears all things means that nothing is excluded. Whatever may come at a person from the outside—whether from the world, from other people, or from fellow Christians—is borne with fortitude and patience. This is by no means easy; for, indeed, only the control of love can keep a person from retaliating. In this connection we may now recall that the last fruit of the Spirit mentioned by Paul is *self-control*. "The fruit of the Spirit is love, joy, peace, patience, kindness, goodness, faithfulness, gentleness, self-control."[109] The constraint of love (the first fruit) is self-control (the last fruit), hence, though they may be viewed separately, it is actually love operating through self-control[110]—thus one basic fruit of the Spirit. Through persistent self-control, made possible by the Spirit, love can indeed bear all things.

The scope of love is thus unlimited. It bears without murmuring or negative reaction all things regardless of their nature or force. Moreover, in this very bearing of all things love operates as a powerful force in the world. For the love that bears up under provocation and irritation—even more, bears up under the attacks of others (whether from friend or foe)—releases a tremendous force for good that can bring about vital change. Such love, truly the love of God in Christ, is a love that knows no bounds.

Love verily bears all things.

2. Love Believes All Things[111]

Love reaches out in belief to all things. Love "always trusts" (NIV), "there is no limit to its faith" (NEB); as such, love "believes all things."

This statement about love is indeed remarkable. If the reference were primarily to God and the things of God—thus believing Him and all things He has given us in His word—it would be immediately understandable. Over and over again the Scriptures attest the importance of such total faith in God; however, Paul here continues to speak about the way of love, namely, in relation to one's fellow man. And this is the remarkable feature: love believes all things in relation to other people. Could this not be the way of deception and folly? A child may believe all things, likewise a foolish person; but does not maturity call for discrimination and judgment? At least from a worldly perspective to believe all things regarding people is surely a gross mistake. If love believes all things, perhaps some counterbalance to love is needed!

Let us pursue this inquiry further. Have not Christians at times been "overbelievers" or, perhaps more accurately, "overtrusters"? The very principle of love seemingly has been a

---

[109]The Greek word is *enkrateia*. Also see Acts 24:25 and 2 Peter 1:6.
[110]Even as love functions through patience and kindness (see earlier discussion).
[111]The Greek phrase for "believes all things" is *panta pisteuei*.

blinder to evil in many situations. Indeed, we are warned in Scripture, "Do not believe every spirit" (1 John 4:1), a warning against false prophets and teachers. How do we reconcile "Love believes all things" with "Do not believe every spirit"? Again, if we believe all things, does not anything and everything become tolerable in the community of faith? Has not such an attitude allowed evil to multiply so that wrong actions of church leaders and members are readily condoned? Paul himself earlier in his letter to the Corinthians instructed them to deliver the incestuous offender "to Satan for the destruction of the flesh" (5:5). How does such an action accord with Paul's words, "Love believes all things"?

Now it is time to answer. Love is not credulous, gullible, blind, unaware of evil; indeed, it sees deeply into every situation—and still believes. Lovelessness is just the opposite: it believes nothing at all. Mistrust thus dominates every situation.[112] Love perceives the total situation and still believes. Surely the primary example of the love that perceives yet still believes is that of Jesus in regard to Simon Peter. John 1:42 reads, "Jesus looked at him, and said, 'So you are Simon the son of John? You shall be called Cephas' (which means Peter)," that is, "a rock."[113] Jesus doubtless saw what was in the man Simon—a long way yet from being a rock; but He also perceived the Peter that Simon could become. Jesus was never deceived by Simon, but believing "all things," even the seemingly impossible, Jesus' faith was finally vindicated and Simon became the Rock of the early church.

So it is that we are challenged in love to believe all things. This means that love "always trusts"[114] and believes for the best. The darkness in the human situation and in people must not be casually overlooked or excused—indeed, at times it must be exposed—but through it all love believes in the possibilities that are always there for the good to finally come through. To the very Corinthians whom Paul chastised severely in his first letter he wrote in his second letter, "I have confidence in you in all things" (2 Cor. 7:16 KJV).[115] This indeed was a love that in spite of what was known continued to believe.

In a very practical sense today love keeps on believing when, for example, a child wanders from the path of truth. Love has no blinders on; it fully recognizes the evil but never fails to believe. Moreover, that very believing can be a tremendous force in bringing about eventual, possibly radical change.[116] Similarly, when a Christian leader, long recognized for his upstanding character, falls into gross sin—sin that calls for punishment—love never gives up. It continues to believe that the person

---

[112]Søren Kierkegaard in his book *Works of Love* writes, "Love is the exact opposite of mistrust and yet is based on the same knowledge . . . where love, for instance, believes everything, it is by no means in the same sense as thoughtlessness, inexperience, and credulity believes everything, which believe everything through ignorance and naïveté. No, love is just as well aware as anyone of everything which mistrust knows, yet without being mistrustful" (p. 185). The title of the chapter containing this quotation is "Love Believeth All Things—and Yet Is Never Deceived."

[113]Both Cephas (Aramaic) and Peter (Greek) mean "Rock" (see NIVmg).

[114]Recall the NIV translation.

[115]Note the parallel to the love that believes "all things."

[116]Augustine attributed his conversion from an immoral life to the many years of believing and weeping prayers of his mother, Monica. A priest once said to Monica, "Go thy way, and God bless thee, for it is not possible that the son of these tears should perish" (*Confessions,* Pusey trans., 3:12). Later Augustine wrote, "To the faithful and daily tears of my mother, I was granted, that I should not perish" (ibid., 189 n. 2).

will eventually repent and be restored. Love believes to the very end.

3. Love Hopes All Things[117]

Hope[118] is the companion to faith. Indeed, it goes even beyond, for when love sees no result in its believing, it still hopes. One of the most vivid biblical illustrations of the relation between faith and hope is the life of Abraham. In Romans 4 Paul speaks first of Abraham's faith: "Abraham believed God, and it was reckoned to him as righteousness" (v. 3). Later Paul added about Abraham, "In hope he believed against hope, that he should become the father of many nations" (v. 18). This suggests that Abraham against all earthly hope continued to hope when there was nothing outward to justify that hope. Hope thus belongs to the outer reaches of faith and enables one to move ahead into the future.

In connection with love, hope knows no disappointment. Paul writes in Romans 5: "Hope does not disappoint, because the love of God has been poured out within our hearts through the Holy Spirit who was given to us" (v. 5 NASB). The love of God floods the believer's heart and reaches out in hope, triumphing over any possible disappointment. According to Proverbs, "hope deferred makes the heart sick" (13:12), but where love abounds, no matter how meager the results, there is no heart sickness or disappointment. For example, one may pray many years for another person's change of heart, but nothing seems to happen. Even so, love does not give up; it continues hoping. There is no disappointment in

such hoping, for love by its very nature never ceases to hope.

This means, further, that love is never pessimistic. Even though love sees utterly no results, it does not become downcast. Indeed, as Paul says later in Romans, "Hope that is seen is not hope. For who hopes for what he sees?" (8:24). Accordingly, when one hopes for some alteration of the human situation, and things only seem to go from bad to worse, love does not stop hoping. Love knows no despair.

Hope therefore is without limits. When flowing out of love, hope reaches far beyond any earthly hope. Love "always hopes" (NIV) and "hopes all things," even to the boundaries of eternity.

4. Love Endures All Things[119]

The love that bears all things, believes all things, and hopes all things is a love that is steadfast and persistent: it endures all things. Love is unlimited in its endurance.[120] Such love perseveres in and through every situation.

Paul writes Timothy, "I endure all things[121] for the sake of those who are chosen, that they also may obtain the salvation . . . " (2 Tim. 2:10 NASB). The apostle had just spoken of his "suffering and wearing fetters like a criminal" (v. 9 RSV). Thus it is endurance through suffering and shame for the sake of others—the endurance of love. Shortly thereafter Paul specifically links love and endurance: "You, however, know . . . my way of life, my purpose, faith, patience, love, endurance, persecutions, sufferings" (3:10 NIV). Love endures all things—"persecutions, sufferings"—and never ceases to love.

---

[117]The Greek phrase for "hopes all things" is *panta elpizei.*

[118]The noun "hope" in Greek is *elpis.* Including the verb *elpizein,* hope occurs 84 times in the New Testament. Paul uses either the verb or the noun 55 times.

[119]The Greek phrase for "endures all things" is *panta hypomenei.*

[120]The NEB reads "There is no limit to . . . its endurance."

[121]The Greek phrase is *panta hypomenō,* almost identical with the *panta hypomenei* in 1 Corinthians 13:7.

The ultimate demonstration of that love was the suffering of Christ on the cross. Christ "endured the cross" (Heb. 12:2)—all the anguish and torment, all the bitterness and evil heaped upon Him. He "endured from sinners such hostility against himself" (v. 3). The endurance of love is the continuation of love regardless of whatever hostility and persecution may be encountered.

The love that endures all things is love in its ultimate expression. We have noted that love always believes for the best and continues to hope, regardless of the human situation. But now we reach the amazing climax: love endures all things that the world may throw against it. Even if faith and hope should seem to be dissipated in the dark night of evil's violent attack, love endures. Never in human history has there been a more haunting cry of utter dereliction than that of Christ on the cross, "My God, my God, why hast thou forsaken me?" (Matt. 27:46; Mark 15:34). *Yet He endured*—to the end!

Such was the love that endured all things: it never fought back, never responded in anger, never sought vengeance. By enduring everything that evil could unleash against Him and absorbing all that evil to Himself, Christ, by His unfailing love, made possible the redemption of a lost world. Love endured—and won the victory.

So we have beheld love in its amazing scope: it bears all things, believes all things, hopes all things, endures all things. This leads to a powerful conclusion: "Love never fails; love never ends"[122] (1 Cor. 13:8). Let us finally view love in this double perspective.

5. Love Never Fails

The love that bears, believes, hopes, and endures all things is a love that can never fail. There can be no defeat for a love that bears the seemingly unbearable, believes when all belief seems in vain, hopes in the midst of the most desperate situations, endures through all time and circumstance. This is the love of God in Christ that reaches out through Christians to all people. Such love can know no failure. In the end it always triumphs.

6. Love Never Ends

Love continues even into eternity. Paul immediately adds, "As for prophecies, they will pass away; as for tongues, they will cease; as for knowledge,[123] it will pass away" (1 Cor. 13:8). The spiritual gifts, for all their importance in this life, will be superseded in the world to come when we see "face to face" (v. 12). But love goes on forever. Faith and hope also continue: "Faith, hope, love abide, these three" (v. 13)—faith as eternal trust in God and His purposes, hope as eternal anticipation of ever-new things. However, greater than both faith and hope is love. For love is the very nature of God: to abide in love is to abide in God both now and in all the ages to come.

"Follow the way of love" is the ultimate imperative for Christian living. It is the way that we have entered upon

---

[122] I have given two translations of the Greek verb *piptei*. *Piptei* literally means "falls" (see, e.g., 1 Cor. 10:8); however, here the better translation is "fails" or "ends" (see BAGD on πιπτω, 1 Cor. 13:8—"become invalid, come to an end, fail"). The NIV and NASB translate this word as "fails"; KJV has "faileth"; RSV, "ends"; NEB, "will never come to an end." Both translations, I believe, contain important elements of truth.

[123] "Knowledge" refers here to the charismatic gift of 1 Corinthians 12:8. So Gordon Fee writes, "Knowledge in this passage does not mean ordinary human knowing or learning, but refers to that special manifestation of the Spirit, the utterance of knowledge" (*First Epistle to the Corinthians*, NICNT, 644). Also see my chapter 13, note 94.

through our Lord Jesus Christ, the way that we are commanded to follow amid all the vicissitudes and challenges of this life, and the way that has no end in the far reaches of eternity. To follow love is to follow God both now and always.

BIBLIOGRAPHY

Achtemeier, Paul J., *Romans*. Atlanta: John Knox, 1985.

Allen, Roland. *The Ministry of the Spirit*. London: World Dominion, 1960.

Arminius, James. *The Writings of James Arminius*. Grand Rapids: Baker, repr. 1977.

Augustine. *Confessions*. Translated by R. S. Pine-Coffin. New York: Penguin, 1961. Translated by E. B. Pusey. New York: Dutton, 1946.

Autry, C. E. *Evangelism in Acts*. Grand Rapids: Zondervan, 1964.

Bainton, Roland H. *Here I Stand: A Life of Martin Luther*. New York: Abingdon, 1950.

Barrett, C. K. *The First Epistle to the Corinthians*. HNTC. New York: Harper & Row, 1968.

————. *The Gospel According to St. John*. Philadelphia: Westminster, 1978.

Barron, Bruce. *The Health and Wealth Gospel*. Downers Grove, Ill.: InterVarsity, 1987.

Barth, Karl. *Church Dogmatics*. Edinburgh: T & T Clark, 1936–69.

Bartleman, Frank. *Azusa Street*. South Plainfield, N.J.: Bridge, 1980.

Basham, Don. *Deliver Us from Evil*. Old Tappan, N.J.: Revell, 1972.

————. *Face Up with a Miracle*. Monroeville, Pa.: Whitaker, 1971.

Bauckham, Richard J. *2 Peter & Jude*. WBC. Waco: Word, 1983.

Bauer, Walter; William F. Arndt; F. Wilbur Gingrich; and Frederick W. Danker. *A Greek-English Lexicon of the New Testament*. Chicago: University of Chicago Press, 1979.

Baxter, Ronald E. *Gifts of the Spirit*. Grand Rapids: Kregel, 1983.

Bennett, Dennis. *Nine O'clock in the Morning*. Plainfield, N.J.: Logos, 1970.

————. *The Holy Spirit and You*. Plainfield, N.J.: Logos, 1971.

Berkhof, Hendrikus. *Doctrine of the Holy Spirit*. Richmond: John Knox, 1964.

Berkhof, Louis. *Systematic Theology*. Grand Rapids: Eerdmans, 1941.

Berkouwer, G. C. *Faith and Justification*. Grand Rapids: Eerdmans, 1954.

————. *Faith and Perseverance*. Grand Rapids: Eerdmans, 1958.

————. *Faith and Sanctification*. Grand Rapids: Eerdmans, 1952.

Bernard, Sister Mary. *I Leap for Joy*. Plainfield, N.J.: Logos, 1974.

Bittlinger, Arnold. *Gifts and Graces: A Commentary on 1 Corinthians 12–14*. London: Hodder & Stoughton, 1967.

Bittlinger, Arnold, and Kilian McDonnell. *The Baptism in the Holy Spirit as an Ecumenical Problem*. Notre Dame, Ind.: Charismatic Renewal Services, 1972.

Bixler, Russell. *It Can Happen to Anybody*. Monroeville, Pa.: Whitaker, 1970.

Bonhoeffer, Dietrich. *Prisoner for God: Letters and Papers from Prison*. New York: Macmillan, 1972.

Bredesen, Harald. *Yes, Lord*. Plainfield, N.J.: Logos, 1972.

Bromiley, Geoffrey, ed. *International Standard Bible Encyclopedia*, rev. ed., 4 vols. Grand Rapids: Eerdmans, 1979–88.

Brown, James. "Signs, Wonders and Miracles!" In *Presbyterians and the Baptism in the Holy Spirit*. Los Angeles: Full Gospel Businessmen's Fellowship International, 1963.

Bruce, F. F. *1 & 2 Corinthians*. NCBC. Grand Rapids: Eerdmans, 1980.

_____. *1 & 2 Thessalonians*. WBC. Waco: Word, 1982.

_____. *The Book of Acts*. NICNT. Grand Rapids: Eerdmans, repr. 1981.

_____. *Commentary on Galatians*. NIGTC. Grand Rapids: Eerdmans, 1982.

_____. *The Epistle of Paul to the Romans*. TNTC. Grand Rapids: Eerdmans, 1963.

_____. *The Epistles to the Colossians, to Philemon, and to the Ephesians*. NICNT. Grand Rapids: Eerdmans, 1984.

_____. *The Epistle to the Hebrews*. NICNT. Grand Rapids: Eerdmans, 1964.

_____. *The Epistles of John*. Grand Rapids: Eerdmans, 1970.

_____. *The Gospel of John*. Grand Rapids: Eerdmans, 1983.

Bruner, Frederick D. *A Theology of the Holy Spirit*. Grand Rapids: Eerdmans, 1970.

Brunner, Emil. *The Christian Doctrine of God, Dogmatics: Vol. 1*. Philadelphia: Westminster, 1950.

_____. *The Christian Doctrine of the Church, Faith, and the Consummation, Dogmatics, Vol. 3*. Philadelphia, Westminster, 1962.

Brunner, Peter. *Worship in the Name of Jesus*. St. Louis: Concordia, 1968.

Butler, Alban. *The Lives of the Fathers, Martyrs, and Other Principal Saints*. New York: Kennedy, 1963.

Buttrick, George, ed. *Interpreter's Dictionary of the Bible*, 12 vols. Nashville: Abingdon, 1962.

Calvin, John. *Commentaries*. Translated by Beveridge. Grand Rapids: Eerdmans, 1948–50.

_____. *Institutes of the Christian Religion*. Translated by Beveridge. Grand Rapids: Eerdmans, 1957. Translated by Battles. Library of Christian Classics, vol. 20. Philadelphia: Westminster, 1960.

_____. *The Acts of the Apostles*. Grand Rapids: Eerdmans, repr. 1965.

Carson, D. A. *Showing the Spirit: A Theological Exposition of 1 Corinthians 12–14*. Grand Rapids: Baker, 1987.

Chantry, Walter. *Signs of the Apostles*. Edinburgh: Banner of Truth, 1976.

Christenson, Larry. *Speaking in Tongues*. Minneapolis: Bethany, 1968.

Clark, Stephen B. *Building Christian Communities: Strategies for Renewing the Church*. Notre Dame, Ind.: Ave Maria, 1972.

Clement, *The First Epistle of Clement to the Corinthians, The Ante-Nicene Fathers*, vol. 1. Grand Rapids, Eerdmans, repr. 1975.

Cole, Alan. *The Epistle of Paul to the Galatians*. TNTC. Grand Rapids: Eerdmans, 1965.

Conn, Charles W. *Pillars of Pentecost*. Cleveland, Tenn.: Pathway, 1956.

Conzelmann, Hans. *1 Corinthians*. Philadelphia: Fortress, 1975.

Cyprian. *The Epistles of Cyprian. The Ante-Nicene Fathers*, vol. 5. Grand Rapids, Eerdmans, repr. 1975.

Dake, Finis. *Dake's Annotated Reference Bible, The New Testament*. Lawrenceville, Ga.: Dake Bible Sales, 1963.

Dale, R. W. *Christian Doctrine*. London: Hodder and Stoughton, 1907.

Dana, H. E., and Julius R. Mantey. *A Manual Grammar of the Greek New Testament*. New York: Macmillan, 1927.

Dayton, Donald W. *Theological Roots of Pentecostalism*. Grand Rapids: Zondervan, 1987.

Delling, Gerhard. *Worship in the New Testament*. Philadelphia: Westminster, 1962.

Dunn, James D. G. *Baptism in the Holy Spirit*. Philadelphia: Westminster, 1970.

_____. *Jesus and the Spirit*. London: SCM, 1975.

Elbert, Paul, ed. *Essays on Apostolic Themes*. Peabody, Mass.: Hendrickson, 1985.

Ensley, Eddie. *Sounds of Wonder*. New York: Paulist, 1977.

Erickson, Millard J. *Christian Theology*, 3 vols. Grand Rapids: Baker, 1983–85.

Ervin, Howard M. *Spirit Baptism*. Peabody, Mass.: Hendrickson, 1987.

Eusebius. *The History of the Church*. New York: Penguin, 1965.

Farah, Charles. *From the Pinnacle of the Temple: Faith vs. Presumption*. Plainfield, N.J.: Logos, 1979.

Fee, Gordon D. *The First Epistle to the Corinthians*. NICNT. Grand Rapids: Eerdmans, 1987.

Finney, Charles. *Charles G. Finney: An Autobiography*. Old Tappan, N.J.: Revell, repr. 1966.

Foakes-Jackson, F. J., and Kirsopp Lake, eds. *The Acts of the Apostles*, 5 vols. Grand Rapids: Baker, repr. 1979.

Foltz, Howard. "Moving Toward a Charismatic Theology of Missions." In *Probing Pentecostalism*. The Papers of the 17th Annual Meeting, Society for Pentecostal Studies, CBN University, Virginia Beach, Va., 1987.

Foulkes, Francis. *The Epistle of Paul to the Ephesians*. TNTC. Grand Rapids: Eerdmans, 1963.

Fowler, Charles J. *Back to Pentecost*. Philadelphia: Christian Standard, 1900.

France, R. T. *The Gospel According to Matthew*. TNTC. Grand Rapids: Eerdmans, 1985.

Frodsham, Stanley H. *With Signs Following*. Springfield, Mo.: Gospel, 1946.

Gaebelein, Frank E., gen. ed. *Expositor's Bible Commentary*, 12 vols. Grand Rapids: Zondervan, 1976-.

Gee, Donald. *Concerning Spiritual Gifts*. Springfield, Mo.: Gospel, 1972.

_____. *Spiritual Gifts in the Work of the Ministry Today*. Springfield, Mo.: Gospel, 1963.

Geldenhuys, Norval. *The Gospel of Luke*. NICNT. Grand Rapids: Eerdmans, 1951.

Gelpi, Donald L. *Pentecostalism: A Theological Viewpoint*. New York: Paulist, 1971.

Gloag, Paton. *A Critical and Exegetical Commentary on the Acts of the Apostles*. Minneapolis: Klock & Klock, 1979.

Godet, F. L. *Commentary on First Corinthians*. Grand Rapids: Kregel, repr. 1977.

Gordon, A. J. *The Ministry of Healing*. Old Tappan, N.J.: Revell, 1882.

Green, Michael. *I Believe in Satan's Downfall*. Grand Rapids: Eerdmans, 1981.

_____. *I Believe in the Holy Spirit*. Grand Rapids: Eerdmans, 1975.

Grosheide, F. W. *The First Epistle to the Corinthians*. NICNT. Grand Rapids: Eerdmans, 1953.

Grossman, Siegfried. *Charisma: The Gifts of the Spirit*. Wheaton, Ill.: Key, 1971.

Grudem, Wayne. *The Gift of Prophecy in 1 Corinthians*. Washington, D.C.: University Press of America, 1982.

_____. *The Gift of Prophecy in the New Testament and Today*. Westchester, Ill.: Crossway, 1988.

Günkel, Hermann. *The Influence of the Holy Spirit*. Philadelphia: Fortress, 1979.

Haenchen, Ernst. *The Acts of the Apostles*. Oxford: Blackwell, 1971.

Hagin, Kenneth. *Bible Faith Study Course*. Tulsa: Kenneth Hagin Evangelistic Association, n.d.

_____. *How to Turn Your Faith Loose*. Tulsa: Kenneth Hagin Ministries, 1983.

_____. *New Thresholds of Faith*. Tulsa: Faith Library, 1972.

Harper, Michael. *Spiritual Warfare*. Ann Arbor, Mich.: Servant, 1984.

_____. *Walk in the Spirit*. Plainfield, N.J.: Logos, 1968.

Harris, Ralph W. *Spoken by the Spirit: Documented Accounts of "Other Tongues" from Arabic to Zulu*. Springfield, Mo.: Gospel, 1973.

Harrison, Everett F. *Acts: The Expanding Church*. Chicago: Moody, 1975.

Henry, Carl F. H. *Basic Christian Doctrines*. Grand Rapids: Eerdmans, 1970.

Heppe, Heinrich. *Reformed Dogmatics*. London: Allen and Unwin, 1950.

Hippolytus (antipope). *The Apostolic Tradition*. Hamden, Conn.: Archon, 1962.

Hodge, C. H. *An Exposition of the First Epistle to the Corinthians*. Grand Rapids: Baker, repr. 1980.

Holman, Charles L. "Titus 3:5–6: A Window on Worldwide Pentecost." In *Probing Pentecostalism*. The Papers of the 17th Annual Meeting, Society for Pentecostal Studies, CBN University, Virginia Beach, Va., 1987.

Horton, Harold. *The Gifts of the Spirit*. Springfield, Mo.: Gospel, 1975.

Horton, Stanley M. *Into All Truth*. Springfield, Mo.: Gospel, 1955.

_____. *What the Bible Says About the Holy Spirit*. Springfield, Mo.: Gospel, 1976.

Hubbard, Ray. *Gifts of Grace*. Bromley, Kent: Foundation Publications, 1971.

Hughes, Philip E. *The Second Epistle to the Corinthians*. NICNT. Grand Rapids: Eerdmans, 1962.

Hull, J. H. E. *The Holy Spirit in the Acts of the Apostles*. Cleveland: World, 1968.

Jeremias, Joachim. *New Testament Theology*. London: SCM, 1971.

Jones, James W. *Filled With New Wine: The Charismatic Renewal of the Church*. New York: Harper & Row, 1974.

Judisch, Douglas. *An Evaluation of Claims to the Charismatic Gifts*. Grand Rapids: Baker, 1978.

Kane, J. Herbert. *Understanding Christian Missions*. Grand Rapids: Baker, 1974.

Keil, C. F., and F. Delitzsch. *Commentary on the Old Testament*, 10 vols. Grand Rapids: Eerdmans, repr. 1983.

Kendrick, Klaude. *The Promise Fulfilled*. Springfield, Mo.: Gospel, 1961.

Kierkegaard, Søren. *Works of Love*. Princeton, N.J.: Princeton University Press, 1946.

Kildahl, John P. *The Psychology of Speaking in Tongues*. New York: Harper & Row, 1972.

King, Pat. *The Jesus People Are Coming*. Plainfield, N.J.: Logos, 1971.

Kittel, G., ed. *Theological Dictionary of the New Testament*, 10 vols. Grand Rapids, Eerdmans, 1964–76.

Koberle, Adolf. *The Quest for Holiness*. Minneapolis: Augsburg, 1938.

Kuhlman, Kathyrn. *I Believe in Miracles*. Englewood Cliffs, N.J.: Prentice-Hall, 1962.

Ladd, George E. *A Theology of the New Testament*. Grand Rapids: Eerdmans, 1974.

Lampe, G. W. H. *Christ and Spirit in the New Testament*. Edited by B. Lindars and S. S. Smalley. Cambridge: The University Press, 1973.

Leith, John. *Creeds of the Churches*. Richmond: John Knox, 1973.

Lenski, R. C. H. *The Acts of the Apostles*. Minneapolis: Augsburg, 1961.

_____. *The Interpretation of First and Second Corinthians*. Minneapolis: Augusburg, 1963.

Lewis, C. S. *Transposition and Other Addresses*. London: Geoffrey Bles, 1949.

Lindsay, Gordon. *Gifts of the Spirit*, 3 vols. Dallas: Christ for the Nations, repr. 1978.

Lippman, Walter. *A Preface to Morals*. New York: Macmillan, 1929.

Lloyd-Jones, Martyn. *Joy Unspeakable: Power and Renewal in the Holy Spirit*. Wheaton, Ill.: Harold Shaw, 1984.

Luther, Martin. *Selections from His Writings*. Edited by John Dillenberger. New York: Doubleday, 1958.

McAlister, W. Robert. *The Dilemma: Deliverance or Discipline?* Plainfield, N.J.: Logos, 1976.

MacArthur, John F., Jr. *The Charismatics*. Grand Rapids: Zondervan, 1978.

McClung, L. Grant, ed. *Azusa Street and Beyond*. South Plainfield, N.J.: Bridge, 1986.

McConkey, James H. *The Three-Fold Secret of the Holy Spirit*. Lincoln, Neb.: Back to the Bible, 1977.

McConnell, D. R. *A Different Gospel*. Peabody, Mass.: Hendrickson, 1988.

McDonnell, Kilian. *Charismatic Renewal and the Churches*. New York: Seabury, 1976.

_____. *Statement of the Theological Basis of the Catholic Charismatic Renewal*. Pecos, N.M.: Dove Publications, 1973.

McDonnell, Kilian, ed. *Presence, Power, Praise: Documents on the Charismatic Renewal*, 3 vols. Collegeville, Minn.: Liturgical Press, 1980.

MacNutt, Francis. *Healing*. Notre Dame, Ind.: Ave Maria, 1974.

_____. *The Power to Heal*. Notre Dame, Ind.: Ave Maria, 1977.

McPherson, Aimee Semple. *The Four-Square Gospel*. Comp. by Raymond L. Cox. Los Angeles: Heritage Committee, 1969.

Marshall, I. H. *Kept by the Power of God*. Minneapolis: Bethany, 1974.

_____. *The Acts of the Apostles*. TNTC. Grand Rapids: Eerdmans, 1980.

_____. *The Epistles of John*. NICNT. Grand Rapids: Eerdmans, 1978.

Martin, Ralph P. *The Spirit and the Congregation*. Grand Rapids: Eerdmans, 1984.

_____. *The Epistle of Paul to the Philippians*. TNTC. Grand Rapids: Eerdmans, 1959.

Meyer, H. A. W. *Commentary on the New Testament, First Corinthians*. Peabody, Mass.: Hendrickson, repr. 1983.

Montague, George T. *The Holy Spirit: Growth of a Biblical Tradition*. New York: Paulist, 1976.

Moody, W. R. *The Life of D. L. Moody*. Westwood, N.J.: Barbour, repr. 1985.

Morgan, G. Campbell. *Acts of the Apostles*. Old Tappan, N.J.: Revell, 1924.

Morris, Leon. *The Epistles of Paul to the Thessalonians*. TNTC. Grand Rapids: Eerdmans, 1984.

_____. *The First Epistle of Paul to the Corinthians*. TNTC. Grand Rapids: Eerdmans, 1958.

_____. *The Gospel According to John*. NICNT. Grand Rapids: Eerdmans, 1971.

Munck, Johannes. *The Acts of the Apostles*. AB. Garden City, N.Y.: Doubleday, 1967.

Murray, Andrew. *The Spirit of Christ*. Ft. Washington, Pa.: Christian Literature Crusade, 1978.

Murray, John. *The Epistle to the Romans*. NICNT. Grand Rapids: Eerdmans, 1968.

Neil, William. *The Acts of the Apostles*. NCBC. Grand Rapids: Eerdmans, 1981.

Neve, L. *The Spirit of God in the Old Testament*. Tokyo: Seibunsha, 1972.

Nicoll, W. Robertson, ed. *Expositor's Greek Testament*, 5 vols. New York: Doran, n.d.

O'Connor, Edward, D. *Pentecost in the Modern World*. Notre Dame, Ind.: Ave Maria, 1972.

_____. *The Pentecostal Movement in the Catholic Church*. Notre Dame, Ind.: Ave Maria, 1971.

Olshausen, Hermann. *First and Second Corinthians*. Minneapolis: Klock & Klock, repr. 1984.

Parham, Charles F. *The Life of Charles F. Parham*. New York: Garland, repr. 1985.

_____. *The Sermons of Charles F. Parham*. New York: Garland, repr. 1985.

Pfeiffer, Charles, F.; Howard F. Vos; and John Rea, eds. *The Wycliffe Bible Encyclopedia*, 2 vols. Chicago: Moody, 1975.

Phillips, J. B. *The Young Church in Action*. New York: Macmillan, 1958.

Prange, Erwin. *The Gift Is Already Yours*. Plainfield, N.J.: Logos, 1973.

Price, Charles S. *The Real Faith*. Plainfield, N.J.: Logos, 1972.

Pytches, David. *Spiritual Gifts in the Local Church*. Minneapolis: Bethany, 1985.

Ranaghan, Kevin and Dorothy. *Catholic Pentecostals.* Paramus, N.J.: Paulist, 1969.

Ranaghan, Kevin and Dorothy, eds. *As the Spirit Leads Us.* Paramus, N.J.: Paulist, 1971.

Rea, John. *Layman's Commentary on the Holy Spirit.* Plainfield, N.J.: Logos, 1974.

Reed, David. "Aspects of the Origins of Oneness Pentecostalism." In *Aspects of Pentecostal-Charismatic Origins.* Edited by Vinson Synan. Plainfield, N.J.: Logos, 1975.

Richardson, Alan. *An Introduction to the Theology of the New Testament.* London: SCM, 1958.

Ridderbos, Herman. *The Epistle of Paul to the Churches of Galatia.* NICNT. Grand Rapids: Eerdmans, 1953.

Robeck, Cecil, Jr., ed. *Charismatic Experiences in History.* Peabody, Mass.: Hendrickson, 1985.

Roberts, Oral. *The Call: An Autobiography.* New York: Avon, 1971.

Robertson, A. T. *A Grammar of the Greek New Testament.* Nashville: Broadman, 1934.

————. *Word Pictures in The New Testament,* 6 vols. Nashville: Broadman, 1930–33.

Robertson, Archibald, and Alfred Plummer. *I Corinthians.* ICC. New York: Charles Scribner's Sons, 1911.

Robertson, Pat. *Beyond Reason.* New York: William Morrow, 1985.

Samarin, William. *Tongues of Men and Angels.* New York: Macmillan, 1972.

Scanlan, Michael, and Randall J. Cirner. *Deliverance from Evil Spirits.* Ann Arbor, Mich.: Servant, 1980.

Schaff, Philip. *History of the Christian Church.* New York: Charles Scribner's Sons, 1882–1910.

————. *The Creeds of Christendom,* 3 vols. Grand Rapids: Baker, 1983.

Simpson, A. B. *The Gospel of Healing.* Harrisburg, Pa.: Christian Publications, 1915.

Stott, John R. W. *Baptism and Fullness.* Downers Grove, Ill.: InterVarsity, 1976.

Strong, A. H. *Systematic Theology.* Old Tappan, N.J.: Revell, 1907.

Stronstad, Roger. *The Charismatic Theology of St. Luke.* Peabody, Mass.: Hendrickson, 1984.

Suenens, Leon Joseph Cardinal. *A New Pentecost?* London: Darton, Longman, and Todd, 1975.

Sullivan, Francis A. *Charisms and Charismatic Renewal.* Ann Arbor, Mich.: Servant, 1982.

Swete, Henry B. *The Holy Spirit in the New Testament.* Grand Rapids: Baker, repr. 1976.

Synan, Vinson. *In the Latter Days: The Outpouring of the Holy Spirit in the Twentieth Century.* Ann Arbor, Mich.: Servant, 1984.

————. *The Holiness-Pentecostal Movement.* Grand Rapids: Eerdmans, 1971.

Thayer, Joseph H. *Greek-English Lexicon of the New Testament.* New York: Harper, 1899.

Thiessen, Henry. "Election and Vocation." In *The New Life: Readings in Christian Theology.* Edited by Millard J. Erickson. Grand Rapids: Baker, 1979.

Tomczak, Larry. *Clap Your Hands!* Plainfield, N.J.: Logos, 1973.

Torrey, Reuben A. *The Baptism with the Holy Spirit.* Minneapolis: Bethany, 1972.

Tourville, Robert E. *The Acts of the Apostles.* New Wilmington, Pa.: House of Bon Giovanni, 1983.

Tugwell, Simon. *Did You Receive the Spirit?* New York: Paulist, 1972.

Unger, M. E. *The Baptism and Gifts of the Holy Spirit.* Chicago: Moody, 1974.

Vaughan, C. R. *The Gifts of the Holy Spirit.* Carlisle, Pa.: Banner of Truth, repr. 1975.

Walvoord, John. *The Holy Spirit.* Findlay, Ohio: Dunham, 1958.

Wesley, John. *A Plain Account of Christian Perfection.* New York: Methodist Book Concern, n.d.

Weymouth, R. F. *New Testament in Modern Speech.* London: James Clarke, 1909.

Williams, A. Lukyn. *The Epistle of Paul the Apostle to the Galatians*. Cambridge Greek Testament. Cambridge: The University Press, 1914.

Williams, J. Rodman. *The Era of the Spirit*. Plainfield, N.J.: Logos, 1971.

_____. *The Gift of the Holy Spirit Today*. Plainfield, N.J.: Logos, 1980.

_____. *The Pentecostal Reality*. Plainfield, N.J.: Logos, 1972.

_____. *Renewal Theology: God, the World & Redemption*, vol. 1. Grand Rapids: Zondervan, 1988.

Williams, R. R. *The Acts of the Apostles*. London: SCM, 1953.

Wimber, John. *Power Evangelism*. San Francisco: Harper & Row, 1986.

_____. *Power Healing*. San Francisco: Harper & Row, 1987.

Wright, G. Ernest. *The Rule of God*. Garden City, N.Y.: Doubleday, 1960.

PERSONS INDEX

SUBJECT INDEX

SCRIPTURE INDEX